SOMALIA

SOMALIA
THE UNTOLD HISTORY 1941-1969

MOHAMED ISSA TRUNJI

LOOH PRESS
2024
Leicester, England
Mogadishu, Somalia

LOOH PRESS LTD.

First Edition, Third Print November 2024

PRINTED & DISTRIBUTED BY
Looh Press Ltd.
Leicester, LE1 2EB
England. UK
www.LoohPress.com
LoohPress@gmail.com

CONTACT AUTHOR:
E: Trunji@yahoo.com

A catalogue record for this book is available from the British Library.
British Library Cataloguing-in-Publication Data

COVER DESIGN & TYPESET
Typesetting by : Mohammed Yusuf (Garanuug Limited)
Cover Design : Looh Press

ISBN
978-1-912411-45-0. (Hardback)
978-1-912411-48-1. (Paperback)

In loving memory of my beloved mother, Araba, and my ever gentle father, Issa.

PUBLISHER'S NOTE

In the past, the academic field that focuses on the Somalis as a people, their culture, land or their politics has been characteristically devoid of the Somali perspective. As a result, much stands to be revisited, examined, and revised. It is towards this objective, that we at Looh Press have decided to produce and distribute works that challenge old dogmas, while paving the way for new narratives and theories that enlighten and enliven the field of Somali Studies. This title exceptionally demonstrates our passion. It is a work that critically re-evaluates a period rarely analysed. The author, Mr Mohamed Issa Trunji, is a veteran lawyer and a witness to many of the events mentioned in this thick volume. He has critically examined British, Italian, UN-Trusteeship and Somali administrations that governed Somalia between 1941 and 1969.

This work has been diligently in production for over eight years, and gives a fresh prespective on the Italian administration and on the turbulences that led to the bloodless military *coup d'etat* in 1969. We are very delighted with this new addition to the Somali Studies library, and are confident you, the reader, will feel the same.

We would like to thank Mohammed Yusuf (Garanuug) who spent a lot of time in typesetting this thick volume. Another person who assisted us in sailing through the stormy oceans of the publishing world is Anita Adams, a veteran publisher and the founder of HAAN publishing—the first publishing house in the West to focus on the Somali Studies. Also the many young and eager Somalis ever present in social media, who constantly engaged with our queries about cover design and preferred layout.

We hope you find this work enriching and intellectually challenging. However, as it is the case with human nature, mistakes and errors are unavoidable, if you come across any, please let us now. Once again, enjoy and sail safely through the pages of history.

Mohammed Abdullah Artan,
CEO of Looh Press
01 November 2015

CONTENTS

MAPS

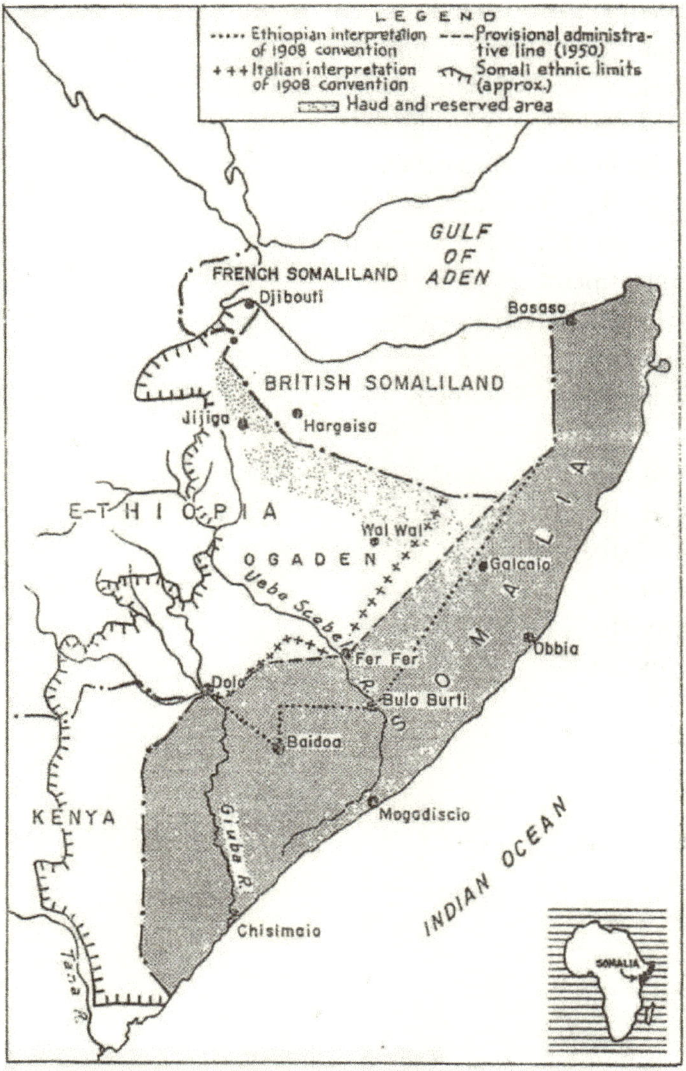

Map 1. Italian vs Ethiopian Border Dispute.

A map clearly showing the following:

- De facto border lines of Somalia known as Provisional Administrative line (1950)
- Somali Ethnic limits (approx)
- Ethiopian Interpretation of 1908 convention,
- Italian Interpretation of 1908 convention.

LIST OF ABBREVIATIONS

AFIS	Amministrazione fiduciaria italiana della Somalia
AOI	Africa Orientale Italiana
ASCM	Archivio Storico Casale Monferrato
ASMAE	Archivio storico del Ministero Affari Esteri
ASM	Associazione Scidle e Mobilen
BAS	British Administration of Somalia
BMA	British Military Administration
CITAO	Compania Italiana Trasporti Africa Orientale
CLAMS	Commissione Liquidazione Arretrati Militari Somali
DC	Democrazia Cristiana
FCO	Foreign and Commonwealth Office
FO	Foreign Office
GSL	Great Somali League
IAOI	Impero Africa Orientale Italiana
LGS	Lega dei Giovani Somali
HDM	Hisbiya Dighil and Mirifle
LPM	Lega Progressista Migiurtinia
MAE	Ministero degli Affari Esteri
MSI	Movimento Sociale italiano
NFD	Northern Frontier District
OETA	Occupied Enemy Territory Administration
PDS	Partito Democratico Somalo
PLGS	Partito Liberale giovani Somali
SANU	Somali African National Union
SNC	Somali National Congress
SNL	Somali National League
SYC	Somali Youth club
SYL	Somali Youth League
TNA	The National Archive
UAS	Unione Africani della Somalia

UNACS	United Nations Advisory Council of Somalia
UNS	Unione Nazionale somala
USP	United Somali party
SNF	Somali National Front
UPB	Unione Patriottica Beneficenza
UNHCR	United Nations High Commissioner for Refugees
WO	War Office

AUTHOR'S NOTE

The idea of writing this book first crossed my mind in December 2007, and I fully anticipated its completion would take a long period of time. In the course of my research, I became aware of how much valuable information on recent Somali history I have overlooked or allowed to slip my mind following the long years of asylum and 'wilderness'. I also discovered how much certain information had been deliberately distorted or invented to serve the particular interests of particular political groups. Some may disagree with some aspects of my research. I make no apologies but rather submit my analysis as a challenge. This book is the culmination of many years' work, and I take full responsibilities for any of its faults.

The initial research took off in January 2008 in London, UK, where I have lived, until very recently, as an asylum seeker – not out of my own choice, but because of the sad circumstances that have made my native country one of the most dangerous places on earth, consequently making a return unadvisable.

It would be remiss if I fail to express my deep gratitude to the British Government and its people for granting me the right to stay in their great country with the enjoyment of full protection of my civil and human rights. I joined the ranks of the growing number of Somali asylum seekers in Britain. Based on the year of arrival, Somali diasporas in the UK can be classified into two main categories: 'old'- and 'new-comers'. The 'old group' includes those who emigrated in the Eighties, before the collapse of state institutions in Somalia. The second group comprises those who came in different waves following the disaster that befell the country in 1991 and in the following years. Having come to Britain in 2005, I thus belong to the latter group.

I was not new in Britain. My first visit to the country dates back to May 1980, following the award by the British Council of a one-year scholarship to pursue a Postgraduate Diploma Course in Shipping and Maritime Law at University College London (UCL). Since then, I have been coming to this country at almost regular annual intervals, both for business and for pleasure.

I left Somalia in 1991 in the wake of the collapse of government institutions at the hands of gangs of looters who vandalized and destroyed whatever public or private property they could get hold of. The Head of State and his once powerful military machinery fled the capital under pressure from ill-equipped and poorly trained mobs who invaded Mogadisho, the country's capital city.

Judging by the behaviour of these undisciplined and trigger-happy groups – most of them without known leaders – it was easy to realize that this volatile situation would soon get out of hand, plunging the country into chaos, with dire consequences for its civilian population, especially the weaker segment of it. With these feelings of fear, I took the decision to embark on a temporary stay abroad which took me first to Italy, a country where, in addition to language and cultural affinity, I could count on numerous friends whose generosity made my stay comfortable and enriching. It had never crossed my mind that what I thought of as a temporary absence would result in a long and, at times, painful inability to return home. I say 'temporary' because the idea to return to Somalia never left my mind. Evidence of this intention is given by the return air ticket via Nairobi that I still keep with me as a souvenir, and that was paid for by an Italian NGO, 'Africa 70', which operated humanitarian relief programmes in Somalia for mainly Ethiopian refugees in the Eighties.

In virtue of my association with the National Refugee Commission (NRC), I made acquaintance and developed contacts with a number of International NGOs as well as the United Nations Refugee Agency, the UNHCR. From beautiful, comfortable Italy, I moved to Geneva in 1992 to join the United Nations High Commission for Refugees as an International Civil Servant – a position I held until my retirement in 2005. Throughout this period, to my utter displeasure, I did not once visit Somalia: the country was listed among the most dangerous places on earth, and as a result, UN staff were advised not to travel there: failure to adhere to this security guidance entailed, amongst other things, forfeiture of the insurance premium in case of any incident arising from visiting the country. It was particularly painful for me to be unable to attend my mother's funerals in Somalia owing to these security rules. Despite the lack of any encouraging indications, I have never abandoned my hope to return to Somalia. This hope was further boosted by the formation of a new government in Kenya in 2004 following a two-year negotiation process involving various Somali groups, with the support of the United Nations and of several countries. Much to the consternation and disbelief of the parties who sponsored the prolonged Somali Peace Conference, a cloud of suspicion and mistrust quickly spread over the Somali delegations, again creating serious doubts about the country's future.

This had been the 14th Somali Peace Conference since 1991—and all of them had ended in dismay. As images of the ugly chair-throwing incidents and scuffles between Somali 'lawmakers' in the Parliament in Nairobi toured the world, few analysts had any doubts that we were heading towards a more sinister and uncertain future. A Member of Parliament interviewed on the matter was reported as saying that the incident "was a sign of democracy." With the shattering of the agreement resulting from the protracted Peace Conference, my hope to return to Somalia and enjoy my retirement also vanished. This is what brought me to Britain.

In Britain, after retirement, I enrolled on a Master's Degree in International Human Rights Law at the University of Essex in 2005, graduating in February 2006. For my dissertation, I wrote a paper entitled 'Prosecution of Past Human Rights Violations'—a subject closely related to the events of the last three decades in Somalia.

Somalia was once celebrated as a democratic oasis in a continent awash with authoritarianism. Today, the East African nation is torn apart and divided into small and unstable tribal cantons, thus ceasing to be a State in any practical sense and becoming a mere 'geographical expression'. More years could elapse before a Somali nation emerges, if indeed it ever will. With time softening the memories of autocratic rule, nostalgia for the overthrown military regime is spreading among Somalis living in Europe. Some even believe that a morally upright dictator could be given *carte blanche* to do whatever he wants, even if that meant breaking the law.

INTRODUCTION

This study covers the period of time between 1941 and 1969—almost three decades which undoubtedly represent a crucial time in Somalia's history, not least for the remarkable events which took place in the country. For the purpose of historical analysis, I have divided this period of time into three distinct phases. In the course of this period, the country came under the rule of three different administrations: British Military Administration, UN Trusteeship and, finally, an independent Somali civilian administration. Each of these administrations, as I will extensively explain, left its imprint not only on the country but also on the lives of its people.

The aim of this study is to shed light on misconceptions held by a large segment of Somalis, and assist them as they become acquainted with major political developments which characterized this period but have been largely ignored, except at the peripheral level. Owing to poor investment in teaching and writing history, the general level of historical knowledge in Somalia society is abysmally low. The existing literature on this important historical period is scanty, shallow and incomplete by nature; it is the work of foreign writers, and consequently does not provide a comprehensive or clear picture of major events. As a result of this paucity of historical information, generations of young Somalis are growing up ignorant of their heritage or exposed to distorted presentations of the history of their country.

This study does not purport to be a comprehensive history of the events which took place during the period it covers. It does, however, focus on major political and social transformations experienced by the country during this period of time. It examines the difficult economic conditions Somalis endured under

British military occupation and the political liberalization introduced by British colonial authorities, which paved the way for the formation of the first social and political movements.

The study covers the long and difficult debates held at the United Nations, with particular emphasis on the conflicting positions and the Four Powers' failure to reach consensus on the future of pre-war Italian colonies in Africa, which eventually resulted in the transfer of the issue to the General Assembly of the United Nations for final decision. An entire chapter is dedicated to the emergence of the first political movements in the territory, and their fierce competition for political primacy, leading at times to bloody confrontations.

As this research will show, the search for independence remained a common creed for all Somali political movements. The political programmes embodied in their respective constitutions and in the repeated requests for independence they each made before the Four Powers Commission of Investigation in 1948 and before the United Nations thereafter, is undeniable evidence of that common goal. Such differences as existed on this issue – and they were slight – referred merely to the procedure through which independence would be achieved. The 'non-Lega' parties pursued clear objectives, designed to eventually ensure independence through a well-articulated process of democratization and modernization which required, in their view, a longer period of preparation than the Lega had planned. For instance, the political programme submitted to the Four Powers Commission of Investigation and to the United Nations by the 'Conferenza' represented a well-articulated agenda compared with the simple and succinct agenda of the Lega.

Some scholars, regrettably, tend to portray non-Lega political parties as negative forces simply because they differed from the Lega in their approach to modalities leading to a smooth, gradual and viable independence. At best, non-Lega political parties were viewed as forces working against Somali national interest.

The performance of the Italian Trusteeship in Somalia, under the aegis of the United Nations, is also examined – with particular attention to the ambitious commitment undertaken by the administering power despite its economic weakness and past colonial legacy, to turn the country into a truly independent African nation within an all-too short period of time. Many, Somalis and foreigners alike, considered the duration of the UN mandate too short and ambitious to accomplish any meaningful achievement. The voices of those denouncing this hypocrisy were ignored or vilified. The study also looks into the rise and gradual disintegration of the traditional political parties as credible political parties (particularly the 'Lega dei Giovani Somali'), most of them eventually ending in disarray and disgrace.

The focus is placed on how the Lega-led administrations ultimately failed to achieve even one of their targets and objectives. In its manifesto, the ruling party promised and preached the eradication of tribalism, the fight against harmful traditions, the adoption of the Osmania alphabet and the liberation and consolidation of territories inhabited by ethnic Somalis in the Horn of Africa. A variety of good reasons, which will be set out in other parts of this book, will explain this failure. The study also looks into how civilian governments followed in the footsteps of AFIS and, before them, of the British military authorities, in creating a breeding ground for the consolidation of tribalism to the point that it became the sole predominant ideology to rule the country.

To this day Somalia remains a stateless country and will probably never again be the same as it was before being pulverized from within. It has gone back to what it was during the pre-colonial era: simply a vast expanse of territory without a central government, inhabited by different clans each under its own jurisdiction.

To call Somalia a failed State seems as generous as it is inappropriate. The country is still without a functioning central government. In 2014, after 23 years of ethnic strife and chaos, Somalia is still ranked as the world's worst failed State by the American Fund for Peace. Somalia is a political paradox: a unified entity on the surface, dangerously divided beneath. The Somalis may boast of having the same religion and culture, but this apparent unity is undermined by clans, themselves further divided into a number of smaller clans and assorted sub-clans.

In common with many African countries, Somalia has never been a politically mature and stable country because of its precipitated independence. In 1960, one of the key questions was whether the new Republic, with all its inherent diversity and ethnicity, would be able to move on from its persistent patterns of conflict. Analysts with deep knowledge of Somalia predicted that the rifts between ethnic groups, between north and south and between nomads and farmers would widen, and that a civil war would be unavoidable. What was predicted in 1960 sadly happened in 1991 – nearly thirty years after the end of the International Trusteeship, and nearly one hundred years since Italian penetration into Somalia in 1890. The brutal wave of ethno-communal clashes in Somalia in 1991 underscores the assertion that it was easier to create the Somali State than to unite its people.

The atrocities beyond description and the scenes portraying the self-destruction of Somali society that the world is witnessing today are the legacy of the way the country was administered since independence. The wounds opened in 1991 have yet to be healed. Many perpetrators of criminal acts are dead or, if alive, unlikely to face justice. Attempts to bring reconciliation to Somali society have to date proven unsuccessful. But however hard Somalia tries to escape its dark past, the ghost of the 1990s cannot be laid to rest. Even if one looks with an indulgent eye at the fourteen years of Lega rule (1956 - 1969), it becomes evident that the merits that have been celebrated are few and very modest.

Lastly, a word on the name of the territory is in order. Although the United Nations and the Four Powers Commission of Investigations refer to the former Italian colony as 'Italian Somaliland', the official name of the Colony which forms the subject of this study was 'Somalia Italiana'. Throughout this study, the former Italian colony is referred to as 'Somalia' and 'Somaliland' (formerly 'British Somaliland Protectorate', now a stable and viable political entity separate from Somalia). The study does not cover the history of and political developments in the Somaliland Protectorate before independence; rather, the reader will find that the question is only discussed inasmuch as it forms part of the Somali context following the ill-fated union with the southern regions in 1960.

Most of the research was conducted at the National Archives at Kew Gardens in London, the Archivio Storico Ministero Affari Esteri (ASMAE) in Rome, Italy, the Istituto Italo Africano in Rome, the Biblioteca Nazionale in Rome, the Biblioteca e Centro di Documentazione Internazionale in Rome, the Archivio Storico Casale Monferrato (ASCM), Italy, the United Nations Library in Geneva and SOAS Library, London.

Regrettably, it has not been possible to consult the many important documents kept in government offices in Somalia before the civil war, which, whether intentionally or unintentionally, were destroyed by the gangs who occupied Mogadisho and other major urban centres at the beginning of 1991.

It is a source of deep disappointment that none of the Somali protagonists of the events discussed in the study have left any written testimony to help us understand the country's history from their own perspective. The only exception was President Aden Abdulla, the Father of the Somali Republic, who kept a personal diary in which major political events are systematically recorded over a long period of time. There were no readers. For the Somali politicians of the time, neither the written nor the printed word existed; everything had to be relayed by word of mouth. Simply they had no education, and most of them went to their graves with their secrets held close to their chests.

I have consulted published and unpublished theses, journals and newspapers, and obtained invaluable information from interviews with individuals who have directly or indirectly witnessed or have at some point been involved in the events which took place during the period under review.

Several people have helped me with my research. I am deeply grateful to them all, but I must make special mention of my very good friend Abdulkadir Aden Abdulla, who encouraged me to start this research. Thanks to him, I had the privilege of becoming the first person to read the rare and jealously kept diaries of his late father (and Father of the Somali Republic), President Aden Abdulla: an invaluable source of information dating back to 1958. Without these diaries, this book would have been very different.

Special thanks also go to General Mohamoud Ghelle Yousuf, who devoted considerable time and energy in providing me with all the UN official records I needed from the Library of the United Nations in Geneva. In the orthography followed in this book, some Somali names and toponyms are left as they were found in the original documents consulted.

Italian occupation of Somalia: historical perspective
Somalia, an Italian invention?

Modern Italy, as a unified state, has existed since 1861. In the years following Italian unification, the newly established Kingdom of Italy was quick to realize that it was late joining the 'scramble for Africa' during which other European powers, notably Great Britain and France, were expeditiously establishing overseas colonies in Africa.

At the time of Italy's arrival, Britain, France, Germany, Spain, Portugal and even little Belgium had already carved out large empires on the African continent. Italy believed that she too had a right to her own overseas empire[1]; the Italians were looking for their 'posto al sole', a place in the sun. One of the last remaining areas open to colonization was the East coast of Africa, and Italy's search for colonies was rewarded in 1885 when she annexed the Red Sea port of Massawa, in Eritrea, that had been part of the crumbling Egyptian Empire. This was accomplished through a secret agreement with Great Britain.

Prior to Italian colonization, the Sultan of Zanzibar had exercised a nominal sovereignty over southern Somalia, better known as the Benadir, with its ports of Merca, Mogadisho and Warsheikh. In the north the two Sultans of Majertenia and Obbia (Hobyo) were jealous rivals, each bidding for control over the Nugal

1 John E. Sandrock, 'Italy's Colonial Empire: a Paper Money Trail', www.thecurrencycollector.com.

Valley. In 1892 the Italian government leased the Benadir ports from the Sultan of Zanzibar, who ceded them for one down payment of 40,000 rupees plus an annual payment of 160,000 rupees.[2]

The Somalis, at that time, did not constitute a single autonomous political unit. They were divided into a number of large and often hostile clans, themselves further split into a wide array of subsidiary kinship groups.[3] Historically, there was no such name as 'Somalia' to describe the geographical region we call Somalia today, just as there was no Tanganyika or Nigeria before the advent of colonialism, as one author notes[4]. For a long period, lack of transport and communications, coupled with the extension of the territory, severely hampered easy and direct contact between the nomadic populations of the North and the farmers in the South. Contact may have existed between nomads during their migrations in search of grazing grounds and water, but such contacts are hard to imagine between nomads and the agro-pastoral communities in the south. These tribal barriers have always presented solid obstacles towards the formation of national conscience and real integration.

It was only after Italian penetration that the country came under one central authority forming one single entity known as 'Somalia'. "Before the arrival of the Italians", writes Nuredin Haji Scikei, "Somalia did not exist as a united political entity. The name Somalia was given to the country by the Italians under decree n. 161 of April 5, 1908."[5]

It is also hard to determine the limits and boundary of the Somali territory given the general nomadic nature of the population, perennially displaced in its search for grazing grounds and water for their herds. To put an end to this phenomenon, in 1909, the British colonial authorities in Kenya introduced measures forbidding Somalis to cross the 'Somali–Galla Line.'[6]

Roughly speaking, the Italian occupation of Somalia was carried out in three distinct stages or phases. In the first period the country was administered through two chartered companies: the Filonardi Company, known as Royal Italian East Africa Company, in 1893–96, and the 'Società Anonima Commerciale Italiana

2 Luigi Robecchi Bricchetti, Dal Benadir. Letter illustrate alla Società Antischiavista d'Italia, La Poligrafica, Milan 1904, p. 48.

3 I.M. Lewis, 'Pan-Africanism and Pan-Somalism', The Journal of Modern African Studies, 1, 2 (1963) p. 147.

4 Godfrey Mwakikagile, The Modern Africa State: Quest for Transformation, Nova, 2001, p. 110.

5 Nuredin Haji Scikei, 'Somalia un'invenzione italiana', Affricana, Miscellanea di Studi Extraeuropei, Associazione di Studi Extraeuropei ESA, 2001, pp 95-108.

6 A.A. Castagno, 'The Somali-Kenyan Controversy: Implementation for the Future', The Journal of Modern African Studies, vol. 2, no. 2, p. 16, 1964.

Del Benadir', commonly known as 'Società del Benadir', in 1896–1905.

During this period, the two commercial companies exercised control over the ports of Benadir: Mogadisho, Merca, Brava and Warsheikh. The companies had full control over customs, taxes and mining rights. In compliance with the convention signed with the government on April 15, 1896[7], the company had to fly the Italian flag, pay the Sultan rent, administer the subsidies to the Sultans of Majertenia and Obbia and apply the General Acts of Berlin and Brussels regarding slavery, alcohol and arms trading.

The Filonardi Company ended in financial failure, as a result of which it was unable to fulfil its obligations. The government and the Benadir Company eventually dissolved their relationship because of the company's failure to abolish slavery under the General Acts of Berlin and Brussels, and the company was transformed into a purely commercial enterprise. The second period began when the Italian Government placed the colony under its direct management in 1905, but the extension of Italian influence beyond the coast of Benadir was painstakingly slow because of a lack of enthusiasm for overseas adventures on the part of Italy's parliament.

In fact, while other members of the government supported the idea of direct rule of Benadir, the Minister of the Treasury of the time, Luigi Luzzati, expressed strong opposition to such a policy. In a letter to Foreign Minister Tittoni, Luzzati, after expressing his concern over the huge costs of the implementation of the new policy regarding the colonies, stated that "The future interest of Italy will never be in Eritrea or in the Benadir, which will not become colonies for settlement, but are destined to represent a perennial economic let-down and consequently political weakness."[8]

However, and despite Luzzati's firm opposition, Tittoni's colonial programme prevailed in the end and Italy purchased the Benadir ports for £144,000. On March 15, 1905, the colony was consigned to the government who acquired the right to maintain commercial installations at Kismayo, in British Jubaland. Nearly 50 years later, in 1941, Luzzati's prophecy came true as Italy was forced to lose her colonies in Africa, with devastating effects. The third period starts in 1923, following the advent of fascism in Italy and the arrival of the energetic and determined Governor Cesare Maria De Vecchi Di Val Cismon, who completed the occupation of southern Somalia, including the Sultanates of Obbia and

7 Hess, *Italian Colonialism in Somalia*, University of Chicago Press, 1966 , p. 58.
8 Letter from Luzzati to Tittoni, August 17, 1904, ASMAI, quoted in Hess, op. cit., p. 86.

Majertenia in 1927, and created what he called 'Somalia Italiana'.

Somali opposition to Italian penetration

Owing to the tribal structure of Somali society, there was no organized large-scale, territory-wide opposition to Italian occupation at any time. "By and large, opposition to the Italians was local in nature", says Hess, adding that it "at no time involved all Somali tribes". The single most important and largest movement, that of the Dervishes headed by Muhammad Abdulla Hassan, was not directed primarily against the Italians[9]. Only when the fascists occupied the northern Sultanates was there an attempt at rebellion, "but Obbia and Majertenia were torn by tribalism and factionalism, and could not present a united front."[10]

In the coastal area, the opposition to the Italians started in May 1904, when Alessandro Sapelli, the last Governor of the Benadir Company, issued an ordinance outlawing the slave trade and permitting the liberation of Bantu slaves, imported from other parts of East Africa and used by the Bimal, a major slave-holding clan, as labour force to cultivate their fields. Merca and Brava were the centres with the highest concentration of slaves. Despite poor records of the actual numbers of slaves in Somalia, Hess cites government sources revealing that, between July 1905 and November 1908, approximately 1,300 slaves had been freed in Mogadisho, 850 in Merca and 150 in Brava[11]. The first Bimal rebellion began on October 27, 1905, when rebel forces attacked Jilib Merca, a coastal village north of Merca, and was the direct result of the issuing of the anti-slavery ordinance[12]. Militant Bimal tribes also blockaded Merca so that relief supplies had to be brought overland under armed escort from Mogadisho to save the town from starvation[13]. The Bimal revolt was easily put down with the aid of Somali allies among the Gheledi. The Gheledi were for a long time the traditional enemies of the Bimal and Wadan.

After crushing the Bimal rebellion, the Italians started moving inland from the coast to extend their colony through a plan called 'Penetrazione Pacifica', or

9 Hess, op. cit., p. 181.

10 Ibid., p. 182.

11 Hess, note 7, p. 88. NB A list of some of the slaves liberated by the Italian authorities at Merca and Brava, found at the 'Centro Robecchi Bricchetti' in Pavia, is with the author.

12 'Colony in Peril: Tribesmen Angered by Stoppage of Slavery Trade threaten Merca, New York Times March 2 1907.

13 Lee Cassanelli, *'The ending of slavery in Italian Somalia: liberty and the control of labour, 1890-1935'*, Suzanne Meiers and Richard Roberts (ed.), The end of Slavery in Africa, University of Wisconsin, 1982, p. 201.

pacific penetration. By 1908, the important centres of Middle Shabelle, Malable, Awdheegle, Berirre and Afgooye were occupied. This successful operation was made possible by the alliance sealed between the Sultan of the Gheledi and the Italian authorities. In less than a year, the centre of Balad, on the river Shebelle, was occupied, after a brief battle with Dervish armed agents in September 1909. The occupation went on to encompass Mahadaay Weyn.

In 1910, with the arrival of the new Governor, Senator Giacomo De Martino, the occupation rapidly expanded to include new territories in the interior. New settlements were thus established at Afgooye, Awdheegle, Balad, Jilib, Margherita, Mahadaay Weyn, Matagoi, and Wanleweyn, in addition to those already in existence at Bardera, Brava, Itala, Jumbo, Merca, Meregh, Mogadisho and Warsheikh[14]. The sequence of operations, completed in 1913, saw the occupation of Bur Hakaba in June 13 and Baidoa in June 25. Other forces moved to Webi Shabelle and occupied Bulo Burti (Bulobarde) in May 1914. Bulo Burti soon became the vanguard post for an offence against the Dervishes who had continued to harass the Shabelle and Macanne tribes along the Webi Shabelle.[15]

While some Somali communities mounted often minimum resistance against the occupying force, others, like the Scidle (Shidle) and Eyle tribesmen around Mahadaay Weyn and Bur Hakaba, whom the Somali tribes regarded as of inferior lineage, welcomed Italian intervention, "because for them the Italian occupation meant additional security and protection for them against the incursion of the GaljalSomali."[16]

With the advent of fascism in Italy and the appointment in 1923 of Cesare Maria de Vecchi as Governor of the colony, the pace of the occupation process assumed new impetus and dynamism. De Vecchi's first task was to disarm the population of Benadir's interior and the Sultanates of Obbia and Majertenia, who had been armed by the pre-fascist administrations in order to ward off incursion from the Dervishes. De Vecchi denounced this 'policy of weakness' which he deemed not only 'un-fascist' but also 'pacifist and Masonic Liberalism.'[17]

On February 2, 1924 De Vecchi gave the order to disarm the Somali tribes of the Upper Webi Shabelle region, where most of the arms of southern Somalia were concentrated. Early in March, the Regional Commissioner of Mahadai

14 Gubernatorial Decree no. 488, May 5, 1910, ASMAI, pos 75/11, f. 122 quoted in Hess, p. 107.

15 Hess, p. 145.

16 De Martino, 'Report to H E. the Foreign Minister', 'The Present and the Future of the Colony', Mogadiscio October 19, 1950 ASMAI, reported in Hess, p. 93.

17 Cesare Maria De Vecchi di Val Cisman, *Orizzonte d' Impero, cinque anni in Somalia*, A. Mondadori – Milano, 1930, p. 25.

informed the Chiefs and elders of the Somali tribes of a government order to surrender all arms and ammunitions within 40 days. While some of the local communities, such as the Macanne, the Hawadle and the Moblen, acquiesced to the new order by surrendering their arms, others seemed reticent to do so.[18]

One of the most recalcitrant among the Somali traditional leaders was Sheikh Hassan Barsane, a cleric of the Galjel tribe, who denounced the governmental order and claimed the right to resist the abolition of slavery on the grounds that Islam sanctioned slavery. To the order given to him to report to the Residente of Mahaddei and surrender the arms held by his people, the rebellious clergy responded with a letter whose content, in view of its importance, is fully reported here. The letter read:

> "To the Residente of Mahaddei, greetings. I have received your letter and understood its contents; in view of its importance however I do not accept your order. We are not coming to you at any cost because you have broken the pact between us. All our slaves have escaped and passed to your side and you have given the order to free them. We are not happy about this action. According to our law, we can put our slaves in prison and subject them to forced labour. For the Prophet and for all Saints, we are very good Muslims. The government has its law and we have ours; we do not accept any law other than our own. Our law is the law of Allah and the Prophet; we are not like other people, you have never seen our people being recruited as Gogles, none of our women came to your side. Now, if you send back all our slaves, both those who joined you earlier and those who came to you at later stage, escorted by 30 or 40 Gogles, and you do all that we are requesting, it is fine. If you do not do that, we are not coming to you as you have requested of us in your letter. We respect all Muslims and the government, but not those who are at war with us. You know the nature of your subjects. Why did you do this to our slaves? If you need tranquillity among your subjects, do us this favour, otherwise you will be held responsible for what happens. If you came to our land to engage in war, we will try to fight back by all means in the same way we fought against the Dervishes. Allah said 'A small group can fight and overcome a bigger group'. The world is about to end, there are only 58 years remaining before its end. We do not want to stay in the world, it is better to die within

18 Ibid., p. 26.

our Islamic law. All Muslims are one compact body.

Signed:
Sheikh Haji Hassan Barsane,
Date: Shaban 5 (March 12, 1924)"[19]

The style and substance of the letter are in stark contrast with the character of the nationalist, anti-colonialist struggle attributed to this clergyman in the Seventies by the Somali military regime. The Sheikh sounded more concerned about the loss of his slaves than troubled by any other considerations. He claimed the right to exploit and dehumanize other human beings born free like him in the name of his religion. Sheikh Hassan Sheikh Nour 'Barsane' was captured and sentenced by the Regional Tribunal of Webi Shabelle to thirty years' imprisonment: the sentence was not entirely served because of Barsane's sudden death from malaria on January 28, 1927 in Mogadisho central prison.[20]

By October 1925, Obbia was occupied and transformed "from a Sultanate into and administrative region with residencies at Obbia, Galkayo, El-Bur and Ilig."[21] It should be noted that the 'peaceful penetration' theory announced by the Italian authorities was, in most cases, far from being peaceful, and in fact was often carried out with the use of military force; this escalated with the arrival of Governor De Vecchi in 1923.[22]

De Vecchi's armies swept through central Somalia overcoming resistance, and finally also vanquishing the forces of Sultan Osman Mohamoud, who had resisted all previous attacks. In November 1927 the formal act of surrender took place in Hurdia, and Bogor Osman dramatically consigned his sword to Governor De Vecchi[23]. With the elimination of the Northeastern sultanates, Somalis became subjects of a state system under the Italian flag and the country was 'united' to become a political entity known as the 'Somalia Italiana' colony. It would continue as such until 1941, when the colony was taken by British forces.

For the first time in its history, through Italian military and political power, Somalia was united into a single society, with a vast territory stretching from the Juba River to the approach of the Gulf of Aden—communities formerly

19 Ibid., p. 27.
20 Ibid., p. 39.
21 Ibid., p. 153.
22 Ibid., p. 89.
23 Bogor Osman was later exiled to Mogadisho.

divided by geographical barriers.[24]

24 Law no. 1587 of July 14, 1926: the colony, incorporating all the territory from Oltre Giuba (Trans-Juba) to Majertenia, took the denomination of 'Somalia Italiana'.

PART ONE

BRITISH MILITARY OCCUPATION

Chapter I

AN UNCERTAIN FUTURE

The Italian African Empire expanded in 1940, during the Second World War, as Mussolini's forces initially pushed the British out of Somaliland. But the Italian victory was short-lived: the British recovered their losses in the field very quickly, reconquered their colony, and then went on to force the Italians out of Somalia, Ethiopia and Eritrea by November 1941. In the same period, the Italians were forced to withdraw from Libya as allied forces swept across North Africa, effectively ending the era of Italian colonization.[1]

Following Italy's defeat in the Second World War, all the former Italian colonies of Somalia, Libya, Eritrea, in addition to the Ogadenia Reserved Area & Haud and to the British Protectorate of Somaliland, fell under British military occupation. Libya and Eritrea were placed under the administrative control of the Middle East Command, based in Cairo, Egypt. Italian Somaliland and the other territories inhabited by ethnic Somalis were placed under the Command of East Africa, based in Nairobi, Kenya: this was known as Occupied Enemy Territories Administration (OETA).

The administration's name was slightly changed in 1942, with the removal of any references to 'enmity', and became the Occupied Territory Administration

1 Scott Rhymer, *The Reluctant Imperialist: Italian Colonization in Somalia,* Kindle edition 2005, p. 104.

(OTA). The name was changed again to British Military Administration (BMA), and, finally, on the eve of placing the territory under trusteeship regime, to British Administration of Somalia (BAS). During this period, the administration was under the responsibility of the War Office and not the Colonial Office.[2]

The British introduced new administrative structures to the territory, which was divided into four Provinces, two fewer than the pre-war number. The territories were:

1. Majertenia, which included the districts of Bender Kassim, Alula, Gardo and Iskushuban.
2. Mudug, which included the districts of Galkayo and El-Bur.
3. Upper Juba, which included the districts of Baidoa, Lugh Ferrandi, Bardera, Oddur and Beledweyne.
4. Benadir, which included the districts of Mogadisho, Afgooye, Merca, Brava, Margherita (Jamama) and Kismayo.

This administrative set-up operated by the British was dictated by and wholly contingent upon military considerations, and did not take into account any of the real political needs or the ethnic and economic nature of any of the populations concerned.[3]

The main concern of the British colonial authority throughout its stewardship of the territory was to maintain strict control of the security situation of the territory – often acting quickly in the mobilization of its forces to deal with armed irregular elements, former Italian servicemen who regularly raided local population areas. Consequently, a gendarmerie force was established after the Italian police force in Mogadisho was disbanded on 16 April 1941.[4]

The top priority accorded to the security question is highlighted by the sheer numbers involved in the gendarmerie force. In fact, by the end of 1943 the Somali Gendarmerie Force consisted of 3,070 Somali and African elements, 120 British officers, some 200 riding and pack camels, 250 horses and mules and a fleet of armoured lorries[5]. Hundreds of trained British gendarmes were unleashed and empowered to capture herds of animals during their patrols or enforcement of

2 Giampaolo Calchi Novati, *Il Corno d' Africa nella storia e nella politica: Etiopia, Somalia ed Eritrea fra nazionalismi, sottosviluppo e guerra*, Sei, Torino1995, p. 90.

3 ASCM 32/9: Ripartizione politico-amministrativa, criteri generali.

4 Lord Rennel of Rodd, British Military Administration of Occupied Territories in Africa During the Years 1941-1947, London H.M. Stationery, 1948, p. 153.

5 ibid., p. 15

law and order, irrespective of whether the owners were in possession of illegal arms or were unarmed poor herdsmen with no association with the disbanded Italian troops.

Collective punishments included such acts as the picketing of the wells where animals would be brought for watering – increasing the chances of seizure of large numbers of animals. By the end of August, 1941, 14,000 Italian rifles and 6,000,000 rounds of ammunitions were collected[6]. Once the camels were collected, they remained in the hands of British forces, secured in an enclosure constructed predominantly of thorns and released only after weapons had been handed in. It is scarcely surprising that, in the process, a number of camels would die in captivity from disease and lack of care, within sight of powerless herdsmen. The practice of keeping the raided camels corralled near a watering hole was known as 'geel ood', meaning camel enclosure.[7]

It is reported that during one of these indiscriminate disarmament campaigns, carried out between December 1944 and April 1945, an estimated 26,000 camels were seized in Ogaden alone and later released in exchange for 1,505 rifles, 202 hand grenades and some 86,000 rounds of ammunition[8]. The Gendarmerie responsible for these heinous acts, under British Commander Colonel R. H. Smith, later Brigadier and Chief Administrator of the former Italian colony, was viewed by the local population with utter contempt and distrust.

Collective punishments were also imposed on innocent villagers under a proclamation issued in 1943 which read: "A Senior political Officer may impose fines on all or any of the inhabitants of a village, area, or district or member of any tribe, sub-tribe, clan or community after due enquiry if he is satisfied that they or any of them have been engaged in any tribal fight, brawl, riots or affray resulting in the wounding or death of any person." [9]

The harsh methods used by the British Colonial Authority prompted Abdulkadir Sakawaddiin to address, in 1946, an open letter to the British Minister of Foreign Affairs, Mr Clement Attlee, in which he vigorously protested against the methods used by the British—especially the collective punishments, which, he wrote, were reminiscent of the previous fascist regime. The costly military operation embarked upon by the colonial authority meant there were little or no

6 ibid., p. 152

7 Barnes, Cedric, '*The Somali Youth League, Ethiopian Somalis and the Greater Somalia Idea, c. 1946-1948*', Journal of Eastern African Studies vol.1, No 2, 2007, p. 9.

8 ibid.

9 TNA WO 230/118, Article 6 of Proclamation n. 6 1943.

funds available for economic and social development, leaving the population not only under constant terror, but suffering severe deprivation.

Pre-war administrative structures on the territory established by Italy were instead based on accords concluded with the different ethnic groups, taking into account ethnic affinity and tradition as well as economic and social considerations. In 1931, the territory was divided into the following 6 regions, with the capital in Mogadisho:

1. Regione Migiurtinia and Nogal which included the 'residenze' of Dante (Hafun), Alula, Bender Kassim, Vice Residenze Candala and Eyl;
2. Regione del Mudugh which included the 'residenze' of Rocco Littoria (Galkayo), Obbia and Elbur.
3. Regione dell'Alto Scebeli which included the 'residenze' of Bulobarde (capital of the province), Beledweyne, Villabruzzi, Balad, Itala (Cadale) and Meregh.
4. Regione del Basso Scebeli, 'residenze' Merca, Afgoi, Awdheegle, Vittorio d'Africa (Shalambood) and Brava.
5. Territorio di Mogadiscio
6. Regione dell'Alto Giuba which included the 'residenze' of Oddur, Baidoa, Lugh Ferrandi, Bur Acaba and Dinsor.
7. Regione del Basso Juba which included the 'residenze' of Kismayo, Jilib, Bardera and Afmedu.[10]

Somalia under two flags

I have borrowed this title from Antonia Bullotta's famous book entitled "Somalia sotto due bandiere". According to British propaganda of the time, British troops in Somalia were presented as a force of liberation from the fascist occupation. However, after the euphoria of the first few months, the Somali had to come to terms with a different reality.

The first proclamation issued by the chief military administrator, Gen. Alan Cunningham, reads as follows: "The powers to be exercised under my authority by the military authorities are intended to supplant and not to supersede the civilian Administration, meaning the pre-existing Italian Civil Administration, and law courts, municipalities, councils and civil officials are hereby requested

10 ASCM, 32/9, Organizzazione Civile 1935-36.

to continue the punctual discharge of their respective duties until otherwise ordered." [11]

British military officials, because of a lack of adequate numbers of experienced personnel and financial resources, had to rely upon the services of many experienced Italian civil servants. "A ridiculously small band of civil affairs officials, many of whom had no previous colonial experience, had arrived in Somalia to deal with the chaos left behind by the fighting", comments Lewis[12] . Scores of Italian civil officials, who had served under the defunct fascist regime in Somalia, were thus hired through a careful selection process. Individuals deemed not to be a security risk were included in the system, while those seen as suspicious were either interned or evacuated to Italy. "The Italian laws have, in general, been respected and great care taken to preserve the fiscal structure to the fullest extent possible. The Mogadisho Municipality has functioned throughout as an Italian department under a 'Commissario Straordinario' appointed under Italian law."[13] The policy was to arrest all Italians who, by their actions, had engendered suspicion or were likely to be at the centre of hostile influence in the event of Japanese activities in the Western Indian Ocean. Rennel gives a total of 140 Italians interned in 1942.[14]

In general, the BMA retained the Italian administrative system wherever possible; the changes introduced were few and concerned personnel and method of administration. Ordinary Somalis did not feel a great difference between the Italians and the British who had replaced them, despite the wartime propaganda of the Allies who portrayed themselves as 'liberators'.

Both the Italians and the British were seen by the local people as gaalo, a Somali term for people of European descent. The Somalis were mindful of the injustice perpetrated by the Italians, especially in imposing forced labour for the benefit of the Italian settlers engaged in agriculture. But neither has the Somali public as a whole ever shown excessive sympathy for the British, as one writer seems to argue[15]. Bitter memories of the brutal methods used by the Gendarmerie under British command, and of the havoc they wreaked by looting and raiding the nomads' herds, still lingered in the minds of many Somalis who

11 TNA WO 230/4, Proclamation n.1 under British Military Government, 1941.

12 I.M. Lewis, *A Modern History of the Somali Nation and State in the Horn of Africa*, James Curry 2002, p. 117.

13 TNA FO 1015/149.Report dated Nov.25, 1946 'An appreciation of the mechanism and probable course of self-determination in Somalia'.

14 Rennel, op. cit., p. 158.

15 I.M. Lewis, op. cit., p. 120.

suffered as a consequence.

This situation created confusion in the Somali psyche. The racial laws, introduced in the first instance by the Italians, had been allowed to remain in place. "In Mogadisho, bars and restaurants reserved only for Europeans are not serving natives", comments Antonia Bullotta[16]. The gravity of the British authorities doing nothing to change anachronistic practices resulted in a number of unsavoury incidents—one involving a group of Somalis, most of them youngsters, invading Italian bars and restaurants in Mogadisho and leading to an angry reaction by the Italian owners, and another the Vice President of the Somali Youth League, (SYL) who attempted to take a seat in the front part of a bus operated by a transport company called CITAO (Compagnia Italiana Trasporti Africa Orientale). The company usually reserved seats at the front of its buses for Europeans, relegating non-Europeans to the crammed back seats. The Italian driver refused to drive on as long as a Somali remained in the front section[17]. In January 1950, a few months before Italy took over the administration of the Trust Territory, a group of Somalis were refused service by the Italian proprietor of a local Hotel in Merca, on specious excuses, although Italians were being served. When the Somalis complained to the District Commissioner, the owner of the Hotel applied for permit to change the hotel into a 'fishing and sailing club', thereby keeping out all Somalis[18]. This was certainly an indication that after several years of colonial service some Italians were finding it difficult to adapt to the changed political circumstances.

There were two racial laws: (a) Law no. 1728 of 17 November 1938, which outlawed marriage between Italian nationals of Aryan race with persons of different race, and (b) Law no. 822 of 13 May 1940, which outlawed the recognition of mixed-race children as natural children by the Italian parent. However, although the fascists ordered strict racial segregation and non-fraternization, this policy was never aggressively enforced. The Italian soldiers and officers formed friendships and romantic liaisons and had children with Somalis—these relationships survived the occupation.

As Hess puts it, "In Somalia there were too few Italians to spread an official racist doctrine."[19] Another author adds: "There were naturally many Italian

16 Antonia Bullotta, *La Somalia sotto due bandiere*, Garzanti, 1949, pp. 135-138.

17 TNA FO 1015/140, Somalia political report no.2, dated May 24, 1947.

18 TNA CO 537/5930, telegram no. 10 from Chief Administrator Brigadier Gamble to the FO, January 20, 1950.

19 Hess, op. cit., pp. 188-189.

officials who, while paying lip service to the bombast of fascism, carried their administrative duties conscientiously and well. And between not a few Somalis and Italians there were frequently bonds of friendship and respect, at least as deep as those between Somalis and expatriate officials in the other Somali territories."[20] The two racial laws were later abrogated under Law no. 25 of 20 January 1944 and under Decree no. 1096 of 3 August 1947 respectively.[21]

From the economic point of view, the territory was plunged into such economic hardship as had never been experienced in pre-war time. As we have seen, in the years immediately after the war, coinciding with British military occupation, much attention was given to the maintenance of the territory's security, leaving other aspect of the population's life unattended. In particular, the British gave little attention to promoting the great economic potential of southern Somalia, preferring instead to wait and see how the turn of events would determine the future status of the territories captured from Italy.

Agriculture, long touted as the cornerstone of Somalia's guarantee of food security, had not been developed to any real extent. Predictably, this brought misery and deprivation to many local communities. A report of the United Nations in 1950 found that three quarters of the cultivated lands were abandoned, farms had lost most of their mechanized agricultural tools, and the irrigation system had become useless through lack of maintenance. To Italy, therefore, Somalia was an economic liability. The justification for holding on to the territory before the war was primarily strategic, inasmuch as Italy had long nourished the ambition of conquering Ethiopia whenever an opportunity would present itself. The invasion was finally ordered in 1935 by the fascist regime.

At the outbreak of the war, there were a number of industrial enterprises, mainly in the transport and building sectors, as well as light industrial companies processing local produce. The Italians introduced public utilities and amenities to the towns, built roads, introduced medical and veterinary services and set an example of modern methods of farming. They also established some relatively modest public services organizations for the supply of clean drinking water, and provided health and education services.

The British Administration, in view of the temporary nature of its occupation and in accordance with the regulations governing occupied territories contained in the 1907 Hague Convention, practised a policy of care and maintenance.

20 I.M. Lewis, op. cit., p. 12.

21 Notes submitted by the Committee representing the Italian Community in Somalia, headed by Barone Beritelli, to the Four Power Commission on 9 February 1948, p. 242.

This meant that long-term programmes could not be initiated and that the Administration limited itself to dealing with the immediate requirements of the Trusteeship and with any problems relating to the security of the territory.[22]

Furthermore the British Administration had a number of existing small industrial plants demolished or transferred out of strategic locations, thus removing vital infrastructure. In 1943 an assortment of machinery, including electric generating plants, lighters and cables etc, was dismantled and removed from the elaborate salt works at Dante (Hafun) for military use and employment in other theatres of war.[23]

The salt deposits of Hafun (Majertenia) were producing more than 200,000 tons annually, most of which was exported to the Far East[24]. The industrial plants demolished or closed down were the Majayahan and Kandala mining quarries[25]. Other infrastructure removed included the 70 miles of narrow gauge railway track linking Mogadisho, Afgooye and Villaggio Duca degli Abruzzi, the Afgooye Bridge on the Webi Shabelle River, the oil storage plant and oil seed crushing plant in Mogadisho. Predictably, these drastic measures produced adverse effects on the Territory's economy and its populations – especially those who, directly or indirectly, were beneficiaries of this most vital means of production and the service industry it supported. The economic structure built by the Italians before the war was degraded over time and destined to collapse with disastrous consequences.

The deteriorating economic situation hit hard at both the Somalis and the Italian community in Somalia, in equal measure. As the latter were the biggest employer of the majority of Somali wage earners, unemployment, particularly within the Somali population, was inevitable. Several workers lost their jobs and most of them remained unemployed during British military occupation. The Protectorate of Somaliland was in a worse economic situation than Somalia under occupation: in contrast to the Italian colony, British Somaliland remained a neglected backwater, Britain having used its colony as little more than a supplier of meat products to Aden. An apt comment from Bullotta on Britain's approach to its colonies and dependencies is that "The colonies always represented for Great Britain only an object to exploit."[26]

---

22 Report of the Four Power Commission of Investigation for Former Italian Colonies, vol. III, pp. 7-40.

23 Rennel, op. cit., p. 170.

24 Hess, op. cit., p. 168.

25 Report of the Four Power Commission of Investigation for Former Italian Colonies, vol. III, pp. 7-40.

26 Bullotta, op. cit., p. 104

Establishing a comparison between the degree of development achieved in the territories inhabited by Somalis, I.M. Lewis wrote: "...Whatever their motives, and notwithstanding the impress of Fascism, decidedly more of benefit to Somalis had been created in Somalia than in British Somaliland, French Somaliland, or, above all, in the northern province of Kenya which for long was destined to remain a stagnant back-water."[27]

The picture of a serious economic situation in the former Italian colony found further confirmation in official colonial documents. Brigadier Scott-Fox, for instance, in one of his reports concludes: "Life was perhaps easier and the means of living more plentiful than they are today."[28] Severe shortages prompted rationing of food and other basic necessities throughout Somalia in some years during the British Military Administration. "People had to queue up for long hours inside barbed wire corridors created in the middle of the Suuk", comments Salah Mohamed[29].

The notion that, as I. M. Lewis wrote, the Somalis had a positive liking for the British and hatred for the Italians should be viewed with skepticism[30]. In reality, the majority of Somalis, already disoriented by the destruction caused by a war not of their making, viewed the British, with their strong military presence in Somalia, composed of Kikuyu, Tanganyikans, Ugandans, Nyassalanders etc, as new colonial rulers: in other words, gaalo replacing other gaalo.

The Somalis were and are mindful of how repeatedly Britain frustrated their aspirations for unification by transferring Haud and Ogadenia to Ethiopia before going even further and unilaterally tracing a new frontier, the so-called provisional administration line, with Ethiopia, shortly before Italy took over the administration of the Trust Territory under UN Trusteeship in 1950. Yet, to do the British justice, the Somalis did receive encouragement to first set up cultural clubs and then to organize themselves into political organizations, a fact that Aden Abdulla, future President of the Somali Republic, eloquently used to embarrass Giuseppe Brusasca, the Italian Undersecretary for Foreign Affairs, who was visiting Somalia in 1950, stating: "The British gave us freedom of expression, freedom to establish political parties, freedom to work for the future of our country, rights the Italians denied to the people."[31]

27 I.M. Lewis, op. cit., p. 112.

28 TNA FO 1015/149 Report dated November 25, 1946'The appreciation of the mechanism and probable course of self-determination in Somalia.

29 Salah Mohamed Ali, *Huddur and History of Southern Somalia*, Nahda Bookshop Publisher 2005, p. 173.

30 I.M. Lewis, op. cit., p. 120.

31 Angelo Del Boca, *Gli italiani in Africa Orientale, nostalgia delle colonie,* Arnoldo Mondadori Editore,

The emergence of political parties

In the wake of the defeat of the Italian fascist regime, the Somalis were unexpectedly ushered into a new era of political consciousness as they had never experienced in the past. They had actively witnessed and taken part in the devastating war between two European colonial powers. Italy, whilst initially having the upper hand in the armed conflict in the Horn of Africa, had lost out to Britain in the end. Like many other Africans involved in a war which was not theirs, the Somalis derived from exposure to the conflict's dynamics a dramatic and lasting psychological effects: a sort of eye-opener which left them with the conviction that their European rulers were not invincible, but weak and vulnerable, like any other human being.

Through the powerful British propaganda tools, the Somalis were aware of the establishment of the United Nations in 1945 and of its programme calling for the independence of peoples under colonial rule. "In Somalia, a striking feature of 1946 was the rapid growth of political consciousness amongst the Somalis, which was particularly manifest in the swift expansion and development of native clubs."[32]

Political movements and any associations having nationalistic connotations or aspirations were banned during the long Italian colonial administration. The only associations permitted to operate in the colony were those of a religious tendency. The Italians were very careful not to antagonize the locals. No political parties existed in Somalia other than the Fascist Party to which only Italians were associated. Nor was there any evidence of the emergence of political groups comparable to those found in British or French Africa. "Political life, such as it was", comments Hess, "existed on two separate levels, the Somali tribal and the Italian administration."[33]

The British Military Administration (BMA) favoured free expression of political opinion in the territory, subject only to certain safeguards to ensure the preservation of law and order. The activities of the parties were regulated under a BMA proclamation, the primary purpose of which was to establish adequate control over these associations during the period of military administration.[34]

Milano 2001, p. 224.

32 TNA CO 537/3641, note on native societies in the Somaliland from Junior Commander I. Myer to I.D. Robertson, Esq., Colonial Office, July 9, 1947

33 Hess, op. cit., p. 182

34 Proclamation n. 4 of 1948

The proclamation required any group wishing to establish itself as an organization to obtain the consent of the district civil affairs officer. His consent was also required in order to organize processions and gatherings, to issue orders to the population, publish any notices or collect any subscriptions other than those provided for in the by-laws. Propaganda for or against any other organization or part of the population, which might create public alarm or lead to a breach of the peace, was prohibited. To quote a British report: "The Policy of the British Military Administration was to guide the clubs as far as possible and to assist their growth along healthy lines rather than repress them and thus drive them 'underground'."[35]

Numerous clubs and societies sprung up during the BMA's lifespan, most of them, though ostensibly standing as social clubs, had political aims. Cedric Barnes explains the awakening of Somali political consciousness in these words: "The reason for this rapid expansion and radicalization was a conjuncture of several factors, but it is most immediately attributable to the international deliberations over the future of the Italian East African Empire."[36]

The associations or clubs that existed before 1947 were more social and charitable than political in character. The parties began to multiply and design political programmes in an effort to prove to the Four Powers Commission that each of them represented the will of the majority. The activities of the political movements were, however, confined to the urban areas, outside of which, as might be expected, there was little interest in political parties.

Of the numerous political movements which came into existence shortly before the Four Powers' mission to Somalia, only two, the Lega dei Giovani Somali and the Hizbia Dighil Mirifle, reached a high level of political development and had a clear political agenda on how to run the territory after independence. The Lega represented the interests of the nomadic population, and the Hizbia represented the agro-pastoralists in the southern regions of the Trust Territory. The remaining parties were small, basically splinter groups of the two main parties, designed only to run in the electoral contest and not worth considering as political parties.

Towards the end of the British occupation of Somalia, an application to form an Islamic party called Somali Muslim League was submitted to the colonial authorities. The application came from certain Barvanese and Ashraf elements

35 TNA CO 537/3641, memorandum on Native Clubs in Somalia, date 27June,. 1947.

36 Barnes, op. cit.,

who, according to British sources, did not seem to have general Muslim support in Somalia, and there was no proof of a connection with the Muslim League in other countries. On these grounds and for this reason, it was considered that the government had insufficient time in which to make such an important decision.[37]

The Somali Youth Club

As we have seen, the impact of a national idea on a people in the throes of violent social changes brought about by war produced the first beginnings of a Somali awakening and a Somali national movement aimed at the creation of an independent State. The first modern Somali social organization, the Somali Youth Club (SYC), was founded in Mogadisho on May 15, 1943, but did not really become active until early 1946 when its membership began to increase.[38] In the beginning, the SYC was primarily actively engaged in promoting social and welfare education and health programmes, targeting particularly the less privileged segments among its affiliates. However, it would be wrong to believe that the promotion of the social welfare of members of the Club could entirely be divorced from political matters.

To help improve the new club, the British allowed the better educated police and civil servants to join, thus relaxing Britain's traditional policy of separating the civil service from political parties "because the new movement was progressive, co-operated with the government, and was anti-Italian."[39] The SYC expanded rapidly and began to open offices not only in the British Protectorate of Somaliland, but also in Ethiopia's Ogaden.

Two differing narratives explain the genesis of the Club. One explanation suggests that in early 1943, when the Italian community in Somalia was permitted to organize political associations, a host of Italian organizations of varying ideologies sprang up with a view to challenge British rule, and agitate, sometimes violently, for the return of the colony to Italy. Faced with growing Italian political pressure inimical to continued British tenure, British colonial officials encouraged the Somalis to organize politically.[40] Solid evidence of active encouragement given to the Lega by the British Military Administration can be found in the speech made by Chief Administrator Brigadier Wikham at the anniversary celebrations of the party on May 21, 1947: "The development and expansion of the Somali

37 TNA WO 230/291 Handover note undated by the Political Secretariat.
38 TNA CO 537/3641 memorandum on Native Clubs in Somalia.
39 I.M. Lewis, op. cit., p. 122.
40 Ibid., p. 121

Youth League during the past four years has been a very remarkable achievement and reflects the greatest credit not only on those who have organized it, but on the larger numbers of Somalis who are ready to devote their money and services to the improvement of the conditions of their countrymen.[41] The aims you have expressed today and which are embodied in your constitution, are worthy of the highest praise, and you may be confident that during the short time which remains to them, the British Military Administration will afford all possible co-operation to attaining them."[42]

The movement spread like wildfire and became very powerful in areas as far apart as Ogaden and British Somaliland. Paradoxically, however, whilst the British administration in Somalia was favourably disposed towards the Lega, the Kenyan colonial authorities proscribed the Kipsingis Central Association and the Garissa branch of the Lega dei Giovani Somali throughout the country on July 13, 1948, deeming them "dangerous to the good of government of the Colony." On June 4, 1948, the Garissa branch of the Lega was declared to be an unlawful society by the Governor;[43] consequently, leaders of the party were exiled to the Turkana Province and not released until 1960.[44]

The second explanation of how the Lega came about, which received wide currency, indicates that the idea of establishing the Lega itself was the brainchild of a group of 13 little-known young urban Somalis. Somali historians place great importance on the date of 15 May 1943, the day when these 13 young Somalis came together, in a small one-room office in Via Cardinale Massaia in Mogadisho, and founded a club they called Somali Youth Club (SYC). The 13 youngsters have since been remembered as the precursors of the Somali independence movement. The group included elements representing the main Somali clans.

There is no consensus among Somalis regarding which person in the group should be considered to have provided the main inspiration. Controversy over this very much debated issue seems to be fuelled by factionalism and devoid of any objectivity. Some maintain that much of the inspiration came from Yassin Haji Osman Sharmarke, the most erudite element in the group by Somali standards of the time. However, this notion is strongly contested by others who attribute credit to Abdulkadir Sakawa-din and Haji Mohamed Hussein, both prominent

41 Report of the Four Powers Commission of Investigation, ch. 5, app. B.

42 Somalia Courier, May 21, 1948.

43 East African Standard, July 1948.

44 A.A. Castagno, '*The Somali-Kenyan controversy: implication for the future*', Journal of Modern African Studies, vol. 2, no. 2, July 1964, p. 174; Ogenga Otunnu, 'Factors affecting the treatment of Kenyan-Somalis and Somali refugees in Kenya: a historical overview, Refugee, vol. 12, no. 5, Nov- Dec 1992, p. 21.

religious figures of ethnic Benadir. Yassin was an ethnic Majerten who served the Italian colonial administration as a clerk. He received a modest level of education at the 'Scuola per figli di capi', a special school for children of Somali paramount chiefs during the fascist regime.[45] Though lacking formal education, he was nevertheless a brilliant man, with sound political awareness. To implement his ideas, he needed two things: a vibrant membership of the Club and a programme which could be incorporated in a statute. He had no difficulty in co-opting 12 persons, selected at random and including his own brother, Dahir Haji Osman 'Dhega-weyne', to become the Club's first members, representing the broader spectrum of Somali clan families. In Somalia, tribalism must be at the heart of everything, and Yassin was well aware of this reality, which he found hard to ignore. The majority of the co-opted members were semi-literate; they earned their livelihood doing menial jobs as shopkeepers, office cleaners, gate-keepers, interpreters etc, and none of them had ever been outside Somalia or come into contact with Western culture and civilization. As for the second requirement, it is widely believed, although there is no hard evidence, that Yassin received benevolent support from little known Italian communist elements in Mogadisho in drawing up the Statute of the Club.

Abdulkadir Sheikh Sakawa-din, grandson of the much venerated religious leader, Sheikh Aweys Al-Qadiria, was elected President of the SYC; Dahir Haji Osman Sharmarke was nominated as its Secretary and Mohamed Hersi Nour and Mohamed Osman were members. The following anecdote, perhaps, best illustrates the low degree of political maturity of the members of the Club. It is said that, when Yassin proposed the establishment of the Club, the term 'Club' itself raised confusion in the minds of some members he approached because of the similarity in pronunciation of Club to 'Kilab' – the Arabic for 'dogs'. Realizing the embarrassment he had created in the minds of his colleagues, Yassin dropped the use of the word 'club' in favour of the more familiar Arabic term 'nadi', widely used in British Somaliland.[46]

The Club's constitution did not refer clearly to the political future of the country. The Club's political aims were limited to two objectives : firstly, to unite all Somalis, particularly the youth, by eradicating harmful prejudices likely to lead to and frequently cause communal and tribal frictions; and secondly, to educate the youth in modern ideas and civilization through cultural circles and through

45 Bullotta, op. cit., p. 101.
46 Testimony released by Mohamoud Aden Yousuf 'Muro' in Leicester, November 4, 2009.

the establishment and expansion of a formal education system based on schools.

The Club becomes a political party: its rise, decline and fall

In April 1947, the Club became a fully-fledged political party; its name was changed from Somali Youth Club (SYC) to Somali Youth League (SYL). In spite of the adoption of a new name, people continued to refer to the League as 'Kulub', a corrupted and shortened reference to the Youth Club. The official newspaper of the time, The *Somalia Courier*, reported the momentous event in its article heralding the changes. It wrote: "On the 1st April 1947 a new era started for the Somali Youth League. In fact it may be said that childhood was over and manhood was reached. On that date the name was changed from Somali Youth Club to Somali Youth League, the latter being more suitable for the widening interests and development. The foundation date of this League is still considered to be the 15th May 1943 but the 1st April is the date that marks the renaming of the Club, the passing of a new constitution and framing of a wider programme. This will be an important date in the history of Somalia."[47]

The new party adopted two additional objectives and appended them to its amended constitution. The first was the elimination of any situation prejudicial to Somali interests and the second was the adoption of Somali as the national language, using an existing script known as 'Osmania', invented by Yassin Osman Kenadid, a Somali nationalist, in 1920, as the national script. The new party was informed that, unless it inserted the words "by constitutional and legal means" after the word "eliminate" in Article (5) (c) of the new party constitution, the Administration would have difficulty in granting approval. To ensure approval of the new constitution, this amendment was accepted.[48]

The Lega differed from the other political parties in two important aspects: firstly, it was led by the best educated elements of the time, and secondly, its financial resources came from monthly contributions from members throughout the territory.

The party had undergone structural reforms and expanded its scope and political programme; however by 1947, of the 13 founding members of the Club, only Haji Mohamed Hussein was actively engaged in the party's business. Yassin Haji did not live long enough to see the evolution of the Club into a political party – the creation of which he had greatly contributed to. The remaining 12

47 Somalia Courier, April 16, 1947
48 TNA FO 1015/140, Somalia political intelligence report no. 2, May 24, 1947

'founding fathers' did not play any significant role in the party's business, being overshadowed, as later events were to prove, by relatively better educated and more active elements who took over the control of the party.

A good number of the 13 'pioneers' had repudiated the Club before it became a fully-fledged political party in 1947. For instance, Dere Haji Dere, one of the founding members of the Club, appeared before the Four Power Commission of Investigation in January 1948 as member of the Hamar Youth Club[49]. Abdulkadir Sakawaddin, the President of the Club, had publicly denounced and repudiated the Club for reasons which remain to this date shrouded in mystery and subject to different interpretations. Some suggest that Sakawa-din was expelled from the party on grounds of alleged contacts with the Italians, the nature of which, however, has never been fully disclosed. Mohamed Awale, a Central Committee member, is reported to have informed the British Police that Sakawaddin had allegedly been coerced "at the point of a pistol" by an Italian medical doctor to sign a pro-Italian declaration, but failed to disclose the contents of the declaration[50]. However, according to British intelligence sources, Abdulkadir had repudiated his former party on the grounds of disagreements over policy: his Islamist teachings clashed with the secular policies of his colleagues. During a religious sermon he delivered at Shangani Mosque, he is reputed to have told his listeners that at its inception, the Lega had laudable aims, but that it had since resorted to violence, and for this reason he had left the party[51].

By the limited evidence available from credible sources, the allegations of betrayal levelled at Sakawaddin call for reserve. Sakawaddin was very influential in the party and was not only highly respected, but also considered a martyr by the other members of the Club.

Apart from Haji Mohamed Hussein, none of the 13 founders played any significant role in pre-independence Somali political life. With regards to the Administration Service, only Dahir Haji Osman and Ali Hassan 'Verdura' held any posts of responsibility in the civil service after independence. Dahir became a top civil servant at the Ministry of Interior and Ali became a top diplomat in the Foreign Service.

Party membership was open to any Somali over the age of 15. It would appear, however, that membership was initially open to men only; women were

49 Commission's Report, Section II, Chapter 4, app. BH3.

50 TNA FO 1015/140, Somalia political intelligence Sitrep no. 4, My 29, 1948

51 Ibid., Secret political intelligence Sitrep no.6, June 16, 1948, from the HQs of the BMA, Mogadisho, to FO.

allowed to join as members and pay subscriptions following the Party Congress of 1950.[52]

Upon joining, new members were required to take a solemn oath to abide by the objectives of the party: "I swear by Almighty God that I will not take action against any Somali. In times of trouble, I promise to help the Somali. I will become the brother of all other members. I will not reveal the name of my tribe. In matters of marriage, I will not discriminate between the Somali tribes and the Midgan, Yibir, Yahar and Tumal." Nothing is said with regard to persons of Bantu descent. Whilst no one would doubt the good intentions of the person or persons who composed these slogans, one would be incorrect in concluding from this that tribalism and personal ambition no longer flourished within the party. Combinations of good intentions and tribally divided societies have never had a happy outcome.

The structure of the party included a unit named 'Horseed' (roughly meaning 'action squad'). The organization, founded on February 7, 1947, was mainly composed of young activists, chiefly responsible for maintaining discipline at party meetings[53]. Virtually a private militia, Horseed was tasked with using any form of intimidation, including physical attacks, against their political adversaries. A British document described the SYL as 'an organization ran very much on fascist lines practising intimidation of political opponents."[54] According to testimonies released to the author, between 1948 and 1949, Horseed elements were used to prevent the opening of branches of the Unione Africani Somali party at Beledweyne by burning down its premises and harassing and physically attacking its supporters.

From available information it would seem that membership of this private militia was made up of young, male and illiterate elements, often from the Majertenia and Mudug provinces. It is said that Hirsi Oker and Hirsi Magan, the former from Muduh and the latter from Majertenia, were known members of the notorious unit. Hirsi Magan is the father of Ms Ayan Hirsi, the Somali-born former Dutch parliamentarian who became a celebrity in her campaign for the liberation of Muslim women from the shackles imposed on them by their menfolk.[55]

Horseed and other elements generally affiliated with the Lega were mostly

52 TNA FO 1915/509 British Administration of Somalia, monthly intelligence report for January 1950.

53 Article 52 of the Statute of the Party.

54 TNA FO 1015/51 Memorandum, with no date, on SYL with particular reference to Mogadisho riots.

55 Ayan is the author of a book entitled Infidel, Ayaan Hirsi Ali. My Life (The Free Press, 2007).

quartered in Iskuraran, an overcrowded, poor neighbourhood situated in the centre of Mogadisho, separated from the modern and residential areas of the city, which were reserved for Europeans. Iskuraran was demolished under a clean-up scheme by the military regime in the Seventies. After independence, many members, disappointed and frustrated by the lack of any reward for the services they had rendered to the party, ended up in oblivion, or joined opposition parties in search of new adventures.

A word may be said about the much debated notion of whether there had been any communist influence on the Lega. It stands on record that a section of the Italian Communist Party, known as 'Partito Comunista', existed legally in Somalia in 1948. According to British reports, it functioned privately with a very limited number of sympathizers, in tandem with scores of other small Italian political parties[56]. This was further confirmed by a public notice reported by the *Somalia Courier* informing the public of a merger between two factions within the same party: the Mogadisho faction and the 'Gruppo Comunista A. Gramsci' faction.[57]

There were many indications supporting the notion that the Italian Communist Party had some influence on the newly established Somali Youth Club (SYC). Firstly, the original flag of the Club with its hammer and sickle was a true copy of the standard of the Italian Communist Party. As a result, British colonial authorities in 1944 withdrew their approval for the Club and authorization for its activities on the grounds of the latter's perceived communist tendencies. To avoid further restrictions and trouble with the authorities, the Club changed its standard. "Since then, the Club is not as it used to be, no more closed fists and no more red flags," comments Del Boca[58]. Secondly, the constitution of the Club was written in Italian, and was believed to have been drafted for the Club by an Italian who may have been one of the local lawyers[59]. Other sources also indicate close contacts between Yassin Haji Osman and a group of 27 Italian communist elements in Mogadisho[60].

The Lega, as an organization, was probably never a communist-oriented party, but at times, as a reaction to the return of Italy to Somalia, voices within the party were often heard publicly advocating that the party embrace communist

56 TNA FO 371/80864 Report on Somalia covering the period from January to December 1949.
57 Somalia Courier, April 16, 1947.
58 Del Boca, op. cit., p. 171
59 TNA FO 1015/140, Somalia political intelligence report, April 10, 1947.
60 Giuliano Pajetta, 'Il cammino della Somalia', L'Unità, August 5, 1971.

ideology. British reports reveal that in January 1950, Mohamed Ahmed 'Ottavio', a member of the party's Central Committee, suggested that the party should become a communist organization. He is reputed to have said that the real reason for the Italian return to Somalia was that Western Powers feared Italy going communist[61].

Another Central Committee member, Ali Hersi Farah, is reported as stating on February 2, 1950 that "Britain's backing for the return of the Italians was due to her fear of Italy going communist and the fear that within one year, the communists would be ruling the world and the British barter plan with Italy would come to naught."[62] Abdirazak Haji Hussein, a former Prime Minister of Somalia, maintains that it would be wrong to conclude from these circumstances that Yassin Haji or any of his party fellows had embraced communist ideology. "For the young inexperienced Somalis it was merely a manifestation of sympathy to the Soviet Union's favourable attitude towards the colonial people," comments the former Prime Minister.[63]

British sources also expressed doubts that there had been any evidence of collusion between the Club and the Italian communist organization in Mogadisho[64]: "Communism had hardly touched the Somali public, at large, nor does this country provide fertile ground field for its growth. Communist activities among the native population are confined to a small clique of urban Somalis. Otherwise, communism in Somalia is so far little more than a topic of discussion in the coffee shops although a number of SYL members hold communist views", reveals a British intelligence report.[65]

By 1956 the party had begun to show signs of strain already pointing to its subsequent disarray. The antagonism and competition between the Darod and Hawiye tribes risked on more than one occasion bringing government activities to the brink of collapse. As a consequence of this state of affairs, Mussa Bogor resigned as a Minister in 1959 after a prolonged quarrel with the Prime Minister. In the central committee of the ruling party, the difficult working relations and the often violent open confrontations between Darod and Hawiye elements

61 TNA CO 537/5930, Telegram no. 10 from Chief Administrator, Brigadier Gamble to His Majesty's Principal Secretary of State for FO, January 20, 1950.

62 TNA CO 537/5930, Telegram no. 24 from Chief Administrator Brigadier Gamble to FO, February 6, 1950.

63 Abdirazak Haji Hussein, notes written to the author, p. 2, February 2010.

64 TNA CO 537/3641, note on native societies in the Somaliland from Junior Commander I. Myer to I.D. Robertson, Esq., Colonial Office, July 9, 1948.

65 TNA FO371/75778 top secret report from British HQs Somalia to Director of Civil Affairs, War Office, London, December 6, 1948.

cast a shadow over the future of the Territory as a united entity. In his detailed diaries, Aden Abdulla convincingly describes how, day by day, the ruling party was derailing from its founding principles and the risk of the country sliding into chaos was looming ahead.

In the early Sixties, towards the end of the Trusteeship period, many historical party figures, for different and often personal reasons, started quitting the party. The first to leave was one of the founders, Haji Mohamed Hussein, followed by a score of other party leaders, the best-known being Sheikh Ali Giumale, Haji Farah Ali and Abdirazak Haji Hussein. All of them formed opposition parties as alternatives to their former party. The loss of high-profile figures was further evidence of a movement crumbling from within. The party also lost the wisdom and guidance of one of its most prestigious members, Aden Abdulla, who was elected President of the Republic. The position required him to be above the parties but he never shied away from playing the role of moderator among the feuding, power-hungry clan leaders present in the National Assembly and in the government. By 1969, as a result of changes of leadership brought about by continuing internal divisions, what remained of the old guard of the party was merely symbolic. The party had lost much of its original nationalistic zeal, values and prestige and reduced itself to a Mafia-like organization in the hands of unscrupulous elements whose main drive was the lust for power and greed for wealth.

The party's popularity had hit rock bottom and, perhaps most importantly, the Somali public at large felt enervated by the behaviour of the political class and incumbents, who through electoral manipulation and corruption were squandering the nation's economic resources for their own benefit. The party's nationalistic values were hijacked by factionalism and sectarian division within the party itself, a circumstance that unfortunately paved the way for the military to seize power. As indulgently as one may look at the fourteen years of Lega rule of the country (1956-1969), it is evident that the Lega's celebrated merits are few and very modest.

The formation of pro-Italian parties, or green parties

British liberalization policy not only brought benefits to the Lega, but also left the door open for the formation of a host of other political-cum-tribal parties which emerged in the Forties, most of them supported by Italy's powerful propaganda machinery designed to strengthen this country's claim to return to Africa. The

Italian government, through the Ministry of Italian Africa, provided funds destined to encourage the political activities of pro-Italian associations in the former colonies. These included associations such as the Istaqlal party, founded in 1948, in Libya; the Veterans' Association and the New Eritrean Pro-Italia Party in Eritrea; and the Conferenza Somala, an association of small political parties, the main components of which were veterans, ex-combatants and local chiefs demanding that Italy return to Somalia as an administering power.[66]

A handful of Italian former civil servants of the fascist regime remained in Somalia after the war. Among this small, but very active group, Vincenzo Calzia and Baron Pietro Beritelli featured prominently at the forefront of the Italian propaganda activities to counter British propaganda[67]. Following the incident of 11 January 1948, Calzia was repatriated by order of the British Military Authorities. After his expulsion from Somalia, Calzia joined the Radio Roma propaganda service, whose target audience was Somalia, in anticipation of Italy's return to its former colony. He would return to Somalia during the Italian Trusteeship Administration, serving as a territorial councillor and remaining in Somalia well after independence.

Italian propaganda also turned its attention to one of the older movements, the Patriotic Beneficence Union (PBU), also known as Jumiyah, founded in 1943. In September 1947 this movement merged with other small parties to form an umbrella organization known as 'Conferenza Somala', which advocated the return of Italy and included the Patriotic Beneficence Union, the Somali Progressive Committee, Hizbia Dighil Mirifle, the Union of Africans in Somalia, the Somali Young Abgal Association, Hidayat Islam Scidle and Mobilen.

As early as 1947, a message was addressed to the Italian community resident in the colonies informing them of steps being taken by the Italian government to return to the colonies[68]. The message sent by Giuseppe Brusasca, De Gasperi's Undersecretary for Africa, reads: "Italians must know that the old colonial system is definitely ended, and that Italy is directed to a colonial politics based on a new method towards the native population." After declaring that Italy was ready to re-administer her former colonies, Brusasca added "this administration will be held intact with its entire staff, but [...] the leadership will be re-entrusted to old

66 Antonio Morone, *'L'eredità del colonialismo per la nuova Italia'*, Vito Francesco Gironda, Michele Nani e Stefano Petrungaro (ed.), 'Imperi coloniali. Italia, Germania e la costruzione del 'mondo coloniale'', Novecento (nuova serie), 1, p. 77.

67 Bullotta, op. cit., p. 174.

68 Towards 1947, a Somali Service directed to Somalia was launched from Radio Rome to report future plans for Somalia on the part of Italy once it returned to its former colony as Administering Power..

colonialists who receive warrants from constituencies after the approval of the population. Natives may participate in the administration of the single colonies, but here too, the selection will be made among the best and most intelligent and those who are worthy of participating in the administration."[69]

The Lega reacted very strongly to the message which appeared in the Mogadisho-based Italian language newspaper Il Popolo on July 6, 1947. For the first time the party signalled publicly and unequivocally its opposition to the return of Italy to Somalia, and submitted the following statement to the Chief Administrator: "The Central Committee of the SYL openly declares that the Somalis are disposed to oppose, at any cost, repeat at any cost, the return of Italy to Somalia."[70]

After the deadly incident of January 1948 and the departure of Calzia and Baron Beritelli from Somalia, the task of leading and promoting contacts with Somali groups passed to Raimondo Manzini, the Italian Liaison Officer in Somalia. Manzini, a career diplomat, was able to capitalize on the changed political environment which resulted in the normalization of the situation in Mogadisho and establish direct contacts with Somali indigenous chiefs and with representatives of various political parties, including the Lega, notwithstanding instructions from Rome to refrain from such contacts. The Liaison Officer viewed these instructions as an obstacle that limited his manoeuvres designed to pave the way for the Italian return to Somalia. The contacts were not always easy: some tribal groups demanded a high price in exchange for their support of an Italian return. This is the case of the Sultan of Majertenia who, in a meeting with Manzini on June 12, 1948, is reported to have claimed reparation for damages his Sultanate had allegedly suffered during the war. The reparation consisted of 66,000 camels, 200,000 sheep, 3,000 cattle, 40,000 dhows, etc.[71] It would seem unlikely that British authorities did not know about these contacts. There are indeed many reasons to believe that these contacts were occurring with their tacit consent.

Contacts were also established with Olol Dinle, the highly respected Sultan of the Sciaveli, very well-known for the vital role he had played in the war with Ethiopia in 1935 to liberate Ogaden. During the Italo-Ethiopian war, Sultan Olol led a guerrilla band of some 4,000 tribesmen against Ethiopia and scored a number of considerable victories. He was personally decorated by Mussolini

69 TNA WO 230/207, Somalia political intelligence report covering the months of May and July, 1947.

70 TNA WO 230/233 Letter of July 7, 1947 from the Civil Affairs Officer, Mogadisho.

71 Telegram from Manzini to the Foreign Minister, reported in Del Boca, op.cit., p. 203.

and given the rank of colonel. A brief announcement later appeared in the newspapers suggesting that the Sultan died on 16 Shawal 1372 of the Islamic calendar while in detention in Addis Abeba.[72]

The HDM and the Conferenza parties regarded Italy as a potential protector against what they perceived as nomadic tribe hegemony represented by the Lega. This explains the roots of the deadly confrontations in 1948 between Somali elements for and against the return of the Italians. The adherents of the Conferenza included individuals who had lost gainful employment after the Second World War and suffered a sort of isolation and despair during British military occupation. They had obviously never given up hope of seeing the return of Italy, their old paymaster, to administer Somalia, which would entail the clear prospect of returning to their much-needed jobs, receiving much-needed salaries or starting a new life. The request put forward by the Conferenza bloc for an extended trusteeship period of 30 years aimed to allow the trusteeship administration sufficient time to enhance their interests and achieve the same modest level of training and experience gained by the nomadic elements during British military administration. As I.M. Lewis explains, "Many Somalis, especially the Hawiye concentrated in and around Mogadisho, tended to regard the Italians as potential allies against further Darod intrusion and pressure into their affairs." He further explains that "For the Rahanweyn, the Darod and the Hawiye were both enemies, in equal measure, to worry about. Similarly, the Dighil and Mirifle tribesmen continued to accept Italian support in an effort to enhance and safeguard their interests against those of predominantly nomadic clansmen from the North."[73]

Hizbia Dighil Mirifle (HDM): its rise, decline and fall

The Hizbia was one of the major political parties in the territory. Like the Lega, this party also went through a process of radical change – bringing it from the humble beginnings of a social club to a fully-fledged political party by 1947. In an essay on the origin of the HDM, Mohamed Haji Muktar remarks that modern political organizations in the inter-riverine area have their origin in a philanthropic movement that appeared in the 1920s under the name of Al-Jamiyyah al-Kheyriyah al Wataniyah (the National Charitable Organization)[74]. In 1947 the

72 *Corriere della Somalia*, Agosto 20, 1953.

73 I.M. Lewis, op. cit., p. 125.

74 Mohamed Haji Mukhtar, '*The Plight of the Agro-pastoral Society of Somalia*', Review of African Political Economy, 1996, p. 453.

Jamiyyah was transformed into a political party known by its tribal name, Hizbia Dighil and Mirifle (HDM), under the presidency of Sheikh Abdullahi 'Beghedi'. Its adherents mainly hailed from the area between the Shabelle and Juba rivers, an important area for agriculture and livestock.

In anticipation of the arrival of the Four Power Commission of Investigation, in 1947 the HDM joined other groups to form the Conferenza Somala, a convention of political associations advocating Italian trusteeship of the territory for a period of 30 years. It should be mentioned however that, although initially supporting the Conferenza's position in favour of Italy's return, the HDM at a later stage distanced itself from the Conferenza bloc and indicated no specific country as trustee, but remained convinced that 30 years would be needed for the Trust Territory to achieve meaningful independence.[75]

The HDM was the second most important political party in terms of its political programme and the constituency it represented. While the Lega derived its support mainly from the arid and sparsely populated northern regions of the territory, the HDM stronghold was in the fertile and agriculturally developed inter-riverine areas. Despite the high potential of these areas, however, their economic opportunities and the social advancement of their people had been neglected throughout the colonial period. The party's programme was to move the country towards total independence on the basis of a federal system. It advocated a federal parliament composed of representatives of the regions in numbers proportional to those of the population of each region, with competence over all matters relating to federal government affairs, including election of the Head of State and the Central Federal Government itself (Article 6 of the party statute). It also supported the idea of regional governments formed by the representatives elected by each region in numbers proportional to the numerical force of the electors (Article 7 of the party statute).

As mentioned earlier, the HDM had initially co-operated with the Italian administration, receiving significant Italian financial backing in its political struggle against the Lega; but soon its relations with AFIS soured and came to an end amid accusations of political manoeuvring against the party. As early as October 1951, i.e. little more than one year from the installation of the Italian administration, the HDM sent a petition to the United Nation's Trusteeship Council accusing Italy of "not showing any convincing programme as to her promises to promote the progress and well-being of the Somali people

75 Report on the Italian Somaliland, Section I, ch. 4, p. 20.

until independence is achieved."[76] The rupture between the party and AFIS is confirmed by a police report referring to a statement made by Abdinour Mohamed Hussein, the leader of the HDM, at a rally held at Afgooye, according to which "the Italians were foreigners in Somalia, and as such, it was necessary to stop asking them for money and awards."[77] By 1954 all the parties risen from the ashes of the Conferenza bloc had redefined their relations with Italy, moving from the patronage system of Forties colonialist propaganda to a more autonomous attitude towards the former motherland."[78]

In the first legislative election in 1956, the party gained 13 seats in the National Assembly, the largest number of seats held by any single party on the opposition benches[79]. Following a law passed by the Legislative Assembly in 1958, making it illegal for political parties to bear tribal names, the party was forced to change its name, but not its political programme[80]. The party, however, found an ingenious way to circumvent the prohibition by changing its name to 'Hizbia Destur Mustaqil Somali' (Somali Independent Constitutional Party) while preserving the acronym HDM and its tribal affiliation.

Ironically, the banning of political parties bearing tribal denominations in Somalia contrasted sharply with the tribally based Somali political system. The daunting task of abolishing tribalism in Somalia required more than just a declaration of good intent; but it seems that the government gave more attention to symbolism rather than substance. Both Abdullahi Issa, who was Prime Minister at the time, and his party fellows lived long enough to realize how unrealistic it was to expect to root out tribalism, a centuries-old institution, in one fell swoop.

Bickering and personal antagonism within the ranks of the party had engendered a lasting split during the run-up to the 1959 general elections. While the party had officially decided to boycott the elections on the grounds of perceived intimidation and violence by supporters of the ruling party allegedly acting under the orders of the government, some HDMS elements, including a former president, a former vice-president and a former secretary general, pursuing personal interests, stood for election on the Lega ticket. Consequently, on winning the elections, the new Lega-led government appointed the former

76 T/PET. 11/109 1 -).

77 Secret Carabinieri report n.64/RP dated August, 1954, reported in Morone, L'ultima colonia, come l'Italia è tornata in Africa,1950-1960, Laterza & Figli, 2011, p. 91.

78 A. Morone, op. cit., p. 91.

79 I.M. Lewis, *'Modern Political Movements in Somalia I'*, Journal of the International African Institute, vol.28, no. 3 (July 1958), pp. 244-261.

80 Article 15 of 1958 Law no. 26 on political elections.

vice-president of the HDMS, Abdinour Mohamed Hussein, to the post of Minister of General Affairs in 1959 (and in 1960, to the post of Minister of Public Works and Communications); whilst the former secretary-general of the party, Abdulkadir Mohamed Aden 'Zoppo', was elected vice-president of the Legislative Assembly. For a long time, the HDMS represented a real opposition party in Parliament. In the second legislative election of 1959, the party gained 5 seats, all concentrated in the Upper Juba region. In the third legislative election of 1964, the party gained 8 seats in the National Assembly, while in the fourth general election of 1969, it gained a mere 3 seats. With most of the legendary 'founding fathers' repudiating their party, its role and its importance as a credible opposition force gradually diminished.

Somali parties and the issue of the Greater Somalia Project

As time passed, Somali political movements went through a period of deep evolution, to the effect that by the mid Fifties all main political parties shared identical points of view with regard to the issue of the Greater Somalia Project. This represented a leap forward and a sense of national consciousness common to non-Lega parties – moving them from a narrow tribal or regional outlook towards support for broad nationalistic objectives. Prior to this new development, the Lega was the only party with a pan-Somali agenda. Its programme on the unification of the Somali territories was reflected in a memorandum submitted to the Four Powers Commission of Investigation in 1948.[81]

The memorandum read: "We wish our country to be amalgamated with the other Somali lands and to form one political, administrative and economic unit with them. We Somalis are one in every way. We are the same racially and geographically, we have the same culture, we have the same language and the same religion. There is no future for us except as part of Greater Somalia. The present international frontiers are artificial and the divisions are placing an unfair strain on the political, administrative and economic welfare of the country. The existence of several foreign official languages within the several territories is enough, in itself, to make aliens out of brothers of the same race, religion and country, and put back our national advancement indefinitely [...] Union with the other Somali lands is our greatest demand which must take priority over all other

81 Report of the Commission, section II, ch. 4, app. P, p. 3, letter addressed to the Senior Secretary of the Four Power Commission of Investigation, January 6, 1948.

considerations."[82] For the Lega, the aim was to assure the independence and the unification of all territories inhabited by Somalis: this included Ogadenia, British Somaliland, Djibouti, and a portion of Kenya known as the Northern Frontier District (NFD).

With regard to the HDM, although it strongly advocated full independence for the country, its original programme, did not include a pan-Somali agenda. Their policy objectives were reflected in the testimony the party gave before the Four Power Commission of Investigation in 1948, when Sheikh Abdullahi Beghedi, President of the party, in answer to a query from the Soviet member of the Commission, stated: "When we asked for the trusteeship, we only meant for the country where the Dighil & Mirifle live, not the rest of the country. We did not mean the rest of Somalia."[83]

Although falling short of a nationalist agenda in its early days, towards the end of the trusteeship period, the party espoused the idea of uniting all Somali inhabited territories under one flag. The HDM constitution promoted "... the unification, through peaceful means, of all Somali territories within a federal system upon attaining their independence." (Article 2) It also espoused the division of the territory into autonomous regions (Article 4), leaving competence on matters relating to defence, international relations, the federal police, and economic development to the central federal government. (Article 5)

In the words of Saadia Touval, "a federal arrangement whereby the component units would enjoy considerable autonomy was viewed as the best safeguard for the special interest of the agricultural population, in an otherwise nomadic society."[84] Geilani Sheikh Bin Sheikh, President of the HDM, reiterated this position in 1958 when he said in a speech at the party convention that "the party has become convinced that the only method for unifying the Somalis is through a federal government which would accord full regional autonomy."[85]

Another political party to emerge during the trusteeship was the 'Partito Democratico Somalo', formerly 'Unione Africani Somalia', which also declared an identical policy *vis-à-vis* Ogaden. At a reception hosted by the new Administrator of Somalia, Ambassador Giovanni Fornari, on April 17, 1950, Councillor Mohamed Sheikh Osman 'Edmondo', Secretary General of the party, had this to say with respect to the Ethiopian-Somali frontier dispute: "The problem which

82 Ibid., p. 15.
83 Report of the Commission, section II, ch. 4, app. N, H15, p. 9.
84 Touval, op. cit., p 96.
85 UN Doc. T/PET.11/583 and UN Doc. T/1372 Par. 61.

at present worries us is that concerning the boundary delimitation with Ethiopia, a problem that we would like to see quickly settled and in a manner such that our feelings and the material necessity of our people are not and should not be trampled on to the extent of undermining our legitimate rights and interests."[86]

On 4 October 1951, during the opening of the third session of the Territorial Council in Mogadisho, Councillor Mohamed Sheikh Osman brought to the attention of Enrique De Marchena, Head of the UN visiting mission, the question of the provisional border with Ethiopia and the economic hardship Somalia would suffer from losing those territories. He said: "I must hasten to declare that no Somali has ever abandoned the Greater Somalia project. In fact, we placed a reservation on the matter at Lake Success during the discussion on the future of Somalia. Nevertheless, before the transfer of power from Britain to Italy, the borders changed three times, none of it done on an ethnic or logical basis. These changes of borders did not receive our consent and, despite our repeated protests, borderlines continued to be frequently changed and drawn. Well, the areas now detached from Somalia proper are areas rich in agriculture and livestock and, most likely, in mineral resources."[87]

The tone of the statement of the leader of the Democratic Party on the issue of Ogaden was similar, if not identical, to a statement made by the Lega's Aden Abdulla three years later at a special session of the Territorial Council attended by a United Nations visiting mission. The Lega leader, speaking in the name of the Council, stated: "In July 1948, the British occupation authorities, in an arbitrary and unilateral manner, negotiated an agreement with Ethiopia on the basis of which territory indisputably belonging to Somalia on geographical, historical and ethnographical grounds was ceded to Ethiopia. In 1950, on the eve of the assuming of power by the Italian Trusteeship Administration, the British Administration traced a new frontier line (which went under the name of Provisional Administrative Line) which, compared to the previous arbitrary frontier, showed a further worsening of the situation to the detriment of the Somali people.[88]

86 *Corriere della Somalia*. Aprile 17, 1950.

87 AFIS Bollettino Mensile no. 7, Octobre - Novembre 1951, p. 7.

88 TNA FO 371108117, confidential report from, British Consulate in Mogadisho to FO, September 18, 1954.

Chapter II

THE ITALIAN FORMER COLONIES
and the Council of Allied Foreign Ministers

Following the creation of the United Nations, President Truman of America, British Prime Minister Mr Attlee and Generalissimo Stalin of the Soviet Union met at Potsdam, July 17–August 2, 1945 and concluded the Potsdam Agreement, in which the three Allied countries decided to form a Council of Ministers.

The first clause of the agreement was the establishment of a 'Council of Foreign Ministers', from Britain, the US, the Soviet Union, France and China. The role of this Council of the 'Five Great Powers' in the world was to prepare peace treaties with the Axis powers, defined in the agreement as the ‹enemy states› (Italy, Romania, Bulgaria, Hungary, Finland and Germany), and settle outstanding territorial questions.[1]

The debate regarding the future status of Italian colonies started in August 1945 at the Potsdam Conference, but because of their conflicting interests the participants were unable to reach an agreement. As a result, the Four Powers decided to postpone consideration of the issue until the meeting of the Council of Foreign Ministers scheduled to take place in London the following month. At the Potsdam peace conference, there was little doubt that each of the four

1 Agreement of The Berlin (Potsdam) Conference, July–August 2, 1945, par. 3 (i).

powers had an agenda and some possible 'solutions' regarding Italian colonies.

Italy had sent a memorandum to the participants of the conference stating her wish to return to all its colonies as a Trusteeship Administration[2]. Substantial discussions on the fate of the colonies were not begun until the first session of the Council of Foreign Ministers (CFM) in London, in September 1945. The foremost territorial problem brought before the ministers of China, Great Britain, France, the USSR and the United States of America was the question of Italy's colonial empire (Libya, Eritrea and Somalia). At the conclusion of the London meeting, there was broad agreement among the Four Powers on the principle of placing the colonies under the trusteeship system of the United Nations Charter.[3]

There was no agreement on the type of the trusteeship and on who the prospective administering power, or powers, would be. It is worth mentioning that Alcide De Gasperi, Prime Minister of Italy at the time, was invited to attend the London conference and submitted a strong argument to claim the return of former colonies to Italy. Australia, Canada, New Zealand, South Africa and India were also invited to the conference – but not the representatives of any of the territories under discussion.

As mentioned earlier, each of the former allies was pursuing its own agenda with regard to the future of the Italian colonies. The USSR, for instance, proposed a single UN trusteeship administration for each of the colonies. Under this plan, the colonies would be divided into four trusteeships and assigned to the Big Powers who would become the administering authority. After a period of 10 years, all the colonies would become independent. The administration of Tripolitania, according to the Soviet Foreign Minister, Molotov, would be shared with Italy[4]. The USSR also requested a naval base in Eritrea which it proposed to administer. Foreign Minister Molotov stated that the USSR needed a base in the Mediterranean for its merchant ships, declaring that the Soviet Union was "extremely interested in the future development of the Mediterranean and Africa and believed that it was fully qualified to undertake the job of trustee"[5] and reassuring the Council that Moscow would not attempt to introduce the Soviet

2 G. Rossi, '*Le colonie italiane alla Conferenza di Potsdam* (luglio - agosto 1945)', Africa XXVIII vol. 4, 1973, p. 512.

3 Benjamin Rivlin, *The United Nations and the Italian Colonies,* Carnegie Endowment for International Peace, New York 1950, p. 9.

4 Foreign Minister V. M. Molotov's press conference, London, September 18, 1945, Soviet News, Soviet Embassy, London, no. 1259, September 20, 1945 quoted in B. Revlin, p. 11.

5 Sulzberger, The New York Times, September 1945.

system in the area.

France, afraid of a dangerous precedent of independence being established in North Africa, supported the proposal to return all the colonies to Italy. Britain made clear its interest in scaling down Italy's role in the Mediterranean and adding former Italian colonies to the British Empire. This plan was endorsed primarily by the Colonial Office but met with some opposition from the Foreign Office, which did not wish to assume responsibility for direct control of the area and preferred it to be a United Nations trusteeship. But after Attlee's Labour government came into power in 1945, the idea seemed to gain ground that the British government ought to maintain its hegemony over former Italian colonies,[6] and Britain rejected the Soviet attempt to get a trusteeship in Africa.

The United States presented a plan for collective trusteeship by the United Nations over all the Italian colonies under Article 81 of the UN Charter. The salient points of the American plan were as follows:

1. That each colony be governed by a neutral (not from the Four Big Powers) administrator with full executive powers, appointed by and responsible to the United Nations Trusteeship Council;
2. That in each colony, an Advisory Committee of seven, composed of representatives of Britain, France, USSR, United States and Italy, plus two residents of the colony, assist the administrator;
3. That Libya and Eritrea be granted independence at the end of ten years, while the trusteeship for Somalia would be of an indefinite duration;
4. That a territorial cession be made in favour of Ethiopia to give her access to the sea through the Eritrean Port of Assab.

From the first meeting of the Council of Foreign Ministers in September 1945, the problem of the Italian colonies' future hardly seemed amenable to easy solution. The London meeting, like the one in Paris, ended in deadlock, with the foreign ministers unable to reach a consensus. The task of continuing the discussions was given to the deputy foreign ministers of the respective member countries of the Council in Paris in April 1946.

At the London conference, the most important development was the United States' detailed proposal over the future of the colonies and the Soviet demand

6 'Umberto Zanotti Bianco and the Mogadisho events of 1948', Modern Italy, vol. 15, no. 2, May 2010, p. 165.

for a trusteeship over Tripolitania. The British did not present a clear proposal on the future of the colonies, only voicing their opposition to all the proposals presented by the other three powers, especially the Soviet request for a trusteeship over Tripolitania.

At the meeting in Paris in April 1946, Bevin, the British Foreign Minister, came up with a proposal of his own calling for the creation of a new united territory to be known as United Somalia, consisting of British Somaliland, Italian Somaliland, the Ogaden and Reserved Area, the latter two being under the sovereignty of Ethiopia, to be placed under British Administration. He conveniently omitted mention of Somalis living in northeast Kenya, a key colony.

Rejecting the American proposal, Soviet Foreign Minister V. M. Molotov condemned it as impracticable. He quoted a Russian proverb: "A child with seven nurses does not get nursed at all."[7] At the meeting in Paris, the Soviet Union, which had vehemently opposed the collective trusteeship proposed by the United States in 1945, introduced a new plan for joint trusteeship. Molotov tabled a new proposal which would place each colony under a trusteeship exercised in each colony jointly by two States – one of the major Allies and Italy – for 10 years. The administrator in each colony could be appointed by the Allied State, his deputy by Italy.

The administration of Tripolitania, according to Molotov, would also be shared with Italy[8]. However, when its bid for joint Soviet–Italian trusteeship over Tripolitania was rejected, the USSR declared its support for the original French proposal for sole Italian trusteeship without any fixed date for independence for all the colonies[9]. The new Soviet initiative was seen as a serious challenge to the United States and Britain in view of the upcoming political elections in Italy, where the strong contest between the democratic forces represented by the Christian Democrat party (Democrazia Cristiana) and the Communist Party dominated the political scene[10]. "The ideological battle being waged in Italy over the general elections of April 18, 1948, became a major factor guiding the trend of the negotiations as both parties spared no effort in exploiting the issues so as to favour their allies in the Italian elections."[11]

The Soviet Union's new move produced a change in the British position:

7 UN Doc. A/C.1/ SR. 239.
8 Rivlin, op. cit., p. 12.
9 The Times of London, May 11, 1946.
10 Rivlin, op. cit., p. 13.
11 ibid., p. 18.

Britain hastened to support the Franco-Russian plan for sole Italian trusteeship without any fixed date for independence for all the colonies—on condition, however, that Cyrenaica be placed not under Italian but under British trusteeship, in view mainly of the British pledge to the Sanussi. The United States were equally malleable to change, and abandoned their original collective trusteeship proposal, in a 'spirit of compromise', stating they would accept the Franco-Russian position if a definite date could be fixed for the independence of Libya and Eritrea.[12] United States' Foreign Secretary James F. Byrnes, however, expressed doubt as to whether Italy was in an economic position to take on the responsibility of the trusteeship and whether the return of the colonies to Italy took sufficient notice of the inhabitants' wishes.[13]

Although the positions of the Four Powers seemed close, no agreement was reached, and as a result discussion of the matter was again referred to the deputy foreign ministers. Ironically, "none of the conferees suggested consulting the native people of the ex-Italian colonies as to their wishes in the matter despite the philanthropic remarks that were made in session", as L.L. Fu-Jen notes[14]. The Council met a further five times before the meeting in London in December 1947, which ended in acrimony, without a date being set for the next meeting.

Bevin's plan for Greater Somalia

As we have mentioned, at the Paris Conference of the Council of Foreign Ministers of the Four Powers in April 1946, Britain unexpectedly introduced a new proposal regarding Somalia. The plan advocated a United Somalia consisting of British and Italian Somaliland plus Ogaden and Reserved Area, placed under British trusteeship, for an unspecified period. This proposal, however, drew sharp criticism from the Soviet Foreign Minister, Mr Molotov, who accused Britain of trying to "expand the British Empire at the expense of Italy and Ethiopia, and consolidating its monopoly position in the Mediterranean and Red Sea."

The two other Western Allies, France and the United States of America, were also against the British plan. The plan was formally elaborated upon by Foreign Secretary Bevin in the speech he delivered before the House of Commons on June 4, 1946, in which he said: "Mr Molotov has been more than unjust in stating that we are trying to expand the British Empire at the expense of Italy and

12 ibid., p. 13.

13 Department of State, Paris meeting of foreign ministers, publication no. 2537, Conference Series 86, pp. 4-5, found at the UN Library in Geneva.

14 Li Fu-jen, 'The Big Four at Paris', Fourth International, vol.7, no. 8, August 1946, pp. 242-245.

Ethiopia and to consolidate what he calls the monopolistic position of Great Britain in the Mediterranean and Red Sea. In the latter part of the last century, the Horn of Africa was divided between Great Britain, France and Italy. At about the time we occupied our part, the Ethiopians occupied an inland area which is the grazing ground for nearly half of the British Somaliland for six months of the year. Similarly, the nomads of the Italian Somaliland must cross the existing frontier in search of grass. In all innocence, therefore, we propose that British Somaliland, Italian Somaliland and adjacent parts of Ethiopia, if Ethiopia agreed, should be lumped together as a Trust Territory, so that the nomads should lead their frugal existence with the less possible hindrance and this might be a real chance of a decent economic life, as understood in that territory. But what attracted Mr Molotov's criticism was, I am sure, that I suggested that Great Britain should be made the administering authority. Was this unreasonable? In the first place, we were surrendering a protectorate comparable in size to the area we hoped that Ethiopia would contribute. Secondly, it was a British force, mainly east African and south African, which freed this area; and it was British, Indian and South African force which bore the main brunt of restoring the independence of Ethiopia and of putting the Emperor back on his throne after several years' sanctuary in this country. We do not seek gratitude on that account but I think it is right to express surprise that our proposal should have met with such unjustified criticism. After all, when we were defeating Italy in East Africa, Britain was open to invasion and we were fighting alone. I hope the deputies at the Paris Conference will now consider a Greater Somalia more objectively.

"All I want to do in this case is to give those poor nomads a chance to live. I do not want anything else. We are paying nearly £1,000,000 a year out of our budget to help to support them – we do not ask to save anything. But to have these constant bothers on the frontiers when one can organize the thing decently—well, after all, it is nobody's interest to stop the poor people and cattle there getting a decent living. That is all there is to it. It is like the Englishman's desire to go into Scotland—to get a decent living. We must consider it objectively. If the conference do not like our proposal, we will not be dogmatic about it; we are prepared to see Italian Somaliland put under the United Nation's Trusteeship."[15]

It is important to say that the genesis of this idea came some years before its official airing in 1946 in the British House of Commons. In fact, a memorandum issued as early as 1944 by the Branch Head Quarters of the East African Command

15 Saadia Touval, Somali Nationalism, Harvard University Press 1960, pp. 79-80.

had outlined proposals based on solid historic and religious considerations for a unified administration of the Somali people. The memorandum stated "the Ogaden people should not be ruled by Ethiopians whose religion is incompatible with that of the Muslim Somali if that is something they do not want. Allowing that will ultimately bring the British into conflict with the Muslim world of the Middle East. Ethiopia is considered a recent interloper with no justification to claim even Harar, let alone the desert region." The memorandum went on to say that the Ethiopian emperor maintained no effective grip over the Ogaden.[16]

Bevin's proposal may have been music to Somali ears, but it would be unwise not to treat it with some skepticism. Firstly, aside from the vague British sympathy for the 'poor nomads', the expansionist aim of putting the whole territory of the Horn of Africa under British control for an unlimited period of time was evident. As Li Fu-jen notes: "behind the pretended concern for the 'poor people' it was clearly Britain's determination not to surrender what she had succeeded in grabbing during the war[17]. Secondly, the British plan fell short of mentioning international trusteeship leading eventually to full independence within a definite period. The Plan purported to only grant grazing rights to Somali nomads, referred to as 'poor people'. Thirdly, it was not a final decision, for its achievement was made conditional on Ethiopian acceptance. In other words, Bevin's plan hinged firmly on the clause 'if Ethiopia agreed'. This tricky clause, making the whole British policy on Somali unification contingent upon Ethiopian blessing, appears not to have captured the attention of many who have written on the subject."[18]

Would anyone in their right mind suppose that Ethiopia would relinquish its claim on Ogaden? Needless to say, Ethiopia rejected the suggestion of renouncing her 'sovereignty'. Commenting on Bevin's Plan, Mesfin Wolde Mariam described the clause 'if Ethiopia agreed' as naïve, raising the question as to how the British could be sympathetic to the 'poor nomads' at the expense of Ethiopia[19]. Fourthly, it would not be unreasonable to fear that, given Britain's breach of its international obligations under her mandate over Palestine, the prospect of Somalia being annexed to Ethiopia remained a possibility.

16 TNA FO 371/41520, Report from the Director of Civil Affairs Branch HQs of East African Command to War Office, May 31, 1944.

17 Li Fu-jen, op.cit.

18 M. Osman Omar, *The Road to Zero. Somalia's self-destruction*, Haan Associates 1992, pp. 18-19.

19 Mesfin Wolde Mariam, '*The Background of the Ethio-Somalian Boundary Dispute*, The Journal of Modern African Studies, vol. 2, no.2, Jul.1964, p. 208.

Bevin's plan divides the Somalis

The peace treaty with Italy

Bevin's proposal on Greater Somalia divided the Somalis, particularly those in the Protectorate. In fact, while the future of Somalia was being discussed at the Council of Foreign Ministers, a group of elders from the Somaliland Protectorate presented a petition to the Principal Secretary of State for Colonial Affairs in which they demanded any unification of the Somali territories be placed under British trusteeship for fifteen years before the granting of independence. The petition, dated August 17, 1946, reads: "We unanimously and strongly desire the amalgamation of the four following Somali territories, the inhabitants of which speak the same language, belong to the same religion, are similar in their general outlook, mode of living and customs:

1. Ogaden territory,
2. The territory presently known as Somalia,
3. The territory presently known as Somaliland Protectorate and
4. All that part of Ethiopia in which the majority of the inhabitants is, and has for time immemorial been, Somali."[20] A number of conditions were attached to the request, including the following:

> "(a) that for religious and cultural reasons, the seat of the government should be in the Somaliland Protectorate, in view of its proximity to the Muslim world, while the amalgamated territories should be under British trusteeship;
> "(b) that the Dominions, British Colonies and other British Dependencies would not take part in the administration of the territories;
> "(c) that the administration would not follow the lines of the modes in existence in Kenya, Tanganyika, South Africa and other African territories, the natives of whom are Negroes;
> "(d) that British officials or other British personnel required to work in the amalgamated territories should be recruited in Great Britain only, and not be men with any previous connection with Negro territories."[21]

20 TNA FO 371/53526 petition signed by 71 elders on August 17, 1946.

21 TNA FO 1015/132, petition dated August 17, 1946, addressed to the Principal Secretary of State for the Colonies.

However, on September 11, 1946, a group of 43 Elders, Sultans, Akils and religious men of Somaliland presented a petition to His Majesty's Principal Secretary of State for the Colonies, angrily rejecting the idea of amalgamating the Protectorate with other territories and other people. The petition reads: "We are strongly opposed to the proposal of amalgamation on the following (among others) grounds:

"We are the descendants of Sheikh Ishak, an Arab, who made Somaliland his home. Documentary evidence shows that 800 years ago our said Arab ascendant came over to this country, known as Somaliland Protectorate, and we have traced our origin to him for the past ten generations.

"Ogaden and the tribes of Somalia trace their origin to Darod, an African. We are therefore two different races in spite of the fact that we have a common language by reason of proximity and neighbourhood." The petition continues: "Take Arabia, for the sake of argument. The Arabs are tied together by one common racial bond. They are all Muslims, Shafites and speak the same language and intermarry, but no amalgamation of all these tribes has ever been possible. Yemen, Hijaz, Irak, Syria and Lebanon remain independent of each other in spite of the Arab language. It has not been possible to keep together Great Britain and Ireland in spite of the fact that their differences are insignificant."[22]

In the former Italian Somaliland, the reaction to the Bevin Plan was reflected in a petition presented by the Lega to the Four Powers Council of Foreign Ministers for the union of all Somali territories, even though the Greater Somalia project had never been on the Council's working agenda.[23]

As mentioned earlier, part of the difficulty in reaching agreement on the future of the colonies was the stillborn peace treaty with Italy. A peace treaty was finally concluded at a conference held in Paris in February 1947. Twenty-one countries took part in the final drafting of the treaty. The relevant article of the treaty dealing with Italy's colonies is Article 23, which reads as follows: "Italy renounces all rights and titles to its former African possessions, i.e. Eritrea, Libya and Somalia. Pending their final disposal, the said possessions shall continue under their present administration, meaning under British occupation. "The final disposal of these possessions shall be determined jointly by the governments

22 TNA FO371/53526 letter dated September 11, 1946, addressed to His Majesty's Principal Secretary of State for the Colonies.

23 TNA WO 230/233, petition dated July 18, 1947 and addressed to the 'Big Four' Council of Foreign Ministers in Paris.

of the Soviet Union, of the United Kingdom, of the United States of America, and of France within one year from the coming into force of the present Treaty, in the manner laid down in the joint declaration of February 10, 1947, issued by the said governments, which is reproduced in Annex XI. "The four nations agree also that, in case they do not agree, the issue will be deferred to the General Assembly of the United Nations for a recommendation. The Four Powers accept and pledge to execute the recommendations. The Treaty provides that the disposal should take into account the wishes and the welfare of the inhabitants and the interest of peace and security."

The settlement elaborated in the peace treaty included not only renunciation of the former colonies but also payment of war reparation and territorial adjustment. Thus, Venezia Giulia was partially annexed to Yugoslavia and the towns of Briga and Tenda, on the western frontier, were annexed to France. The treaty also limited Italian rearmament.

The reparation and border adjustments were perceived in Italy as a major injustice: hence, the treaty was known in Italy as 'Pace punitiva', or 'Punitive peace'. Italy, for all intents and purposes, was considered a vanquished country. Pietro Nenni, Foreign Minister at the time, informed the Four Powers in a diplomatic note that the treaty, and especially the clauses dealing with the territories, had dealt a devastating blow to Italian national spirit, and raised the prospect of revisiting the treaty. "Not even one single Italian request was accepted" he concluded[24]. The treaty provoked widespread criticism in Italy over the way the government had handled the negotiations with the Four Powers, leading eventually to the resignation of the government led by Alcide De Gasperi.[25]

Following stipulation of the peace treaty with Italy, the task of further discussing the future of the colonies was assigned to the deputies, who were given responsibility for making recommendations to the Council of Foreign Ministers (CFM) as to the disposal of the colonies. The deputies were also tasked with sending a commission of investigation to the three colonies and consulting with the other participating 'interested governments' who had signed the peace treaty with Italy. The so-called 19 'other interested governments' included Australia, Belgium, Brazil, Byelorussia, Canada, China, Czechoslovakia, Egypt, Ethiopia, Greece, India, Italy, the Netherlands, New Zealand, Pakistan, Poland, Ukraine, the Union of South Africa, and Yugoslavia, who all were given the opportunity

24 The Somalia Courier, January 21, 1947.
25 ibid.

of expressing their views on the question of the Italian colonies.

These states came under two categories: (1) those having territorial claims on the colonies and (2) those having an interest but no claim to any territory. Ethiopia, Egypt and Italy fell under the first category: they were governments with claims on the colonies[26]. Ethiopia had a claim over the entire territory of Eritrea, based not only on her need for an outlet to the sea but also on the affinity of the population of the Eritrean highlands with the Ethiopians of the Tigrai Province. With respect to Somalia, although she originally laid claim to the colony, Ethiopia expressed the readiness to "accept any solution freely expressed by the inhabitants" on condition that Italy not be accorded any responsibility for administering the territory.[27]

The Treaty did not cover Ethiopia, as the latter was never an occupied enemy territory in the true sense of the term. British policy towards Ethiopia had always been clear and in favour of the Emperor. "His Majesty's government would welcome the reappearance of an independent Ethiopian State and will recognize the claims of the Emperor Haile Selassie to the throne", reads a British document[28]. As soon as conditions permitted, Emperor Haile Selassie returned not only to his throne but to his power.[29]

The Four Powers Commission of Investigation

The peace treaty fell far short of the full hopes of the Somalis but did nevertheless give them much. A Four Powers Commission of Investigation was sent to ascertain the Somalis' views on the future of their country, in compliance with the provision of Annex XI of the Italian Peace Treaty. The terms of office of the Commission were to report to the deputy foreign ministers on the economic, social and political conditions of the colonies and to ascertain the views of the local population over the future of their respective countries. It was not required to submit any recommendation on the final disposal of the colonies.

The Commission consisted of representatives from Britain, France, the United States and the Soviet Union. The heads of delegation were Mr F. E. Stafford for Britain, Mr John E. Utter for the United States, M. Burin des Roziers for France

26 Benjamin Rivlin, The United Nations and the Italian Colonies, Carnegie Endowment for International Peace, New York, 1950, p. 17.

27 UN Doc. A/C. 1W8.

28 TNA WO 230/4, Note on policy and practice in respect of occupation.

29 The First to be freed. British Military Administration in Eritrea and Somalia, 1942-1943, Ministry of Information, London 1944, p. 6.

and Mr Artemy Feodorov for the U.S.S.R.

The British delegation had five members, the US five, the Russian and the French delegation each had seven members. There were also seven members of the Secretariat. In total, there were thirty-five representatives[30]. As expected, evaluation of the data gathered was split on ideological and national grounds[31], but "the Commission seemed to agree upon a number of basic questions and facts concerning the social and economic situation of the local population in all three territories. Socially, the indigenous population was suffering from a high degree of illiteracy and they were lacking necessary experience and training for independence. Economically, the colonies were poor, heavily dependent on foreign assistance for their basic needs."[32]

The Commission arrived in Mogadisho on January 6, 1948. Sadly, however, the visit was marred by serious disturbances between Somali rival groups in the course of which several people were killed on January 11, 1948. Alerted by the insecurity of the atmosphere prevailing in the capital city as a result of the riots, the Commission, in a letter addressed to the Chief Administrator, asked for details of any steps the Administration might have put in place to ensure the freedom of the population to speak and express their views at the hearings.

The letter reads: "The Commission considers it necessary to draw your attention to the fact that the conditions in the town as a result of the pogrom and terror of January 11th and consequent atmosphere of fear and lack of confidence of the population prevent the Commission from freely determining the views of the population regarding its future and generally interfere with its normal working. The Commission would like to be informed as to what steps to take to ensure in the future a free hearing and expression of the views of the population regarding the future of Somaliland."[33] In his reply to the Commission, the Chief Administrator gave an undertaking that he would take "such steps as he considered best suited – including strengthening of the forces of law and order to ensure that there were no obstacles to a free hearing and expression of the views of the population."[34] However, and in spite of the deteriorating security atmosphere created by the incident of 11 January, the Commission continued undeterred with its activities – including the holding of separate meetings

30 Somalia Courier, January 7, 1948.
31 Rivlin, op. cit., p. 18.
32 Ibid.., p. 19.
33 TNA WO 230/231, letter to the Chief Administrator of Italian Somaliland, January 14, 1948.
34 Ibid., letter from Brigadier R.H. Smith to the Senior Secretary of the Commission, January 16, 1948.

with the existing political parties and other non-Somali organizations present on the territory. The Commission expressed its sympathy for all victims of the unfortunate event and warned the Administration against repetition of these disorders, further stating that no action of retaliation would be taken against those who freely expressed any views.

The procedure adopted by the Commission for the hearings was based on submission of written statements combined with direct questions that Commission members may address to any individuals representing the parties[35]. Along with Italian, Arab and Indian associations, some eleven Somali organizations, including a few who had practically no influence outside Mogadisho and little standing based on a credible political programme, presented the Commission with their views about the future of the territory.

The final Report consisted of 4 chapters, mainly covering areas such as the economy, politics, social and other issues likely to affect the population. The incidents certainly had serious repercussions throughout the territory, and the delegation was not able to come to any definitive conclusion as to what extent they had affected the expression of opinion by the people. The French and Russian delegations considered that the Mogadisho incident of 11 January had hindered free expression, while the British and US ones did not.[36]

During the course of its investigations, the Commission held 13 meetings at which 756 people were heard collectively or separately and visited 26 villages and localities, including Beledweyne, Bulo Burti, Merca, Jenale, Villabruzzi, Galkayo, Afgooye, Wanleweyn, Balad, Jelib, Margherita, Kismayo, Afmedu, Isha Baidoa, Hoddur, Wajit, Lugh Ferrandi, Bur Hakaba, Dinsor, Mahadai, Brava, Bender Cassim and Gardo[37]. In certain areas of Somalia the Commission observed that people were afraid to express opinions for fear of the Somali Youth League, and received a number of complaints against the interference, corruption and arbitrariness of the Somali Gendarmerie who were often identified with this party.

Predictably, this was a daunting task to accomplish – further complicated by the political interests pursued by each of the four countries represented in the Commission. "The work was not easy. There were language difficulties in the commission and in the field [...] The task of the Commission was further complicated by the different approach to colonial matters pursued by each of the

35 Report of the Four Powers Commission, section II, ch. 4.

36 Somalia Courier, August 25, 1948, quoting the London Times of July 31, 1948.

37 Report of the four Powers Commission. Section V, p. 110.

Four Powers."[38] The Commission held its last meeting on 19 February and left by plane in two flights on 20 and 22 February.[39]

Massacre of Italian civilians on January 11, 1948

Events leading to the incident

Towards the end of 1947 feelings were running high and people were growing increasingly anxious in anticipation of the announced arrival in Somalia of the Four Powers Commission of Investigation. Despite of the terms of the peace treaty whereby Italy renounced all claims to her former colonies, Italian elements mounted a propaganda campaign geared to persuading the local population to request the Four Powers Commission to return the territory to Italian administration. This campaign, mainly organized and orchestrated by former officials of the Ministry of Italian East Africa, was beginning to reach alarming proportions. Individuals like Dr. Calzia, Sig. Occhipinti, Sig. Peschieri, Dr. Biasi and Col. Alberto Mazzi were some of the most prominent activists behind it.[40]

On December 20, 1947, a few days before the arrival of the Commission, Giuseppe Brusasca sent a message to the Somalis (later produced as evidence of Italian propaganda activities in Somalia in the Court of Enquiry) in which he praised the work of Italy's pre-war administration of her colonies, describing it as a solid foundation for the future of the new Somalia. Predictably, in an already highly charged general atmosphere, the campaign aroused anger among the section of the local population with nationalistic aspirations, represented by the Lega.

In anticipation of the arrival of the Commission, numerous parades of Somalis, advocating the return of Italy, took place in the capital. The Italian community and a number of Italian-language newspapers published in Mogadisho contributed to the promotion of the case for the return of Somalia to Italian administration. In addition to the parades, there appeared to be an active process of mobilizing to the cause a number of former servicemen and combatants, as well as the section of the Somali population who placed their trust in the Italians. Other activities included campaigns in support of the Hawiye population in and around

38 F.E. Stafford, The' Ex Italian Colonies' in International Affairs, Royal Institute of International Affairs (1944-), vol. 25, no. 1, Jan. 1949, p.51.

39 TNA WO 230/251 Annual report of the Administration of Somalia for the period January 1, to December 31, 1948.

40 Ibid., Annual report of the Administration of Somalia for the year ending 31 December 1947.

Mogadisho, who had seen their status and welfare diminish under the British Military Administration (BMA) with a growing 'intrusion' of Darod elements in their territory.

On or around 19 December 1947, writings such as 'Morto Italia' appeared on the walls of public buildings and elsewhere in Mogadisho[41]. On January 3, 1948, a Mills bomb in a petrol-soaked wrapping smashed through a window of the Catholic printing press (Stamperia Missione). The police had intercepted a letter addressed by Dr. Calzia to Dr. Antonio Biasi, an Italian national serving as a clerk of the British Military Administration in Beledweyne, which confirmed the existence of an active Italian propaganda network in areas outside Mogadisho. According to Italian sources, the double agent Mussa Barre had handed over the letter to the police; details of the letter were leaked to the Lega[42]. On the night of 2 January 1948, at about 20.10 hrs, in Beledweyne, Antonio Biasi was attacked by four people who shot and wounded him as he made his way to his place of residence. In Mogadisho, an anti-personnel bomb was thrown into 'Bar 900' on January 6, and a Mills grenade thrown into 'Bar Italia' on January 7. No one was arrested in connection with any of these incidents.

On 6 and 7 January, 1948, at times coinciding with the arrival of the Commission, illegal processions took place in Mogadisho. The processions were headed by diesel lorries, driven by Italians and filled to capacity with Somalis. "In most instances, each lorry had an Italian 'cheerleader' with a large Italian flag on either side of the canopy of the cab or the front of the lorry. In a matter of a few minutes, 20 to 30 lorries were going round the town with Italian flags being waved to accompanying shouts of 'Viva Italia'".[43]

The activities of the Clubs on 6, 7 and 11 January, 1948 were an attempt by the various rival political organizations to display to the Four Power Commission the respective strengths of their movements. According to British sources, "The Lega sent a group of 15 holy men and Sheikhs to the Conferenza on the evening of the 10th to request the Conferenza take no action against a Lega procession planned for the 11th. They failed to achieve their objective after six hours' discussions as the Conferenza refused their request, insisting that the Lega had no right to hold a procession in Mogadisho."[44]

41 TNA FO 1015/45, findings of the Court of Enquiry which assembled at Mogadisho on January 22, 1948 to investigate demonstrations which happened in Mogadisho on January 11, 1948, p. 3.

42 TNA WO 230/123 Testimony of Lieut. Col. B. K. Thorne, Deputy Commandant of the Somali Gendarmerie, p. 24 of the findings of the Court of Enquiry.

43 Thorne, findings of the Court, p. 26.

44 Statement of Major A.O. Smith, Civil Affair Officer (C.A.O. before the Court of Enquiry).

Antonia Bullotta, witness of the tragic events of January 11, has a different version of the facts: "On Saturday January 10, 1948, I received a visit by a group of Lega leaders who begged me to inform all Italians to try to stay away from all kind of demonstrations and principally to keep out of any possible fray."[45] She also claimed to have phoned Baron Beritelli in the presence of her visitors, giving him a summary briefing of the situation. "He gave me assurance that he would do his best to persuade also the two rival groups to reach an agreement on tomorrow's procession. 'We too will do our best', promised my visitors."[46] According to Bullotta the two parties, Lega and Conferenza, agreed to stage the processions on the same day on the basis of a plan agreed between them. "It was Thorne who, angered by the failure of his plans, denied the Conferenza the right to participate in the demonstrations. The Conferenza, in spite of the absence of the requisite request and notice, insisted upon its right to hold a procession on that day and attacked the Lega HQs. "The Conferenza came under attack by swarms of Lega adherents, imported and sent by Thorne. Enraged, they reacted and repulsed the assault, attacked the adversary's HQs, seized it, pulled down the red flag and hoisted the tricolor instead."[47] "We had the right to hold a procession with or without permission because we are the local people and the Lega were coming from distant places like Harar and Berbera" stated Islao Mahadalla, President of the Conferenza group, in his testimony before the Court of Enquiry in Mogadisho.[48]

On 11 January, the Lega, known for its anti-Italian sentiments, requested and obtained permission from the military administration to organize a massive demonstration to show the Commission's delegation the strength of popular demand for independence. The Lega invited the Commission of Investigation to watch their procession: the Commission answered in non-committal terms, meaning that they would not watch it officially.[49]

Early in the morning of Sunday 11 January the Lega commenced to assemble near the Italian cemetery, now the site of the Saudi donated Mosque, in preparation for the afternoon's procession. They were estimated to be several-thousand strong, consisting "not only of local Somalis but also of troublesome

45 Bullotta, op. cit., p. 187.
46 ibid., p. 188.
47 ibid., p. 190.
48 TNA WO 230/123, Proceedings of Court of Enquiry.
49 Ibid., letter from the Senior Secretary of the Commission to the President of the Lega dei Giovani Somali, January 9, 1948.

groups brought in from outlying districts to take part in the demonstration."[50] According to some sources, the demonstrators converged on Mogadisho from places as far as Majertenia and Somaliland on board lorries reportedly provided by the British military authorities[51]. At the same time, Conferenza adherents were making their plans to frustrate the Lega's procession on that day, and organized a group of armed men carrying stones, spears, bows, arrows and clubs, who "appeared to be people from the Abgal tribe", as revealed by the Court of Inquiry.[52]

The reaction of the Lega was swift, with indiscriminate assaults against Italian nationals and attacks on their dwellings in Mogadisho. The incident took a heavy toll: 51 Italians killed and 48 injured. Out of those killed, 3 were female and 5 were children 16 years and under. Of the injured, 32 were male and 19 female – 6 were under the age of 16. According to the Court, the British colonial authorities had warned Baron Beritelli, Commissario Straordinario and leader of the Italian community, of the imminent security risks; however, it seemed that the warning was not taken seriously.

One hundred and seventy-seven Italian homes were looted[53]. Most of the Italian victims were caught at Zoni villas — colonial bungalows usually occupied by Italian families at the time, located today in an area near Sheikh Hassan Barsane Secondary School. This was an easy target because of its proximity to Lega HQs. "If they could not be easily carried away, the contents of these bungalows were destroyed. Any Italians who were at home at the time of the attack were massacred indiscriminately or left for dead where they lay."[54] Bullotta blames elements she describes as 'outsiders' for the massacre, ruling out the possibility of it being the work of local Lega elements[55]. "I was profoundly shocked by the nature of some of the killings. Bodies were badly slashed, in some cases obviously after death" stated Thorne testifying before the Court of Inquiry.[56]

No one was arrested in connection with the looting and killings. Italian sources produced a list of individuals highly suspected of having taken part in the pogrom, all affiliated to the Lega party. Many of them, in diverse capacities, served the trusteeship administration after receiving training in Italy. The list

50 Findings of the Court of Enquiry, p.6.
51 Bullotta, op. cit., p. 181.
52 Findings of the Court of Enquiry, p. 6.
53 Report of the Four Powers Commission of Investigation, section II, chapter 7, app. B.
54 Bullotta, op. cit., p. 192.
55 ibid., p. 193.
56 Thorne, Findings of the Court of Enquiry, p. 35.

included well-known personalities like Dahir Haji Osman, Ali Dhorre Shiddo, Mohamoud Mohamed 'Faccia di Falegname', Farah Sugulle, Elmi Gelle 'Dhungale', Haji Mohamed 'Boracco', Haidar Mohamed Illivi, Mohamed Sheikh Nour, Mohamoud Hassan Adde 'Qalfan', Daud Timayare, Sheikh Hussein Marehan, Farah Ali Omar, Haji Mohamed Hussein and Ali Hassan 'Verdura'.

Hearing of the Lega on January 20, 1948

Expressing the views of the Lega before the Four Power Commission were:

1. Haji Mohamed Hussein, President
2. Abdullahi Issa, Secretary General
3. Sherif Mohamoud Abdurrahman, Member
4. Mohamed Ahmed, Member
5. Haji Farah Ali, Member and
6. Haji Bashir Ismail, Member.[57]

The Chairman of the Commission:

"Gentlemen, we have come here to find out your wishes for your country, ex-Italian Somaliland. We have not power to decide anything. We shall take our report to the Four Powers. Say what you have to say freely and without fear. Answer questions freely and openly. We assure you full protection against any harm from this Administration or any other government."

Spokesman's statement:

Abdullahi Issa "In the first instance we thank the Four Big Powers for giving us the opportunity to appear before the Commission. We have been selected by the Committee of the SYL to represent them on their behalf. Besides we represent 90 per cent of the population of the country of Somalia. This is the capital and of necessity a cosmopolitan town, therefore, there are all sorts of people, but you will be able to verify the truth of our statement when you go into the interior. The SYL has been established for four years, and during that time its objectives have been to promote the welfare and interests of the people of this country. How much we have discharged our aims is proved by the number of followers we have, therefore, we state that we are not only a political association,

57 Report of the Four Powers Commission of Investigation, sect. I, ch. 4, app. A H2.

but we represent the Somali people of their own free will, and we want ample opportunity to be able to put forward any other matter we consider of interest in the national welfare. The express wishes of the SYL are contained in the memorandum forwarded to you."[58]

Questions and Answers:

US Delegate's questions

Mr Utter

I would like to address my first question to the President of the SYL. I noticed in the statement that the SYL mentions ten years as the time limit which they wish for trusteeship after which they expect independence. Do you consider ten years as sufficient time for education and training of a number of Somalis adequate for the administration of this territory?

Haji Mohamed

We feel that, if the administering powers do the maximum to train us and educate us we shall be in a position within ten years to be able to do our internal administration.

Mr Utter

You have asked for Four Powers trusteeship. Do you want one of them to be given the administration entirely or do you expect to have a committee of the Four Powers to reside in the country?

Haji Mohamed

We want a committee of the Four Powers to reside in the country so that all the Four will know what is going on in our territory. We want the Four Powers together.

Mr Utter

Would you agree to be placed under the general trusteeship of the UN Organization?

Haji Mohamed

No, the UN Organization is composed of too many nations. We desire the responsibility for our country to be limited to certain countries.

Mr Utter

Why you don't ask for one power as a trustee?

58 TNA WO 230/231Hearing of the party on January 20, 1948.

Haji Mohamed

We have already had experienced the administration of one government over fifty years and Somalis have no progress and have nothing to show for it.

Mr Utter

Would you accept a prolongation of time if it were deemed necessary by the UN or whoever was looking after the trusteeship?

Haji Mohamed

We desire that all should be done to accelerate the Somali administration, but if at the end of that period we are not yet in a position to work for our internal government, we shall agree to any prolongation that may be recommended.[59]

Mr Utter

Do you realize that Great Britain is obliged to furnish about £500,000 a year towards the running of the territory over and above the revenue which is taken from the country?

Haji Mohamed

The Somalis are not well aware of the fact that the expenditure is towards the welfare of the Somalis.

Mr Utter

You realize, I suppose, if a real programme of education and development of the country were undertaken that would cost a lot of money?

Haji Mohamed

Yes, we realize this.

Mr Utter

Perhaps you will tell me how and where you expect the necessary funds to come from.

Abdullahi Issa

We have already stated in the memorandum to the Commission we desire a commission to be appointed to make a preliminary survey and study what is the best way for getting the finance for the country.

Mr Utter

In case the trusteeship which you desire was not accepted, would you be willing to accept the rule of Ethiopia?

59 Report of the Four Powers Commission of Investigation, section II, chapter 4, app. A H2, pp. 1-2.

Haji Mohamed

No, never.

Mr Utter

Supposing that the United Nations or the Four Powers recommended that the trusteeship under the UNO be administered by Italy, would you accept?

Haji Mohamed

No, never.

Mr Utter

Would you be willing to accept the trusteeship of Great Britain?

Haji Mohamed

If we were unable to get our most immediate independence to get the Greater Somalia, we would accept the trusteeship which would make it possible for us.

French Delegate's questions

M. Burin Des Roziers

We have just heard that the SYL claims to speak on behalf of 90 per cent of the population of the country. Figures have been given us by the League that they have 93,000 actual members and 300,000 followers. It does not seem to me that this represents 90 per cent of the country. How are these two statements to be reconciled?

Haji Mohamed

When we say our supporters are 300,000 we mean actual members.

M Roziers

What do you understand by 'followers', is it somebody who accepts the programme of SYL?

Haji Mohamed

Yes, and on that point, the tribes in the interior said that they are in agreement with the aims and ideals of the SYL.

M. Roziers

Has the following gradually increased since the movement started in 1943?

Haji Mohamed

Yes, there has been a gradual increase.

M. Des Roziers

I see the membership of the League is open not only for residents in former Italian Somaliland, but also to residents outside, in other Somali territories, is this correct?

Haji Mohamed

Yes.

M. Des Roziers

Are these residents also allowed to be members of the Central Committee and Central Direction?

Haji Mohamed

If the members happen to be in Somalia they are allowed, though they come from other Somali territories, to be members of the Central Committee.

M. Des Roziers

I have carefully read the Statutes of the League, those of May 1943 and those of the last April 1947. In those Statutes nothing is said about the political programme of the League about the future of Somalia. When was this programme formulated?

Haji Mohamed

Our present programme was built on our aims that were already there. Our purpose is to bring about the union of the Somalis. It was in the previous statutes and the present one that the aim of the SYL is to bring the Somalis together and to create brotherly love between them.

M. Des Roziers

That goes for the union of all Somali people, but the programme regarding the trusteeship, to rule the country for ten years by the Four Powers was not in the Statutes. When was that part of the programme formulated?

Haji Mohamed

Our present request for UNO trusteeship was formulated by the SYL when we came to know the Four Powers would come to know the desire of the Somali people.

M. Des Roziers

Could you, or the Secretary General, tell us what funds are in the bank now which belong to the SYL?

Abdullahi Issa

The cash in the bank is about 20,000 shillings. I have not the book with me and that is subject to corrections. The funds of the SYL are not only kept at the HQs; the branches have a certain amount too. Our purpose is not to gather money but to spend it in education.

M. Des Roziers

Do you know what rent the SYL pays for the house and the HQs here in Mogadisho?

Abdullahi Issa

The rent paid for the League's HQs is 265 shillings through our own initiative per month, but we had to do a lot of improvements and repairs in the structure.

M. De Roziers

To whom does the house belong?

Abdullahi Issa

We rent the house from the Custodian of Enemy Property.

M. Des Roziers

Can you tell us whether you think, with time, this country could live on itself economically to an appreciable extent?

Abdullahi Issa

If the country is developed, and people are encouraged in their own interests, we feel there will be appreciable improvement. For instance, all the time of Italian occupation, foodstuffs were imported from outside, but now, on account of the encouragement the Somali agricultural communities have received, they have developed many foodstuffs for their local needs and foodstuffs are even exported.

UK Delegate's questions

Mr Stafford

Do you realize that Great Britain is obliged to furnish about £500,000 a year towards the running of the territory over and above the revenue which is taken from the country?

Haji Mohamed

We do not know that fact.[60]

Mr Stafford

Does any contribution come from outside Italian Somaliland or from any

60 H2 Hearing, January 20, 1948.

other source?

Abdullahi Issa

The only contribution we get is from other Somali SYL members outside Somalia.

Mr Stafford

How many fully paid officials have the League?

Abdullahi Issa

There are about a hundred full time workers for the League.

Mr Stafford

I will now address my questions to one of the ordinary members, Haji Farah Ali. Where do you come from?

Haji Farah

From Obbia, in Somaliland, but for the last 25 years I have been living and working around Mogadisho and Merca.

Mr Stafford

What do you think will be the capital of Greater Somalia?

Haji Farah

It is a matter which would be decided later on by the people in consultations with the Administering Power, if we get an administering power.

Mr Stafford

Would the SYL be in favour of direct taxation of Somalia to obtain the money that would be necessary for the additional expansion of education that they need?

Haji Farah

Yes, the SYL should be in favour of that and any other measures that we know are for the true welfare of our country.[61]

Mr Stafford

I would like to ask you whether you think the Greater Somalia movement has the general support of Somalis in the other territories.

Haji Farah

Other Somalis outside Somalia are in great support of this desire for a Greater Somalia.

Mr Stafford

Do you think it is the general desire of all other Somalis?

61 TNA WO 230/231. Hearing of the party on January 20, 1948.

Haji Farah

Yes.

Mr Stafford

I understand that there are certain so-called low-caste tribes in this country, such as the Midgan and Bon. What is the attitude of the League to such so-called low cast tribes?

Haji Farah

The SYL feels that the aim of education should be in Somali, and these differences between classes are a contributory cause of the backwardness and lack of improvement of the people.[62]

Mr Stafford

When was Osmania invented and by whom?

Haji Bashir Ismail

About 30 years ago by a man named Osman Yousuf.

Mr Stafford

I would like to get more information about it.

Abdullahi Issa

The Italian government felt if we had a language of our own which was strange to them, it would be a political weapon against them, and therefore as a matter of policy they stopped it.

Mr Stafford

How exactly it was stopped, by order?

Abdullahi Issa

Any Somali caught writing or reading it was put in jail.

Mr Stafford

But the Somali Youth League wishes to encourage its use?

Abdullahi Issa

SYL would like it to be promoted and the administering authority should promote its spread to the other Somalis and facilities made available.

Mr Stafford

I would like to address a question to another ordinary member, Sherif Abdurrahman. Where do you come from?

Sherif Abdurrahman

Isha Baidoa (Baydhabo), in Somalia; I am a trader by profession and a religious leader.

62 Ibid.

Mr Stafford

I would like to put the same question to Haji Bashir.

Haji Bashir

I live in Obbia. I am trader by profession. I am one of the active members of the SYL, an active volunteer worker for the aims of the SYL.

Mr Stafford

Have you been in the SYL since its inception?

Haji Bashir

I have been a member only for the last two years.[63]

Mr Stafford

Does the Secretary General wish to address us?

Abdullahi Issa

We wish to stress our greatest demand and the matter of greater importance to us is the question of Greater Somalia. This is the matter not only felt in Somalia proper; it is something felt by Somalis in other Somali territories. When the Commission of Investigation was established in 1948 to gauge the wishes of the population of the former Italian colonies its terms of reference did not include the Greater Somalia scheme. This was the first hurdle against the idea and will be followed by more difficult odds.

Soviet Delegate's questions

Mr Feodorov

First of all why your League is called Youth League?

Abdullahi Issa

Because at the beginning, it was founded by the youth of the Somalis.

Mr Feodorov

Therefore, we can argue that there is a difference between its original formation and what it is at the present time?

Abdullahi Issa

Yes, there is a decided difference between its first formation and now. At the beginning, it was desired to leave out the reactionary elders who did not understand what modern requirements are and our objective was limited to the details in our report.

63 Ibid.

Mr Feodorov

In what circumstances did the transition come about in the political aims of your society?

Abdullahi Issa

When the people saw that we had the interest of all Somalis at heart and they had proof of the aims we were bringing about, then the general Somali population started becoming to be part of our organization

Mr Feodorov

Can you tell us the number of members the League has got in former Italian Somaliland and in other Somali territories?

Abdullahi Issa

The number is already reported by us: 93,000 members in Somalia proper, and 30,000 outside Somalia. But there are large numbers of people who have joined recently, the total of which we have not got available.

Mr Feodorov

Why is it that you need the trusteeship of four and not only one, like Great Britain?

Haji Mohamed

We ask for a joint trusteeship because we would like the four great powers to be equally aware of what was being done for our country. We found in our experience that we have been under one government and have little to show in the way of progress.[64]

Mr Feodorov

Can you tell me how many people in the League have had a European education?

Abdullahi Issa

I have not got the details, but I believe it is about 500 persons who have had some European education in Somalia.

Mr Feodorov

In regard to your statement about education in your memo, I would like to know what the degree of literacy of your members is. Are there many schools in which the Somali language is taught?

Abdullahi Issa

Literacy in Somali language is not practicable. There is a written Somali language started 30 years ago which was stopped forcibly by the Italians.

64 Report of the Four Powers Commission of Investigation, sect. II, ch. 4, p. 15.

Now, for lack of material as well as facilities, there is not much progress. The people know more Arabic.

Mr Feodorov

In your memo you demand the Somalization of the administration. How do you envisage that in keeping with the demand for trusteeship of the Four Powers?

Abdullahi Issa

We envisage that the trusteeship be operated on behalf of the Somali people and we should be given every opportunity to fill up every post within the administration we can get, and to train us so that we can take more and more posts.

Mr Feodorov

I would like to ask a question to Sherif Abdurrahman Mohamoud. What are the political activities of the League?

Sherif Abdurrahman

The foremost aims are education of the Somalis and promotion of modern ideas of civilization and general welfare of the Somalis.

Mr Feodorov

These are the aims of the League which you stated in your memo which I have read, but how these aims are promoted in practice. Do you have educational classes, how many, where, what happens?

Sherif Abdurrahman

Schools have been opened in most branches of SYL; there are also regular meetings every Saturday night in every SYL branch where instructions and lectures are given by Somalis to their brothers, and there are inspectors who tour around the various areas giving different information and putting their ideas to the people.[65]

Mr Feodorov

In point six of the letter, dated January 18, the League states there should be no discrimination of a political and social nature. Why has this question cropped up? Is there any political and racial discrimination in the country at the moment?

Sherif M. Abdurrahman

There is no racial discrimination in existence now, but it existed under the Italian Administration. Racial discrimination to a very bad degree existed

65 TNA WO 230/231Hearing of the party on January 20, 1948.

under the Italian Administration.

Mr Feodorov

I am not talking about racial discrimination, but in your letter you state no discrimination in the political, social and economic sphere.

Sherif M. Abdurrahman

Before the present Administration, it was an order of the Italian government that any Somali meeting a white man should salute him. He had no freedom of speech. There were no clubs, no associations, and no bodies in which we could give our own opinion. What freedom of expression we got, we got under the British Military Administration, not before. From the employment point of view, trade is not going normally as before, but in regard to discrimination in economy, towards the end of the Italian Administration, no Somali was permitted to export goods direct or import goods direct. No Somali owned land which he cultivated in his own interest of any great value. Within the country itself, there were restrictions of movement. If a Somali wanted to go from Mogadisho to neighbouring place, Brava, for instance, he had to get permission.[66]

It should be noted that the programme the Lega submitted to the Four Powers was drafted with the advice of Mr Alex J. Salole, a Somali lawyer resident in Aden, and of Michael Mariano, a former employee from the North. Both men were Catholics and in the case of Mariano, Christian faith did not prevent him playing an important role in Somali politics. Elected in the list of the National Union Front (NUF) party in the electoral district of Erigavo in 1964, Mariano became Minister of Planning in Egal's second government in 1969. After the military coup of 1969, he served as the first Somali Ambassador in Lusaka, Zambia.

The Lega is known to have advanced a number of requests, both in Mogadisho and New York, with regard to the future of the country: at the beginning they asked for immediate independence; this position was later modified, apparently because it was found unrealistic. The hypothesis of a shorter period of UN trusteeship, not exceeding three or five years and finally ten years, was then advanced as an alternative to immediate independence.[67] It is hard to fathom the wisdom and rationale for the decision to limit the length of the trusteeship to ten years given the fact that the territory was insufficiently developed socially,

66 Ibid.

67 UN Doc. A/C.1/SR.270.

politically and economically.

Chief Administrator Brigadier Drew, commenting on the solution proposed by the Lega, had this to say: "The solution of the SYL, a Four Power trusteeship, is utterly impracticable. All Four Powers know that and recognize this and would never agree on such a solution. The members of SYL have been badly served by their leaders who put forward this fantastic proposal to the Four Power Commission. A trusteeship can only be exercised by a single power."[68]

The British member of the Commission made the following more sarcastic comment with regard to the answer given by Haji Mohamed in favour of joint Four Power administration: "It was naively explained that Four Powers were preferred to a single Power because four milch camels were better than one. A larger number than four would need too much looking after. If one Power tried to oppress, the others would protect, and so on."[69]

Hearing of Hamar Youth Club on January 20, 1948

The Club was founded in April 1945 and claimed to have 1,507 members of Hamar youth in Mogadisho. Appearing before the Four Power Commission to represent the Club were:

1. Haji Muhiddin Haji Ali, President,
2. Sheikh Omar Haji Yusuf, Member,
3. Aweys Dheere Diinle,
4. Dheere Haji Dheere,
5. Mohamed Abukar Aboka and
6. Ahmed Sherif.[70]

The Club had no supporters or branches outside Mogadisho. According to its statute, the Club had no political purpose, but its aim was to promote friendly relations between the young men of the Rer Hamar and to give assistance to those in need.[71]

The Club stated that it held classes in Arabic and English to abolish illiteracy amongst its members, and claimed that it had effected reconciliations within the Hamar community, as well as in many other minor disputes amongst Hamar

68 TNA FO 1015/27 top secret report, May 19, 1948.
69 Stafford, op.cit., pp. 47-55.
70 Report of the Four Powers Commission of Investigation, sect. II, ch. 4, app. B H3.
71 Ibid., p. 12.

tribesmen. In the hearing of January 20, 1948 before the Four Power Commission, on the question of the future of Somalia, the Hamar Youth Club aligned itself with the Lega dei Giovani Somali, requesting a Four Power trusteeship for ten years and favouring a Greater Somalia. If Four Power trusteeship were impossible, the Club would accept whatever was decided, barring Ethiopian or Italian trusteeship.[72]

Hamar Youth Club spokesman's statement

Mohamed Abukar Aboka: "Before starting to give our speech, I thank you very much for coming as a Commission to this territory. We have one desire, the Greater Somalia, because after the Italian occupation time here in Somalia, we were never allowed to any political matters. However, since the British occupied here, we learned about political matters and many classes and organizations were opened in Somaliland. We understand now that every one wishes to help his brother. We ask now for Greater Somalia; we did not ask it before because we did not understand it. Now we feel it is good for us to get Greater Somalia. The Somali nation is not very large. I don't think there will be more than four million especially we want to get Greater Somalia and we ask you to grant our wish."[73]

US Delegate's questions

Mr Utter

I shall address my first question to the President of the Hamar Youth Club. Can you tell me why the Hamar Youth Club, which has the same essential programme as the SYL, has set itself up as a separate organization and has not joined the SYL?

Haji Muhiddin Haji Ali

We have our own club called Hamar Youth Club (HYC) and we wish to join or to share the life of the SYL because we understand they are doing their best for the country.

Mr Utter

Why then does the Hamar Youth Club not join definitely with the SYL?

Haji Muhiddin

Because we are only in Mogadisho and the SYL live in out stations

72 Ibid.

73 TNA WO 230/231Hearing of the party on January 20, 1948.

everywhere in Somaliland.

Mr Utter

I understand the SYL has its organization in Mogadisho and in all the other places. Why is it that Hamar Youth Club does not join with the local organization of SYL?

Haji Muhiddin

We have our own name in this town and we wish to go with our neighbour.

Mr Utter

Can you tell me whether the Hamar Youth Club would be willing to accept any alternative to trusteeship by the Big Four?

Haji Muhiddin

We put our request in writing. We suggested the Big Four should govern us here.

Mr Utter

If that is not possible would you accept any other solutions for the future government of this country?

Haji Muhiddin

Still we would like to have very much the Big Four.

Mr Utter

You would like it very much, but if it were not possible would you accept any other arrangement for the future of this country?

Haji Muhiddin

We should like the governments to do their best and give us what we request, but if that is not possible, we will accept what we are given.

Mr Utter

Would Hamar Youth Club accept the rule of Ethiopia?

Haji Muhiddin

We would not.

Mr Utter

Would you accept Italy as a trustee?

Haji Muhiddin

We would not.

French Delegate's questions

M. Burin Des Roziers

It is stated in the first article of the Statute that it is clearly understood that "our organization has not any kind of political purpose. It is not interested in political reference, even indirectly."

Haji Muhiddin

Yes, these articles were produced when the war was on.

M. Burin Des Roziers

This was produced in August 1945?

Haji Muhiddin

We are still following the regular articles that started the Club.

M. Burin Des Roziers

When did the Club decide to adopt ideas regarding the future of Somalia such as trusteeship by the Four Powers; when was this decided on?

Haji Muhiddin

Since they got the idea that the Commission are coming to visit this country.

M. Burin Des Roziers

I have now the paper sent by the Club that there are 8,000 followers of HYC, are they also followers of SYL?

Mohamed Abucar Aboca

They are, there is great friendship between us.

Soviet Delegate's questions

Mr Feodorov

In your letter you said that you wished the establishment of English and Arabic education, why?

Haji Muhiddin

Yes, because we want to be educated and learned.

M. Feodorov

Why have you chosen Arabic and English languages?

Haji Muhiddin

We chose Arabic because we are Muslims the same as they are. English is useful for the entire world.

M. Feodorov

In your letter you spoke about the necessity for the development of the whole country. Has the deputation here any idea in what direction this development should take place?

Haji Muhiddin

For the programme of the party, we have started studies.

M. Feodorov

In your letter you say it would be desirable to develop agriculture, commerce, trade, industry, etc. Does the organization realize it will require a lot of money to do this? Where it does propose the money to come from?

Haji Muhiddin

The governments should assist the poor.

M. Feodorov

But where is the government going to get the money from to help?

Haji Muhiddin

The governments are governments and the government can raise the people who live under them.

UK Delegate's questions

Mr Stafford

I would like to address my question to Dheere Haji Dheere. I heard that there are 8,000 followers of Hamar Youth Club.

Dheere Haji Dheere

Yes.

Mr Stafford

Do they all live in Mogadisho?

Dheere Haji Dheere

Yes.

Mr Stafford

There are no supporters or followers out in the provinces?

Dheere Haji Dheere

We have no Club outside Mogadisho, but some of our people do go sometimes outside.

Mr Stafford

But they usually live in Mogadisho?

Dheere Haji Dheere

Yes.

Mr Stafford

Do I understand that the 8,000 also belong to the Somali Youth League?

Dheere Haji Dheere

The 8,000 people we mean they are members of the Somali Youth League, but the Hamar people are more than 8,000.

Mr Stafford

Do any of these 8,000 members of the HYC as far as you know belong to the SYL?

Dheere Haji Dheere

No.

Mr Stafford

Are you quite sure?

Dheere Haji Dheere

Yes.

Supplementary questions of US delegate

Mr Utter (USA)

I would like to put a question to Aweys Diinle. Do you consider 10 years a long enough time that your people will be prepared to be independent at the end of 10 years?

Aweys Diinle

That would be sufficient.

Mr Utter

Supposing that at the end of 10 years it was found there were not enough trained Somalis, would you be willing to have the trusteeship continued for another period?

Aweys Diinle

I consider that 10 years will be enough for us to be educated: within 10 years we will be able to become independent.

The Club would soon distance itself from the Lega to form a separate political party. The community from which it drew its support is generally referred to as 'Reer Hamar', or the people of Mogadisho. As the term itself denotes, the Reer Hamar are original settlers of Mogadisho before the successive influx of migration of Somali nomadic tribes from the north of Somalia. They are considered as being of Arab descent; however, unlike the Bantu, they are not despised or relegated to a lower stratum of the social scale.

Hearing of the Conferenza Somala on February 4, 1948

The Conferenza Somala was founded on 18th September, 1947, at a conference of representatives of the Patriotic Beneficence Union, the Somali Progressive Committee, Hizbia Dighil Mirifle, the Union of Africans in Somalia, and the Somali Young Abgal Association; it also claims to have been joined later by the Bimal Union and Hidayat Al Islam.[74]

The Conference was represented by:

1. Islao Mahadalla, President
2. Ahmed Kahie, Acting President
3. Kahie Haji, Political Secretary
4. Mao Osman, Advisor
5. Rabi Ugas, Advisor
6. Sheikh Mohamed, Advisor, and
7. Hillo Mohamed[75]

The Conference considered that Italian trusteeship could be accepted provided Italy fulfilled the 23 points adopted by the Conference itself.

Spokesman's statement

Islao Mahadalla

We like to ask whether we have freedom to speak because we are prisoners.

M. Burin Des Roziers (France)

We want the representatives to speak their mind as frankly and openly as possible, no unpleasant consequences will result from their open speaking.

74 Report of the Four Powers Commission of Investigation, ch. 4.

75 Ibid., sect. II, ch. 4, app. H16.

Islao Mahadalla

But we are still in prison because we want Italy.

M. Burin Des Roziers

You have five minutes amplifying the documents submitted by the Conferenza Somala. .

Islao Mahadalla

We apply for an Italian administration because Italy has done many things in favour of Somalis and kept peace with justice. Colonel Thorne and Major Smith are the friends of SYL and SYL belongs to the British Administration. When we declared ourselves in favour of the Italian Administration our chiefs, our fathers were put in prison or confined at Galkayo. The list of detainees under the Public Security Proclamation 1943 from the Conferenza include Sig. Di Biasi, Sig. Occhipinti, Sig. Baschieri, Sig. Calzia, Mohamed Jumali, Mohamed Mohamoud Agane, Mohamed Mohamoud 'Fodle', Haji Omar Ambure, Islao Mahadalla, Mussa Samantar.[76] On behalf of the Conferenza Somala, we apply for an Italian administration, because Italy who has been here for fifty years has done many things in favour of Somalia and kept peace with justice. Seven years of British Administration and we have had no peace whatsoever, because by night while sleeping thieves steal our properties and there is no intervention on the part of the justice.

On the contrary they assist the criminals who appeared during the last days especially Colonel Thorne, the Commander of the Gendarmerie and the present Political Officer, Major Smith. They are the friends of the SYL. Those who do not belong to the SYL are threatened with imprisonment and confinement. All SYL belongs to the British Administration. A person who is not SYL cannot belong to a service of the British Administration. The Askars and the Gendarmerie who are not members of the SYL are ill-treated and put in prison because this was the order of Colonel Thorne. In the last year, we have been ordered to give our opinion as to the future of the administration of Somalia. When we have decided ourselves in favour of Italian administration, our chiefs, and our brothers, were put in prison or confined to Galkayo. Those who have killed the Italians are free

76 TNA WO 230/23, letter from Legal Adviser of the Chief Administrator to the Commission of Investigation, January 22, 1948.

in their houses. Those who have looted, nobody puts in prison because they are SYL.

Soviet Delegate's questions

Mr Feodorov

I would like to ask the President the reason for the formation of the Somalia Conference?

Islao Mahadalla

It was the wish of the Somali population.

Mr Feodorov

In your document you said the Somalia Conference was formed by seven separate organizations. Can you tell me how it was that these seven organizations were united; was it voluntarily or was there any other kind of propaganda carried on?

Islao Mahadalla

It consists of seven organizations, plus tribes. For many years we have been divided. We have noticed that the British Administration helped the members of SYL. This was the reason we made a union of brotherhood whereby we should act with sorrows and happiness. It was always our hope that the Commission would come and see the present situation of Somalia, because before the British occupation, a woman could leave Mogadisho and go Addis Ababa without taking even a stick and without being molested or ill-treated while during the days of the British administration we are not even safe in our houses where we do not sleep safely.

Mr Feodorov

When you were formulating your demand for the return of Italian administration, did you fully understand the political and economic position of the country?

Islao Mahadalla

Yes, because during the Italian time, there was freedom of work and of agriculture because most of the Somalis spoke Italian.

Mr Feodorov

Several of the representatives who spoke before us had stated that there was forced agricultural labour during the Italian administration.

Islao Mahadalla

Those who say that are SYL, nobody else in Mogadisho because they are well considered and assisted by British administration.

Mr Feodorov

At present you are under detention, what are the reasons for it?

Islao Mahadalla

Only because I am in favour of Italy, I did not kill. I was arrested on the 12th after the attack against the Italians. Those who killed the Italians are at large; those who have killed and looted are in their houses because they are SYL members.

Mr Feodorov

Tell me, on 11th did you try to organize some sort of resistance or intimidations to the SYL?

Islao Mahadalla

Absolutely no, we could not do so. We let the people be attacked because we feared that the Gendarmerie was in favour of the SYL. We could not do army attack because we feared to walk in the roads and streets because all the Gendarmerie were members of the SYL.

Mr Feodorov

Can you tell us who the President of HDM was when you accepted the declaration of the party?

Islao Mahadalla

Formerly Sheikh Abdullahi was the President of Hizbia, then he became a traitor at the last moment, when he came in front of the Commission, this is the letter of his resignation. A copy was sent to the political officer, Mogadisho.

Mr Feodorov

Did the whole HDM resign from the Conferenza or only the President?

Islao Mahadalla

The President and two or three of his followers. We have his signature whereby he first adhered to the Conferenza.

UK Delegate's questions

Mr Stafford

I should like to ask the President what the conference regard as the Somali people; are they inhabitants of the Italian Somalia or do they include the inhabitants of other Somali territories?

Islao Mahadalla

Exclusively Italian Somaliland, excluding British, French Somaliland and Ethiopia.

Mr Stafford

Who were the people who were deported; can you give me their names?

Islao Mahadalla

Islao Omar Ali, Hussein Ali Idur, Yeberro Omar and Haji Hersi 'Gurei'.

Mr Stafford

When were these people deported?

Islao Mahadalla

About three months ago when we heard the Commission was coming to Somalia. It was alleged by members of the SYL if these people were deported, nobody will apply for an Italian administration.

US Delegate's questions

Mr Utter

Can you tell me on whose initiative was the Somalia Conference formed?

Islao Mahadalla

Salah Sheikh Omar.

Mr Utter

Was he the founder?

Islao Mahadalla

Yes, I was at the time the Secretary General of the Patriotic Beneficent Party.

Mr Utter

Will you tell me whether the Somalia Conference had anything to do with the demonstrations which took place in Mogadisho on the 6th and 7th January?

Islao Mahadalla

Some of them.

Mr Utter

But the Conference, as an organization, did not itself go to the demonstrations?

Islao Mahadalla

As a regular one, no, since that was organized by some young persons.

Mr Utter

Now, will you tell me whether the 23 points which have been circulated to us by the other members associated to the Somali Conference; were they formulated by the Conference itself?

Islao Mahadalla

Yes.

Mr Utter

Will you tell me how long you wish for Italian trusteeship?

Islao Mahadalla

30 years.

Mr Utter

Tell me why have you chosen 30 years?

Islao Mahadalla

Because we believe that Italy civilized the world and we think that in a period of 30 years she can give us a government.

Mr Utter

By that you mean independence?

Islao Mahadalla

Yes.

Mr Utter

How do you explain that Sheikh Abdullahi of the HDM appeared before the Commission recently as the President of the association, accompanied by Abukar Kassim and other members to be accepted by all the members present as their President?

Islao Mahadalla

It can't be.

Mr Utter

What I want to know is how you explain that Sheikh Abdullahi appeared as President of the Association a short time ago accompanied by all these members of the association?

Islao Mahadalla

I know, but it can't be; this was a disguised thing.

Mr Utter

Will you explain why Abukar Kassim and the other members who came with him recognized him as President when they came before the Commission?

Islao Mahadalla

They were threatened they would be arrested.

Mr Utter

Would the Somalia Conference accept Italy on any conditions without Italy recognizing the 23 points?

Islao Mahadalla

No. We would not accept Italy if she did not accept the 23 points.[77]

UK Delegate's questions

Mr Stafford

Who do the Conferenza regard as the Somali people?

Islao Mahadalla

Exclusively Italian Somaliland, excluding British and French Somaliland and Ethiopia (Ogaden) Somaliland.[78]

Mr Stafford

So when you talk about the Somali people you mean only the inhabitants of Italian Somaliland?

Islao Mahadalla

The question of Greater Somalia is a question raised by the SYL, which led to request that because Foreign Minister Bevin talked about a Greater Somalia.

Mr Stafford

Who were the people deported, can you give me their names?

Islao Mahadalla

Islao Omar Ali, Hassan Ali Idur, Yeberro Omar and Haji Hersi 'Gurei'

---

77 Report of the Four Powers Commission of Investigation on the Somaliland, sect. II, ch. 4, app. O, H16, p. 7.

78 Ibid., p. 3.

Mr Stafford

When were these people deported?

Islao Mahadalla

About three months ago when we heard the Commission was coming to Somalia. It was alleged by members of the SYL if these people were deported, nobody will apply for an Italian administration.

Mr Stafford

In the formation of the Somalia Conference, did you have financial or other assistance from the Italian community?

Islao Mahadalla

No.

The 23 points or conditions advanced by the Conference

The Conferenza party requested the return of Italy as an Administering Power under the supervision of the United Nations for 30 years, but subject to radical reform of the country and its economic and social development, detailed in 23 points submitted to the Four Powers Commission, known as the '23 conditions'. The conditions, in view of their importance, are reproduced below in full.

1. Full independence and admission on equal terms to the community of free peoples.[79]
2. Recognizing that this is not immediately possible, socially, politically or economically, request for a sincere and disinterested guidance by a European Nation, to enable them to govern themselves within 30 years.
3. An independent state conforming to the principles of the Muslim religion, but allowing the practice of other religions.
4. Parity of right and duty between the Somalis and the subjects of the Trustee Nation.
5. Schools on European lines with Islamic teaching for the Somalis and the right to enter any other schools.
6. The greatest possible impulse to be given to education in every branch.
7. Increased participation of the Somalis in the government to be assured.
8. Gradual admission into the public administration of Somalis possessing the necessary qualifications and capacity, on equal terms with Europeans, especially in the public administration which will be autonomous.

79 Report of the Four Powers Commission of Investigation, sect. II, ch. 4, app. B.

9. Somalis to be admitted to all grades of the civil administration, the army and the police.
10. Somalis to be admitted to the universities and assisted by government grants during their studies.
11. Existing Islamic schools to be maintained.
12. An Upper Islamic school to be established for Somalis who should be sent to El-Azhar courses.
13. All schools and other questions of interest to the Somalis to be studied jointly between them and the Government.
14. Professional and commercial education also to be provided.
15. Local and central assemblies to be established, at first consultative, but exercising increasing powers until the Central Assembly becomes a true Legislative Chamber.
16. Liberty of association, press and opinion.
17. Development of public health and sanitation facilities.
18. Liberty to select and engage in any employment and profession.
19. The right to reside anywhere in the territory, except any special areas restricted by law.
20. Liberty to sojourn for study, business or other matters in the territory of the European Nations.
21. Development of rural economy and veterinary assistance.
22. Respect for the religion and customs.
23. Assistance to orphaned children, invalids and foundlings.
24. All pending claims for payments by Italy's former military and civil employees to be settled and all damages arising from the last war to be paid by Italy.
25. Italy to "warrant that no revenge or retaliation will be perpetrated against the Somali people for their behaviour during and after the war up to the cessation of the present administration and that the territory will be democratically governed and administered."
26. No racial discrimination to be practiced; in this connection, the Italian government should give the largest warranty.

The above are known as the 'twenty-three points', although the Declaration of the Somalia Conference reflects more than twenty-three points[80]. The Somalia

80 Ibid.,.app. R.

Conference sought to arrive at independence by means of evolution along reasonable lines, in accordance with the traditions and historical development of the Somali people.[81]

The Conference, claiming to represent the population of the southern regions, saw Italy as the most appropriate administering power to prepare the country for total independence under strict conditions. Although the Conferenza acknowledged abuses committed by Italians in Somalia in the past,[82] they realized that a democratic Italy would not repeat similar abuses under the auspices of the United Nations. Italy's obligation to fulfil the 23 points embodied in the written manifesto was a condition sine qua non the return of Italy could not be accepted. The representatives of the Conference requested the Commission to expedite the decision on the future of Somalia so as to end existing feelings of uneasiness anduncertainty.[83]

At close scrutiny, the programme of the Conferenza was a well-elaborated political agenda, far more detailed and coherent than the condensed programme the Lega presented to the Four Power Commission. The Conferenza agenda reflected nationalistic aspirations such as the first condition, which demanded "Full independence and admission, on equal terms, to the community of free people."

Hearing of Hizbia Dighil Mirifle on January 24, 1948

The party was represented by:

1. Sheikh Abdullahi Sheikh Mohamed "Beghedi", President
2. Abukar Kassim, Vice President
3. Hassan Yero', Secretary
4. Mursal Mohamed, Member
5. Sheikh Mustaffa Sheikh, Member and
6. Sheikh Ali Ibrahim, Member[84]

On 18th September, 1947, the party joined the Somalia Conference, which advocated Italian trusteeship subject to fulfilment of 23 conditional articles.[85]

81 UN Doc. A/C.1/SR. 286, par. 56.
82 Ibid.
83 Report of the Four Powers Commission of Investigation, sect. II, ch. 4, p. 13.
84 Ibid.
85 Ibid.,. app. B.

The Spokesman of the organization, Sheikh Abdullahi Beghedi, made the following statement: "We are greeting you and thanking you. We are called Dighil and Mirifle. We have already told you in writing about the country we live in. We live in that part of Italian Somaliland which is more comfortable and fruitful than the rest, and we can produce all sorts of food in this place, maize and banana. We always stop other people who wish to make trouble or rob. Wherever we live there is no thieving or robbing. I wish to request three things: (a) We wish to have peace and tranquility, (b) Secondly, we want the country in which we live in be always regarded as belonging to us, and if the government who live with us wishes thing from us, we want them to be discussed first, (c) The other people who are not Dighil and Mirifle people they may live and stay with us, but we want them behind us recognizing the land as belonging to us and not to them."

US Delegate's questions

Mr Utter

There are two letters submitted by Hizbia Dighil and Mirifle, one dated January 7, 1948, signed by Abukar Kassim, the second one dated January 21, 1948, signed by the Sheikh. To which of these two sets of documents do you refer?

Sheikh Abdullahi

The latter one.

Mr Utter

I would like to ask the Sheikh how many members are there in all of the HDM.

Sheikh Abdullahi

60,871. In the Mogadisho branch there are 1,500.

Mr Utter

Do the remainder of your members normally live around Isha Baidoa?

Sheikh Abdullahi

Mostly they do live in Isha Baidoa, but we start from Afgooye to Isha Baidoa.

Mr Utter

The Statutes of the HDM of April 1947 contain no political programme. When did they decide on a political programme?

Sheikh Abdullahi

Before you arrived, we were called and informed of your coming by the Administrator. We started to work out the idea we now have.

Mr Utter

Did the HDM have anything to do with the Conferenza Somala?

Sheikh Abdullahi

Yes, when the meeting took place, we were called by them and spoke to them.

Mr Utter

When did you decide not to go along with the Somali Conference?

Sheikh Abdullahi

We were not satisfied with the programme of the Conferenza Somala and thought harm would come of their decisions. We did not agree, and we thought they might take even worse plan.

Mr Utter

How long do you think the trusteeship would be necessary, for how many years?

Sheikh Abdullahi

We thought that ten years should be sufficient for us to be educated; later on we understood that that was too short. Many things have to be studied and ten years would not be long enough.

Mr Utter

How long do you think would be necessary?

Sheikh Abdullahi

Thirty years.[86]

Mr Utter

Would HDM accept Italy if it accepted the 23 conditions of the Conferenza Somala?

Sheikh Abdullahi

We were told there are 40 governments united together (UN) and any of those considered good for us we would accept.

Mr Utter

That includes Italy as well?

Sheikh Abdullahi

Any government except black people.

86 Ibid., app. N H15, p. 3.

Mr Utter

In other words you would not accept Ethiopia?

Sheikh Abdullahi

No.

Mr Utter

In the letter of January 21 you spoke of the fact that the Italian government used methods of slavery. What do you mean by that?

Sheikh Abdullahi

During Italian government the country was safe, but the labour was forced.

Soviet Delegate's questions

Mr Feodorov

Does the President know about the activities of the League, and does he know about them?

Sheikh Abdullahi

I do not.

Mr Feodorov

Have you never heard about the League?

Sheikh Abdullahi

I have seen them always and we live together in the town.

Mr Feodorov

Does he know anything about their activities?

Sheikh Abdullahi

I do not know anything about their programme.

Mr Feodorov

In other words, you are not interested in the political activities in the country?

Sheikh Abdullahi

I have interest only in Dighil and Mirifle territory.

Mr Feodorov

If he has no interest in the country generally, how can he then support that political program of the trusteeship of the Four Powers?

Sheikh Abdullahi

When we asked for the trusteeship, we only meant the country where the

Dighil and Mirifle live. We do not mean the rest of Somalia.[87]

UK Delegate's questions

Mr Stafford

Does the Sheikh himself have any fear of reprisals?

Sheikh Abdullahi

No.

Mr Stafford

Does he think that the members of the Club have any fear of reprisal?

Sheikh Abdullahi

I do not think that they have any fear.

The HDM initially supported the Conferenza Somala's proposal for Italian trusteeship, but at its hearing and through its letter of January 21, 1948, the party requested joint trusteeship by the Four Powers for the duration of 30 years subject to the fulfilment of the 23 points. The request for a longer period of trusteeship advanced by the Hizbia stemmed mainly from recognition that the inhabitants of the south found themselves in a disadvantaged position compared to the relatively higher standard of education enjoyed by the nomadic populations affiliated with the Lega. In addition to this, followers of the Conferenza in general, and those living between the two rivers in particular, were conscious of the great potential in agricultural output offered by their land. To develop this economic potential and to open schools, public works and other vital infrastructure, a longer trusteeship administration was essential, hence the ten-year period advanced by the Lega was seen as insufficient to accomplish the needed economic development and prepare the territory for real independence.

Hearing of the Patriotic Beneficence Union on January 21, 1948

The Union was founded on 5 June, 1943, with branches in Mogadisho and outside the capital; the Commission could not verify the number of branches. The Union's programme was to further the welfare and civilization of the Somali population through morally and socially acceptable activities, including religion, politics, education and aid. The Union was a member of the Conferenza Somala,

87 Ibid., app. N, H15, p. 9.

adhered to the same programme and requested Italian trusteeship over thirty years.[88]

Appearing before the Commission on behalf of the Union were:

1. Salah Omar, Amoudi, President,
2. Alasso Addawi, Abgal, Wa'esle, Vice President,
3. Haji Abdi Hirabe, Abgal, Eli Omar, Secretary,
4. Mohamed Khediye, Habargidir, Member,
5. Hassan Alasso, Abgal, Wa'esle, Member,
6. Omar Ga'al, Eli Omar, Member.[89]

The representatives of the Patriotic Beneficence Union requested the Commission to guarantee security; that there be no reprisals for the representatives, and also that the Commission leave behind its representatives on departing from Somaliland, and that those arrested be released.[90]

The President of the organization, Salah Omar, made the following statement: "We thank you for coming from Four Powers and giving us the opportunity for making our speech freely. We are very much pleased to have you here in this country. Also the population of the town is pleased too. The reason you have come to this country is to ask the people their opinion and what they wish; for that we thank you too.

Our party, the Jamia people, has decided that we wish to have the Italian government, while the British government is here, we were living in difficulty, no safety no security. At the time when the Italian government was here, a man who had under him four families, the pay he received in a month was sufficient for them."

UK Delegate's questions

Mr Stafford

What do you mean four families?

Salah Omar

Four children.

88 Ibid., p. 13.
89 Ibid., app. E.
90 Ibid., p. 13.

Mr Stafford

And the pay he got was sufficient for him to live on?

Salah Omar

Now people have to sell their gold, their property, their houses, they are selling all they have earned in order to eat.

US Delegate's question

Mr Utter

Your new statute was approved on October 7, 1947, and contains no political purpose. When did you decide to support the political programme of the Conferenza Somala?

Salah Omar

The time we printed the statute was the time we started to get out our political programme.

Mr Utter

When was that?

Salah Omar

We have written it here on October 7, 1947.

Mr Utter

How many members are there in the Mogadisho branch?

Salah Omar

8,000 people in Mogadisho.

Mr Utter

If the 23 conditions stated in the Statute which you forwarded with the letter are not respected by Italy would you still favour this country as a trustee?

Salah Omar

We would have Italy back with conditions.

Mr Utter

For how long a period do you wish Italy to act as trustee?

Salah Omar

Thirty years.

Mr Utter

Why you selected thirty years?

Salah Omar

Because during these thirty years we wish the Italians to provide schools for us, and to train us as well.

French Delegate's questions

M. Burin Des Roziers

When the party formulated this programme, how long has this programme been known?

Salah Omar

When the British occupied here, after six months of the British stay we got the idea it would be better to have Italy.

M. Burin Des Roziers

You have said a great many of your members are of the Abgal tribe. Can you explain in what other parts your recruitment is particularly strong?

Salah Omar

In Gosha tribe at Margherita and Jilib.

M. Burin Des Roziers

You mention some people of [Jamia] have been put in jail. Can you give any figures, how many of them?

Salah Omar

On October 29, 1947, a man named Kassim Ali Agon was arrested. He was sent away to Galkayo. Islao Omar Ali and Yebero Omar Abukar were arrested on October 30, 1947.

M. Burin Des Roziers

Have you been told if you showed your feelings for Italy there might be bad things for you?

Salah Omar

What we understood was whoever was in favour of the Italian government coming here was arrested.

Soviet Delegate's questions

Mr Feodorov

You just mentioned the fight that took place between the Arabs and Somalis. Between which Somalis and which Arabs was the fight?

Salah Omar

The SYL and the Arabs.

Mr Feodorov

You stated that the political activities of your organization started shortly before the arrival of the Commission. Why did they not start before, were there any difficulties?

Salah Omar

We were frightened before. The fear we still have.

Hearing of Unione Africani in Somalia on January 23, 1948

The organization was founded on 5 July, 1947 with no clear political agenda. Its aims were mainly to co-operate with the local authorities for common interests, to attain brotherhood between people eliminating strife and enmity, and to promote general welfare, peace, freedom and progress.

The Union was a member of the Conferenza Somala and requested Italian trusteeship for thirty years, subject to the 23 conditions drawn up by the party.

The Union was represented by:

1. Ahmed Kahin Omar, President
2. Mohamed Hassan Gure (Usbeye), Secretary
3. Hassan Yevero', Member
4. Ali Hassan, Member
5. Haji Abdi Hussein, Member and,
6. Badi Awale, Member

The spokesman of the organization, Ahmed Kahin Omar, made a statement: "Our President is in prison. We do not know what he did. We heard it was because he was in favour of the Italians. All heads of the Conferenza are detained. All are in favour of Italy."

US Delegate's questions

Mr Utter

I would like to address the Secretary, what the number of your membership is?

Mohamed Hassan Gure

Between 5,600 and 5,700

Mr Utter

Do you have branches up-country?

Mohamed Hassan Gure

No, there are no branches outside because we do not receive permission.

Mr Utter

Will you tell me why you call yourself the 'Union of Africans'?

Mohamed Hassan Gure

Because any African who is in this country may become a member.

Mr Utter

Have you many or any members who came from other countries of Africa?

Mohamed Hassan Gure

Not so far, for the time being not, but we wait for it.

Mr Utter

What do you mean by 'getting in contacts' and hoping for an answer soon?

Mohamed Hassan Gure

Because they are Africans as well.

Mr Utter

Do you intend to correspond with any other country?

Mohamed Hassan Gure

Yes.

Mr Utter

Which countries, for example?

Mohamed Hassan Gure

All Africans up to Egypt, Tunis and Tripoli.

Mr Utter

When do you expect to put that extensive programme into practice?

Mohamed Hassan Gure

When we find freedom because we are today prisoners.

Mr Utter

You did not state in your letter, you attached a programme. Is that your own programme or the programme of the Somalia Conference?

Mohamed Hassan Gure

We are like branches. The Conferenza Somala rules the whole of Somalia, except Darod. This is Sub and Somali. There are two brothers; their land is Eyl down to Kismayo.

Mr Utter

Would the President tell me for how long you wish an Italian trusteeship?

Mohamed Hassan Gure

Thirty years.

Mr Utter

Would you accept Italy without these conditions, or would you insist on such conditions?

Mohamed Hassan Gure

No, we want the Italian government with the programme which we made and we want also your supervision.

The President and three of the Union's members, chosen to appear before the Commission, were under arrest at the time of the Commission's visit to Mogadisho. The Union expressed fear of the Somali Youth League, the police and the authorities.[91]

Soviet Delegate's questions

Mr Feodorov

It is said that your organization is subsidized by the Italians, is that true?

Mohamed Hassan Gure

It is not true.

French Delegate's questions

M. Burin Des Roziers

I will address myself to the Secretary. Has the Union been in favour of Italian administration since its foundation?

Mohamed Hassan Gure

We did not think at the foundation to have Italy; we thought of our interests.

91 Ibid., p. 14.

M. Burin Des Roziers

When did you join the Conferenza Somala?

Mohamed Hassan Gure

The Conferenza Somala was opened about three months ago, before the Commission was expected.

M. Burin Des Roziers

And they joined the Conference as the Commission arrived?

Mohamed Hassan Gure

Yes, all the parties went to them, except SYL.

M. Burin Des Roziers

They joined the Conferenza because they were in favour of the return of the Italians?

Mohamed Hassan Gure

Yes, when we heard of the Commission, it was then that we entered into an agreement.

Hearing of the Somali Young Abgal Association on January 21, 1948

The Association was founded on 3 February, 1947. Membership was confined to tribes of the Abgal. They also had two branches outside Mogadisho. The programme of the Association was mainly the enhancement of the "moral and cultural education of the youth of Abgal, and the attainment of brotherhood." The Association descended directly from the Progressive Committee of Somalia and adhered to the programme of the Conferenza Somala. With the aid of the Italian Government, the Association intended to attain independence and self-government. It requested Italian trusteeship for Somaliland.[92]

In the course of the hearing the representatives of the Association requested the Commission to order the release of thirteen detainees, eight of whom were Abgal, being held in custody "on suspicion of Italian sympathies." The representatives stated that "for a considerable time" the country had been in a prevailing state of fear and insecurity" which had worsened on the arrival of the Commission."

The representatives of the organization were:

1. Sheikh Mohamed Ahmed,

92 Ibid., p. 15.

2. Ahmed Nour,
3. Hassan Mohamed,
4. Hussein Mungie,
5. Abtidon Omar, and
6. Mohamed Mohamoud

The spokesman of the association, Sheikh Mohamed Ahmed, made this statement: "We are tied up with the Committee for Somali Progress. This is the letter which has been prepared by the Committee for Somali Progress which it is sending to the Commission. There are nine persons and each person represents his own tribe inside the Abgal. You should call them because the British and others do not want these people to be heard. We are young people, but there are also the elders and those should be heard as well. We were like children and we have our chiefs. Our chief is detained in the Majertenia area. This was to prevent us defending our rights before the Four Power Commission. We want to get assurances that we can speak freely because the askars come every night to prevent us defending our rights, in front of the Commission."[93]

Mr Stafford (UK) replied: "You had already been given assurance that the Commission will take steps to ensure that you are not subjected to ill-treatment because you came here today. Now the Commission will put questions to your deputation."

US Delegate's questions

Mr Utter

I would like to ask the President how many members the Somali Young Abgal Club has.

Sheikh Mohamed Ahmed

30,000

Mr Utter

Is this only in the Mogadisho branch?

Sheikh Mohamed Ahmed

No, all over the country where there are Abgal.

Mr Utter

How many branches of the Club have you?

93 TNA WO 230/231Hearing of the party on January 21, 1948.

Sheikh Mohamed Ahmed

Three big sections.

Mr Utter

How many are there in the Mogadisho section?

Sheikh Mohamed Ahmed

There are about twenty-five thousand.

Mr Utter

Could I now address my next question to the President. Do you intend to speak for all the sections of the Club, or only for the Mogadisho section?

Sheikh Mohamed Ahmed

I am answering on behalf of all the people who wear the badge. You will find the section of Villabruzzi (Jowhar) who will answer there. You will find also a Secretary in Itala (Adale). But now the HQs is here I am answering for them.

Mr Utter

No mention is made of the political aim of the society in their statutes. When did you adhere to the programme of the Conferenza Somala?

Sheikh Mohamed Ahmed

It was about a month ago when the office of the Somali Conferenza Somala opened.

Mr Utter

Is it true that Imam Mohamed Imam Abdulle, the Chairman of the Comitato, joined the SYL on the 11th of January 1948?

Sheikh Mohamed Ahmed

Yes, that is true.

Mr Utter

Has that in any way affected the membership of your organization?

Sheikh Mohamed Ahmed

The Imam is finished because he took another law, because a king cannot be a king without his people.

Mr Utter

How long do you want Italian trusteeship and under what conditions?

Sheikh Mohamed Ahmed

It is written in the programme that you have received.

Mr Utter

You do not know how long that 'it' is?

Sheikh Mohamed Ahmed

We want it indefinitely, because from the day the Italians went away, we can neither sleep nor eat.[94]

Mr Utter

You have no idea of the length of the time they propose for an Italian trusteeship?

Sheikh Mohamed Ahmed

30 years

Mr Utter

Do you know under what conditions?

Sheikh Mohamed Ahmed

Yes, I approved all of them. If the Italian government does not fulfil the conditions, the Four Power Commission is responsible to see the Italian government does so.

Mr Utter

Who wrote the letter which you sent to the Commission, the first letter in Italian?

Sheikh Mohamed Ahmed

It was the Conferenza who wrote it for us.

French Delegate's questions

M. Burin Des Roziers

How many people are there in the Abgal?

Sheikh Mohamed Ahmed

How can we say that, may be one million or even more.

M. Burin Des Roziers

Do you think most of Abgal are in favour of the return of the Italians?

Sheikh Mohamed Ahmed

You are here to see.

M. Des Roziers

How do you think we are going to see that?

Sheikh Mohamed Ahmed

You will go to Villabruzzi, El Bur.

94 TNA WO 230/231 Hearing of the party on January 21 December, 1948.

Soviet Delegate's questions

Mr Feodorov

Can you tell me why you objected to the two interpreters that we had?

Sheikh Mohamed Ahmed

Because they were against me; I went to the Political Officer that is the Civil Officer. I waited there from 7 o'clock in the morning until 1 o'clock and these people did not let me go in.

Mr Feodorov

Is that the only reason, or are there any others?

Sheikh Mohamed Ahmed

Yes, there are other reasons.

Mr Feodorov

What are they?

Sheikh Mohamed Ahmed

The other reasons are that I am in favour of Italy and they are in favour of the government.

UK Delegate's questions

Mr Stafford

If the Abgal tribe has millions of members, why is it only thirty thousand belong to the Abgal Club?

Sheikh Mohamed Ahmed

There is no question of being compulsory. The people they are welcome who like to come with us because they enjoy being with us. Why do you want to know the number of the members of our Club?

Mr Stafford

I merely want to find out those who joined the Club because they have such a good programme.

Sheikh Mohamed Ahmed

Do you do this for all political parties or for the Abgal only?

Mr Stafford

I only want to see the membership roll to see how it is maintained. Will you now answer, my question is: the other members of the millions of Abgal do not want to join the Club?

Sheikh Mohamed Ahmed

They will come, they will come.[95]

Hearing of the Hidait Al Islam Shidle & Mobilen on January 23, 1948

The Hidait Al Islam Shidle & Mobilen was founded on 5 October, 1947, in Villabruzzi (Jowhar), with Headquarters in Mogadisho and six branches outside the city. Its representatives before the Commission of Investigation were:

1. Abdulkadir Nour, President
2. Osman Hussein, Vice President
3. Amoush Maalim, Secretary
4. Abukar Hussein, Member,
5. Dirie Malak, Member, and
6. Mudei Maalim, Member.

The party's programme was the promotion of the welfare of its members in the Mobilen and Shidle tribes. On 30 December, 1947, the party joined the Conferenza Somala and supported its requests for Italian trusteeship for 30-40 years.[96]

Abdulcadir Nour made the following statement: "We were very glad when we heard the Four Powers Commission was coming. Before there was tranquillity and now we are very narrow. I wish to know whether I am allowed to speak or not." Mr Stafford (UK) replied "We have invited you to speak and told you there would be no unpleasant consequences if you did."

Abdulkadir Nour

If I speak freely when I go out they will take me and put me in jail. Our name is Sub and Somali, that is, this land is ours. The Sub and Somalis are brothers, we are seven parties and we are in agreement with the Conferenza.

Mr Stafford

You must confine your remarks to the Hidayat ul-Islam. You can explain you belong to the Sub, but you must speak on behalf of the Hidayat.

95 TNA WO230/231Hearing of the party on January 21, 1948.

96 Ibid., p. 16.

Abdulkadir Nour

The purpose of opening the Club was to defend our land. Our land produces every kind of produce, fruits and so on and we are here to defend our land and our king.[97] Now I will not speak any more but to express our wish that we want the Italians.

US Delegate's questions

Mr Utter (USA)

Your HQs is in Villabruzzi (Jowhar) and not in Mogadisho?

Amoush Maalim

Mogadisho.

Mr Utter

Is the President empowered by all those branches?

Abdulcadir Nour

Yes, the whole.

Mr Utter

Will you tell me when you adhered to the political programme of the Conferenza?

Abdulkadir Nour

One month ago, on the December 30, 1947.

Mr Utter

Will you tell me for how many years you want Italian trusteeship?

Amoush Maalim

Until such time as we learn well and we know how to drive cars, airplanes, to be engineers, doctors and so on.

Mr Utter

How long you think that will take?

Amoush Maalim

More or less thirty or forty years.

Mr Utter

The Conferenza Somala has a programme consisting of 23 points, are you aware of these points?

Abdulkadir Nour

97 A clear reference to King Vittorio Emanuele III of Italy, who abdicated on May 9, 1946, succeeded by Crown Prince Umberto. Vittorio Emanuele died in Egypt in 1947.

We are in full and complete agreement.

Mr Utter

Can you tell me one of the points? I do not want you to read it, just give me one point?

Abdulkadir Nour

I must have a look of it.

Mr Utter

Have you not read it before accepting it?

Abdulkadir Nour

Yes, I read it.

Utter

You as President do not know what is in it?

Abdulkadir Nour

Yes, I know, we have all read it.

Mr Utter

Will you give me one point among the 23 points of the Conferenza Somala?

Abdulkadir Nour

We asked for the Italians because at the time there was peace and tranquillity.

Mr Utter

I will not press that any further as I see I am not getting anywhere.

French Delegate's questions

M. Burin des Roziers

Ever since it was founded the Hidayat Ul-Islam has favoured the return of the Italians?

Abdulkadir Nour

Yes, we always wanted the Italians.

Burin Des Roziers

Can you tell me if all the members of Shidle and Mobilen tribes want them?

Abdulkadir Nour

Yes, we all do.

Fearing persecution, the deputation requested the Commission to leave one of its representatives in Somaliland after its departure.

Foreign associations in Somalia

1. Hearing of the Comitato Rappresentativo Italiano on January 22, 1948.

An Italian Representative Committee, known as "Comitato Rappresentativo Italiano" (CRI) was formed in February 1947, just seven days before the arrival of the Four Powers Commission of Investigation, to represent the Italian community and express its wishes on the future of Somaliland, bringing them to the attention of the Four Powers Commission.[98]

The President of the Committee was Barone Pietro Beritelli, with Vincenzo Calzia (President of the Chamber of Commerce), Carlo Rosso (Health Inspector), Camillo Decina (Veterinary Inspector), Antonio Falcone (an official of the Civil Engineering Department), and Marcello Felicori as members. "Despite being established at the eleventh hour, the CRI was able to produce a 300-page long typewritten report and submit it to the Commission of Investigation on January 21,1948."[99]

"The report summarizes, in a coherent way, all the Italian work in Somalia, from the early explorations to the character of the Italian penetration, from the health organization to the meteorological services, from livestock and agriculture development to taking stock of the industry and commerce."[100] The document rejects, in particular, the accusations levelled against the past Italian administration (imposition of racial laws, lack of education for the natives and enforcing of a system of coercive labour), praising instead the work done by Italy in Somalia in favour of the native population.[101]

On the question of the future of Somaliland, the CRI stated that all the Italian parties requested the return of the territory to Italian administration. At the same time it agreed on the necessity not only of United Nations supervision of Italian trusteeship but also of development of Somaliland in accordance with the new

98 Del Boca, op. cit., p. 173.
99 Ibid., p. 174.
100 Ibid.
101 Report of the Four Powers Commission of Investigation, pp. 227-245.

principlesof democraticItaly.[102]

The members of the Representative Committee and representatives of the Italian parties stated that they had not engaged in propaganda in favour of Italy amongst the local population, and that their only form of propaganda was the publication, in Italian, of articles on the work carried out by Italy in Somalia[103]. Representatives from some Italian political parties, like the Christian Democrat and the left-wing parties (Communists and Socialists), were also heard by the Commission.

2. Hearing of the Arab Community on January 20, 1948

The Local Born Young Arab Association formed on 21 May, 1947. Its aims included raising the moral and cultural level of the Arab youth, helping them to obtain education, etc. On the question of the future of Somaliland the organization limited itself to requests for such a government as would guarantee security, free trading and protection of property.[104]

It was represented before the Four Powers Commission by:

1. Sherif Mahdi Mohamed
2. Haji Salim Abdalla
3. Haji Ahmed Masaid
4. Hassan Mohamed El-Safiani
5. Abdul Hamid Salim and
6. Mohamed Obeid.

US Delegate's questions

Mr Utter

May I ask you how many Arabs are there in Italian Somaliland?

Mohamed Obeid

25,000.

Mr Utter

Of these 25, 000 Arabs – how many members are of this organization, this community?

102 Ibid., sect. II, ch. 4, p. 17.
103 Ibid., p. 17.
104 Ibid., sect. II, ch. 4, p. 18.

Sherif Mahdi Mohamed

The 25,000 includes women and children.

Mr Utter

My question was do all the Arabs belong to the organization, this Arab organization?

Sherif Mahdi Mohamed

The Arab community embraces all the Arabs.

Mr Utter

Can you tell the 14 countries of origin of most of the members.

Sherif Mahdi Mohamed

Mogadisho.

Mr Utter

In that case are many of them settled here for many generations?

Sherif Mahdi Mohamed

Yes, there are many of them who have been residing here for 70 to 80 years.

Mr Utter

If this country were given any form of government of its own, would you take its nationality or remain aliens?

Sherif Mahdi Mohamed

We would like to remain aliens.

Mr Utter

Even if there was a definite nation and government here, would you still want to be aliens?

Sherif Mahdi Mohamed

We would sooner stay here because many of us have estates and friends here.

Mr Utter

But you would not like to become citizens of this country?

Sherif Mahdi Mohamed

We would be compatriots.

Mr Utter

I take it that you would still wish to remain a foreign community?

Sherif Mahdi Mohamed

Yes.

Mr Utter

How do you think the commerce of this country could be developed?

Sherif Mahdi Mohamed

It depends on the development of the communications, to be able to export the things that are produced.

Mr Utter

Do you consider there is sufficient produce of export from this country to increase the foreign trade?

Sherif Mahdi Mohamed

The increase of export is dependent on agriculture and industry.

Mr Utter

What industry you think can be developed in this country?

Sherif Mahdi Mohamed

I cannot express my opinion on this; it is on the government.

Mr Utter

Do you think this country could become self-sufficient; could it produce enough to feed itself and to support the government for its own revenue?

Sherif Mahdi Mohamed

Every territory needs help. No territory can support itself.

French Delegate's questions

M. Burin Des Roziers

In the memorandum we have received it is stated that conditions generally have been difficult of late: can you explain in what way they are more difficult?

Sherif Mahdi Mohamed

I can only explain in regard to Arabs.

M. Burin Des Roziers

What are the difficulties regarding the Arabs?

Sherif Mahdi Mohamed

For full explanation I need time.

M. Burin Des Roziers

It is stated in this paper that security is difficult at the present time. Is that your opinion?

Sherif Mahdi Mohamed

The important thing is security. No one can deal without it.

M. Burin Des Roziers

Why is security not good now as it was previously?

Sherif Mahdi Mohamed

This needs no explanations, you may have seen.

M. Burin Des Roziers

The paper refers also to the riots which took place in October in which many Arabs were killed. We are interested to find out what was the principal object that caused these riots?

Sherif Mahdi Mohamed

The questioner has more knowledge than the questioned. The only one with more knowledge is the Principal Administrator; he is responsible, the government is responsible of what happened.

M. Burin Des Roziers

I return to the question mentioned in the paper which is important. Have you or any of your fellow members of the Arab community any explanation to give of the unfortunate incidents of last October?

Sherif Mahdi Mohamed

Do you ask about secret things or open things?

M. Burin Des Roziers

I would like to have both.

Abdul Hamid Salim

I cannot say anything about secret things, but those members of the Arab community while they were in procession, with official authority of the Administration, on October 26 1947 was attacked suddenly.

M. Burin Des Roziers

Do you know who attacked you?

Abdul Hamid Salim

First of all we were unprepared; if we had been prepared for such an attack we would have taken arms with us. Such an incident has never happened before.

M. Des Roziers

In the past, before the war, had there been such riots against the Arab people?

Abdul Hamid Salim

Five or six times before the last attack.

M. Des Roziers

Before the war?

Abdul Hamid Salim

Never, they have developed since the war.

M. Des Roziers

Why is the Arab community being attacked now if it was not before?

Abdul Hamid Salim

There may be secret things which we understand and which we could not explain.

M. Des Roziers

Is the reason why you are reluctant to give the real explanation for the disorders the fact that the explanations might make situation worse?

Abdi Hamid Salim

Probably.

M. Des Roziers

Is this fear of making thing worse by giving reason shared by the whole Arab community?

Abdul Hamid Salim

Anyway I cannot explain.

M. Des Roziers

Would the Arab community prefer to be administered as they were before the war?

Abdul Hamid Salim

In certain things like security they would, but on other matters it had improved since.

M. Des Roziers

Before the war, were the Arab communities doing good business?

Abdul Hamid Salim

They were doing good business.

M. Des Roziers

Before the war, were there restrictions on their trade?

Abdul Hamid Salim

It was only since the war between Italy and Ethiopia.

M. Des Roziers

Were there any restrictions on the business carried out by the Arabs during Italian time?

Abdul Hamid Salim

There were restrictions on currency exporting.

M. De Roziers

Was there great competition between Italian traders and Arab traders?

Abdul Hamid Salim

This existed in the whole world.

Based on the programmes the political parties and organizations had submitted to the Four Power Commission on the future of the country, there emerged a consensus on one key point – ultimate independence of the country, but only after a certain period of time that would allow the administration to prepare the trusteeship for self-government. Major differences continued to exist on a number of other equally important points related to the issue of independence.

The Lega dei Giovani Somali and Hamar Youth Club expressed their wish for a ten-year Four Powers trusteeship followed by independence; if this was impossible, a United Nations trusteeship would be accepted as an alternative to the suggested Four Powers joint administration. Both organizations rejected trusteeship of Italy or Ethiopia.

The 'Conferenza Somala' and its constituent parties and organizations, excepting Hizbia Dighil Mirifle (HDM), expressed preference for Italian trusteeship for 30 years under UN supervision, followed by independence and subject to the 23 conditions advanced by the Conferenza.

Why was Britain not favoured as an administering power?

The two European countries which expressed an interest in taking up the responsibility of administering Somalia were Britain and Italy[105]. Both powers maintained close ties with Somali political organizations and groups. The British initially supported the Lega, while Italy enjoyed a special relationship with political parties whose creation and financial viability it heavily contributed to. One simple question frequently asked was why the Lega leadership did not request British administration which, under any circumstances, was the most convenient at the time, not least because of the advantage of continuity. To this simple question,

105 For Britain, refer to the Bevin Plan of 1946 over Greater Somalia.

a number of answers have been given. According to one opinion, Britain had been dropped, *a priori*, on grounds of possible negative reaction from the nomadic population who would withdraw their financial support to the party had Britain been chosen as trustee. The nomadic population was resentful for all the suffering it had endured under British military occupation[106]. However, it is hard to accept this argument as valid and convincing, for the nomadic population was not politically mature enough to fully understand the political game being played on their behalf concerning the future of the country. In fact, outside the towns, there was little evident interest in political parties and the modern political ideals they propagated.

The conclusion reached by the Four Powers Commission of Investigation on the poor level of social and political awareness of the rural population is firm: "The population, as a whole, is politically immature and people are essentially accustomed to looking to their leaders for views on matters of major concern. The majority, when asked, stated that the future of the country had not been discussed at tribal meetings, but said their people would support anything they said to the Commission."[107] The poor level of political awareness of the Somali population at large was further reflected in a British document which reads: "On the whole, the Bushmen were politically disinterested; they were like simmering milk which could be made to boil if sufficient flame was fanned, but could soon cool down without flame."[108] Given the poor level of political maturity of the nomads, it was the responsibility of the Lega leadership to take an informed decision on what the future best interest of the territory was to be.

According to another opinion, the Lega leadership saw the British as untrustworthy agents who might have a sinister hidden agenda. "The SYL leadership was distrustful about the British; they believed that Great Britain, an old colonial power, would try, once given the mandate to administer Somalia, to level down Somalia to the status of her colonies in Africa."[109]

There is no better confirmation of this fear than in Haji Mohamed's response to the USSR member of the Four Powers Commission of Investigation when the latter sought to know why his party supported a trusteeship of four and not only one. The answer was short and precise: "We ask for a joint trusteeship because we would like the four great powers to be equally aware of what was being done

106 Abdirazak Haji Hussein, written testimony, February 2010, p. 4.
107 Report of the Four Power Commission of Investigation on Somaliland, sect. II, p. 110.
108 TNA FO 371/241, minutes of meeting held at the H.Q. B.A.S. on August 27, 1949.
109 Salah Mohamed Ali, op. cit., pp. 320-21.

for our country."[110] This fear would soon fade away, as explained in this chapter, and the Lega would tardily present an official request for British administration.[111]

Many Somalis believe that the British surrendered Ogaden to Ethiopia out of spite after the Lega 'let them down' by not choosing them as future trustees. This conviction may be ascribed to ignorance of history. The true reasons for ceding Ogaden to Ethiopia had nothing to do with the issue of trusteeship, for Britain had never made a secret of her wish to restore to the Ethiopians all the territories comprised in the 1933 frontier prior to the Italian-Ethiopian war of 1936.

Nearly eight months after the arrival in Mogadisho of the Four Powers Commission of Investigation in January 1948, the Lega realized the risk inherent in insisting on a request for a collective Four Powers administration. Reversing their previous decision, they now came out in full support of British trusteeship of Somalia. The move apparently sought to achieve one major objective: the undermining of Italy's growing manoeuvres at the United Nations to return to Somalia as an administering authority. To this end, in a petition addressed to the British Secretary for Foreign Affairs, Mr Bevin, they stated their decision to withdraw the previous request and submit a new demand for British administration. Needless to say, owing to changed circumstances, the request came too late to be considered and was rejected outright by the British. The letter read:

> Your Excellency
>
> We realize that our demand for Four Powers Administration, vide letter reference no. 4923/STAT/85 and various memoranda submitted to the Four Powers Commission of Investigation, is all together impracticable, the international situation makes such demand extremely difficult. We, therefore, beg to state that we have decided to withdraw our previous demand for Four Powers Government and we herewith request solely for British Administration for Somalia. The reasons which have led us to alter our previous demand are as follows:
>
> a. Our greatest aim is the unification of the Somalilands and we are fully aware that the British Somaliland, and the northern Frontier District of Kenya are British-held territories, the placing of our territory, Somalia, under British administration would be a step

110 Report of the Four Powers Commission of Investigation, sec. II, ch. 4, p. 15.

111 TNA FO 1015/51 petition to Mr. Bevin, signed by 14 members of the Central Committee of the SYL.

towards that unification.

b. We believe that the British Administration, more than other European governments, lays great emphasis on education which is undoubtedly the greatest asset for the advancement of backward people like ourselves. The British Administration, more than other European governments, assure political advancement. Such fact is amply evidenced by reference to Great Britain's record in connection with most of the young nations of today in Asia and Africa.

We desire to inform the Secretary General of the United Nations of the alteration of our decision. We trust that Great Britain will accept our request for British Administration in our territory of Somalia. Such notice of acceptance could be communicated to us either through our branch in the UK with the following Address:

> Doalla Mohamed, Esqr.
> Secretary General - Somali Youth League (UK)
> 7 Nelson Street,
> Cardiff

Or through the appropriate authority in Somalia.
We urge Your Excellency to accept our request at which we have arrived after careful scrutiny and deep consideration. We are always willing and prepared to co-operate with the British Administration here and also with His Majesty's Government in the United Kingdom. We are fully aware of the fact that it is Great Britain alone that can afford us, willingly and generously, that education and subsequent political advancement, without which our efforts in nation-building would be of no avail. We need hardly stress that education and political progress are more important for us than any other considerations.

Thanking Your Excellency
We remain,
Your obedient servants
The Central Committee of the Somali Youth League

The petition, dated September 19, 1948, was signed by all fourteen members of the Central Committee of the party: Haji Mohamed Hussein, President; Ahmed Shire Addawi, Vice-President; Abdullahi Issa, Secretary General; Osman Mohamed, Assistant Secretary General; Sheikh Issa Mohamed, Treasurer; Mohamed Awale Liban, Member; Abdi Rashid Ali, Member; Ali Moallim Mohamed, Member; Osman Sheikh Mao, Member; Dahir Haji Osman, Member; Ali Hersi Farah, Member; Sheikh Mohamed Osman, Member; Mohamed Ahmed 'Ottavio', Member; Sheikh Mohamoud Mohamed Farah, Member.

This rather apologetic and desperate appeal was totally ignored by Mr Bevin. It is difficult to say whether the slight was intentional. The only reply received in connection with the petition was a telegram from the Secretary for Foreign Affairs addressed to the Chief Administrator and instructing him to inform the petitioners of the following points: (a) that His Majesty's government was not in a position to administer Somalia; (b) that the future of Somalia would be decided by the United Nations, and (c) that the Lega should respect international decision, whatever they may be, and give any future administration the same support and co-operation as given to the BMA.[112]

The September petition followed a similar one submitted to the British Government in early June 1948, in which a request was made for British trusteeship over Somalia. The petition explained the reasons why an application for British administration was not advanced during the Four Powers Commission of Investigation in January. The Lega had estimated that the British were undergoing a serious economic crisis at the time (January 1948) and felt that "Great Britain alone would not be able to advance their economic conditions fastenough."[113]

The Commission of Enquiry and its recommendations

The January incident aroused strong emotion in Italy against the British Military Administration, accused of doing little or nothing to safeguard civilian populations placed under their protection. The British Administration came under fire for failing to take the required security measures to prevent the carnage in such a charged atmosphere at the time. The former 'Casa del Fascio' building, which hosted the HQs of the Gendarmerie, was only at stone's throw from the

112 TNA FO 1015/51, top secret telegram of September 24, 1948 from the War Office to Civaffairs Mogadisho.

113 Ibid., petition to Mr. Bevin, signed by 14 members of the Central Committee of the SYL.

Zoni villas, where the pogrom occurred. "The troops who were not in shortage of guns, machineguns, and armored vehicles witnessed passively the atrocities being committed," accuses Bullotta.[114]

A special Court of Enquiry was established in January 1948 to shed light on the events which led to the incidents of January 11: this was a panel of three military officers chaired by Colonel H.J.M. Flaxman, assisted by two other army officials. An Italian diplomat, Renato Della Chiesa, was later accepted to attend the works of the Court as an observer. Della Chiesa was at the time the Italian Ambassador in East Africa.

Antonia Bullotta, who spent a considerable period of time in Somalia as a journalist and witnessed the killings, points an accusing finger at certain elements she deems responsible for the massacre and describes them as 'foreigners' rather than members of the local people associated with the Lega in Mogadisho. "In anticipation of the arrival of the Four Powers Commission, at accelerated pace," she writes, "hundreds of people from Majertenia, British Somaliland and Ogadenia started converging into Mogadisho. There is good reason to believe that British colonial officers were not passive onlookers, but provided material assistance to ferry these people to the capital."[115] This unusual movement of people converging into Mogadisho to boost the ranks of the Lega is confirmed by many people, including prominent Somali politicians[116], as well as several oral testimonies from people directly involved in the looting of Arab and Italian properties in Mogadisho. Bullotta accuses the British colonial authorities of direct involvement in the carnage of which the Italian community in Mogadisho bore the brunt.

She cites a case in which a British colonial officer, Lieutenant Colonel Thorne, provided lorries and weapons to the members of the Lega who converged into the capital and watched passively whilst an Italian national was killed at the Central Police Station. Lt. Col. R.M. Thorne, who was serving as Deputy Commander of the Somali Gendarmerie at the time of the disturbances, became the subject of grave charges aired by the radio and the Italian press and including complicity in and abetment to loss of Italian lives and property.

Bullotta is not the only observer to accuse the British of wrongdoing. There were eye witnesses, among them some colonial officers who accused the colonial authorities of negligence in not stopping the atrocities against innocent civilians.

114 Bullotta, op. cit., p. 191.
115 Ibid., p. 181.
116 Abdirazak Haji Hussein, written testimony, February 2010, p. 3.

In fact, testifying before the Court, R.R Wisher, Finance Officer of the BMA, stated: "I could see gendarmes armed with truncheons, either watching the looters without attempting to stop them, or actively helping them to move furniture through the doors of the houses being looted."[117] Other witnesses spoke of direct involvement of the Somali Gendarmerie in the massacre. A. T. Bevan, of the British South African Police attached to the Somali Gendarmerie, stated before the Court: "A Somali, sitting in the front seat of a green Vanette, was firing at the natives in the street. I chased the vehicle and finally caught up with it and stopped it. I pulled the passenger out and disarmed him. He was a Gendarmerie Warrant Officer, not wearing badges. I handed the Warrant Officer to the duty officer at the Central Police Station."[118]

Major A.O. Smith, the Civil Affair Officer posted in Mogadisho, was even more specific in blaming the Somali Gendarmerie when he stated before the Court that: "It was reported on January 13 that a gendarme had been observed on the 11th shooting at an Italian. On 14 January, the Commandant of the Somali Gendarmerie reported that a Gendarme of the 'H' Company was suspected of being one who had shot at an Italian. At a later date, the Deputy Commandant of the Gendarmerie reported to me that eight Somali gendarmes had been found with looted property in their possession and action was being taken against them."[119]

Although instructed not to investigate in full detail, the Court of Inquiry had nevertheless recognized the role that a section of the Somali Gendarmerie had played in the events of 11 January, 1948. "It is abundantly clear that a section of the Force played a more than discreditable part in the events of 11 January, 1948. They were as members or supporters actively on the side of the Lega."

Between 60 and 80 % of the Somali members of the Gendarmerie were alleged to be affiliated to the Lega[120]. The party undoubtedly appeared to have had much support from the Administration, for reasons of policy, and in the minds of its opponents was a government-sponsored institution. However, the Court refuted allegations that British officials took part in or instigated the attacks[121]. Italian losses as a result of the disturbances have been calculated at about £275,000.[122]

117 TNA WO 230/123 Testimony of Witness no. 32, Findings of the Court of Enquiry to investigate disturbances at Mogadisho on 11 January 1948, pp. 73-74.

118 Ibid., pp. 13-15, Testimony of Witness no. 2.

119 Ibid., p. 16, Testimony of Witness no. 1.

120 Ibid., p. 27.

121 Proceedings of Court of Enquiry.

122 TNA FO 1015/45 Telegram n. 913 of May 28, 1948 from Rome to the FO.

Having remained in session for thirty-three days and heard one hundred and one witnesses, the Court reached two major conclusions: (a) that the Italians had played a major part in causing the disturbance and hence had to take an equal share of responsibility for its arising and its consequences, and (b) that the Administration had failed to appreciate the situation and act firmly by forbidding demonstrations by either party.

It is interesting to note that the Court found not only both the Italians and the Administration, but also the Commission of Investigation to blame. In particular, the delay in hearing any of the parties for at least a week after its arrival was considered part of the cause of the outbreak of violence. The Administration maintained that had the parties been heard without delay, or the Commission heeded the Administration's warning of "the danger of procession and agreed to its ban, it is probable that, for the time at least, feeling would have subsided" as the Court of Inquiry noted.[123]

The Court recommended measures be taken to improve relations between the Italian community in Somalia and the Administration, as well as a curtailment of the powers of the Lega "which has been fostered and encouraged to an extent which seems out of reasonable proportion to any political necessity or expedient."[124] The Court added that "The part played by the Lega supporters, whether with, or without the tacit encouragement of its leaders on 11 January, raises grave doubts as to their fitness to be trusted with responsible government, but its supporters may see, in this totally unpunished massacre of Europeans, a sign of encouragement."

The Court concluded that "in order to prevent occurrence of future grave disorder, the national aspirations of the Lega must be kept within proper bounds, and better relations with the European community should be cultivated by the Military Administration."[125] The Court further recommended that the percentage of non-Somali members in the police force should be raised and that the association of members of the force with any of the numerous clubs and societies existing in the country should be discouraged[126]. Further, it should be ensured that police personnel swear loyalty to the BMA and take an oath renewing their contract with the service, and that they should be compelled to

123 Findings of the Court of Enquiry to investigate disturbances at Mogadisho on 11 January 1948, p. 15.
124 Ibid., p. 29.
125 Ibid.
126 TNA FO 1010/51, secret Memo by D.C. Cumming, Major General, Chief Administrator of June 1, 1948, p. 27.

resign from membership of any political party. By the end of 1948, the BMA had taken further action to review the composition of the gendarmerie, leading to the disbandment of 13 Somali infantry companies.

It was felt that the Administration needed a shake-up because the incidents of January 1948 had disorganized several years of peaceful administration. A number of top colonial officers in charge of the administration of the territory were removed as a result of recommendations by the Court of Inquiry. The first head to roll was that of Brigadier Reginald H. Smith, the Administrator, who was replaced by Brigadier Drew, former Chief Administrator for Eritrea[127]. This was followed by the dismissal of Lt. Col. Thorne, who was removed from his appointment as Deputy Commandant of the Somali Gendarmerie on the grounds that "he had failed to appreciate properly the situation which was developing the morning of the disturbances."[128] Major A. O. Smith, the Civil Affairs Officer (C.A.O.) of Mogadisho, was another 'casualty' – transferred to an outpost province of Somalia.

For Calchi Novati "The incidents of 1948 were the product of a turbulent phase of transition in which at least three factors clashed: the Italian propaganda designed to return to Somalia, the desire of Great Britain to annex Somalia, the emergence of Somali nationalism."[129] This conclusion, however, seems to obscure the broader problems of Somali tribalism which played a crucial role in the tragic incidents of January 1948. On the diplomatic front, Italy was successful in getting an Italian diplomat placed in Mogadisho as a liaison officer.[130]

What were the benefits for Italy of a return to Somalia?

All Somali parties, irrespective of their political or tribal affiliations, recognized the necessity for European tutelage for some time under the international trusteeship system before full independence was achieved. The overriding interest of the Somalis and Somalia was that whatever authority taking over Somalia should be prepared to spend money in the country for education, economic development etc. "The governing Power needs to make serious administrative efforts, but she would have also to pay, for the country can pay nothing", as Longrigg wrote.[131]

127 Telegram n. 194 from London to Rome, 1 April 1948 (Mae, 19/1)

128 Findings of the Court of Enquiry to investigate disturbances at Mogadisho on 11 January 1948.

129 Calchi-Novati, *'Gli incidenti di Mogadisho del gennaio 1948, rapporti italo-inglesi e nazionalismo somalo',* Africa, Anno XXXV - no. 3-4, Settembre- Dicembre 1980 p. 355.

130 Raimondo Manzini, Ambassador in Léopoldville, was appointed to serve as liaison officer in Mogadisho on May 14, 1948.

131 Stephen H. Longrigg, *Disposal of Italian Africa'* International Affairs, Royal Institute of International

Without this, neither the welfare of the people nor their political aspirations could progress. Any administering authority should be ready to undertake these obligations. The question was to decide which power was best qualified and ready to take over the trusteeship of the former Italian colony. Ethiopia, Italy and Great Britain expressed interest in Italian Somaliland. Ethiopia was not seeking trusteeship administration over Somalia, but rather pursuing an old claim to annex Somalia, a position that had little chance of winning support from the United Nations.

Among the Four Powers, only Britain expressed an interest in administering Somalia, but after its ill-defined Greater Somalia project was dismissed in 1946 as imperialistic and land-grabbing, she abandoned the idea of administering Somalia on economic grounds[132]. British official sources reveal that the British, because of serious economic concerns, were not ready to continue spending money in Somalia. "The British taxpayer is already paying ten shillings per head per annum for each Somali in Somalia, man, woman and child, and he is not prepared to continue with this commitment. If not Italy, then who?" asks Chief Administrator Brigadier Drew[133]. Another top British officer in Somalia, Major General Cunningham, is reported as saying: "No one in his right mind supposes that we should want to add yet another area of light sandy soil to the Empire's long list of liabilities."[134] The United States, for historical reasons, were not interested in engaging in an African adventure. France remained constant in her long-standing position in support of Italy returning to all its former African colonies.

Italy regarded the reacquisition of its former colonies as a crucial step, for the purposes not only of international rehabilitation, but also of reintegration into the Western alliance system as a credible partner. After all, the Italians continued to consider the African Horn as their traditional sphere of influence[135]. Consequently, in the absence of a major power willing and able to assume international trusteeship responsibilities in Somalia, the conclusion that a non-fascist Italy wishing to return to Africa should assume these responsibilities seemed inevitable.

Affairs (1944-), vol. 21, no. 3 (July, 1945), p. 366.

132 TNA FO.1015/51 top secret telegram from the War Office to Civaffairs, Mogadisho, September 24, 1948.

133 TNA FO.1015/27 top secret report from Brigadier G. F. Drew, May 19, 1948.

134 William Roger Louis, 'The British Empire in the Middle East 1945-1951', Arab Nationalism, the United States and Post-war Imperialism, Oxford University Press,1984, p 280.

135 Okbazghi Yohannes, *The United States and the Horn of Africa*, Westview Press, Oxford 1997, p. 202.

Under the terms of the Peace Treaty of 10 February 1947, Italy was obliged to unconditionally renounce all right and titles to her former colonies, but she argued that she had not renounced her right to claim the restitution of this sovereignty, or to obtain trusteeship. Italy based its claim on the arguments that: (a) it fought on the side of Allied forces following the collapse of the fascist regime, (b) the colonies were all acquired before the advent of fascism and had been under legitimate Italian sovereignty for decades, (c) pre-fascist Italy never considered the colonies as tools of imperialistic exploitation but rather as a means for absorbing Italy's surplus manpower, (d) present democratic Italy should not be held responsible for the iniquities of the fascist regime.[136] The request was not that Italy should be permitted to return to an ancient and anachronistic form of imperialism, but rather that it should be allowed "to carry on its constructive efforts in Africa in accordance with the principle of the United Nations Charter."[137]

Italy hoped that her post-1943 belligerency on the Allied side and the contribution given to the victory by her anti-fascist Resistance would give her valid credentials, winning her favour and granting some concessions from her former enemies. Italy did not claim the right to return to those colonies which had fallen prey to fascist aggression, i.e. Ethiopia and Albania. Italian Foreign Minister Count Sforza practically demanded that Italy be entrusted with trusteeship of Tripolitania, Somalia and Eritrea. The length of the trusteeship would depend on the rapidity with which the people of the territories could be prepared for independence.[138]

On the occasion of the entry into force of the Peace Treaty on 19 September 1947, Brusasca sent a message to the population of the former colonies. The message claimed for Italy the right "to guide again those people to the highest degree form of political structure for the common interest of the people living in those territories with the hope to resume the common work for the prosperity and the political well-being of Libya, Eritrea and Somalia."[139]

Between Somalia, Eritrea and Libya, it was especially on Somalia that Italian expectations were concentrated. Somalia was seen as unprepared for immediate independence and, in case of trusteeship administration, Italy had

136 Letter from Alcide De Gasperi to Secretary of State James Byrnes, Department of State Bulletin, vol. XIII, no. 333, November 11, 1945, pp. 764-5.

137 C. Grove Haines, '*The Problem of the Italian Colonies*', Middle East Journal, vol. 1, no. 4 (Oct. 1947) p. 430.

138 Christopher Seton-Watson, '*Italy's Imperial Hangover*', Journal of Contemporary History, vol. 15, no. 1, Jan. 1980, p. 172.

139 Bollettino settimanale della stampa coloniale ed estera, n°. 2, 8 gennaio 1948.

sufficient credentials to advance her candidature to assume such a responsibility. For Libya, the chance of Italian return, even under the guise of a trusteeship, was slim, because the strong Arab lobby at the United Nations was actively working for immediate independence for the country. Eritrea was torn apart by Ethiopian claims, the ambitions of Sudan and the nationalistic voices calling for independence.[140]

An important support for the government in its claims came from the Italian political parties: even those on the left supported the campaign to return to Africa. The issue of the colonies featured prominently in the political platform of all political parties in the crucial general elections of April, 1948. The territories became an important electoral issue for all political forces and no-one wanted to be seen as neglecting this issue.[141]

A large section of Italian public opinion, including the antifascist political parties, matured the conviction that "it was fascism which lost the war, not Italy."[142] Consequently, it is not surprising that exponents of such varied political persuasions as Ivanoe Bonomi, Giuseppe Saragat, Pietro Nenni and Alcide De Gasperi should have pressed Italian claims during the treaty negotiations[143]. Predictably, during the debate on ratification of the Treaty in the Italian Constituent Assembly, the Government came under scathing criticism from the opposition right-wing party for its handling of the issue, with the extreme right-wing party repeatedly accusing De Gasperi of 'treason'.

From the very beginning, Somalia, as a single political and economical unit, presented huge financial difficulties. There were large deficits in the colonial government's budgets and balance of payments, and Somalia lacked the means to support a central administration.

Prior to 1941, metropolitan Italy paid about two thirds of the country's expenses. Large-scale colonization by Europeans, the object of much past effort and expense by the Italians, misled by 'demographics' and strategic mirages, was never practicable[144]. The country that Italy was requested to bring to independence within a definite period of ten years was, economically, one of the poorest country in the world, and, socially, one of the most underdeveloped. In 1950, the illiteracy rate stood at the staggering level of 99.4%. There was one

140 Calchi Novati, op. cit., p. 329.
141 Ibid., p. 258.
142 A. Morone, *'L'eredita' del colonialismo per la nuova Italia'*, Novecento, 2009. p. 73.
143 Haines, op. cit., p. 430.
144 Longrigg, op. cit., p. 365.

medical doctor for every 60,000 people and 1, 254 beds in the ten small hospitals spread across the country.[145]

According to a study conducted by Professor Ferdinando Bigi, in 1953 the economic activities of the Somali population, estimated at 1,263,584, presented the following picture: Pastoral 42%, agro-pastoral 28.1%, agricultural 19%, traders 3.2%, artisan 1.0%, others 4.8%[146]. As we have seen, a 1950 United Nations report found that three quarters of the cultivated land were abandoned, farms had lost most of their mechanized agricultural tools, and the irrigation system had become useless because of lack of maintenance.

The Egyptian member of the United Nations Advisory Council, Kamal-u-Din, sharing his impressions on the situation he found in Somalia in 1954 with friends and relatives in Egypt, gave a shocking assessment of the economic and social degradation prevailing in the Trust Territory. He wrote: "The state of poverty the people in this territory languish in is shocking. Many of them conduct a life similar to that which existed the time Adam was descended on the earth. The tens of thousands of persons living in the bush and in the farming land are semi-nude, wearing only rags to cover their private parts. They feed themselves with what they hunt in the bush in addition to the milk they get from camel, cattle and goats. In the desert areas of the territory and on the farmlands, the people live in the open without shelter. Only the Sultans of the tribe and the paramount chiefs may have shelters, huts made of bamboo and tree branches. In the capital city itself, the locals live in poor and overcrowded slums. Despite the availability of vast cultivable land, the majority of the local people disdain the art of working; they have no clear understanding of the method of cultivation. The people are convinced that the agriculture is not possible without the mechanized means used by the Italians. They ignore the simple agricultural implement used by the Egyptian to till the land.[147]

Earlier in 1949, during the discussions on the future of Somalia, Enrico Cerulli, an Italian scholar of Somali and Ethiopian studies, colonial official, diplomat and a member of the Italian delegation at the Trusteeship Council, admitted that "Somalia, with its equatorial climate and barren resources, offered Italy no opportunity for colonization for her surplus population or for economic

145 Ministry of Foreign Affairs, Rapport du gouvernment italien à l'Assemblée Generale des Nations Unies sur l'administration de la Somalie placée sous la tutelle dell'Italie, avril-decembre 1950, Roma, Istituto Poligrafico dello Stato, 1951.

146 Ferdinando Bigi, '*Situazione e prospettive economiche della Somalia alla vigilia dell'indipendenza*', Africa, Anno XV, n°3, 1960, p. 133.

147 Ahmed Bahu-Din, Muamarat Fi Ifriqiya, Cairo, Isa al-Babi al Halabi, 1958, p. 18.

exploitation", adding that "it will cost us ten billion lire annually to administer theterritory."[148]

Predictably, Italian economy was not in good shape as a result of the devastating effects of the Second World War. In 1954 its industrial production had dropped to one quarter of what it was in 1938, and the agricultural production had shrunk to half its size over the same period[149]. The disastrous state of the economy was highlighted by Prime Minister Alcide De Gasperi in a radio broadcast speech in 1947 addressed to the Italian public, in the following terms: "Italy needs foodstuffs, raw material, and sources of energy (coal, diesel and electricity), and capital for financing."[150]

If this was the state of affairs in both the Trustee and Trust territory, what interest was there for Italy to return to Africa and take up the responsibility of a costly trusteeship administration? "Nobody has provided an explanation of what irremissible national interest pushed Italy to come back to Somalia in 1950", comments Pietro Petrucci[151]. An explanation was, however, given by Italian political leaders who, despite conceding that trusteeship was a financial burden, raised arguments of foreign policy and international prestige. "The Italian people do not live on bread alone" wrote Count Sforza, who played a key role, as Foreign Minister, in the protracted diplomatic negotiations leading to the return of Italy to Somalia.[152]

Giuseppe Brusasca, Undersecretary for Foreign Affairs in charge of the AFIS dossier, is quoted as saying: "We were going back to Somalia to demonstrate that we were able to inaugurate a new politics in Africa, not one of exploitation anymore, but of collaboration."[153] Italian political leaders were unanimous in their affirmations, showing that they were very much aware of the political importance of returning to Africa, not to gain any economic benefit, but in search of prestige and new alliances outside Europe. In a statement made during the Parliament debate on the acceptance of the trusteeship mandate for Somalia in February 1950, Premier De Gasperi said that "to accept the administration of Somalia means to work for a new world, to earn friendship among all the people longing for liberty and progress by returning to the old Italian Risorgimento."

148 UN Doc T/PV. 207.

149 U. Triulzi, *'L'Italia e l'economia somala dal 1950 ad oggi'*, Africa, vol. XXVI, dicembre 1971, p. 442.

150 Somalia Courier, May 15, 1947.

151 Pietro Petrucci, Mogadisho, Nuova ERI , Torino, 1971, p. 94.

152 C. Sforza, *Cinque anni a Palazzo Chigi*, Rome, Atlante 1952, University of Michigan, pp. 97-99.

153 Patrizia Palumbo (ed.), *'A Place in the Sun': Africa in Italian Colonial Culture. From Post-Unification to the Present, 1997*, 2003, pp. 30-31.

Italy was using Somalia as the first great display of 'virtuous power' after the collapse of fascism.

The legacy of 11 January

At close scrutiny, the incidents of January 11, 1948 appear to have damaged rather than improved the Lega's position. The disturbances in Mogadisho had shattered long years of peaceful administration, and the prestige of the British colonial authorities, accused by the Italian press of failing to protect the life of civilians, had badly suffered as a result. If the aim the Lega wanted to achieve was to gain sympathy and support from the United Nations, that aim had been missed. On the contrary, the incident had put the party at loggerheads both with the Administration and with the Arabs, whether in Somalia or in the neighbouring Arab countries with which they traded, as well as finally leading to improved relations between the Italian community and the British Administration. The first signs of changed circumstances clearly came when the new Chief Administrator, Brigadier Drew, met the Somali Community in Mogadisho at Cinema Hamar on May 12, 1948, and delivered an important speech in which he unveiled the new policy of the Administration. He made it clear to his Somali audience that, as of May 1948, processions and demonstrations were forbidden throughout the territory: "Should any club or party disobey the order, the president and the committee members of such a club or party will be held individually and collectively responsible."[154] In compliance with this new policy, the party was banned, for the first time, from holding a procession on 15 May 1948, the fifth anniversary of its foundation, and was only allowed to celebrate on its own premises.[155]

New measures were introduced, placing the police and the field force of the gendarmerie under separate commands. The police force was placed under the control of the Chief Administrator through a Commissioner of the Police, and the field force under the control of the Officer Commanding Troops[156]. Brigadier Drew was instructed to adopt an impartial but firm attitude towards the various communities and "to use force if the Lega tries to challenge the authority of the

154 TNA FO 1015/45 Text of the address delivered by the Chief Administrator in the Hamar Cinema at Mogadisho, 12 May, 1948.

155 TNA FO 1015/140, Political intelligence Sitrep no. 2, May 14, 1948.

156 TNA FO 1015/45 Text of the address delivered by the Chief Administrator in the Hamar Cinema at Mogadisho, 12 May, 1948.

Administration."[157] However, although the authorities were ready to take firm action in case of any breach of law and order, it was never considered to declare the Lega an illegal organization: "it would be most unwise for us to attempt to break up a so widely distributed and disciplined organization", reads a British secret report[158]. When Brigadier G.F. Drew, at the end of his tenure as Acting Chief Administrator for Somalia, returned to Eritrea to resume his previous position as Administrator, his departure was saluted with much jubilation in Lega circles, which attributed to him the failure to implement what they believed was the British policy of support for their party.[159]

Furthermore, the British colonial authorities admitted, for the first time before the United Nations, that the Lega was not the only representative of the local population, thus recognizing the presence and the role of other political formations whose importance and weight the British had ignored or minimized inthepast.[160]

The Undersecretary of State for Foreign Affairs, Mr Mayhew, announced in the House of Commons that the Greater Somalia project had been withdrawn because it had "not met with the support of other powers."[161] But the real rupture between the BMA and the Lega occurred when on September 24, 1948 Britain concluded an accord transferring Ogaden to the full sovereignty of Ethiopia. The Somalis announced they were ready to fight to the last drop of blood.[162]

Having lost the British support they had enjoyed for a long time, the Lega shifted their attention to the United Nations, with petition after petition to the Secretary General. When the case of former Italian colonies was referred to the United Nations, the party sent an envoy to the United Nations to further their plea for independence and against the return of Italy. At Lake Success, however, the envoy was to battle violently with representatives from the Conferenza Somala, which as we have seen was a convention of associations demanding that the country be placed under the Italian trusteeship before achieving independence.

The envoy's mandate was simple and clear: to insist that any trusteeship arrangement the UN may adopt for Somalia should not last more than ten years, and to oppose the return of Italy, a position that was never reviewed or

157 TNA FO 1015/51, Secret memo to the Director of Civil Affairs, June 1, 1948,

158 TNA FO 1015/51 Top secret report from Major General D.C. Cumming, Chief Civil Affairs Officer, June 1, 1948.

159 TNA FO 1015/51, HQ East Africa Command monthly intelligence review, May 1948.

160 UN Doc.A/C.1/SR. 288.

161 TNA FO 1015/51 Monthly intelligence newsletter no. 21, December 1948.

162 TNA CO 537/3641 Letter of R.H. Smith to the Ufficio Affari Civili, August 6, 1947.

abandoned until the end, even in the face of changes taking place at the UN, and even when it became clear that Italy was highly likely to be assigned the task of administering the trusteeship for Somalia.

The disposal of the Haud and Ogaden

After the invasion of Ethiopia in 1935, the Italian government had incorporated Eritrea, Ethiopia and Somalia into one regional bloc, forming the Italian East Africa Empire (IEAE).

The Italian East African Empire, under Marshall Pietro Badoglio, was divided into five administrative governorates: Eritrea, Harar, Galla & Sidamo, Showa and Somalia. One of the most significant adjustments the Italians introduced was the creation of a much larger Somali administration by detaching the Ogaden region from Ethiopia and combining it with Somalia, creating thus La Grande Somalia, or 'Greater' Italian Somalia[163]. However, while Ogaden became part of the Governorate of Somalia, with Mogadisho as the provincial capital, Harar became part of the Hararghe Governorate.

General (later Marshall) Rodolfo Graziani, who succeeded Pietro Badoglio as Viceroy of Ethiopia, found the way the regions were divided unfair to the Somalis. In fact, he wrote the following telegram to Mussolini, spelling out his disagreement with the situation: "Separating Harar from the Governorate of Somalia would sound like severing the head from the body of Somalia. Harar is a Muslim centre to which the Somali population had aimed during the difficult military campaign paying a high price in blood. For all these reasons, and considering that the Galla population gravitating around Harar constitutes a minority compared to the Somalis, I am of the humble but firm opinion that the frontier of the Governorate of Somalia must be extended to include Hararghe up to Diri Dawa".[164]

In 1942, after occupying the Horn of Africa, Britain signed an agreement with Ethiopia under the terms of which it recognized Ethiopia's independence. However, there was one important clause attached to the Agreement: the right of Britain to control the Ogadenia and Haud areas, two regions inhabited by Somalis[165]. On close scrutiny, the Anglo-Ethiopian Convention of 1942 did not specifically provide for the transfer of Ogaden, which happened later

163 Barnes, op. cit., p. 3.

164 Del Boca, op. cit., pp, 234-5.

165 Article 2 of the Agreement.

under Ethiopian rule after the war[166]. It was under the second Anglo-Ethiopian Convention of 1944 that Britain recognized Ethiopian sovereignty over the two territories of Ogaden and Haud and, while they were still under its control, allowed the Ethiopian flag to be hoisted in parallel with the Union Jack on government buildings to symbolize Ethiopian sovereignty.[167]

The Somalis were undoubtedly given some hope and stimulus immediately following World War II when the British administered all of the five Somali lands except French Somaliland and proposed a Greater Somaliland under British trusteeship. They were led to believe that, as a minimum, Britain might hold on to the Ogaden. This did not happen, and Ogaden was handed over to Ethiopia in 1948, thus formalizing, as it were, the death of the Greater Somalia project. The Lega's declared intention to meet the Ethiopian advance into Ogaden with armed resistance did not materialize, and its strongholds in Gabridaharre, Warder and Shilabo did not interfere with the handover of the territory to Ethiopia.

The handing of Ogaden to the Abyssinians was completed on September 12, 1948, when Mustahil was transferred, without incident, to the Ethiopian Administration – the date coinciding with the submission of the future of Somalia to the United Nations, following the disagreement of the Four Powers over the issue of the former Italian colonies. "This moderation on the part of the Lega may be ascribed to fairly large sums of Ethiopian money finding its way into the pockets of influential members of the native community", as a British intelligence report comments[168]. A sum of £91,000 was allegedly offered by the departing British "as disbursement amongst the Ogaden clansmen in settlement of all outstanding blood dues and claims incurred during the British rule."[169]

On 29 September 1954, while Ethiopia and Italy were still engaged in inconclusive negotiations on the border demarcation between Ethiopia and Somalia, Britain had returned the Reserved Areas to Ethiopia under a bilateral agreement referring to an unpublished Anglo-Ethiopian treaty dating back to 1897. Article One of the new Agreement reads: "The full and exclusive sovereignty of Ethiopia over the territories which are set forth in the attached schedule (hereinafter referred to as 'the territories'), recognized by the Anglo-Ethiopian Treaty of 1897, is hereby reaffirmed."

The Anglo-Ethiopian 1945 agreement provides: "The right of tribes coming

166 Rennel, op. cit., p. 95.
167 Ibid. , p. 495.
168 TNA FO 1015/51 HQ East Africa Command monthly intelligence report, September 1948.
169 I.M. Lewis, op. cit., p. 150.

respectively from Ethiopia and Somaliland Protectorate to cross the frontier for the purpose of grazing, as originally set out in the Anglo-Ethiopian Treaty of 1897 and the letters annexed thereto is reaffirmed by the two Contracting Parties who shall take steps to ensure that as far as possible tribal grazing rights in the area shall be protected."

In 1960 Ethiopia terminated grazing rights, thus nullifying the Treaty of London that had permitted Somali herders to move freely in and out of Ogaden: "The agreement provides also that, as from February 22, 1955, British Military Administration for which temporary provisions were made under the Anglo-Ethiopian Agreement of December 19, 1944, shall be withdrawn from the Reserved Area as defined in the schedule to the Agreement and from that part of the Ogaden which is at present under British Military Administration. The Imperial Ethiopian Government shall from that date resume jurisdiction and administration of, and over the territories."[170]

The transfer was viewed by the Somalis as a betrayal of the protectorate treaties that Britain had signed with traditional leaders in 1884-1886. The Somali tribes had in fact challenged both the agreements of 1897 and that of 1954 between Britain and Ethiopia, and claimed that their own 1884 agreement with Her Majesty's Government overrode these – urging the case be referred to the International Court of Justice "for an advisory opinion on the legal validity of the Anglo-Ethiopian treaties". The United Nations Charter did not give representatives of British Somaliland any right to petition the United Nations, since the Somaliland Protectorate was neither a member of the United Nations nor a Trusteeship Territory.

News of the agreement had given rise to widespread feelings of anger, and a delegation comprising Michael Mariano, Abdirahman Ali and Mohamed Dubeh was sent to London to protest against the agreement and to secure a postponement of its implementation. During their visit to London, they formally met and discussed the issue with the Secretary of State for the Colonies, Alan Lennox-Boyd. Somalia's arguments were based on three points:

1. That the two treaties disregarded early agreements made with the clans, that had put them under British protection;

170 Agreement between the government of the United Kingdom of Great Britain and Northern Ireland and the government of Ethiopia relating to certain matters connected with the withdrawal of British Military Administration from the territories designated as Reserved Area and Ogaden, London November 29, 1954, Treaty Series no. 1 (1955-).

2. That the Somalis were not consulted on the terms of the treaties between Britain and Ethiopia and in fact had not been informed of their existence; and
3. That the treaties violated the self-determination principle.

Secretary of State for the Colonies Mr Lennox-Boyd stated in the House of Commons that the delegation put their points of view "with dignity and force and made abundantly clear the value they attach to being under British administration", adding: "I have had no alternative but to inform them that Her Majesty's government must abide by their obligations in international law. I have made clear to them what those obligations are, and have told them there is no question of Her Majesty's government's repudiating international agreements."[171]

Commenting on the highly questionable handover, I.M. Lewis wrote: "As the victim of fascist aggression, Ethiopia had naturally every right to the most consideration and generous treatment. But, it was unfortunate that in the process of satisfying her claims to reparation for the events of the past, protesting

171 British Somaliland (Anglo-Ethiopian Agreement) HC Deb 23 February 1955 vol. 537 cc1281-9.

Somalis should be sacrificed and the collective Somali desire for national self-determination be cast aside as soon as it had achieved an articulate existence."[172] The transfer of Haud had marked a moral defeat for Somali nationalism.

172 I.M. Lewis, op. cit., p. 151.

Chapter III

THE ITALIAN COLONIES BEFORE THE GENERAL ASSEMBLY

The disposal of the Italian colonies proved to be one of the most vexing and difficult problems the victorious Four Powers faced in the post-war era. A welter of conflicting claims emanating from six different stakeholders had emerged to complicate the matter: Ethiopia claimed Eritrea and Somalia, thus pursuing its policy and its dream of expanding its empire, end its landlocked state and get an outlet to the sea. The Arab States called for the independence of Libya in solidarity with their Arab brothers. France laid claim to Fezzan, in the south-western part of that colony, to protect its interests in the neighbouring North African colonies. Britain was seeking to bolster its weakening position in the Eastern Mediterranean by retaining control over Cyrenaica, the colony's eastern half. The native inhabitants of all the colonies, in varying degrees, were crying out for freedom. And last but not least, the defeated enemy state, Italy, put up a determined struggle to prevent the loss of her colonies.[1]

One year after the coming into force of the Peace Treaty with Italy and after three years of discussions among the Big Four, the future of Italian colonies in Africa remained undetermined. The Allied deputy foreign ministers submitted their respective recommendations, characterized by disagreement not only

1 Rivlin, op. cit., vol. 3, no. 3, Aug. 1949, pp. 460-461.

between the Soviet Union and the Western Powers, but between the Western Powers too. The work of the deputies was difficult and inconclusive as they could not even agree on procedural matters, such as the number of Commission officials to be dispatched to the colonies or the itinerary and composition of the Commission itself, let alone any substantial matters.

The report of the Four Power Commission of Investigation was submitted to the Council of Foreign Ministers at their Paris meeting in September, 1948. On September 24, the governments of France, the Union of Soviet Socialist Republics, Great Britain and the United States of America jointly addressed a communication to the Secretary General informing him that, in conformity with Article 23, paragraph XI of the Treaty with Italy, the question of the disposal of the former Italian colonies was being referred to the General Assembly of the United Nations.[2]

The Assembly was thus given the role of arbiter in a dispute that had defied solution despite protracted and intricate negotiations among the leading powers of the world. "The role which the Assembly assumed", comments Rivlin, "was very similar to the role it was asked to play when the British turned over to it the problem of Palestine", with one important difference: whereas on the Palestine issue the General Assembly's recommendation was not binding, with respect to the Italian colonies the Assembly was given the unique function of making a final and binding recommendation."[3]

The General Assembly, on the recommendation of the Bureau (A/653) in the course of its 142nd ordinary meeting held on September 24, 1949, decided to pass the issue to the First Committee for consideration and report. However, when the first part of the third regular session of the General Assembly opened in Paris at the Palais de Chaillot on 21 September, the issues on the agenda were many and not all the delegations had had enough time to 'digest' the abundant documentation transmitted by the Council of Ministers[4]. The last-minute inclusion of the question on the Assembly's agenda left delegates with hardly enough time to consult with their governments on the matter.

The Assembly placed discussion of the issue on the last point of its agenda — behind a number of important questions such as the Reports of the Atomic Energy Commission, the Palestine question, the political independence and

2 A/645 and A/645/Add.1.

3 Rivlin, op. cit., p. 459.

4 Rossi, op. cit., p. 398.

territorial integrity of Greece, and the independence of Korea[5]. Due to the pressure of business, it was not possible to make a decision on the question during the Paris session of the General Assembly; therefore, examination of the issue was deferred until the second part of the third regular session of April 1949 in Lake Success, New York.

Consideration of the matter began during the second part of the session, at the 238th meeting of the First Committee held on April 6, 1949. In the course of this period, the United States came out heavily in support of Italian trusteeship of Somalia. The US policy to support the Italian claim over trusteeship of Somalia was made public by US Secretary of State John Foster Dulles in early April, with the advancing of a number of arguments in these terms: "the area is without major strategic importance, from the standpoint of international peace and security. In view of the revival of democratic government and institutions since the overthrow of Fascism in Italy and the demonstrated willingness and ability of the present government of Italy to assume the obligations of a peace-loving state in accordance with the Charter, we feel that Italy should be invited to undertake the responsibility of administering the Italian Somaliland under the UN Trusteeship system[...] The Italian nation has a surplus of population of people who have demonstrated in many part of the world their capacity to develop waste places into productivity. We believe that the natural welfare of the Italian people and the inhabitants of Africa can be advanced, by co-operation under sound administration."[6] However, the Soviet Union, which in the past had favoured the Italian claim with regard to all its former colonies, had by now changed its position, proposing instead a plan by which all former colonies would be placed under direct United Nations trusteeship.[7]

The Bevin–Sforza compromise plan

The Somali political parties invited to the UN

While the Assembly was in recess, it was suddenly announced that British Foreign Secretary Mr Bevin and Italian Foreign Minister Count Carlo Sforza[8], meeting in London, had come to a compromise plan on the future of the Italian

5 UN Doc. A/C.1/SR.143.
6 Department of State bulletin, April 17th, 1949, p. 485, (in Azbaghi, op. cit., p. 203).
7 A/C.1/433/Rev..
8 Sforza served as Minister of Foreign Affairs from February 2, 1947 to July 19, 1951.

colonies. This became widely known as the Bevin–Sforza Plan[9]. The Plan was signed in London on May 4, 1949 and reflected the desire of the two countries to apportion the colonies between them without considering the positions of the populations concerned, or that of the other three allies. The Bevin–Sforza Plan was a compromise reached outside the United Nations process; it was a bilateral agreement between Britain and Italy and as such it was liable to meet with defeat at the UN. The new Anglo-Italian deal advocated the division of Libya into three different provinces:

1. Tripolitania: to be placed under Italian trusteeship in 1951 assisted by a Consultative Committee composed of France, India, Italy, USA, Egypt (or any other Arab country) and a representative from the local population.
2. Fezzan: to be placed under trusteeship assigned to France.
3. Cyrenaica: to be placed under trusteeship assigned to Britain. All of Libya would be granted independence at the end of ten years.

For Eritrea, the Plan envisaged the following arrangement: with the exception of the Western provinces, Eritrea would be annexed to Ethiopia through a treaty with the UN, giving guarantee of special status for the cities of Asmara and Massawa. The terms of such a guarantee would be established by the UN in consultation with Italy. The western provinces would be incorporated with neighbouring Sudan.

Somalia would be placed under trusteeship with Italy as administering power; no mention was made of any date for independence.

The Bevin–Sforza Plan is a further demonstration of the continued disagreement among the Four Powers regarding the disposal of Italian colonies. It also reflects changing patterns of relationship between former enemies Britain and Italy, confirming further that the efforts of the Italian Foreign Minister Count Sforza were successful in winning Mr Bevin's assent to a compromise plan. "The results of the 1948 Italian elections, in which the democratic forces emerged hugely victorious, appear to have produced the effects of diminishing Britain's doubts about Italy's democratic credentials", comments Seton-Watson[10]. Mutual understanding between Italy and Britain was facilitated not only by the results of the Italian elections of 18 April 1948, but also by Italy's joining of the

9 United Nations Press Release, GA/PS/217, May 10, 1949.

10 Seton-Watson, op.cit., p. 177.

north Atlantic Treaty Organization, NATO, as a full and equal member. In fact, on April 4 1949, Sforza signed the North Atlantic Treaty on behalf of Italy as an equal founding member.[11]

The provisions of the Anglo–Italian plan were incorporated in a resolution submitted by Britain to the General Assembly of the United Nations[12] and referred to the First Committee, known as Political and Security Committee and appointed by the General Assembly, which debated the issue between 6 and 13 May, 1949. The Plan was categorically rejected by the Somali League; however, it received enthusiastic support by the leaders of the Conferenza Somala. In fact, in a telegram addressed to Brusasca few days before the rejection of the Plan by the General Assembly, Somali leaders expressed their satisfaction with the plan in these terms: "Pregovi rendervi interprete governo italiano rallegramenti popolazione somala Accordo Sforza–Bevin conferma idea nostra, firmato Islao e Yassin." ("We kindly urge you to pass on to the Italian government the congratulations of the Somali people, Sforza–Bevin Plan in line with our idea. Signed: Islao and Yassin".)[13]

After the massacre of 11 January 1948 in Mogadisho, political confrontations between Somali rival groups over the future status of their country moved to New York, a neutral site where the parties were able to present their views in a peaceful atmosphere. Like the Lega, the political association known as Conferenza Somala was invited to dispatch its own envoys to Lake Success to present their views on the future of the territory. On the basis of this invitation the Conferenza Somala sent as its representatives Islao Mahadalla and Yassin Ali Sharmarke, brother of the late Abdirashid Ali Sharmarke, the last civilian President of the Somali Republic.

The fact that the Conferenza sent two of its members to the United Nations was a shock for the Lega, who feared that representatives from the rival group might present themselves at Lake Success as delegates not just chosen by the Conference, but also representing all Somali tribes. To prevent this happening, leading notables within the Darod clan in Mogadisho petitioned the Administrator against allowing Yassin Ali to travel to New York, arguing that he might present himself as qualified to speak for all the Darod tribes, in addition to representing the Lega Progressista Migiurtina. The Administrator declined the request to forbid Yassin's departure, but at the behest of the petitioners signalled

11 Morone, op. cit., p. 78.

12 UN Doc. A/1C.446, May 12, 1949.

13 ASCM, 34/65, Maggio 15, 1949.

to the Foreign Office to make it known that the delegates were representing the Conferenza.[14]

As feared, the Conferenza sent a cable to the United Nations stating that Islao Mahadalla Mohamed would also represent the Hawiye tribes, and that Yassin Ali would represent the Lega Progressista Migiurtina and the Darod tribes. The same British source speaks of strong rumours that Yassin Ali would be physically liquidated either before his departure or even during his journey to the UK. He was, in fact, the victim of a minor assault as he was entering his house on the evening of April 18, 1949. "The assailant escaped and Yassin was immediately provided with bodyguard among his supporters who, by the night previous of his departure, numbered 40, posted in strategic positions around his house."[15] All its efforts to stop the Conference delegates' departure for New York having proven unsuccessful, the Lega made a last and desperate attempt, on April 21, on the eve of the delegation's departure for London, by summoning at least 48 Sheikhs "to pray that the plane would crash."[16] Needless to say, Allah did not accommodate the Lega's prayers, and Yassin and Islao Mahadalla arrived safe and sound at the United Nations HQs in New York. A British intelligence report suggests that the funds put at the delegation's disposal by the Italian government totalled 45,000 shilling[17]. This was ample funding compared with the very modest amount of £750 that the Lega had requested permission to transmit to London to cover its representative's expenses on the trip to the General Assembly sessions in Lake Success.[18]

Hearing accorded to the Somali Youth League

When the General Assembly reconvened at Lake Success (New York) in April 1949 for the second part of the third session, the question of the disposal of the former Italian colonies received immediate attention. In fact, it was the first item on the agenda of the First Committee. Immediately after convening, a sub-committee of Committee I (Sub-Committee 15) was established, with the task to consider the various proposals.[19] The Sub-Committee immediately turned its attention to the Bevin–Sforza compromise plan on the future of the

14 TNA FO 1015/188 Political intelligence report: Somalia for period ending April 22, 1949.
15 Ibid.
16 Ibid.
17 Ibid.
18 Ibid., Somalia for period ending March 4th, 1949.
19 UN Doc. A/C.1/466, May 12, 1949.

colonies, rather than the resolutions previously presented to Committee I, as the Bevin–Sforza seemed to several delegations the only plan that might possibly muster the necessary two-third vote. Before opening the debate on the question, Committee I approved a resolution, submitted by the United States of America, inviting the government of Italy to appoint a representative to sit, without vote, in the Committee's discussions, in accordance with its request[20]. Enrico Cerulli, the Italian observer at the United Nations, was allowed to take part in the discussions on the colonies.

On April 11, 1949, at its 242nd meeting, the Committee adopted a resolution submitted by the United Kingdom. There was a proviso that a sub-committee (Sub-Committee 14), composed of Brazil, Egypt, France, Haiti, India, New Zealand, Norway, Poland, the Union of Soviet Socialist Republics, the United Kingdom and the United States of America examine the requests presented by political parties or organizations of the territories concerned not later than April 23, 1949, and report to the Committee on the extent to which those bodies represented substantial sections of the opinion in those territories[21]. Following the recommendations of Sub-Committee 14, the Committee heard the representatives of the following political parties for Somaliland:

1. The Conferenza Somala
2. The Lega Progressista della Migiurtinia
3. Unione Gioventù Hamar[22] and
4. Lega dei Giovani Somali.

It should be noted that the emergence of strong pro-Italian political parties such as the Somali Conferenza, which came into existence after the visit of the Four Power Commission of Investigation, represented a serious challenge to the Lega's claim to represent the overwhelming majority of Somali people.

On April 21, 1949 Abdullahi Issa, representative of the Lega dei Giovani Somali and Hamar Youth[23], explained that the purpose of his organization in appearing before the Committee was to express the categorical opposition of the overwhelming majority of the inhabitants of Somalia to the restoration of Italian

20 A/C.1/430.

21 UN Doc. A/C.1/435.

22 The Unione Gioventù Hamar did not in fact send a representative of its own to Lake Success, but was represented by the Lega envoy.

23 UN Doc A/C.1/SR.248, April 21, 1949.

administration in any form or guise whatsoever. He urged the Committee to act in accordance with that opinion and drew their attention to the principles contained in paragraph 2 of Annex XI of the Italian Peace Treaty. Mr Issa explained that he was speaking on behalf of the Somali people because he was "the leader of a strong progressive nationalist movement which was likely to be the dominant factor in local politics for some time to come." He had "a following of some 300,000 persons at the time of the Four Power Commission of Investigation's visit to Somalia."[24] Other than Abdullahi Issa, the other Lega delegates present at Lake Success were Ali Nour and Ismail Hassan, both citizens of the British Protectorate of Somaliland, who volunteered to give a hand to the Lega envoy.

The envoy stressed that, during the fifty years of Italian rule, the population had been kept in slavery, deprived of education, of commercial opportunities, and of possibilities for social and political advancement. He stated that their lands had been seized and, under the dreaded colonia system, the people had been pressed into forced labour under conditions of almost incredible cruelty. Mr Issa appealed to the Commission, exhorting it to be guided not by the principle of political expedience but by the interests of the inhabitants. He added that "if, contrary to the expressed desire of the Somali people, the United Nations should decide to return the territory to Italy, then the Somalis could not be expected to have faith in the United Nations."[25]

In reply to a question from Mr Cooper of Liberia as to what form the Somali opposition to Italian trusteeship would take, the Lega envoy stated that the Somali people would offer physical resistance in spite of their limited resources because they "preferred death to the return of Italian rule."[26] On the notion that Italy was now a democratic country, different from the fascist regime, he said that "no persuasion could convince the Somali people that the new Italian regime would behave any better than the preceding ones." He claimed that Italy based its desire to share in the administration of the former colonies "upon the necessity of procuring an outlet for its surplus population."

He stated that the programme of his organization, as presented to the Four Power Commission of Investigation, had been: (a) A collective trusteeship under the United Nations of no more than ten years leading to the establishment of complete independence; and (b) Strong opposition to the restoration of Italian administration in any form.

24 Ibid.
25 UN Doc. A/C.1/SR. 248.
26 Ibid.

On May 12, 1949, precisely one week before the closure of the regular third session of the General Assembly, the Lega envoy, appearing again before the First Committee of the General Assembly, quoted excerpts from a letter addressed to the Chairman of Sub-Committee 15, in which the Somali Youth League vehemently protested against the new proposal before the Sub-Committee and demanded self-government and independence for the people of Somaliland as provided for in the United Nations Charter.[27] Mr Issa quoted the SYL's position on a decision in favour of a trusteeship—that it would be favourable to direct United Nations Administration for a period not exceeding ten years, designed to lead the Somalis to self-government followed by complete independence.

Issa's broadcasts from America

During his visit to Lake Success, the Lega emissary had been broadcasting four times a week from the stations WRNA, WRNI and WOOC in New York to his audience in Somalia, from 18:25 to 18:35 hours GMT – at the estimated cost of £1.00 a minute.

On May 10, 1949 he told his listeners: "If Italy returned, it would never leave the country again, and if she came back the same thing would happen in Somalia as had happened in the Union of South Africa. The white population would increase, the black population would decrease and the former would swallow the latter. As long as the white men remained in Somalia, the Somalis would be always the victims."[28]

In a subsequent message, on May 13, 1949, after the Sub-Committee had accepted the British proposal that Somaliland and Tripolitania should be placed under Italian trusteeship, he made a scathing attack on the British, calling them thieves and accusing them of betraying their agreement with the Lega that Italy should never come back to Somalia. His message made reference to the fighting between the Arabs and Jews in the course of which Britain pretended to be friend of the Arabs, but betrayed them to Israel[29]. In the same message of May 13, the Lega emissary repeated again that in the USA there was no justice because there were many pro-Italian Jews, and that everything was done by force, similar to the force applied against the Palestinian Arabs. In a bid to alleviate the frustrations of his listeners, he said that the decision of the Sub-Committee was not the

27 UN Doc. A/C.1SR/270, May 12, 1949.
28 TNA FO 371/73795, translation of Issa's message, May 10, 1949.
29 Ibid., translation of Issa's message, May 17, 1949.

opinion of the United Nations but was merely an agreement between Mr Bevin and Count Sforza. He reminded his listeners that the people of Tripolitania had rioted on hearing that Tripolitania would be placed under Italian trusteeship, and had smashed Italian buildings, fought the British and torn the British flag. He cited countries like Indonesia, Burma and China, who were all fighting to secure freedom. For the Lega emissary "it would be better to fight for two or three hundred years than to be under Italian domination [...] it would be better for all Somalis to be killed than to have Italians in Somalia. The Somalis would be treated as 'natives, as the black South Africans were being treated in the Union of south Africa."[30]

On two separate occasions he cited two Italian nationals whom he blamed for ruining Mogadisho: Dr. Dall'Olio and Sig. Francesco Boero. Dr. Dall'Olio was an Italian judge serving under the British Administration and Signor Francesco Boero a leading businessman. Mr Issa did not indicate what the two Italians were being blamed for. He called on the Somalis to resist, by force if necessary, any UN decision in favour of Italy. These anti-British and anti-Italian messages raised fears in the mind of the British colonial authorities in Somalia that these broadcasts may represent an incitement to violence. The British colonial authorities sought ways of stopping these messages being aired[31]. The difficulty was, however, that these broadcasts were generated from private stations and no official representations could be made to the United States Government about them.[32]

Hearing accorded to the Somalia Conference

With direct Italian financial assistance and guidance, a four-strong delegation representing the Conferenza Somalia party attended United Nations debates at Lake Success on the future of Somalia. According to British intelligence reports, the total sum put at the delegation's disposal was Sh45, 000 including Sh16, 000 for payment to BOAC agents for fares. The report adds: "On paper the sum represented a Sh.So5,000 subscribtions paid by each of the nine Conferenza Clubs. However, it is believed the actual cash paid was collected from Dott. Benardelli, from three of the leading Italian industrial concerns, namely S.A.I.S. De Vincenzi and Boero."[33]

30 Ibid.

31 73795 telegram from Mogadisho addressed to FO, May 14, 1949.

32 Ibid., telegram from FO to Mogadisho, June 2, 1949.

33 TNA FO 1015/188"Political Intelligence Report-Somalia no.7/49 for period ending 22nd April, 1949.

The members of the delegation included Islao Mahadalla Mohamed, Yassin Ali Sharmarke, Abukar Kassim, and Mohamed Sheikh Osman 'Edmondo'[34]. Delegation members were selected with the utmost care and consideration so as to include the three major Somali tribal groups: the Darod, Hawiye and Dighil Mirifle. Yassin Ali Sharmarke, Secretary General of the Lega Majertenia, represented the Darod; Abukar Kassim, Vice President of the Dighil and Mirifle Party, represented the Sab, and Islao Mahadalle, President of the Conferenza Somala, jointly with Mohamed Sheikh Osman 'Edmondo', the Hawiye. The delegation was truly representative of all Somali clans, carrying with it 173 credentials signed by 3,256 persons[35] divided as follows:

1. Darod race: 53 credentials signed by 960 persons,
2. Hawiye race: 70 credentials signed by 1,438 persons,
3. Sab race (Dighil and Mirifle): 30 credentials signed by 693 persons,
4. Political organization and former servicemen: 11 credentials signed by 165 persons.

The selection and composition of the Conferenza delegation was carefully effected to demonstrate the ideal that tribal affiliation is far more important than affiliation to any political party.

Appearing before the Political Committee of the General Assembly of the United Nations on May 3, 1949, Islao Mahadalla Mohamed said that, as President of the Somalia Conference, he was speaking on behalf of a coalition of seven parties formed in September 1947. The parties were the Patriotic Beneficence Union, the Hizbia Dighil Mirifle, the Somali Young Abgal Association, the Union of Africans in Somalia, the Bimal Union, the Hidayat Al-Islam Shidle & Mobilen, and the Somali Progressive Committee. He added that he had been asked to represent the Hawiye and Sab tribes which between them formed two thirds of the population of Somaliland and which had been unable to send a special representative[36]. In his statement, Islao Mahadalla defined and elaborated on the political programme of his organization, supported by religious leaders and other dignitaries. The same programme had been placed before the Four Power Commission of Investigation in 1948 – with the request that the trusteeship of

34 ASMAE, 9/11, Secret document no. 1176 di prot. to the Foreign Ministry, Rome, September 20, 1949.
35 Ibid.
36 Information about Somalia's population has always been obscured by a myriad of figures. To this day, no-one knows which one is accurate.

Somaliland be entrusted to Italy.

The President of the Conferenza Somala, explaining the grounds upon which his organization favoured Italian administration, said that Italy brought great administration and economic progress to Somaliland. The Italian language and civilization were more widely spread throughout the country than any other European language or civilization. The Italian government had promised to administer Somaliland in accordance with the principles of the Charter and the wishes of the inhabitants. That was, according to the representative of the Conferenza, "the desire of two thirds of the people of Somaliland as well as the Darod who, with the exception of the Mogadisho section and the Somali Youth League, formed the remainder of the population." Islao Mahadalla added that "the Majerten population were particularly in favour of an Italian trusteeship, and had sent on their behalf Yassin Ali Sharmarke, representative of the Lega Progressista Migiurtina, to New York. The Sultan of the Majerten, Mussa Yousuf Bogor, had sent a telegram to the United Nations declaring himself in favour of a democratic Italian trusteeship, recalling what had been accomplished by that country."[37]

Appearing again before the Committee on May 12, 1949, the representative of the Conferenza Somala stated that his party gave its full support to the draft resolution provided by Sub-Committee 15 in respect of Somaliland. As he had explained in his previous statement, it was the cherished desire of the Somali people to attain complete independence, but they realized that the time was not yet ripe and that an interim period of administrative guidance was essential.[38]

The Conferenza Somala representative added that his delegation fully believed that trusteeship under the United Nations offered the best solution for his country. He advised the Committee against placing undue importance upon the opposing views expressed by the spokesman of the Somali Youth League, which "represented only a small minority group living in or near Mogadisho." Replying to questions posed by Mohammad Zafarullah Khan, representative of Pakistan, Mr Mahadalla stated that Italian rule had lasted for almost fifty years and that that period had been characterized by peace and justice, adding that about 500 Somalis held official government posts, many of them in the Justice Department.[39]

In reply to further questions from the Pakistani representative as to the role played by the Somalis in the administration of Justice, Mr Mahadalla explained

37 254th meeting of the Committee held at Lake Success, New York on Tuesday, 3 May, 1949.

38 UN Doc. A/C.1SR/270, May 12, 1949.

39 Ibid.

that there were two kinds of Courts in Somaliland: the Muslim and the Italian Courts. In the former, the majority of judges belonged to the indigenous population, and many of the latter were also assistant judges in the Italian Courts. As for the High Courts, it was true that no Somali had ever been President, but Somali nationals had performed ancillary functions. He added that remuneration of Somali judges and court officials had been approximately the same as that of Italians performing the same functions. Approximately fifty Somali judges received a salary of 3,000 lire per month.[40]

In reply to further questions from the same Pakistani representative as to the number of universities and institutions of higher education established under Italian regime, the representative of the Conferenza Somala replied that there were educational establishments of all kinds – institutions teaching Islamic Law and religion, medicine, and general and technical subjects. As to civic administration, there were four municipalities apart from Mogadisho, each of which was administered by an Italian and assisted by a Somali. The Conferenza representative further explained that "under Italian rule there had been eleven political associations. It was true that only one newspaper was published in the territory in both Arabic and Italian, but that was due to the recent social developments in Somaliland."[41]

Addressing questions from the representative of Poland, Mr Drohojowski, as to why, after fifty years of the progressive rule which the representative of the Conferenza Somala had described, the people of Somaliland did not yet deem themselves ready for independence, Islao Mahadalla explained that Somaliland's unpreparedness for self-government was not due to any lack of progressiveness on the Italian government's part during the past fifty years. When Italy assumed the administration of the country, the indigenous population had been largely nomadic and much of the early Italian efforts had been devoted to the establishment of communications and the creation of towns and communities. "The fascist rule" commented Islao Mahdalla "had interrupted the progressive development of the country."[42]

The Conferenza delegation to the United Nations General Assembly returned to Mogadisho on December 26. During their stay in Rome, en route from the United States, the delegates were received by Italian Prime Minister Alcide De Gasperi, and were reported to have been highly praised for their part in securing

40 Ibid.
41 Ibid.
42 Ibid.

a favourable decision by the General Assembly.[43]

The First Committee accepts a resolution based on the Bevin–Sforza Plan

Various draft resolutions were submitted to the First Committee, the most important one being that presented by the United Kingdom reflecting the Bevin-Sforza agreement on the future of the three pre-war Italian colonies.[44]

The United States delegate presented on May 9 a draft resolution[45] recommending the establishment of a sub-committee (Sub-Committee 15). This Sub-Committee would "consider the various proposals which have been submitted or may be submitted to the Committee, draft a resolution for the Committee's consideration and report to the Committee not later than Thursday noon, May 12, 1949."[46]

The sub-committee held four meetings on 10 and 11 May. At its first meeting, Mr Padilla Nervo (Mexico) was elected as chairman, and Mr Hermod Lannung (Denmark) as rapporteur. After an exchange of views on the best and speediest approach to the various proposals concerning the former Italian colonies, the sub-committee broadly agreed to decide on the principles contained in the said proposals rather than on the proposals themselves[47]. On the basis of that deliberation, it was agreed to separately examine the question of the disposal of each of the three territories: Libya, Somalia and Eritrea.

With regard to Somalia, the sub-committee noted that none of the proposals submitted envisaged immediate independence for Italian Somaliland. By nine votes against four, with three abstentions, the sub-committee rejected the proposal to place Somalia under direct United Nations trusteeship. By ten votes against three, with three abstentions, the sub-committee rejected the proposal to place Somalia under collective trusteeship. By nine votes against six, with one abstention, the sub-committee adopted the proposal to place Somalia under Italian trusteeship.[48]

The sub-committee approved the Anglo-Italian plan and submitted it to the

43 TNA FO 1915/509 British Military Administration Somalia, monthly intelligence report for December 1949.

44 UN Doc. A/C.1/446, May 11, 1949.

45 UN Doc. A/C.1/458.

46 UN Doc. A/C.1/459.

47 UN Doc, A/C.1/466, May 11, 1949.

48 Ibid.

First Committee[49]. The 15-nation sub-committee reviewed all the proposals but preferred the Bevin–Sforza plan for the former Italian colonies. Vote on the Bevin–Sforza plan was 10 for, with 4 against and 1 abstention. The plan was then submitted as a package to the First Committee.

In the full Committee 1 meeting, the Bevin–Sforza Agreement approved by Sub-Committee 15 sparked a prolonged and heated debate. With regard to Somalia, Sir Zafarullah Khan, of Pakistan, bitterly noted that "fifty years of Italian rule had not prepared Somali people in the slightest way for independence. The Territory did not even have a newspaper in the language of the people from which they could derive information and political instruction." He wondered whether fifty more years of Italian rule would bring the Somalis any closer to the attainment of independence[50]. In recognition of his strong support for the Lega's position, Sir Zafarullah Khan was awarded with the First Star of the Somali Republic, First Class, during his visit to Somalia in January 1963.

Criticism of the resolution also came from the Saudi Arabia delegate, Mr Aousley W. Dejani, who said: "It was alleged in the Sub-Committee's report that the recommended proposal represented a compromise. If that was so, many delegations would be bitterly disappointed, for the compromise would have been reached at the expense of the population whose fate was being decided."[51] The Soviet delegate commented "History, or rather diplomatic tragedy, had rather unfolded itself behind the back of the First Committee. Its members were being called upon to set the seal on a fait accompli, that is to say, an agreement reached between United Kingdom and Italy, with the tacit consent of the United States."[52]

The Egyptian delegate, reacting to the Anglo–Italian Plan on the future of the Italian ex-colonies, recalled that riots had broken out among the Somalis when they had heard of the possibility of the return of Italy to their country. He read the following quotation from a cable received from Italian Somaliland: "The unfortunate decision of the Sub-Committee was based exclusively on political and imperialistic considerations framed outside the United Nations. In fact, the whole debate of the Sub-Committee was based on the discussions in Whitehall, the seat of the British government in London, between Count Sforza and Mr Bevin."[53]

49 Ibid.
50 UN Doc. A/C. 1/SR 270, par.17.
51 UN Doc. A/C. 1/SR/ 271, May 12, 1949.
52 Ibid.
53 UN Doc. A/PV. 218, May 17, p. 194.

With the strong backing of the USA, UK, France and the Latin American Republics, the resolution based on the Bevin–Sforza Plan was adopted by the First Committee, despite bitter opposition within the Committee. The vote was 34 to 16, with 7 abstentions, which exceeded the two third vote required to ensure adoption in the General Assembly. However, the paragraph-by-paragraph vote indicated that adoption at the General Assembly of all provisions of the compromise was in doubt, since the proposal to place Tripolitania under Italian trusteeship was adopted by a vote of only 32 to 17 with 8 abstentions.[54]

British troops open fire on demonstrators

Despite the diplomatic success scored by Italy in winning the support at the United Nations with regard to possible Italian return to Somalia, the prospect was still far from clear, and further complicated by disorders which were taking place in Mogadisho. Lega supporters were known to be listening intensely to radio news of United Nations discussions on the future of Somalia[55]. As the news of a possible Italian return filtered in, huge anti-Italian demonstrations were organized on October 5, 1949 despite the ban imposed on such activities by the British military authorities. The British authorities were well aware that any decision the UN may take would be unpopular with a segment of the local population, and disturbances were anticipated from the time of the announcement until the incoming Governing Authority was installed. The demonstrations appear to have been triggered mainly by the broadcasts aired by the leader of the Lega in New York.[56]

The demonstrators submitted a letter to the District Commissioner of Mogadisho warning the local security agencies to avoid any disruption as they would have to take responsibility for anything happening. The letter was constructed in such a way as to imply that the demonstration was an expression of disaffection by all of Somalia's tribes rather than a Lega-inspired one. It bore the signature or fingerprint of 70 Somali tribesmen together with an identification of the tribe from which they came. However, one thing that could not escape the attention of the authority was the presence among the signatories of leading Lega exponents like Haji Mussa Bogor and Haji Farah Ali.

For the authority, the procession was illegal on the grounds that the petition

54 Rivlin, op. cit., p. 39.

55 TNA WO 276/146 report of the Chief Administrator, Somalia, on events of Mogadisho on October 5, 1949.

56 TNA FO 371/73796 PM/WS/49/140 of October 8, 1949.

was submitted in breach of the statutory time-frame of seven clear days required by the Peace and Order Proclamation to apply for authorization to organize a procession. The petition read: "We, the undersigned Somali Chiefs, Sheikhs, Elders, Notables and men of standing and influence hereby inform you that we are today going to make a demonstration in order to protest Italian return in our country as suggested by various Nations of the United Nations Organization. The demonstration will be a peaceful one and no trouble will be caused. The British Administration is requested to: safeguard shops and other private properties, leave the Somalis make their demonstration peacefully and not cause trouble to them which otherwise the British Administration will be held responsible."[57] The colonial authorities responded with a warning that the procession was illegal and that it could not be authorized.

On the same day, 5 October, the Conferenza party submitted a letter to the Chief Administrator demanding "the same right to be granted to them in order to show what their wishes are in respect of the future of Somalia now being debated at the United Nations."[58] Ignoring the order from the authority, the Lega started its procession at about 1 o'clock from the outskirts of Mogadisho, carrying banners bearing anti-Italian slogans. Crowds of some 2,000 men refused to disperse although warned by the authorities to do so within fifteen minutes. As soon as the protesters' stance grew more violent, the British colonial authorities' previously benign attitude turned hostile. The police riot squad charged the crowd with batons but was forced to withdraw under a hail of stones. The crowd surged forward and the police opened fire, killing one person and wounding thirteen. Most of the crowd dispersed but reconverged a quarter of an hour later. After being warned by police officers to disperse within ten minutes, the crowd still refused to obey the order and "military force assisting the Police shot a selected ringleader on the spot."[59]

Mindful of the bloody incidents of 11 January 1948, the British military authorities did not want to take any chance, but got tougher with the demonstrators and, albeit in an apparently peaceful manner, violently suppressed the procession, causing deaths, injuries and arrests.

In his report to London, the Chief Administrator wrote: "I sent for the Italian Liaison Officer and his Assistant and told them what had happened during the

57 TNA FO 1015/397, letter dated October 5, 1949 bearing the signature of 70 persons.

58 Ibid.,, letter dated October 5, 1949, jointly signed by the Vice President, Ahmed Cahie and Mohamed Mohamoud Fodle, Secretary General of the Conferenza.

59 Ibid. , telegram cypher/OTP no. 87, from Mr. Gamble, of October 5, 1949 to Foreign Affairs.

afternoon. They expressed great satisfaction upon our handling of the situation."[60]

By October 17, the casualty list had grown to include six people dying of wounds suffered on October 5, and 13 injured[61]. The security force suffered only minor injuries, including one British officer and six native constables wounded by stones and knives[62]. Some 300 people were arrested for breach of curfew regulations, of which some 200 were convicted and about 100 acquitted or cautioned.[63]

The premises of the Lega and Conferenza Somala were searched but no weapons were found. Six persons considered to be the ringleaders were put on trial and given prison sentences ranging from 6 to 12 months. At 14:40 hrs of October 5, 1949, a curfew was ordered and arrangements were made for the arrest or deportation of known leaders who had made inflammatory speeches. A number of prominent Lega elements including Sheikh Mohamoud Mohamed Farah 'Malingour', Mohamed Ahmed 'Ottavio', Haji Dirie Hersi, Ali Hersi Farah and Dahir Haji Osman were deported to the interior of the country with an obligation to reside at El-Bur town, some 450 km from Mogadisho. The deportees were released on December 18, 1949 and arrived in Mogadisho on the same day[64]. Of the six ringleaders arrested (Haji Mussa Bogor, Sultan of Majertenia, Haji Jim'ale Barre, Chief Abgal, Wa'esle; Haji Ali Abdi, Chief Hawadle; Issa Galan, Chief Ali Saleban; Farah Ali, Chief Omar Mohamoud, and Haji Mohamed Abdulle, 'Qurmone', an influential trader), two were acquitted and one sentenced to six months' imprisonment on account of his age. Two, Haji Mussa Bogor and Haji Jumale Barre, were each given a 9-month prison sentence with hard labour[65]. The Lega had decided to employ an Arab lawyer from Aden, Mohamed Ali Lugman, to prepare the appeal against the conviction and sentences against the notables[66]. However, after various delays, Mr Lugman apparently decided not to come, allegedly because not enough money was offered, and the Lega briefed Mr W.C. Nicoll, a Lawyer from Nairobi who was visiting Mogadisho, to prepare their appeal[67]. The appeal against conviction and sentences imposed on the notables in connection with the October 5 incidents was made to the chief

60 Ibid., secret report from the Chief Administrator, Somalia on the events of Mogadisho of 5th October 1949.

61 Ibid., telegram from Gamble to FO, October 17, 1949.

62 Ibid., telegram from Gamble to FO, October 7, 1949.

63 Ibid.

64 TNA FO 1015/509 monthly intelligence report, December 1949.

65 TNA FO 1015/397 telegram from Gamble to FO, October 7, 1949.

66 Ibid., telegram from Gamble to FO, October 12, 1949.

67 TNA FO 1015/189 monthly political intelligence report, November 1949.

administrator—it was dismissed, but all the sentences were reduced[68]. All those who had been imprisoned as a result of the demonstrations of October 5, 1949, were released before the British handover of April 1, 1950. The demonstration of October 5, 1949, entered Somali history as 'Dhagah tuur', meaning stone throwing. "The plan of a show of force fails, mainly because the Lega no longer enjoys the protection of the British authorities and the complicity of the Somali Gendarmerie", comments Angelo Del Boca.[69]

First Committee discusses Mogadisho disturbances

Reports of the disorders in Mogadisho reached Commission I of the United Nations as it was considering the future of pre-war Italian colonies. The first news about the situation in Mogadisho was relayed to Abdullahi Issa and to the Secretary General of the United Nations by a young Somali activist, Mohamoud Yousuf Aden 'Muro'[70]. In his messages, Muro demanded the Chief Administrator and other British colonial officers be tried before the International Court of Justice for four crimes including "massacring coldly our people."[71]

The text of the message, addressed to the Chairman of the First Committee, was read out by the Liberian delegate, H.F. Cooper, on October 7, 1949.[72] The message reported information regarding anti-Italian demonstrations in Mogadisho and British troops using live ammunition on the demonstrators, resulting in seven deaths and several injuries. The letter also referred to the imprisonment of hundreds of persons, including many tribal chiefs, and the deportation of political leaders affiliated to the Somali Youth League. It urged the First Committee to recognize the serious nature of the situation and to intervene without delay[73]. However, the British representative within the Committee, Mr Hector McNeil, downplayed the intensity of the disorders in Mogadisho and accused the Lega of trying to impose their views on the entire Somali population[74]. For the first time the British authority had publicly recognized the political role of non-Lega parties in Somalia, putting the Lega and its rival organizations on equal footing.

68 TNA FO 1015/509 British Military Administration Somalia, monthly intelligence report, December 1949.

69 Del Boca, op. cit., p. 206.

70 Mohamoud Yousuf, widely known as 'Muro', was elected deputy in the electoral district of Galkayo following the general elections of 1959; he became Minister of Education in Abdullahi Issa's second government before independence. After independence he served as ambassador in Addis Abeba, Ethiopia..

71 TNA FO/1015/397, telegram from Gamble to FO, October 10, 1949.

72 UN Doc. A/C.1/SR.288.

73 Ibid.

74 Rossi, op. cit., p. 532.

He concluded that "the United Kingdom Administration was trying to avoid the recurrence of demonstrations such as had taken place some time ago and that had resulted in the death of some 40 Italians."[75]

A second letter accusing Britain of taking repressive measures against peaceful procession was read out by the representative of Byelorussia, Mr Kuzma V. Kiselev. The letter expressed deep disappointment that the Committee had not taken effective action, but had limited itself to asking the British representative for information. The letter accused the British of taking repressive action against the SYL, closing their headquarters and jailing or exiling their leaders.[76]

Reacting to a question by the representative of Yugoslavia as to whether the British Administration in Somaliland considered it a crime to demonstrate against assumption of trusteeship by Italy or any other European country, the representative of Britain replied that it was not a crime for the Somali people to express their political views. However, it was the duty of the Administration to maintain law and order. The recent disorders, the extent of which, he believed, had been exaggerated, had not resulted from simple expression of opinions but from an attempt by a certain group to enforce its political views upon the entire community. The British representative again recalled that Somaliland had been the scene of serious disturbances in the past and stated that the British Administration did not intend to permit a repetition of such events through dereliction of its duty[77]. The representative of Britain made a further statement in which he said that in view of the violent anti-Italian riots of 1948, the British authority only attempted to prevent those levelled against the Italian minority. He refuted the claim that restrictions that had been imposed as temporary measures were directed exclusively at the Lega.[78]

The incidents of 5 October and the repressive security measures taken by the colonial authorities, including the temporary closure of Lega HQs and the deportation of some of its members, had led to the resignation of a group of leading elements of this party, who addressed a letter to the Chief Administrator in which, after expressing their frustrations, they announced their decision to relinquish membership of the Central Committee. The resignation letter, dated October 24, 1949, bore the signatures of Ahmed Addawe, Haji Farah Ali,

75 United Nations Press Release GA/PS/247, 7 October 1949.
76 UN Doc. A/C.1/SR.288.
77 Ibid.
78 UN Doc. A/C.1/SR. 292.

Abdirashid Ali, Osman Sheikh Mao and Mohamed Farah Siad[79]. They demanded that they should not be held responsible for any demonstration that elements associated with the Lega may stage against the Italian return. The way the demonstration had been handled by the British authorities in Somalia placed the UK in an awkward position at the United Nations. Consequently, the British government recommended that their colonial authorities not only reopen the Club buildings, but also reduce security measures to the very minimum.[80]

Bevin–Sforza Plan narrowly defeated in the General Assembly. The crucial vote of the Haitian Delegate. Italy's turnabout

Predictably, the Bevin–Sforza Plan, approved by the Political Committee, was met with strong criticism from various quarters when it came up for discussion in the General Assembly of the United Nations.

Soviet Minister Jacob Malik denounced the planned disposal of the former Italian colonies as a move by the United Kingdom and the United States of America to maintain their hegemony and domination. The Russians, supported by the other Eastern European States and many Arab and Asiatic States, declared that the resolution failed to reflect the views and the interests of the peoples of the colonies themselves. The USA, United Kingdom, France and Latin American countries claimed that since it was not possible to find a solution that would completely reconcile all the various suggestions, the Bevin–Sforza plan was the best that could be expected under the circumstances.[81]

The heated plenary session on the issue took place as the General Assembly was driving hard towards adjournment. However, "when at late evening of May 17, the voting process started, the result confirmed the Italian fears: while the paragraph relating to Britain's trusteeship over Cyrenaica was adopted by 36 in favour, 17 against and 6 abstentions and French trusteeship over Fezzan by 36 in favour, 15 against and 7 abstentions, obtaining thus the required majority, the paragraph concerning Italian trusteeship over Tripolitania was short by one vote to obtain the required two-third majority in the General Assembly having obtained 33 votes in favour to 17 against with 8 abstentions."[82] Haiti, which was not expected to vote against the Bevin–Sforza package on former Italian colonies, did instead vote against the plan. "This uncertainty about Tripolitania

79 TNA FO 371/73797 Letter of disclaim signed by some syl members, October 20,1949.

80 TNA FO 1015/397 cypher/OTP from New York to FO, October 7, 1948.

81 UN Doc. A/PV. 217 and A/PV 218.

82 Rossi, op. cit., p. 468.

jeopardized the whole resolution, for Italian trusteeship over Tripolitania was the concession that swung the Latin American States behind the compromise", comments Rivlin.[83]

Again when the question of Italian trusteeship over Somalia was put to the vote, the Haitian delegate to the United Nations, Senator Emile St. Lot, voted against the plan. 35 delegates voted yes, 19 no, and there were 4 abstentions; it was only one vote short of the required two-third majority. This was a big shock to the USA, the UK and Italy with its large Latin American bloc.[84]

After the votes on single paragraphs, some delegates from Central and South America, in addition to France, unhappy about the rejection of the paragraphs on Tripolitania and Somalia, announced they were going to vote against the entire resolution of the Political Committee.[85]

When the rest of the resolution came up for the final vote, it was overwhelmingly defeated by a combination of Latin American, Arab, Asian and Soviet States, each group for its own reasons. In a final vote on the package, the Bevin–Sforza Plan was, ironically, rejected by 37 votes against, 14 in favour and 7 abstentions[86]. As the defeat of the compromise resolution came five days after the date originally set for the Assembly's adjournment, the delegates were left with no alternative but to postpone a final decision until the fourth regular session of the General Assembly[87]. At its meeting held on 18 May, 1949, a resolution presented by the representative of Poland to postpone further consideration of the question until the fourth regular session of the GA was adopted by 51 votes to none with 6 abstentions.

The vote of Haiti was decisive in the failure of the Bevin–Sforza Plan. Haiti's delegate broke ranks with the position of other Latin American States, known for their support for the return of Italy to her former African colonies. Contradicting explanations were advanced with regard to the behaviour of the Haitian delegate. According to Count Carlo Sforza, St. Lot "was drunk and not in possession

83 Rivlin, op. cit., p. 39.

84 The countries voting in favour of the resolution were: Argentina, Belgium, Bolivia, Brazil, Canada, Chile, Colombia, Costa Rica, Cuba, Denmark, Dominican Republic, Ecuador, El Salvador, France, Greece, Guatemala, Honduras, Iceland, Luxemburg, Mexico, the Netherlands, New Zealand, Nicaragua, Norway, Panama, Paraguay, Peru, Union of South Africa, United Kingdom, United States of America, Uruguay and Venezuela. Voting against: Burma, Byelorussia, Czechoslovakia, Egypt, Haiti, India, Iraq, Lebanon, Pakistan, the Philippines, Poland, Saudi Arabia, Syria, Ukraine, USSR, Yemen and Yugoslavia. Abstaining: China, Ethiopia, Iran, Israel, Liberia, Siam (Thailand), Sweden and Turkey.

85 Rossi, op. cit., p. 469.

86 UN Doc. A/PV. 218.

87 UN Doc. A/PV. 219.

of his full mental capacity at the time of voting."[88] Some alleged that he had been bribed by Arab delegates who opposed the delay to grant independence to Libya. Others, by contrast, gave positive comments on the personality of the Haitian diplomat, portraying him as a person who, unlike other Latin American delegates, had always made known his opposition to Italy's trusteeship over any of its former African colonies.[89]

In fact, after rejecting the Bevin–Sforza Plan, Saint-Lot made the following comments before the General Assembly on 18 May 1949: "Given the affinities with the African people, it was impossible for Haiti to support the draft resolution of the First Committee, which might have had nefarious consequences for those peoples."[90] Saint-Lot voted against the Bevin–Sforza plan in disregard of his government's instructions. The Italians might have seen him as villainous, or mad, but for the Somalis he was a saviour. In fact, in a show of gratitude and in recognition of the honourable position he took *vis-à-vis* the Bevin–Sforza plan, Mr Emile Saint-Lot was decorated with the Order of the Somali Star, Second Category, on 27 August, 1961[91], and later hired to serve as legal advisor for the Somali Permanent Mission at the United Nations in New York, for a monthly fee of $400.[92]

The growing pressure from within Italy on the colonial issue, particularly from the right-wing parties within the Constituent Assembly, did not allow De Gasperi's government to abandon the hope of retaining some foothold in North Africa despite the defeat of the compromise Bevin–Sforza solution at the General Assembly of the United Nations. However, after long insisting on trusteeship for her former African territories, and in the face of the rejection of the Anglo–Italian plan, Italy came out in favour of full and immediate independence for Eritrea and Libya[93], performing, as one author put it, "una vera e propia capriola diplomatica": a real diplomatic somersault.[94]

The first sign of this new policy was given when Count Sforza told the Italian Parliament that Italy was ready to "listen to other proposals" for a solution of the question[95]. Explaining this change of heart, Count Sforza said that the Italian

88 Sforza, op. cit., p. 161.
89 Rossi, op. cit., pp. 468-469.
90 UN Doc. A/PV. 219.
91 Diary Aden Abdulla, August 27, 1961.
92 Ibid., June 30, 1962.
93 UN Doc.A/C.1/SR. 279, par. 8.
94 Morone, op. cit., p. 41.
95 The New York Times, May 27, 1949.

people were now convinced "they must actively seek the friendship of the new states coming to life in the territories where Italians brought civilization."[96] In October, the Foreign Minister made a further declaration in which he announced that the Italian government had decided to support the idea of immediate independence of "the two most progressive territories, Eritrea and Libya"[97] and the withdrawal of Italy's request for trusteeship over Tripolitania and Eritrea "because she has recognized that what is important for the economic and civil life of the two countries is that the present provisional regime should come to an end."[98] However, with regard to Somalia, Italy renewed its request for trusteeship because it wanted "to continue the work it started in that part of the world and that was not completed."[99]

Following this new development, the Arab–Asian States now became less hostile towards the idea of Italian trusteeship over Somalia, considered as the least advanced among the three territories in question. As was to be expected, Latin American States supported the new Italian position without hesitation[100], and, as a further show of solidarity with Italy, also approved a proposal submitted by the head of the Brazilian delegation which linked the question of independence for Libya with Italian administration of Somalia. Under this joint proposal, Latin American States would not vote for Libyan independence unless the Assembly agreed on Italian trusteeship over Somalia[101]. The Americans supported the establishment of Italian trusteeship, but they proposed that the General Assembly and the Trusteeship Council of the United Nations be granted powers to review the progress and development of this territory from time to time with a view to determining whether it was ready for independence.[102]

A resolution was also introduced by Pakistan suggesting for Somalia a ten-year trusteeship administered with "a view to its incorporation into a united independent Somaliland", with the proposal that the General Assembly and the Trusteeship Council review the progress and development of the territory from time to time in order to determine whether satisfactory progress was being made towards preparing the country for independence[103]. The third resolution was

96 Pittsburgh Post Gazette, October 4, 1949.
97 UN Doc.A/C.1/SR. 279, par. 8.
98 Rivlin, op. cit., p. 51.
99 Sforza, op. cit., p. 180.
100 UN Doc. A/C.1/SR. 278 through A/C.1/SR/285.
101 The New York Times, October 7, 1949.
102 UN Doc. A/C.1/497.
103 UN Doc. A/C.1/499.

from Liberia, and called for Somalia to be independent after five years under direct United Nations trusteeship.[104]

The issue of the Colonies comes before the Fourth General Assembly

The views of the Somali organizations

As we have seen, the question of the disposal of former Italian colonies was inconclusively examined during the second part of the third regular session of the General Assembly. When the General Assembly of the United Nations convened its fourth ordinary session, on the recommendation of the General Committee at its 224th plenary meeting of September 22, 1949, the General Assembly referred this item to the First Committee for consideration and report. Consideration of the question by the First Committee was begun at the 278th meeting held on September 30, 1949. At that meeting, the Committee adopted a proposal by the Chairman to invite the government of Italy, in accordance with its request, to appoint a representative to sit without vote on the Committee while the question was under consideration.[105]

At its 279th meeting on October 1, 1949, the Committee approved a second draft resolution[106] by the Chairman providing for the request of representatives of political parties or organizations in the territories concerned, presented not later than October 10, to be referred to a sub-committee (known as Sub-Committee 16). Sub-Committee 16 was also tasked to report to the Committee on the extent to which these parties or organizations seeking to be heard may represent substantial sections of opinion in the territory in question.

In this connection, the Sub-Committee presented three reports to the First Committee[107] concerning the various requests received and the preliminary information obtained on the three ex-Italian African countries. Following the recommendation of the Sub-Committee, like in the previous session, two organizations from Italian Somaliland, namely the Somali Youth League and Hamar Youth Club, as well as the Conferenza Somala, were granted hearings by the Committee[108]. Following are the main points raised by the two contending Somali political organizations before the Commission.

104 Ibid.
105 UN Doc. A/C.1/478/Rev.1.
106 UN Doc. A/C.1/438.
107 UN Doc. A/C.1/494, A/C.1/495 and A/C.1/496.
108 A/1089, November 15, 1949.

(a) Statement of the Lega representative

At the Fourth ordinary session of the General Assembly of the United Nations, appearing before the First Committee of the General Assembly on October 7, 1949, the representative of the Lega stated: "At the opening of the previous session of the General Assembly of the United Nations, when the question of the disposal of former Italian colonies had come before the General Assembly, for the first time the Somali people had been imbued with great confidence and faith in the United Nations. However, that confidence and faith was considerably reduced in light of subsequent developments which resulted in the so-called Bevin–Sforza Agreement." He expressed his "deepest thanks" to all those nations which, at the last session, had made possible the rejection of the Bevin–Sforza plan. The Bevin–Sforza plan, Mr Issa declared, would have meant "survival of colonialism of the worst type."[109] He spared no criticism to his political rivals who, appearing before the First Committee in the last session, expressed support for the Bevin–Sforza Agreement, calling them 'quislings' who represented ineffective or non-existing parties. These 'traitors', as he also called them, were far more interested in receiving eight years' back pay due to them as ex-servicemen claiming that Italy had formally promised to grant this back pay to all servicemen in case Somalia be returned to Italian administration.[110]

The Lega envoy claimed that his party enjoyed the unanimous support of the Sultans, tribal chiefs, elders and religious leaders of all tribes living in the former Italian Somaliland. "The Somali Youth League", he said, "was expressing the greatest desire of our people in demanding the immediate independence of Somaliland. However", he added, "the Somali Youth League was reasonable enough to state that, if the General Assembly would consider it best to place Somaliland temporarily under trusteeship, the party would not object provided that the restoration of Italian administration in any form and guise, even as a trustee under the supervision of the United Nations, be completely excluded."[111]

Referring to the recent Italian pronouncement with regard to Libya and Eritrea, Mr Issa expressed his disappointment that while these two countries were now considered ready for independence, delegations did not see fit to reconsider their attitude with regard to Somaliland. The Somalis, Mr Issa declared, preferred "complete extermination" to Italian rule, adding that, if

109 Press release GA/PS/247, October 7, 1949.
110 UN Doc. A/C.1SR/287, October 7, 1949, par. 10.
111 Press release GA/PS/247, October 7, 1949.

there was even the slightest doubt in the truthfulness of this statement, the best and most just solution would be to send a new Commission of Investigation to Somaliland to ascertain the true wishes of the people. It was better to delay a solution for another year than to condemn the whole population of Somaliland to "total extermination." In the event that a new Commission of Investigation would be sent out to Somaliland, Mr Issa asked the United Nations to select the Commission members "among the strictly neutral member states."

In a subsequent testimony before the Committee, the Lega envoy reiterated that his organization would react violently if the General Assembly re-established Italian rule in spite of the presence of the British troops[112]. However, history records that, rhetoric apart, after the incident of 5 October, the Lega kept a low profile and staged no serious anti-Italian demonstrations, and Mr Issa himself became one of the closest friends of Italy during the Trusteeship period and thereafter.

(b) Statement of the Conferenza representative

Speaking before the General Assembly's Political and Security Committee on October 7, 1949, the representative of the Conferenza Somala, Islao Mahadalla, renewed his appeal for a prompt and just decision for the future of his country still under military occupation. He called for an Italian trusteeship over Somalia until the country was ready for independence. "At the very least," he said "Italy should be included among the administering powers if the United Nations voted formultipletrusteeships."[113]

In a fresh move seen as a departure from the earlier demand for a thirty-year period of trusteeship, he signalled his acceptance for the independence of Somalia to be granted within the time limit strictly necessary to achieve the level of progress which would ensure wise administration and stable democratic liberties. The Conferenza would oppose collective administration or alternate administrations by several nations under the control of the United Nations. The party further recommended gradual but rapid Somalization of the administration on an equal basis for all Somalis.[114]

Islao Mahadalla contested the Lega's claim to representation of the majority of the Somali population. He referred, in particular, to the Somali Sab community who, although they were the first to fall victim to fascist oppression, were now

112 UN Doc. A/C.1/SR.290, par. 30.

113 The New York Times, October 7, 1949.

114 UN Doc. A/C.1/SR.286, October 6, 1949, par. 21.

convinced that democratic Italy would not repeat the mistakes of the past. In reply to the representative of the Ukrainian Soviet Socialist Republic, Islao Mahadalla referred to his rival party, the Lega, as an extremist and 'terrorist' organization.[115]

Reacting to a question asked by the same Ukrainian representative about the educational benefits which the Somalis had derived from the Italian administration and how many had learnt to read during Italian rule, Mr Kassim, another member of the Somalia Conference delegation, replied: "after thirty years of Italian administration, it could be claimed, generally speaking, that all the people of Italian Somaliland spoke Italian."[116]

The representative of Pakistan, Sir Zafarullah Khan, sarcastically congratulated the Somali Conference delegation for "the well-prepared statement which evidenced a remarkable standard of political ability", asking him at the end what were the positions the members of his delegations held in private life. To this Mr Kassim replied that two of the representatives including himself were employed by the British Administering Authorities; the rest were businessmen and tribal chiefs. One of the two employees was a legal advisor in the Department of Justice and the other a revenue collector in the service of the Municipality of Mogadisho[117]. Mr Kassim further stated that about 30 per cent of the population was of similar educational and social standing[118]. Sir Zafarullah Khan, observing that the previous reply showed that Somalia had reached a higher level of literacy than India and Pakistan had at the time they obtained independence, asked what further requirements were lacking for self-rule. Mr Kassim replied that the principal reason for which the Somalia Conference did not consider the country ready for independence was an economic one. He admitted, however, that there were also educational and social obstacles. He believed that a number of stages would have to be passed through before the country could be ready for independence, which could only be achieved when certain racial and group prejudices had been overcome.[119]

The representative of Syria, Mr Rifat, noting that the provision in the Sub-Committee 15 draft resolution, based on the Bevin–Sforza compromise in respect of Somaliland, did not specify any time limit for the proposed trusteeship, asked

115 Ibid.
116 Ibid.
117 UN Doc. A/C.1/SR.286, par. 32.
118 Ibid.
119 Ibid.

whether the representative of the Conferenza Somala thought that his country needed indefinite guidance on the part of Italy. The Conferenza envoy explained that his organization sought Italian guidance until the people of Somaliland were ready for self-government. He thought that the period of preparation might last for perhaps thirty years. He was convinced that Somalia was not ready for immediate independence; this was agreed during the works of the Four Power Commission of Investigation. "Naturally", Mr Kassim observed, "if the country was offered its independence, the Somali Conference would not refuse that."[120] He further stated that there was a need for a period of administration to prepare the country for real self-government, and that his party was in favour of trusteeship accorded to Italy under the supervision of the United Nations.

Responding to a question posed by the Iraqi representative, Mr Al-Jamali, on the number of Somalis having higher education in law, medicine, agriculture etc, Mr Kassim stated that, in the interior of the country, all the doctors and heads of infirmaries were Somalis and possessed appropriate university qualifications. The same applied to the other branches of the liberal professions[121]. Replying to a more direct question by the Yemeni representative in the Committee, Mr Sayed Al Qadi Mohamed Al Amri, as to whether the Conferenza Somala would consider accepting independence should the Commission decide in that sense, Mr Kassim replied that if the Somali people were to act in accordance with their conscience and in the knowledge of the stage of progress reached, they would refuse it because they were not ready for absolute independence, and that he nonetheless regarded liberty and freedom as highly desirable.[122]

Intervening in the discussions, Mr Clutton of the United Kingdom dismissed the statement made by Mr Kassim that any member of the Conferenza Somala delegation was employed by the British Administration. The head of the Conference delegation was not an employee of the Department of Justice of the British Administration; he was employed as a clerk for one of the Italian judges.[123]

At its 291st meeting on October 11, 1949, the First Committee established a sub-committee (known as Sub-Committee 21) composed of the representatives of Argentina, Australia, Brazil, Chile, China, Czechoslovakia, Denmark, Egypt, Ethiopia, France, Guatemala, India, IRK, Liberia, Mexico, Pakistan, Poland, Union of South Africa, Union of Soviet Socialist Republics, United Kingdom

120 UN Doc. A/C.1/SR.290, October 10, 1949, par. 1.
121 UN Doc. A/C.1/SR.286, par. 59.
122 Ibid.
123 Ibid.

and United States of America, with the purpose of studying all drafts and suggestions submitted to the First Committee or which might be submitted to the sub-committee, or to propose a draft resolution or resolutions to settle the question of the disposal of the former Italian colonies in Africa[124]. The sub-committee held 29 meetings between October 11 and November 1, 1949, under the chairmanship of Dr L. Padilla Nervo (Mexico), with Mr J.D.L. Hood (Australia) as its rapporteur. It was presented with six draft resolutions which had been submitted to the First Committee by India (UN Doc A/C.1/491), Iraq (UN Doc A/C.1/489), Liberia (UN Doc A/C.1/490), Pakistan (UN Doc A/C.1/499), the Union of Soviet Socialist Republics (UN Doc A/C.1/487) and the United States of America (AC.1/497). The sub-committee examined the question of the disposal of each of the three territories separately and in the following order: Libya, Italian Somaliland and Eritrea. A drafting committee of five members, namely the representative of Australia, rapporteur of the Sub-Committee, and the representatives of Argentina, Czechoslovakia, India, and Iraq, was entrusted with the task of preparing one or more draft resolutions incorporating the principles and concepts embodied in the six draft resolutions submitted earlier to the First Commission.

Recommendations of Sub-Committee 21

In addition to the six draft resolutions earlier submitted to the First Committee on the disposal of Italian Somaliland, three new draft resolutions were presented to the sub-committee by Argentina. India and Iraq[125]. All these draft resolutions were thoroughly examined and provided for by the sub-committee taking decisions on all the principles embodied in each of them.[126]

The first question examined with regard to Somalia was whether independence should be granted to Italian Somaliland. By a unanimous vote, the sub-committee adopted the principle that Italian Somaliland should be accorded independence.

The second question considered was at what date Italian Somaliland should be granted independence. By a vote of 8 in favour, 11 against and 2 abstentions, the sub-committee rejected the proposal by the Union of Soviet Socialist Republics that Italian Somaliland should be granted independence after five years.

The third question examined was whether Italian Somaliland should become independent after a period not exceeding ten years. By a vote of 10 to 11, the

124 UN Doc. A/C.1/522, November 1, 1949.

125 UN Doc A/C.1/SC.17/L.5), India (A/C.1/SC.17/L.6) and Iraq (A/C.1/SC/L7).

126 UN Doc. A/C.1/522, November 1949.

sub-committee rejected the principle contained in the proposals by Iraq and Pakistan that Italian Somaliland should become independent after a period not exceeding ten years.

The fourth question examined was whether independence should be granted to Italian Somaliland after a period of ten years. By a vote of 9 in favour and 11 against and 1 abstention, the sub-committee rejected the principle contained in the proposal by Liberia that Italian Somaliland be granted independence after a period of ten years.

The fifth question considered was whether Italian Somaliland should be granted independence after a period of ten years unless at that time the General Assembly decided otherwise. By a vote of 15 in favour, 3 against and 3 abstentions the sub-committee approved the principle contained in a proposal of the United States of America that Italian Somaliland should become independent after a period of ten years, unless the General Assembly decided otherwise.[127]

The sixth question considered was whether Italian Somaliland should be placed under the International Trusteeship System with the Organization as the Administering Authority. A vote was taken by roll-call upon the proposal with the organization as Administering Authority. The proposal was rejected by 12 votes against 9.

The seventh question considered was whether Italian Somaliland should be placed under the International Trusteeship System with three States as Administering Authority. By a vote taken by roll-call upon the proposal with a collective Administration with three Sates as Administering Authority, the proposal was rejected by 12 votes to 4, and 5 abstentions.

The eighth question considered was whether Italian Somaliland should be placed under the International Trusteeship System with one State as the Administering Authority, the latter being Italy. The proposal for a single Power trusteeship, with Italy as the Administering Power, was adopted by 12 votes to 8 with 1 abstention.

The ninth question considered dealt with a Declaration of Constitutional Principles designed to guarantee the rights of the people of Italian Somaliland and to establish and develop self-government in the territory. By a vote of 14 in favour, none against, and 6 abstentions, one member being absent, the sub-committee decided to recommend that a Declaration of Constitutional Principles should be annexed to the Trusteeship Agreement.

127 UN Doc. AC.1/497.

The tenth question examined dealt with the modalities concerning the conclusion of the Trusteeship Agreement. By a vote of 13 in favour, 3 against, and 4 abstentions, one member being absent, the sub-committee adopted an Argentine proposal to the effect that the Trusteeship Council negotiate with the Administering Authority the draft of a Trusteeship Agreement for submission to the General Assembly, if possible during the present session and in any case no later than the first regular session of the General Assembly.

The eleventh question considered was concerned with the delimitation of the international boundary of Italian Somaliland, to which reference was made in paragraph 3 of the resolution drafted by Pakistan[128]. In view of the refusal of the representative of Ethiopia to join the Commission for the delimitation of the Ethiopian-Italian Somaliland boundaries proposed by Pakistan and the United States of America, pending the satisfaction of Ethiopia's claims in Eritrea, the representatives of the latter countries withdrew their proposals. The representative of Pakistan, however, stated that the matter could be taken up when the Eritrean question had been settled.

Briefly, Sub-Committee 21 recommended the following solutions with respect to Italian Somaliland:

1. That Italian Somaliland should be an independent, sovereign State.
2. That this independence should become effective at the end of 10 years from the date of the approval of the Trusteeship Agreement by the General Assembly, "unless at the end of that period the General Assembly decides otherwise."
3. That during the period mentioned in paragraph 2, Italian Somaliland should be placed under the International Trusteeship System with Italy as the administering authority.
4. That the Trusteeship Council should negotiate with the Administering Authority the drafting of a Trusteeship Agreement for submission to the General Assembly, if possible during the present session, and in any case no later than the fifth regular session.
5. That the Trusteeship Agreement should include an annex containing a Declaration of Constitutional Principles guaranteeing the rights of the inhabitants of Somaliland and providing for institutions designed to ensure the inauguration, development and subsequent establishment of

128 UN Doc. A/C.1/499.

full self-government.

6. That in the drafting of this Declaration, the Trusteeship Council and the Administering Authority take into account the annexed text proposed by the Indian delegation.[129]

With a vote of 10 in favour, 9 against and 2 abstentions, the sub-committee finally decided that its recommendations to the First Committee should be incorporated in one draft resolution covering the three territories.

The work of Committee I

The Philippines' proposal

The First Committee examined the report of Sub-Committee 21 on the three former Italian colonies between 4 and 8 November, 1949 and then proceeded to vote upon the various draft resolutions placed before it. In voting on the report, Committee I voted on each paragraph, accepting in the process a number of amendments while rejecting several others.

The Committee adopted three key amendments of section 2 of the report dealing with Somalia. First was an oral amendment by the Philippines suggesting deletion of the last phrase of paragraph two, proposed by the United States of America and reading "unless the General Assembly should subsequently decide otherwise." (AC.1/497) The qualifying clause was, as proposed by the Philippines, deleted in a vote which saw France, the United Kingdom and the United States, among 22 other States, in opposition to the majority.[130] Second was a Lebanese proposal[131] with respect to paragraph 3, according to which an Advisory Council should be set up to aid and advise the Administering Authority. This was adopted.

Third was an Argentine recommendation[132] proposing to invite Italy to undertake the provisional administration of Italian Somaliland "pending approval by the General Assembly of a trusteeship agreement for that territory." An amendment to the Argentine proposal was introduced by Chile[133] suggesting that Italian provisional administration should begin after the Trusteeship Council and

129 UN Doc. A/C. 1/522, November 1, 1949.

130 Lawrence S. Finkelstein, Somaliland under Italian Administration: a Case Study in United Nations Trusteeship, Carnegie Endowment for International Peace, 1955, p. 4.

131 UN Doc. A/C.1/530.

132 UN Doc. A/C.1/541.

133 UN Doc. A/C.1/545.

Italy had negotiated the draft trusteeship agreement, but not before its approval by the Assembly, "on condition that she undertakes to administer the territory in accordance with the provisions of the Agreement and the International Trusteeship System." The Argentine amendment, as modified by Chile and Mexico, was adopted.

A Liberian amendment, which suggested postponing the disposal of Somalia until after the Commission of Investigation proposed for Eritrea examined the question, was rejected, as was a Polish amendment calling for Somalia's independence in three years.[134]

The Indian proposal on the Constitutional Principles was taken as a set of recommendations which would serve as guiding principles to the Administering Authority; consequently, it was inserted as an annex to the draft resolution.[135]

The majority of the committee members supported Section B of the resolution regarding Somalia. However, concerns soon emerged over the future attitude of the local population towards working with the Italian authorities. The most stringent criticisms to Section B came from Ethiopia and Liberia, the only two African countries to be members of the United Nations. The Italian representative, Ambassador Alberto Tarchiani, intervening on a number of occasions in the debate, had given assurances to the Political Committee as to the honesty and reliability of Italian intentions[136], attempting to dissipate any fears about possible Italian intentions to extend the trusteeship period[137] and also give assurance on the intention of the Italian government not to discriminate against those Somali leaders who opposed the return of Italy to Somalia.[138]

The Arab states supported the resolution on Somalia; however, *per contra*, they requested solid guarantees to safeguard the local population. The representative of Lebanon stated that, although some Somali groups were apprehensive of Italy as the administering authority of Somaliland, the text of the present draft contained genuine guarantees against any abuse on the part of the administering authority that could be summed up as follows:

The prospect of definite and ultimate independence after ten years' trusteeship;

The prospect of the proposed Trusteeship Agreement whereby members of the Trusteeship Council would avail themselves of the opportunity to plead the

134 Rivlin, op. cit., p. 57; A/1089, November 15, 1949.

135 UNGOAR IV 1/SR 321, November 10, 1949.

136 UNGAOR IV, A/C 1/RS p. 314, as reported in Rossi, op. cit. , p. 554.

137 UNGAOR I4, A/C SR, p. 318, 320, November 10, 1949.

138 UNGAOR I4, A/C SR 321, November 10, 1949, as reported in Rossi, op. cit., p. 555.

cause of the Somali people with a view to securing adequate guarantees for the inhabitants of Somaliland;

The inclusion in the Trusteeship Agreement of constitutional principles safeguarding the fundamental human rights of these people;

The proposed Advisory Council which would participate in the debates of the Trusteeship Council regarding the administration of the territory;

The inclusion in the Advisory Council of some Asian and African countries which would have the interest of the people of Somaliland at heart;

The assurance that the Trusteeship Council itself would be continuously watching the development of the territory towards full independence; and finally,

The need for the Organization to have faith in the new and democratic Italy by entrusting it with the task of administering the territory of Somaliland.[139]

The voting on each section and on the resolution as a whole within the Committee indicated a safe majority over the required two thirds:

	YES	AGAINST	ABSTENTION
SECTION A (LIBYA)	50	0	8
SECTION B (SOMALIA)	47	7	4
SECTION C (ERITREA)	47	5	8
RESOLUTION AS A WHOLE	49	1	8

The key to the success of the resolution lay in the Italian government's new policy announced immediately after the defeat of the ill-fated Bevin-Sforza compromise. The final decision mainly reflects a political compromise, painstakingly worked out in the General Assembly over two years, in which the positions of the Arab-Asian and Latin American blocs were united for a solution of the Somali question. The actual acceptance of the ten years as a limit came about more because "it was politically acceptable than because it was theoretically justified in consideration of the state of underdevelopment and political and social immaturity of the population of the Trust Territory", comments Finkelstein.[140]

However, despite the apparent general acceptance, the resolution continued to be subjected to criticism from a number of countries. For instance, Ethiopian

139 UN Doc. A/C.1/ 320, Lake Success, N.Y., November 10, 1949, par. 33.

140 Finkelstein, op. cit., p. 3.

Foreign Minister Aklilou Habt-Wold denounced the resolution as a "policy of injustice and opportunism". He noted that Italy was reportedly considering the dispatch of highly trained troops to Somalia[141]. The Ethiopian minister added that his country felt threatened by such a prospect. Liberia, the only other Black African country member of the United Nations, supported the Ethiopian position calling for a reconsideration of the section of the resolution dealing with Eritrea and Somalia. No action, however, was taken on the Liberian request, as it was not put into the form of a resolution.[142]

The Lega found an odd ally at its side at the United Nations: Ethiopia. The two parties shared one common concern: the return of Italy to Somalia under any form or system. Another source of criticism to the resolution came from France, who considered that the time limit laid down for both Libya and Somalia was unrealistic and not justified in the light of information available on the actual preparation of the two territories for independence[143]. However, in the face of the large entente between the Asian–Arab blocs and the Latin American Republics, any attempt to question the decision of the Political Committee was doomed to fail.

By September, Mr Issa's extreme confidence that Italy could not muster the required majority in the General Assembly gave way to a sense of despair when he realized that the trend at the United Nations was going in favour of Italian return to Somalia. In the bargaining for votes in Committee I, the Arab and Asian blocs appeared to have let down his party in their opposition to the Italian return. In one of his cables from New York to Mogadisho, he vents his anger against Great Britain. The cable reads: "Please forward the following message to SYL local Committees in Somaliland, British Somaliland and elsewhere (.) My congratulations for valuable efforts you achieved for the sake of the beloved motherland (.) Notorious Imperialist Britain intends to suggest again the restoration of the hated Italian rule in Somalia (.) Please inform Somalis everywhere to be ready as Day of Jihad approaching (.) My best salaams and Somalia Ha noolaato. Abdullahi Issa."[144]

141 The New York Times, November 18, 1949.
142 Rivlin, op. cit., p. 60.
143 Ibid.
144 TNA FO10156/189 monthly political intelligence report by British Military Administration, September 1949.

The future of the ex-colonies decided by the General Assembly

On November 11, the First Committee recommended the adoption by the General Assembly of the following resolutions with regard to Somalia:

> That Somaliland will become an independent and sovereign State;
>
> This independence shall become effective at the end of ten years from the date of approval of the Trusteeship Agreement by the General Assembly. During this period, mentioned in paragraph 2, Italian Somaliland shall be placed under the International Trusteeship System with Italy as the Administering Authority;
>
> The Administering Authority shall be supported and advised by an Advisory Council composed of representatives of the following states: Colombia, Egypt and the Philippines. The Headquarters of the Advisory Council shall be in Mogadisho. The precise term of reference of the Advisory Council shall be determined in the Trusteeship Agreement;
>
> That the Trusteeship Council negotiate with the Administering Authority the drafting of a Trusteeship Agreement for submission to the General Assembly, if possible during the present session, and in any case no later than the fifth regular session;
>
> That the Trusteeship Agreement shall include an annex containing a Declaration of Constitutional Principles guaranteeing the rights of the inhabitants of Somaliland and providing for institutions designed to ensure the inauguration, development and subsequent establishment of full self-government;
>
> That Italy is invited to undertake the provisional administration of the territory.[145]

Finally, after all-night discussions on November 21, 1949, the General Assembly of the United Nations, after section by section approval, overwhelmingly accepted the draft resolution by a vote of 48 to 1 and 9 abstentions, placing Somalia under Italian Trusteeship. The lone dissenting voice being that of Ethiopia, the abstaining Powers were: Byelorussia, Czechoslovakia, France, New Zealand, Poland, Sweden, Ukraine, USSR and Yugoslavia. It is interesting to note that Soviet Union and the Eastern European States, despite their strong opposition to the resolution, decided not to vote against it[146]. All the stakeholders had acted according to the changing political circumstances of the time. Britain departed

145 UN Doc. A/1089, November 15, 1949.

146 Rivlin, op. cit., p. 61.

from its original pro-Lega attitude, allying its position with that of Italy. The United States and France made no secret of their policy – to place Somalia under Italian administration. The Soviet Union, as we have seen, changed positions on the issue of the former Italian colonies on a number of occasions depending on the circumstances, at times favouring the Italian return to Somalia, only to reverse their position at will. The signals coming from the Four Powers *vis-à-vis* the future of Somalia and the position of the numerically important Latin American bloc at the United Nations, favourable to Italy's claim over her former colonies, were too obvious to be underestimated. However the Lega, instead of adopting new positions matching the changing circumstances, remained clinched to their old anti-Italian rhetoric which, as time passed, seemed to have lost most of its original appealing force.

In the end, and after nearly one year of intensive debate, the decision of the General Assembly of the United Nations resulted in failure to satisfy the expectations of any of the Somali political groups. The Lega felt deceived by the international body who overwhelmingly decided that Italy should return to Somalia as administering authority. The pro-Italian group, on their part, saw the decision of the United Nation as contrary to their well-articulated demand for a longer UN trusteeship mandate. Regrettably, however, the big losers were the inhabitants of the Trust Territory, whose future was being decided by foreign powers in New York without giving due consideration to the country's best interest. It was not easy to determine the wishes of the population over their future; during its stay in Somalia, the Four Power Commission of Investigation found enough evidence that the population as a whole was politically immature, and that people were accustomed to looking to their tribal leaders for views on matters of major concern. Matters related to the future of the country had not been discussed at tribal meetings.[147]

In general, resolutions on the former Italian colonies catered for Western military strategy interests in the Mediterranean and Red Sea areas. As a result, after independence, King El-Sanousso of Libya ceded a military air-base on Libyan soil to Britain and the United States in recognition of their support for the independence of his country. On the other hand, the United States, because of their support for the resolution calling for a federation of Eritrea and Ethiopia, gained a special relationship with the Emperor which paved the way for the conclusion in 1953 of a pact for the use of the important radio communication

147 Report of the Four Powers Commission on the Italian Somalia, sect. II, p. 110.

centre of Kagnew, near Asmara (Radio Marina during Italian time).

Finally, for all her demands for trusteeship administration in her former African colonies, Italy managed to recover only Somalia, considered by many as the least important in terms of economic development and also, compared to Eritrea and Libya, having an insignificant number of Italian settlers to be protected. However, Italy gained recognition by the international body that it was fully qualified to participate in the Trusteeship System at a time when it was not even a member of the United Nations. "Although Italy obtained limited success with the United Nations, it gained the prestige of placing itself in the international political and economic system, ending the state of isolation created by fascism and the war", wrote Giampaolo Calchi Novati.[148]

Instituting the Trusteeship Arrangement

Ethiopia attempts to delay the process

In its resolution of November 21, 1949, the General Assembly of the United Nations had called upon the Trusteeship Council to negotiate with the Administering Authority over a draft trusteeship agreement to be submitted for approval by the General Assembly no later than its fifth regular session in 1950. The resolution recommended, inter alia, that Italy should be invited to undertake the provisional administration of Italian Somaliland. In the meantime, the Italian government, in a communication addressed to the Secretary General of the United Nations on 22 February 1950, undertook to administer the territory in accordance with the provisions of the Charter relating to the International Trusteeship system while the Trusteeship Agreement for the territory was awaiting approval by the General Assembly.[149]

Two weeks after the General Assembly made its recommendations, initial steps for carrying out the provisions on Somalia were taken by the Trusteeship Council by establishing a special committee with the task of preparing a draft Trusteeship Agreement. The committee was composed of France, Iraq, the Philippines, the Dominican Republic, the United States of America and the United Kingdom[150]. In all previous cases, the Administering Authority had submitted its draft

148 Calchi Novati, op. cit., p. 88.

149 TNA FO 1015/556 Note no. 1511/285/50, March 21, 1950; Count Sforza's reply, no. 3/5004, of March 21, 1950.

150 Among these States, France, Great Britain and the United States of America had trusteeship responsibilities..

proposal for consideration directly to the General Assembly or the Security Council and, in effect, retained full control over its contents[151]. In the case of Somalia, since the decision to place the territory under the trusteeship system had stemmed from the United Nations, the latter also had the responsibility to play an active role in the drafting process of the Trusteeship Agreement. The responsibility to prepare a trusteeship agreement was not left to Italy, who was invited to participate, without vote, in the deliberations on Italian Somaliland, as were Egypt and Colombia by virtue of their membership of the Somalia Advisory Council. A fourth country invited to participate in the deliberation of the drafting committee, without vote, was Ethiopia, which claimed to have a 'special interest' in East Africa invoking article 79 of the Charter of the United Nations. India was also invited because of her authorship of the Constitutional Principles annexed to the Resolution.[152]

The Drafting Committee was also empowered to allow representatives of the political parties and organizations in Somalia to express their views before it, if they so desired[153]. However, the decision, taken on the motion of the Philippines, to invite native inhabitants, met with strong British objections on the feasibility of consulting local opinion. In any case the argument proved somewhat academic as no representative of any Somali political party appeared before the Committee to express the party's views.

The invitation extended to Somali political parties to attend the meetings of the Drafting Committee represented an opportunity for them to insert whatever conditions or clauses they may have seen to serve the interest of their country. This opportunity was lost. The absence of the Lega envoy from Geneva during the drafting process was later explained as based on the fear that "his presence there might be interpreted as a sign of the Lega's acceptance of the United Nations decision on Somalia."[154] However, in a memorandum to the Secretary General of the United Nations, Trygve Lie, on October 18, 1950, and on behalf also of the Hamar Youth Club, Lega representatives requested "the right to participate in the forthcoming debate on the Draft Trusteeship Agreement for Somaliland by the Fourth Committee." The memorandum was signed by Abdullahi Issa and Ismail Hassan[155]. In the same memorandum the Lega advanced the proposal to

151 Finkelstein, op. cit., p. 6.
152 Rivlin, op. cit., p. 68.
153 UN Doc.T/442, par. 68.
154 TNA CO537/5930, secret dispatch from Gamble to FO, January 27, 1950.
155 Ascm Gb. b. 81, f. Onu.

incorporate in the Trusteeship Agreement a declaration calling for "the unification of Somalia, artificially divided, whose inhabitants represent one single race and language, the same faith and Islamic culture and conducting the same tradition across the Somali Peninsula which forms an entity geographically indivisible."[156]

The Somaliland Committee held an organizational meeting on December 13, 1949 at Lake Success, electing Max Henriquez-Urena of the Dominican Republic as chairman. The Committee reconvened in Geneva on January 9, 1950 and in the course of the following ten days prepared a draft text for presentation to the Trusteeship Council. The draft agreement was chiefly based on two drafts submitted by Italy and the Philippines respectively. There were basic points of disagreement between the Italian and Philippine drafts.

One of the points of controversy concerned efforts by Italy to secure an agreement as favourable as possible to herself, while the Philippines and Iraq, as self-appointed spokesmen for colonial people, strove determinedly to make the draft agreement "a model expression of trusteeship, containing detailed guarantees for the native population and sharp curbs on the administering authority's freedom of action."[157] Another point of disagreement was over the question of military establishment and armed forces. Italy, in her prepared draft, asked for the power to establish in the territory whatever military, naval and air installations were deemed necessary for defence, to maintain her own armed forces and to raise volunteer contingents in the territory[158]; the Philippine draft, on the other hand, specifically prohibited the administering authority from establishing military, naval and air bases and from stationing or employing its own armed forces in the territory.[159]

On December 5, 1949, the Ethiopian Minister of Foreign Affairs, Abte-Wold Aklilou, appealed to the Secretary General of the United Nation Trygve Lie "to take all appropriate steps to ensure that the Trusteeship Agreement for former Italian Somalia should not be prepared without the participation and agreement of Ethiopia."[160] Ethiopia refused to participate in the work of the Trusteeship Council unless her right to vote as a 'State directly concerned' was recognized. When the Trusteeship Council went ahead with its plan to draft the agreement ignoring Ethiopian objections, Ethiopia sought to delay the works. In a cablegram

156 Ibid.
157 Rivlin, op. cit., p. 71.
158 UN Doc. T/429, art. 6.
159 UN Doc. T/440, art. 4.
160 UN Doc.A/C.1/w8/Add.2. par. 164.

to the Trusteeship Council, Ethiopia requested that "sufficient time be allowed to clear and elucidate certain points." Ethiopia referred first to the fact that the Ethiopian–Italian Somaliland border was not demarcated, and second, raised doubts over the legality of Italy, a non-member of the United Nations, assuming the functions of Trustee. Ethiopia declared that she was considering submitting the case to the International Court of Justice (ICJ) for an advisory opinion[161]. Obviously, the Ethiopian claim lacked solid legal argument because, under Chapter XII of the UN Charter, the authority which would exercise the administration of a Trust Territory might be one or more States or the Organization itself. In fact, Article 81 of the Charter clearly refers to 'one or more States' and not to members of the United Nations. For this reason, it had never been stated, either by the Four Powers or by any other government consulted, that the fact that Italy was not a member of the United Nations excluded her from participation in the trusteeship system[162]. Consequently, the Ethiopian threat of legal action did not deter the Trusteeship Council from proceeding with the drafting of the agreement, and Ethiopia, in an effort not to prejudice her position, refrained from taking part in the works of the Council without a vote, but merely sent observers to the committee's sessions.[163]

A brief account of Italy's non-membership of the United Stated Nations is in order. Due to its role during World War II, and despite its fighting alongside the Allies at the end of the war, Italy was refused admission, even as an observer, to the San Francisco Conference of April-June 1945. After the signing of the Peace Treaty on February 10, 1947, the Italian government made a formal request for admission to the United Nations on May 7, 1947[164]. The bid was supported by the Western and Latin American nations. The Soviet Union, on the other hand, was in favour of admission of a number of its satellite countries – Bulgaria, Hungary and Romania. Western countries felt that these satellites lacked the prerequisite for admission set out in Article 4 of the United Nations Charter, which provides that "membership of the United Nations is open to all other peace-loving countries which accept the obligations contained in the present Charter and are able and willing to carry out these obligations."

The Soviet Union vetoed Italian admission first in 1947 and later in 1948[165].

161 UN Doc. T/430.

162 Records of the 239th Meeting of the First Committee held at Lake Success, New York, on Thursday, 7 April 1949, p. 8.

163 UN Doc. T/441 and T/452.

164 The Somalia Courier, May 15, 1947.

165 Gabriella Venturini, 'Italy and the United Nations', Hamline Law Review, 1966, p. 627.

"In 1949, Italy was still kept in state of 'quarantine' as a result of the war it had lost", comments Luigi Gasbarri[166]. At the United Nations Italy only had observer status, and would not become a fully-fledged member of the UN until 1955 – five years after the UN's decision to award her the trusteeship of Somalia.

The Trusteeship Agreement, as drafted by the Committee with a few changes introduced by the Trusteeship Council itself, was approved by the Council at its meeting of January 27, 1950.

The Trusteeship Council report, comprising the draft agreement, was submitted to the General Assembly, after which the Fourth Committee considered the question during the period 10–16 November, 1950. Following an extended debate, the Committee adopted an Iraqi proposal to accept the request of the Lega and to invite it "to participate without vote in the work of the Committee" during the debate on the drafting of the Trusteeship Agreement for Somaliland. Subsequently, an invitation was also issued to the Conferenza Somala to be represented in the Committee[167]. The Fourth Committee approved the draft by a vote of 44 to 5 with one abstention on November 16, 1950. The Soviet bloc powers opposed the approval of the draft agreement, and Liberia abstained. "In coming to their conclusion, the Fourth Committee overrode strenuous efforts by the Ethiopian delegation to question the legality of the Committee's approval of the proposed agreement", comments Finkelstein[168]. The Agreement was subsequently approved by the General Assembly at its plenary meeting on December 27, 1950 by a vote of 44 to 6. "Their decision reflected mainly a political compromise worked out painfully in the General Assembly over two years in which the vote of the Arab-Asian bloc and the Latin American blocs were now for a solution for the Somaliland."[169]

It was not until 3 February, 1951 that the Italian government submitted a bill on Somalia to its Parliament with the view to securing approval for the despatch of troops to Somalia. The bill was passed by the Chamber of Deputies on February 4 by 287 votes to 153 (the Socialist and Communist Party opposing the bill), and by the Senate on 8 February, with a show of hands.[170]

166 Luigi Gasbarri, *'L'AFIS (Amministrazione Fiduciaria Italiana della Somalia, 1950-1960), una pagina di storia italiana da ricordare'*, Africa, anno XLI, n° 1, marzo 1986, pp. 73-88..

167 Finkelstein, paper given at a Carnegie Endowment for International Peace seminar on February 25-26, 1955, p. 10.

168 Ibid.

169 Ibid., pp. 25-26,.

170 Saul Kelly, Cold War in the Desert: Britain, United States and the Italian Colonies, 1945-52, Macmillan 2000, p. 147.

The ratification of the Trusteeship Agreement by law no. 1301 of November 4, 1951 entered into force on December 22, 1951. The delay in intervening on the matter was due, among other reasons, to the political crisis which developed in Italy following the resignation of Prime Minister Alcide De Gasperi in January 1950.

Peculiarity of the Somali trusteeship regime

In 1945, under Chapter XII of the Charter, the United Nations established the International Trusteeship System for the supervision of trust territories placed under it by individual agreements with the States administering them. The Charter introduced a new principle recognizing to the United Nations the right to intervene in the internal affairs of self-governing territories. The principle departs from the idea, prevailing at the time, that relations between colonizing powers and the peoples under colonization were mere bilateral relations between the two parties. With this relationship now being considered public, the United Nations acquired the right to intervene on behalf of the international community.[171]

The Trusteeship Council, one of the main organs of the United Nations, was established to supervise the administration of trust territories and to ensure that governments responsible for their administration took adequate steps to prepare them for the achievement of the Charter's goals. The Charter authorized the Trusteeship Council (Article 5) to examine and discuss reports from the administering authority on the political, economic, social and educational advancement of the peoples of trust territories; to examine petitions from the territories and to undertake special missions to the territories themselves.

Under Article 77 of the Charter, the Trusteeship System applied to three kinds of territories which were eligible for UN trusteeship:

a. Territories held under mandates established by the League of Nations after the First World War;
b. Territories detached from 'enemy States' as a result of the Second World War; Somalia, together with the rest of the Italian former colonies, falls under this category.
c. Territories voluntarily placed under the System by States responsible for their administration.

171 Ahmed Baha'al-Din, *Mu'amaratun fi Ifriqia (Plot in Africa),* Cairo, Isa al-Babi al Halabi, 1958, pp. 12-13.

In the early years of the United Nations, 11 territories were placed under the Trusteeship System. The basic objective of the System was to promote the political, economic and social advancement of the territories and their development towards self-government and self-determination. The System also encouraged respect for human rights and fundamental freedoms and recognition of the interdependence of the peoples of the world.

Today, all 11 territories have either become independent States or have voluntary associated themselves with a State. The Security Council in 1994 terminated the United Nations Trusteeship Agreement for the last territory – the Trust Territory of the Pacific Islands (Palau), administered by the United States, after it chose self-government in a 1993 plebiscite. Palau became independent in 1994, joining the United Nations as its 185th Member State. With no territories left in its agenda, the Trusteeship System had completed its historical task. The eleven territories which came under the Trusteeship System were:

Togoland (under British administration), united with the Gold Coast (Colony and Protectorate), a non-self-governing territory administered by the United Kingdom, became independent in 1957 to form Ghana;

Somaliland (under Italian administration) united with the British Somaliland Protectorate in 1960, became independent to form the Republic of Somalia;

Togoland (under French administration) became independent as Togo in 1960;

The northern territory of Cameroon (under British administration) joined Nigeria, while the southern territory became an independent Cameroon in 1961;

Tanganyika (under British administration) became independent in 1961. In 1964, Tanganyika and the former protectorate of Zanzibar, which had become independent in 1963, united as a single State under the name of the United Republic of Tanzania;

Ruanda-Burundi (under Belgian administration) voted to divide into the two sovereign States of Rwanda and Burundi which became independent in 1962;

Western Samoa (under New Zealand administration) became independent as Samoa in 1962;

Nauru (administered by Australia, New Zealand and the United Kingdom) became independent in 1968;

New Guinea (administered by Australia) united with the non-self-governing territory of Papua, also administered by Australia, became the independent State of Papua New Guinea in 1975;

The Federated States of Micronesia became fully self-governing in free association with the United States in 1990;

The Republic of the Marshall Islands became fully self-governing in free association with the United States in 1990;

The Commonwealth of the Northern Mariana Islands became fully self-governing as Commonwealth of the United States in 1990.

A brief comparison between the system of the Permanent Mandates Commission of the League of Nations and that of the Trusteeship Council of the United Nations may not be out of place. This comparison is particularly important in light of the problems the system raised between the Administering Authority and the United Nations Consultative Council on Somalia (UNCAS) based in Mogadisho. Two important points of difference call for comment. Firstly, the United Nations Trusteeship Council is essentially a political body. The representatives of those states which are its members sit not as individuals but as governmental representatives. This is a very different state of affairs from that which existed in the Permanent Mandates of the League of Nations, where members were appointed as individuals and technicians, and once appointed they were free to study and comment on the annual reports and other information submitted to them in a quasi-judicial capacity, rather than being expected to follow instructions from their respective countries.

Secondly, the Trusteeship Council of the United Nations is again different from the Permanent Mandates Commission of the League of Nations because of the increased control role it exercises through two important instruments: (a) the missions to the trust territories to control the work of the administering power, and (b) the petitions lodged by the local people to the Trusteeship Council.

The trusteeship regime placed on Somalia presents a unique feature, for it was the only case in which trusteeship responsibility was assigned to a defeated former colonial power which was not even a member of the United Nations. This particular situation led to the approbation of stringent trusteeship arrangements for Somalia in comparison to the existing Trusteeship Administration. These strict conditions included a specified duration of ten years set for the mandate given to Italy, followed by independence after this period[172]. "For the first time in the history of the UN a target date was imposed on a Trusteeship Power",

172 Art. 3 of the Trusteeship Agreement of the Territory of Somaliland under Italian Administration, adopted by the Trusteeship Council on January 27, 1950.

wrote Alphonso Castagno[173]. Other trustee countries (Australia, Belgium, Britain, France, New Zealand and the USA) were given indefinite duration and the Trusteeship Agreement made reference to 'self-government' and not to full independence as an alternative solution.

Another unique feature of the Trusteeship Agreement for Somalia was the provision for an Advisory Council to assist the Administering Authority in the control of affairs in the Trust Territory. "No other Trust Territory has been watched over so jealously by its guardians as has Somalia, which has long been viewed as the special ward of the United Nations," comments A. Castagno[174].

The effect of this UN presence in Somalia was also further strengthened by the provision of regular visiting missions which, like the Advisory Council, reported to the Trusteeship Council of the United Nations (see Article 5 (3) of the Trusteeship Agreement in conjunction with Article 87 of the Charter of the United Nations). Throughout the period of the mandate, three missions visited Somalia between 1951 and 1957.

However, these political and civil guarantees did not make for smooth Italian-Somali relations at the beginning. The Lega, or more precisely, the Lega's radical wing, distrusted the new Administration, suspecting it of having a hidden colonial agenda despite the fact that a process of decolonization of non-independent territories had been put in place by the United Nations Organization and the Atlantic Charter. On the other hand, the Administration found other Somali political parties which did correctly see the Italian Trusteeship as an agency acting on behalf of the United Nations and accountable to it, and were therefore ready to offer collaboration and co-operation to the new administration.

Somali reactions to the UN decision

The UN's decision left the Lega with a difficult choice: either 'swallow the bitter pill', or challenge the international body's decision. The radical wing of the party was utterly against any form of co-operation with the incoming administration, and contemplated approaching the Ethiopian government with a view to make sure of their help should a form of resistance to the Italian authorities be adopted. Earlier contacts of Abdulkadir Sheikh Sakawaddin, the first President of the party, with the Emperor of Ethiopia in August 1946 indicate that the Emperor was in full sympathy with the principles of the Somali party and

173 A.A. Castagno, op. cit., p. 339.
174 Ibid., p. 513.

expressed his readiness to accord them any assistance in his power. It is reported that the Emperor seized the opportunity to state that "the flag of Ethiopia was the banner of all Africans."[175]

British intelligence reports indicate "increasing evidence of contacts established between Lega leadership and Ethiopia at several centres." According to the same sources, the Somali Youth League considered, among other issues, the possibility of exodus to Ethiopia in the event of Italy returning to Somalia[176]. The radical faction went further, requesting Ethiopian administration as alternative to the Italian option. "It is now the wish of the Somali people that I should make on their behalf the following petition to the Assembly, namely, that the Administration of Somalia should at once be transferred to and vested in Ethiopia, or alternatively, Great Britain and Ethiopia jointly" wrote Ali Nour Elmi, one of the representatives of the SYL and Hamar Youth Club on December 1949 to the Secretary General of the United Nations.[177]

However, the official position to be adopted vis-à-vis the UN decision was discussed in a meeting in Mogadisho in November 1949 to which all branch secretaries of the party were invited. Three options were on the table: (a) to remain in Somalia and fight it out with the Italians; (b) to transfer HQs to Ogaden and link up with the Ethiopians, (3) to co-operate with the Italians and capture the best positions under the Trusteeship so as to be leaders of the country when independence would be granted.[178]

The opinion of the moderates, led by Aden Abdulla, prevailed at the end of the discussions. The remarkable leader reminded his party fellows that the public was ill-prepared for armed resistance and for challenging the decision of the world body on behalf of which Italy was coming to administer Somalia as a trustee. The best course of action, he suggested, was to 'wait and see' how the new Administration would respect its international obligations under the Trusteeship Agreement.[179]

By virtue of this decision, the party decided not to oppose the Italian administration with violence. It is reported, in fact, that the President of the Lega, Haji Mohamed, in his tour to the Upper and Lower Juba Provinces, called on Lega members to behave well during the period of handover and to "collaborate

175 TNA, CO 537/3641.
176 TNA FO 1015/188 telegram n. 53 from Mogadisho to the FO, April 18, 1949.
177 UN Doc. A/C./179 of November 11, 1950, p. 10.
178 TNA FO 371/73797, telegram to from Gamble to Foreign Office, November 1949.
179 Interview with Mohamoud Yousuf Aden 'Muro' on 9 August 2009 at Louvien, Belgium.

with the incoming Italian Administration if they respected the obligations under the Trusteeship Agreement."[180] The same British intelligence report adds that the SYL Committee itself drafted a letter for circulation to all SYL branches north of Beledweyne, in which members were instructed to avoid any disturbance of the peace or anti-Italian acts, but also to "not go out of their way to be friendly." Members were also encouraged to accept employment if offered on sufficiently good terms. "The majority of the League Committee and members have taken up a sane viewpoint which reflects to their credit" comments a British source in Mogadisho.[181]

It is significant to remember that, although the Lega's anti-Italian campaign had had some success and influence in the past, before the incidents of January 1948, there had never been universal anti-Italian feelings in Somalia. This argument is illustrated by the petitions sent to the United Nations by groups that were well-disposed towards Italy, representing important tribal leaders across the territory. Perhaps the most significant among the messages is the petition sent by the Bogor of the Majerten, Bogor Moussa Yousuf, to the United Nations, Britain, France, the USA and Russia.

The Bogor's message was given prominence in the Italian press, which described it as a declaration of support for Italy from the Sultan and Majerten Chiefs. The text of the Bogor's message, as reported in the Italian press, reads: "We, Sultans, Chiefs and Sheikhs of the Majerten, turn to you to declare that the Four Power Commission did not refer to us or in any way consult us. This was on account of the present government (i.e. the British Military Administration) which kept us apart. We, Sultans and Sheikhs, were prepared to receive the Commission in the town of Gardo, situated between Galkayo and Bender Kassim where they interrogated little boys who pretended to be Majerten Chiefs, and by intimidation and menaces, expressed wishes which were not our claims. We therefore think it is opportune to send you this document so that you can understand our desire. We have been united and free for over 800 years until 1928, when the fascists assumed power. We request that the United Nations return to ['] our Majertenia government, entrusting, however, the trusteeship to democratic Italy, based on rights and conditions to be laid down [']." The petition was given in the town of Gardo on 10th of Jamadu Al-Tani, 1367 (10.4.1948).[182]

180 TNA CO 537/5938B monthly intelligence report for month ending February 1950.

181 TNA FO 1015/553 Report on the Transfer of Administration in Somalia from the United Kingdom to Italian Trusteeship 1950,.

182 TNA FO 1015/140, Political Intelligence Sitrep no. 8 from HQs BMA, Mogadisho to FO, July 5, 1948.

Italian claims to return to Somalia received a major boost from fresh political developments which took place in Majertenia. A new political party, resulting from a major schism in the ranks of the Lega branch in Majertenia, was established in 1948, with its main HQs at Bender Kassim (now Bosaso). The policy of the new party, which was sponsored by the Bogor of the Majerten clan, was to favour the return of Italy as Administering Power for Somalia.[183]

Furthermore, when it had first been rumoured that the Italians were coming back, "a number of notables, even if they were ostensibly supporting the Lega, began to make secret contacts with the Italian Liaison Officer in Mogadisho" as revealed by a secret report from the British Military Administration HQs in the capital[184]. In addition to this, a number of prominent members of the party, who in the past were opposed to the Italian return to Somalia, became salaried chiefs on the AFIS payroll. They included, among others, Haji Mussa Bogor and Haji Ali Abdi Hawadle, who had both been involved in the bloody anti-Italian demonstration on October 5, 1949.[185]

Italy, as we have seen, counted many other friends in Somalia, represented by the Somali Conference party, who laid no smaller claim than the Lega to the right to represent the people of the territory. Pro-Italian political parties, under the umbrella of the Conferenza, whose active members included prominent tribal chiefs (traditionally well-disposed towards Italy) as well as former servicemen, hailed the return of Italy with enthusiasm and a sense of pride for their victory over their rival parties at the United Nations. In 1950, the Conferenza, under the leadership of Islao Mahadalla, included: Comitato Progresso Somalo (CPS), Unione Patriottica Beneficenza (UPB), Gioventù Abgal (GA), Hizbia Dighil Mirifle (HDM), Unione Africani Somali (UAS), Scidle e Mobilen (SM), Giamiya Bimalia (GB) and Lega Progressista Migiurtina (LPM).

183 TNA FO 1015/140, Political intelligence report, Somalia, July 5, 1948.

184 Ibid., Secret report from the political advisor office, B.M.A. Asmara to the FO, February 22, 1948.

185 Decreto n° 105 rep., Ottobre 1, 1950. Bollettino Ufficiale Afis, Supplemento 1 al n° 8, Mogadiscio, Novembre 30, 1950.

PART TWO

ITALY RETURNS TO AFRICA

Chapter IV

INCIDENT-FREE HANDOVER

At a time when no decision had yet been taken on the future of Somalia, a handover plan was discussed and agreed upon between Britain and Italy. The formal proclamation of the termination of British administration was made by the Chief Administrator on March 30, 1950.[1]

On 1 April 1950, as provided by the General Assembly Resolution, the transfer of administration from the British to the Italians was formalized with a solemn ceremony. The handover process took place without incident all over the Territory. "Fortunately, it was accepted calmly by the population, and it is hoped that the anti-Italian parties will now collaborate with the new administration in the task of preparing Somalia for independence" reads a report from Brigadier F.G. Drew, the Chief Administrator, to the Foreign Ministry.[2]

In Mogadisho, the ceremony of lowering and hoisting flags took place in the courtyard of the Governor's Palace, known as 'Palazzo del Governo'. It is significant that, the last Italian flag in the Horn of Africa having been lowered at Gondor, in north-western Ethiopia, on November 27, 1941, that flag was again hoisted in East Africa on April 1, 1950.[3]

1 UN Trusteeship Council Official records, seventh session, vol. 1.
2 TNA FO 371/80864, report on the administration of Somalia, dated December 31, 1949.
3 Hess, op. cit., p. 175.

A large crowd of Somalis, including religious and tribal chiefs, attended the historic ceremony. Top officials from Britain and Italy were present to witness the event. The former nation was represented by Gen. Dowler, Commander in Chief of the East African Troops, and Gen. Geoffrey Gamble, Chief Administrator of Somalia; the latter, by Acting Administrator Pompeo Gorini, and the Commander of the 'Corpo di Sicurezza' [Security Corps], Gen. Arturo Ferrara, in addition to the Italian Liaison Officer in Somalia, Ambassador Raimondo Manzini.[4]

With the same modality, the transfer of power took place in all parts of the Territory, and the day passed without incident, except for a brawl which broke out between elements of the Conferenza and the Lega dei Giovani Somali at Bardera (Upper Juba). The brawl, which later degenerated into shooting, claimed the lives of three persons; a few more were slightly injured.[5]

The handover of the Territory was to take place from the front to the rear according to the plan prepared earlier for this purpose[6]. Alula, in the Majertenia Province, was the first district to be handed over on March 17, 1950. The handing over of the Majertenia Province was completed on March 26, 1950. The handing over of Mudug Province was completed on March 25 and that of the Upper Juba on 27. In the Lower Juba area and Kismayo district, the handover was completed on April 1st, 1950. The remainder of Benadir Province and Mogadisho were handed over on the same date.

In its editorial comment, the official daily newspaper *Corriere della Somalia* wrote triumphantly: "Nine years of British administration over the territory of Somalia ended this morning in accordance with the decision of the General Assembly of the United Nations at Lake Success on 21 November 1949. Above the administrative buildings in the capital, Mogadisho, there now flies the tricolored flag of the Republic of Italy. The Union Jack is lowered. With dignity and simplicity, in harmony and friendship, Britain transferred, at the wish of the United Nations, the administration of Somalia to the Republic of Italy. All was completed without incident and in harmony."[7]

Brigadier Gamble, who was present in Mogadisho on April 1, 1950, said the handover was "very impressive, punctual and dignified."[8] In certain areas of

4 *Corriere della Somalia*, Aprile, 1,1950.

5 Telespresso 3/5176/C from Manzini to Zoppi, Aprile 1, 1950, as quoted in Del Boca, op. cit., p. 217.

6 TNA FO 1015/553, Report on the transfer of administration Somalia from the United Kingdom to Italian trusteeship. 1950.

7 *Corriere della Somalia* Aprile 1, 1950.

8 TNA FO 1015/553, Report on the handover of Somalia, file no. R/P.I.46 by Brigadier Gamble, April 8, 1950.

Somalia, such as Baidoa, the arrival of the Italians was welcomed with particular enthusiasm as a heavy downpour of rain on March 23, the same day as the handover, eased a severe water shortage. This fortuitous rain, after months of drought and hardship, was interpreted by the local population as "a mark of the favour of Allah at the return of the Italians."[9]

The perceived danger was that some extremist elements associated with the Lega, disappointed and fearing for their future, might try to stir up trouble either before or after the arrival of the Italians, or that elements of the pro-Lega Somali police might go as far as staging a mutiny. Nothing of the predicted disorder or unrest happened; the situation remained calm and promising. "The atmosphere was much more tranquil than had been expected, and none of the upheavals and resistance expected in some quarters materialized" comments Saul Kelly.[10]

Kelly raises a number of suppositions as to what might have contributed to this relaxed atmosphere: more Somalis than expected welcomed the return of the Italians, perhaps through indifference or fear. While the suppositions raised by Kelly may be valid to some degree, one should not ignore the efforts of persuasion made by the British colonial authorities among the population at large and designed to cool down the tension. In fact, between the announcement of the Trusteeship and the formal handover, British authorities on many occasions encouraged the local population to serve under and co-operate with the incoming Italian administration.

Brigadier Gamble, the Chief Administrator, on December 20, 1949, seizing the occasion of Sheikh Soufi's annual pilgrimage to Mogadisho, addressed an important speech to the public in which he said: "The people of Somalia should be thankful there exists no longer, as was the case last year, uncertainty as regards the future of their country.

"Whilst doubts existed regarding the future, many, very naturally, spent valuable time in arguing and discussing what should and should not happen to Somalia instead of applying their efforts to agriculture, trade and professions to the benefit of themselves and the whole community. Now the future is clear.

"As you know, the time approaches when I and my Administration will be handing over the care of Somalia to the representatives of Italy. I am confident that their beneficent direction and control of your country will help you forward to a happy and contented future, provided they receive your co-operation.

9 TNA WO 230/291, Report on the handover of Upper Juba Province, March 31, 1950.

10 Saul Kelly, op. cit., p. 150.

"In ten years' time, Somalia obtains its independence and until that occurs, the great responsibility of the duty of trustee power passes to Italy, guided and helped by representatives of three other Nations and hearing the views and the wishes of the people of the country as voiced by their selected representatives.

"There have, we all know, been many who have actively opposed such a situation. Everyone is entitled to his own opinion, so it could not have been otherwise. Now, however, the decision has been made and it is the clear duty of all patriotic men and women to put away from them discussion and argument and to work together for the bright future of their country."[11]

Lieutenant Colonel Alfredo Arnera, who served in Somalia during the AFIS period as commander in chief of the Somali police force and who was present at this important event, wrote: "No Somali protests, no one disobeys, no one has the slightest thought of doing anything which is not in line with what is going on."[12] Arnera added that the carabinieri "were ready to intervene with firm determination should the Somali police show signs of 'défaillance' or the enemy of our country dare put their hidden threats into action."[13] The British authorities were also instructed to intervene in the event of disturbances during the handover ceremony. "In the event of disturbances which endanger the safety of British, Italians, Indians or other families, you are responsible for taking all the necessary steps to ensure their safety" reads a directive given to General Dowler by the Command Force on January 11, 1950.[14]

The demonstrations of 5 and 7 October 1949, in which 6 people were killed and a dozen injured[15], were the last mass attempt on the part of the Lega to influence the decision of the General Assembly of the United Nations, and since those objectives were not achieved, there were no further demonstrations worth mentioning. But, while violent confrontations did not occur, the radical wing of the Lega did not spare strong denunciations of the new administration through the foreign press and during the weekly meetings of the party. These verbal attacks, however, fell short of producing popular agitation such as to seriously undermine the public order. At Lake Success, before the First Commission of the General Assembly, the Lega representative solemnly declared: "The Somali

11 Brigadier Gamble's speech at the annual pilgrimage to the tomb of Sheikh Soufi at Mogadisho, Somalia Courier, December 20, 1949.

12 Arnera, op. cit., pp. 46-47.

13 Ibid.

14 TNA WO 230/270 Directives of the Commander-in-Chief Middle East for General Arthur Dowler, January 11, 1950.

15 INA FO 371/80864 Report of the Chief Administrator, dated December 31, 1949.

Youth League was positive that, should the General Assembly decide to restore the 'hated Italian rule' in Somaliland, the people will resist to the last man." "Immediate reaction to such an unfortunate decision" stated the envoy "would be inevitable notwithstanding the fact that the British bayonets, Tommy guns, thousands of heavy tanks and planes stationed in Mogadisho and in other centres throughout the territory are ready to subdue our people forcibly."[16]

However, when the 'hated Italian rule' was established on April 1, 1950, the Lega did keep a low profile in Mogadisho as well as in the rest of the country, creating no reason for Britain to use bayonets, tanks or military aircraft to establish public order. According to British sources it was noticeable, however, that immediately after the formal handover ceremony, in Mogadisho, strong patrols of carabinieri police, armed with Thomson sub-machine guns and pistols and accompanied by native police in groups, varying from four to twelve, appeared in all main streets. Public buildings were carefully guarded and armoured cars and lorries carrying armed troops also patrolled the streets. "It seemed that as though the Italian authorities intended to show their strength so as to prevent trouble in the future" reads a British report.[17]

Deployment plan of Italian troops in Somalia

Operation Caesar

The deployment of Italian troops in Somalia was considered at a time when it was not even clear whether the administration of Somalia would in fact be transferred to Italy. In order to have a plan ready to be put in place at short notice in the likely event of a United Nations decision in favour of Italy, the two governments, Italian and British, reached a preliminary arrangement concerning the handover of power between the outgoing British administration and the incoming Italian one. To this end, a preliminary plan, code-named Operation Trousseau, was first prepared in December 1948, and later approved in London on May 13, 1949 under the new name of Operation Caesar. The plan provided for a 2,000-strong contingent of Italian troops to be deployed in Somalia.

In April 1949, the administration of Somalia passed from the British Military Administration (BMA) to the Foreign Office Administration of African Territories, and became known as British Administration, Somalia (BAS). After

16 Press Release GA/PS/247, October 7, 1949.

17 TNA FO 1015/553 Report on the transfer of administration in Somalia from the United Kingdom to Italian Trusteeship. 1950, pp. 15-16.

the rejection of the Bevin-Sforza compromise plan, the British government felt that the six battalions contemplated in the original Operation Caesar were no longer sufficient against possible violent reactions from Somali nationalists in the event of a UN decision in favour of Italian return to Somalia. The British then proposed to increase the size of their troops to a total of 5,000. However, soon after the General Assembly of the United Nations decided to accord the trusteeship of Somalia to Italy, the Italian government felt the need to reduce the number of troops to be sent to Somalia to avoid unnecessary military expenses weighing on the national budget, and also because large numbers of troops would give the mission the character of a military occupation, incompatible with the new role of Italy in Somalia.

Italian Prime Minister Alcide De Gasperi, as well as his ministers of Foreign Affairs (Count Carlo Sforza), of the Treasury (Giuseppe Pella) and of Italian Africa (Giuseppe Brusasca), were convinced of the adequacy of "a strong garrison, well-armed, based at Mogadisho where the representatives of the United Nations were posted."[18] De Gasperi was also of the opinion that the fact that the Trusteeship was sanctioned by a decision of the United Nations and not imposed by an Anglo–Italian accord considerably reduced the likelihood of violent opposition from Somali nationalists. The British, however, considered the military reduction unsound, making it clear they "could not accept responsibility for any failure as a result of this reduction."[19] However, not everybody within the Italian government was in agreement with the troop reduction. Randolfo Pacciardi, Minister of Defence, and the Army Chief of Staff insisted on keeping the troop levels agreed upon earlier with the British unchanged. Their worries were mainly focused on safeguarding the honour of the troops by having enough of them on the ground to deal with any violent opposition. "It would be disastrous for Italian prestige and presence in Somalia, as Administering Power, if our forces, because of numerical insufficiency, were to suffer a humiliation in some parts of Somalia" Pacciardi commented[20]. The 5,000 troop level agreed upon took into consideration the unstable security situation and the protection of Somali borders with Ethiopia. Commenting on the troop levels to be deployed in Somalia, Michele Pirone, a leading expert in Somali affairs, makes the following

18 ASCM 32/9 Appunti della riunione per la Somalia (minutes of the meeting for Somalia held on November 26, 1949 at 17:30hrs at the Ministry of Italian Africa), p. 9.

19 TNA FO1015/549, telegram no. 5 from Gamble to Foreign Office, January 11, 1950.

20 ASCM 32/9 Appunti della riunione per la Somalia (minutes of the meeting for Somalia held on November 26, 1949 at 17:30hrs at the Ministry of Italian Africa), p.3.

observation: "It would be unfortunate to go back to the former colony with a sort of occupying army of 5,000 men."[21]

An advanced team, led by General Arturo Ferrara, was dispatched to Somalia in January 1950, tasked with analyzing the situation on the ground and exploring the possibility of reducing the size of the troops to be deployed in the Trust Territory. The need for sending such a technical and military mission was triggered by economic concerns related to the military expenses Rome wanted to contain. Following his extensive visit, which covered the entire country, General Ferrara concluded that it was possible to cut down the size of the troops, from the 12 battalions advised by the British to 9[22]. British sources suggest that Ferrara informed the British authorities in Mogadisho that the Italian government was proposing a reduction: the forces would now consist of five battalions plus ancillary troops: army 4,665, navy 321, and air force 682. Total: 5,668, which was a reduction of 1,098 on the planned figures agreed upon in Rome in 1949.[23]

The Italian authorities also prepared a plan for the recruitment and training of native levies – the number of which was to be divided between the districts of the territory on a tribal basis. Itala (Adale), Warsheikh and Danana were designated as recruitment centres[24]. The British also opposed the idea of counting the locally recruited native elements as part of the troop levels agreed upon under Operation Caesar[25]. Twelve hundred levies were to be recruited by the incoming Administration prior to the handover.

When the first announcement was made of such recruitment in Mogadisho, some Lega members complained that all the levies would be taken from Hawiye tribes rather than from the Darod. When it was announced that this was not to be the case, and that recruitment would be evenly distributed among tribal groups, the Lega decided that they would support the move and pledged assistance to get as many of their members as possible into the ranks.[26]

The deployment of Italian troops in the Trust Territory was sanctioned by the Trusteeship Agreement between Italy and the United Nations. In fact, under

21 M. Pirone, *Appunti di storia dell'Africa, Somalia*, Edizioni Ricerche", Roma 1960-1961, pp. 146-47.

22 Arturo Ferrara, *'Note sulla preparazione dell'esercito somalo della Somalia indipendente. Dal 1 Aprile 1950 al 30 Luglio 1953'*, p. 2, as quoted in Del Boca, op. cit., p. 210.

23 TNA WO 230/270 Record of Conference held at British Administration H.Q., Somalia Mogadisho, January 10, 1950.

24 Ibid., Sheet 2 attached to letter no. 196 from the Rappresentanza Italiana in Somalia to the BAS Political Secretary, Mogadisho, February 1950.

25 ASCM, 33/23, report from Benardelli to MAI and MAE, December 9, 1949.

26 TNA FO 1015/509 British Administration Somalia, monthly intelligence report for the month ending February 28, 1950.

article 6 of the Agreement, Italy had an obligation to deploy a small army to maintain law and order in Somalia.[27]

Arrival of Italian troops

The movement of the 'Corpo di Sicurezza' from Napoli to Somalia was completed within a period of two months, starting 2nd of February and ending 2nd of April, 1950, to coincide with the start of the trusteeship administration period[28]. Nine ships were used to transport a total of 5,791 men, 793 lorries, light armoured cars and tanks, four calibre 100/17 howitzers, six boats, four airplanes, 5,813 tons of various material and 1,077 tons of ammunitions.[29]

The first advanced contingent of Italian troops (1,133 men) and consignment of goods arrived at Mogadisho port on February 20, 1950 on board the ship Auriga. The troops were encamped, temporarily, at Campo Bottego, a military camp in the outskirts, north of the capital (now Camp Halane). Towards the end of March, military ship Cherso docked at Mogadisho carrying air force materials, including a number of Douglas Dakota 53 for transportation use.

The task of the 'Corpo di Sicurezza' was predictably arduous: maintaining the unstable security in the urban areas, where pockets of anti-Italian resistance still persisted, coupled with the long standing tribal conflicts in the vast territory stemming from competition for water and grazing, in addition to the need to protect security along the unmarked border line with Ethiopia, a country with whom Italy had no diplomatic relations at the time of assuming responsibilities in Somalia.[30]

The landing of Italian troops at the port of Mogadisho took place smoothly; similarly the movement of troops to various localities in the hinterland to replace British forces faced no hindrance. Only one incident without consequence was registered at Bender Kassim (Bosaso), some 1,500 km north of Mogadisho, where some dockers, believed to have links with the Lega dei Giovani Somali, refused to unload material and equipment belonging to the Italian troops destined to be based in the Majertenia region[31]. According to General Ferrara, the dockers' reaction had been foreseen and precautions had been taken in advance.

27 Art. 6 of the Agreement reads: "The Administering Authority may maintain police forces and raise volunteers contingents for the maintenance of peace and good order in the Territory.".

28 A. Arnera, 'I carabinieri in Somalia durante l'Amministrazione Fiduciaria Italiana in Somalia', Il Carabiniere, no. 5 (1980), p. 46.

29 Del Boca, op. cit., p. 210.

30 A. Arnera, op. cit., p. 46.

31 Ibid.

In fact, a unit of underwater swimmers, equipped with specialized equipment, was incorporated in the battalion. It was, therefore, this unit that undertook the operation of unloading the material from the ship, Giovanna C., under the most difficult conditions caused, among other things, by a very rough sea[32]. By contrast, the Italian troops were welcomed enthusiastically in Mogadisho. On their arrival, Islao Mahadalla, Chairman of the Conferenza Party, wrote this message of congratulations to Brusasca: "On the occasion of the landing of your troops we urge Your Excellency to represent our constant faith and love to democratic Italy."[33] The 'Corpo di Sicurezza' was disbanded in 1956 and its members (all Italian troops) were repatriated[34], while the Somali components of the disbanded force joined the Somali police force established in the same year.

The Italians were very conscious of the delicate relations with Ethiopia and careful not to further exacerbate their relations with the oldest State in Africa. The Italian concern towards Ethiopia is better illustrated in the following statement of Count Sforza: "To be in Somalia means to be in Africa, to collaborate in the peaceful development of this continent; therefore, we are not going to keep Somalia in antithesis with Ethiopia, but as a base for the resumption of friendly relations. The 25,000 Italians in Eritrea are telling me that it is in their supreme interest that Italy gets along with Ethiopia; otherwise it will be their death. Somalia, as a colony, is worthless, but it is a very important pawn in foreign policy, this is the point of view of my Ministry. In order not to alarm Addis Abeba it is therefore necessary to remove from the return of Italy to Somalia any character of military occupation. We have to go to Somalia with the absolute certitude to avoid disorder, but to agree together that Italy is not but the gendarme of the United Nations."[35]

Establishment of the Provisional Administrative Line

When Somalia became a Trust Territory in 1950, the General Assembly of the United Nations recommended that "the portion of the boundary between the Trust Territory of Somaliland under Italian Administration and Ethiopia, not already delimited by international agreement, be delimited by bilateral negotiations

32 A. Arnera, as quoted in Del Boca, op. cit., p. 216.

33 ASCM, 34/65, telegram no. 1786, from Mahadalla to Brusasca, Febbraio 20, 1950.

34 Decreto n° 16 Gennaio 1, 1956, Bollettino Ufficiale N. 1 al N. 3, Marzo 1956.

35 ASCM, 'Brusasca', 32/9, ASCM 32/9 Appunti della riunione per la Somalia (minutes of the meeting for Somalia held on November 26, 1949 at 17:30hrs at the Ministry of Italian Africa, pp. 1-2.

between the government of Ethiopia and the Administering Authority."[36] The Trusteeship Agreement stipulated that "The Territory to which this Agreement applies is the Territory formerly known as Italian Somaliland, hereinafter called the Territory, bounded by the Somaliland Protectorate, Ethiopia, Kenya and Indian Ocean. Its boundaries shall be those fixed by international agreement and, insofar as they are not already delimited shall be delimited in accordance with a procedure approved by the General Assembly."[37]

The Ethiopian representative made a formal reservation by declaring that his government did not recognize any international agreement between Italy and Ethiopia fixing their respective frontiers and that, therefore, he could not accept a text referring to the existence of such agreements[38]. However, during the course of the Trusteeship Council discussion of the draft of Trusteeship Agreement, Ethiopia did finally, in discussion with the British government, decide on a provisional frontier up to which the Italian government was to take over.

Following that decision between Britain and Ethiopia, the UK representative[39] presented a letter to the Trusteeship Council with information regarding a new provisional frontier line to which the British government proposed that the Italian government should adhere when it took over administration of the territory. The details of the provisional line were set out in the enclosure of the letter and on the map attached to it; the letter stressed that the arrangement was provisional and without prejudice to the final settlement of the demarcation of the frontier between Ethiopia and Somalia.

The proposed frontier line is defined in the said letter as the "line going from intersection of 48 degrees east longitude and of 8 degrees north latitude, thence south-west to a point six kilometres to the south-east of Gherou, thence 3 kilometres to the south of Balli Abdi Ali, thence between Dabarueine and Gheligir, thence to Fer-Fer, leaving Fer-Fer to the Ethiopian Administration, thence to a locality designated as Casiagur, thence approximately due west between El Grasle and Dudun Har, thence between El Durrei and El Neghet to Bag Berde, leaving Bag Berde to the Ethiopian Administration, thence in a west-south-west direction to south of El Candar to Bur Nohle through Bur Udalei, thence to the south of Dal Gaandalei to Uacsen, thence to Yet, leaving Yet to the Italian Administration, thence in a south-south-west direction between Abdi

36 G.A. Res. 392 (V), Dec. 15, 1950.
37 Art.1 of the Trusteeship Agreement.
38 A/AC. 18/105 of January 27, 1950.
39 UN Doc. T/484, of March 2, 1950.

Nor and El Garap, thence between Ber Curale and Sanca Bissach, to a point 3 kilometres north of Last Cho Rehanuein, thence between Did Anan and El Did Anan, thence 3 kilometres to the north of Ega Dale, and then to Dolo. At Dolo, the line follows the already demarcated frontier dividing the locality between Ethiopia and Somaliland."[40]

In a letter to the Trusteeship Council, the Italian government pointed out that the provisional line had been fixed without consultation with Italy and therefore reserved its position on the legal and other aspects of the question. The Ethiopian government, likewise, reserved its rights on the question.

British sources reveal that even after this decision had been announced the Ethiopian government was still raising claims of ownership of various localities along the 'Straight Line'. The three most important of these were Fer Fer, Yed and Dolo. Fer Fer was a small village (about 40 Km north east of Beledweyne) at which three roads converged, one from the south, one to Hargeisa, through the Ogaden, and a third to Callafo via Mustahil. It was finally decided that the village of Fer Fer should pass to Ethiopian control, but the road juncture just south of the village should come under Somali administration. This made it necessary to remove a police post from Fer Fer to the road juncture. Yed, it was finally decided, would remain as Somali-administered territory. Dolo consisted of three villages, two of which are under Ethiopian jurisdiction and the other in Somalia: the Ethiopians claimed that the whole of this locality should pass to them, but their claim was rejected, and the situation at Dolo remained as it was at the time, with the frontier being formed by the Dawa Parma river through the point at which the confluence of the latter river and the Ganale Doria form the Juba River, and then in a straight line running east from that point.

In accordance with Operation Caesar, it was necessary for the parts which were to pass to Ethiopian control to be handed over before March 19, 1950. In point of fact, some localities such as Mustahil, Godder and Bug Berde were handed over on March 14 after a meeting at Beledweyne between the Chief Administrator and General Asafu Wolde Giorgis[41], in which details of the handover of these posts were discussed. During this meeting, General Asfau again raised the question of the legitimate ownership of Yed and Dolo but "at the end, he agreed that a decision made at a higher level should be honoured", as the Chief Administrator, Brigadier Gamble, wrote.[42]

40 UN Doc. T/484 of March 2, 1950.

41 Governor of Ogaden and Commander of 3rd Division based in Ogaden.

42 TNA WO 230/291, Frontier Demarcation, from the Political Secretariat, March 31, 1950.

The most inexplicable aspect of the matter was the fact that the Somalis, the inhabitants of the land Britain was unilaterally handing over to Ethiopia, were not consulted. Consequently, rather than remaining passive onlookers to what was happening, they reacted to this injustice and made their voice heard. In fact, on March 16, 1950, a deputation of some eighty traditional chiefs met the district commissioner of Beledweyne to protest against the handover of Mustahil, Sul Sul and Fer Fer to Ethiopia. "Only four of them spoke, but the rest expressed full agreement with what was said." As the district commissioner wrote in his report to the chief administrator, the four spokesmen were: Ahmed Gure 'Sandol', Moallim Hussein, Shuriye Yousuf and Abdulle Aden[43]. The points made by the petitioners were as follows:

1. The territory in question was taken by the British from the Italians by force of arms and had been administered by the British for nine years;
2. While the territory was still under British administration, the United Nations had given trusteeship to Italy for ten years;
3. Ethiopia had never in the past attempted to exercise any efficient administration over the area and the Somali people would not allow her to do so in the future;
4. It appeared that, at the last minute, and before the arrival of the Italians, Great Britain was trying to curry favour with the Ethiopians and 'double cross' both Italy and the Somali people, with the result that Italy would be deprived of the ten-year trusteeship and the Somali people in the area would be deprived of their share in the ultimate self-government accorded to the reminder of the territory.

The protesting Somali notables had been told by the district commissioner that any adjustment made to the frontiers had been decided by consultations between the British, Ethiopian and Italian governments, and that, in any case, such adjustment would only mean that the frontier would follow the old international frontier existing prior to the Italian–Ethiopia war of 1935[44]. Here the bad faith and misrepresentation of facts on two points on the part of the British colonial officer in Beledweyne is worth noting: firstly, there was no fixed frontier between Ethiopia and Somalia as recognized by Ethiopia and Italy; secondly, Italy was not

43 TNA WO 230/296 letter from Smith, DC Belet Uen, on protests launched by Somali Notables against the handover of Fer Fer, Sul Sul and Mustahil to Ethiopia, March 16, 1950.

44 TNA WO 230/296 Confidential letter from Brigadier G. M. Gamble to Foreign Affairs, March 24, 1950.

consulted in the adjustment to the frontier unilaterally operated by Britain. At Galkayo, similar protests by Somali notables were organized against Ethiopian takeover of the wells of Dudub.[45]

Difficult negotiations between Ethiopia and Italy

The exact line of the boundary between ex-Italian Somaliland and Ethiopia has never been properly agreed and demarcated. The current frontier between Ethiopia and Somalia, as mentioned before, is a provisional one, determined unilaterally by the British in 1950, at the time of withdrawing from Somalia, for mere administrative purposes.

In 1908 Italy and Ethiopia attempted to reach an accord providing for definitive demarcation of the frontier, and a few years later an Italo–Ethiopian Commission was appointed to establish the line on the ground. But conflicting opinions on the territorial limits of certain tribes mentioned in the treaty and different interpretations of trigonometric points of reference led to a cessation of the Commission's activities. Negotiations between Ethiopia and Italy proved initially complicated, mainly because of an absence of diplomatic relations between the two countries; but even after relations between Ethiopia and Italy were restored late in 1951, no progress was achieved.

"It would be unfortunate if, in addition to many serious problems which will unavoidably exist as the trusteeship terminates, the independent State contemplated by the trusteeship arrangement likewise inherits unresolved boundary questions" reads a United Nations report.[46] It was clear since the beginning that Italy and Ethiopia were not very much determined to come up with a mutually agreeable solution of the problem they themselves had created in the past. "The Ethiopians have no intention of taking any steps in the matter before 1960, while the Italians, always mindful of their nationals in Ethiopia and Eritrea, have no interest in crossing swords with the Ethiopians for the benefit of the Somalis, and are only concerned with keeping the United Nations happy" comments a British source.[47]

Since the beginning, the Ethiopians, invoking Articles I, II and III of the 1908 Treaty which states that the frontier starts from Dolo and proceeds eastwards to

45 Ibid.

46 UN Doc. T/1033, United Nations Visiting Mission to Trust Territories of East Africa, 1951 Report on Somaliland under the Italian Administration..

47 TNA FO 371/108095, confidential dispatch form the British Consulate at Mogadisho to FO, March 17, 1954.

the sources of the Maidaba, claimed that the frontier should pass through Isha Baidoa, some 100 miles to the south of the present provisional frontier. The Ethiopian arguments were that Isha Baidoa was formerly known as 'Maidaba' by the local Ethiopian tribes and that the Rahanweyn tribes mentioned in Article I of the 1908 Treaty live to the south of the line Isha Baidoa-Bulo Burti[48]. The Italians had formally rejected the Ethiopian claim for this large slice of territory lying inside the present frontier of Somalia, and no progress could be made on the solution of the border question in the initial stage of the negotiations.

The first definite action taken by the General Assembly on the Somali–Ethiopian border question came in December 1954 — five years after the first Resolution of December 1950 – in the form of a plea for the two powers to arrive at a solution through direct negotiations and, should they fail to achieve any results by July 1955, to agree on mediation[49]. The Ethiopians expressed their opposition to the pressure of the deadline established by the GA Resolution.[50]

Acting under pressure from the General Assembly, the two powers started negotiations in 1955. In the course of the negotiations, Ethiopia, for the first time, relinquished its original claim to the boundary allegedly established by the Treaty of 1908 agreed between Major Nerazzini, of Italy, and Emperor Menelik, and offered to accept the provisional administered line as a compromise. When Italy rejected the proposal, Ethiopia returned to its original claim[51]. Italian diplomatic documents show that there has never been a clear and definite delimitation of the boundary between Ethiopia and Somalia. Rather, the stipulation between Major Cesare Nerazzini and Emperor Menelik was only an entente between the two parties without a signed agreement[52]. Attempts to reach an agreement failed amid difficulties over a number of key questions of a legal and geographical character.

Realizing that no progress was being made in the negotiation process, the General Assembly again passed a resolution[53] calling on Italy and Ethiopia to continue negotiations and to report to the twelfth session of the General Assembly on their progress. If there were no substantial results by that time, the

48 TNA FO 371/125691, confidential report from British Embassy in Addis Abeba to FO, August 29, 1950.
49 General Assembly res 854 (IX), 14 December 1954.
50 Aide-memoire from the Department of State to the Ethiopian Embassy, Washington, November 5, 1955.
51 Mesfin Wolde Mariam, '*The Background of the Ethio-Somalian Boundary Dispute*', Journal of Modern African Studies, vol. 2, no. 2, (Jul 1964), p. 210.
52 TNA FO 371/108117, Letter no. 221427/95 from the Italian Ministry of Foreign Affairs to the British Embassy in Rome, July 1932.
53 Resolution 1068 (XI), February 26, 1957.

two nations were urged to resort to mediation or arbitration.[54]

Throughout the drawn-out negotiations, the Italians kept the opinion that the present frontier line, fixed by the British Authorities on their departure from Somalia in 1950, was not compatible with the wishes of the Somali tribes who lived on the borderline, and that, if the principle of self-determination were accepted, the majority of the border tribes under Ethiopian jurisdiction would wish for a revision of the frontier in favour of Somalia. The Ethiopians, for their part, attached extreme importance to the territorial integrity of their empire, and were not ready to concede any territory over which they held sovereignty. Therefore, it was clear from the beginning that they would not accept any agreement with the Italians on these terms, or any solution or arbitration by the United Nations which required them to give up any of their territory. As a result, "all attempts to arrive at an agreed solution have failed, largely owing to the dilatory tactics of the Ethiopian Government."[55]

By 1957, the Ethiopian government forwarded two alternative proposals for the solution of the problem and declared at the same time that these constituted, from the Ethiopian point of view, the only acceptable issue. The proposals were as follows:

- the present administrative boundary to become the definitive frontier between the two countries; migrations, grazing rights, the use of water wells etc to be negotiated by an additional protocol;
- alternatively, the whole matter to be submitted to the International Court of Justice (ICJ).

The proposals were not acceptable to the Somali government, which suggested in its reply that the new border should run along the line 180 miles from the coast mentioned in the Ethiopian Memorandum of 1934; alternatively, a solution should be sought by having recourse to a mediator, in compliance with Resolution 392 (V) of December 1950. The Somali government made it clear that they were opposed to a ruling of the International Court of Justice.[56]

54 Memorandum of conversation, Addis Abeba, March 12, 1957, 610 Foreign Relations 1955-1957, vol. XVIII.

55 TNA FO 371/125691, confidential report from British Embassy in Addis Abeba to FO, August 29, 1950.

56 Ibid , letter from the Italian Embassy in London, October 27, 1957.

The Somalis sidelined in the discussions on the boundary question

The General Assembly Resolution, calling for a negotiated solution on the boundary question, gave to the direct interested party, the Somalis, no role in the negotiation process; consequently, Ethiopia and Italy were treating the boundary issues as purely bilateral matter. Both Ethiopia and Italy appeared to have been frustrated by the lack of progress in the negotiations in the face of procedural difficulties, in particular a difference of opinions over Somali representation in the negotiation process. Ethiopia held that as a matter of principle it must deal primarily with Italy, and objected to a role for Somalis even as experts or advisors on the Italian side of the negotiating table[57]. It was not until mid-1956 that Somalis began to participate officially in the negotiations. They had felt that their case was not being presented adequately. This feeling was expressed by the Somali negotiator, Haji Farah Ali, when he stated that "the principles and treaties on which the negotiations between Ethiopia and Italy were being conducted had not been fully endorsed by the Somali government, inasmuch as [they] contrast with the rights, aspirations and interests of the Somali people."[58]

With no results forthcoming, Aden Abdulla, the President of the National Assembly of Somalia, speaking at the 642nd meeting of the Fourth Committee during the 11th session of the General Assembly, stated that the members of the Somali Parliament and government who had carefully studied the reports of the Italian and Ethiopian governments on the conduction of negotiations had concluded that such negotiations would serve no useful purpose in view of the essential differences in the reports concerned. Aden Abdulla said that "the Somali people saw no alternative but to proceed to the second stage provided for in the General Assembly's Resolution 392 (V)", and they formally requested the General Assembly to instruct the Secretary General to appoint a mediator.[59]

On the difficulties experienced by the Italians with the Ethiopians, Prince Colonna of the Italian Ministry of Foreign Affairs, who participated in the direct negotiations with Ethiopia on the border dispute, said that "Italy had come against a stubborn resistance on the part of the Ethiopians and they must ask themselves what was the reason for that resistance." Colonna further added: "At the risk of appearing pessimistic, it seemed difficult to avoid the conclusion that

57 Somalia, Aide-Memoire from the Department of State to the Ethiopian Embassy, Washington, November 5, 1955, Foreign Relations 1955-1957, vol. XVIII.

58 GAOR 12th sections fourth committee, 734th MGT 6 December 1957, par. 39, pp. 389–390 (Haji Farah has acted as unofficial Somali representative at the United Nations since 1957.).

59 UN Doc. T/1311, par. 49, pp. 22-23, April 22, 1957.

Ethiopia decided to advance the frontier as far as possible achieving in this way the partition of the present Somali territory as the Ethiopians had maintained in the course of the direct negotiations which we had had with them in Addis Abeba."[60] The intransigence of the Ethiopians during the negotiations with Italy is confirmed also by British sources. "Ethiopia was often guided by the rigid attitude of its legal advisor, who was an American, and seemed to think and act like a legal advisor for a business concern engaged in a law suit." This was the comment of Mr Watson of the British Foreign Office, present at the Italo-British conversations on Somalia.[61]

When it became apparent that the parties could not reach an agreement, the General Assembly specifically recommended "the parties to establish, if possible, within three months, an arbitration tribunal consisting of three jurists, one to be appointed by Ethiopia, one by Italy and one by agreement between the jurists so appointed or, failing agreement between them, by His Majesty the King of Norway, to delimit the frontier in accordance with the terms of reference to be agreed upon between the two governments, with the assistance of an independent person to be appointed between them."[62]

In this way, the General Assembly circumvented the mediation procedure, taking into consideration that the period remaining for the trusteeship was too brief to go through the intermediate step. Castagno explains that the arbitral technique was favoured by Ethiopia, who contended that the dispute was restricted to different interpretations of the Treaty of 1908. "The Somalis," he states "who had wanted the more flexible technique of mediations, accepted arbitration after the Somalia Prime Minister, upon persuasions from several friendly governments, flew to Addis Abeba on a 'good neighbour' visit in December 1957."[63] By December 1958 the arbitral tribunal had been selected, but no agreement had been reached on the *compromise d'arbitrage*[64] as the parties were unable to agree on an "independent person" to assist the drawing up of the tribunal's term of reference. The Italians nominated a Swiss, Mr Plinio Bolla, as their arbitrator[65]. As the General Assembly had recommended an 'independent

60 TNA FO 371/131463, Italo-British conversations on Somalia, record of the second meeting held at Palazzo Chigi, Rome, on March 3, 1958.

61 Ibid.

62 General Assembly res. 1213 (XII), 14 December 1957.

63 A.A. Castagno Jr, Anne Winslow and Agnese N. Lockwood (ed.), Somalia: International Conciliation, no.522, March 1959, pp. 388-9.

64 Ibid., p. 390.

65 TNA FO 371/131463 Italo-British conversations on Somalia, record of the meeting held on March 3, 1958 at Palazzo Chigi, Rome.

person' to be nominated by the King of Norway[66], the king duly nominated the former Secretary General of the United Nations, Trygve Lie. A draft compromise submitted by Lie was first accepted by the two parties late in 1959, as a basis for discussions; both Ethiopia and Italy presented amendments to parts which they found unacceptable.

It should be noted that the 1948 Protocol under which Britain handed Ogaden over to Ethiopia was neither published in the Treaty Series nor registered with the United Nations because it was felt at the time that it was only of a provisional nature and unsuitable for publication. Because of this omission, the Protocol could not be invoked before any organ of the United Nations in the Somali-Ethiopian territorial dispute.[67]

The two parties, Italy and Ethiopia, adopted two different and irreconcilable positions *vis-à-vis* the demarcation line to be placed on the ground. The Italian position is outlined in a memorandum presented to the United Nations, which advocated that the Tribunal should consider the question and give its decision on the basis of all international conventions relating thereto, and of the interests and well-being of the populations *ex aequo et bono*[68]. Italy also insisted that the third person be prominent in 'public affairs', expressing preference for the Secretary General of the United Nations, or a person appointed by him, rather than an 'international jurist'. Clearly the Italian position satisfied the Somalis as it took into considerations ethnic and non-legal factors in the solution of the boundary question.

The Ethiopian government, on its part, insisted that the Treaty of 1908 must be rigidly interpreted and be the only basis for arbitration[69], on the grounds that Ethiopia could not be bound by agreements between Italy and other colonial powers to which Ethiopia itself was not party. The Somalis responded to this argument by saying that if this was a valid point, then there was no reason they should be bound by any agreements at all, since none of them were drafted with Somali consultation[70]. According to Castagno, the Ethiopian position, which prevents a third party from being heard, was probably intended to preclude the United Kingdom from submitting evidence.[71]

The Italians were well aware of the importance of Ethiopia in the Horn of

66 G.A. Res.1245 (XIII), December 13, 1958.
67 TNA FO 371/108117, confidential memo from Foreign Office, May 13, 1954.
68 U.N. Doc. A/4030, 5 December 1958, p. 3.
69 U.N. Doc. A/4031, 5 December 1958 and add. 1, 10 December 1958.
70 A.A. Castagno, op. cit., p. 390.
71 Ibid., p. 391.

Africa; but neither were they ready to ignore the validity of the Somali claims. "Italy knew that Ethiopia was the bulwark of the West in the Horn of Africa and it took account of Ethiopia's importance and function, but it was not possible to allow this at the expense of Somalia", commented Count Straneo, an Italian diplomat, during the Italo-British conversations on Somalia in 1958.[72]

As no solution seemed in prospect prior to Somalia becoming independent, the parties informally agreed in December 1959 that the provisional administrative line should remain in force until a final settlement was made[73]. The failure of the two sides to reach a solution has its roots in an emotionally charged background. Ethiopia had vigorously opposed the return of Italy as the administering authority in Somalia.

Fornari appointed administrator

The UN established the Italian Trusteeship Administration, known by its Italian acronym AFIS (Amministrazione Fiduciaria Italiana della Somalia). Following the United Nations' decision on the Somali trusteeship, the Italian government was faced with the difficult task of preparing itself before returning to Somalia. Delicate issues such as finalization of the discussions with Great Britain on a timely and smooth handover of power, troop deployment and civilian staff to be engaged in Somalia needed immediate attention. While all these matters were being discussed in a joint ministerial meeting chaired in Rome on November 26, 1949 by Prime Minister Alcide De Gasperi, the problem of who to entrust with the responsibility to run the Trust Territory as 'commissario straordinario' loomed large in the minds of Italian politicians.

Although the Italian representative in Somalia, Raimondo Manzini, had on different occasions voiced warnings against sending to Mogadisho any officials previously involved with the fascist regime, the government selected Guglielmo Nasi, a retired army general who had served as governor of Harar during Italian occupation of Ethiopia[74]. Nasi had also served as military governor of British Somaliland from August 19 to October 1940. The General's tenure would be temporary: he was supposed to remain in Mogadisho only up to the end of the handover of powers between Britain and Italy, and then be replaced by a civilian

72 TNA FO 371/131463, Statement of Count Straneo, Italo-British conversations on Somalia, record of the second meeting held at Palazzo Chigi, Rome, on March 3, 1958.

73 UN Doc.A/C4/SR.10001.

74 ASCM, 267, telegram from the Italian Delegation at Geneva to the Commissario Trapasso Amministrazione, January 19, 1950.

administrator.

According to Italian sources from Mogadisho, Nasi was seen as an acceptable choice for the position of administrator. "In Hargeisa, in British circles, as well as in Mogadisho, among native circles" wrote Ferrara "I heard unanimous appreciation of the Italian government's decision to appoint Nasi as Administrator of Somalia."[75] Other Italian sources from Mogadisho also spoke of the high esteem and consideration the General seemed to enjoy in Somalia both from the British authorities and the Somali notables[76]. However, this choice raised controversy in the Italian Parliament and was vigorously opposed by the Ethiopian government[77] for reasons linked to the General's past association with the defunct fascist regime.

Emperor Haile Selassie sent a formal protest against the appointment of General Nasi as Administrator for Somalia. The Ethiopian opposition to Nasi was based mainly on two arguments: firstly, Nasi's 'proven' reactionary attitude in the matter of native education, and, secondly, the fact that as a Governor of Harar he had been the fascist ruler of Somalia too[78]. Nasi also served as a top military officer in the military establishment in Somalia; his designation as 'commissario straordinario' for Somalia also became the subject of heated debate in the Italian Parliament where Giancarlo Pajetta, from the Communist Party accused the General of alleged criminal acts against Ethiopian resistance movements and of killing several patriots during the time he had served the fascist regime in Ethiopia[79].

Count Sforza, the Foreign Minister, explained that the choice of General Nasi was made on grounds of technical considerations because of his knowledge of the local situation. However, coming under growing pressure, both internal and external, the government took the decision to recall Nasi from Mogadisho and at the same time abolish the position of 'commissario straordinario' in favour of that of 'administrator'. But the selection of the civilian chief administrator for Somalia also became a daunting task. The long list of potential candidates for the office of administrator for Somalia included Francesco Saverio Caroselli[80], Fornari, Brosio and Senator Tessitori. Even the Mogadisho branch

---

75 ASCM, 33/16, telegram no. 191509, from General A. Ferrara to Brusasca after his mission to Somalia, Marzo 10, 1950.

76 ASCM, 33/16, telegram no. 0383 from Gorini to MAI, March 3, 1950.

77 Telegram no. 3/3503 from MAI to the Italian delegation in Geneva, January 28, 1950.

78 TNA FO1015/549, Telegram from Addis Abeba to FO, January 18, 1950.

79 A. Morone, op. cit., p. 58.

80 Francesco S. Caroselli was the last Governor of Somalia and author of the remarkable book Somalia

of the Democrazia Cristiana (the Christian Democrats) threw itself into the fray, suggesting the future administrator should be of their political persuasion and not involved in the previous fascist regime.[81]

The choice finally fell on Giovanni Fornari, a career diplomat serving as Italian ambassador in Santiago del Chile. He was appointed on 31 March 1950[82]. Fornari was born in Rome in 1903 and served as diplomat in France, Spain, Greece, Holland and Argentina before being appointed full ambassador in Chile in 1948. He arrived in Mogadisho to take up his office as administrator on April 6, 1950[83]. Pompeo Gorini, a top official from the Ministry of Italian Africa, who was in charge of the administration of the Territory during the transfer of power before Fornari's arrival, was appointed as Secretary General of the Administration. Another diplomat, Pier Pasquale Spinelli, was appointed as Chef de Cabinet. Upon assuming the administration of the country, the acting Administrator Pompeo Gorini addressed a warm proclamation to the people of Somalia in which he spelled out Italian commitment to the obligations provided for in the Trusteeship Agreement with the United Nations[84]. To prevent any disorders, British laws and regulations were to remain in force until further notice, but soon some of these laws and regulations, seen as incompatible with the new regime, were abrogated.

In fact, in a clear policy to assert its new role in Somalia, AFIS hastily repealed a series of proclamations issued by the British military occupation and regulating different aspects of the administration of the Territory, the most important of which were:

Proclamation no. 1 of February 1, 1941 ('Military Jurisdictions');
Proclamation no. 2 of February 21, 1941 ('War Crimes');
Proclamation no. 17 of October 10, 1941 ('Application of Italian Law');
Proclamation no. 19 of October 24, 1941 ("Juvenile Offenders");
Proclamation no. 6 of March 6, 1942 ('Enemy Trading');
Proclamation no. 12 of February 1, 1942 ('Bank Accounts');
Proclamation no. 19 of May 15, 1942 ('Oaths and Witnesses');

ferro e fuoco..

81 Del Boca, op. cit., p. 60.

82 Bollettino Ufficiale dell'Amministrazione Fiduciaria Italiana della Somalia, Anno 1, Supplemento n° 1 al n° 1, Mogadiscio, Aprile 19, 1950.

83 Somalia Courier, April 7, 1950.

84 Proclama di assunzione dell'Amministrazione Fiduciaria, Bollettino Ufficiale dell'AFIS, n°1, April 1, 1950.

Proclamation no. 15 of May 4, 1943 ('British Military Administration');
Proclamation no. 27 of August 1943 ('Kadis');
Proclamation no. 33 of October 16, 1943 ('Enemy Property').

These proclamations, together with others, were considered incompatible with the new juridical aspect the Trust Territory had assumed under the International Trusteeship System. In the same vein, certain expressions with racial connotations used in the past to identify the native population and reflected in judiciary law (R.D. n. 1638 of June 20, 1935) were repealed. Thus the expression 'sudditi coloniali od assimilati' ('colonial or assimilated subjects') was replaced with 'somali e stranieri giuridicamente ad essi equiparati' ('Somalis and foreign persons juridically equal to them').[85]

Relations between AFIS and the United Nations Advisory Council

From the beginning, there had been confusion about the exact character of this anomalous organ. In fact, on the very day of the handover ceremony at Mogadisho, a question arose over the location of the UN flag and the presence of the UN representatives on the balcony. The UN Advisory Council had proposed that the chairman of the UNAC and representatives of the Secretary General should take their place on the balcony alongside the representatives of Britain and Italy at the handover ceremony. However, Italian Liaison Officer Gorini objected, on the grounds that the United Nations was not directly concerned with the transfer of the Administration, its role being limited to that of observer[86]. "The atmosphere existing between the Italian Administration and the United Nations representatives is electric" reads a British document[87]. After some discussions as to where they and their flag should be positioned, the UN representatives stood on a separate balcony with their flag draped on the balustrade[88]. Relations between the Italian Administration and the Council were, at times, arduous and confrontational. Owing to its anomalous character, the Council was soon exposed to various pressures from local individuals and political parties aiming to involve it in conflicts between the people and the Administration. In the first few years of

85 Ordinanza n° 7 Aprile 12, 1950, Bollettino Ufficiale AFIS, suppl. n°1 al n°1, 19 aprile 1950.

86 TNA CO 537/5720, telegram from Gamble to FO, March 29, 1950.

87 TNA FO 1015/553 file n. CMG /1/376 from Gamble, personal and confidential, to Major General R.G. Lewis, Director General F.O.A.A.T. London, March 31, 1950.

88 TNA CO 537/5721, short interim report on the handover of Somalia, from Gamble to FO, April 8, 1950.

the trusteeship period, the Somalis were under the impression that the Advisory Council had supervisory functions – which was not exactly the case. As a result, "this wrong interpretation of the role of the Council pushed some political leaders to pit the Advisory Council against AFIS, thus complicating problems of co-operation between the Administration and the Somalis", as Castagno wrote[89]. According to Castagno, one of the areas where misunderstandings arose was the flow of petitions lodged by local people directly and examined by the Council without first involving the administering authority in the matter. The issue caused a deep split within the Council itself.

The Philippine delegate, Mr Carpio, who advocated broadest possible powers for the Council, proposed in the General Assembly of the United Nation that the Advisory Council be authorized to deal with the petitions[90]. The Philippine delegate was frequently suspected of encouraging people to step up the submission of petitions denouncing the Administration.[91]

The issue broke into the open in a venomous exchange between the Colombian and Philippine members of the Advisory Council during the 415th meeting of the Trusteeship Council in June 1952. The Colombian delegate declared that he was opposed to any attempt by any member of the Council to promote personal policies, adding that there had been serious differences of opinion between him and the Philippine delegate on the examination of petitions. In a bid to settle the controversy, the Trusteeship Council issued a deliberately worded resolution explaining that "The role of the Advisory Council as defined in Art. 12 of the Trusteeship Agreement is to aid and advise the Administering Authority."[92]

Of the three countries represented by delegates on the Advisory Council, two could not be less interested in Somalia. The third, Egypt, had very different aims. Through her delegate, Egypt had been working very hard to influence the Trust Territory so that it would eventually fall under what was known as the 'Arab bloc'. The Philippine delegate went to such extreme lengths in anti-Italian activity that the Italian government had to request his recall[93]. The delegate from Colombia was reputed to harbour pro-Italian sentiments, but it was with the representative of Egypt that the Administration had the most difficult relations.

89 Ibid., p. 398.

90 Report of the UN Advisory Council for the Trust Territory of Somalia under Italian Administration, covering the period from April 1, 1951 to March 31, 1952.

91 ASMAE, AP 1953, File 917.

92 Report of the Trusteeship Council covering its Fourth general session and its 10th and 11th session.

93 TNA FO 371/102561, annual report on the Trust Territory of Somalia under Italian Administration for 1952.

"Egypt, in view either of its leading role within the non-aligned movement and the Arab World, or its ambition to politically penetrate the areas south of the Red Sea, on which Somalia is situated, interpreted its presence in the Advisory Council as one possible channel of influence", wrote Morone[94]. For instance, it was common knowledge in Somalia that the Egyptian member of the Council, Mohamed Kamal-u-Din Saleh[95], exercised his office as delegate to the Advisory Council in order to serve the policy aims of his government—e.g. by attempting to prevent representation for agencies such as International Cooperation Assistance (ICA), Sinclair Somali Oil Corporation and the Somali Development Agency which AFIS had set up.[96]

Furthermore, the insistence of the Egyptian representative on the adoption of Arabic as the medium of education, to the detriment of the Somali language, was a reflection of Egypt's policy to 'arabize' Somali society. The heavily intrusive Egyptian interference in the domestic affairs of Somalia became the subject of criticism from government and opposition parties alike. In fact, the Somali government saw this attitude and the Egyptian manoeuvres as interference in their internal affairs, which lead to a formal protest[97]. Similarly, some political parties, as well as individual Somalis, saw the activities of the Egyptian member of the UNACS as aimed at advancing the interests of his country to the detriment of Somalia. In fact, in a petition[98] to the UN, Mohamed Sheikh Osman 'Edmondo', Secretary General of the Partito Democratico Somalo and member of Parliament, accused the representative of Egypt on the Advisory Council of interference in the political and economic life of Somalia, and in particular of using teachers appointed and paid for by the Egyptian government to spread propaganda among political parties, chiefs and holy men in order to persuade them that their future belonged either in the Arab League or within a confederation with Egypt. These revelations were seen as damaging Egyptian policy in Somalia. "No petition has ever been forwarded by the Secretariat to New York of such embarrassment", comments a confidential report from British sources in Mogadisho[99]. The Egyptians, in a bid to repair the damage, persuaded a number of Somali Democratic Party members to sign a petition to the United

94 A. Morone, *'L'ONU e l'Amministrazione Fiduciaria Italiana in Somalia, dall'idea all'istituzione del trusteeship*, Italia Contemporanea n° 242, marzo 2006.

95 He was assassinated in Mogadisho by a Somali national in April 1957.

96 Baha'al-Din,op. cit., pp., 45-49.

97 *Corriere della Somalia*, Dicembre 4, 1958; Diary Aden Abdulla, October 31, 1959.

98 T/PET.11/668) of February 14, 1956.

99 TNA FO 371/ 118674 Monthly summary for February 1956, by the British consulate, Mogadisho.

Nations repudiating their Secretary General.

The Council was plagued by inherent weaknesses which often paralyzed its function as UN watch-dog. One of these weaknesses was represented by the high turnover of Council members and their frequent absence from the Trust Territory, "as few of them were happy to be stationed in an area like Somalia which was outside the mainstream of diplomatic life."[100] This circumstance was confirmed by the frequent and protracted absence of the delegates from their duty station. "Over long periods one or more of the members of the Council have not been represented in Mogadisho", according to a report of the first UN visiting mission to the Trust Territory[101]. The same report reveals "During two periods totalling six months and a half, a quorum of two members could not be continued": the absence of one or two members of the Council from the Trust Territory was a common occurrence. One exception was the Colombian representative, Edmondo de Holte Castello, who stayed in Somalia throughout the mandate period and held his position for ten years; the representatives from Egypt and the Philippines were subjected to frequent turnover: for Egypt, Amin Rostem Bey (March–May 1950); Talat Mohamed Ragheb (June 1950–January 1951); Salah El-din Fadel Bey (February 1951–September 1952); Mahmoud Moharram Hammad (October 1952–January 1954); Mohamed Handy (February–October 1954); Kamal Eddine Salah (November 1954 –April 1957); Mohamed Hassan El Zeyyat (May 1957–June 1960), while for the Philippines, Manuel Escudero (March–September 1950); Victorio D. Carpio (October 1950–May 1952); Vicente L. Pastrana (June 1952–March 1955); Cosme P. Garcia (April 1955–March 1956); Mauro Baradi (April 1956–June 1960).

In addition to scant financial resources and limited staff, the Council was also plagued by a considerable degree of disharmony and open enmity between the delegates, which restricted its effectiveness and credibility[102]. "There is no regular day for meetings which are arranged ad hoc, conditioned by the hangover of Castello, the whim of the Philippine or the other preoccupations of the Egyptian delegate", comments a British diplomatic source in Mogadisho.[103]

The municipality of Mogadisho decided in February 1958 to honour the UN and the State members of the Advisory Council by renaming certain streets in

100 A.A. Castagno, op. cit., p. 397.

101 UN Doc. T/1033, United Nations Visiting Mission to Trust Territories in East Africa 1951, Report on Somaliland under Italian Administration, par. 63, p. 8.

102 TNA FO 371/1022561, annual report on the Trust Territory of Somalia under Italian Administration for 1952, from British Consul-General, Mogadisho to FO, London, February 6, 1953.

103 TNA FO 371/102567, restricted report from British Consulate, Mogadisho, to FO, June 11, 1953.

the city centre: hence United Nations Avenue, Colombia Avenue, Avenue of the Philippines and Avenue of Egypt (widely known as Viale delle Nazioni Unite, Via Colombia, Via Filippine and Via Egitto).

Administrative structure

The Italians had evolved a system of administration which they could easily apply to the whole territory, the basis of which was the trusteeship agreement. The administrative system introduced by AFIS was not entirely new. Of necessity, much of it was an outgrowth of the system employed during the fascist regime. The first set of administrative regulations gave the administrator free hand in legislating for the Trust Territory, and the provincial commissioners and residents, most of them former colonial officials, enjoyed considerable freedom in their executive and judicial powers.

At the head of the administrative system was the administrator, who was chief executive and possessed powers of legislation in accordance with article 4 of the Declaration of Constitutional Principles annexed to the Trusteeship Agreement. He represented the Italian government in the Trust Territory[104]. He was assisted by a secretary general, who might act on his behalf, and an administrative staff divided into seventeen departments: the Office of the Administrator, the Office of the Secretary General, the Security Corps Headquarters, the Department of International Affairs, the Department of Internal Affairs, the Office of Personnel and General Affairs, the Department of Finance, the Department of Agriculture and Animal Husbandry, the Department of Industry, Internal Trade and Labour, the Department of Currency and Foreign Trade, the Department of Law and Justice, the Department of Education and Public Health, the Department of Public Works and Communications, the Department of Information and Statistics, the Printing Press Office, and the Department of Accounts.[105]

Largely as a result of the greater efficiency of the administrator and the need for economy, in 1953 the administration was reformed and the departments reduced in number. As a result of this reform process introduced by Administrator Martino, the number of departments was reduced from seventeen to seven, namely: the Cabinet of the Administrator, Department of Internal Affairs, Department of Financial Affairs, Department of Legislative and Judicial Affairs, Department of Personnel and General Affairs, Department of

104 Art 1 of Italian Presidential Decree no. 2357, December 1952.
105 UN Doc T/1033, par. 53; Ordinance no. 47 of July 22, 1950; Ordinance no. 47 of July 22, 1950.

Economic Development, Department of Social Development[106]. This structure was to become the basis for the future Somali administration after independence. It should be noted that during the trusteeship period, the Italian government took charge of international relations concerning Somalia; citizens of the Trust Territory in foreign countries enjoyed the protection of the Italian diplomatic and consular services.[107]

During the colonial period, the organization of the civil departments of the territory was modelled on different criteria and consisted of the following offices:

1. The Governor
2. Ufficio del Segretario Generale (Office of the Secretary General)
3. Direzione Affari Civili e Politici (Civil and Political Department)
4. Direzione Affari Economici e Finanziari (Economic and Financial Department)
5. Direzione di Colonizzazione (Department of Colonization)
6. Direzione del Personale e Affari Generali (Department of Personnel and General Affairs)
7. Ragioneria Centrale (Central Accounting Department)

A new organization of regions and districts was also introduced whereby the territory was, in the beginning, divided into 5 'commissariati regionali' (namely Majertenia, Mudug, Benadir, Upper Juba and Lower Juba, each under a 'commissario regionale') and 21 'residenze' (districts)[108]: a division broadly reflecting the characteristics and tribal nature of the inhabitants.

The first commissari regionali were: C. Lucchetti (Majertenia), M. Tomaselli (Mudug), L. Gasbarri (Benadir), U. Copasso (Upper Juba) and G. Ruggieri (Lower Juba).

The Commissariato of Majertenia included the following districts: Bender Kassim, Alula, Gardo and Iskushuban. In July and September 1950, two new districts, Candala and Eyl[109], were created and added to Majertenia.

The Commissariato of Mudug included the districts of Beledweyne, Bulo Burti, Galkayo, El Bur and Dusa Mareb. In July 1950, the new district of Obbia

106 ASCM, 33/17, Circular no. 26920, Maggio 10, 1953.

107 Art. 3 of Italian Presidential Decree no. 2357, December 1952.

108 Ordinanza n° 8 aprile 12, 1950, 'Ordinamento amministrativo della Somalia', Bollettino Ufficiale AFIS, suppl. n°1 al n°1950.

109 Ordinanza n° 49 luglio 28, 1950, Bollettino Ufficiale N. 5, Agosto 1, 1950, Ordinanza n° 57 rep 1° settembre 1950, Bollettino Ufficiale N. 7 Ottobre 1, 1950 .

was added to the Mudug Province[110]. In July 1951, the Commissariato of Mudug was split into two separate regions, as a result of which a new region, which included Beledweyne, Bulo Burti, Villaggio Duca degli Abruzzi and Itala was established and called Commissariato dell' Uebi Scebeli (Webi Shabelle)[111]. In the same year, the regional capital of Mudug was moved from Beledweyne to Galkayo. Later on, in 1954, the Commissariato as Uebi Scebeli was renamed Hiran, which included Beledweyne and Bulo Burti[112]. The Commissariato of Benadir included Mogadisho, Afgooye, Villaggio Duca degli Abruzzi, Merca and Brava. In July, two new districts were added: Balad and Itala.[113]

The Commissariato of Alto Giuba (Upper Juba) included the districts of Baidoa, Bur Hakaba, Oddur, Lugh Ferrandi and Bardera.

The Commissariato of Basso Giuba (Lower Juba) included the districts of Kismayo and Margherita (Jamama). During the colonial period, the regions were 8: Majertenia, Nugal, Mudug, Upper Shabelle, Lower Shabelle, Mogadisho, Upper Juba and Lower Juba.

For quite some time, the commissari regionali, in addition to their executive and political functions, also exercised judicial functions under the juridical organization approved by Royal Decree on June 20, 1935, n. 1638, in force at the time. Wishing to ensure the independence of the judiciary from the political and executive power, the Administration abrogated the relevant provisions of this judicial organization, establishing instead regional tribunals chaired by professional judges in all regions of the territory; thus the commissari no longer exercised any judicial functions[114]. The denominations 'commissari regionali' and 'residenze' were later changed into 'regioni' and 'distretti'.

Fear of retaliation

The decision of the United Nations to assign the responsibility to administer Somalia to Italy had generated in a number of people a fear of retaliation on the part of the incoming administration on account of past anti-Italian activities and alleged involvement in other crimes, worst of all the massacre of Italian civilians in 1948. However, even before receiving the trusteeship mandate for Somalia,

110 Ibid.

111 *Corriere della Somalia*, Luglio 2, 1951.

112 Ordinanza n° 12 giugno 22, 1954, Bollettino Ufficiale N. 7, Luglio 1, 1954.

113 Ordinanza n° 49 luglio 28, 1950, Bollettino Ufficiale N. 5, Agosto 1, 1950.

114 Ordinanza n° 13 rep 2 agosto 1954, Bollettino Ufficiale 16 agosto 1954, suppl. n° 1 al n° 8;Ordinanza n° 7 maggio 22, 1953, Bollettino Ufficiale suppl. n° 2 al n° 8, Mogadiscio, 20 giugno 1953.

the Italians had been careful not to be seen as harbouring ill-feelings or any intention to discriminate against local people who opposed their return to the country. Along with other Italian politicians, Giuseppe Brusasca, Undersecretary for the Ministry of Italian Africa, had taken pains to make it clear that Italy was far from wishing to persecute its Somali opponents. In fact, in a message addressed in 1947 to the Italian communities who had remained in Africa after the war, Brusasca wrote: "No punishment will be given to those who operated against Italy." The message also carried the undertaking that Italy would fulfil its commitments towards its ex-servicemen. "The rights of those who served under the Italian government will be recognized and all outstanding payments will be settled." Brusasca ended his message by declaring: "Italy is coming to promote freedom for all, and the population will rapidly proceed towards the form of self-government they deserve."[115]

At every opportunity, Brusasca and concerned Italian politicians missed no chance to reiterate that Italy was in Somalia not as colonial power but rather as an agent of the United Nations with the task to prepare the territory for independence. In fact, addressing the second batch of Italian personnel departing for Somalia on February 25, 1950, the Undersecretary gave them clear and unequivocal directives:

"You are going there with a new, great and delicate duty having international and domestic purposes. Italy will no longer exercise its direct sovereignty on that country. This concept has totally ceased to exist. We are going to Somalia as representatives of the United Nations with a well-defined mission which is to create, within ten years, a new independent Somali State. You will be officials of the Italian State, but you will be carrying out an international mission of our country. The Administration will be civilian and should be as such. The 'Corpo di Sicurezza' must collaborate with the Administration to ensure public order and work. The mandate given to Italy assumes crucial importance both for the world and for us. For the world, in that all is set, for the first time, to create a new State in a depressed area, within a very limited period of time. If we, as trustees representing the civilized nations, will give them credit for successfully achieving their target, we will offer those motives of major confidence to the people of the world. By creating political and economic independence in Somalia, which is one of the most depressed areas in the world, we will have the chance of becoming like a great enterprise specialized in the great international duty to

115 TNA WO 230/233 Letter of July 7, 1947 from the Civil Affair Office, Mogadisho.

elevate depressed areas. We will thus acquire the right to be called to compete where there is a need to bring evolution and civilization."

"The natives", added Brusasca, "are no longer those people you left. The ten years of the post-war period have deeply changed them. You must absolutely not consider as opponents those who espoused opinions different from ours. As long as they are performing their duties for the common interest and for the achievement of the obligations deriving from our mandate, no discrimination should be applied. It is necessary to take into account and understand the legitimate right that the Somalis have exercised in manifesting their own opinion and their desires for their future. Of course, in return for the trust that you will accord on a case-by-case basis, you should expect loyalty, honesty or skill, keeping in mind that all the inhabitants of the Territory are entitled to all rights. No privilege and favouritism should be accorded to our nationals who, however, should be sure of the possibility to work and enjoy all the rights contemplated in international conventions."

Addressing, in particular, personnel destined to be stationed in the border areas of the territory, the Undersecretary requested they maintain "the most comprehensive and scrupulous objectivity", adding that "the Italian government wishes all efforts to be made to entertain closer and friendly relations with Ethiopia."[116]

Again, in the speech he gave on June 2, 1950 during his first visit to Somalia, widely covered by the local media, Brusasca returned to the same subject: "The mandate given to us has not been agreeable to all the inhabitants: as I have already declared many times, those who are opposed to us have the right to display their feelings freely." In a bid to set to rest any suspicion the Lega may hold he added: "We will not on that account discriminate against anyone, provided that all collaborate loyally and sincerely in the solving of the tasks which have been entrusted to us and which the vast majority of the population, to whom we are profoundly grateful, has requested should be entrusted to us."[117]

In its editorial of November 18, 1950, the *Corriere della Somalia* published an article entitled Let us return to the realities, in which it stated: "…it is necessary to remind Somali political parties and all Somalis that, if they have the future of

116 Agenzia Nazionale Stampa Associata, Servizio Italiano: ANSA 53. Le Direttive del Governo Italiano ai funzionari partenti per la Somalia, (Directives from the Italian government to officials levaing for Somalia), Roma, 25 febbraio 1950..

117 TNA FO 371/80887, secret report of September 19, 1950, from British Consulate Mogadisho, quoting *Corriere della Somalia* of September 15, 1950.

their country at heart, if they really believe in its independence, if they really want to create a State within ten years, they must stop tilting at windmills with fruitless combativeness, useless after the approval of the Trusteeship Agreement by the United Nations."[118] Echoing the Undersecretary's statements on the new role of Italy in Somalia, the Administration made every effort to explain its policy in Somalia. In fact Dr. Benardelli, Director of Civil and Political Affairs, sent a long circular letter to all regional commissari and residenti with clear instructions to be impartial and not divide the population under their jurisdiction by discriminating "between those in favour of AFIS and those against it."[119]

The commissari and residenti were instructed to assist pro-Italian parties but to avoid giving them stipends. The kind of support recommended was by way of awarding them lucrative public contracts and other services[120]. The circular, designed to serve as a guide to the regional authorities—many of them probably having little or no past experience in Africa – consisted of 15 points containing instructions, recommendations, and a code of conduct to be observed in interacting with the local population under their respective jurisdictions. A key component of the circular is the slogan: "Italy is in Somalia to be a guide to the Somalis; the latter are all equal before it."[121]

The commissari were strongly advised not to demonize the Lega. "It is highly probable that this party may become a major political partner of the Administration—hence the need to encourage this evolution in our favour"[122], wrote the Director of Civil and Political Affairs. Significantly, Benerdelli's prediction came true: in the space of less than four years since the circular was issued, a new era of close co-operation between AFIS and the party took shape.

There were still some among the most radical members of the Lega, including a few elements serving in the police force, who may have entertained fears of possible retaliation from the new Administration on grounds of their presumed role in the incidents of January 11, 1948 in Mogadisho. However, records show that many individuals suspected of involvement in the massacre of Italian civilians in Mogadisho and known for their anti-Italian attitude joined the service of the new Administration, and many of them were sent for studies and training

118 *Corriere della Somalia*, Novembre 18, 1950.

119 ASMAE, AFIS, box 19, file 34. The five-page circular shows no date, but most probably was written in early 1950, soon after the Administration was established..

120 Asmae "Afis"19/47, Circolare segreta from Benardelli to all Commissari and Residenti, Marzo 30, 1950.

121 Ibid.

122 Ibid.

to Italy without discrimination.

The right of petition

The right of petition was a clause enshrined in the Trusteeship Agreement: it derived from a provision in the UN Charter giving the Trusteeship Council of the United Nations power to accept petitions emanating from the inhabitants of the trust territories and to examine them in consultation with the Authority administering the territory concerned[123]. By interpretation, the provision came to mean that any person, anywhere in the world, who wrote to the Trusteeship Council with a complaint about any or all of the trusteeship territories could count on having his case examined and acted upon.

Exercising this right, not only Somali political parties, but also individuals and other groups, particularly in the early years of the trusteeship regime, did submit hundreds of petitions to the UN denouncing Italian behaviour against them. The Lega, for example, alleged that heavy-handed measures were taken by the Administration. In certain cases the Italian Administration was accused of "encouraging an atmosphere of division between the local population and of arbitrarily terminating the contracts of any of its employees found to be affiliated to the Lega, replacing them with individuals affiliated to organizations close to the Administration": a clear allusion to the Conferenza Somala[124]. Petitions were filed citing cases of arrest, fines and deportation of Lega members who had refused to disclose their ethnic origin, as well as manipulation of the Conferenza Party against the Lega[125]. According to official figures, there were 106 Somalis arrested and given prison sentences for politically-related activities.[126]

In an attempt to win the hearts and minds of the population, Ambassador Fornari issued an ordinance in June reducing the prison sentences of those already serving time for crimes committed before the transfer of power to Italy[127]. This was followed by another act of clemency aimed to allay tension during Ramadan by granting general amnesty for all politically-related offences committed in the territory during and after the transfer of power.[128]

123 Art. 87 of the UN Charter.

124 Unor, T/ Petit, 11/16. Petition from the Lega, Bardera Branch, to the Trusteeship Council.

125 Unor, T/14, from Mogadisho HQs to the Trusteeship Council.

126 Rapport du gouvernment italien a l'Assemblée Generale des Nations Unies sur l' Administration de la Somalie placée sous la tutelle de l'Italie, avril-decembre 1950, Istituto Poligrafico dello Stato, Roma, 1951, p. 235.

127 Ordinanza n° 29 rep. dell' 8 giugno 1950, Bollettino Ufficiale, suppl. n° 2 al n° 3, 16 giugno 1950.

128 Ordinanza n° 40 luglio 17, 1950, Bollettino Ufficiale, suppl. n° 2 al n°4, 20 luglio 1950.

Records show that, from April 1950 to 31 December 1959, the number of petitions presented to the Trusteeship Council stood at 815, of which 62 were presented in 1959 [129]. In the face of the growing number of petitions originating from the trust territories, the General Assembly invited the Administering Powers to consider "positively" the possibility for the indigenous population to participate, as part of their respective delegations, in the works of the Trusteeship Council in New York[130]. As a result, Mohamed Farah Siad 'Kid' was sent to New York in his capacity as councillor. However, he did not take part in the discussions of the Trusteeship Council: rather, his role was that of a mere assistant to the Italian delegation at the United Nations.

Before assuming administration of the Trust Territory, the Italian government undertook to maintain in its service all civil servants employed by the British Administration, known as ex-BAS, on the same rate of pay and service conditions as under British administration. A hefty majority of these elements, who served under the British Administration, particularly the police, were known to be associated with the Lega, which as we have seen was a political movement opposed to the return of Italy. This anomaly was tolerated, if not encouraged, by the British during their occupation; it was however a source of embarrassment for the Italian Administration to continue to employ and maintain in their active service some individuals who manifestly identified with political parties.

In a move to clean up the police from unwelcome elements, a number of servicemen had their contracts terminated on grounds of partiality, indiscipline or inefficiency. The Lega complained that these dismissals were carried out on political grounds[131] and the Administration conceded that cases of dismissal of civilian and police staff suspected of links with the Lega had occurred, but claimed this was not a systematic pattern[132]. "There have not been any definite cases of victimization of ex-BAS civil servant employed by AFIS, but some of them, particularly the Police, were not allowed to belong to the Lega and if they were had been dismissed", reads a British document[133].

There were clear directives from the Ministry of Italian Africa to cleanse the

129 Rapport du gouvernment italien à l'Assemblée Generale des Nations Unies sur l'administration de la Somalie placée sous la tutelle de l'Italie 1959, p. 111.

130 Resolution no. 554 of 18 January 1952.

131 TNA FO 371/80887, letter signed by Dr. Benardelli and dated August 15, 1950, in response to the letter of the Lega, dated July 25, 1950.

132 ASCM, 'Brusasca', Relazione politica del 10 Maggio 1950.

133 TNA FO 371/89887, extract from a letter to Brigadier Gamble from Barry, British Consul, Mogadisho, June 1, 1950.

force from elements which, because of their past and present conduct, were considered unwelcome and inefficient[134]. "Eliminate without indulgence those who do not deserve to be part of AFIS", wrote Brusasca to Fornari.[135]

Disciplinary action was taken, for instance, against ex-Inspector Mohamed Abshir and Inspector Issa Jama, resulting in suspension from duty; both were however reinstated later with full back-pay; both submitted petitions to the Trusteeship Council[136]. All those affected by the disciplinary measures lodged petitions with the Trusteeship Council. It would nonetheless be wrong to conclude that, although holding the record in terms of the number of petitions submitted to the Trusteeship Council, the Lega was the only political party making its voice heard at the United Nations. Other political organizations also petitioned the Trusteeship Council on a number of occasions.

Petitions presented directly to the Trusteeship Council in New York, or through the Advisory Council based in Mogadisho, were generally raised in such a manner that, except in few cases, no action was taken to remedy the complaint because of its vagueness or inarticulate voicing. Responses from the Trusteeship Council were generally very slow, sometimes taking as long as a year and the Council often tended to accept the explanation of the Italian Administration.

Tribal intolerance in Baidoa: Kulubey Dhawa riots

When Italy assumed the administration of the Trust Territory in 1950, the structure of Somali society remained as ethnically divided as it was before the war. The situation had further been exacerbated by the formation of a string of small competing political parties and organizations, hastily organized on the eve of the Four Powers Commission's visit in 1948.

The new era of freedom of expression and formation of political parties inaugurated during British rule unleashed, especially in the capital, Mogadisho, a wave of publicly expressed hostilities and intolerance towards ethnic Somalis hailing from the nomadic northern regions of the Trust Territory. The most evident slogan expressing this intolerance, widely circulating in Mogadisho at the time, was: "Dabaalataa ama doon kortaa, Darood Dalkeeyga iiga guur", which means "O people of ethnic Darod pack up and leave my land. It is up to you how you move out: either swimming or by boat."

134 ASCM b.47, f, 272, relazione politica del MAI a Mogadisho.

135 ASCM, 46/263, letter no. 158003/25 from Brusasca to Fornari, Aprile 18, 1951.

136 T/PET 11.21: Petition from Mr. John C. Gee.

Tribal intolerance reached its climax when, just one month before Italy assumed administration of the Trust Territory, Haji Mussa Bogor and Haji Dirie Hersi, both prominent Lega members and businessmen, were attacked on the streets of Mogadisho on March 6, 1950 by tribesmen of the Hawiye tribe[137]. A British intelligence report reveals that "A band of Habargidir, a mostly pro-Italian tribe, attacked two Darod notables who were prominent in the Lega. Neither of the two was much hurt, but for a day or two feelings ran high."[138] One claim made by the Habargidir was that the attack came as a reprisal against those who had two days previously attacked Mohamed Sheikh Osman 'Edmondo', a prominent pro-Italian and member of the Habargidir[139]. An 8pm to 5am curfew was imposed on Mogadisho the next day. Six people were arrested in connection with the attack. The incident is connected, according to British authorities, with moves by the Conferenza, culminating in the submission of a petition for deportation from Mogadisho of, amongst others, the two men attacked. The petition was refused[140]. However, the Lega maintained the view that the incident was politically motivated, excluding any tribal connotations.[141]

The feeling of intolerance and hostility towards ethnic groups from the northern part of the territory was not an isolated phenomena limited only to Mogadisho, but it was deeply felt also in the agricultural areas of the south. In Somalia, natural resources are not evenly distributed among all areas of the country. The fertile and agricultural lands are situated in the southern part; the only two perennial rivers are in the south – hence the waves of population moving from the northern regions to the south for their survival and to escape the hostile environment and poverty of their homeland.

Rahanweyn resentments against Somali nomads ran deep. The feeling was mutual. The pastoralist Samaali population were seen by the local Dighil and Mirifle as invaders who encroached on the areas between the two rivers with the Italian occupation and would, if allowed, overrun the territory and dominate the less warlike indigenous inhabitants of the area, who are the majority. Mention should be made also of the fact that the population of Dighil and Mirifle regarded the nomadic Somali tribes as foreigners, as illustrated in their testimony before the Four Power Commission in 1948.

137 HC Deb, 21 April 1950 vol. 474 cc45-6W.

138 TNA FO 1015/553, Report on the Transfer of Administration in Somalia from the United Kingdom to Italian Trusteeship. 1950.

139 TNA CO 537/5938B Political Intelligence Report n 3/50 for the period 1-18 March 1950.

140 TNA FO 371/80886, Telegram from Gamble to FO, London, March 7, 1950.

141 ASCM, 34/60, telegram no. 1025, from Gorini to MAI, March 20, 1950.

The feeling of intolerance towards the nomadic population was expressed in the following popular slogan: "Hunguri dhamaantiis unni hukunee, aaw surwal dheedheerow may amaasaan?" which roughly translates as: "I am the supplier of the food you eat. O people wearing long trousers (the Lega), what will be your destiny if I stop feeding you?"

On April 17, 1950, just two weeks after the Italians had officially taken over the administration of the Trust Territory, bloody tensions erupted in Baidoa, the provincial capital of Upper Juba, where the Lega section came under attack from a group of local people and a number of houses and business premises belonging to non-Dighil elements were looted or set ablaze. This riot, which passed into Somali legend as 'Kulubei dhawa' or 'Hit the Lega adherents', was the ugliest riot of that period in Somalia. Official reports from Baidoa indicated that the fracas, which had started in the morning, lasted until 2pm. Two persons associated with the Lega were killed. The party blamed the Authority for doing little to stop the violence.[142]

According to the Italian authorities, who denied accusations of doing little to quell the riots, the cause of the incident lay in the ill-feeling which the Dighil and Mirifle bore against certain elements of the Lega, for whom the period of British military administration (BMA) had allegedly been advantageous in numerous ways[143]. It was reported that 60 families, totalling between five to six hundred people, had fled the city in the wake of the incident. The rioters targeted only those ethnic Somalis belonging to the Lega; others remained unharmed.

The Administration did not agree that those who had suffered losses were entitled to compensation to be paid for by the government, but as a gesture of good will offered help to those who suffered during the disturbances by either granting special import licenses to enable them to renew their stocks of goods or helping repair damaged premises[144]. Each family affected by the violence received an ex-gratia payment of Sh.So100. The Administration covered the repair costs of the damaged huts or shops. In 1951, claims for further compensation were received by the Administration, which then allotted to the 'residente' a sum of Sh.So 60,000 in final and as ex-gratia settlement of all outstanding claims.[145]

Since all the claimants belonged to one political party, the residente decided to

142 T/PET.11/40, dated May 3, 1951.

143 UN Doc. T/923, Report of the United Nations Advisory Council for the Trust Territory of Somaliland under Italian administration covering the period April 1950 to 31 March 1951.

144 TNA FO 371/80887, secret report from British Consulate General, Mogadisho to FO, October 12, 1950.

145 UN Doc. T/923.

call on that party's leaders to form a commission to advise him on the criteria for distribution of the money. The commission received seventy claims and rejected 45; the compensation sum of Shilling 60,000 was divided among the 16 applicants whose claims were accepted as genuine[146]. British sources suggest that a number of people belonging to tribes under British protection, such as the Dulbahanta and Warsangeli, some of them living in the Trust Territory for 30 years, had approached the British Consulate in Mogadisho to complain of injuries sustained and losses suffered in the wake of the Baidoa disturbances. They claimed to be "unable to get redress from the Italian authorities and terrorized by the members of Rehanweyn tribes if they tried to go to court."[147]

In a bid to calm the situation, the district commissioner of Baidoa and the officer in charge of the local police station were removed following a joint visit by a UN-AFIS mission led by Dr Benardelli, Head of the Political Office of the Administration, who recommended the measure.

The Lega always denied or ignored the truth: i.e. that Somalia was sitting on a tinderbox that could at any time explode and plunge the country into civil war and tribal strife. Instead of urgently addressing ethnic problems through a reconciliation process, improved economic conditions for rural inhabitants and good governance, successive Somali civilian governments preferred to boast that the Somali population was 'united and compact'. The dormant volcano on which the country was sitting erupted suddenly in 1991, precipitating the current civil war exactly after 30 years since the country came under Lega administration in 1956, and 60 years since Governor De Vecchi forcibly established what he called 'La Grande Somalia' in 1927.

Brusasca-Aden Abdulla showdown

On May 25, 1950, less than a month after the establishment of the Administration, Giuseppe Brusasca arrived Mogadisho – the first high profile visit to Somalia by an Italian official since the end of the war.

At the start of his mission, Brusasca explained once more Italy's new policy in Somalia. In his own words: "We were going back to demonstrate that we were able to inaugurate a new politics in Africa, not one of exploitation, but of collaboration."[148] Top of the agenda for Brusasca's maiden mission to Somalia

146 UN Doc. T/L. 347, June 19, 1953.

147 TNA FO 371/80887, confidential report of June 6, 1950 from British Consulate Mogadisho to FO.

148 Palumbo (ed.), op. cit., p. 31.

was to "ascertain the social, political and economic conditions of Somalia and to convince the incredulous elements of the Lega that the Italian government had the intention to carry out the trusteeship in good faith."[149]

During his mission, Brusasca visited all the important centres of the territory, meeting with traditional chiefs and Somali politicians, conferring with the most loyal among them and awarding State honours to the chosen few.

Among the notables and traditional chiefs (from Mudug Province) who received honours were: Dahir Set (Rer Aden), Haji Ali Balle (Beidian), Sheikh Mohamoud Yousuf (Omar Mohamoud), Farah Godagode (Omar Mohamoud), Duale Kahie (Sa'ad), Nour Ali Omar (Sa'ad), Giama Set (Sa'ad), Ahmed Nour (Soliman), Salad Ahmed Qarei (Soliman), Haji Mohamed Afrah (Sarur), Sheikh Hassan Adde Fighi (Sa'ad), Haji Gurhan Egal (Wagardha'), Haji Ahmed Dallan (Omar Mohamoud), Sheikh Warsame Abdi (Lelkasse), Giama Hassan Ghibin (Rer Mahmud), Hassan Giama (Meheri), Ali Barre (Omar Mohamoud, Rer Abdulle), Warsama Auden (Omar Mohamoud, Rer Abdi Issa), Ismail Giama Gis (Omar Mohamoud), Mussa Samatar (Osman Mohamoud), Abdi Mussa (Omar Mohamoud), Shire Egal (Wagardha'), Mahmoud Gurei Elmi (Omar Mohamoud, Rer Abdulle), Ersi Arab (Omar Mohamoud, Rer Ersi), Ali Mohamed (Beidian), Abduraman Ali (Beidian), Bihi Nour (Omar Mohamoud, Rer Aden), Ali Barre Botan (Omar Mohamoud, Rer Mohamed Omar), Giama Warsama Islan (Rer Mahad), Islan Abdulla (Omar Mohamoud), Haji Warsama Ali (Rer Calaf), Haji Giama Issa (Rer Ersi).

In Mogadisho, Brusasca received important personalities from Benadir, including Islao Omar Ali on behalf of the chiefs and notables of Mogadisho, Islao Mahadlla (President of the Conferenza Party), Haji Mohamed Hussein (President of the Lega dei Giovani Somali), Yassin Ali Sharmarke (Lega Progressista Somala), Salah Sheikh Omar (Unione Patriottica Somala), Haji Muhiddin Ali (President of Club Hamar), Mohamed Sheikh Osman (Unione Africani), Abdalla Hamed Salim (representing the Arab Community), Cav. Uff. Hamed Fadel (from the Pakistani Community), Cav. Sheikh Nour Hussein (representing the Eritrean Community), Sheikh Mohamoud Kadi (on behalf of the religious leaders), Sheikh Abdullahi Sheikh Mohamed (for the Hizbia Dighil and Mirfle Party). Among those decorated with the Order of National Solidarity was Ahmed Kharbash, a Yemeni national who had been prominent during the Arab–Somali riots in October 1947 and had returned to Somalia after being

149 Ibid.

deported to Aden by the British Administration.[150]

The Italian government, in fulfilment of its undertakings, had settled claims for back pay in favour of former servicemen. The settlement sum covered the period between 1 February 1941, the date on which British forces occupied Somalia, and 15 September 1947, the date on which, following the Peace Treaty, Italian sovereignty on Somalia ceased. The Committee in charge of the payment of arrears was known as 'Comitato per la Liquidazione degli Arretrati per Militari Somali'(CLAMS).[151]

The largesse of the Administration towards its supporters went beyond material and other symbolic recognition to include concessions in the religious sphere when the Administration sent 58 Arabs and Somalis, chiefly the latter, all well-known Conferenza supporters, on a free pilgrimage to Mecca. Two special aircraft were used to transport them.[152]

During his mission in Somalia, Brusasca met with some exponents of the Lega dei Giovani Somali in Mogadisho. Drawing on Brusasca's notes, Del Boca reveals a showdown between Brusasca and Aden Abdulla. "At the beginning, the dialogue between Aden Abdulla and Brusasca was not easy, as the Lega delegation soon assumed an attitude of reservation, if not of criticism. The conversation between the two men was terse and uncompromising. In a brusque, matter-of-fact manner, Aden Abdulla started the conversation by asking: "Vogliamo sapere che cosa è venuta a fare l'Italia in Somalia." ("We want to know what Italy has come to Somalia for".) Brusasca's response was calm and concise: "We are here on behalf of the United Nations with the task to organize your State." Aden Abdulla's riposte was: "Non farete di questo mandato un pretesto per poi rimanere come colonizzatori?" ("You are not going to use this mandate as a pretext to remain as colonizers?")

"Poi il dialogo si fa sempre più acceso. Con estrema durezza, i somali rinfacciano a Brusasca tutti i torti d'Italia, dai genocidi al lavoro coatto, dall'aver coltivato il tribalismo all'aver mantenuto i somali nella più completa ignoranza." ("The dialogue then becomes more and more heated as the Somalis harshly remind Brusasca of all the wrongs Italy had committed, ranging from the genocide to forced labour, from encouraging tribalism to keeping Somalis in utter ignorance.")[153] Brusasca tried to defend himself from this barrage of

150 TNA FO 371/80887 secret report from the British Consulate Mogadisho, June 21, 1950.

151 Ordinanza n° 20 maggio 20, 1950, Bollettino Ufficiale, suppl. n° 2 al n° 2, 24 maggio 1950,.

152 TNA FO 271/80887 secret report of August 30, 1952 from British Consulate Mogadisho to the FO.

153 Del Boca, op. cit., p. 224.

accusations by pointing out the improvements achieved by Italy during its tenure as administrator of the territory. "All that is here has been done by Italy: roads, hospitals, public services, waterworks and sanitation—in short, everything." "This is true," Aden Abdulla responds "but those who came after you granted us something immensely much more important than that. They gave us freedom of expression, freedom to establish political parties, freedom to work for the future of our country."

After the difficult initial round, the meeting ended in a less tense atmosphere. "Despite having some reservations, the Lega delegation gives assurances of loyal co-operation with the Italian administration. These understandings receive the blessing of the Central Committee whose entire membership goes to the airport to see off Giuseppe Brusasca who returns to Italy."[154]

On the eve of Brusasca's visit to Somalia, the Central Committee of the Lega had dispatched a circular to all its sections in the territory instructing local leaders on how to present the party's policy during Brusasca's visit in their respective areas[155]. The circular focused on a number of concerns to be raised, mainly regarding the manner in which Italian authorities had dealt with various issues. These included the Baidoa incident and the choice of former fascist personnel as AFIS administrators. However, despite the strongly-worded circular, Brusasca received a warm welcome in all the areas he visited in Somalia. For instance, in his welcoming address to Brusasca, the President of the Lega, Haji Mohamed, exhibited a less than hostile attitude: "Your Excellency, we assure you that the Lega has as its first priority the interest of Somalia and the Somalis, and, consequently, AFIS can count everywhere on the SYL's support in all that is intended to be done in the country's interest."[156] Even warmer, overly friendly was the welcome message addressed to the distinguished visitor by the secretary of the local section of the Lega at Belet Uen: "Your Excellency, the Lega dei Giovani Somali of Beledgweyne is fully convinced of how serious Italy is about the trusteeship administration of this Territory; it has faith in what you have repeatedly said over the radio and the press in the interest of Somalia and the Somalis. Your Excellency can therefore surely count on the full support of the SYL in the field of education, as well as in pacification among all Somalis."[157]

154 Ibid.

155 ASCM, 34/65, Circular n. Reg. I.G.8A to all outpost sections from the party HQs at Mogadisho, 24 May, 1950.

156 ASCM, 60/57, letter from Haji Mohamed to Brusasca, Maggio 25, 1950.

157 ASCM, 60/57, letter from Sceik Ali Giumale, Secretary of the Lega's Belet Uen section, to Brusasca, during the latter's visit to Belet Uen, Maggio 29, 1950.

The warm welcome Brusasca received in all the places he visited, including areas considered Lega strongholds, belied the widely held opinion that the Lega was absolutely hostile to Italian administration. Before ending his mission, Brusasca, accompanied by all senior civic and military officers, paid his respects to those killed on January 11, 1948 by placing a wreath on their resting place at the local cemetery.[158]

Kismayo incident, August 2, 1952

Relations between the local Lega leadership of Kismayo and the regional AFIS authorities had never been smooth, especially in the early years of the establishment of the trusteeship regime. This situation derived from mistaken interpretation of instructions regulating the flying of the Italian flag alongside the standards of political parties on buildings hosting Party HQs in the territory. Whilst the requirement to fly both flags side by side was a mere recommendation, the provincial commissario of Lower Juba, Aldo Wagner, was exerting strong pressure on political parties for the Italian flag to be hoisted at the provincial HQs of all political parties, a position the Lega strongly resisted.

In order to submit their arguments, a three-member delegation representing the Lega requested through the provincial Commissioner a meeting with the AFIS Secretary General, Mario Canino, who was visiting Kismayo on August 2, 1952 with Gualtiero Benardelli, Chief of Political Affairs[159]. However, the commissario rejected the request and asked the applicants to submit their complaint in writing instead. Public anger intensified when it emerged that the Lega was being denied the opportunity to meet the visiting top AFIS officials. Within a few minutes, an angry crowd, estimated at between 100/150 persons and including women and children, gathered in the area and started hurling stones at the carabinieri (non-commissioned Italian policemen) and local policemen who had come to disperse the crowd[160]. The ensuing confrontations claimed the lives of two carabinieri, Inspector Mario Salaconi and Luciano Fosci, together with a Somali police inspector, Auod Salem. One carabinieri officer, one NCO and eight Somali policemen were seriously injured. The demonstrators

158 TNA FO 1015/189 secret of June 1950 from British Consulate Mogadisho to FO.

159 ASCM, 'Brusasca', 46/263, letter from Fornari to Undersecretary of Foreign Affairs, Paolo Emilio Taviani , Agosto 12, 1952.

160 ASMAE, AP 1950-1957, Somalia, Busta 917, top secret report from Fornari to Taviani, Agosto 12, 1952.

suffered no casualties[161]. The killing of the two Italian soldiers raised a storm of indignation in the territory. Telegrams of condolence from De Gasperi and other Italian leaders were published daily in the local newspaper alongside articles and editorials condemning the murderers and exculpating all Somalis other than the Lega dei Giovani Somali. According to Lt. Colonel Alfredo Arnera, the incident was condemned by the Somali public opinion at large[162]. In fact there was massive popular condemnation of the incident by all Somali political parties and organizations, except for the Lega. Messages from tribal and religious leaders addressed to the Administration not only condemned the incident, but also advocated severe retribution against the perpetrators of the killing of the policemen in Kismayo.[163]

Commenting on the Kismayo incidents, British diplomats in Somalia reported that "There is a good deal of truth in the Administration's claim that Italian rule in Somalia is generous towards native interests in keeping with the spirit of the Trusteeship Agreement. Unfortunately, however, Signor Wagner has little sympathy with present policy and there is no doubt that his harsh administrative methods were directly responsible for the outbreak of violence."[164] The Provincial Commissario of Lower Juba appears to have had a history of harsh administrative methods, and his critics blamed him for the outbreak of violence. Serious disorders had taken place at Galkayo, where he was posted before being moved to Kismayo, and it was reported that the Lega was strongly opposed to his continuing in office[165]. Wagner, who had served as district commissar at Bulo Burti during the fascist period, became a liability and an embarrassment to the Administration. The prevailing opinion was that he had been very negligent in his handling of the incident, and that had he acted judiciously from the beginning the damage could have been averted. He was removed from his post as commissario for Lower Juba and repatriated on grounds of inefficiency and insubordination shortly before the start of the trial for the Kismayo incident.[166]

Convinced that the demonstrations in Kismayo had been organized by the Lega, the Administration concluded that the Central Committee of the party must be held responsible for the killing and must take the consequences. Accordingly,

161 Il Giornale d'Italia, Agosto 3, 1952; FO 371/96646, confidential report 4/15, from British Consulate Mogadiscio to Her Majesty's Principal Secretary for FO, August 12, 1952.

162 A. Arnera, op. cit., p. 38.

163 *Corriere della Somalia* , Agosto 12, 1952.

164 TNA FO 371/96646, confidential report, from British Consulate Mogadisho to FO, August 9, 1952.

165 Ibid.

166 ASCM, 33/17, letter from Martino to Brusasca, March 1, 1953, and Brusasca's reply, Aprile 17, 1953.

the Headquarters of the party in Mogadisho were seized and temporarily closed down. This measure was revoked after 5 days, but Lega sections in Kismayo, Afmedu, Margherita (Jamama) and Jilib, all in Lower Juba, remained closed for a longer period, from August to November. Margherita was reopened on 11 September, Jilib on 3 October, Kismayo and Afmedu on 11 November 1952[167]. It was reported that none of the UN Advisory Council members were present at Mogadisho at the time of the incident. The Administrator refused to see the party's leadership and went on "to snub the Lega for the rest of the year", comments a British source in Mogadisho[168]. For the British Consul General, "The Administration's refusal to talk with the President of the party and the moderate leaders was a mistake."[169]

By the middle of August Haji Mohamed, the leader of the party, left for Cairo "and with him went a good opportunity of influencing the moderate members of the party," as a British report states[170]. However, Italian authorities both in Rome and in the Trust Territory felt the need to handle the matter with moderation in order to avert further outbreaks of violence. In fact, the Undersecretary of the Italian Ministry of Foreign Affairs, Paolo E. Taviani, strongly recommended that the local authority act with moderation and avoid anything that might be seen as mass retaliation against the Lega dei Giovani Somali. "I urge you to prevent our reaction being described as precipitous and excessive" Taviani warned in a message to the Acting Administrator, Canino, in the absence of Fornari who was on holiday in Italy[171]. Prime Minister De Gasperi added his voice, urging the trusteeship authorities to treat the matter with firmness and justice but avoid generalized repression in their search for culprits[172]. De Gasperi was specific in pointing out that the notion of regarding the Lega as a 'subversive' organization was a mistake to be avoided; in his view, it was instead necessary to quickly associate with the most intelligent leaders in political life and administration, and wisely foresee which party would be at the core of the future self-government of Somalia. De Gasperi feared that the fight against the Lega could lead to the emergence of fanaticism and create situations similar to those existing in other

167 Enrico Martino, Due anni in Somalia, Mogadiscio 1955, p. 101.

168 TNA FO 371/2561, Annual report on the Trust Territory of Somalia under Italian Administration for 1952.

169 TNA FO 371/96646, confidential report from the British Consulate Mogadisho to FO, August 9, 1952.

170 Ibid.

171 ASMAE, AP, 1952, File 917, August 22, 1952.

172 Ibid.

Islamiccountries.[173]

Referring to mistakes made by some senior Italian officials in relation to the Kismayo incident, De Gasperi singled out AFIS Secretary General Canino and Aldo Wagner, Commissario of Upper Juba Province. "Unfortunately" he wrote" there are in Somalia officials with a colonial mentality like that Wagner of Kismayo who in the past has provoked violent reactions in other duty stations where he was posted. Had Canino not made a mistake by failing to receive the public, alleging as a justification that he was at Kismayo in a private capacity? A secretary general cannot strip himself of his tutorial authority in the presence of primitive people", De Gasperi concluded.[174]

Against this background, police started criminal investigations which ended with the arrest and conviction of 10 people charged with manslaughter and 38 more charged with resisting arrest. The Italian press reported the names of Sheikh Mussa and Ibrahim Abdi among those arrested in connection with the incident[175]. The Court of Assizes closed the hearing of the appeal filed by 55 of the people charged in relation to the Kismayo incident against the verdict of the Regional Court by confirming the ruling of the Regional Court of Kismayo, which had sentenced one person, Aden Artan Mussa, to 24 years in prison, and given terms of 16 years and 4 months each to 10 of the defendants (Mohamed Abdullahi Dirshe, Hussein Yahia Ali, Fatma Fahie Auod, Nour Mohamoud Issa, Kalif Ismail Auod, Mohamed Illaho Mohamed, Mohamed Hassam Mohamed, Aboukar Abdi Moumin, Abdi Mohamed Godir and Salah Yousuf Issa Liban) as well as prison terms ranging between 3 years and 6 months and 2 years and 4 months to 35 other defendants. Four of the defendants received hefty fines (Sh. So 500) in connection with their role in organizing the demonstration that led to the fatal incident[176]. It took 44 sessions, the hearing of 900 witnesses and 9 hours' deliberation for the court to deliver the final verdict.[177]

Echoes of fascist activities in Somalia

Much has been said and written about the number, background and political affiliations of senior Italian personnel serving AFIS. By the end of 1950, there

173 Remo Roncati, *Alcide De Gasperi: partecipare alla ricostruzione del mondo,* Rubattino, 2012, p. 184.

174 'Scritti e discorsi politici', ID., vol 4 cit. t. it. p. 2557, as reported in Roncati, op. cit., p. 185.

175 Il Quotidiano, Il Secolo d'Italia, Agosto 8, 1952.

176 *Corriere della Somalia*, Agosto 17, 1953; ASMAE, AFIS, box 4, File 16. Bollettino informazione, agosto 1953, p. 2.

177 ASMAE, AP, 1953, box 917. Notiziario settimanale n° 17853 dall' 11al 17 agosto 1953.

were 4,426 personnel in the civil administration, of which 760 were Italian nationals, 3,641, Somalis and 25 from different nationalities. Of the 760 Italian personnel, 380 had come from Italy between April and December 1950; 82 were kept in service in Somalia during the British occupation; and 370 were the so-called 'ex-BAS' who had served under the British Administration Service[178]. Some of these Italian personnel, including the administrator, were officials from the diplomatic service; others had come from the defunct Ministry of Italian Africa ('Ministero Africa Italiana'), while a third group was hired occasionally according to need. This combination of men of different political background and experience, constituted an element of friction and was often the main reason for discordant views among senior officials of the Administration, which also had to deal with the problems caused by the small but influential Italian community in Somalia. This community was mainly made up of individuals whose long connection with the territory dated back to the fascist period; most of them had difficulties in keeping pace with changed circumstances.

The Italian community in Somalia, at the start of the new administration, was divided according to political loyalty to Italian political parties. Italian political parties with branches in Mogadisho included, among others, the Christian Democrats (DC), the Socialists (PSI) and the Movimento Sociale Italiano (MSI), the latter being a party of fascist tendencies. Although the administrator had been the main source of information, Brusasca still sought an independent source of information in order to have a complete picture of the Trust Territory. To this end, he received regular reports from Giacomo Bona, a lawyer, and L. Massimini, a leading businessman based in Mogadisho, providing information on alleged fascist activities in Somalia. Giacomo Bona, who served at Mogadisho as secretary of the Christian Democratic Party branch in Somalia, wrote in one of his communications to Brusasca: "Owing to misunderstandings between the newcomers and the old guard, which soon developed into fierce argument, a clash became inevitable [...] this was not the only reason for the friction, but the different economic treatment between newcomers and 'residuals' from the outgoing administrations played a role in the confrontation."[179] Indeed, the salaries of Italian functionaries coming from Italy were three times higher than those of their Italian colleagues of the same grade hired locally in Somalia.[180]

178 Del Boca, op. cit., p. 223, note 8.
179 ASCM, 60/53, letter from Bona to the HQs of the Christian Democratic Party (DC), Rome, June 15, 1950.
180 Del Boca, op. cit., p. 227, note 26.

Bona, who was a good and reliable source of information for Brusasca, also stated that 'strange phenomena' occurred, consisting of "a recurrence of fascism, accentuated by the attitude of the new personnel who do not hesitate to level public criticism, which is typical of fascists, at the Administration; [...] complete lack of democratic spirit in the new personnel."[181]

As to the strength of the Fascist Party, Bona reported that the party counted 250 members and denounced what he saw as an 'increase in fascist publications' originating from Italy, via Asmara, containing literature hostile to the new Italian policy in Somalia. Bona did not limit his well-documented observations to simply denouncing fascist presence in Somalia, but also suggested drastic measures be taken to curb the activities of fascist elements in Somalia[182]. Bona's frequent reports and reflections on the fascist presence in Somalia are further confirmed by detailed police reports. One of these reports states: "The Movimento Sociale Italiano (MSI), a neo-fascist organization, is the most active political party in Somalia, the party which gives the clearest sign of its presence in Somalia [...] it is necessary to keep an eye on this movement and its adherents who spare no criticism to the Administration."[183]

That the spirit of fascism had not been completely exorcized from the Trust Territory is illustrated by the fact that a group of ex-fascists in Mogadisho, calling themselves 'Ex Reparti Coloniali', sent a telegram of congratulations to Gen. Graziani on his release.[184]

Luigi Massimini, another confidant of the undersecretary, was more specific in denouncing fascist activities in Somalia and the role of the police: "The police focus their attention exclusively on three categories of people: frightened group of communists, Italians considered as having collaborating with the British, and leading Lega members. All these activities are praiseworthy, but, in addition to controlling the British Consulate in Mogadisho and the residence of the Consul General as well as those of members of the Lega, it is also important to keep an eye on the growing fascist activities."[185]

Ambassador Fornari himself was too concerned with the negative attitude of

181 ASCM, 60/53, letter from Bona to the HQs of the Christian Democratic Party (DC, Rome, June 15, 1950.

182 ASMAE, AP 1953, Somalia box 2, File 4. Letter from Bona to Taviani, Aprile 4, 1953.

183 ASCM, 37/105, notes no. S. -345/7 R.P. from the Comando Gruppo Territoriale to Brusasca, June 11, 1951.

184 TNA FO 371/80887 file n. 9/8 of September 14, 1950 from British Consulate Mogadisho to FO, London.

185 ASCM, 48/284, letter from Massimini to Brusasca, October 7, 1950.

some members of the Italian community in Somalia, many of them farmers, *vis-à-vis* the progressive policy undertaken by the AFIS, particularly in relation to the participation of Somalis in the administration of the Trust Territory. The chief administrator felt hampered by the rivalry between the Italian Foreign Ministry and the Ministry of African Affairs. He considered that it was wrong for the Italian government to assign officials who had been part of the pre-war Italian administration in Somalia to posts within the Trusteeship. "Mostly their ideas of administration are out of date and not compatible with the idea of Trusteeship", he commented[186]. Fornari further vented his frustration in a letter to Brusasca on 16 February 1951, stating that "the Italian community in Somalia does not want to accept that they are no longer the boss."[187] However, Fornari watered down concerns about neo-fascist activities in Somalia[188]. Another senior AFIS official, Count Bacci di Capacci, is reported to have referred to some Italians in Somalia in unflattering terms. "They did not realize that the world had changed since 1939 and that Somalia was not now a colony and would not be treated as one."[189]

Italian Prime Minister Alcide De Gasperi, who was reading the repeated reports on fascist activities in Somalia, did not hide his conviction that fascism was operating in the Trust Territory. "I regret to agree with certain unfriendly media, but it is perfectly true that there are still many fascists and that, in certain private gatherings, even attended by Administration staff, the anthem Giovinezza is sung." (this was the anthem sung by the fascists during the 'march on Rome', which led to its being considered the official anthem of the fascist regime.) De Gasperi sent a strong warning to the administrator: "This is something of which the Governor has to be wary, as it may raise double concerns, among both the Somalis and the UN..[190]

The reaction of the Lega

In the eyes of the Lega, the new Italian Administration in Somalia was identical in structure to the old administration active during the fascist regime. With the exception of the chief administrator and few others, the bulk of the Italian administrators, especially the top ranking officials, were staff of the 'Ministero

186 TNA FO 371/80887, secret report from the Governor of Aden to the Secretary of State for the Colonies, June 3, 1950.

187 ASMAE, AFIS. Letter from Fornari to Brusasca, box 2, file 4, Febbraio 16, 1951.

188 ASMAE, AFIS. Letter n° prot. 1038/S from Fornari to Brusasca, box 2, file 15, Aprile 7, 1951.

189 TNA FO 371/80887, secret report no. 3, 1950, from the British Consulate to FO 7, June 21,1950.

190 'Scritti e discorsi politici', ID., vol. 4 cit. t. it. p. 2557, as reported in Roncati, op. cit., p. 185.

dell'Africa Italiana'.[191]

Among the senior AFIS officials sent to Somalia were: Benardelli, Gasbarri, Chapron, Copasso, Gonella, Ducati and Soleri, all of them ex personnel of the Ministry of Italian Africa. While lauding the administrator for his favourable attitude towards Somali aspirations, the president of the Lega complained that not all subordinate authorities were moved by the same spirit[192]. In a letter addressed to the administrator, the president of the Lega bemoaned the behaviour of certain AFIS officials in these terms: "Despite Your Excellency's efforts and good intentions, we are certain that your officials are of the old fascist system, whose character will not allow them to adapt to new conditions. Your task will not be made easy and you will never be able to know the real situation."[193]

In a petition addressed to the UN, the Lega requested the replacement of the officials who had served under the fascist regime with officials from the Foreign Ministry[194]. The Lega was disturbed by the number of ex-fascist administrators returning to Somalia and doubted 'the leopard's ability to change its spots'. The issue of Italian officials who had past links with the fascist regime was brought to the attention of the Italian government in Rome. The Italian weekly magazine Epoca, in its issue of March 28, 1954, published an extract of discussions held in Rome in 1954 between Aden Abdulla, then President of the Lega, and Prime Minister De Gasperi. The magazine reported that the Somali leader had made the following appeal to De Gasperi: "Your Excellency, if Italy really wants to show good faith towards the Somalis, call home those who are putting obstacles in the way of collaboration between us and the Administration, those who have baksheesh, paternalism and a kick in the pants as a system of government. The rest will go of its own accord."[195]

However, among Italian officials were some inspired with a progressive democratic spirit and alien to outmoded colonial methods. One of them, Luigi Gasbarri, has been blamed for his exceedingly liberal attitude towards the Lega dei Giovani Somali[196]. According to British reports, the Chief of Political and Security Affairs, Dr Benardelli, remained by far the most successful Italian official serving under the AFIS in Somalia. "Indeed the only man who maintained respect

191 ASCM, 'Brusasca', 81/ONU, Memorandum to the General Assembly of the United Nations from the Somali delegation, Lake Success, N.Y. October, 1950.

192 TNA FO 371/90328, secret report from the British Consulate in Mogadisho, to FO January 18, 1951.

193 TNA FO 371/80887, letter from the President of the Lega to the Administrator, July 25, 1950.

194 T/PET.11/40, May 3, 1951.

195 Epoca, Marzo 28, 1954.

196 TNA FO 371/96646 confidential report of August 27, 1952 from British Consulate Mogadisho to FO.

for the Administration in the eyes of the Somalis is Dr Benardelli, who managed to run the political side, as distinct from the economic and administrative sides, largely on his own with considerable success", comments a British secret document[197]. Benardelli is also remembered as an able and gallant leader of the Marehan irregulars between 1940 and 1941, with the rank of major in the Italian army, before surrendering in Jimma, Ethiopia, with General De Simon's forces. Known as 'Twinkle Toes' in British military circles because of his small size boots[198], Benardelli was a master of the Somali tongue and of the complex inter-relationships of Somali clans.

According to the jokes widely circulating in Mogadisho, the acronym for the Administration's name (AFIS), meant not 'Amministrazione Fiduciaria Italiana in Somalia' but Ancora Fascisti In Somalia (Again Fascists In Somalia) or Abbiamo Fregato gli Indigeni Somali (All Frigged for Indigenous Somalis). While the Lega maintained its strong opposition to the return to Somalia of former fascist personnel, the Conference party expressed their preference for some while objecting to the return of others.[199]

In his end of mission report, before leaving his post as Administrator of Somalia, Fornari reveals that "There were some who hoped to declare the Lega an illegal organization on the grounds that, by its hindering of the activities of the Italian Administration aimed at preparing this country for independence, it could be considered as a movement working against independence itself. The majority of Italians residing in Somalia are of this opinion. [...] The Lega is not a movement to suppress; the Administration's policy towards this party is driven by this vision, namely a policy of non-persecution but not of weakness or compliance; rather a policy channelled towards a major understanding of the moderate faction and the isolation of the extremists."[200]

A few months after Italy assumed administration of the country, Fornari sent to all commissari and residenti clear and firm directives on "absolute and loyal guarantee towards the local population under their jurisdictions without any discrimination based on politics or ethnicity, total respect of their personality

197 TNA FO 371/108095, confidential dispatch from British Consulate Mogadisho to FO, March 17, 1954.

198 W.E. Crosskill, *The Two Thousand Mile War*, Robert Hall, London, 1980, p. 59; PRO, 'FO' 1015/140, Somalia Political Intelligence Sitrep. no. 6, June 16, 1948.

199 ASCM, 34/65, undated letter to Brusasca, jointly signed by Islao Mahadalla, Mohamed Sheikh 'Edmondo' and Yassin Ali Sharmarke, without date, addressed to Brusasca.

200 Ascm, Gb b. 47 f. 273, rapport segreto n. 44337/1717 from Fornari to MAE, September 27, 1952.

and liberty, whose exercise constitutes a reason of pride for democratic States."[201] In a letter to Brusasca, the Administrator explained that "The Lega, on one hand, includes some core moderate leading elements who understand the meaning of collaboration; but, on the other, it also includes extremist elements, particularly in the periphery. For my part, I personally entertain the required contacts geared towards appeasement and collaboration. On the other hand, I have decided not to confuse goodwill with weakness and to adopt with the necessary firmness any measures required in order to determine and denounce those suspected of violating the law."[202]

AFIS faces financial constraint

Fornari's woes were not only problems of a political and security nature. In fact, little more than one year after taking up his position as chief administrator, he faced wider financial pressure. The Italian Ministry of Treasury had initially allocated 8 billion Lire to AFIS for the financial year 1951-52, but that amount had been drastically reduced to 6 billion as part of a policy to contain public expenditure[203]. With this decision taken in Rome, the chief administrator and his staff found that their efforts and original plan to better social conditions for the local population were being challenged, as they were left with hardly enough resources to cover administrative costs, let alone any manoeuvres to address development projects.

Fornari described as excessive and unacceptable this reduction amounting to a quarter of the initial budget allocation. He launched a blunt warning to Rome against this move, emphasizing that "with this budget, no improvement on the economic and social fields is possible."[204] For Fornari, a budget of only 6 billion Lira was hardly enough to cover administrative costs, excluding any possibility of promoting social and economic development of the country Italy was meant to help achieve economic and social progress under the Trusteeship Agreement. In a desperate message to Undersecretary Brusasca he wrote: "I would appreciate it if you could bring all this to the attention of President De Gasperi and Minister Sforza [...] I do not feel able to continue leading this Administration with 6 billion Lira, and it would be dishonest if I remained holding my present position

201 ASCM, 47/272, Circular no. 290/SP/S from Fornari to all Commissari and Residenti, July 15, 1950.

202 ASCM, 46/262, letter from Fornari to Brusasca, April 24, 1950.

203 ASCM, 37/106, meeting at MAI, March 13, 1950.

204 ASMAE, Afis, letter no. 1038 from Fornari to Brusasca, box 2, file 15, April 7, 1951.

after June 30" [205]. Reacting further to the budget reduction, Fornari wrote again to his friend Brusasca: "It is my firm decision to renounce my responsibility without the situation first being fixed as it would be impossible to run the Administration without the required financial resources."[206]

The shortage of money forced the Administration to introduce a gradual reduction of military expenditure by repatriating Italian military personnel from the 'Corpo di Sicurezza' and hastened the process of 'Somalizing' the administration by replacing expatriate civil service and police staff with native elements, a policy the Administration adopted to save money for social development. Despite public order problems still lingering, the first 1,870 unit of the 'Corpo di Sicurezza' were repatriated in October 1950, thus saving Lire 197,191,570 [207]. By July 1951, the 5,688 Italian troops that had initially landed in Somalia in March 1950 were reduced to 2,012 and further curtailed to 1,108 by the end of the year. By 1953, the number of expatriate troops was brought down to 692 elements, and this led to the organization of the first training academy for policemen. After this reduction in the number of troops, the 'Corpo di Sicurezza' became heavily Somalized, with 1,348 Somali against 692 Italians. The departing Italian personnel was being replaced by newly trained Somali police officers[208].

However, many expressed serious concern over the hurried process of troop reductions on grounds of potential deterioration of internal and external security in the Trust Territory.[209]

In spite of these drastic cuts in budget, Fornari was able to realize important social projects including building new schools and hospitals as well as renovating existing ones. The aeronautical school announced courses for wireless operators, wireless mechanics and meteorologists. An agricultural school (Collegio Agrario) was opened at El-Mugne, south of Merca, on November 16, 1952, starting with 25 students. In Mogadisho, a college for the children of Somali soldiers, known as 'Collegio Figli Militari' or 'Collegio Ferrara' was established. Other educational institutions built included a Commercial School, a School of Fishing and Marine Studies and a School of Islamic Studies, followed by a School for Health Inspectors.

Further reductions in AFIS expenditure, amounting to 300 million Lira, were

205 Ibid.
206 ASCM, 46/263, telegram no. 212117 from Fornari to Brusasca, May 15, 1951.
207 ASCM, 37/102, notes taken by Brusasca during the meeting at MAI, October 5, 1950.
208 A. Arnera, op. cit., pp. 36-37.
209 ASCM, 37/106, telegram no. 01921 from Gorini to MAI, October 16, 1950.

planned for the fiscal year 1952-53. But Enrico Martino, who replaced Fornari at the beginning of 1953, in a long telegram to the Foreign Ministry warned that such a reduction "will make it impossible to prepare the economic development plan expected to be submitted to the next session of the United Nations."[210] He concluded his telegram by emphasizing that "Any reduction affecting the current fiscal year as well as the coming years would trigger strong political and social backlash."[211]

Institution building

The immediate task of the Administering Authority, as stated in the Trusteeship Agreement, was "to foster the development of free political institutions and promote the development of the inhabitants of the territory towards independence; and to this end give the inhabitants of the territory a progressively increasing participation in the various organs of government."[212]

The foundation of the future State had to start not from the centre but from the periphery, in the outpost districts and regions. The first step towards local government was the establishment of 'Residence Councils' (Consigli di Residenza) in all the territory's twenty-seven districts, or 'residences', as they were then called (Circular no. 22809 of July 27, 1950).

Three categories of people were eligible to become Residence Council members: hereditary chiefs of tribes (Ugas, Wabar, Malaq, Islan, Iman, etc); those elected in customary tribal assemblies and recognized by public opinion as persons of particular culture and standing; and representatives of political parties. The composition of the Residence Councils was modified by the ordinance of October 20, 1951[213], which also made provision for increased representation of the branches of the political parties within the district. For the purpose of determining political representation in Residence Councils in 1951, only those branches existing and recognized by September 1, 1951 were taken into consideration. Recognition of a branch required presentation of a list of names of at least 200 members (Article 2 of Ordinance). A Residente's decision could be appealed by addressing the regional commissioner in the first

210 ASMAE, AP, 1953, telegram no. 2284 dated 5.3.1954, from Martino to Foreign Ministry, Rome, File 917.

211 Ibid.

212 Trusteeship Agreement, art. 3, par. 1.

213 Ordinanza n° 18 rep ottobre 20, 1951, 'Riforma dei Consigli di Residenza e del Consiglio Territoriale', Bollettino Ufficiale AFIS, suppl. n° 1 al n° 10, 25 ottobre 1951.

instance and the chief administrator in the second instance[214]. Representatives of the parties and notables were appointed for one-year terms by the chief administrator. Their functions were chiefly of a consulting nature on all matters of interest to the district, particularly regarding agriculture, animal husbandry, transhumance, public works, taxations and education.[215]

With little or no experience in the complexity of the matters they were expected to discuss and provide advice on, residence councillors had little influence, existing more than anything else as a sort of 'window dressing'. An additional function of the Residence Council was to select delegates for the regional assemblies, where regional representatives to the Territorial Council were designated[216]. The effectiveness of rural councils was undermined by the wanderings of the nomads on their search for watering holes and pastures, a circumstance that made stable political organization difficult to sustain. Consequently, the Administration's plan to use rural councils as bridges to development turned out to be unworkable, a situation that enabled AFIS-appointed commissars to become the focus of power and political action.

Towards the end of 1950, a second important step was taken with the establishment of the Territorial Council, popularly known as 'Consiglio Territoriale': in fieri, the future Somali Parliament[217]. The Council was a consulting body meant to assist the Administration in all public functions except foreign and defence affairs. However, advice from the Territorial Council was not binding except on questions relating to the acquisition by non-Somalis or organizations controlled by non-Somalis of right over land, other than concessions on lease, which the chief administrator decided according to the agreed opinion of a 2/3 majority of Council members.[218]

The first Territorial Council was composed of 35 members, of whom 28 were Somalis. Twenty-one seats were held by tribal representatives, seven by Somali political parties, four by the Italian community, two by the Arab community, and one jointly by the Indian and Pakistani communities. Of the seven councillors representing the political parties, four were nominated by the Conferenza Somala

214 Ibid. art. 2.

215 UN Doc.T/1033. United Nations Visiting Mission to Trust Territories in East Africa, 1951, Report on Somaliland under Italian Administration.

216 Ordinanza n° 18 rep 20 ottobre 1951, 'Riforma...', Bollettino Ufficiale AFIS, suppl. n° 1 al n° 10', art. 4, 25 ottobre 1951.

217 Ordinanza n° 144 rep dicembre 30, 1950, Bollettino Ufficiale Afis, Anno II, suppl. n° 1 al n° 1, Mogadiscio, Gennaio 2, 1951.

218 Declaration of Constitutional Principles attached to the Trusteeship Agreement, art. 14.

and three by the Lega dei Giovani Somali[219]. This step represented an expression, for the first time in Somalia, of direct involvement of the local population in the administration of their country.

Opening the first session of the Territorial Council on December 30, 1950, Fornari said: "In a few hours' time, the news of our meeting will cross over the frontier of the Territory to convey to all neighbouring and distant countries alike that Somalis of each group and party have started meeting together in an assembly, jointly with exponents of the minority community. This is still a small assembly, but you should bear in mind that all modern States derive their democratic origin from assemblies like yours."[220]

In 1951 a reform had been introduced in the democratic institutions created in the territory. The method of selecting regional representatives had been modified to give less emphasis to tribal representation. Each of the 'commissariati' was allotted one seat for every 70,000 inhabitants. A 'commissariato' composed of three districts was allotted a minimum of three seats, or small villages exceeding 30,000 people[221]. Membership of the Territorial Council was open to the following categories:

Regional representatives
Political representatives
Economic representatives
Education/culture representatives and
Representatives from small communities

Selection of tribal representatives was made through an established mechanism. Each residence council chose five of its members to represent the population in a regional assembly which met in each region. Each assembly submitted to the administrator a list of candidates consisting of twice as many names as the number of the seats to be filled, and from those lists the Administrator selected the required number of Council members. The six regions were assigned seats as follows: four to Benadir, two to Lower Webi Shabelle, two to Lower Juba, five to Upper Juba, five to Mudug including Hiran, and three to Majertenia[222]. The

219 Rapport du gouvernment italien à l'Assemblée Generale des Nations Unies sur l'administration de la Somalie placée sous la tutelle de l'Italie, avril 1950-decembre 1950, p. 41-42.

220 Del Boca, op. cit., p. 235.

221 Ordinanza n° 18 rep ottobre 20, 1951 'Riforma...', art. 3.

222 UN Doc. T/1033, par. 66.

formula appears as a compromise between the principle of assigning tribal seats by district and that of assigning seats on a territorial basis in proportion to the size of ethnic groups. Each legally recognized political party, having at least 5 regional branches in the interior of the territory, received one seat. Additional seats were allotted on the basis of one seat for over 25 branches.[223]

Under this new scheme, representation of political parties increased by four seats. The Conferenza, once an umbrella organization which had received four seats under the previous system, was no longer recognized as single entity, and seats were allocated to individual political parties formerly grouped under it. Hizbia Dighil Mirifle received 2 seats; Lega dei Giovani Somali 5; Lega Progressista Somala 1; Unione Africani Somalia 1, and Unione Nazionale Somala 1. Political party candidates were to be designated in lists presented to the administrator by the central committee of the respective party, with each list containing twice as many names as the number of seats allotted to the party concerned.

For 'minority communities', candidates were to be designated by their respective communities and through the commissariato of Benadir and Lower Juba provinces[224]. The Arab, Italian and Indo–Pakistani communities were allotted three seats each. Under the new ordinance, the number of seats allotted to political representatives should not, in any case, be less than half that allotted to regional representatives, and the number of non-Somali members should not, in any case, exceed $^{1}/_{6}$ of the full strength of the Council.[225]

The members of this advisory body were appointed annually by the administrator among the candidates designated by concerned parties. Persons designated to the Territorial Council were required to be able to read and write in Italian or Arabic. In 1951, of the 18 councillors representing the parties, twelve were members of the Conferenza and six belonged to the Lega dei Giovani Somali; two to economic categories; two to the Italian community; two to the Arab community and one to the Indo–Pakistani community. A restricted committee composed of 4 councillors from the Conferenza, 1 from the Lega, 3 from the clans, 1 Arab and 1 Italian was formed to function during the Territorial Council recess.

In 1952, the composition of the Council was increased from 35 to 44 members. The number of seats allocated to the political parties (Lega dei Giovani Somali, HDM, Unione Africana Somala, Lega Progressista Somala, Unione Nazionale

223 Ordinanza n° 18 rep ottobre 20, 1951 'Riforma...', art. 3.
224 Ibid. art. 4(e).
225 Ibid. art. 3.

Somala, Lega Nazionale Somala, Bimal, Beneficenza and Lega Democratica Somala) went up to 18 due to the number of new branches opened, while the economic category went up to 8 and the number of seats allotted to traditional representatives remained unchanged[226]. In 1953 the number of Council members was further increased from 44 to 53. In compliance with the administration policy designed to introduce reforms in the election of its members, the tenure of the Territorial Council for the year 1953 was extended until the planned general elections which were held in 1956 [227]. Similar steps were taken with respect to the 'ConsigliodiResidenza'.[228]

Criticism was raised about the way council seats were distributed among eligible categories and organizations. In a petition addressed to the administrator, the Lega vigorously protested against the criteria adopted for the allotment of seats and the selection of territorial councillors.

The Lega lamented, in particular, that due consideration had not been given to its size and importance as a party, while members of the Conferenza parties were allotted seats both as tribe representatives and, at the same time, as representatives of political parties. As proof of this the Lega referred to the case of Islao Mahadalla, President of the Conferenza, who had been appointed representative of the Hawiye tribe on the Territorial Council; Salah Omar, President of the Unione Nazionale Somala, one of the Conferenza components, appointed representative of the Rer Hamar tribe; Sheikh Abdullahi Mohamed, President of the Hizbia Dighil Mirifle, appointed on the Territorial Council as representative of the Hizbia and Dighil tribes of Mogadisho[229]. The Lega also raised objections to the fact that six members of the Territorial Council for Majertenia Province were affiliated to the Lega Progressista Migiurtina Party, coming under the Conferenza umbrella, and that five of them belonged to the same tribe as Osman Mohamoud. The six councillors were: Bogor Mussa Yousuf Bogor, Khalid Yousuf Bogor, Abdi Haji Yousuf, Mohamed Mussa, Arsce Aw Mussa and Ismail Haji Yousuf.

The Lega petition concluded: "A further factor, which is in our opinion very troubling, is that many of the persons indicated as future councillors are illiterate, and therefore unfit for the task they will have to discharge. Undoubtedly, this is a

226 Rapport du gouvernment italien à l'Assemblée Generale des Nations Unies sur l'administration de la Somalie placée sous la tutelle de l'Italie, 1954, p. 31.

227 'Ordinanza n° 22 rep. 21 dicembre 1953 Mogadiscio, Bollettino Ufficiale, Gennaio 2, 1954.

228 Ibid.

229 T/PET.11/40 Annex 4, December 12, 1950.

fact that will help neither the Administration's task nor the evolution of the Somali people."[230] Reference was made, in particular, to the exclusion from the Council of paramount chiefs, such as the Iman of the Omar Mohamoud[231]. Complaints over the way seats had been allocated also came from the Indian community, who felt unhappy that a Council member representing the Indian and Pakistani communities was a Pakistani national. Territorial Council members were unpaid; an allowance of Sh.So 15 a day for each session was paid to councillors present. Those living outside Mogadisho had their travel expenses reimbursed.[232]

230 Ibid.

231 TNA FO 371/90328, report from the British Consulate to FO, February 1, 1951.

232 'Ordinanza n° 3 rep, 6 febbraio 1951, Bollettino Ufficiale AFIS n° 3, art. 1, March, 1, 1951.

Chapter V

MARTINO REPLACES FORNARI
Steps towards appeasement

Fornari was promoted and appointed Ambassador to Egypt at the beginning of 1953; he was replaced by another career diplomat, Enrico Martino, who arrived on February 14, 1953 to take his position as administrator[1]. Before his appointment as chief administrator of the Trust Territory of Somalia, Martino was ambassador in Belgrade, in what was then Yugoslavia. With Martino's term of office, the Trusteeship ushered in a somewhat troubled era, characterized on one side by divisions within the Lega leadership, split between collaborationists and 'radicals', and on the other by uneasy relations between the Administration and the Lega.

Of the four administrators who ruled the territory, Martino was the one who spent most material time there. Mindful of the volatile political situation prevailing in the Trust Territory, and capitalizing on the groundwork laid by his predecessor, Martino made all efforts designed to ameliorate relations between AFIS and the major political party in the territory. At the time of his arrival in Somalia, the Administration was convinced that the Lega was a force to reckon with, a force which could not and should not be suppressed. Martino's first priority, therefore, was to lay down the basis for a new relationship with the major political party

1 Rapport du gouvernment italien à l'Assemblée Generale des Nations Unies sur l'administration de la Somalie placée sous la tutelle de l'Italie, 1953, p. 17.

in the territory, directing his attention to its moderate wing, represented by the widely respected and far-sighted vice-president of the Territorial Council, Aden Abdulla. A shrewd politician, Abdulla was convinced from the beginning that the Lega had nothing to lose if it co-operated with the Administering Power. Pier Paolo Spinelli and Luigi Gasbarri, two top AFIS functionaries, were instrumental in engaging Lega members who were considered mature and open-minded in constructive dialogue. Gradually, the Lega came to realize the advantages of moderation and constructive dialogue with the Administering Authority, and started opening out from its initially rigid positions.

Before engaging in any dialogue with the Administration, the party posed a string of conditions. These included requesting AFIS to distance itself from the previous colonial government and its programme, take concrete measures to abolish tribalism and collective punishment and conduct a population census ahead of future political elections[2]. It is significant to note that asking the Administration to abolish centuries-long institutions such as tribalism and collective punishment was tantamount to asking for the moon: tribalism and the practice of collective punishment survived even after independence, and a population census was never seriously considered by post- independence Somali governments.

The first signs of improved relations emerged in May 1953 during the anniversary celebrations marking the 10th anniversary of the foundation of the party on May 15, 1943. On that occasion, Vice President Sheikh Mohamed Sheikh Osman made a long speech, very moderate in tone, recognizing the existence and the need "to complete the process of appeasement between the Administration and the Lega."[3] The Administration, represented at the ceremony by Dr Benardelli, Director of the Political Office, gave a forthright reminder of the immensity of the task confronting the Somalis, and went on to sum up its own achievements in the last three years and some of its immediate plans. Benardelli spoke about the progress achieved in agriculture, the pastoral field and fishing, as well as the process of Somalization of the public service[4]. Further signs of improved relations had also been noticeable in the government newspaper, which gave considerable coverage to the Lega's celebrations in the provinces

2 ASMAE, DGAFIS box 9, file 2, Memorandum of the Lega, Aprile 1950, as reported in Morone, L'ultima colonia: come l'Italia è tornata in Africa, 1950-1960, Laterza & Figli 2011, p. 71.

3 TNA FO 371/102566, Vice-president's speech, May 15, 1953.

4 Ibid., restricted report from British Consulate, Mogadisho, to FO, May 17, 1953.

after a policy of complete boycott.[5]

But all was not as it appeared on the surface. While efforts to create entente between the party and the Administration were gaining momentum in the territory, at the United Nations the Lega envoy continued to attack the Administration's policy as though unconcerned with or unaware of the improved relationship between his party's and the Administration itself, taking issue against the latter for using in Somalia past Italian legislation dating back to the fascist period as well as numerous proclamations made by the war-time British Military Administration. The envoy also blamed the present Administration for not doing enough for the economic development of the territory and for recruiting Italian nationals in lieu of native Somalis in the public service, and urged the General Assembly's solemn decision of November 21, 1949 be reaffirmed during the current session.[6]

However, several other Somali political organizations (Unione Africani Somalia, Lega Progressista Somala, Hizbia Dighil and Mirifle, Unione Nazionale Somala, Lega dei Giovani Benadir, Giovani Abgal and Hidayat-El-Islam, Scidle and Mobilen Youth League), in a memorandum of December 1, 1953 addressed to the Fourth Committee of the General Assembly, spoke positively about the achievements realized by the Administration in the three years since its inception. The memorandum reads: "Fortunately, the country is moving ahead; situations are evolving and initiatives which before were only simple aspirations have today become, or are on the point of becoming reality." The memorandum was signed by Mohamed Sheikh Osman (Segretario Generale Unione Africani Somalia), Aden Shire (President, Lega Progressista Somala), Haji Salah Omar (President, Unione Nazionale Somala), Abdi Nour Mohamed (President, Hizbia Dighil e Mirifle), Sherif Mohamed Hussein (President, Unione Giovani Benadir) and Haji Ahmed Farrei, and identified a number of achievements, including the favourable climate of security prevailing in the territory, the municipal elections scheduled for March 1954, the empowerment of the Territorial Council to discuss the national budget and the appointment of Somali Vice-residents and police officers in many districts.[7]

The Italian representative at the United Nations, Ambassador Guidotti, surprised by the continued hostile attitude of the Lega envoy towards the work of AFIS in Somalia, wrote: "Abdullahi Issa took almost no account of his party's changes of policy and the instructions he might have received [...] his attitude in

5 Ibid., May 23, 1953.
6 UN Doc. A/C.4/253, November 23, p. 3.
7 UN Doc. A/C.4/256, December 1, 1953.

the present session of the IV Commission marked a regress with regard to what Mr. Issa himself held at the Trusteeship Council."[8]

For Ambassador Guidotti, the only way to silence the Lega envoy was to remove him from the United States. "The best way would be to send him to his country. I think it will not be difficult to obtain from the Americans to send him back soon; and later on, if he did return to Canada, thought should be given to how to chase him from there too."[9]

To give the appeasement process a chance to succeed, the party instructed its envoy to the United Nations to drop his anti-Italian rhetoric at the Trusteeship Council and not to press complaints submitted in petitions regarding the suppression of political parties and the use of force by the Administration "since the arrival of a new Administrator, Martino, has led to a much more satisfactory relationship between the Lega and the Administration."[10] The Administration also received a boost from the Territorial Council when this advisory body decided to send its two Somali vice-presidents to New York to express support for the economic initiatives taken by the Administration in favour of Somalia.[11]

According to Italian diplomatic sources, US authorities invited the Lega envoy to leave American soil on grounds of suspicions against him[12]. It is not clear, however, what the specific nature of the reported suspicion might have been. Most probably, the Lega envoy was not kicked out from the US, but he was quietly recalled by his party when it became clear that his continued presence at Lake Success would not help the normalization of relations between the Administering Authority and the most popular political party in the territory. He was replaced by Abdirazak Haji, a rising star destined to become party leader in 1956 and Head of Government in 1964.

To frustrate any attempt by Mr. Issa to undermine AFIS's agenda, the Administration drew up a plan designed to entice him to remain in Italy before his return to Somalia. On his way back from New York, the Lega leader made a stop-over in Rome. Enrico Martino, seizing this opportunity, made a number of suggestions to his government, all designed to delay Issa's return to Mogadisho until after March 28, 1954, the date set for the first municipal elections in the territory. The plan was to make arrangements for Abdullahi Issa to meet top

8 ASMAE, AP 1953, Somalia, File 917. Telespresso from Guidotti to FO Rome, p. 1, December 10, 1953.

9 Ibid.

10 UN Doc.A/C.4/254 of November 24, 1953; FO 371/102566, telegram no. 125 from the UKDEL, N.Y. to FO, London, June 24, 1953.

11 *Corriere della Somalia*, April 14, 1954.

12 ASMAE, AFIS, box 4, file 16. Bollettino informazione, October 1953.

level Italian officials, as well as organizing private visits to tourist attraction sites in Italy where his ego could be sufficiently massaged. In the event that this plan might not work, Martino suggested that alternatively a story should be concocted about the 'unavailability' of seats on Alitalia flights in order to delay Issa's arrival in Mogadisho.[13]

In Rome, however, the Lega leader kept a low profile and did not report to the Foreign Ministry; moreover his travel plan could not be changed simply because "he was flying on a British Airline ticket."[14]

The assassination of Councillor Ustad Osman Hussein

The highest-profile politically motivated physical attack was the attempted murder of Mohamed Sheikh Osman 'Edmondo', leading light of the Conferenza and member of the Territorial Council. Mohamed Sheikh Osman 'Edmondo' (not 'Il mundo' or 'El Mondo' as he is sometimes erroneously called), was born in a village on the outskirts of Mogadisho in 1913. At the age of 5 he was left in an orphanage and was adopted by an Italian officer who sent him to Italy where he attended school for four years. From 1931 to 1935 he was a clerk at Mustahil, and later at Brava and Merca. In 1937 he was employed by the Italian Consulate in Calcutta (India). Early in 1939 he was transferred to the Italian Consulate at Aden where he stayed until 1940 before returning to the Secretariat at Mogadisho. When the British forces entered Mogadisho, he moved to Mustahil. In 1943 he became a district clerk at Gabridarre (Ogadenia) and later in Warder, Ogaden, where he was dismissed. After dismissal he made his home in Beledweyne until 1946 when he moved to El-Bur.[15]

On the night of 6 March 1952, the territorial councillor was accosted on his way home by four men. While one was talking to him another shot at him with a pistol and hit him in the leg and the head. Luckily, he escaped without serious injuries. According to British sources in Mogadisho, some 700 persons were rounded up by the police in connection with the aborted assassination attempt[16]. While the figure reflected in the Consulate's report sounds grossly exaggerated[17],

13 ASMAE, AFIS, 1953, file 917. Secret telegram dated 10.3.1954, from Martino to the Foreign Ministry, Rome.

14 Ibid., secret telegram of 13.3.1954, from Franca to Martino.

15 TNA FO 1015/189, Monthly Political Intelligence Report from British Military Administration for September 1949.

16 TNA FO 371/96646, dispatch of 27th March, 1952, from British consulate , Mogadisho;.

17 The British Consulate depended heavily on Somali informants, many of them ex British servicemen in the Consulate's service..

it is nevertheless believed that scores of people were rounded up by the police in connection with the incident. Many were arrested for questioning and released next day, while others, especially those with no fixed abode, were deported from Mogadisho. The councillor had no doubt that his assailants were a gang of ruffians linked to the Lega and wearing the party's badge. The Lega distanced itself from the crime, which their leadership deplored, though it was widely believed that the attempted murder was their work. The attack on Mohamed Sheikh 'Edmondo' followed an incident on the previous day in which Sheikh Noor Hussein, the Eritrean representative of culture on the Territorial Council, was beaten up with a stick by an elderly supporter of the Lega in a public place.[18]

One year later, and precisely on May 26, 1953, Ustad Osman Mohamed Hussein, exponent of the HDM party and member of the Territorial Council, was gunned down. For a long time the Hizbia had warmly supported the constitution of a federal system for Somalia consisting of three autonomous provinces and largely corresponding to the main three Somali races: Darod, Dighil Mirifle and Hawiye. The Hizbia arranged to send a 30-year old, named 'Ustad' Osman Mohamed Hussein, to Lake Success to point out to the UN a solution in that sense for the future Somali state. He was a territorial councillor and spoke Arabic, English and French[19]. In addition, rumours that were never confirmed suggested that the main purpose of the Hizbia envoy's mission was to formulate a request to the UN designed to prolong the trusteeship mandate on Somalia by an additional 20 years, seen as necessary to make the territory self-sufficient and genuinely independent.[20]

Ustad Osman Hussein was murdered outside his home in the Hamar Weyn district of Mogadisho one day ahead of his planned departure for Lake Success. His body bore twenty-three knife wounds[21]. The Central Committee of the Lega issued a strong statement utterly condemning the brutal crime. Nevertheless, many dismissed this statement. The police made three arrests in connection with the murder, two of them members of the hit squad known as 'Horseed'. Hussein's assailants, all hailing from the nomadic tribes of the northern part of the territory, were 24-year old Mohamed Ali Haji Abdurahman, Qabila Lelkasse, a laundryman, 30 year-old Aden Abdurahman Farah 'Gurei', Qabila Omar Mohamoud, employee of the 'Farmacia Imperiale', 29-year old Mohamoud

18 TNA FO, 371/96646, dispatch no. 15 of 11th April 1952, from British Consulate, Mogadisho.

19 ASMAE, AFIS, box 4, file 16. Bollettino informazione del mese di maggio 1953, p. 1.

20 Ibid.

21 TNA FO 371/102566, restricted report from British Consulate Mogadisho to FO, May 28, 1953.

Mohamed Gouled 'Gagale', and Qabila Marehan, employee of the AFIS print works known as 'Stamperia AFIS'[22]. Feelings ran very high in Mogadisho and other parts of the territory. In Baidoa, the Hizbia stronghold, the local members of the party were prepared to take mass revenge on the local Lega branch, but Dr Benardelli, the Director of Internal Affairs, issued firm instructions for the maintenance of order[23]. Unlike the incident in which Mohamed Sheikh Osman 'Edmondo' was involved in 1952, this time the Administration exercised restraint, and did not carry out any mass arrests or enforce any deportation orders. The Hizbia dispatched their president, Abdinour Mohamed Hussein, to New York in place of the murdered councillor, amid rumors that he would ask for an extension of the trusteeship period for a further ten years. (I could not find any evidence of initiatives taken by the HDM at the United Nations to prolong the trusteeship mandate.)

The murder of Ustad Osman Hussein Mohamed entered into history as the first politically motivated assassination ever committed in Somalia, as opposed to the many other cases of killings occasioned by tribal feuds. The killing caused great consternation in the Hizbia camp, which issued the following communiqué: "The party and committee members of the Hizbia Dighil Mirifle are firmly convinced that Ustad Osman Hussein fell victim of a vile, premeditated and intentional political plot. The Executive Committee of the HDM acquiesced in the collaboration of all citizens for the tracking down of the perpetrators and exhorted all party members, wherever they may be, to exercise restraint and remain calm, placing their faith in the work of the Police and the Justice system." The communiqué was signed by the President of HDM, Abdinour Mohamed Hussein, Vice-president of the Territorial Council. A reward of Somali Shilling 5,000 was offered by the HDM for information leading to the capture of the murderers of Ustad Osman[24]. The crime became something of a *cause célèbre* and further strained the relations between the Lega and the Administration. The seat vacated by Ustad Osman as territorial councillor was taken up by Sheikh Abdullahi Sheikh Mohamed Osman.[25]

On June 27 1953, the Administrator paid an emotional tribute to the slain councillor on opening the second session of the Territorial Council, using the occasion to remember the rare qualities of Councillor Osman Hussein. In this

22 ASMAE, AFIS, box 4, file 16. Bollettino informazione del mese di maggio 1953.
23 TNA FO 371/102566, restricted report from British Consulate Mogadisho to FO, May 28, 1953.
24 Somalia Nuova, May 31, 1953.
25 'Decreto n° 99 del 20 giugno 1953'. Bollettino Ufficiale AFIS n° 7, Mogadiscio, July 1, 1953.

inaugural speech, the Administrator told his audience that he was "certain that every one of you, at this moment, has remembered the capacity and talents of Osman Mohamed, but above all, his quality in the educational and spiritual fields for which he was known in Somalia as 'Ustad', – that is 'Professor'. The greatness of his personality puts in full relief the shameful crime of his murderers who waited for him, at night, on a street corner, while he was absorbed in his work and in the future of his beloved Somalia, returning to his home, where his wife and beloved sons awaited him. But, whatever his assassins' intention might have been, they were deceiving themselves if they thought that by killing one man they could kill an idea. I hope I am interpreting your wishes when I say that an everlasting marker should be erected at the place where Osman Mohamed was murdered. The place which today holds memories of blood and shadow will thus become a beacon of light and life. If a project of this kind is decided upon, the Administration will facilitate its realization."[26]

To commemorate the Councillor's memory, a street in the capital, formerly known as Via Vincenzo Gioberti and located near his house in the Hamar Weyn district, was named after him, becoming Via Ustad Osman[27]. In paying tribute to Ustad Osman before the Territorial Council, Martino did not ascribe the crime to the Lega but to what he called "extremist elements linked to that party whose acts have not been disowned."[28]

Perhaps few people know that Ustad Osman was in the past politically associated with, and a member of, the Lega party. He was recruited as an Arabic teacher for the Lega's privately-run schools in Galkayo. Italian intelligence reports suggest that, in view of his political maturity, ability and good linguistic skills, a requirement hardly possessed at the time by any other Lega member, he was seen as the best candidate to represent the Lega at Lake Success during the debate on the future of former Italian colonies. He was fluent in Arabic, English and French, and spoke a decent Italian. However, despite his cultural advantage over his fellow party members, he had been side-lined and "a different envoy was sent in his place on purely tribal considerations."[29] A politician with an extremely sharp mind, he switched sides, joining the Hizbia Dighil Mirifle, thus making enemies and risking his own security.

26 TNA FO 371/102567, Enrico Martino's speech made at the opening of the second session of the Territorial Council on June 27, 1953.

27 *Corriere della Somalia*, July 30, 1953.

28 E. Martino, op. cit., p. 36.

29 ASMAE, AFIS, box 4, file 16. Bollettino informazione del mese di maggio 1953.

The 1954 municipal elections. Census of urban population

The first municipal administration, known as 'Organizzazione dell'Amministrazione di Mogadisho', was established in Mogadisho in 1951 under the responsibility of a 'commissario' appointed by the Administrator and assisted by a 'consulta' made up of six Somalis, three Italians, one Arab and one representative of the Indo-Pakistani community, all appointed by the Administrator on the basis of proposals made by the Residence Council for a duration of one year[30]. This was followed in 1951 by the institution of municipal services, known as 'Amministrazione dei Servizi Municipali', in all districts and sub-districts of the Trust Territory under the direction of a Head of Districts and Sub-districts selected by the traditional chiefs, minority communities and economic and professional categories, appointed by the Regional Commissioner and assisted by a 'consulta' made up of a number of members ranging between a minimum of 6 and a maximum of 12 according to the size of the population.[31]

The first regular municipal election law was enacted in 1953[32]. Prior to the date of the elections, the Administration conducted a census of the urban population of the Trust Territory and their economic activities. The survey started in 1952 and was meant to collect data on several aspects of the life of the urban population such as number of families, number of ethnic groups, gender, date and place of birth, place of residence, main and secondary occupation, etc. The municipal elections of 1954 represented the first step in the difficult democratization process and the first opportunity to test the degree of maturity achieved by the local population less than 4 years from the establishment of the trusteeship regime.

The elections held on March 28, 1954 were based on universal male suffrage: voting right was not extended to women. Voting was on the basis of electoral certificates distributed by municipal officials to persons registered on general lists of voters which were compiled on the basis of the population register[33]. Persons of 21 years of age having resided in the municipality for at least one year prior to the date of the election and with no criminal record for crimes carrying more

30 'Ordinanza n° 9 rep. giugno 6, 1951. Bollettino Ufficiale AFIS, suppl. n° 1 al n° 6 , June 1951.

31 Ibid.

32 'Ordinanza n° 18 dicembre 20, 1953, "Elezioni delle Consulte Municipali"'. Bollettino Ufficiale AFIS, suppl. n° 1 al n° 12, Dicembre 24, 1953.

33 Gilbert Ware, *'Somalia from Trust Territory to Nation, 1950-1960'*, Phylon (1960-), vol. 26, no. 2 (2nd qtr. 1965), p. 178.

than 3 years of imprisonment were eligible to vote. Candidates were required to be 25 years old and literate in Italian or Arabic. Individuals condemned for a crime that local tradition regarded as serious, and those serving in the military or paramilitary bodies, were not eligible to be elected as councillors[34]. No election took place in certain municipalities where only one list was presented; in such instances, the candidates won by proclamation and the rural population was not called to take part in the municipal elections. Actual elections took place only in twenty-seven municipalities. The reader may be interested to learn that in Mogadisho, the capital, out of 12,081 registered voters, only 8,819 cast their vote.[35]

Fifteen political parties took part in the electoral contest. The results gave the Lega a comfortable majority of 141 out of 281 councillors. "Save the HDM, most of the other Conferenza parties, at the first test, have shown their inconsistencies, disproving the Conferenza's "claim, harboured for long years, to represent the majority of the population", as Morone comments[36]. The main opposition party, the (HDM), gained 57 councillors. The third party, representing a substantial part of the urban electorate, was the newly-established Partito Democratico Somalo, formed by a merger with the Lega Progressista Somala. The PDS gained 22 municipal council seats, the Unione Africani Somalia 28, the Unione Nazionale Somala 9, the Unione Patriottica Somala 4; the Associazione Gioventù Abgal, Scidle (Shidle) and Mobilen and a number of minor parties, all together, gained 69 municipal council seats.[37]

The Administrator contested the notion that the Lega had made significant gains in the election, highlighting areas where it had fared badly and exalting, instead, the election results obtained by the opposition parties. "Although the Lega won 141 out of the 281 elective seats, it cannot claim to have supremacy in all the municipalities. In fact, on the basis of the election results, in 16 municipalities, among them Merca, the other parties have obtained the majority, while in three municipalities, including Mogadisho, these parties have obtained 50% of the seats", the Administrator commented[38]. The elections were conducted amid a passionate campaign run by AFIS and the Somali political movements in the

34 Rapport du gouvernment italien à l'Assemblée Generale des Nations Unies sur l'administration de la Somalie placée sous la tutelle de l'Italie, 1954, p. 34.

35 *Corriere della Somalia*, Marzo 29, 1954.

36 Morone, op. cit., p. 89.

37 UN Doc T/1143 and Corr.1 par. 29, p. 4.

38 ASMAE, AFIS, 1953, file 917. Telespresso no. 557923/421 from Martino to the Foreign Ministry, Rome, March 30, 1954,.

main urban areas: out of the estimated population of 237,632, the number of registered voters was 50,740; those who actually cast their votes on election day numbered 38,119.[39]

Following the municipal elections of 1954, AFIS took further steps designed to accelerate the process of building a structure for the future State. Among these measures, two initiatives worth mentioning are: granting municipal councils deliberative powers over vast activities within the administrative services, and removing competence for municipal affairs from district commissioners to assign it to one commissario, appointed by the Administrator as head of the municipal administrations. This paved the way for capable Somalis to become heads of local administrations.[40]

Extension of the trusteeship: an empty claim

During the first three years of AFIS Administration, the Lega, or more precisely a fraction of it, hardly hid its fear that the Trusteeship Agreement adopted by the General Assembly might not be successfully implemented and that Italy might seek an extension of the period so as to retain her hold on the territory for longer than envisaged. Whether an extension of the trusteeship period was possible or not, or whether Italy had ever seriously considered such an option, and what interest might be behind it is hard to say[41]. The desirability of this plan was ruled out in the early days of the trusteeship regime. In a long report to Rome at the end of his tenure as Administrator, Giovanni Fornari made this comment on the issue: "It does not seem that we have any particular interest in the extension of our mandate, there being no economic benefit except for a political benefit deriving from our presence in Africa and, in the future, for having helped a country to attain independence."[42] Ambassador Martino, who succeeded Fornari, was even more categorical in playing down this option. Speaking at the Italian–African meeting organized in Milan on April 26, 1954 by the 'Gruppo Bottego', he reminded his audience of "the necessity to dispel the notion that Italy is not intentioned to grant independence to Somalis in 1960."[43] The notion of an extension of the mandate was further discredited by British sources in

39 Rapport du gouvernment italien à l'Assemblée Generale des Nations Unies sur l'administration de la Somalie placée sous la tutelle de l'Italie, 1954, p. 38.

40 Del Boca, op. cit., p. 244.

41 Any alteration to the Trusteeship Agreement, under article 21, requires the support of the administering authority and of a 2/3 majority of the General Assembly of the United Nations.

42 ASCM, 47, 273, report n. 44337/1717, December 23, 1952.

43 Martino, op. cit., p. 37.

Rome, which revealed that Italy regarded it as "an expensive, unprofitable, and potentially embarrassing responsibility."[44] "If Italy wishes to retain her hold on the territory, she will use other methods with less risk of failure,"[45] comments the same British source.

Fears stemmed mainly from the reports submitted to the United Nations in which the territory was routinely described as an extremely poor country requiring immense foreign investment and aid to be economically viable. This kind of reports and statements, though reflecting the reality on the ground, had been transmitted back by Abdullahi Issa as "a plot by the colonial powers to extend the trusteeship period."[46] The Lega representative in New York, in his statement before the Trusteeship Council's 577th meeting on November 23, 1953, made the following remarks: "Economic and social conditions of the Territory and its inhabitants are frequently raised to justify the move aimed at extending the rule of Italy over Somalia."[47] He was referring to statements made by the representatives of France, Belgium and Great Britain in the Trusteeship Council about economic development and the size of the efforts required in this respect. He referred, in particular, to similar observations made earlier by the representative of Colombia, a member of the United Nations Advisory Council on Somalia, describing the economy of the territory in the following terms: "If in addition to the grinding poverty of the Territory, we add the fact that nine-tenth of its inhabitants live under a tribal system dating back from biblical times and that, owing to the standard of education, there is not a single University graduate in the whole Territory, the Council will at least understand our doubts. We think that everybody is sharing these doubts in silence."[48] The Lega saw things differently, and its representative at the United Nations made a statement containing the following remarks: "From these observations, we can clearly see the thinly veiled attempt to secure extension of the Trusteeship period."[49]

In 1953 the international press was virtually silent about Somalia and its future. However, towards the end of 1957, some foreign media suddenly started expressing doubts that Somalia could be qualified for independence within the

44 TNA FO 371/131463, confidential telegram from British Embassy Rome to FO, April 19, 1958.

45 TNA FO 371/108101, confidential report from the British Consulate Mogadisho to R.G.I. Elliott, Esq., S.L.D. Aden, June 16, 1954.

46 Ibid.

47 UN Doc. A/C.4/253, November 23, 1953.

48 UN Doc. T/PV, 463, par. 65: Statement made before the Trusteeship Council by Mr. De Holte Castello, the Colombian Delegate of the UN Advisory Council for Somalia, June 18, 1953.

49 UN Doc. A/C.4/253 of November 23, 1953.

time limit set for by the UN. In fact, the British press had devoted a number of articles on the future of the territory, some of them bearing the signature of leading authorities in the field of colonial studies, like Margery Perham, writer and lecturer on African Affairs, and Sir Gerald Reece, former Governor of Somaliland[50]. In a leading article on Somali affairs published in *The Times* on December 23, 1957, Margery Perham and Sir Gerald Reece agreed that "the United Nations' decision to grant independence to Somalia, within 1960, was premature and irresponsible."[51]

The *East Africa and Rhodesia* newspaper went further, calling the United Nations' decision an 'act of folly'[52]. The articles deeply displeased the Prime Minister of Somalia and led him to have two leading articles published under his name in the official Italian-language daily *Corriere della Somalia* on 18 and 20 January 1958 respectively.

The leading article depicted Perham as "wrapped up in her colonial studies that in the long run produce a certain mentality" and Sir Reece as "obviously moved to nostalgia by thoughts of the times when he could order Somalis about as he liked." As for *East Africa and Rhodesia*, the article dismissed it as a publication for 'old fogey' reactionaries[53]. The Somali Minister of Economy, Haji Farah Ali, who was in London at the time, made representations to the British government about these press reports and was told that the views expressed by the writers did not represent those of Her Majesty's Government.

Then it was the turn of the *East African Standard*, a leading Nairobi daily newspaper which in an unprecedented criticism described the Somali government as 'fascist' and the Somali people as an 'immature race'[54]. Another foreign newspaper which focused its attention on Somalia was the authoritative French daily *Le Monde*, which, after expressing doubts on whether Somalia was a politically and economically viable country, suggested that, rather than an extension of the Italian mandate, the best solution would be "to accord Somalia full independence with regard only to internal affairs, but to assign to the government in Mogadisho a United Nations Trusteeship Council which will assist it, for ten years, on foreign and financial matters, and to contribute in its economic reforms up to the time when the new State will become viable." *Le*

50 Governor of the British Protectorate of Somaliland between November 1948 and February 1954.
51 *Corriere della Somalia*, Gennaio 18, 1958.
52 TNA FO 371/131460, Confidential report from British Consulate Mogadisho to FO January 22, 1958.
53 Ibid.
54 *Corriere della Somalia*, Gennaio 18, 1958.

Monde went on to suggest countries like Italy, France, Britain, Ethiopia and one or two others (having no vested interest in the area) as potential members of the proposed Council, and concluded: "The United Nations could thus give a proof of wisdom by averting the risks associated with haste."[55]

Some also made themselves heard in Italy calling for the prolongation of the trusteeship regime, which in their view was necessary to prepare the territory to become self-sufficient. Gregorio Consiglio, writing in *Affrica*, the magazine he directed, said that Somali people had "not yet gained the cultural, technical, social and civic capacity indispensable for self-governance" and did not as yet "have the economic structure necessary to survive."[56] On the basis of these considerations, Consiglio recommended that the Italian government submit the question to the UN in clear terms and seek a second mandate 'for a minimum of twenty years' in order that Somalia may "stand on its own two feet."[57]

As expected, the suggestion generated a wave of protest from the Somalis, which eventually forced the Italian government to distance itself from the author's views in the same magazine and stress its indisputable commitment to granting political independence to the Somalis in 1960. The official position of the Italian government *vis-à-vis* Mr Consiglio's suggestions was clearly expressed by Vittorio Badini Confalonieri, Undersecretary for Foreign Affairs: "I and the Italian government do not share your opinion."[58] Angelo Del Boca comments that "despite the criticisms and suggestions for extension of the trusteeship, the government in Rome was not in doubt, nor had it changed its mind about its plans for the Territory and would indeed grant independence to the Somalis six months ahead of the date of expiry of the trusteeship regime."[59]

Martino's last hurdles: the economic plan

In a spirit of collaboration, before leaving Somalia, Ambassador Martino undertook significant initiatives which would have a considerable impact on the future political life of the territory. On September 6, 1954 a decree instituting the Somali flag (a blue rectangle with a five-point white star in the middle) was presented to the United Nations by the Italian President of the Republic[60].

55 *Le Monde*, March 5, 1959, as quoted in Del Boca, op. cit., p. 272.
56 Del Boca, op. cit., p. 271.
57 *Affrica*, n° 3, Marzo 1955, as quoted in Del Boca, op. cit. p. 271.
58 *Corriere della Somalia*, Maggio 25, 1958.
59 Del Boca, op. cit., p. 273.
60 'Ordinanza n° 17 settembre 6, 1954'.

Martino then began preparing the ground for the general elections scheduled for 1956 to elect members of the Legislative Assembly, with substantial political powers to replace the Territorial Council, whose function was that of a mere consulting body.

To commemorate the institution of the flag, Ambassador Martino made a brief statement: "O Somali people. In a few minutes' time and for the first time in your history, rising up in the sky will be the symbol that you have chosen to manifest the ardent wish to be a free and independent nation and in whose shadow you wish to march united, as a people, in order to achieve material and spiritual progress." Concluding his speech he said: "O people of Somalia, after twenty-four months of work in this Territory, it will shortly be a moment of deep emotion for me as I see the blue flag with the five-point white star being hoisted. With a felicitous intuition you chose the unequalled colour of your sky and the blazing lights of your nights as a symbol and guide for you. Viva la Somalia!"[61] The Somali flag was hoisted for the first time side by side with the Italian and UN flags on October 12, 1954.

By the end of 1955, a time coinciding with Martino's end of mission in Somalia, the Italian Trusteeship Administration had apparently succeeded in convincing the Lega that it was only a temporary agency committed to adhering to its international obligations as contemplated in the Trusteeship Agreement. In that year "the Lega dei Giovani Somali executed a *volte-face* and announced a policy of collaboration with the Trusteeship Administration."[62]

The 'arranged marriage' between Italy and this party, brokered by the United Nations, thus became a relationship based on mutual understanding and love. It was a slow and difficult process: it took nearly four years for the two parties to come to terms with the facts and to realize that the rapidly approaching target date for independence did not permit the luxury of sterile confrontations. The new relationship survived, in spite of a couple of tricky moments—one when Osman Hussein was murdered and the other when Abdullahi Issa in New York made strong attacks on the Administration, violently countered by Martino who lashed out at the Lega on accounts of Issa's exaggerated criticism of the Italian Administration in the Fourth Committee of the United Nations[63]. The lack of co-operation and meaningful dialogue between the Administration

61 E. Martino, op. cit., pp. 87-88.

62 Hess, op. cit., p. 193.

63 TNA FO 371/108095, confidential dispatch from the British Consulate Mogadisho the FO, March 17, 1954.

and the Lega caused valuable time to be lost in the first crucial years of the new Administration, leaving the latter with no option but to depend on advice from the United Nations Advisory Council for Somalia (UNACS) in respect of economic and social plans to be promoted in the territory.

One of the direct effects of the collaboration between AFIS and the Lega was the end of the special relationship of the Italian Administration with the Conferenza, which eventually led to the latter's disintegration. New political entities sprung up from the ashes of the Conferenza, a coalition of small parties created in 1947 with Italian political and financial support. However, the HDM maintained its original character, while the Lega Progressista Somala (LPS) and the Unione Africani della Somalia (UAS) gave way to the Partito Democratico Somalo (PDS), and the Gioventù Abgal originated the Partito Liberale Giovani Somali (PLGS).

The Conferenza expressed resentment at what it considered the conciliatory attitude adopted by Dr Benardelli towards its rivals, the Lega. Civil and Political Director Benardelli had always been the guiding spirit behind the Conferenza group, and there had been a bitter comment about the fact that he, "having used the pro-Italian elements before the granting of the Trusteeship, is now ready to forsake them."[64] Conferenza people feared being abandoned, losing aid and relevance and being hemmed in by their former foes. As mentioned earlier, the understanding between AFIS and the Lega had resulted in the so-called pro-Italian parties losing the political and financial support they had traditionally received from Italy[65]. Although available records show evidence of understanding between AFIS and the Lega dating back to times earlier even than the official return of Italy to Somalia, a real co-operation between the two sides took shape only after the political elections of 1956 which led to the formation of the first Somali government.

During his tenure, Martino had promoted the setting up of a number of key institutions designed to back up his policy of *rapprochement.* One of these was the Credito Somalo, the other was the Institute of Social Science, Law and Economics. Martino claimed that the creation of these institutions "made a significant contribution to improving the relationship between the Administration

64 TNA FO 1015/553, Report on the Transfer of Administration in Somalia from the United Kingdom to Italian Trusteeship, 1950.

65 Paolo Tripodi, *The Colonial Legacy in Somalia: Rome and Mogadishu from Colonial Administration to Operation Restore Hope,* 1999, Macmillian Press Ltd & St. Martin's Press, Inc., p.73.

and the Lega."[66] However, the list of events believed to have contributed to the improvement of relations is long and includes the setback in relations between the Lega and the British that occurred when the latter handed over Ogaden and Haud to Ethiopia in 1954.[67]

The election for president of the Lega, held in the territory in November 1954, resulted in a sweeping victory for Aden Abdulla, who gained sixty per cent of the seven thousand five hundred votes cast. Abdullahi Issa was elected as secretary general of the party[68]. To many observers, Aden Abdulla's overwhelming victory was seen as a very good sign that the party had come to recognize the advantages of a policy of moderation, and could appreciate "a man of real ability who is capable of holding independent views."[69] Aden Abdulla's moderation and co-operation with the Administration over the previous years had been a success for the party as a whole, as a British source noted.[70]

The return of Abdullahi Issa as secretary general was seen by analysts as somewhat unexpected: Issa had been completely inactive since his return from New York the previous March, and was generally thought to be temporarily retiring from the political limelight. However, the appointment of Mohamoud Yousuf Aden 'Muro', his close associate, as assistant secretary general, was considered as an indication that the Lega did not expect Abdullahi Issa to work full time. "It is possible that the appointment is a gesture to placate the more ardent nationalists in the party without great significance", comments a British diplomatic source.[71]

The return of the radical Lega secretary general to Somalia was seen as a sign of greater influence of the radical group within the ranks of the party and an indication of difficult times ahead for the Administration. However, within the Lega there was a considerable body of opinion favourable to the idea of co-operation with the Administration. With no alternative approach to this line of action, the secretary general came to the conclusion that his political position was no longer sustainable in the face of the rapid progress the territory was making towards independence. It is reported that he requested to be allowed to

66 ASMAE, AFIS, box 2, file 3, top secret report from Martino to Gaetano Martino, April 9, 1955.

67 Tripodi, op. cit., p. 63.

68 TNA FO 371/108096, confidential monthly summary for November 1954 from British Consulate Mogadisho.

69 TNA FO 371/102567, restricted report of 21/27/53 from British Consulate Mogadisho to African Department, FO, November 21, 1954.

70 TNA FO 371/108101, confidential report from the British Consulate Mogadisho to the FO, May 18, 1954.

71 Ibid.

resign from his position on the grounds that his presence in that capacity made relations between the Administration and the Lega difficult[72]. History shows how Abdullahi Issa later abandoned his anti-Italian stance, joining the camp of the 'collaborators' within the party and eventually becoming one of the Somali politicians closest to Italy during the UN trusteeship mandate period and beyond.

The 7-year economic plan (1954-1960)

During its first years, the Administration focused its attention on laying the foundations for the social and political institutions of the future Somali State. In 1954 it produced the first blueprint for Somali economic development, known as 'Piani di sviluppo della Somalia' or 'Economic Development Plan for Somalia'. It was not until the fourth year that, under pressure from the United Nations, AFIS started building an economic programme to be completed by the 1960 termination date of the trusteeship regime.[73]

The plan was mainly drawn on the technical study conducted by Italian economist G.F. Malagodi[74]. The United States International Cooperation (ICA), later United States Agency for International Development (AID), had an important role in the implementation and financing of this project, having undertaken a series of technical assistance surveys in Somalia. In consideration of the importance of the programme, South Dakota State College was awarded a contract to develop a detailed plan regarding livestock accumulation, which was carried out under the guidance of the college itself.[75]

In order to ensure timely implementation of the plan, the United States and Italy set up the Somali Development Fund. The US made a further contribution of $4.4million to the fund, while Italy added another $7.6 million over the first four years of the plan. About 60% of the total advance budget was assigned to projects designed to benefit pastoral economy and the indigenous agriculture[76]. The remainder was allocated to improvement of roads and ports and the promotion of crafts, industry, commerce and urban development. The projects envisaged for pastoral economy mainly included the excavation of shallow wells, the drilling of deep wells and the construction of water catchment basins.

For the development of indigenous agriculture, construction of various

72 Ibid.

73 U.N. Docs A/3170, p. 299; U.N. Doc.T/1033, p. 20.

74 G.F. Malagodi, *'Linee programmatiche per lo sviluppo della Somalia'*, Roma 1953.

75 Department of State Bulletin, August 9, 1954, as reported in 'Domesticating Somalia', Yohannes, op. cit.

76 Mark Karp, *The Economy of Trusteeship in Somalia,* Boston, 1960, p. 130.

irrigation works for some 30,000 hectares of land in Middle and Lower Shabelle were planned. For Middle and Lower Juba, the plans included an improvement of the irrigation system by utilization of excess river water and construction of modern storage facilities for grain (silos) on each farm. The creation of 240 reservoirs for rain water was also planned[77]. The budget for agricultural development in 1954 – 60 was 20,844,000 Somali shilling, roughly US$3,000,000[78]. The livestock programme was centred on an extension of well drillings already begun with US financial and technical assistance at the end of 1953. A total of 400 shallow and 200 deep wells were to be dug by the end of 1959 to provide for 330,000 heads of livestock a day.[79]

The plan also envisaged the establishment of a special Bank, known as 'Credito Somalo' (Somali Credit Institute) with an initial capital of $800,000, from which native farmers could obtain short to medium-term credit at low interest rates[80]. The long-term objective of the Credito Somalo was to move Somalia towards self-sufficiency by means of food production and stockpiling of essential foodstuffs. To strengthen the institution even further, the United States Development Loan Fund lent it $2 million for the purpose of extending cheap credit to Somali farmers and businesses.[81]

Chronic deficits in the administration budget precluded the use of domestic revenue for financing the Plans. In 1951, the second year of the trusteeship, ordinary budget income was Sh.So34 million, while the estimated budget for 1960, year of independence, was about Sh.So86 million, almost four times the projected income[82]. The 'Somalo' was authorized by the Trusteeship Administration under Ordinanza no. 14 of 16 May 1950[83]: it replaced the East African shilling at par, also replacing the small amount of Italian lire in circulation at the rate of 1 Somalo = Lit 87.49. It was given an IMF parity of 124.414 mg fine gold, equal to one shilling sterling. Internationally, this currency became known as the 'Somali shilling' when Somalia became independent on 1 July 1960.

77 Speech given by Administrator Enrico Martino before the XIV Session of the United Nations Trusteeship Council, June 4, 1954.

78 Martino, op. cit., p. 56.

79 The Economy of the Trusts Territory of Somaliland. Report of a Mission organized by the International Bank for Reconstruction and Development at the request of the Government of Italy, Washington, D.C. January 1957, p. 4.

80 'Ordinanza n° 3 febbraio 22, 1954'.

81 Department of State Bulletin, April 23, 1959, p. 565.

82 ASMAE, AFIS, box 9, file 2: Speech given by Ambassador Mario Di Stefano, Administrator of Somalia, on April 30, 1960, during the inauguration of the first session of the Legislative Assembly for 1960.

83 Bollettino Ufficiale, suppl. n°1 a ln° 2, Mogadiscio, May 18, 1950.

In 1950, the Territory was running a budget deficit of 74% which by 1958 had been reduced to 52% and was estimated to be equal to 36% in 1959 [84]. Professor U. Triulzi[85] explains that during its ten-year administration of Somalia the Italian government did not succeed in improving Somali economy, citing as reasons for this failure the limited time available to realize a valid economic programme and the country's scarce resources, as well as the limited levels of external aid donated and the ways in which it was invested.

Struggling as she was with her own reconstruction in the difficult post-war period, Italy was not in a position to solve all the problems of one of the poorest countries in Africa. Yet Triulzi suggests that some basic mistakes were made by AFIS in its planning and daily running of the country's economy. To give one example, the return to the pre-existing regime of monoculture, coupled with excessive support given to Somalia's banana production, had created a basic one-crop structure which forced the country into an uneconomic, unhealthy and productively unbalanced output. Aside from bananas, no other products such as maize, cotton, groundnuts etc had any economic and commercial relevance for Italy[86]. Thus, rather than diversifying existing cultures by using land abandoned as a result of the war while encouraging economic activities such as agricultural production or labour-intensive small industries, which might have created more adequate bases for long-term economic development, the Italian Administration proceeded with vertical economic policies which led to forced bilateralism with Italy.[87]

Such a method proved to run counter to Somalia's independent development. Bananas remained the prime product at the core of national economy, representing 65% of the total value of Somali exports. The only alternative staple was livestock (meat and hides), which would take a couple of decades to build up to a point where it could replace bananas. Owing to budget limitations and the lack of natural resources like oil, there was little development work done by Italy. "Available funds were barely enough to cover administrative costs", concludes Triulzi.[88]

The following table shows the trend of income budget, in Somali shillings,

84 TNA FO 371/131466, speech delivered by Di Stefano on occasion of the opening of the second session of the Legislative Assembly for the year 1958 on October 25, 1958.

85 Professor of Political Economy and International Economy, Faculty of Political Sciences, La Sapienza University, Rome.

86 U. Triulzi, *'L'Italia e l'economia somala dal 1950 ad oggi'*, Africa, vol. XXIV, no. 4, 1971, p. 452.

87 Ibid., p. 459.

88 Ibid., p. 461.

during the ten-year trusteeship period:

YEAR	BUDGETED INCOME
1951	34,270,000
1952	34,034,000
1953	30,713,000
1954	36,820,000
1955	41,624,000
1956	44,221,000
1957	48,875,000
1958 (8 MONTHS)	39,121,000
1959	60,500,000

Chapter VI

ANZILOTTI REPLACES MARTINO
Further steps towards self-government

The year 1955 saw important changes involving top AFIS officials: Enrico Anzilotti replaced Martino as administrator, and Piero Franca replaced Pier Paolo Spinelli as secretary general of the Administration. Anzilotti was born in Florence in 1898. He served as an artillery officer during the First World War. After legal training, he was appointed secretary to the Italian delegation to the League of Nations at Geneva in 1920. He embarked upon a diplomatic career in 1925, serving in Cairo and Alexandria. From 1937 to 1944 he was consul in Algiers, Oran and Melbourne, and for a few months he served as first secretary in Kabul. In June 1944, he returned to the Foreign Ministry in Rome, and early in 1946 was appointed counsellor at the Italian Embassy in China. From there he was transferred in 1948 to London, and in 1949 was appointed minister in Tel Aviv. From 1952 until his nomination as Administrator of Somalia, he served as ambassador in Vienna, Austria.

While the appointment of Anzilotti passed without controversy, Franca's nomination sparked off polemics stirred up by the Ethiopians. Since Minister Franca had served in Eritrea, Somaliland and Ethiopia during the fascist era, the Ethiopians made strong representations about his appointment, as they had done in the past over General Nasi's appointment as commissario for Somalia in 1950. Franca's appointment became an international issue when it was raised by Sir F. Medicott, a member of the British House of Commons, who put a question to the Secretary for Foreign Affairs as to whether he was aware of what he called the "anxiety felt concerning the proposed appointment of Franca, a former fascist official, as secretary general of the Italian Trust Administration in Somalia." Responding to this question, Secretary of State for Foreign Affairs Mr Turton stated: "since taking up his duties at Mogadisho in April last, Franca, who was appointed by the Italian government, has shown concern for the advancement of the Somalis in full accordance with the trusteeship obligations assumed by the Italian government."[1] Franca entered the Italian colonial service in 1928 and served in Eritrea, Somalia and Abyssinia. Since the War he had served in Rome as director of the Office of Former Italian colonies and subsequently as director general of the Foreign Ministry department dealing with the Trusteeship Administration in Somalia.

Anzilotti's arrival ushered in the third phase of the trusteeship regime: a crucial period in which the somewhat troubled past relations between the Lega and the Administration might be seen to be easing. Anzilotti, a seasoned diplomat, built his appeasement process on the work done by his predecessors through further dialogue with the political parties. Anzilotti oversaw further steps towards the territory's independence, including organization of the first political elections, set for 1956, and formation of the first Somali government. His critics say that as an administrator he was "seldom seen in Somalia except on very important occasions occurring three or four times in a year, administering the Trust Territory, most of the time, from his personal villa at Pescia in Tuscany."[2] Franca was the 'agent of the absentee landlord', and Anzilotti only paid rare and brief visits to Somalia[3]. However, on the grounds of his liberal policy, he was decorated by the Somali government with the Order of National Solidarity, a privilege not granted to any of the other three Italian diplomats who governed the territory during the trusteeship mandate.[4]

In anticipation of the 1956 political elections, the Administration hastened to introduce reforms which resulted in the abolition of the Residence Council (established under Circular no. 22809 of July 27, 1951) and the creation of District Councils. The policy of the Administration was designed to make

1 *New Times and Ethiopia News*, January 7, 1956.
2 Del Boca, op. cit., p. 246.
3 Ibid.
4 *Corriere della Somalia*, Agosto 4, 1958.

this body a more democratic organ, with deliberative powers, elected through universal suffrage.

A draft ordinance submitted to the Territorial Council for discussion laid down the procedure for the election of district councillors through traditional gatherings known as *shir*[5]. Under this ordinance, each administrative district was divided into tribal areas, each of which would hold a *shir* and elect its traditional chief to represent it in the District Council. Because of the tribal nature of this body, no provision was made for the inclusion of representatives from political parties[6]. However, special provision had been made to enable certain traditional chiefs, whose prominence derived from hereditary and religious prestige, to take place without loss of dignity. Approximately twenty such leaders were involved where "the Chief's leadership was so indisputable that to elect him at a *shir* would merely cause offence."[7]

As a result, paramount chiefs, owing to their influence and prestige within their communities, were automatically included as members in the District Council. Such was the case of Ugas of Desciscia (Deshishe) (Bosaso), Beldaje of Siwaqron (Alula and Iskushuban), Ugaas of Ali Soleiman (Candala), Sultan of Majerten, Islan of Issa Mohamoud (Nugal), Islan of Omar Mohamoud (Galkayo), Ugas of Marehan (Dusa Mareb), Ugaas of Murusada (Elbur) Ugaas of 'Ayr (Elbur), Ugas of Duduble (Elbur), Iman of Abgal (Itala); Iman of Abgal (Mogadisho) Ugas of Hawadle (Beledweyne), Uabar of Gegele (Beledweyne), Ugas of Galgel (Bulo Burti), Ugaas of Daut (Itala), Ugaas of Issa Harti (Itala), Ugas of Mobilen (Balad), Uabar of Illivi (Balad), Sultan of Bimal (Merca), Sultan of degli Elai (Bur Hakaba), Garad of Gassargudde (Lugh Ferrandi), Ugas of Awlyahan (Bardera), Ugaas of Mohamed Zuber (Kismayo).[8]

The Administration also put forward a motion calling for shir election of traditional chiefs every two or three years in order to give people more of a say in the management of their affairs. This initiative was, however, heavily defeated, the Lega representatives alone being in its favour[9]. The idea of creating a body of an exclusively tribal nature was vehemently opposed by the Lega members of the Territorial Council. As a result, the original ordinance prepared by the Administration's Department of Political Affairs in anticipation of the

5 'Ordinanza n° 5 marzo 20, 1955, "Istituzione dei Consigli Distrettuali"'.

6 *Corriere della Somalia*, Marzo 10, 1955.

7 TNA FO 371/113455, restricted letter from British Consulate Mogadisho to the FO, March 25, 1955.

8 ASMAE, AFIS, box 9, file 9, Circolare n° 76474 dell' 11 febbraio 1955, "Elezione del Consiglio Territoriale e istituzione dei consigli distrettuali", from Benardelli to all regional and district commissioners.

9 TNA FO 371/96646, secret report from the British Consulate in Mogadisho to FO January 16, 1952.

future general elections was amended by the inclusion in the District Councils of representatives of the political parties, as well as shir elected chiefs. As mentioned earlier, the Lega's proposal was accepted after much heated debate in the Commission, with Lega groups in the Territorial Council threatening to stage a walk-out[10]. The Commission further proposed the inclusion in District Councils of representatives from the economic sector and from religious and cultural institutions, and for all these members to be appointed by a decree of the administrator. The amendments proposed by the Territorial Council and accepted by the Administration were so numerous and substantial that at the end there was not much difference in either composition or functions between the new District Councils and the old Residence Councils they were supposed to replace.

One particular problem, to which there was no easy solution, was the distribution of seats among electoral districts in the general elections scheduled for 1956. Although the number of electors in municipality areas was known, figures for the tribal areas were a matter of conjecture and a source of fierce argument[11]. The original plan drawn up by AFIS for the distribution of seats was rejected outright by all political parties. Under this plan, municipalities and rural areas were to be regarded as separate electoral divisions, and seats distributed on the basis of one for every 25,000 heads of population in rural areas, and one for every 5,000 in the municipalities. The Administration was anxious to prevent any possible accusation that they were 'rigging' the distribution in favour of any particular party. The scheme did not pass because of questions arising from the estimation of numbers of people in the various areas and the inevitable insistence on the part of territorial councillors that "their areas were much more densely populated than they actually were."[12]

1956 general elections

The indirect vote

The first general election law was issued on 31 March 1955 (Ordinance no. 6 of March, 1955). This was a daunting task, not only because it was a new experience for the Somalis, but most importantly because it was scheduled to take place

10 ASMAE AFIS, box 9, file 9, Breve cronostoria di come si è giunti alla tenuta degli 'scir' per l'elezione dei capi (istituzione dei consigli distrettuali) e per l'elezione del Consiglio Territoriale, p. 3.

11 TNA FO 371/113455, confidential letter from the British Consulate, Mogadisho to FO, April 1, 1955.

12 Ibid. Conversation between Guido Natali and the Acting British Consul, April 21, 1955.

without a clear picture of the size of the population called to participate in the election process. In the face of the difficulties involved in organizing a credible census of the nomadic population, AFIS had introduced a mixed election system under the terms of which residents living in the cities and in possession of an electoral card could directly cast their vote, while nomadic populations living in the rural areas expressed their vote through their tribal leaders. The difference between the two categories of population figures consisted in the former being registered in the municipal electoral roll, politically more mature, with past experience acquired in the 1954 municipal elections; while the latter was not registered, illiterate and politically immature.

As for running 'second-degree elections' among the rural population, the Administration felt that the most appropriate system was to apply the traditional Somali shir system, through which each tribal unit would nominate one electoral representative who would subsequently present himself at an electoral college on a date set for the voting.[13]

For this purpose, shir were organized for all tribal units, which *grosso modo* corresponded to the actual number of salaried chiefs. The purpose of the *shir* was to make as close as possible a head-count of the tribesmen present at the gathering. Detailed procedures and regulations were put in place to organize the nominations, provide a time frame for the completion of the operation, specify the role of the observers, establish penalties for those contravening the law and provide guidance on the publication of the results.

Traditional assemblies to designate electoral representatives for the nomadic population were organized from August 1 to November 30, 1955 throughout the territory[14]. A total of 616 *shir* were organized between August and November 1955 for a population of 772,000 – a figure greatly exceeding that which was expected from an estimated population of 1,270,000, considering women and persons under the age of twenty-one did not have the right to vote.[15]

The manifestly exaggerated number of rural voters had to be accepted and was added to the 86,000 municipal electors to give a total of 858,122 potential voters nationwide[16]. Then on the day of the election, electoral representatives and municipal electorate voted together. While it was 'one man, one vote' for voters

13 'Circolare n° 76474 dell'11 febbraio 1955...' from Benardelli to all regional and district commissioners.

14 'Decreto n° 93, maggio 27, 1955.

15 Report of the United Nations Advisory Council for the Trust Territory of Somaliland under Italian Administration in UN Doc. T/1245, May 1, 1956, p. 12.

16 Rapport du gouvernment italien à l'Assemblée Generale des Nations Unies sur l'administration de la Somalie placée sous la tutelle de l'Italie, 1955, p. 25.

registered on the municipal electoral roll, electoral representatives had a block vote equivalent to the number of votes they had received in the tribal *shir*. Each electoral representative could either ask the electoral committee for a number of ballots equal to the number of people on whose behalf he was to vote, or cast only one ballot requesting the committee to confirm the number of votes he had obtained in the *shir*. To calculate the total number of votes, the number of municipal electors was added to the number of rural and nomadic electors who had voted through electoral representatives. The indirect vote clearly favoured the areas which had the most inflated figures relative to tribal voters. In a number of cases, it was necessary to invalidate the *shir* vote owing to efforts on the part of the tribes concerned to inflate their own importance by magnifying their figures.

The Administration advanced a number of detailed arguments in favour of the indirect vote for the rural population: the lack of a credible population census with no electoral certificates necessary to determine the size of the electorate made it difficult to control how the rural population would cast their vote: hence the necessity to resort to the *shir* system, seen as the only imaginable mechanism apt to determine the size of the rural population eligible to vote. It was not appropriate or even possible to make participants to the *shir* vote directly for the election of Territorial Councils because of the lack of political maturity of the rural population.

Despite these arguments, the Lega, in agreement with other political parties, persisted in its strong opposition during Territorial Council discussions over the matter, suggesting the postponement of the political elections until it would be possible to conduct the elections through a direct vote system[17]. However, to allay these concerns, AFIS proposed, and the Lega accepted, a compromise formula on the basis of which new municipalities were created and the jurisdictions of some already existing were enlarged in order to allow as many voters as possible to take part in the 1956 direct elections. To this effect, eight new municipalities were established and four existing ones were expanded, bringing the number of new electors casting a direct vote to 35,000[18]. The rural communities were for the most part completely incapable of exercising political judgment and could have but the vaguest idea of what 'the government' is. "Their entry into the political sphere may not in practice be a good step forward", commented a

17 ASMAE, AFIS, box 9, file 9, 'Breve cronostoria di come si è giunti alla tenuta degli 'scir' per l'elezione dei capi (istituzione dei consigli distrettuali) e per l'elezione del Consiglio Territoriale, p. 4.
18 Ibid., p. 5.

British report.[19]

Mogadisho and the single seat

Seats were eventually allocated in an arbitrary manner to different electoral districts. In this haphazard method, Bulo Burti and Bur Hakaba, for instance, were allocated the highest number of seats (5 each). One question frequently asked is why Mogadisho, the most populous urban centre of Somalia, was so underrepresented in the first general election of 1956. Under the election law of 1958, one additional seat was assigned to Mogadisho. The answer to this question is simple, but not necessarily convincing. In Mogadisho, there were no tribal voters or communities of the rural population taking part in the election process, as was the case in the outlying districts where overzealous Somali local officials had inflated the number of voters. As far as Mogadisho was concerned, only voters registered in the municipal electoral roll could cast a vote: consequently, with only 18,153 registered voters, Mogadisho got one single seat open for competition between five political parties: Lega dei Giovani Somali (6,605 votes), Giovani Benadir (2,530); Hizbia Dighil & Mirifle (2,015); Partito Gioventù Hauia (1,841); Partito Democratico Somalo (162).[20]

In the 1956 general elections, the Lega had chosen, through primary elections, Abdullahi Issa as their candidate for Mogadisho. He received 7,158 votes. Competing with him were Haji Yousuf Egal, a leading businessman politically close to the Egyptians, who received 382 votes, and Osman Ahmed Roble, a member of the Central Committee, who received 882 votes.[21]

The candidates of the other four parties for the single seat of Mogadisho were: Sherif Mohamed Hussein (Giovani Benadir); Haji Mohamoud Borraco (Hawiye Party); Geilani Malak (Hizbia Dighil & Mirifle); Alasso Addo' Go'oso (Partito Democratico Somalo).

It was in the elections of 1956 that voting irregularities first presented serious problems which the administering authorities failed to address. The event, which had been expected to be the beginning of a true democratic process in Somalia, marked instead the beginning of a disaster that continued to haunt the country even after independence. "The electoral system was farcical thanks to the recurrent weakness of Italians in their desire to please rather than face up to

19 TNA FO 371/113455, confidential report from British Consulate, Mogadisho to FO, April 1, 1955.

20 *Corriere della Somalia*, Marzo 1, 1956.

21 TNA FO 371/118674, summary monthly report for December 1955 from the British Consulate Mogadisho.

the responsibilities of Trustee", comments a British source in Mogadisho.[22]

Based on figures collected following the *shir* process, the 60 Territorial Council seats allocated to the districts at the rate of one seat for every 14, 502 voters were considered by many, including the United Nations, as a very low proportion of the population of the territory[23]. Where a district had insufficient voters, it was merged with its neighbours. Five districts were affected by these mergers: Alula-Candala, Balad–Villabruzzi, Afgooye–Dafet, Margherita–Jilib and Nugal–Daror (Eyl and Iskushuban), making 25 electoral districts in all. Grossly inflated figures were given in many rural areas, particularly where local officials were Somalis belonging to the same tribe or group as the voters, with the connivance of salaried chiefs. Many outsiders were encouraged to attend the *shir* – thus swelling the numbers of tribesmen present at the *shir* in breach of the electoral system.

The stakes for the Italian Administration had become conspicuously higher following the embarrassing setback in the 1954 municipal elections, when the Somali political parties backed by the Administration were vanquished by the Lega. The Administration, alerted by the landslide victory of the Lega and by the poor performance of Conferenza parties in the first municipal elections, encouraged the small parties to merge into one party with some policy behind it, which could stand on its own feet and compete with the Lega in future general elections. According to British Diplomatic sources, Spinelli, the secretary general of the Administration, spelt out the prospect of halting the financing of these small parties, indicating that as from June, 1953, the Administration "could cease to pay the expenses of the parties' HQs, including rent, electricity, orderlies, telephone, etc, etc."[24]

The Administration was mainly worried about the prospect of leaving behind the spectre of a one-party system after independence. As a result of this pressure, a new political party was created under the name of 'Partito Democratico Somalo' or Somali Democratic Party—uniting the Unione Africani Somalia, Unione Nazionale Somala, Unione Patriottica Somala, Associazione Gioventù Abgal, Scidle e Mobilen, and a number of minor parties.

The HDM did not join this pact, considering they were strong enough to stand alone and preferring to preserve their characteristics as the party of the

22 TNA FO 371/135675, confidential document no. 2 (1059/57).

23 Report of the United Nations Advisory Council for the Trust Territory of Somaliland under Italian Administration: April 1955 - 31 March 1956. UN Doc.T/1245, May 1, 1956.

24 TNA FO 371/102566, restricted report from British Consulate, Mogadisho, to FO, May 23, 1953.

agro-pastoral population living between the two rivers[25]. The new party was led by Abdullahi Haji Mohamoud 'Insania', a school teacher; other office holders included Mahamed Moussa Farah (vice-president), Mohamed Sheikh Osman 'Edmondo', a territorial councillor and former head of the Unione Africani Somali party (secretary general), and Haji Yahia Mohamed, of the Personnel Department at AFIS (treasurer)[26]. The party advocated gradual abolition of the traditional social system, a unitary republican form of government with a decentralized administration and Greater Somalia. The party's programme was to abolish the tribal system through gradual economic, social and political reforms.[27]

Election results

The 1955 electoral law was heavily criticized by both the Lega and the United Nations Advisory Council, which insisted on the need to conduct the elections after the citizenship law was approved and a reliable population census was available. With the adoption of the tribal *shir* and the indirect voting system, a clan institution was being formalized, attaching different tribes to designated electoral districts artificially created by the Administration.[28]

An element of division and fragmentation was therefore added to an already divided Somali society; this has proven hard to eliminate up to the present time[29]. As Paolo Tripodi puts it, "the population were forced to find a party representative of the clan and the coincidence between clan and party became intense."[30]

Although electoral law shaped on Western principles was passed by the Legislative Assembly to discipline the elections, there was still a question of political elections being contested on a party basis. "They are conducted on lineage-group principles, members of lineage-group supporting their candidate in opposition to a candidate of a rival lineage-group", comments Lewis.[31]

Of the 25 constituencies, 6 had no contest at all, since only Lega candidates

25 Rapport du government italien à l'Assemblée Generale des Nations Unies sur l'administration de la Somalie placée sous la tutelle de l'Italie, 1954, p. 39.

26 TNA FO 371/108101, restricted document no. 43.13/54 of July 26, 1954 from the British Consulate in Mogadisho to the FO.

27 SDP manifesto, art. 5.

28 Tribal boundaries virtually coincided with those of electoral constituencies..

29 For a detailed explanation of the procedural aspect of the 1956 elections, cf. Guido Natali, Le prime elezioni politiche in Somalia, AFIS, 1957.

30 Tripodi, op. cit., p. 79.

31 I.M. Lewis, *Modern Political Movements in Somaliland II'*, Africa Journal of the International African Institute, vol. 28, no. 4 (Oct. 1958), p. 348.

registered and presented lists. The districts where no election had taken place were: Dinsor, taken by HDM; Afmedu, Adale, Beledweyne, Bulo Burti and Obbia, won by the Lega dei Giovani Somali. Elections took place in the remaining 19 districts. (Bosaso, Candala-Alula, Sol (Gardo), Nugal-Daror (Eyl and Iskushuban) Galkayo, El-Bur, Dusa Mareb, Villabruzzi-Balad, Mogadisho, Afgooye–Dafet, Merca, Brava, Bur Hakaba, Baidoa, Oddur, Lugh Ferrandi, Bardera, Margherita-Jilib, Kismayo). The sixty seats in the National Assembly were allocated to electoral districts on the basis of 14,302 votes per seat. Accordingly, the distribution of seats between political parties whose candidates were elected was as follows:

PARTY	NO. OF SEATS
LEGA DEI GIOVANI SOMALI	45
HIZBIA DIGHIL E MIRIFLE	13
PARTITO DEMOCRATICO SOMALO	3
UNIONE MAREHAN	1

The results marked the eclipse of the pro-Italian parties which had been generally regarded by the Administration as the country's future government. However, when Parliament met, members of the Partito Democratico Somalo and the Marehan Union crossed the floor of the House and joined the Lega dei Giovani Somali, leaving the HDM as the sole opposition group in Parliament[32]. Despite the support it received from the Administration and the broad base of its constituency, the Partito Democratico Somalo failed to elect more than 3 candidates nationwide: Arsce Aw Musse, (Gardo), Mohamed Sheikh Osman 'Edmondo' (El-Bour) and Hassan Abukar Ahmed (Afgooye–Dafet). Most of the seats were, without doubt, won by judicious expenditure. In this way, through fraud, and taking advantage of the complicated electoral system, the Lega obtained the majority of the seats. There was a lot to be worried about, for the prospect of a Legislative Assembly dominated by one party would provide a disastrous start for Somalia.

The 1956 general elections brought about a new development in the sense that they transformed the Territorial Council into a fully-fledged elective legislative body, with full statutory powers over legislation dealing with domestic affairs[33],

32 UN Doc. T/1372, April 22, 1958, par. 58, p. 24.

33 Ordinanza n° 6 gennaio 5, 1956.

composed of 70 seats, ten of which were reserved for foreign ethnic minorities living in the territory, the Italian and Arab communities being allocated four seats each and the Indian and Pakistani groups one seat each. For the election of representatives of the foreign communities living in the territory, a separate electoral system was envisaged[34]. Each candidate was to be selected by an Electoral College chosen through a primary election in which all the members of the minority concerned had the right to vote. The candidate was required to be over twenty-one years old and have been twelve months in the territory.[35]

All the four Italian representatives elected as Members of Parliament were well-known as ardent fascists. Avvocato Carlo Quaglia, a solicitor elected as Member of Parliament to represent the Italian community of Mogadisho, had a record of having betrayed to Mussolini an anti-fascist plot in which he was involved in 1925, saving his own neck at the cost of his friends'. Dr Vincenzo Calzia, a former official of the Italian Ministry of Africa, representing the Italian community of Villabruzzi (Johar), was one of the main agitators in the incident of 11 January 1948 in Mogadisho. Colonnello Camillo Giorio, representing the Italian community of Merca, was a member of the military establishment prior to 1941. Only Francesco Boero, a leading businessman representing the Italian community of Mogadisho, had held no government positions during the fascist era.

Haji Mohamed Ali Bin Quer and Haji Nasser Ali represented the Arab community of Mogadisho, Said Mohamed Salim represented the Arab community of Margherita (Jamama) and Ali Maiub Ali the Arab community of Baidoa. Damador Tribhonar Shah represented the Indian community and Ahmed Fadel Hasham the Pakistani community.[36]

According to British sources, Italian MPs usually voted with the government; the Arabs also voted with the government, except when religious factors were involved; the Indians and the Pakistani rarely spoke and were watchdogs of their communities' interests[37]. "The Italians, Arabs and Indians were elected, but they were expected only to contribute towards resolving economic and social problems and not to engage in partisan debate on political questions", comments Castagno.[38]

34 Ordinanza n° 6 marzo 31, 1956, art. 2.

35 TNA FO/371/118674, Monthly summary for December 1955 from British Consulate Mogadisho.

36 *Corriere della Somalia*, Marzo 1, 1956.

37 TNA FO 371/131460, Secret report from British Consulate General Mogadisho to FO, January 22, 1958.

38 A.A. Castagno, op. cit., p. 351.

The new Legislative Assembly was to be housed in the building known as the 'Casa del Fascio', originally built in 1938 for the Italian Fascist Party. The newly elected members, or 'deputati', as they were known, seemed not to have changed in any way from the old Territorial Councillors, except for the jackets and neckties many of them wore. The Legislative Assembly looked like a tribal assembly; a large number of its seats were filled by persons who were certainly capable in tribal matters in the bush, but "with little or no experience in the complexity of modern legislations", comments a British source in Mogadisho[39]. The Territorial Council, which opened its doors for the first time on February 18, 1951, held its last meeting on January 7, 1956 and was formally dissolved on January 31 of the same year to give way to the newly elected Legislative Assembly.[40]

The first session of the Legislative Assembly was chaired by Haji Omar Sheegoow, in his capacity as the most senior Member of Parliament. During the session, Aden Abdulla was elected President and Haji Omar Sheegoow and Abdinour Mohamed Hussein (HDM) Vice-president. At the National Assembly inauguration ceremony, Aden Abdulla made an important statement in the presence of the Administrator, Ambassador Anzilotti, and other foreign dignitaries. "The date of 30 April 1956 will remain engraved in golden characters in the first pages of the history of this country, but will also remain engraved in the hearts and minds of all Somalis grateful and appreciative of Italy and the United Nations who have made such a big step possible."[41]

Abdullahi Issa appointed Prime Minister

The Hawiye-dominated government

During Anzilotti's term of office, the territory's progress towards self-government had proceeded at a speedy rate, and further steps had been taken with a view to preparing the territory for full independence by the target date. In fact, a political development of considerable significance took place with the establishment in 1956 of the first five-member Somali government, enjoying very wide powers with regard to internal administration of the territory[42]. Abdullahi Issa Mohamoud, former Lega envoy to the United Nations and known for his strong

39 TNA FO 371/118675 Report from British Consulate Mogadisho, Febbraio 8, 1956.

40 *Corriere della Somalia*, Gennaio 9, 1956.

41 Extract of statement made on 30 April 1956 during the inauguration ceremony of the National Assembly.

42 Legge n° 1 maggio 7, 1956.

anti-Italian stand, was designated as Prime Minister. His designation was the result of informal consultations the Administrator had carried out with different political leaders, including, in addition to the Lega party, the opposition parties, represented by the HDM and the Partito Democratico Somalo, as well as the leaders of the minority communities represented in the Legislative Assembly.[43]

The formation of the government represented a turning point in the hitherto uneasy relations between the major political party in the territory and the Italian Trusteeship Administration. "By the time Abdullahi Issa assumed the office of Prime Minister, little trace remained of the earlier antagonism between the Administration and the Lega; a good working basis had now been reached between the two sides", comments Lewis.[44]

As a result of this new development, the ruling party, under the influence of Abdullahi Issa, assumed a more conciliatory attitude towards the Trusteeship Administration, and consequently the Italian Administration put full trust in the person of the Prime Minister of Somalia. Abdullahi Issa, now Prime Minister, took special pains to acknowledge the substantial contributions of Italy, which he said "had returned to the noble tradition of the Risorgimento, a tradition rooted in the brotherhood of man and in the support of oppressed peoples struggling to gain their independence."[45] Mr. Issa's statement was in stark contrast to his past position *vis-à-vis* the Italian return to Somalia – a position he continued to defend even after the United Nations had placed Somalia under Italian Trusteeship. He was once quoted as saying that if the Italians came back they would kill him and other young men who were outstandingly anti-Italian[46]. Now that Issa had government responsibilities, gone were the days when he had stressed, before the General Assembly of the United Nations, that "Somalia preferred death to Italian rule."[47]

The Administrator continued to have full administrative and legislative powers, including that of vetoing any legislation and issuing decrees in cases of urgency and necessity. These, however, were to be submitted as soon as possible to the Legislative Assembly for enactment. The Administrator also had the power to dissolve the Assembly and call for new elections in the event that the Assembly should be unable to discharge its functions or do so in such a way as to

43 *Corriere della Somalia*, May 8, 1956.
44 I.M. Lewis, op. cit., p. 14.
45 *Il Messaggero di Roma*, March 3, 1957, as quoted by Castagno, op. cit., p. 352.
46 TNA FO 1015/51, secret letter from Robert Mason to The Rt. Hon. Ernest Bevin, M.P., June 26, 1948, .
47 U.N. General Assembly, official Records (GAOR): 4th session 1st Committee, 288th Mtg., October 7,1949, par. 25; ibid., 290th Mtg., October 10, 1949, p. 352).

endanger the normal conduct of the legislative process. He continued to take full responsibility for matters relating to international affairs and defence. However, although relations with foreign countries were the concern of the Administering Authority, the Somali government had always had the possibility of maintaining contacts with the outside world in order to make known its views and to discuss its problems, especially that of obtaining financial assistance.[48]

The programme presented to the Legislative Assembly centred mainly on domestic issues, foreign policy being still outside its purview. Immediate attention was given to stipulations relative to the precarious economy of the territory, with particular emphasis on the fields of agriculture, livestock and small industry, and on the attraction of foreign capital and aid. The long-standing question of the script for the Somali language also received attention. Regarding social affairs, the government pledged to find ways of introducing full universal suffrage, with the inclusion of women. The latter move was met with strong opposition by conservative elements in the Legislative Assembly who saw as un-Islamic any form of female emancipation, including voting rights. To win support from Parliament, the Prime Minister went into detail, explaining the benefits of granting women the right to vote and citing examples of a number of Islamic countries where women already did enjoy that right[49]. The government obtained the confidence of the Legislative Assembly by 44 against 10 votes on October 3,1956.[50]

The government was composed of the Prime Minister, selected from the majority party in the Legislative Assembly, and ministers appointed by the Administrator, all from the ruling party. It should be noted that Aden Abdulla, President of the Lega, advocated a multi-party cabinet so that other parties could gain experience in executive responsibility, but the party congress voted down the proposal because "it felt that to bring in HDM members would imply an acceptance of tribalism."[51]

Behind the nationalist facade, the composition of the government was clearly based on clan logic, but not every Somali clan was represented. The HDM for instance, representing the farming population of the south, were not given any government position and the party leaders immediately accused the new

---

48 UN T/1396, July 10, 1958.

49 Statement by the Prime Minister before the Legislative Assembly on September 26, 1956, Bollettino Ufficiale, suppl. N° 1 al n° 11, November 13, 1956.

50 *Corriere della Somalia*, Ottobre 4, 1956.

51 A.A. Castagno, op. cit., p. 532.

government of favouritism towards the nomads.

The Legislative Assembly decided to limit the number of ministries to five: Domestic Affairs, Social Affairs, Economic Affairs, Financial Affairs and General Affairs. The ministers appointed were: Haji Mussa Bogor, Haji Farah Ali, Sheikh Ali Giumale, Salad Abdi Mohamoud and Mohamoud Abdinour 'Juje'. Those appointed as ministers were ill-prepared in terms of educational and professional experience. In fact, none of the new ministers, including the Prime Minister, had any formal education or administrative experience. Before entering politics, they were small businessmen, propelled to power by sheer ability. Given that the Assembly was composed largely of uneducated old-timers, it was indeed difficult to find anyone with even a pretence of the capability required of a minister. As a result, "when the Administrator decided to form a Somali government, it was with difficulty that six Somali members of the Legislative Assembly could be found, sufficiently capable to begin on the task of becoming Ministers: and if they resigned, today, it would prove almost impossible to find another six", comments a British source in Mogadisho[52]. None of the ministers knew what the job of a minister was. As a result, for the first few months, the former Italian directors, now operating as advisors, continued to run the departments. To each Somali minister a personal advisor was appointed: Gualtiero Benardelli for the Minister of Interior, Fulvio Rizzetto for the Minister of Social Affairs, Luigi Gasbarri for the Minister of Economic Affairs, Giulio Ricoveri for the Minister of Finance and Menotti Tomaselli for the Minister of General Affairs.[53] As the proverb says: "In the country of the blind, the one-eyed man is king". In the Somali context, a man of even limited ability was a great advantage in the company of those less able. The advisors would attend the meetings of the Council of Ministers, without the right to vote. Later on, in 1957, the advisors were replaced by Italian experts reporting directly to their Somali superiors. Somali cabinet ministers were heavily dependent on substantial advice, but this did not interfere with their independence of decision. The experts would do all the work and simply get the ministers to put their signatures on the papers. Attempts to appoint technocrats as ministers were strongly discouraged by the Administration on the grounds that such a move may adversely affect the efficiency of the public administration.[54]

With the establishment of the Somali government and the election of the

52 TNA FO 371/125675, Confidential report from the British Consulate General, Mogadisho, to FO January 4, 1957, p. 2.

53 Decreto amministrativo del 7 maggio 1956 n° 7, rep Bollettino Ufficiale.

54 *Corriere della Somalia*, Maggio 9, 1956.

Legislative Assembly, the Somali people acquired a wide measure of self-government and autonomy, consistent with the undertaking assumed by the Administering Authority to "foster the development of free political institutions and promote the development of the inhabitants of the Territory towards independence and give to the inhabitants of the Territory a progressively increasing participation in the various organs of government." In the same year, three important steps were taken: (a) dissolution of the 'Corpo di Sicurezza' followed by repatriation of the Italian military personnel and incorporation of the Somali components of the force into the police force; (b) establishment of the Somali Police Force under the command of Lt. Colonel Umberto Ripa di Meana[55], and (c) enactment of new judicial regulations, known as 'Ordinamento Giudiziario'[56]. Commenting on this important development, Vincenzo Mellana, who served in Somalia as State Counsel ('Avvocato Erariale'), wrote: "Thus principles have been put in place that are essentially consistent with the introduction into Somalia of a three-tier justice system like Italy's, while preserving both the ordinary and Islamic jurisdictions."[57]

When the Somali government was first established in 1956, the President of the Legislative Assembly happened to be from the Hawiye clan-family; the Prime Minister, too, was Hawiye. In the Council of Ministers, Hawiye members were the majority in the government formed by the Lega: "a party generally identified by members of other parties with the interest of the Darod clan-family." comments I.M. Lewis[58]. What Lewis, however, seems unaware of is that the nomination of Aden Abdulla and Abdullahi Issa to the top positions of State institutions came through a free and democratic election process. Notwithstanding the full confidence accorded to the two leaders, the "Hawiye predominance in the government and the party aroused dissatisfaction among the Darod which came to a head on a number of occasions and eventually contributed to the split within the party in 1958", comments Saadia Touval with a certain degree of accuracy.[59]

The leading members of the government, in addition to the President of the Legislative Assembly, were drawn from the central region of Hiran. The

55 Decreto n° 19 gennaio 1, 1956, Bollettino Ufficiale, suppl. n°1 al n°3, 8 marzo 1956.

56 An 'Ordinamento Giudiziario' of 118 articles was enacted to replace the old fascist regulations approved by D.L. no.1638 of June 1935.

57 Vincenzo Mellana, Ministero Affari Esteri: *L'Italia in Africa. L'amministrazione della giustizia nell'Africa Orientale,* Vincenzo Mellana, Ministero Affari Esteri: L'Italia in Africa. L'amministrazione della giustizia nell'Africa Orientale, Soc. Abete, Roma 1972, p. 452.

58 *'Modern Political Movements in Somaliland II'*, IM Lewis, Africa Journal of the International African Institute, vol. 28, no. 4 (Oct. 1958), p. 352.

59 Touval, op.cit., p. 89.

President of the Legislative Assembly and the Minister of Social Affairs were elected by the electoral district of Beledweyne, and the Minister of Economic Affairs came from the Bulo Burti district. The rise of Hawiye members was particularly irritating for the Majerten, who aspired to top leadership.

Not only did the Hawiye dominate the executive, they also made up the majority of the central committee of the ruling party. In 1954, for example, the president, vice-president and secretary general of the party were all from the Hawiye clan-family; more than two thirds of members of the central committee were Hawiye, six of them coming from the same sub-clan of Abgal.

Census of the population residing outside the municipal areas

One of the most difficult tasks, which required urgent attention, was the issue of the population census of the Trust Territory, particularly regarding rural dwellers. The issue had been a subject of intense debate since the early years of the trusteeship administration and before the 1956 general elections. However, while all the concerned parties, including the United Nations, the Administering Authority and the Somali political parties, were in full agreement as to the necessity of carrying out an official population census, they seemed to be lacking a clear idea of how such a complicated process could best be executed.

Acting under growing pressure, the government introduced a draft law in 1956 on population census limited to the rural population. The Somali Legislative Assembly approved the law with minor amendments on September 6, 1956 by 33 votes for, 25 against and 1 abstention[60]. In practice, the survey required by law was a mere registration of population rather than a real census of the population residing outside the municipal areas, and the process, as predicted, ended in total failure[61]. More than a census, it was considered to be the means of identifying those elements among the nomads entitled to vote in the political elections scheduled for 1959 and to whom an electoral certificate would be issued in order to overcome the unsatisfactory indirect system of voting through electoral representatives. Both AFIS and the Somali government made conscientious and costly efforts to secure a registration of the nomads and complete the exercise within the time limit assigned to it.

It was clearly an ambitious and complicated operation and many, including the

60 UN Doc. T 1311, April 22, 1957, par. 106, p. 45.

61 Legge n° 10 dicembre 30, 1956, 'Rilevazione demografica delle popolazioni extra-municipali', Bollettino Ufficiale, Ottobre 1, 1956.

United Nations, expressed reservations about its success from the outset. One obvious shortcoming was the absence of qualified personnel to carry out such a sophisticated operation. The census law provided for a registry office for the extra-municipal population to be set up in each district and for the census-taking operation to be completed in 12 months. Beginning January 10, 1957, it was to have been completed on December 31 of the same year. The exercise was to be conducted in three phases: direct survey carried out by salaried tribal chiefs acting as census-taking chiefs; registration and control carried out by the district officers; revision and inspection entrusted to regional officers. The documents to be compiled would be: the census list, compiled by the census takers, which would include various data (sex, name, patronymic name, paternal grandfather); and the population registers, filed on a card index system, which would be kept in the district offices.[62]

The law provided for a periodic notification, to be given every three months at least by the census takers to the district offices, of all modifications made to population registers as the result of births, deaths, movement of persons, marriage and divorce that took place within the ethnic group or areas allotted to each census taker for survey.

As predicted, and despite the efforts made by the Ministry of the Interior, the census count was not successful in all six regions. At the very outset, it was realized that the operation would be fraught with many serious difficulties, particularly if the chiefs did not give their full co-operation. In three regions (Benadir, Hiran and Upper Juba) there was a considerable degree of success; in the other regions (Majertenia, Mudug and Lower Juba), there was a failure to obtain accurate results[63]. The census, intended to allow the preparation of electoral rolls for an individual and secret vote to be given to every qualifying Somali during the next year, had been a farce.

The United Nations Advisory Council for Somalia (UNCAS) confirmed the failure of the census operation and reported: "It is significant to note that the most sparsely settled region, Majertenia, by November 1957 had recorded no fewer than 889,000 persons." Another UN document reported that the most sparsely settled regions together (Majertenia and Mudug) had listed more persons (1,295,000) than the rest of Somalia, where population was estimated to stand at 1,070,000[64]. The only known census conducted in 1931 showed that

62 UN Doc. T 1311, April 22, 1957, par. 106, pp. 45-46.

63 Ibid., par. 77, p. 29.

64 Ibid.

the lowest population density was registered in Majertenia and Mudug because of the aridity of the terrain (0.8 persons per km^2), while the highest level of density was registered in the inter-riverine areas (3.5 persons per km^2)[65]. According to analysts, the failure of this exercise was caused by "reasons of prestige and [...] failure to understand the significance of census taking. Chiefs in the nomadic areas were eager to report impressive numbers of tribesmen. Many of them filed lists containing the names of non-existing tribesmen."[66]

The emperor's call

Although Ethiopian claims over Somalia had in the past failed to gain support at the United Nation, Ethiopia had not abandoned her desire to incorporate Somalia into her vast empire. In fact, while negotiations between Ethiopia and Italy on the demarcation of the border were going on, Emperor Haile Selassie, between 2 and 29 August 1956, visited the cities of Gabridaharre, Callafo and Dagahbour, all sited in the Ogaden region. He took this opportunity to remind the local population that they "are by race, colour, blood and customs, part of the great Ethiopian family" and invited the ethnic Ogadens to combat what he called all kinds of propaganda aimed at undermining the freedom and unity of Ethiopia – a veiled jab at those calling for Greater Somalia.

In the second part of his speech, the emperor addressed the inhabitants of Somalia under Italian trusteeship, exhorting them to follow the example of the Eritreans who had rejoined the motherland and were now satisfied that unity is force. With regard to the idea of the Greater Somalia scheme, the emperor stated: "We believe that all the Somali people are economically linked to Ethiopia, and consequently, we do not believe that a State of that kind could survive by remaining outside and separated from Ethiopia."[67]

The Prime Minister of Somalia reacted to the emperor's statement with a measured speech given before the Legislative Assembly on September 25, 1956, in which he said: "It is clear, honourable colleagues, that reference is to a Somalo–Ethiopian federation along the lines of that between Eritrea and Ethiopia. And it is on this point that I feel obliged to say immediately, in the name of the government I represent, and in the name of all of you, supreme representatives of this country, that the Somali people do not share the

65 Malagodi, op., cit., p. 30.
66 Ware, op. cit., p. 178.
67 Speech delivered by the Emperor at Qabridaharre, August 1956.

representations or the aims of the Emperor of Ethiopia. I also feel obliged to say that, while the Somali people truly and firmly wish for friendly and cordial relations with Ethiopia, first of all they wish equally firmly and absolutely for liberty and absolute independence, which are irreconcilable with any form of federation with anyone. On the question of 'Greater Somalia' we wish to express our warmest good wishes for it because people of the same race, same language and same religion can soon be united under a single, free and independent state."[68] The Prime Minister's speech was followed by a more radical motion passed in the Legislative Assembly, which ran as follows:

"The people of Somalia consider any idea of federation irreconcilable with their own aspirations to the most absolute form of liberty and independence and declare henceforth that they will not accept any move aimed at putting such a sacred principle under question. The Somali people also wish to make known that they do not share the opinion expressed by the Emperor of Ethiopia about community of race, blood and language with the Ethiopian population which might be claimed to justify the federation which was hinted at. The people of Somalia vow that, as from this moment, 'Greater Somalia' shall become a concrete and shining reality to unite under."[69] The Legislative Assembly urged the Italian Administration to forward the motion approved by the Assembly to the Italian government and to the United Nations.[70]

In 1957, the Ethiopian government sought to accommodate the Ogadeni by allocating $7 million for Ogaden development, and opened several schools that taught in Amharic, the national language mostly unknown to Somalis[71]. Further steps were taken a few years later to appease the Somalis when Addis Abeba named Somali advisors to the Amhara governor of Ogaden, appointing Somali governors for three of the four regions and for the twenty-three districts under administration. Abdurahman Sheikh Abdi, a nephew of the rebel Sayyid Mohamed Abdulla, was later made Vice-minister of the Interior. However, as Harold Marcus notes, "the Ethiopian government could not overcome the pull of Somali nationalism."[72]

Once more, towards the end of November 1963, in a radio broadcast message, Emperor Haile Selassie invited the Ogaden people to come out of the bush and

68 TNA FO 371/118710; ASMAE, AFIS, box 9, file 6, Text of Prime Minister's speech before the Legislative Assembly on September 25, 1956.

69 Ibid., Declaration by the President of the Legislative Assembly.

70 ASMAE, AFIS, box 9, file 9, Letter from Anzilotti to Aden Abdulla, September 26, 1956.

71 Marcus, Harold G. *A History of Ethiopia*, Berkeley, University of California Press 1994, p. 94.

72 Ibid.

collaborate with the government in the economic and social development of their region to defeat what he called 'certain elements incited by foreign forces.' In the message the emperor invited the Ogaden to let him know the needs of their region, but predictably enough those needs did not include the need to be left free. Commenting on the emperor's pronouncement, Aden Abdulla notes in his journals: "The emperor seems to be naive (or playing dumb) if he believes anyone will listen to him. The emperor should know the Somali proverb: 'only water and food can quench a thirsty and hungry person'."[73]

On the same subject, in 1948, the Foreign Minister of Ethiopia, Ato Aklilu Habt Wolde, referring to the Somali question, said: "I have pointed out the long-standing bonds of racial origin, the sentiments of culture, religion and economic interdependence, and the mutual struggle against Italian aggression on which my government has based its case in regard to Somalia. Furthermore, it should be remembered that the war with Italy commenced with an invasion from Italian Somaliland."[74]

Somalization process and its problems

One of the obligations Italy had assumed under the Trusteeship Agreement was to gradually increase the participation of the indigenous population in the various branches of the administration. The efforts of the Administering Authority to accelerate the training of Somalis for advancement in the administrative service had taken the form of a special education programme designed to provide Somalis with what was often termed as a broad cultural background.[75]

A School of Political Administration, where administrative staff and others took courses after working hours, was established in Mogadisho in September 1950[76]. Candidates for admission were selected through submission of an essay written in Arabic, English or Italian.[77]

One hundred and seven candidates sat the written test: 75 chose Italian as their medium of expression, 22 Arabic and 10 English. Of those who sat for the entry examination, 39 were successful. According to their political affiliations, 20 belonged to the Lega dei Giovani Somali, 16 to the Conferenza, 5 to Hizbia Dighil

73 Diary Aden Abdulla, December 3, 1963.

74 *News Times and Ethiopian News*, August 14, 1948.

75 UN Doc. T/1143 and corr. 1, p. 8.

76 Ordinanza n° 61 del 1° ottobre 1950, 'Istituzione di una scuola di preparazione politico-amministrativa', Bollettino Ufficiale Afis, n°7.

77 *Corriere della Somalia*, Ottobre 26, 1950.

and Mirifle, 3 to the Lega Progressista Somala (LPS), 5 to the Unione Africana, 4 to Jimiya, 1 was neutral and 2 were Arabs[78]. A different figure was given by the Lega, who put the number of candidates at 120, about 100 of which belonging to their party[79]. The training programme was chiefly designed to train administrative staff. In the eyes of many, however, this much-advertised school was in reality nothing but an adult night school of a special nature, with a glorified name. "I do not think it needs to be taken seriously as a nursery of future Somali statesmen", commented a British source in Mogadisho[80]. The students' schedule comprised between two and three hours' study per day, from 6pm to 9pm, designed to turn individuals with no formal education into top executives in a very short time. The school provided a three-year course ranging over such subjects as history, international law, public law, Islamic institutions, elements of civil and criminal law and of public financing and accounting, political and economic geography.

The poor level of preparation achieved by students after three years vindicated the school's critics, many of whom expressed reservations about the curriculum taught and the manner in which it was delivered. At a certain point, the students'association ('Allievi Scuola di Preparazione Politica Amministrativa') made representations to the Administration about the poor teaching methods and the valuable time wasted because of the absence of teachers – most of them were full-time staff of other branches of the Administration, but some ran their own businesses or worked as employees of private firms. In a petition addressed to the Trusteeship Council, the students also complained of the limited time at their disposal to seriously pursue their studies: they all worked from 7am to 3pm for the Administration before attending the courses starting at 5pm[81]. The first group of eight graduates of the School of Political Administration were sent to Italy for further study.

Though the Italians pointed with pride to the training schools they had opened for the preparation of the future Somali elite, the level of preparation of the Somali students, after they received degrees both at home and in Italy, was equivalent to secondary school education rather than to a university or even a high school degree.

Most of the students trained to be the future elite of the territory after independence were in their forties, had no previous formal education and were

78 TNA FO 371/90528 Report from British Consulate Mogadisho to FO January 5, 1951.
79 Ibid., letter from Acting Secretary General of the Lega to the envoy at Lake Success, November 3, 1950.
80 TNA FO 371/90328, secret report, from British Consulate Mogadisho, to FO, January 3, 1951.
81 UN Doc. T/PET.11/99 signed by Ahmed Shire Lawaha and 22 other students, October 4, 1951.

handicapped by poor knowledge of the Italian language. According to some analysts, the School of Public Administration was an instrument used by AFIS to influence the students – many of them Lega militants – rather than providing serious training opportunities for future top civil servants. During his tenure as Prime Minister, Abdirashid Ali Sharmarke, who himself had graduated from that school, expressed his disappointment over the poor level of training and command of the Italian language of the Italian-trained civil servants, compared to their British-trained colleagues from the north, and deplored the fact that few of them were capable of writing an official letter in good Italian.[82]

The United Nations also joined in criticism of the way the school was organized. For Mr Cebes Haberskey, Principal Secretary of the UNACS, "The School of Political Science was something organized very quickly and not seriously. It produced too many 'dottori', too many dropped out."[83] The Somalization process advanced slowly during 1950-1954 because, at the beginning of the mandate, there were no Somalis well enough trained to take up certain executive responsibilities within the Trusteeship Administration. For this reason the Administration, at the beginning, followed a slow and cautious policy of 'Somalization', mostly implemented by the appointment of veteran clerks to minor posts. The customs and postal services were assigned to Somali personnel. The first Somali postmaster was put in charge of the Brava Post Office in 1951. "Such an important appointment marks the beginning of a process by which all posts of the Administration will be occupied by Somalis", the *Corriere della Somalia* wrote triumphantly.[84]

However, by 1954 the Somalization process was moving at a good pace, to the point that Martino was able to report to the Territorial Council on March 8, 1954 on the progress made. "The process of the appointment of Somali elements in the managerial positions of the public administration has made progress. As of today, there are 6 Somali heads of districts and 15 heads of sub-districts, an important achievement if we consider that there are a total of 30 districts in the Territory. [...] In the police force, forty-eight police stations out of sixty-nine are under the command of Somali officers and NCOs. Almost all postal and customs offices are run by Somalis. Five Somali officers are receiving on-

82 Diary Aden Abdulla, February 10, 1963.

83 Interview released by Haberskey to Angelo Del Boca on June 26, 1960, reported in Del Boca, op. cit., p. 287.

84 TNA FO 371/90328, secret report of September 24, 1951, from the British Consulate Mogadisho to FO,

the-job training as assistants to Italian directors in different branches of the public administration. If we consider that we are now halfway to the country's independence date, these data are encouraging. The remaining five years will see a further acceleration in the Somalization process as the training of young people through the various types of disciplines and through on-the-job experience is being developed."[85]

The training and Somalization process was not only criticized for its poor results, but also denounced as unavailable to large segments of the population. In fact, in a petition addressed to the Italian Prime Minister[86], the Central Committee of the HDM, together with the Territorial Councillors of the party, complained vigorously about the Somalization process which, they said, was not giving them their legitimate share in the police, security and civil services. In the petition, they asked for equal participation in the administration of the country and for the appointing of qualified elements of their group, especially in the security and police force. The absence of elements of their ethnic group in the police ranks raised fears within the HDM that the political elections scheduled for 1956 might take place in an atmosphere which was neither free nor fair.

The Italian Foreign Ministry was inundated with messages denouncing AFIS's allegedly biased policy against HDM. "Current Somalization criteria do not have our consent. We urge equal treatment be given to elements of our group, who represent an active part of the population of the territory", reads one of these messages from the HDM[87]. Similar messages of protest, from Dighil and Mirifle chiefs and notables in Dinsor, Kismayo and Bur Hakaba[88] respectively, were submitted to the attention of the Italian Ministry of Foreign Affairs in Rome.

It appears from the messages that the Dighil and Mirifle population did not trust the Somali police: they were particularly worried about the role of this force, whose component elements were largely driven by the nomadic population of the country (all loyal to the Lega), and who they thought would play a major part in rigging the outcome of the 1956 elections. "Owing to lack of tribal balance in the police force, the coming political elections could not be free and fair" was the concluding remarks of all these messages sent to the Italian authorities.

85 E. Martino, op. cit., p. 131).

86 T/PET.11/583, 26 August 1955.

87 ASMAE, AP, 1955, file 1037, telegram no. 12310, of 12.8.1955 from the HDM Committee in Lugh Ferrandi to the Italian Ministry of Foreign Affairs.

88 ASMAE, AP, 1955, file 1037, telegram no. 111305, of 13.7.1955, from the chiefs and notables of Dinsor to the Italian Foreign Ministry; telegram no. 11924, dated 26.7.1955); Awdheegle, telegram no. 11936pc of 26.7.1955 and telegram no. 11142 of 13.7. 1955.

After independence, the HDM made similar complaints to the President of the Republic, emphasizing the poor share of representatives of their ethnic group within the civil administration as well as in the high ranking positions in the army and police forces[89]. However, it would be misleading to conclude that this lack of tribal balance in the armed forces was the product of government policy meant to discriminate against the Dighil and Mirifle communities. As early as 1952, AFIS reported that the only region where it had proved impossible to fill the quotas for civil service and police appointment was the Upper Juba, predominantly inhabited by Rahanweyn, known for being less disposed to join government service. "In the southern regions of Somalia, formerly Italian Somaliland, the Darod, who live in the poorer areas, are more readily disposed to join government service than are the slightly better-situated Hawiye; and among the agricultural Dighil and Rahanweyn the proportion of those interested in joining government service is the lowest of all", wrote Saadia Touval.[90]

As part of the Somalization process, in 1955, Piero Franca, AFIS Secretary General, appointed a young Somali, Mohamed Sheikh Hassan, to the important and highly complex position of head of his personal secretariat: this raised some eyebrows, especially in Italian circles[91]. Other senior appointments followed, including that of Abdirashid Ali Sharmarke as assistant in the legal department—"He was regarded as the most able of the Administration's Somali employees", comments a British source[92]. By 1956, the Somalization process had reached its zenith: all heads of districts were Somalis. The first Somali district commissioners appointed in 1955 were: Ali Shiddo Abdi (Beledweyne), Ali Omar Sheegoow (Afmedu), Osman Omar Sheegoow (Obbia), Aden Shire Jama (Lugh Ferrandi), Issa Eimoi (Balad), Ahmed Sheikh Mohamed Issa (Jilib), Bile Mussa Sciamal (Margherita), Hassan Mohamed Hassan 'Waqoyi' (Villaggio Duca degli Abruzzi) and Mugne A. Sheikh (Bardera). The first Somali prefect (provincial governor) was Hassan Nour Elmi, appointed on June 17, 1955 as Prefect of Hiran.[93]

On the Somalization process, Ambassador Anzilotti had this to say: "The Somalization process I announced on June 23 last year before the Territorial Council has been surpassed by the chain of events. All the districts and all the

89 Diary Aden Abdulla, April 12, 1962.

90 Touval, op. cit., p. 86, 197n1.

91 TNA FO 371/113455, confidential letter from British Consulate Mogadisho to FO, June 22, 1955.

92 Ibid.

93 Rapport du gouvernment italien à l'Assemblée Generale des Nations Unies sur l'administration de la Somalie placée sous la tutelle de l'Italie, 1955, p. 17.

regions are currently run, or will shortly be run, by Somali officials."[94] By the end of 1958, Somali personnel controlled fifteen of the nineteen government departments. The other four, mainly technical, such as the Veterinary Department in the Ministry of Social Affairs, and the Department of Foreign Exchange and Foreign Trade in the Ministry of Financial Affairs, remained under Italian control.[95]

The speed of this political transformation provided new perspectives on a wide range of problems and raised a new question as to whether Somalia was going too slow or too fast. The United Nations Advisory Council for Somalia (UNACS), while commending the Administering Authority's efforts in establishing a completely Somali civil service, nevertheless expressed concerns that the rate of withdrawal of Italian personnel may have a negative impact on the efficient functioning of the various services[96]. Other observers believed that the early withdrawal of Italian personnel was dictated by financial considerations. "For the Administration it was a way to reduce the administrative costs involved and shun all actions that could embroil it in the internal affairs", comments a British report.[97]

It should be noted that the police force was 'Somalized' earlier than the other branches of the civil administration. In 1958 a Somali officer, Lt. Colonel Mohamed Abshir, was appointed chief of police[98]. The new commander was an ethnic Darod and so, to attenuate growing tribal feelings, a Hawiye officer, Daud Abdulla, had to be promoted to the same rank as Abshir and appointed vice-commander of the force. In addition to poor training, another problem posed by the Somalization process was the appointment of officials to their own tribal districts, which made them naturally subject to communal pressure, particularly in inter-clan disputes. As Castagno put it, "even those Somalis who have taken the plunge into modernity have found themselves inextricably bound with their diya-paying group."[99] Another author, writing on the same subject, wrote: "Even the most westernized Somalis, the most ardent nationalists, who violently oppose tribalism, are not oblivious to their tribal connections."[100] The answer was to post

94 Extract of statement made on April 30, 1956 during the inauguration ceremony of the first session of the Legislative Assembly, elected following the first general elections in Somalia of March 1956.

95 UN Doc. T/1444, 14 April 1959, p. 13.

96 UN Doc. T/1372, April 22, 1958, par.66, p. 26.

97 TNA FO 371/131457, report from the British Consulate in Mogadisho to FO February 25, 1958.

98 *Corriere della Somalia,* Dicembre 16, 1958.

99 A.A. Castagno, op. cit., p. 512.

100 Touval, op. cit., p. 86.

them to districts where tribal loyalty would not clash with duty, but this rule did not always prove possible to strictly observe.

Chapter VII

HAJI MOHAMED ELECTED PRESIDENT OF THE PARTY

The first ministerial crisis

Haji Mohamed became the first president of his party in 1947, a position he was elected to in successive years up to August 1952, the date on which he left for Egypt. During his stay in Egypt, which lasted some five years, he used the political platform offered to him by the Egyptian government in Cairo to accuse the Somali government of being too close to the West, and to Italy in particular, and doing little to realize the national goal of reconstituting Greater Somalia. His anti-Western and anti-AFIS tirades through the Egyptian media, including radio broadcasts, were closely monitored by the Italian Embassy in Cairo, which regularly reported to Mogadisho and Rome on the utterances of the Lega leader.[1]

This hostile propaganda against the Somali government, at variance with the official party policy conducted in a foreign country, predictably irritated the ruling party. However, despite his departure from the party line, Haji Mohamed was elected president of the party in 1957 even before his return from Egypt. This was seen by analysts as a distinct victory for the pro-Egyptian wing of the party.[2]

A brief illustration of the tense atmosphere which followed the election of

1 Telespresso no. 514216/420 of 30.3.1954, from Martino to Foreign Minister.

2 Aden Abdulla became vice-president.

the new president is in order. The first signs of friction between the central committee of the party and the newly elected president emerged immediately when, after his election, the latter was instructed to return to Mogadisho. He replied by saying that he needed some time to take examinations in the studies he had been pursuing and also that he would like to go to Syria and Bahrain and to other countries in the Middle East on behalf of the party in order to get funds, etc[3]. He was granted only the time absolutely necessary to take his examinations (a month or little more), but before going anywhere, in the name of the party or of Somalia, he was required to retake the oath of office and become president. Not only did Haji Mohamed not return to Somalia until December 4, 1958, four months after he had been elected, but contrary to the will of the Central Committee, he also travelled to the countries he had said he would visit. "He finally arrived on December 4, the day after the Prime Minister and the President of the Legislative Assembly had left for Addis Abeba, to receive an uproarious welcome from a clearly organized crowd in which anti-American banners were prominent."[4]

Available records show that, prior to his departure for Egypt, his attitude towards the new Italian administration had seemed to be showing all signs of moderation and openness. In fact, on May 26, 1950, during an official reception held at the official mansion of the chief administrator to welcome Giuseppe Brusasca, in the presence of scores of other political and traditional leaders, Haji Mohamed, speaking on behalf of his party, made the following remarks: "Your Excellency, on behalf of the Lega dei Giovani Somali, I have the honour to extend to you our most sincere welcome to Somalia anticipating that your visit will mark the beginning of an era of peace and understanding between Somalia and AFIS. Your Excellency, the Lega would like to point out that it has as its prime objective the interest of Somalia and the Somalis and consequently AFIS may fully count on the Lega's support in all what is being done for the interest of the territory. Once more, you are welcome."[5]

British sources described him as a moderate politician. "By the middle of August 1952, Haji Mohamed had left for Cairo and with him went a good opportunity of influencing the moderate members of the party," British sources

3 TNA FO 371/131465, Central Committee letter of June 25, 1958 addressed to the branch sections and explaining the reasons that made the expulsion of the former President necessary.

4 TNA FO 371/125676 Confidential report, monthly summary of October and November 1957 from the British Consulate Mogadisho to FO.

5 *Corriere della Somalia*, Maggio 27, 1950.

in Mogadisho commented.[6]

By the time Haji had returned from Egypt, the country had changed a great deal. There was a functioning government, led by his own party, in charge of the domestic affairs of the territory; his party held the majority of seats in the Legislative Assembly; the process of Somalization had gone faster than many had predicted and the political atmosphere between AFIS and the Lega was one of co-operation, with a focus on the target date of independence and a smooth transfer of power even ahead of the date originally sanctioned by the United Nations.

However, Haji had returned from Egypt a much-changed person, at odds not only with the Administering Authority, but also with members of his own party who had elected him as their leader. His first criticism was launched against those he called the 'Italian hyenas' and those who had accused of serving their selfish aims – a reference to the two Lega leaders who had gone on a visit to Ethiopia. The Prime Minister and the President of the Legislative Assembly had been invited to visit Ethiopia by Emperor Haile Selassie. "His 5 years in Egypt had left a deep mark on him and, for the time being, he was unable to see things except through Egyptian-made glasses," comments a British source in Mogadisho.[7]

The newly elected president of the Lega soon found himself out of step with the thinking of mainstream party members and the government. He started delivering inflammatory statements against the AFIS and the government, accusing them of 'betrayal' of the party principles. Since his return from Egypt he had been a thorn in the Administration's side and an embarrassment to those party fellows who did not share his radical views. Haji Mohamed's attitude also seriously challenged the efforts made by the Italian government for a smooth transfer of power to the future independent Somali State.

Taking advantage of the absence of the Prime Minister and the President of the Legislative Assembly, on mission abroad, Haji demanded that Acting Prime Minister Sheikh Ali Jim'ale, Minister of Social Affairs[8], consult him on all State affairs. The Acting Prime Minister refused to have anything to do with him and, after consultations with Haji Farah (Minister of Economic Affairs) and Mohamoud Juje (Minister of General Affairs), went to see Haji Mussa Bogor, the Minister of the Interior, to enlist his support against interference from Haji

6 TNA FO 371/96646 confidential report of September 6, 1952 from the British Consulate Mogadisho to FO.

7 TNA FO 371/131462, secret telegram of March 1958 from British Consulate Mogadisho to the FO.

8 Decreto Amministrativo n 3 rep; Bollettino Ufficiale della Somalia, n° 1, 3 dicembre 1957.

Mohamed. The Minister of the Interior reportedly pleaded sickness, declined to intervene, and asked not to be disturbed, "although he had spent three hours the previous evening with Haji Mohamed", reveals a British intelligence report[9]. Sheikh Ali then called on Acting Administrator Piero Franca to tender his resignation; the Ministers of Finance and General Affairs followed suit, albeit reluctantly. Franca asked them to stay on in their posts until the Prime Minister and the President of the Legislative Assembly returned to Somalia.

On returning to Mogadisho, the President of the Legislative Assembly hastened to meet with the Minister of the Interior, who had been 'hiding in hospital' since 3 December, and demanded his written promise of support for government policy – a request the Minister rejected. According to British sources in Mogadisho, the Minister, at the last minute, decided against travelling with the President of the National Assembly and the Prime Minister to Addis Abeba at the invitation of His Majesty the Emperor of Ethiopia, giving medical reasons as a justification for not showing up. The Prime Minister, on his part, demanded and obtained loyalty pledges from his other ministers; all agreed except the Minister of Finance, Salad Abdi, a relative of Haji Mussa's. The Prime Minister, reacting to the attitude of the two ministers, took personal control of the internal and financial affairs and, without consulting the Minister of the Interior, published in the official newspaper an order for the dismissal or transfer to remote provinces of all prefects and sub-prefects known to be sympathetic to Haji Mohamed and Minister Haji Mussa[10]. The Prefect of Benadir, Hassan Nour Elmi, was transferred to Majertenia Province, while Nour Ahmed 'Castelli', Prefect of Lower Juba, was put on reserve.[11]

The Acting Administrator's suggestion to the Prime Minister to resign in order to ease the tension and then form a new cabinet was thought to be counterproductive[12]. After some time, Franca decided to approve the orders the Prime Minister had given, provided that the latter persuaded Haji Mussa voluntarily to resign from office or, failing that, obtained a vote of confidence from the Legislative Assembly.

In a bid to solve the crisis, the Parliamentary group of the Lega, together with a group of tribal elders, met on the night of 29 December to examine the

9 TNA FO 371/131459, confidential report from British Consulate Mogadisho to FO, December 23, 1957.

10 Ibid., Confidential report n. 25 (1018/57) from British Consulate Mogadisho to Selwyn Lloyd, December 23, 1957.

11 Decreto amministrativo n° 36 del 18 dicembre 1958, 'Movimento di prefetti', Bollettino Ufficiale, n°3, 1° marzo 1958.

12 Diary Aden Abdulla, January, 2, 1958.

situation with a view to finding a way out of the crisis. According to British sources, this meeting lasted until 03:30 hours and was resumed at 09:30 hours on the 30th December. The same British sources indicate that "by 20:00 hours, Haji Mussa Bogor agreed to resume his duties, provided there was no interference in his department by the Prime Minister and that the Prefects of Kismayo and Mogadisho whose transfer to other posts had been published in the press were allowed to remain in their posts."[13] The Prime Minister ceded on these points and went to inform the Acting Administration that the crisis had been resolved. However, the ministerial crisis may have temporarily been patched up but the deepened national crisis and tribal antagonism towards the government persisted for a long time to come. Relations between Darod and Hawiye had become tense on account of the bad relations between the Prime Minister (Hawiye) and his Minister of the Interior (Darod).

Western concerns

The Americans, who had been closely following the growing and repeated anti-western utterances of the President of the Lega, saw this new development as likely to lead the pro-Western wing of the ruling party to lose ground to the pro-Egyptian faction, with consequent loss of Western prestige in the Horn of Africa. The Americans and their Western allies feared, in particular, that Haji's newfound political power might pave the way for Soviet penetration in the Territory. These fears prompted an immediate meeting between the American Consul General in Mogadisho, Mr. Lynch, and Haji Mussa Bogor, the Minister of the Interior. The American Consul General raised with the Minister the possibility of introducing anti-communist literature into Somalia to combat both communism and positive neutralism. However, the Minister appeared not to share the American's concerns, ruling out the view that communism represented a real menace to Somalia. He stated that any hasty introduction of such material into the territory would only serve to offer the Somalis the opportunity to explore non-Western values and alternatives. The Somali Minister maintained the view that "potential Ethiopian aggression against Somalia, coupled with American military assistance to Ethiopia, has already aroused Somali suspicion with respect to the American role in Horn affairs, which could perhaps supply the necessary

13 TNA FO 371/131459, confidential report from British Consulate Mogadisho to FO, December 31, 1957.

environment for breeding anti-Western sentiments."[14] In the words of Okbazghi Yohannes, "from the American vantage point, the Minister's underestimation of Haji Mohamed's powerful pro-Egyptian attitude and pro-neutrality orientation was less than reassuring."[15]

As an orator, Haji Mohamed was a firebrand and chose to attack the Italians with such virulence that his speeches often led to riots and posed danger to the life of Italians and other foreigners in the Territory. Attempts to persuade him to moderate his utterances had failed and the relations between Haji Mohamed and the government further deteriorated when he made damaging statements at the African-Asian People's Solidarity Conference in Cairo in 1958 in his capacity as leader of his party. He is reported to have made an appeal to the States participating in the Conference to cover the deficit of the Somali annual budget in lieu of the colonialists, a clear reference to the Italians, to avoid the possibility that "the colonialists will ask us for part of our sovereignty in addition to requesting us to join the European Economic Market."[16] This statement and other criticisms he launched against the Western powers were considered out of line with the official policy of the ruling party and the government.

According to police intelligence reports, Haji Mohamed, in a public speech he made at the Afgooye section of the ruling party on February 1, 1958, incited the Somalis to "retake forcibly the agricultural land the Italians confiscated from the Somali farmers."[17] This kind of statement and other similar provocative utterances, typical of the President of the Lega, led Anzilotti, the Administrator, to conclude that this was the prelude for a vast programme of nationalization of foreign property in Somalia, to be introduced soon after independence[18]. On another occasion, Haji Mohamed is quoted as inciting the public to violence: "If you do not shed blood you will not be able to secure the independence of your country." Pamphlets were circulated in Mogadisho extolling Haji Mohamed's political virtues while accusing the Lega leadership of sycophancy and sheepish capitulation to the West.[19]

As mentioned earlier, the Italians were not the only target of the Lega leader's tirades after his return from Egypt. His criticism put the Western powers most

14 DOS 777, 00/1-2858, 'Election of Haji Mohamed', cited in Okbazghi, op. cit., p. 209.

15 Ibid.

16 Diary Aden Abdulla, January 22, 1958.

17 ASMAE, AFIS, box 9, file 2. Excerpt of series of speeches made by Haji Mohamed Hussein from December 1957 to 1958 and recorded by the police.

18 Diary Aden Abdulla, February 6, 1958.

19 DOS 777, 00/8-257, 'Election of Haji Mohamed', as quoted in Yohannes, op. cit., p. 208.

involved in Somali affairs on alert. The British government showed early signs of preoccupation in relation to the Lega President's growing attacks against the West and was the first to seek a common strategy with Italy, France and the United States of America, the three western powers with historical ties with Somalia. A concerted action was necessary in order to avoid an unceremonious exit of the West from Somalia because of Egyptian pressure on a 'shaky' Italian Administration.[20]

The British consul in Mogadisho, who was closely monitoring the internal political situation in Somalia, had this to say: "I am afraid that the situation created here by the President of the Lega, is going to have immediate repercussions on our relations with Somalia, whether or not the Administration and the government can control the widespread agitations he has caused since his return from Egypt."[21] Unlike the Italians, the British seemed to have overestimated the ability of the newly elected Lega President to greatly influence and determine the future course of events in Somalia. The seemingly exaggerated British assessment of the situation is reflected in a telegram from their Consul General in Mogadisho to the Foreign Office. The telegram reads: "Should the local situation develop in a way such as to render Italian position in any way untenable, could the United Nations be persuaded to appoint a Somali, say Aden Abdulla, Administrator for Somalia for the remaining period until December 1960. This would give a breathing space until then, rendering the anti-colonialist campaign of the President of the Lega nonsense and effectively preventing him until 1960 from irresponsible action even if he manages to get himself elected as Head of State."[22]

The Italians, however, though admitting the existence of the problem, did not see Haji Mohamed as a real threat to future Western interest in Somalia. Acting Administrator Piero Franca believed that the 'venom' of Haji Mohamed's propaganda would "produce no durable effects; accordingly, the best way of dealing with him was to take no action as any disciplinary action against him would likely provoke violent repercussions and push the government to espouse the President's nationalistic ideas."[23]

However, Britain and Italy, recognizing the political and strategic importance

20 TNA FO 371/131460 confidential report from the British Consulate Mogadisho to FO, December 28, 1957.

21 Ibid.

22 Ibid., telegram from British Consulate Mogadisho to FO, London, February 6, 1958.

23 Ibid., report dated January 27, 1957 from the British Consulate General in Mogadisho to the FO, covering conversations between Minister Franca and the British Consul General.

of Somalia, agreed to be more vigilant and to co-operate closely in preventing a possible expansion of Egyptian and Soviet influence in the Horn of Africa after the Territory's independence. "It is clear that the Egyptians are having success, and that the 'progressive' pro-Western wing of the Lega is losing ground to the pro-Egyptian faction who will probably get the upper hand at the forthcoming elections", reads a British document[24]. The West thus felt it was necessary to make every effort to influence events in Somalia in a favourable direction, in order to counterbalance Soviet interest, likely to considerably increase in the area.[25]

The common Anglo-Italian strategy on Somalia was discussed in three rounds of talks, the first held in Rome in February 1958, the second in London in April, and the third again in Rome in May of the same year.

In the course of the talks held in London, Italian Undersecretary for Foreign Affairs Alberto Folchi, who was leading his country's delegation, is reported as saying that "while Somalia's relations with the West have been cordial in the past, there has been a deterioration in the internal situation after 1956 as a result of the Egyptian influence and the activities of the 'extremists' in the Lega dei Giovani Somali stirred up by the President, Haji Mohamed Hussein." Folchi was convinced that 'assurances' by the West about continued provision after independence of the economic aid needed by Somalia, estimated at $6 million, was the most effective way of supporting the 'moderates' in the elections of 1959. However, Folchi made it clear to his British counterpart that Italian aid to Somalia would be contingent upon the 'moderates' returning to power at the forthcoming elections. "If the 'extremists' gain power, he stated, "aid assistance would obviously be reconsidered."[26]

Nevertheless, the British representative present at the discussions, Mr Ross, seemed not to be in full agreement with Folchi, and pointed out one inconvenience in making an offer of economic aid conditional on a friendly Somali government remaining in power after 1960. He cited as an example the case of Azhari in the Sudan, who was anti-Western before he became Prime Minister but "modified his ideas when in power."[27] At the end of their successive discussions on the Horn of Africa in general, and Somalia in particular, Britain and Italy agreed "to take action to retain the area in the Western orbit and to prevent its sliding under

24 Ibid., telegram from FO London to Washington, February 3, 1958.

25 TNA FO 371/131463, record of Anglo-Italian discussions on the Horn of Africa on April 1 and 2, 1958 at London.

26 Ibid.

27 Ibid.

foreign influence."[28]

However, while the Western powers agreed, in principle, to give economic incentives to the moderate wing of the ruling party in time to influence the elections scheduled for 1959, there was no consensus over the portion each of them was required to contribute in the financial and economic support to Somalia. The Italians maintained that they could not do more than keep up the banana subsidy (amounting to $2 m) and provide technical assistance (amounting to $1m), while hoping that somebody else – in fact the United States of America – would find the remaining $3 m. The British urged the Italians to shoulder a substantial part of the aid to Somalia[29], to bear the greater part of the $6 million burden, half from budget deficit and half as development. Although the US might be able to provide some technical assistance, there were practical as well as constitutional difficulties over obtaining congressional approval for direct budget subsidy. A British contribution was not expected in view of Britain's heavy commitments elsewhere in the world[30]. Furthermore, the British were already committed to spending in the Somaliland Protectorate a sum equal to the subsidy needed in Somalia[31]. The Americans, like the British, exerted pressure on the Italians to bear the greater part of Somali economic aid, especially the budget deficit. France expressed interest but made it clear that there was no question of contributing any money, although they 'might possibly offer some *bourses d'études*, their interest being in the Addis Abeba–Djibouti railway which they hoped to operate as a joint French–Ethiopian concern.[32]

Egypt tried to challenge the Western strategy, particularly that of the United States, which they saw as "taking up the former colonial positions."[33] Eventually, convinced that the means available to them to confront the West were very limited, the Egyptians sought solace in proposing the creation of a Somali fund at the United Nations, with multilateral contributions, from which Somalia could receive economic assistance while avoiding being heavily dependent on one of the two blocs. However, owing to scant interest and lack of funds, this move, too, failed, and the Egyptian proposal was doomed to vanish before seeing the light.

28 Ibid., Anglo-Italian discussions on Somalia at the Palazzo Chigi, March 4, 1958.
29 Ibid., telegram from the Foreign Office, London, no. 434, April 1, 1958.
30 Ibid., second Anglo-Italian discussions on the Horn of Africa on April 1-2, 1958.
31 TNA FO371/131460 telegram from FO to Washington, February 19, 1958.
32 TNA FO 371/131463, secret report from British Embassy, Rome, to FO, London, April 18, 1958.
33 Nae, Mfa b, 49, f 72/1; letter n. 17/2/1/S from Mohamed Hassan El-Zeyyat to Cairo, January 10, 1958, as reported in Morone, L'ultima colonia: come l'Italia è tornata in Africa 1950-1960, laterza & Figli, 2011, p. 12.

Italy threatens to relinquish the trusteeship mandate

While the moderate faction of the Lega, led by Aden Abdulla and Abdullahi Issa, had softened its early hostile position towards the Administering Authority, especially after the political and municipal elections of 1954 and 1956, the more radical faction of the party, led by its new President, continued its virulent attacks not only on the Administering Authority but also on the government. The criticisms were levelled especially at the President of the Legislative Assembly and the Prime Minister, both from the Lega, for their collaboration with the Administering Authority. The President of the Legislative Assembly was dubbed 'Shamoun', after the Falangist pro-Western president of Lebanon in 1958[34]. The newly elected President of the Lega had continued to make public speeches which openly conflicted with the assurances given by the Legislative Assembly and the Somali government regarding the protection of the life and property of foreigners residing in the Trust Territory[35]. The Italian government grew impatient and wondered whether the party itself had radically altered the official policy it had hitherto pursued.

The first to ring alarm bells was Piero Franca, the Acting Administrator. Following the election of Haji Mohamed as President of the Lega, Franca, in a telegram to Anzilotti, who was in Rome at the time, gave a detailed analysis of the difficulties the man could pose for future relations between the Administration and the ruling party, suggesting, in conclusion, a number of options that Italy might take, including that of surrendering the mandate to the United Nations.

Franca wrote:"The main political party in Somalia has elected, as its President, an individual who until recently has waged, and probably will continue waging, a hostile anti-Italian campaign. This situation offers us the justification to draw whatever conclusion might please us, including that of renouncing the trusteeship mandate. I do say anti-Italian and not pro-Egyptian because the two expressions are not synonymous or, at least, we should officially pretend that they are not. It remains now to be seen what Haji Mohamed is going to do. If he is intelligent, he will decline the leadership of the party and remain in Cairo and enjoy the prestige of the electoral victory. If he is stupid, he will come and will continue to do in Mogadisho what he used to do in Cairo, in which case either he is neutralized, or we will leave, the latter scenario being, in my view, the most favourable as far as

34 I.M. Lewis, op. cit., p. 158.

35 Document T/1372 of 22 April 1958, p. 22, par. 52.

we are concerned, but, probably, not for the Somalis."[36]

Haji's populist calls to expropriate Italian-owned land, without compensation, had become a source of frustrations for Italy, at a time when she was even ready to put the independence date forward, should the Somalis requested so.

In October 1957, Administrator Anzilotti declared before the Legislative Assembly the need for collaboration between the ruling party and AFIS, referring also to the possibility of Somalia attaining its independence before the date of December 2, 1960. In his statement he said: "Should such collaboration between the Administering Authority, the Somali people and the political parties disappear, it would only remain for the Administering Authority to inform the United Nations of the impossibility of honouring the contractual obligations that the Italian government stated not long ago it would completely fulfil until the expiration of the mandate." He added: "the same would be all the more true should the Somali people manifest expressly through legitimate channels their will to obtain full independence before 2 January 1960."[37]

In this difficult moment, Anzilotti clearly expressed to Aden Abdulla the dismay of his government *vis-à-vis* the anti-Italian statements publicly reiterated by the president of the ruling party. Anzilotti spoke plainly to Aden Abdulla: "We seek clarifications as to whether the ruling party associates itself with Haji Mohamed's policy," he said, and further added: "Italy does not believe it deserves the continued and gratuitous accusations levelled against it by the President of the ruling party, at a time when Italy is convinced that it has satisfied the expectations of the Somalis by putting in place a government responsible for all domestic affairs". Using his meeting with the most prestigious and pragmatic Lega leader, the Administrator made it clear that the Italian government could not continue to exercise its trusteeship mandate without being sure of support from a substantial majority in the political parties.[38]

On February 7, 1958, the Somali Prime Minister received a chilling letter stating that clear action by the Somali government was essential to clarify its official policy towards Italy and restore confidence in foreign investors. This stern warning was from Enrico Anzilotti, the Administrator[39], who wrote: "As it is evident, the President of the Lega dei Giovani Somali, after his return to

36 Asmae, Dgafis, b 19, f, 5, Letter from Franca to Anzilotti, August 18, 1957, as reported in Morone, op. cit., pp. 104-5.
37 T/1372, April 12, 1958 page 2.
38 Diary Aden Abdulla, May 30, 1958.
39 Document T/1372 of 22 April, 1958, p. 23, par. 52.

Somalia, continued doing what he used to do through Cairo Radio, making public speeches in open contrast not only with the commitments and the assurances given by the party in its electoral platform, but also with the Legislative Assembly and the Government, with regard to the protection of the life and property of aliens resident in Somalia, and to the guarantees offered to foreign capital investment in Somalia; furthermore these statements constitute a threat to public order."[40]

Anzilotti made it clear that, if the present uncertain situation was to continue, the Italian government would be obliged to report to the United Nations on the situation that was developing in Somalia[41], and further urged the Prime Minister to obtain from the Legislative Assembly "an unequivocal statement regarding the value of the assurance which the same Assembly formally reaffirmed on various occasions concerning the protection of the life and property of foreigners residing in Somalia and the guarantees afforded to investments of foreign capital in the Territory."[42] The strong Italian position raised the real prospect of the Territory being abandoned without direction. The government, reacting to Anzilotti's request, addressed a letter to the Central Committee requesting clarification of the party's position vis-à-vis the statements of the newly elected President[43]. Faced with the prospective that Italy might surrender the mandate before the target date for independence, the Central Committee of the ruling party hastened to take measures to avert the worst.

Anzilotti's carefully worded but firm letter to the Prime Minister and his frank *tête-à-tête* talks with the President of the Legislative Assembly did pay off. In fact, on 15 February, 1958, the Legislative Assembly passed a motion reiterating its assurances about foreigners and foreign investments in the Trust Territory[44]. British sources in Mogadisho suggest, however, that the government failed to obtain the necessary support for the first motion submitted to the Legislative Assembly, which was tantamount to a repudiation of the President of the Lega for his attacks against the foreigners. The same sources refer to "a compromise reached on February 15 after three days of secret negotiations which provided for confirmation of resolutions passed by the Territorial Council and Legislative

40 ASMAE, AFIS, box 9, file 2, Letter no. 22092, from Anzilotti to Abdullahi Issa, Febbraio 7, 1958.

41 Ibid.

42 Document T/1372 of 22 April, 1958, 23, par. 52; ASMAE, AFIS, box 9, file 2. Letter no. 22092, from Anzilotti to Abdullahi Issa, February 7, 1958.

43 Diary Aden Abdulla, February 2, 1958.

44 Document T/1372, Annex V, Motion by the Legislative Assembly of Somaliland confirming assurances in regard to foreign residents and capital, approved unanimously on February 15, 1958.

Assembly guaranteeing the life and property of foreign residents but omitting denunciation of the President."[45]

The party on the brink of a split

While the four Western powers directly involved with Somali affairs were busy planning a common strategy for the future of Somalia, the internal crisis within Lega ranks had further deteriorated, reaching a breaking point. Within the party leadership, the debate grew increasingly bitter: the 'moderates' accused the 'extremists' of being tools of the Egyptians, while the 'extremists' retorted that the 'moderates' were stooges of the Italian colonialists and American imperialists[46]. The two camps seemed to be drifting inexorably towards a split.

An extraordinary party congress was convened in Mogadisho from 28 March to 26 June, 1958, with this crisis at the top of the agenda. Some 116 persons took part, including 19 Central Committee members, 43 deputies and 47 branch secretaries[47]. There was a delegate from British Somaliland and several delegates from the Ogaden tribes, none of whom had a right to vote.[48]

The first to speak in the congress was the party's President – an extract of his speech is reported here:

> "We do not call upon the people to use terrorism or to make a bloody revolution in order to expel the Trusteeship Administration from Somalia before the end of the mandate in 1960. Neither I nor you have any intention of killing, ransacking, spilling blood or casting law-abiding people out of our country. It would be unnecessary to say this at all if exasperated colonialists had not spread lies about us which have finally upset intelligent foreigners and worried ourselves.
>
> "We insist that the Trusteeship Agreement between Italy and the United Nations be carried out precisely and fully under international guarantee that full independence will be attained and full liberty of action enjoyed within the date laid down unless, by friendly agreement, the mandate comes to an end sooner than stipulated.

45 TNA FO 371/131460, telegram from the British Consulate Mogadisho to the FO, February 17, 1958.

46 TNA FO 371/138306 Confidential dispatch from British Consulate to FO, April 4, 1959.

47 TNA FO 372/131464, letter of transmittal from SYL Headquarters issued by the office of the president of the party, June 19, 1958.

48 TNA FO 371/131463 confidential report of 1018/58, from British Consul Mogadisho to FO, April 1, 1958.

"We shall accept no postponement of the date of our independence beyond 1960; neither shall we accept the substitution of this Agreement by any military or political pact or arrangement imposed on us. We shall not allow any political, military, economic and financial tutelage after 1960 by any powers. We heard a declaration by the Administrator of this Territory in October last, a declaration he has since repeated on various occasions and that he repeated, in fact, personally to me quite recently. He said that Italy was ready to give up the mandate in Somalia and to declare our complete independence when we asked her to do so. There is not one single Somali alive who would not ask that this be done. We shall be helped by world opinion, by our neighbours, by our co-religionaries. If the Trusteeship Administration is honest in its intention to give us full independence, then we demand it now. We have nothing to fear. No country would have gained its independence in the last one hundred years if it had waited until all its problems were settled before asking for it.

"In case independence does not come before 1960, we must repeat our firm intention to insist that the Administration should continue to give us a good administration and transfer offices into our hands in two and half years' time. We shall vigorously oppose any change of the Trusteeship Administration whether in form or substance, because this would replace the trusteeship with a form of protectorate, a hidden colonial system. I shall never agree to be President of the Lega once there is, under a new form perhaps, an Italian supervisor who would, in fact, wield the power. There are three roads to follow. We may take the first and the second but I will never agree to the third. The first leads to complete independence now, by peaceful means, on the basis of the Administrator's promise. The second is to insist upon full independence by 1960 and complete Somalization between then and now. I shall be with you on either of these two roads. But I will never accompany you on the third road which means to act as Head of State with all the real power in the hands of Italians. This would be tantamount to a Somali government under Italian protectorate. This we will not accept.

"We are prepared fully to collaborate with the Italian Administration and the United Nations until independence in 1960 but we shall refuse to work with anybody who tries to withhold our rights.

"We shall be glad to have any experts who live among us or who offer to give us the benefit of their technical skills but only if this does not imply any limitation of our sovereignty.

"We shall accept aid whencesoever it may come provided it is channelled through the United Nations and provided there are no tags attached.

"It is evident that the Italians attempted to increase our import trade at the expense of our export. They have tied our economy to their agricultural and industrial monopoly, which has seriously lowered our standard of life. All the proceeds of our exports of cattle and meat are seized by the Italians, who thereby effectively prevent us from trading elsewhere than Italy at lower price. For example, we have been forced to import rice from Italy though we could produce it ourselves or buy it from our neighbours. I hope to see Somalis and foreigners setting up trading companies and later to see Somalis setting up trading companies alone. We shall not accord foreigners worse treatment than they receive in Italy, for example, but we cannot forget that the colonialists originally came to Somalia through concessions granted to foreigners in our ports. We shall not be ungrateful to those who are prepared to help us and to collaborate with us.

"We hereby declare that the frontier question between Ethiopia and Somalia must not be allowed to delay our independence. We are a small country and we present no danger to anybody. The Ethiopians have often aired their fear that Somalia might once more become a base for operation against them. We understand their fears and believe that the best guarantee against repetition of past events is that we should collaborate and form a united front against foreign conquerors. If Ethiopia fully recognizes our rights, they will be able to win our friendship and count on us to help defend their independence.

"Islamic culture leads the fight against colonialism. It alone can help us to attain full independence and carry us along the path to modern progress. Our sons must be educated in its spirit and that is why we demand that all school programmes should be revised and brought into line with Islamic laws and culture."[49]

The second speaker was the vice-president of the party, Aden Abdulla. In

49 TNA FO 371/131463: Extract of the speech made by the President of the Lega dei Giovani Somali at the opening of the Extraordinary Congress.

the course of the debate Aden Abdulla made a passionate intervention which determined the end of Haji Mohamed's presidency of the party. In view of its importance, Abdulla's speech is partially reported here:

> "It is true that from the beginning until the last elections of Haji Mohamed to the presidency, this happy organization (the Lega) has always been managed in a comradely way and there has never been any necessity for us to defend ourselves against the ambitious deviations and 'personality cult' that seem to be the chief aim and tactics of Haji Mohamed.
>
> "The current President left Somalia for Egypt in 1952 of his own free will, abandoning the post of president that he had held for several years. It is the opinion of many that he ran away from difficulties. He did not ask himself whether he should remain to help in the fight. He followed his personal interest.
>
> "In 1957 once again the question of the presidency of the party was raised. Nobody opposed his nomination although he was abroad. He was elected and the first thing he did, by means of Egyptian radio, was to make believe that all the leaders in Somalia were traitors paid by the colonialists whom they served, and that our people were living under the worst kind of colonialism.
>
> "According to Mohamed Hussein, to work in politics means to scheme against one's own friends in one's own party, as he did over the Egyptian radio and has done since his return.
>
> "Till now I have refrained from contradicting him publicly as I hoped the members of the party should condemn him, but nobody can have patience with this man.
>
> "I have twice made speeches without first consulting the Central Committee and I am ready to suffer the consequences. I did it to provoke the reactions of the President's I followed and obeyed. Haji Mohamed Hussein has not reacted, and his bad faith is manifest.
>
> "The President continued to do this because evidently, as he declared in Aden and Hargeisa, he was not afraid of the government or the Central Committee in which he had no confidence, but counted on the people who he pretended had given him their confidence, and had no confidence in the others.
>
> "It is not by inciting the people against foreigners that we can gain the

confidence of those foreigners. It is not by awakening the jealousy and envy of the masses that the interests of Somalia will be advanced.

"If, as is meant to be, and justly so, we wish the majority of Somali firms to be owned by Somalis, this can be realized by means of a law that we can pass, but no other way can succeed. Haji Mohamed has used a battering ram on open doors. For example, he has said that any contributions from individual foreign states towards aid to Somalia must be given through the United Nations: Haji Farah Ali, Minister of Economic Affairs, had already said this to the United Nations on instructions from the Somali government. He has said that the independence of Somalia must be declared after the election and the mandate ended: this is a matter that was already decided and it is quite clear that the Administrator made his memorable declaration only after consulting the Lega dei Giovani Somali.

"According to such declarations, that Administrator Anzilotti had naturally made with the full consent of his government, and which we are counting on, the anticipated independence of Somalia is already endorsed and can materialize without any difficulty.

"But if Italy, as she threatened to do, renounces the mandate for the Somalis' fault, have you thought of the risk we are running?

"In every country of the world, for imperative monetary reasons, the State tries to compel the country from which it buys to give an amount equal to what it has spent. Italy, therefore, is thus within its rights if in exchange for our exports it asks that we respond with equal imports from Italy.

"On the border question, Haji Mohamed said, if I am not mistaken, that England told us that without her the Abyssinians would not spare us. Are we inferring this or have we any proof of such a thing? We have had several talks with English personalities, as with personalities from several other countries, and nobody has yet told us to seek the protection of his country against the Ethiopians or anyone else; nor have any of them shown any preoccupation at the danger of Ethiopian aggression against Somalia. And I remember very well several of them advised us to do our utmost so that we and Ethiopia can cut in half our mutual mistrust.

"To speak like that is, in my view, dangerous for Somalia and amounts to nothing less than trying to discredit the policy of independent powers who have their own good reasons for following a certain policy.

"If, in reality, Haji Mohamed wishes to follow a neutral policy, why speak evil of certain powers and well of others. Is this neutrality?

"One last word: I have already pointed out to Haji Mohamed one of the results that could emerge from his conduct, a result none of us would like to see. We are grateful to Egypt for all she is doing and do not wish the Somalis to be divided into pro- and anti-Egyptians. But, as Haji Mohamed began his campaign in Egypt and has now come from that country, rightly or wrongly, it will be inevitable that someone will blame Egypt for what he says and then create enemies for Egypt herself. You must judge."[50]

The Central Committee ejects Haji Mohamed

Aden Abdulla emerges leader of the party

In compliance with articles 30, 33 and 47 of the statute of the party, concerning disciplinary sanctions, the Central Committee expelled the President from the party on May 21 by a vote of 7 for the expulsion and 4 against, with 8 members absent. The matter was then taken to the Congress where, by a vote of 42 for and 38 against, the expulsion was confirmed. It is reported that about 30 delegates were absent and did not know the vote was taking place.[51]

Haji Mohamed was expelled from the Lega on the grounds that he "impaired the unity of the party, allowed dictatorial tendencies, and acted contrary to the party statute."[52] The resolution read: "Taking into consideration the fact that the current President does not intend to observe the democratic practice which is the essence of the life of the party; taking account also of the attitude assumed by Mr. Haji Mohamed Hussein, not only in the capital city, but also up-country, where he delivered speeches and made declarations, with no consideration for general interests not only of the Party, but also of the country of which the Party is a vigilant protector; in consideration of the demonstration organized by Mr. Haji Mohamed Hussein, designed to influence the decision of the Congress currently in session, and of the speech he delivered to the demonstrators in which, with no consideration for the consequences that could derive to the country, already on the verge of independence, he used the phrase 'shed blood'..."[53]

As a result, the longest serving leader of the party since its inception in 1943,

50 TNA FO 371/131463 confidential report dated April 1, 1958 from British Consulate Mogadisho to FO.

51 Ibid., telegram from the British Consulate, Mogadisho to the FO, May 23, 1958.

52 *Corriere della Somalia,* Maggio 26, 1958.

53 Asmae, Afis, box 9, file 2, resolution adopted by the Central Committee of the Lega dei Giovani Somali.

a man who had dominated the party's life for dozens of years, lost not only the leadership but also his membership of the party. Subsequent to this, riot squads surrounded the Lega HQs building in Mogadisho to prevent any popular demonstration in favour of the President of the Lega. Following the President's speech, a member of the Central Committee, Ahmed Mohamed Ali 'Allora', insisted upon asking questions. He was ruled out of order. The following day, he gained entrance into the party's headquarters where he assaulted the President, giving him a pounding with his fists. Later that day, it is alleged that the Haji Darod group[54] sent a semi-blind man, Arrabey Indhole, led by another man, to assault Ahmed 'Allora'. The Disciplinary Committee of the Lega fined the President 50 shillings and 'Allora' 20 shillings for 'affray'.[55]

In June, the party congress elected Aden Abdulla to succeed Haji Mohamed as party leader. This was the second time Aden Abdulla was elected as party leader. His election was a surprise because of the way it came about and the unusual process it took. To start with, Aden Abdulla did not run for the position— he was, at the time, holding the office of president of the Legislative Assembly and was tormented by two main preoccupations: firstly, that the accumulation of the two functions of president of the party (if he were elected) and president of the Legislative Assembly might undermine the efficiency of one or both bodies; secondly, as one of the strongest critics of Haji Mohamed's policy, he did not want to be seen as coveting party leadership[56]. Notwithstanding the clear arguments he put forward, his name was included in the list of candidates.

In a secret ballot which took place on June 9 1958, the Congress, by 44 votes, elected him president of the party[57]. His closest contender, Sheikh Mohamoud Ahmed Mohamed Addan 'Kutuba-Hor', received 42 votes. In a written communication to the Committee of the Congress, in charge of the organization of the election process, Aden Abdulla reiterated his decision not to accept the responsibility to lead the party. However, following increased pressure brought to bear on him from many quarters and groups, he reluctantly accepted, with the proviso that the election process be repeated so that he might get a full vote of confidence from the Congress, and that sections of the party in the provinces, still loyal to the ex-President, manifest their support to him or, at least, stop

54 A group of four of five influential Darod tribesmen politically close to the Egyptians.

55 TNA FO 371/131463 confidential report from the British Consulate Mogadisho to the FO, April 1, 1958.

56 Diary Aden Abdulla, June, 9, 1958.

57 ASMAE, Afis, box 9, file 2, Rapporto segreto da Mogadisho al Ministero degli Affari Esteri, Direzione Generale per gli Affari dell'Afis, Roma, undated.

their exaggerated campaign in favour of the latter[58]. When the election process was repeated for the second time on the night of June 11, by open ballot, Aden Abdulla received a quasi-unanimous vote: 66 votes out of some seventy voting members of the Congress.[59]

Members of the Central Committee were also elected. Ali Hersi Farah became vice-president, Mohamed Haji Sobrie secretary general and the 'usual' Sheikh Issa Mohamed was treasurer. With regard to their political tendencies, the members of the new Central Committee were regarded as pro-western. "Fifteen of the Committee members are described as politically western-minded and tailor-made for the current government", comments Piero Franca.[60]

Formation of the Greater Somali League Party

Although he maintained that the Central Committee of the party was not legally empowered to expel him from the party, Haji Mohamed did not challenge the decision of the Committee against him through the existing party appeal mechanism[61]. Mediation efforts, sponsored by some up-country branches of the party, particularly in Benadir province, to readmit him into the party failed to generate consensus.[62]

On Thursday July 24, 1958, Haji formed a new party, the Greater Somali League, (GSL) generally known as Great. At the inaugural ceremony, Haji Mohamed strongly attacked his former colleagues of the SYL, without however mentioning any one of them by name, but describing them as intruders who betrayed the fundamental principles upon which the party was founded in 1943. He said: "If I say that the GSL is a new Lega it would not be a correct definition. Superficially, it is new in form, name and appearance, but in actual fact it is an old one. The principles and objectives of the GSL are the same as those for which the old Somali patriots strove over a long, long time. In 1943, a Somali society was formed of which I had the honour of being a member. This group established the Somali Youth Club which later came to be known as the Somali Youth League. The aims of the SYL were to free Somaliland from imperialist bonds and reunite all the territories. We worked for those aims but saw with

58 Diary Aden Abdulla, June 11, 1958.
59 Ibid., June 12, 1958.
60 Asmae Afis, box9, file 2, Telespresso n° 7547, from Piero Franca to Ministry of Foreign Affairs, Rome, June 26, 1958.
61 Article 11 of the Statute of the Party provides for an appeal mechanism.
62 Diary Aden Abdulla, June 4, 1958.

deep regret that the party got infiltrated by a number of intruders who worked to promote their personal interests at the expense of the country. They deviated from the fundamental principles on which the League was based. These led to our separation. We have now formed this new League which I am honoured to inaugurate now. It bears the standard which those intruders brushed aside, and perseveres in pursuing the principles of liberty, justice and freedom which the intruders evaded. In this time in which the trusteeship mandate is nearing its end, we are establishing this new party which is committed to work solely for the good and interest of Somalia. We must return to the path from which we have been swayed, the road of freedom, justice and independence."[63]

In his speech, Haji Mohamed listed four main objectives the party would pursue: the top priority was the attainment of independence, followed by the unification of all Somali territories, a foreign policy of positive neutrality and the eradication of tribalism. The new party adopted a pro-Egyptian policy as manifested in its campaign for the adoption of Arabic script for the Somali language, and in its promotion of Arabic culture and conviction that Arabic should be the national language of the country. Recognizing the will of the people as supreme, the State should empower the working class and the peasants through the promotion of economic development and the de-tribalization of the Somali society. The struggle to free Somalia from colonialism was inseparable from the national urgency to achieve the unification of all Somali-speaking inhabitants. The Lega dei Giovani Somali was criticized for being too closely associated with the Italian Trusteeship Administration and for permitting 'economic exploitation' by certain Italiancompanies.[64]

A Central Committee of 13 members was formed. The members were Haji Mohamed, Omar Haji Abdalla Banafunzi, Abdurahim Haji Mohamed, Mohamed Hassan Hersi 'Hippo', Aboukar Mohamed, Abdi Mohamed Ossoble Abdurahman, Mohamed Sheikh Yousuf (Deputy for Afmedu), Yousuf Hassan Roble, Muhiddin Burhot, Ali Abdurahman Haji Osman, Mohamed Ali Hassan Hussein, Hassan Mohamed Warsheekh and Haji Ali Hersi. The Great Somali League claimed to have inherited the original radicalism of the Lega dei Giovani Somali of the past, rejected Western assistance, adhered to the Afro-Asian movement and called for unification of the Somali territories, no matter if to

63 TNA FO 371/131465, Haji Mohamed's Speech on the inaugural ceremony of GSL, translation from original text in Arabic.

64 G. Costanzo, op. cit., p. 91.

achieve this one might have to team up with the devil.[65]

Haji Mohamed's comments sparked serious concern in the SYL leadership. He made an appeal to the dissidents within his former party who supported him for his election as president of the Lega, in a bid to win their support for his new party. His action was specifically directed to the Majerten members of the Lega who he knew were dissatisfied with the government. Thanks to its dynamic and efficient organization, the new party soon attracted a considerable following, especially in Mogadisho and Lower Juba province. The bulk of support for the party came from merchants who considered themselves victimized by government corruption, young students who had failed to obtain government posts on completion of their studies and a segment of Darod tribesmen who resented Hawiye predominance in the government.[66]

In an endeavour to allay the rumours, current at the time, about alleged Darod support of the newly established Greater Somali League Party, prominent Darod members of the ruling party published an appeal to what they called 'people of good sense'. The appeal was addressed to the Darod tribes at large. It read:

> "In this difficult period which our people are now going through, in the name of our country, in the name of our citizens, in the name of the most sacred thing which unites us, in the name of all these ideas, we beg you not to be the cause of the division of the united people of Somalia by forming other parties, by creating organizations on a tribal basis. O brothers, we warn you against passing to the new party, meaning the Great Somali League, which has assumed a tribal character; currently it is known as Darod party.
>
> "Brothers, if we examine the issue from the tribal perspective, it emerges clearly that we have the lion's share in our current government. In the economic field, for instance, the Darod are the only clan who has the monopoly of the economy of the country. In fact, we can ask ourselves: which of the six regions of our territory enjoys better economic treatment than the two regions of Mudug and Majertenia after the opening of the trade links with Aden?[67]
>
> "The same argument can be brought up with regard to the trade links that Lower Juba province has with Kenya. It is a fact that other regions of

65 Del Boca, op. cit., p. 277.

66 TNA FO 371/138306 Report n. 1019/59 of April 4, 1959 from the British Consulate, Mogadisho to FO.

67 Decreto n° 69 aprile 21, 1956, 'Agevolazione fiscale a favore degli abitanti del Mudugh e della Migiurtinia'.

> the country do not enjoy similar favourable treatment with respect to free trade. Up to now, the government has drilled 12 wells at Galkayo and Dusa Mareb, whilst at Obbia, El Der and El Bur, only 2 wells have been drilled. Therefore, what more can we ask the government after this demonstration of generous benevolence towards the regions inhabited by Darod tribes?[68] What are the tribal practices the government is accused of? Ask yourself, instead, about the advantages we might forgo by dividing ourselves into tribes and small parties! Don't we realize that the Dighil and Mirifle and their 'rogue party' will capitalize on the situation to get the majority of vote. Would that be in our interest?[69]
>
> "Brothers, we beg you also to bear in mind that, if a person belonging to the Darod tribe holds the office of the president of the Council (Prime Minister) and president of the Assembly (Legislative Assembly), they cannot do better than the present government."[70]

The appeal was signed by Haji Dirie Hersi (President) and the following members: Salad Abdi Mohamoud, Aden Shire Jama, Haji Giama Mahmoud, Haji Abdullahi Scirua (Shirwa'), Haji Yousuf Haji Ali, Osman Haji Hussein, Ali Hersi Farah, Ibrahim Osman Ibrahim and Sugulle 'Habsei'.

In the beginning, Haji Mohamed tried to exploit the solidarity he personally enjoyed in the Territory in view of his past political record, and to manipulate the political clashes masked in East–West terms. Initially, hopes that this might trigger a wave of further defections and the weakening of the Lega as a party proved optimistic. However, despite intense propaganda and the pomposity of his speeches, Haji Mohamed was unable to strip the Lega of more than a handful of followers. In fact, in the municipal elections of November 1958, the Lega gained a landslide majority of 416 out of 663 seats; the GSL obtained only 36 seats. Although his firebrand politics continued to worry the Lega leadership, Haji Mohamed never managed to cut deeply into the party's constituency as there was no major, serious policy challenge to pose as an alternative to that of the Lega.

Following the schism in the Lega, and the establishment of the GSL with a

68 TNA FO 371/ 131465, letter of September 17, 1958 from the British Consulate Mogadisho to the FO, app. B.

69 ASMAE, AFIS, box 9, file 2, Letter no. 1018/58 of 13.8.1958.

70 TNA FO 371/ 131465, letter of September17, 1958 from British Consulate Mogadisho to the FO, app. B.

Marxist tendency, the Lega-led government, in an endeavour to allay the worries of the West, published in the *Corriere della Somalia* of August 20, 1958 an article which stated: "The Somali government absolutely refutes giving an anti-western orientation to its foreign policy". The editorial, which normally reflected the position of the Prime Minister, added that being "anti-western is tantamount to a lack of gratitude, and would be a policy against our national interests."[71]

In his comment on the government's clear foreign policy leaning towards the West, Angelo del Boca wrote: "How distant seems Fornari's time, in reading this document, when between AFIS and the Lega there was an open war and the Italians of Mogadisho used to put pressure on the Administrator to declare the Lega an illegal organization! Now, there is not a single Italian among AFIS staff or the old Italian community in Mogadisho who is anti-Lega since the Lega became pro-Western and softened its chauvinistic programme."[72]

In its November 1960 party congress, the GSL split into two factions, when Haji Mohamed Hussein, after returning from China, advocated a socialist state and a pro-communist foreign policy. One faction in the party accused him of dictatorial tendencies and administrative irregularities[73]. The conservative and religious-oriented faction insisted that the party programme must remain nationalistic, democratic and Islamic. "In April 1962 Haji Mohamed was able to use the remnants of a party seriously debilitated by schism to form a new party called the Somali Democratic Union (SDU), which was composed mainly of unemployed townsmen, discontented leaders of the SNU and the USP of Somaliland", comments Castagno[74]. He was elected as member of the Parliament following the 1964 general elections on an SDU ticket from the city of Merca, Lower Shabelle. In the following general elections of 1969 he was not elected.

71 *Corriere della Somalia*, Agosto 20, 1958.
72 Del Boca, op. cit., p. 275).
73 Touval , op. cit., p. 9.
74 A.A. Castagno, op. cit., p. 549.

Chapter VIII

DI STEFANO REPLACES ANZILOTTI
The 1958 municipal and 1959 political elections

Ambassador Anzilotti left Somalia in 1958 following his request to be relieved of his post on grounds of ill-health[1]. He was replaced by Mario Di Stefano, another career diplomat. Di Stefano had served in the Italian Foreign Service, holding different positions such as Director of the Americas and of the Far East departments. He had also worked in different capacities at the Italian embassies in Canada, United States and U.S.S.R. Before assuming his responsibility as administrator for Somalia, he was Italian ambassador in Moscow for more than six years.

Ambassador Di Stefano arrived at a time when the Trust Territory had gone a long way down the road to independence, with all State institutions, Parliament and executive branches already in place and functioning. He arrived in Mogadisho on October 9, 1958[2]. His tenure, though not free from controversy, was made easier by the groundwork done by his three predecessors. Among the urgent tasks before him was the organization of the second municipal elections in the Territory, to be held in October 1958, and the general elections planned for 1959.

A municipal election law was passed by Parliament in preparation for the 1958

1 TNA FO 371/131467, letter 1516/310 of June 25, 1958 from the British Embassy in Rome.

2 Rapport du gouvernment italien à l'Assemblée Generale des Nations Unies sur l'administration de la Somalie placée sous la tutelle de l'Italie, 1958, p. 6.

municipal elections. In comparison with the elections of 1954, the 1958 law[3] introduced new innovations under the following main principles: every elector had one vote which he/she had to express freely and directly; voting was for lists of candidates presented in each constituency by political parties; women also had the right to vote and to stand for election (article 7 of the law); voting was on the basis of electoral certificates handed out by municipalities to persons registered on general lists of electors; only Somalis over 18 years of age could participate in the elections.[4]

Based on the size of the municipality, the number of councillors to be elected for a term of office of four years ranged from 25 in the main cities to 11 in municipalities with less than 3,000 inhabitants. 663 seats were allotted in the 45 municipalities[5]. All six political parties contended in the elections. The LGS presented lists in all the 45 municipalities; the HDMS in 21; the (GSL) in 9; the (PLGS) in 8; the (UGB) in 2; and the Giovani Fichirini Somali (GFS), a local group of fishermen on Bagiuni Islands off the coast of Kismayo, in one municipality.

Actual voting took place on 20 October 1958 in twenty-seven municipalities, out of the 45 nationwide. In eighteen municipalities, no voting took place inasmuch as only Lega lists were presented and the new councillors, all belonging to the Lega lists, were proclaimed elected. In the Majertenia, Mudug and Hiran regions, only Lega candidates were admitted, "there being", according to the government, "no opposition".[6]

The number of voters registered increased threefold from 50,740 in 1954 to 156,636 in 1958[7]. This was due to the establishment of new municipalities, the granting of the right to vote to women and the lowering of the voting age from 21 to 18 years. The vast and active participation of the public to the campaigns organized by the political parties was evident everywhere in the country. "There was evidence of lavish expenditure by all parties, so that the question of the origin of their respective funds was not raised seriously by any of them", comments the British Consul General in Mogadisho.[8]

The ruling party, conscious that it had been greatly weakened by the split of May 1958, took oppressive action against the opposition. Certain district

3 Legge n° 15 giugno 25, 1958, Bollettino Ufficiale, n° 3 al n° 6.

4 In the 1954 municipal elections, the voting age was 21 years..

5 UN Doc. T/1444, 14 April 1959, par. 92, p. 23.

6 TNA FO"371/138306, Report from British Consulate Mogadisho to FO, April 4, 1959, p 2.

7 UN Doc. T/1444,14 April 1959, par. 93, p. 23.

8 TNA FO 371/131466, letter of October 15, 1958 from the British Consulate Mogadisho to FO.

commissioners were accused of organizing certain lists and obstructing others. Rumours of irregularities were gathering pace and complaints poured into the United Nations Advisory Council. It was alleged that district commissioners in a number of municipalities had, after accepting Lega lists, suspended all other political parties because of possible breach of the peace and therefore would not accept any further lists from the temporarily banned parties. In other municipalities, lists of the opposition parties were allegedly found to be incorrectly completed and necessary corrections could not be made in time before the last date for the submission of the lists. In municipality centres where opposition parties were contesting, their known supporters claimed that they had difficulties in registration, being asked to produce documentary proof of age in a country where birth certificates were non-existent.[9]

The districts where opposition parties faced particular harassment and intimidation included Dusa Mareb, Bosaso, Beledweyne, Baidoa, Margherita, Afgooye, Villabruzzi, Hawadlei, Merca and Gardo and Dol Gab. In the municipality of Dusa Mareb, no election took place for reasons of public order and by virtue of Decree No. 131 of 2 September 1958 an extraordinary commissioner for the municipality was appointed. At Dusa Mareb, the activities of the GSL and PLGS were forbidden and their respective lists rejected by the authority[10]. At Bosaso, the judge rejected the list of the GSL whilst at Baidoa the prefect cited the absence of the judge and district commissioner as a reason for declining the lists. At Beledweyne, the chairman of the PLGS was forced to leave the city after his party's list was rejected by the authorities. However, although they unscrupulously made use of their positions to manipulate the electoral machinery, the Lega did less well than they had hoped. They did win an absolute majority of 27 over 45 municipalities and remained the strongest party in several others; but in the southern regions, where the elections were contested, they lost considerable ground, mostly to the Hisbia Destour Mutaqil Somali, the HDMS, which obtained 175 against 57 in the 1954 municipal elections. In the capital, Mogadisho, the candidate of the Partito Liberale Giovani Somali, Ahmed Mudde, was elected 'sindaco' (mayor) with 14 votes against 11 in favour of his closest contender, Hassan Barre Toho, of the Somali Youth League[11]. The newly established Greater Somalia League made a poor showing in the nine districts

9 Ibid.

10 ASMAE, AFIS, box 4, file 9, Meeting of the representatives of the four opposition parties with the Administrator, November 20, 1958.

11 *Corriere della Somalia*, Novembre 17, 1958.

they contested, failing to win absolute majority in any of them. The GSL made its best showing in Kismayo, obtaining 956 votes.

The distribution of seats among the various political parties was as follows:

PARTY	NO. OF SEATS
LEGA DEI GIOVANI SOMALI, INCLUDING UNCONTESTED SEATS	416
PARTITO COSTITUZIONALE INDIPENDENZA SOMALA (HDMS)	175
GREAT SOMALI LEAGUE (GSL)	36
PARTITO LIBERALE GIOVANI SOMALI (PLGS)	27
UNIONE GIOVANI BENADIR (UGB)	6
UNIONE GIOVANI FICHIRINI SOMALI	3

Strong representations were made to the Administrator by opposition parties. On November 20, 1958, one month after the municipal elections, a delegation representing four political opposition parties was received by Administrator Mario Di Stefano.

The president of the GSL Haji Mohamed, the president of HDMS Geilani Sheikh Bin-Sheikh, the president of the PLGS Haji Mohamed Mohamoud 'Boracco', the president of the UGB Abukar Hamoud 'Soccoro' and the inspector general of the GSL, Mohamed Sheikh Yousuf 'Derbi' requested a meeting with the Administrator. They complained about the way the government had handled the municipal elections of October 1958 and urged his personal intervention so that a similar situation would not be repeated in the coming political elections scheduled for early 1959. They claimed that the judicial and administrative authorities up-country were biased against opposition parties. Di Stefano listened carefully to the grievances of the opposition parties, but did nothing to rein in the government's unfair practices and restore the rule of law. The Administrator said to his interlocutors that the Somalis were now in charge of the domestic affairs of their country and that there was little he could do to tackle their grievances.[12]

12 ASMAE, AFIS, box 4, file 9 Meeting of the representatives of the four opposition parties with the Administrator, Novembre 20, 1958.

Prolongation of the term of office of the Legislative Assembly

The issue of the population census came up again for discussion on 26 May 1958, when the Legislative Assembly, while discussing a draft law on the forthcoming 1959 general elections, chose to prioritize a motion presented by a cross-party group of 50 MPs, mainly but not solely from the ruling party[13], inviting the government to prolong the term of office and activity of the Assembly, originally expected to end on 30 June 1958, up to December 31, 1959. The reasons for requesting the extension were stated in the preamble of the motion as follows: a registration of the population was considered necessary in order to guarantee the accuracy of the popular consultation by direct suffrage; the holding of election in 1959 would necessarily imply a second electoral consultation in 1960, when the trusteeship period was due to end, thus placing an undue burden on the Territory's finance; there was a need to approve a comprehensive law on citizenship, defining persons who might vote or be elected.[14]

The motion was approved by 51 votes, out of 60 present, 2 against and 7 abstentions[15]. It should be noted that the abstentions came from the 7 members of the government present in the assembly hall[16]. The government was thus requested to withdraw the election bill and resubmit it to the Legislative Assembly by the end of 1959, after the population census had been completed and the citizenship law passed. Reasonable as the proposal may sound, the reality was that the government did not consider it as an attractive option, not least because time was running out for the legislature, with barely six months left before its official expiry. The Prime Minister, in a letter to the Acting Administrator, made clear that his government was not ready to present a law prolonging the term of office of the Legislative Assembly. "Without ignoring the decision of the Assembly", he wrote, "it is a fact that the government will not present a bill relative to the prolongation of the Legislative Assembly up to 31 December, 1959, unless such a prolongation meets Your Excellency's favour."[17]

As a result of a subsequent compromise between the government and Parliament, the motion was later superseded by a new bill suggesting the

13 ASMAE, AFIS, box 9, file 2, Text of the motion attached to letter no. 460985 of May 26, 1958 from Aden Abdulla to the Prime Minister and the Administrator.

14 UN Doc.T/1444 Report of the UN Advisory Council for the Trust Territory of Somaliland under Italian Administration covering the period from April 1, 1958 to March 30, 1959, April 14, 1959, par. 73, p. 19.

15 ASMAE, AFIS, box 9, File 2, Minutes of meeting of the Legislative Assembly no. 5/R of May 26, 1958, p. 4.

16 Ibid., letter No 027/Ris. of May 28, 1958, from Abdullahi Issa to Piero Franca.

17 Ibid.

extension of the Assembly up to December 31, 1958[18]. By virtue of this law the office of presidency of the assembly was to function until the meeting of the next assembly[19]. The law also provided for the payment of a final allowance, equal to three months, to the deputies "for obvious reasons of equity."[20]

By Administrative Decree no. 171 of December 31, 1958, the National Assembly was then dissolved[21]. Following the compromise between the government and the Parliament over the extension of the duration of the Legislative Assembly, the government submitted a bill to the Legislative Assembly prior to the general election scheduled for March 1959[22]. The new electoral law was passed without the crucial issues of population census, revision of the electoral boundaries and registration of voters being resolved. However, the law contained three important innovations in comparison with the 1956 electoral law. Firstly, the previous political elections were based on universal male suffrage only; women had no right to vote. Under the elections of 1959, citizens of both sexes were entitled to vote (Art. 9) and to be elected. Secondly, the indirect voting system (through the electoral representatives for the nomadic population) was abolished and every elector, whether rural or urban, was casting his/her vote directly without electoral certificate. Thirdly, the qualifying age was lowered from 21 to 18 years (Article 9). The verification of elector status was carried out in each case by the polling officers through a summary process after consultations with the representatives from the lists of each political party.

It is, however, obvious that without voter registration (and with the ink easily erasable) voters were tempted to abuse the system by casting their vote on more than one occasion. Any Somali who was twenty-five or older was eligible to become candidate, provided that he was literate in Arabic or Italian (Article 11). The law required the list of candidates be signed by no less than two hundred and no more than three hundred voters and accompanied by a deposit of Sh.So1,000 for each list. Civil servants were allowed to run as candidates for elective office. In the former British Somaliland, civil servants were forbidden to stand for elective office and discouraged from engaging in political activities.

18 Legge n° 24 dell' 1 agosto 1958.

19 Legge n° 31 del 29 dicembre 1958, 'Mantenimento in funzione Ufficio di Presidenza Assemblea Legislativa e indennità di liquidazione ai Deputati', Bollettino Ufficiale, suppl. n°3 al n°1, 20 gennaio 1959.

20 UN Doc.T/1444, Report of the UN Advisory Council for the Trust Territory of Somaliland under Italian Administration covering the period from April 1, 1958 to March 31, 1959, April 14, 1959, par. 75, p. 20.

21 'Scioglimento dell'Assemblea Legislativa', Bollettino Ufficiale, suppl. n°3 al n° 1, 20 gennaio 1959.

22 Legge n° 26 dicembre 12, 1958, Bollettino Ufficiale, suppl. n° 2 al n° 12.

By contrast, in the Southern region, by prevailing tradition, civil servants were party members or even party leaders, and were permitted to stand for election to the Legislative Assembly. Accordingly, a number of civil servants were elected members of Parliament and placed on leave without pay for the duration of the elective office.

The country was divided into 30 electoral districts with the creation of the 5 new districts of Alula, Iskushuban, Balad, Wanleweyn and Jilib. The number of seats to contest for was raised from 60 to 90, distributed before the elections on a regional basis: Majertenia 13, Mudug 13, Hiran 12, Benadir 18, Upper Juba 22, and Lower Juba 12. The UN and AFIS were both of the opinion that seats should be distributed after the election, adopting the system of national quota. Similarly, the increase in the number of deputies from 60 to 90 (Article 3), considered excessive, raised objections from different quarters, including the UN Advisory Council in Mogadsicio, the Administering Authority and the opposition parties[23]. It was considered that such a high number of members of parliament would substantially burden the Territory's future budget. However some MPs, although recognizing that this number was rather high for a country like Somalia, maintained this would have the effect of reducing the defects of the unicameral system.[24]

In the run-up to the elections, the ruling party felt that it was facing strong challenge from the opposition parties in the general elections planned for 1959 as it was rumoured that the opposition parties were being subsidized by foreign consulates based in Mogadisho. In order to counter any influence, real or fictional, from foreign agents in the internal affairs of the Territory, two motions were introduced to Parliament on December 15, 1958 by a group from the ruling party. The first called upon the government to take steps to invite the foreign community "to observe scrupulously the principles of hospitality and non-interference" and the second called upon "Consulates established in the Territory" (at the time, Egypt, Ethiopia, France, United Kingdom, the United States of America and Yemen were represented by Consulates) "to observe absolute and unquestionable neutrality and also observe scrupulously the principle of non-interference on the part of foreign powers in the internal affairs of the country."[25]

It was widely believed that certain foreign powers had been subsidizing Somali

23 UN Doc.T/1444, 14 April 1959, par. 104, p. 25.

24 Ibid., par. 106, p. 26.

25 *Corriere della Somalia*, Dicembre 16, 1958.

political parties for their own ends. Although no foreign countries were named, it was generally thought that the motions were directed at the Egyptian Consulate for allegedly supporting the GSL and the Ethiopian Consulate for allegedly supporting the HDMS and the Liberal Party in the Municipal elections of 1958. British sources reveal that Aden Abdulla had denounced the conduct of the Ethiopian and American Consulates in Mogadisho as incorrect, accusing them of subsidizing 'certain elements'[26]. The Egyptians were believed to have paid large sums to the Greater Somali League, the Ethiopians to have financed the Liberal party and the Italians to be "generously contributing to the Lega coffers."[27] There was little question that close contacts existed between Ethiopia and the HDM and PLGS. The existence of such relations is evinced by Ethiopian diplomatic sources in 1958 suggesting that "a decision was passed to grant a total of 117,000 Birr for the upcoming general elections to the PLGS and HDM for a period of sixmonths."[28]

At the same time, the government made the Assembly pass the emergency law giving the police sweeping power in dealing with security matters including the power to detain individuals suspected of undermining security for a maximum of one year without being charged[29]. Another bill was passed practically giving the government a monopoly on the press and the printed word, while a third one barred foreign consulates from interfering in the internal life of the country and Somali citizens from visiting the offices of such consulates without good reasons. Media freedom was on the slide despite a better political climate. "Once the Somali government was established, the SYL, because it had borne the brunt of the nationalistic struggle, could not avoid regarding itself as the exclusive guardian of nationalism and national goals. It could permit opposition and criticism, but any threat to the power position of the party itself was viewed as an act of treason against Somali nationalism," comments Castagno.[30]

'Il patto del diavolo' (Devil's pact)

An anti-Lega coalition of four parties (HDMS, GSL, PLGS and SANU), worried

26 TNA FO 371/131463, telegram from British Consulate Mogadisho to FO, March 31, 1958.

27 TNA FO 371/138307 confidential dispatch from British Consulate Mogadisho to FO, December 20, 1958.

28 Minutes of a meeting at the Ethiopian Prime Minister's office on September 22, 1958, as quoted in 'Ethiopia in African Politics, 1956-1969', a doctoral dissertation by Belete Belachew Yihun, April 2012, p. 111.

29 UN Doc. 1444, April 14, 1959, par. 97, p. 24.

30 A.A. Castagno, op. cit., p. 362.

that the proposed electoral law would leave them at the mercy of the government's whims, hurried to form what they called a United Front and threatened to boycott the elections unless this discriminatory law was withdrawn. This new anti-Lega coalition was soon to be dubbed by its critics 'Patto del diavolo' or 'Devil's Pact'.[31]

A joint manifesto of the four opposition parties was published, requesting the putting in place of a mechanism necessary to ensure free and fair elections. In particular, the four parties requested the UN to supervise the election process from January 1959, stating that supervisors should not have vested interests in Somalia and should be assisted by representatives of each political party, the government, AFIS and the Advisory Council of the United Nations. In case of unavailability of UN personnel, supervisory tasks should be handled by the UN Supervisory Council, empowered to cancel any elections deemed irregular. The joint requests also included the setting up of an interparty committee to ensure safety of voters and non-intervention of Italian officials in influencing the voting freedom of the political assembly. Use of media channels such as the *Corriere della Somalia* and Radio Mogadisho, as well as government-owned equipment such as cars or other vehicles should be restricted, and a special body, independent both from the government and the parties and in contact only with the UN Advisory Council, should be set up to directly supervise the casting of votes.[32]

Within the Legislative Assembly, the opposition objected also to two other main points of the draft electoral law, namely the proposed five-year term of the new Assembly and the assignment of seats to districts before the elections in absence of definite figures for the number of electors or actual voters in each district. Arguing that a parliament elected during the Trusteeship period could not be considered as truly representative, the opposition pleaded for the Assembly term to be reduced to two years. It was further argued that it would certainly be possible, during these two years, to take an accurate census of the population on the basis of which new and more valid elections could be held after independence.[33]

The two main reasons for boycotting the elections were presentation of the list on a district basis rather than a national list, and the amount of the cash deposit requested for each seat, which the opposition considered too high[34].

31 The expression was coined by Aden Abdulla..

32 TNA FO 371/138308 Letter from the British Consulate Mogadisho of February27, 1959.

33 UN Doc. T/1444, April 14, 1959, par. 106, p. 26.

34 Rapport du gouvernment italien à l'Assemblée Generale des Nations Unies sur l'administration de la Somalie placée sous la tutelle de l'Italie, 1959, p. 24.

However the government went ahead with its plan, despite criticism from the United Nations and objections from the opposition parties, who worried that the electoral law would deprive some persons of the right to vote, meaning that those living in districts where only one party list has been submitted might fail to disclose the number of voters in all districts, thus encouraging people in whose districts no elections were held to vote in another district[35]. The political climate of the electoral campaign was characterized by controversy and protests mounted by the opposition parties against the Somali government and Italy on the way the electoral process was being handled.

A delegation from the opposition parties met with Administrator Mario Di Stefano on 9 January 1959 in the presence of Minister Piero Franca (AFIS Secretary General), Dr Benardelli (Deputy AFIS Secretary General) and Dr Carlo Fettrappa-Sandri (Administrator's Chief of Staff). The delegation included Abdulkadir Mohamed Aden 'Zoppo' and Salah Mahadu Abdi, Secretary General and member of the Central Committee of the HDMS, Omar Haji Banafunzi, Deputy Chairman of the GSL Abukar Hamoud 'Soccoro', Chairman of the Unione Nazionale Somala (UNS) Haji Mohamed 'Borraco', and Ahmed Mudde Hussein, Chairman and Deputy Chairman of the PLGS.

In the meeting, the opposition flagged up some irregularities and voiced concerns about the general situation of intimidation prevailing in the country, which, in their view, was not conducive to fair and free elections. What most worried the opposition was the role of the police and of the local authorities hired by the government as obstacles to the opposition. The representatives of the GSL complained particularly about the detention of the president of their party and his group during their electoral campaign in Majertenia[36]. Haji Mohamed was arrested in Majertenia in December while touring there to open some new sections of the party and charged with 'incitement to rebellion' under the new emergency law. Many believed that the government was using the charges as a pretext to prevent the GSL opening any branches in the outlying provinces. But Majertenia was not the only province where local authorities exercised pressure to avoid the opening of GSL branches.

The Prefect of Hiran is reported to have issued an ordinance banning the opening of a Greater Somali League section in Beledweyne and, when a section was opened despite the ban, ordering demolition, with no compensation, of the

35 UN Doc.T/1444, 14 April 1959, par 109, p. 27.
36 Ibid., par 115, p. 28.

two-room structure used as an office. This dramatic event was confirmed by a number of persons present who directly witnessed the occurrence. The owner of the demolished structure was a member of the ethnic Macanne who, despite their considerable number and their status as the first settlers of Beledweyne, have historically been underrepresented in the public administration, sometimes by their own choice, but often because of prejudice. HDMS and PLGS representatives referred to serious difficulties, intimidation and hindrance on the part of the local authorities during the process of in the presentation of the lists in the districts of Baidoa, Bur Hakaba, Oddur, Brava and Dinsor.[37]

As they had previously done in other circumstances the opposition parties set a number of conditions for their participation in the electoral process. These were: a 25-day extension for presentation of lists in the electoral districts; freedom of political activity; freedom of movement of political leaders; presence in the voting process and counting of the ballots by UN observers; ballot boxes to be entrusted to UN observers.[38]

As in 1958, the opposition parties again urged the Administrator to intervene and ensure free and fair elections. But the official policy of AFIS was to interfere as little as possible in an internal matter it considered to be within the competence of the Somali government. The Administrator was convinced that the Somali government, since its establishment in 1956, had "enjoyed a large autonomy in the administration of all that concerns internal matters."[39] He seemed to give the impression that he had 'abdicated' much of his authority and that the Somalis were now virtually self-governing. It was an open secret that Di Stefano supported the Lega-led government, irrespective of moral considerations. "With healthy cynicism, Di Stefano pointed out to western officials that the only alternative to the Lega was a government dominated by Haji Mohamed, a situation as unpalatable to the western world as it was to himself. He was determined to destroy Haji Mohamed's influence and remove this virus, once and for all, from the Somali body politic", comments a British diplomat in Mogadisho[40]. It is further reported that, when the American Consul General in Mogadisho, in a meeting with the Administrator, expressed his worries about possible external criticism of the way the elections were being conducted, Di Stefano wondered

37 Ibid.

38 Letter dated January 12, 1959 to the Administrator, signed by Abdulkadir Mohamed Aden (HDMS), Omar Haji Abdalla Banafunzi (GSL) Haji Mohamoud Borracco (PLGS) Abukar Hamoud 'Soccoro' (UNS).

39 Top secret telespresso no. 1333, from Di Stefano to Foreign Ministry, Rome, March 5, 1959.

40 TNA FO 371/138306 Confidential report from the British Consulate Mogadisho to the FO, April 4, 1959.

"whether the West would like to accept a Somali government headed by Haji Mohamed." Under pressure from the UNACS, the government only accorded a 3-day extension for the opposition party to submit a list of candidates in the electoral districts, disregarding the UNCAS request of a 5-day delay.[41]

Under pressure from every quarter, and in a bid to safeguard its own image, the government decided to push the opposition to take at least a symbolic participation in the elections. To achieve this, it encouraged splits within the ranks of the opposition, successfully persuading some prominent elements of the loose United Front to present their lists of candidates. Consequently, at the last moment, before the closure of the electoral lists on January 13, 1959, the united front of the opposition parties was broken, with a few HDMS and liberal candidates taking advantage of the extension to submit lists in some districts in breach of party line.[42]

As a reaction to this development, a hurriedly convened Congress of the HDMS on January 19-21 promptly disowned those members who had agreed to participate in the elections and passed a resolution expelling the Secretary General Abdulkadir 'Zoppo' from the party and suspending Geilani Sheikh, the President of the party himself. The latter, a civil servant who had in the past been 'exiled' to Galkayo, was recalled to Mogadisho: a move seen by the government as a purely political manoeuvre meant to encourage the split within the ranks of the HDMS.[43]

The Congress then presented the government with a fresh set of demands which included the following: reopening of the electoral lists for a further ten days; assurance that genuine HDMS lists would be accepted in the main HDMS strongholds (Baidoa, Bur Hakaba, Merca, Brava and Gelib); guarantee as to the democratic conduct of the elections and particularly a restriction on the Lega using government transport for election purposes. These legitimate demands were promptly turned down by the Somali government and the Administrator refused again to intervene in what he considered as 'Somali internal affairs.' Adding confusion to the political situation, on February 2 the *Corriere della Somalia* published a notice signed by Geilani Sheikh Ben Sheikh expelling three party members (including Abdulla Yousuf 'Meygag') who had been leaders of the movement for the boycott of the elections. In all fairness to the government,

41 Telegram from Mussa Bogor, January 10, 1959.
42 FO 371/146954 confidential report from the British Consulate Mogadisho to FO, February 17, 1959.
43 TNA FO 371/125676 Monthly report for the month of March 1957 from the British Consulate Mogadisho.

it should be noted, however, that there are records indicating that the regional authorities were given formal directives to act impartially towards the competing parties and, in some cases, to correct certain decisions they had taken and that seemed to be damaging the opposition.

Indeed, in a telegram addressed to the district commissioner of Merca, the Minister of the Interior sent the following directives: "For political reasons and justice there is no justification for the closure of HDMS branch."[44] In a subsequent telegram, the Minister gave further instructions to all district commissioners to respect the law and act impartially towards the contending parties. "I do recommend once more that no obstacles should hinder the presentation of the lists and that there should be no resort to any illegal expedients not in line with the liberal spirit of the electoral law."[45]

Six days later, the Prime Minister himself issued clear instructions to regional and district commissioners urging them "to facilitate the submission of the lists of candidates from all competing political parties and to waive, if necessary, certain unnecessary formalities", adding that "any excessive restrictions in this regard run counter to the spirit of the electoral law and the clear intention of the government."[46] At the end of the period set for the presentation of the lists of candidates, the ruling party had lists presented in all electoral districts; the HDMS in eight electoral districts (Bur Hakaba, Oddur, Wanleweyn, Merca, Afgooye, Lugh Ferrandi, Jilib and Kismayo); the PLGS in four (Mogadisho, Balad, Merca and Villabruzzi). The Greater Somalia League presented candidates in only few constituencies (including Galkayo and Eyl) and withdrew them before the elections.

Disturbances in Mogadisho ahead of the elections

Before the general elections, a tense situation developed in many parts of the territory. In Mogadisho, on the evening of 20 February 1959, a clumsily-made hand grenade was thrown in front of a restaurant but did not explode; an Italian national was attacked and wounded. In both cases police arrested the offenders, who were identified as militant members of the Greater Somali League party. One week before the disturbances, Ambassador Di Stefano, who was closely monitoring the situation, wrote the following telegram to Rome: "Some extremist

44 ASMAE Telegram no. 350140, from Mussa Bogor to DC Merca, January 5, 1959.

45 Ibid., Telegram no. 350079/11EP, from Mussa Bogor to all district commissioners, January 6, 1959.

46 Ibid., Telegram no. 350411/17, from Abdullahi Issa to all regional and district commissioners, January 11, 1959.

elements of the Greater Somali League possibly with some troublesome belonging to opposition parties may be planning to stir up disturbances and may be preparing acts of violence against Italians, Americans and their property."[47]

Riots broke out in Mogadisho during the pre-election campaign in which one person was killed, and nine people between demonstrators and police officers were wounded, including the capital's district commissioner, Ahmed Haji Afrah, alias Ahmed 'Sciuqul', who received stab wounds. The casualty was a female protester called Awa Aden Mussa who died from gunshot wounds[48]. "The government behaved with considerable hysteria and carried out mass arrests. About 280 people were arrested, including 112 women", commented Angelo Del Boca, who was in Mogadisho to report on the events[49]. Among the arrested were Haji Mohamed Hussein and the President of the (SANU).

A curfew was imposed on the capital, and the local branches of GSL and SANU were closed and gatherings of these parties were banned as consequence. The curfew was lifted on March 1, 1959 to avoid holding elections while a curfew was in force. The mass arrest of GSL adherents, including Haji Mohamed, unleashed a string of condemnations and appeals to AFIS, the Italian Parliament and the UN Advisory Council on the part of the GSL itself. The issue of the sweeping measures taken by police against opposition members was raised at question time in the Italian Parliament on February 26 by communist deputies Boldrini and Giancarlo Pajetta.

In reply, Di Stefano explained that "the Somali government, since its establishment in 1956, enjoys vast autonomy and real self-government in all that concerns policy and internal administration and, in any case, there have not been any arbitrary arrests or political persecutions, but only arrests executed in compliance with the law."[50] It was true that the Italian Administration had formally already transferred much of the administrative powers to the newly born Somali institutions. However, "the risk was also evident, even in the respect of the spirit of the Code, of the mandate ending in political failure, for which the Italian government would be accountable to the Italians, the Somalis and the United Nations", as Antonio Morone correctly points out.[51]

The trial of Haji Mohamed Hussein, imprisoned on trumped-up charges

47 ASMAE Telegram n. 1567 from Di Stefano to Ministry of Foreign Affairs, February 13, 1959, quoted in Morone, op. cit., p. 121.

48 *Corriere della Somalia*, Febbraio 27, 1959.

49 Del Boca, op. cit., p. 278.

50 ASMAE Telespresso n.1333, March 5, 1959, from Di Stefano to the Foreign Ministry, Rome.

51 A. Morone, op. cit., p. 122.

of public violence, finally started on September 3, 1959. In May the group of prisoners started a hunger strike which was duly announced, through a visit from the UNACS and dispatches sent to all the Foreign Consulates in Mogadisho, as a protest against the illegal detention of innocent victims. The strike however, collapsed on May 5.[52]

The Egyptian newspaper El-Gumhuria in its May 27, 1959 edition reported news that the Secretariat of the Afro-Asian Solidarity Conference had arranged defence counsel for Haji Mohamed, who had been arrested and detained since January by a 'colonial government'. This sparked strong reaction by the Somali government and the ruling party alike[53]. The lawyer nominated as Haji's defence counsel was the Italian communist senator Mario Palermo, assisted by a leading Mogadisho lawyer, Carlo Quaglia, whose former fascist activities caused the visiting *Time Life* correspondent, James Bell, to describe the fascist-communist union in defence of Haji Mohamed as a 'unholy alliance' in an article by that title. Shortly before the start of the trial, the defence counsel was joined by the arrival from Italy of another lawyer, a socialist member of Parliament, Lucio Mario Luzzato[54]. The opening of the trial was delayed owing to Haji Mohamad's demand that he should be handcuffed before appearing in court. "The authorities refused to provide him with this martyrdom", comments a British source in Mogadisho[55]. Twenty-eight of the accused were found guilty and given sentences ranging from 16 months' to nine years' imprisonment with hard labour, Haji Mohamed himself being given a suspended sentence of one year's imprisonment, conditional on good behaviour in the future.[56]

Election results

The elections started on 4 March 1959 and were spread out over the following four days because of the largely nomadic or semi-nomadic character of the population who cast their votes without electoral certificates. In place of electoral certificates, the government introduced the system of marking the hands of the voters with indelible ink: this was meant to discourage electoral fraud, but the ink proved easy enough to erase with lemon, soda and sand.

52 TNA FO 371/138309 confidential report of May 6, 1959 from the British Consulate Mogadisho to the FO.

53 Diary Aden Abdulla, June 5, 1959.

54 TNA FO371/138314 confidential report from the British Consulate Mogadisho to FO, September 3, 1959.

55 Ibid., September 9, 1959,.

56 *Corriere della Somalia*, Settembre 22, 1958.

Out of the 30 constituencies, nationwide, 19 had registered only the Lega lists of candidates (Lista Unica). The districts where no election took place were: Bosaso, Alula, Candala, Gardo, Iskushuban, Eyl, Galkayo, Obbia, El-Bur, Dusamareb, Beledweyne, Bulo Burti, Itala, Brava, Baidoa, Bardera, Dinsor, Margherita, Afmedu. Elections did take place in 11 districts: Mogadisho, Merca, Afgooye, Villabruzzi, Balad, Wanleweyn, Lugh Ferrandi, Oddur, Bur Hakaba, Kismayo and Jilib.

In areas where only one list was registered, the Minister of the Interior was empowered to enact provisions in order to prevent electors from one area going to vote in other areas. On the face of it, that sounded reassuring, but these provisions were defined in such a loose way as to render them almost meaningless. In fact, as feared, massive numbers of voters moved from the districts where only one list was presented and even from beyond the provisional border line to districts where elections were taking place, a phenomena often encouraged by the political parties, particularly the ruling party.

The government made all efforts to secure re-election of the members of the Cabinet. Thus the 12 Lega seats of Hiran, being 'unopposed', showed in the re-election of the Prime Minister, the Minister of Social Affairs and the Minister of Economic Affairs. The Minister of the Interior, elected from the districts of Alula and Iskushuban, had opted for the tribally contested Alula seat, ignoring his party's plea[57] to opt for Iskushuban seat in order to placate the grievances of the Siuaqron (Siwaqron) ethnic clan who strongly resented the candidature of Haji Mussa in Alula, their home base. By opting for the Alula seat, Haji Moussa paved the way for his kinsman, Haji Moussa Samatar, to take the Iskushuban seat.

In the face of growing pressure from the Abgal, who claimed Mogadisho as their tribal base, the Prime Minister, who in 1956 had been party candidate for the single seat in the capital, chose this time to link the Minister of Social Affairs to the much safer seat of Beledweyne, where only the Lega list was 'unopposed'. Only the Minister of General Affairs appeared momentarily to have the courage to accept a contest when he entered his candidature at Baidoa, the center of HDMS strength, "but admiration faded when it was learned that the Lega list was returned 'unopposed'", comments a British source based at Mogadisho[58]. Disagreement fuelled by tribal motivations broke out between the Central Committee and the Mogadisho local committee over the party's candidate for the

57 TNA FO 371/138314, confidential report from the British Consulate Mogadisho to FO, September 23, 1959.

58 TNA FO 371/138308 confidential report from British Consulate Mogadisho FO, March 28, 1959.

elections in Mogadisho. Two candidates were considered: one was the veteran member of the party, Sheikh Issa Mohamed, a Bernardino, and the other was Ahmed Dahir Hassan, a Darod. The latter was nominated, but not elected: the two Mogadisho seats were taken by two candidates who, although belonging to the same Abgal clan, represented two different political parties.

The elections themselves could be little more than a formality once the Lega gave itself 83 seats out of 90 by declaring a number of constituencies to be 'unopposed'. The ruling party won again, amid sharp accusations of electoral improprieties, through the use of public resources and slush funds. When ballots were counted, distribution of seats across the parties emerged as follows:

PARTY	NO. OF SEATS
LEGA DEI GIOVANI SOMALI	83
HIZBIA DIGHIL E MIRIFLE	5
LIBERALI GIOVANI SOMALI	2

It should be emphasized that Somalis do not attach particular interest to the winning political party, simply because each tribal group had voted for candidates of their tribe and not necessarily for a party. What really mattered was the tribal composition of the elected membership of the Legislative Assembly. Thus, of the 90 seats, 39 went to Hawiye, 32 to Darod; and 19 to Dighil and Mirifle[59]. What was elected was then a tribal assembly under the mantle of party names. As a result of the restrictions imposed on opposition parties, the political game was left open for the Lega leading the country towards a one-party system. Commenting on the election results, Aden Abdulla, an absolutely upright man, noted in his journals: "I am glad of the electoral victory for my party, but at the same time, I would have been equally glad had there been strong opposition and had the 'lista unica' not been a product of fraud."[60]

In a succinct but comprehensive report to Rome on the post-electoral situation in Somalia, Piero Franca, AFIS Secretary General, gave a bleak picture of the situation in the Territory less than a year before the end of the trusteeship mandate. "From the result, which is unsatisfactory", he wrote, "it is clear that the new Assembly does not exactly represent the real force of the political parties in the Territory. The result well confirms the criticisms and attacks levelled

59 Ibid., March 25, 1959.
60 Diary Aden Abdulla, March 11, 1959.

during the elections against the ruling party, the government and the Italian Administration."[61]

It is reported also that the Egyptian member of the Consultative Council, alarmed by widespread electoral fraud, reported to the UN Trusteeship Council on the whole extent of the problem he had witnessed and suggested fresh elections be held under close UN monitoring. The Trusteeship Council hoped that the government of Somalia would consider submitting the holding of general elections to the Legislative Assembly as soon as tractable after independence as a means of furthering political stability in the Territory. Sadly, neither the UN nor the Administering Authority seemed perturbed by the voting irregularities denounced by the opposition parties and by the Egyptian member of the Consultative Council. As a result, Italy lost the opportunity to intervene with determination by banning the 'lista unica' and annulling election results at least for the constituencies in which votes had been grossly rigged, in the same way it had disregarded, with good reason, the grossly inflated figures of the population census carried out in 1957. One cannot help but agree with an author who wrote: "Italy abandoned Somalia to its destiny before the official end of its commitment in the country."[62] It could be added here that Italy had little appetite for pressing Somali government to conduct fair elections, fearing such a course of action may cast negative judgment on her work in Somalia over the previous ten years.

The first session of the second and last Legislative Assembly of the Trust Territory of Somalia under Italian Administration was opened by the Administrator, Mario Di Stefano. The opening of the Assembly took place in a tense political atmosphere "due to the inability of the Lega deputies of agreeing among themselves on the composition of the government and to the bitterness between Darod and Hawiye following Haji Musa Bogor's exit from the Cabinet."[63]

When the new Parliament held its first meeting on May 26, Aden Abdulla was, for the second time, elected President of the Legislative Assembly, obtaining 76 votes out of 87[64]. Abdulkadir Mohamed Aden 'Zoppo' and Haji Bashir Ismail were elected Deputy Presidents, obtaining 46 and 39 votes respectively[65]. The division of functions within the presidency of the Legislative Assembly clearly reflects tribal balance, as the President belongs to the Hawiye and his two

61 ASMAE Telespresso no. 2071, from Franca to D.G. Somalia, Foreign Ministry, Rome, Aprile 14, 1959.

62 Tripodi, op. cit., p. 100.

63 TNA FO371/138311, dispatch from the British Consulate Mogadisho to FO, May 29, 1959.

64 *Corriere della Somalia*, May 27, 1959.

65 Ibid.

Deputies to the Rahanweyn and Darod respectively.

Meanwhile, in the neighbouring protectorate of Somaliland, following the constitutional development introduced by the British government, legislative elections were held in February 1960. The members of the Somaliland Assembly had been elected in February 1960 by universal adult male suffrage in the single constituency system[66]. The voters had been registered in the five main urban centres, but registration was not required in the rural districts. The Somali National League (SNL) gained twenty of the thirty-three available seats, the United Somali Party (USP), representing the Darod and Dir clans, twelve and the National United Front (NUF), in alliance with the Lega, one. The NUF's defeat is clearly attributable to the Christian affiliation of its leader Michael Mariano, of which his political opponents had made a prominent campaign issue.[67]

The result of the 1959 elections which gave the NUF one seat came as a rude shock to the Somali government. According to British sources, the Lega government of Somalia had openly lent support to Michael Mariano and the NUF of Somaliland for some years and confidently believed Mariano's prediction that the party would return, at least, 12 members of the Somaliland Legislative Council.[68]

A party with a double soul (Un partito con due anime)

As we have seen, the opposition having been destroyed or driven underground, Somalia had virtually become a one-party territory. Nevertheless, not all was rosy for the Lega, which had fallen prey to its own internal dissensions. In fact, soon after the general elections of March 1959, a serious, unexpected crisis emerged again within the ruling party leadership over the President's proposal for the convening of an extraordinary Congress with the participation of representatives from the regional branches of the party, the party's parliamentary group and the Central Committee.

The idea was to involve the party members up-country so they would have their say in the selection process of the future Prime Minister and the president of the Legislative Assembly following the general election. "It is not fair to resort to them when we need their force and exclude them from taking part in important

66 Legislative Council election. Ordinance n. 9 of 1958 as amended, reported in Contini, The Somali Republic, an Experiment in Legal Integration, Frank Cass & Co 1969, p. 19.

67 I.M. Lewis, op. cit., p. 154.

68 TNA FO 371/146955, confidential report from British Consulate Mogadisho to FO, March 1960.

political decisions", notes Aden Abdulla in his journals[69]. The idea of urgently convening a party convention was not shared by all Central Committee members, particularly those politically close to the Prime Minister. When the proposal was put on vote, it was rejected by 10 votes, 7 in favour and 2 abstentions.[70]

The Central Committee members who voted against the proposal were Haji Jim'ale Barre Toho, Hassan Barre Toho, Osman Ahmed Roble, Osman Sheikh Mao, Abdinour Mohamed Hussein, Mohamed Ahmed 'Ottavio', Ali Mohamed Ali Afrah, Haji Abdisamed Mohamed and Sheikh Issa Mohamed. Voting in favour of the convening the Congress were: Aden Abdulla, Ali Hersi Farah, Abdirazak Haji Hussein, Mohamed Ossoble Walaio, Hussein Abdi Abdulla 'Farmacia', Mohamoud Ahmed Mohamed Addan 'Kutuba-Hor' and Ahmadei Mohamed Nour. The two abstained were Sheikh Mohamoud Mohamed Farah and Mohamed Haji Sobrie.[71]

Similarly, within the government there were divergent views over the convening of the Congress. Mohamoud Abdinour 'Juje', Sheikh Ali Jim'ale and Sheikh Omar Sheikh Hassan 'Lugey', together with the Prime Minister were against the idea of convening a congress. On the other hand, Haji Mussa Bogor, Salad Abdi Mohamoud and Mohamoud Ahmed Mohamed Addan 'Kutuba Hor' were in favour. Haji Farah's position was not clear as he was on mission abroad.

The disagreement over the convening of the party congress led to a gridlock. Opponents of the proposal shared the concern that the congress might exacerbate the already sharp divisions within the ranks of the party following the expulsion of the ex-president one year earlier[72]. In reaction to this result, Aden Abdulla resigned from party leadership, later withdrawing his resignation on the condition, however, that "the reasons which caused it were eliminated."[73]

A communiqué printed by the government's official newspaper, the *Corriere della Somalia*, announcing the end of the crisis caused by Aden Abdulla's resignation, read: "The Central Committee of the Lega announces that it has resolved the internal crisis existing since March 26, 1959. The leader of the party has in fact withdrawn his resignation. [...] The Committee re-examined the reasons that prompted the crisis and adopted measures including the convening of a congress limited only to a single representative from each of the outpost districts."[74]

69 Ibid.
70 Ibid., Telespresso no. 2071, from Franca to D.G. Somalia, Foreign Ministry, Rome, Aprile 14, 1959, p. 3.
71 Diary Aden Abdulla, March 24, 1959.
72 Ibid.
73 Ibid., April 3, 1959.
74 *Corriere della Somalia*, Aprile 25, 1959.

This was not the first time Aden Abdulla disagreed with the party leadership. In 1958 he resigned from his position as vice-president of the party after publicly denouncing the bickering, radicalization and dangerous polarization of the Central Committee between Darod and Hawiye, the latter ethnic group forming the majority of members ready to support the government for good or bad. "I absolutely must quit the Central Committee as it is not possible for me to continue working with people like these", wrote Aden Abdulla in his journals[75]. Another serious worry for the far-sighted political leader from Beledweyne was the pro-communist Egyptian policy of the President of the Party, Haji Mohamed Hussein, and his overtly anti-western hostility at a crucial time when wisdom would have dictated the maintenance of a more balanced policy *vis-à-vis* major foreign powers. The resignation was later withdrawn following pressure from fellow party members on the proviso that the President of the party changed his policy and returned to the fold.

With the participation of 30 representatives from outpost districts, the highly anticipated Congress of the party was convened on May 22, its immediate task being, among other things, to designate the future president of the Legislative Assembly and the future Prime Minister, two positions which had become vacant following the general elections in March[76]. At the end of a marathon session lasting from 09:30 am to the following morning at 00:35, the results of the vote for the premiership were: Abdullahi Issa 68; Aden Abdulla 52; Abdirashid 1; spoiled votes 4[77]. According to British reports, the Americans and the Italians were accused of having spent tens of thousands of pounds to ensure sufficient support for Issa[78]. The British Consulate can be a good source of information, though as with any other foreign diplomatic body, its reports must be weighed for factuality and analysis.

At the same session, the Congress designated Aden Abdulla as President of the Legislative Assembly; the results of the voting were: Aden Abdulla 65; Abdullahi Issa 38; Gabio 13; Abidrazak 2; Nour Hashi 1; Sheikh Ali Jim'ale 1; Abdirashid 1; Haji Mussa Bogor 1; spoiled votes 3[79]. The first important debate during the Congress session was concerned with the composition of the new government. On May 19, a motion was passed in favour of a single party, a Lega

75 Diary Aden Abdulla, January 14-15, 1959.

76 ASMAE Telegram no. 15488, from Franca to Foreign Ministry, Rome, April 26, 1959.

77 *Corriere della Somalia* ,May 23, 1959;.

78 TNA FO 371/138/310 Confidential report from British Consulate Mogadisho, to FO, May 23, 1959.

79 Ibid confidential letter no.1017/59 from the British Consulate Mogadisho, to FO, June 2, 1959: Diary Aden Abdulla, May 22, 1959.

government as against a coalition. The voting in favour of the motion was 65, with 43 against and 19 abstentions.[80]

Closure of the GSL and UNS HQs

Second ministerial crisis

A sudden widespread revival of tribal enmity had reached into the government itself and made a mockery of the Lega's claim of having stamped out tribalism. The struggle pitted against each other two of Somalia's most powerful clans, the Darod of Haji Mussa and the Hawiye of Abdullahi Issa. Conflict between these two 'super clans', as well as internecine battles among myriad of sub-clans in the interior on account of pasture and water, have always represented an element of internal unrest. "The Prime Minister, a Hawiye, was hardly on speaking terms with the Minister of the Interior, Haji Mussa Bogor, who was a Darod", comments a British source in Mogadisho[81]. Haji Mussa was the son of the last Sultan of the Majerten, Bogor Osman, and had migrated with his father to Mogadisho in 1927. In 1950 he was appointed territorial councillor and then elected from the constituency of Galkayo in the first general elections of 1956, before moving to the hotly contested constituency of Alula. He had always had a difficult working relationship not only with the Prime Minister, but also with other cabinet colleagues, notably the Minister of General Affairs and Personnel, Mohamoud Abdi Nour 'Juje' and the Minister of Social Affairs, Sheikh Ali Giumale.

Haji Mussa Bogor's new feud with the Prime Minister came to a head during the week April 27–May 2, 1959 when the Minister ordered the Provincial Governor of Benadir, Ali Omar Sheegoow, to allow the reopening of GSL and SNU premises in Mogadisho, seized under Gubernatorial Ordinance no. 1/959 of February 23, 1959 following a decision taken by the government. This move put the Minister on collision course with the Prime Minister. The Provincial Governor, finding himself in a difficult situation, referred the matter to the Prime Minister, who countermanded the order[82], whereupon the Minister suspended the Governor for insubordination. This was, in turn, countermanded by the

80 Diary Aden Abdulla, May 19, 1959; FO 371/138310, confidential report no 1017/59, from the British Consulate Mogadisho to African Department, FO.

81 TNA FO372/125676, monthly summary report for the period October-November 1957, December 1, 1957.

82 ASMAE Riservato, urgent letter no. 300433 del 29 Aprile, 1959, from Abdullahi Issa to Ali Omar Sheegoow.

Prime Minister, but the Minister ordered the police to release the premises of the two parties[83]. This order was carried out, thus challenging a political decision already taken by the government with his concurrence.[84]

In response to the Prime Minister's request for a delay in execution of the order given to the police for fear of an unexpected situation that might arise from the reopening of GSL and UNS premises, Haji Mussa wrote: "For the same reasons I exchanged with you verbally in our last meeting, I am deeply sorry I have to inform you that, despite my all good intentions, I cannot and absolutely do not wish to adhere to your invitation to postpone the order I gave for the reopening of the HQs of GSL and UNS[85]. I am convinced that the measure I have taken is fully compatible with the superior interests of the Territory, particularly if we take into consideration the current international situation concerning Somalia and the imminent session of the Trusteeship Council." He then added "On the other hand, I don't think I could back-track a decision I have taken on a matter falling under my exclusive competence without my name and my personal prestige being made to suffer."[86]

The reasons why the Minister acted at such variance with a policy decision of the government of which he was a member remain unclear. Two theories are advanced to explain his behaviour. According to some sources, the Minister was acting under pressure from the Egyptian member of the United Nations Advisory Council[87]. . Egypt was known for its active support for the GSL party founded by Haji Mohamed Hussein after a split within the Lega ranks in 1958. Others believe that Haji Mussa assumed the government would again order the closure of the premises of the GSL, widely considered as the party of the Darod, a measure that would have further poisoned Darod–Hawiye relations and as a result of which he would emerge as a defender of Darod interests and a leader of his community[88]. That was not to be: the government chose not to order the closure of the premises of the two parties, but the Prime Minister requested the Minister resign from his ministerial position. The quarrel drove a wedge between the two heavyweight politicians. The Minister refused to step down.

83 Letter no. 354665 of April 28, 1959, from Haji Mussa to the Police HQs, Mogadisho: by Ordinance no. 1/354664, dated April 28, 1959, the Minister abrogates Gubernatorial Ordinance no. 1/959 of February 25, 1959 contemplating the closure of the two parties HQs in Mogadisho.

84 TNA FO 371/138309, confidential letter from the British Consulate Mogadisho to the FO, May 6, 1959; Diary Aden Abdulla, April 28, 1959.

85 ASMAE Letter no. 432, from Abdullahi Issa to Haji Mussa Bogor, April 28, 1959.

86 ASMAE Letter no. 354662, from Mussa Bogor to Abdullahi Issa, April 28, 1959.

87 I.M. Lewis, op. cit., p. 158.

88 Diary Aden Abdulla, April 30, 1959.

This new development, likely to undermine the internal peace of the country, pushed some more moderate Lega exponents such as Aden Abdulla, Haji Farah Ali (Minister of Economic Affairs), Abdirazak Haji (Central Committee member, former party President and newly-elected deputy), and Abdirashid Ali (a newly-elected deputy), to seek a 'behind the scenes' compromise. The mediation team appreciated that, unless something was done quickly, the planned party congress might result in a further split within the ruling party and would cause a large Darod exodus towards a new party or, worse still, the (GSL). A pre-congress conference was thus called, under the chairmanship of Aden Abdulla: it was composed of all Lega Legislative Assembly deputies who were in Mogadisho in order to reach some sort of preliminary agreement on settling Darod–Hawiye differences.[89]

The resignation of Minister Mussa Bogor

The crisis turned nasty and the matter was in the end debated at the Central Committee of the Lega, which recommended the resignation of the Minister in order to avoid the collapse of the entire Government at a delicate time nearing the independence date. After some prevarication, Haji Mussa finally resigned from his post as Minister of the Interior on 4 May, 1959, probably cajoled into doing so by some of his colleagues (Abdirashid Ali, Haji Farah Ali and Salad Abdi). The resignation was handed over to the Prime Minister by Haji Farah, Aden Abdulla, Abdirashid Ali and Salad Abdi[90]. In the letter of resignation he addressed to the Prime Minister, Haji Mussa wrote: "Mr President, in relation to the difficulties arising between me and Your Excellency stemming from the instructions I have given to the Governor of Benadir for the reopening of the HQs of the concerned two political parties, and your lack of confidence in me, it is necessary, for my own dignity, for me to tender my resignation from the ministerial post. Despite my resignation rest assured, Mr President, that the sense of friendship and the esteem I harbour for you are not diminished and will never diminishes." The style and language of the letter contrast sharply with the deteriorated personal relations between the two Lega giants, and the concluding remarks of the letter are very formal and reassuring. It is highly likely that Mussa was made to believe that his resignation would be rejected, but to his surprise, the Prime Minister accepted it, excluding any possibility of reinstating the Minister

89 TNA FO371/138310, confidential report from British Consulate, Mogadisho, to FO, May 20, 1959.
90 Diary Aden Abdulla, May 4, 1959.

in his former position.[91]

The government-run Italian language daily newspaper, *Corriere della Somalia*, on May 9, 1959 carried a brief communiqué from the office of the Prime Minister announcing the latter's acceptance of the resignation of the Minister of the Interior tended to him on May 4, 1959. The Acting Administrator Piero Franca, however, refused to endorse Haji Mussa Bogor's resignation on the grounds that it would upset the inter-tribal balance and that the Prime Minister had acted unconstitutionally in accepting the resignation of a Minister without the Administrator's prior approval or even knowledge.

The political crisis further deepened with the unexpected resignation of another Darod Minister, Salad Abdi, on May 9, 1959 but the Prime Minister expressed his intention not to accept it. The Minister, who was member of a 'reconciliation committee', felt strong resentment against the Prime Minister's decision to ignore the committee's conclusions on the issue[92]. "The stage was thus set for a complete split between the Darod and Hawiye elements within the SYL, and various extremists were suggesting a mass resignation or a mass dismissal of all Darod in the government services", reveals a British source in Mogadisho[93]. Once again moderate Lega exponents (Aden Abdulla, Haji Farah Ali, Abdirazak Haji and Abdirashid Ali) sought to resolve matters 'behind the scene'. These conflict-resolving methods, attempting to solve state affairs in the same way tribal disputes are settled, are very fashionable in Somali politics. The four wise men succeeded in persuading the Prime Minister not to accept Salad Abdi's resignation and also to persuade the latter to remain in the government. The Prime Minister remained unmoved by calls to reject the resignation of Haji Mussa, threatening to resign rather than retaining him in his previous position.

Franca, in the end, reluctantly accepted the resignation of Mussa Bogor and signed the relevant decree on May 12, 1959 after this was recommended by the Central Committee of the ruling party in order to avoid the collapse of the entire government. He then rejected the resignation of Minister Salad Abdi[94]. It was widely believed that Franca favoured Haji Mussa's position, while the Administrator was generally thought to support the Prime Minister's point of view. Indeed the Administrator, on his return to Somalia from home leave, did

91 ASMAE Letter no. 300448, addressed to Haji Mussa, Maggio 8, 1959.

92 ASMAE Telegram no. 15531, from Franca to the Foreign Ministry, Maggio 10, 1959.

93 TNA FO371/138310 Confidential report from the British Consulate Mogadisho to the FO, May 20, 1959.

94 ASMAE Telegram no. 15436, from Franca to the Foreign Ministry, Rome, Maggio 11, 1959.

endorse the position of the Prime Minister.[95]

Since then, Haji Mussa was relegated to the position of 'king-maker', a role he played very well during the presidential elections of 1961 and 1967. He emerged at the forefront in 1969 when, following the sudden death of President Sharmarke, his party chose him to replace the slain President. However, this was a short-lived plan, frustrated by the unexpected advent of the military take-over on October 21, 1969. Mussa was killed in 1991 in mysterious circumstances in Mogadisho amid the chaos which marked the beginning of the civil war. At the time he was engaged in the peace process between Siad Barre's ending regime and the uncompromising Hawiye rebel groups, the USC.

Darod tribesmen claim the two seats of Lugh Ferrandi

Murder of Councillor Moallim Omar Maio

As mentioned earlier, the election results were the product of systematic and widespread fraud perpetrated by the officials in charge of polling stations, with the obvious blessing of the government. The opposition, as expected, cried foul, asking the Court to annul the electoral results of a number of districts including Lugh Ferrandi (Upper Juba). The electoral results for Lugh Ferrandi were invalidated by the judicial authorities on grounds of irregularities following a judicial recourse lodged by the HDMS.[96]

Prior to the judicial revision of the results, the two seats were allocated to the ruling party, represented by two Darod deputies. The invalidation of the electoral results of this district could not have happened at a worse time, and added tension to the already strained Darod–Hawiye relations. The judge found a violation of Articles 1 and 2 of Electoral Law no. 12 of 12.12.1958 based on the evidence of movement of electors from the electoral district of Bardera, who had intended to support the ruling party by casting their votes in the locality of Saranlei which falls under the electoral district of Lugh. The judge also heard evidence of irregularities involving cases in which electors cast their vote more than one time in the electoral section of El-Wak[97]. Article 1 of the electoral law provides for each elector to have one vote in his electoral district, and article 2

95 TNA FO 371/1469 In bitter disagreement with Di Stefano, Franca left Somalia for good on May 18, 1958 as the former returned to Mogadisho.

96 Article 58 of the electoral Law no. 26 of 12 December 1958 as amended by Law no. 4 of August 1, 1959.

97 ASMAE, AFIS, box 4, file 9, Ruling of the Regional Judge of Upper Juba, Dr. Furino, of April 9, 1959, invalidating the results of Lugh election.

provides for each district to constitute one electoral constituency.

As the consequent developments surrounding the matter show, the actual losers were the Darod and not the Lega as a party. The Lega, the party holding parliament majority and destined to hold the reins of power after the end of the trusteeship mandate, mainly derived its support from the Darod and Hawiye tribes, a coalition of convenience between nomadic clans in continuous rivalry and competition, not united by a common political ideology that could transcend tribal horizons.

Despite the absence of an accurate census, each ethnic group claimed numerical superiority over the other. The cancellation of the two seats of Lugh left the Darod with only 30 deputies against 32 for the rival Hawiye clan[98]. Many were surprised that only the results of Lugh elections were called into doubt, then annulled notwithstanding the fact that practically throughout the Territory votes were systematically rigged and irregularities committed and denounced. The invalidation of the Lugh election results rekindled old grudges and animosity, leading to accusations that the Hawiye-dominated government was biased against the Darod. Whether the accusations are genuine or not has no importance, it simply reflects the state of tension amid growing polarization within the ruling party. Meanwhile, prominent Darod businessmen, members of the Lega, unleashed a campaign of propaganda aimed at regaining the two seats of Lugh Ferrandi.

As a result, an angry Darod tribal group met Aden Abdulla in his office at the Legislative Assembly to claim the 'right' of their tribe to have the two seats of Lugh Ferrandi invalidated by the Court. On April 11, 1959, Aden Abdulla gives the following account in his journals of the atmosphere which prevailed in the meeting with the group: "This morning at 10 o'clock I received in my office at the National Assembly Haji Dirie Hersi, Agi [Haji] Mohamed Abdulla Dirir, Agi Mohamed Abdi Dere, Sugulle Habsei, accompanied by Agi Mussa Bogor. Agi Mussa had phoned me at 9 o'clock informing me in advance of their wish to see me together with Abdullahi Issa. Abdullahi could not be found. On behalf of the Darod, they spoke to me threateningly about how the invalidation of the Lugh elections decreed by the district judge of Upper Juba must be reversed, whether that's right or wrong. If I've understood them well, as Darod they would speak against the elections as a whole. I tried to explain to them that it is inappropriate to present the question that way, that what happened was nobody's fault because

98 ASMAE Telespresso no. 2071, from Franca to D.G. Somalia, Foreign Ministry, Rome, p. 4.

the Hisbiya had the right to seek redress from the judge and [it was] for him to decide the matter after ascertaining the facts. Anyway, I told them to bring the matter to the attention of the Prime Minister, but if possible not in the way they had presented it to me i.e. on behalf of the Darod! I was unable to conceal my disappointment and went as far as telling them I could not intervene in the matter unless they first recognized that the two seats were to go to the Lega and not to the Darod. After I made my position clear, they changed their attitude and reverted to a more reasonable tone[99]. [...] On the following day, in the presence of the Prime Minister, Haji Dirie and his kinsmen changed the menacing attitude they had displayed earlier and agreed to follow the legal way to claim the two parliamentary seats on behalf of the Lega."[100]

New elections for the Lugh Ferrandi district were scheduled for 11-15 January 1960, instead of from 6 to 10 December, 1959 as previously decreed[101]. However, less than a week to the elections, in an already charged political atmosphere, the HDMS candidate Councillor Moallim Omar Maio was stabbed to death in Lugh on 5 January, 1960. The incident sparked a wave of condemnations across the country, and Parliament adopted a unanimous and strongly worded resolution deploring the assassination of the former councillor and calling the government to bring the perpetrators to justice[102]. In a vast police operation, the perpetrator of the criminal act, Farah Hassan Mohamed ('Farah Barrei') was apprehended. He was 34-year old, of the Marehan clan family, born in Dusa Mareb and with no fixed abode[103]. In view of the gravity of the crime, a number of persons suspected of having direct or indirect links with the crime were arrested or detained by the police for questioning. Almost all of them belonged to the killer's clan family and were politically associated with the Lega dei Giovani Somali[104]. This was the second high-profile political assassination in Somalia, after the barbaric killing of Ustad Osman in 1953. The two victims had one common denominator: they were both from the Dighil Mirifle clan family, peace-loving and well-educated politicians. In both cases, the attackers turned out to be of nomadic origin, from Mudug, politically linked to the Lega dei Giovani Somali.

Six political parties competed in the Lugh by-election, and the results were as

99 Diary Aden Abdulla, April 11, 1959.

100 Ibid., April 12, 1959.

101 Decreto Amministrativo n°118 del 10 Agosto 1959.

102 *Corriere della Somalia*, January 27, 1960.

103 ASMAE Telegram no. 90 S/9, from Lugh to the Ministry of Interior, January 5, 1959.

104 ASMAE Secret telespresso no. 500180, from Dr.Gasbarri to the Foreign Ministry D. G. Somalia, Rome, January 7, 1960.

follows: HDMS 3,177 votes; Somali Union 1,263; Liberali Giovani Somali 2,726; SDU 1,600 votes; Lega dei Giovani Somali 2,036 votes; Partito Repubblicano Somalo 703 votes. The two seats went to non-Darod elements: Abdikarim Hussein Malak of the HDMS and Mohamed Elmi Burale of the Partito Liberale Giovani Somali (PLGS).

Abdullahi Issa reconfirmed

Scramble for leadership

The first and direct effect of the political crisis which engulfed the Lega was the prolongation of the gestation of the new government. Tribal rivalry and personal jealousies had held up the formation of the new government since the March elections. Abdullahi Issa, endorsed by the Party Congress, was designated by the Administrator as a Prime Minister for the second time and formed a new government in July 1959, five months after the ruling party won controversial electionsinMarch.[105]

Ending the country's political gridlock, on June 16, 1959, Issa formed the new government, a 15-strong Cabinet that was in fact a coalition of clan representatives bearing the titles of ministers and undersecretaries. The broad-base government gave proportional share to all three major contending clan families represented in the Parliament: Five posts went to the Darod: (1) Salad Abdi Mohamoud, (2) Mohamoud Yousuf Aden 'Muro', (3) Sheikh Mohamoud 'Malingour', (4) Mohamed Ali Da'ar, (Undersecretary), (5) Aden Shire Jama 'Aden Low' (Undersecretary). Four positions went to the Dighil and Mirifle: (1) Abdinour Mohamed Hussein, (2) Haji Omar Sheegooq, (3) Sheikh Muktar Mohamed, (Undersecretary) and (4) Sheikh Omar Sheikh Hassan 'Lugey' (Undersecretary). Four, in addition to the Prime Minister, who reserved the Portfolio of the Interior for himself, went to the Hawiye: (1) Sheikh Ali Giumale, (2) Osman Ahmed Roble, (3) Haji Farah Ali (4) Abdurahman Haji Moumin, (Undersecretary) in addition to Mohamed Sheikh Gabio, who would, at a later stage, be appointed Minister without Portfolio for Constitutional Affairs. One position (Mohamoud Abdinour 'Juje') went to the Dir clan family. The composition of the cabinet reflected a victory for the Prime Minister's faction. However, immediately after the formation of the government, a 17-strong

105 Decreto amministrativo n°44 del 24 giugno 1959, rep. Bollettino Ufficiale, suppl. n° 4 al n° 6 del 26 giugno 1959.

faction within the parliamentary group of the governing party staged a rebellion against the Prime Minister and the way he had formed the Cabinet, accusing him, among other things, of forming the government on strictly tribal base. Little argument is needed to demonstrate that in Somalia, no Prime Minister can survive if he fails to distribute portfolios according to the strength of the various clan families represented in the Legislative Assembly. However, critics of the government said that the three Darod ministers were regarded by their tribesmen as 'renegades and weaklings'. Salad Abdi, whose resignation had been refused by the Prime Minister the previous May, was rewarded by a 'demotion' from Finance to Agriculture. Sheikh Mohamoud 'Malingour' was an Ogadeni Darod and a government 'pensioner', while 'Muro' was regarded as an 'opportunist' and personal friend of the Prime Minister.[106]

As a result, in 1959, a new political development emerged, marking the Lega's departure from their long-standing position of refusing to share the spoils of political power with their political adversaries such as HDMS and others[107]. In the absence of clear ideological differences between the Somali political parties, the Prime Minister accepted in his government elements once described as 'traitors' and on the 'lista nera' (black list). Their past political activities were no longer important; what mattered was the clan family they represented. It should be remembered that the pro-Italian parties challenged the Lega, not only in Somalia, but at Lake Success, too, in the course of the debate on the future of Somalia at the United Nations, calling them a 'terrorist' organization.[108]

As a result of this new policy, a number of long-time opposition party members joined the governing party in search of ministerial positions. They included, among others, Abdinour Mohamed Hussein, former President of the HDM, who, after repudiating his former party officially on January 25, 1958[109], was rewarded with a cabinet post in the new government as Minister of General Affairs. Other leading politicians who crossed the line were Aden Shire Jama, 'Aden Low', former President of the Lega Progressista Somala[110], becoming Undersecretary of the Ministry of Home Affairs. Aden Shire had served in the Italian army, from 1933 to 1947, joining the Italian Resistance movement. As recognition of his participation in the guerrilla activities of the Italian Resistance

106 TNA FO 371/138312, confidential letter from the British Consulate Mogadisho, to the FO, July 1, 1959.

107 A.A. Castagno, op. cit., p. 369

108 UN Doc A/C.I/SR 286, par. 24.

109 Diary Aden Abdulla, January 28, 1958.

110 *Corriere della Somalia*, January 25, 1953.

partisan group ('partigiani'), a road was named after him: Via Aden Shire in Rome. He left the pro-Italian Partito Democratico Somalo in 1956 to join the Lega[111]. Abdullahi Haji Mohamoud 'Insania', former Secretary General of the Somali Democratic Party[112] became Undersecretary of the Ministry of Education in 1960.

Abdulkadir Mohamed Aden 'Zoppo', former HDM Secretary General, joined the ruling party and was elected vice-president of the Legislative Assembly in 1959, before becoming Minister of Finance in the first government after independence. Abdinour and Abdulkadir 'Zoppo' shifted their long-standing position to become part of a political process they had disparaged for decades. Haji Bashir Ismail, former Vice-president of the Lega Progressista, joined the governing party and was elected Vice-president of the Legislative Assembly in 1959.

As mentioned earlier, unlike other opposition parties, the HDM did not end in dissolution, but remained for a long time the only credible opposition party before independence, a party which represented the most productive regions of the country, in addition to occupying more than one-fifth of the seats in the Assembly.[113]

Revolt of the Majerten parliamentarians

The Administrator dismisses the dissidents out of hand

As the country became increasingly jittery on the eve of independence, rival factions within the ruling party started scrambling for leadership of the post-trusteeship regime. A powerful group of Darod MPs, led by Abdirashid Ali Sharmarke and Abdirazak Haji Hussein, continued to campaign for a change of leadership. The group staged a rebellion against the Prime Minister. The criticism to the Prime Minister focused on three key points: the way the government had handled the elections, which they thought had been rigged in many areas; the number of ministers, which in their view was excessive and a burden on the meagre national budget; and the moral and professional standard of the ministers, considered to be below normal requirements.

111 TNA FO 372/131459, Confidential. Dispatch from the British Consulate Mogadisho to FO November 13, 1958.

112 UN Doc.T/1143 and Corr.1, Report of the United Nations Visiting Mission 1954 on Somaliland under Italian Administration, par. 29, p. 4.

113 Costanzo, op. cit., pp. 86-87.

Reacting to the argument raised in relation to the financial burden, the Administering Authority provided an account of the estimated expenditure necessary to maintain the enlarged government. The salaries, allowances and miscellaneous expenses of the new ministries and their undersecretaries amounted to approximately Sh.So21,000 per month or about Sh.So200,000 per year, a level of expenditure the Administration considered a matter of relatively little concern[114]. Dissatisfaction may have been genuine to a certain degree, but there was an element of 'sour grapes' for those deputies who had failed to gain high offices because of the increase. This may be true, especially with regard to Abdirashid and Gabio. In fact, in November, when Gabio was appointed Minister without Portfolio, in charge of the Constitutional Affairs, he broke off with the dissident group.

Abdullahi Issa, who was once the international face of the Lega in late Forties and early Fifties, faced the biggest challenge since his appointment as Prime Minister in 1956. Commenting on the political situation the Prime Minister was facing, Piero Franca had this to say: "The current Prime Minister is heavily criticized not for his direct responsibilities (he is generally considered only a weak person), but for his entourage, considered responsible for maladministration, squandering and corruption."[115] Some would have liked to see Issa removed. Many called on him to get rid of at least some of the old ministers of his government, if not all of them. The most frequently mentioned personalities, according to Franca, were Sheikh Ali Giumale, Minister of Social Affairs, Mohamoud Abdinour, Minister of General Affairs, and Salad Abdi Mohamoud, Minister of Finance. Others added to the list even Mussa Bogor, Minister of the Interior, and Haji Farah Ali, Minister of Economic Affairs: the latter, whose long absence from the Territory had raised a wave of antipathy against him, was seen as an opportunist who enjoyed avoiding internal bickering by staying abroad.[116]

There was also little prospect of the Prime Minister being able to satisfy all aspirants to high office without increasing the new cabinet to a ridiculous number of ministers. On June 11, he offered the posts of counsellor of non-ministerial rank for Parliamentary and Foreign Affairs to Abdirashid and Gabio, respectively. "The offers were refused and further consultations had to be hurriedly undertaken."[117] Other disappointed aspirants, headed by Nour Hashi Alas, a SYL

114 Statement made by Luigi Gasbarri, in UN Doc. T.C.1021st meeting of July 21, 1959.
115 ASMAE Telespresso n. 2071, from Franca to D.G. Somalia, Foreign Ministry, Rome, 14 April 1959.
116 Ibid.
117 TNA CO 371/138311, confidential report from the British Consulate Mogadisho to the FO, June 17,

deputy, member of the Central Committee of the Party, Haji Musa Bogor, Gabio and Mohamoud Ahmed Mohamed Addan 'Kutuba-Hor', threatened to form a new party to include "all good Somalis, irrespective of tribe". They accused the Prime Minister of bad faith in declaring at every opportunity that tribalism was dead while forming the government on strictly tribal lines.[118]

It was also rumored that the Administrator, in a bid to cool down the tension, had suggested to the Prime Minister to drop Salad Abdi and Osman Ahmed Roble from the list in favour of Gabio and Abdirashid, whose recent return from Rome with university degrees was given so much publicity. But the Prime Minister remained committed to his list of ministers. Di Stefano confided to Aden Abdulla that the two new graduates were frustrated for not achieving their dream to become members of the Cabinet: both had hoped to become deputy prime ministers[119]. Abdirashid is quoted as saying "The rising class of Somali 'intellectuals' must be given representation in the government", and that it was "nonsensical to give expensive training abroad to Somalis and then not to make use of their education."[120]

Di Stefano also shared with Aden Abdulla some intelligence reports suggesting that Abdirazak considered the appointment of Mohamoud Yousuf Aden 'Muro' as minister as an affront to him and to his rer, on grounds of his rer's numerical superiority over that of Minister Muro; however Aden Abdulla did not believe this report[121]. Both Abdirazak and Muro hailed from the Majerten, Omar Mohamoud clan, but of different sub-clans.

On June 19, the Prime Minister submitted his list of ministers to the Central Committee of the ruling party for approval, but the Central Committee refrained from expressing its views on the new government on the grounds that, having elected a Prime Minister, they had delegated the work of forming the Cabinet to him and that the final decision rested with the Legislative Assembly[122]. On the following day, June 20, the dissident group wrote a letter to the Prime Minister and the Administrator, protesting against the composition of the new government on the following grounds: the Cabinet was excessively large and

---

1959; Diary Aden Abdulla, June 19, 1959.

118 Ibid.

119 Diary Aden Abdulla, June 27, 1959.

120 TNA FO 371/138312, conversation at a luncheon given by the Acting American Consul in Mogadisho on 24 June, 1959.

121 Diary Aden Abdulla, July 18, 1959.

122 TNA FO 371/138312, confidential report from the British Consulate Mogadisho to the FO, July 2, 1959.

imposed an unnecessary strain on Somali economy; it was tribalistic in character and would not heal the rift in Somalia's national unity; it gave no recognition to Somalia's 'intellectuals'.[123]

On June 23 the Administrator received the dissident group in the persons of Abdirashid Ali, Abdirazak Haji, Dahir Nour, Mohamed Ossoble and Mohamed Sheikh Gabio. What was discussed in the meeting was reported in detail in a note written by the British Consul who met the Administrator afterwards, which was recorded by Aden Abdulla in his journals:

"The Administrator assured me that he had taken great pains to persuade these men. He, as the Head of the Trusteeship Administration, had had no say whatsoever in the choice of the ministers and, if those chosen were really unfit for office, it was the dissidents' duty to find support for their campaign to remove them among all the deputies, and not seek to achieve their ends by means that are improper and harmful to the national interest. When appeals to reason produced no useful results, Di Stefano adopted a sterner line with the group. After explaining that the Prime Minister had 65 deputies with him, whereas the dissidents group could only mobilize 14 deputies in the Assembly, the Administrator told his critics he would stand by the Prime Minister and that they would carry a heavy responsibility if they sought to depose him in any but a democratic way. He stated that threats would not deter him, and that as a Sicilian, he knew more about tribalism and its workings than they did."[124]

"After uttering this warning, he dismissed them and they proceeded to the Post Office to dispatch their telegram of protest to the government in Rome and to the Trusteeship Council in New York", the British Consul General adds[125]. The text of the telegram sent on June 27 to the United Nations reads: "We the undersigned Legislative Assembly and Somali Youth League members on behalf of other colleagues and Somali people strongly protest against Chief Administrator Di Stefano for having formed new Somali government on tribal basis with unjustified superfluous number of ministers and undersecretaries beyond our modest budgetary means. Such policies endanger our national unity and reduce the ability to be self-supporting strictly connected with our political independence. We further submit this appeal with request that you intervene and recall Ambassador Di Stefano in order to avoid further consequences which

123 Ibid., July 1, 1959.

124 Diary Aden Abdulla, June 26, 1959; 'FO 371/138312, secret letter no. 1018/59, dispatch no. 36, from British Consulate Mogadisho, to the FO July 10, 1959 .

125 Ibid.

may cancel brilliant work done by his predecessor." The signatories to this petition to the United Nations Trusteeship Council included Mohamed Ossoble Adde (Hawiye), Nour Hashi Alas (Darod, Majerten) Abdirazak Haji (Darod, Majerten), Ahmed Egag (Darod, Majerten), Abdirashid Ali (Darod, Majerten) Dahir Nour (Darod, Majerten), Mussa Bogor (Darod, Majerten), Said Mussa (Darod, Majerten), Yassin Nour (Darod, Majerten), Mussa Samantar (Darod, Majerten), Ibrahim Haji Mussa (Darod, Majerten), and Sugulle Mohamed (Darod, Lelkasse).[126]

A similar telegram, though longer and more detailed, was sent to the Italian Foreign Minister, Giuseppe Pella, with 18 instead of 15 signatories[127]. To guard against the possibility of postal censorship, the rebels handed a copy of the message to J. Cebe-Habersky, a Czechoslovak serving as Principal Secretary for the UNACS who was leaving Mogadisho for New York that day[128]. Mediation efforts between the dissident faction and the Prime Minister, promoted by the President of the Legislative Assembly in close collaboration with the Central Committee of the ruling party, ended in disarray[129]. The majority of the Central Committee endorsed the position of the Prime Minister, calling the dissidents to adhere to the party line to no avail[130]. The group was advised to use their constitutional powers and challenge the government in the Legislative Assembly when discussing its programme, but they were not open to compromise. There were plenty of good reasons to attack the government programme in the Legislative Assembly, ranging from the poor state of the economy to rampant corruption and maladministration. Eventually, the dissident faction was suspended from membership for breaching party rules.[131]

To counter the moves of the dissidents, a group of Mogadisho tribal chiefs, notables and religious leaders, all from the Hawiye clan family, went to call on the Administrator on July 4 to ensure him of their unwavering confidence and support for the Prime Minister. The group was formed of 18 people but claimed to represent 84 of the Somali leaders in Mogadisho, including some public administration staff.

The Central Committee of the Lega dismissed the allegations of the dissident

126 UN Doc.T/Pet.11/L45, 1 July 1959.
127 TNA FO 371/138312, confidential report from the British Consulate Mogadisho, to the FO July 2, 1959.
128 Ibid., July 1, 1959.
129 Diary Aden Abdulla, July 10, 1959.
130 Ibid., July 17, 1959.
131 Ibid.

faction as "absurd accusations cabled to the Trusteeship Council by a small group of deputies belonging to the Party concerning the formation of the Somali government" and expressed its full confidence in the "enlightened and farsighted work of His Excellency Ambassador Di Stefano."[132]

In his long and detailed notes covering his conversation with the Administrator, the British Consul General, Mr Kendall, enumerates a number of factors contributing to this critical situation. First and foremost was the fact that "tribalism had prevented people from seeing things through the eyes of a Somali rather than those of a Darod, Hawiye or Rahanweyn. Secondly the Lega dei Giovani Somali which, for too long, had enjoyed a monopoly of political power was unable or unwilling to tolerate opposition in every shape and form, those envious Somalis not sharing in the spoils of political power."[133]

Kendall's summary of the situation is probably very close to the facts when he says: "I find it difficult to believe that the rebel group within the SYL will settle down into 'healthy' opposition. Tribal feelings are involved, much personal bitterness exists between contending factions, and they are moved by different interests and different aims."[134]

The Lega's bickering moved to the United Nations

In 1949, Abdullahi Issa had been bitterly challenged at Lake Success by the Conferenza Somala; in 1959, ten years later, he faced a wave of criticism not only from the traditional opposition parties, but also from a section of his own party, blaming him, inter alia, for the way he had handled the general elections of March 1959 and the way he had formed the government. When all attempts to solve the crisis failed to generate agreement, the Lega's bickering landed eventually at the United Nations when a defiant Abdirazak, together with his colleague Mohamoud Ahmed Mohamed Addan 'Kutuba-Hor', travelled to New York in July to challenge the legitimacy of the Somali government before the United Nations Trusteeship Council. This potentially damaging move, at this crucial time, caused many eyebrows to be raised. Many feared that such an act might call into doubt whether the country was ready for independence, and this was the last thing Somalis wanted to happen.

To counterbalance the rebels' manoeuvre, the government, in addition to

132 UN Doc. T/PET.11/L.44, 1 July 1959.
133 TNA FO 371/138312, dispatch from the British Consulate Mogadisho to FO July 10,1959.
134 Ibid., July 3, 1959.

a delegation already present in New York, dispatched urgently to the United Nations two members of Parliament, Ali Mohamed Hirabe 'Hagarey' and Abdullahi Haji Mohamoud 'Insania', accompanied by a police officer, Lt. Colonel Daud Abdulla, to defend the government's position. The irony was that the two men the Lega sent to New York to take its defence were in the past well-known prominent members of an anti-Lega front. The two were carrying with them written statements, bearing many signatures of ordinary persons to prove the popular support the new government was allegedly enjoying.

Protesting before the United Nations against the Somali government were also representatives from the traditional opposition parties. Opposition leaders including Abukar Hamoud 'Soccoro' (Somali National Union), Sheikh Mohamed Ahmed Mohamed 'Yero' (HDMS) and Abdullahi Abukar Sheikh Ahmed 'Gacma-dheere' (GSL) appeared before the UN Trusteeship Council to air their grievances[135] directed against both the Somali government and the Italian Administration.

For the Somali National Union, former Unione Gioventù Benadir, the terms of office of the Legislative Assembly elected in 1959 were unacceptable because the five years for which it had been elected exceeded the period of the Trusteeship Administration. After denouncing violations of freedom and civil liberties allegedly committed by the government, 'Soccoro' appealed for new elections to be held under international supervision and for immediate release of all political detainees. For the HDMS party, the 1959 general elections were conducted in a climate of intimidation and curtailment of individual liberty: hence their decision to boycott it. The 5 members elected on a HDMS ticket did not represent the party line: they had already been expelled from the party on January 29, 1959, i.e. before the elections.

For the GSL representative, the elections were marred by systematic violations of individual liberty and freedom, followed by massive vote rigging. He, too, appealed for the 1959 elections to be made null and void, and for new elections to be organized under the supervision of the United Nations before the expiry of the trusteeship mandate; for the present Constitution to be considered provisional; for immediate release of all political detainees; and for the issue of the frontier dispute with Ethiopia to be solved on the basis of ethnic considerations, thus raising a strong nationalistic agenda not shared by the other opposition parties[136].

135 UN Doc.TC 1014th meeting of July 16, 1959.
136 Ibid.

The representative of the GSL made the strongest and fiercest of the statements explaining amongst other things that Administrator Di Stefano seemed to "enjoy the sight of blood in the streets of Mogadisho when he has caused massacres."[137] The debate on the petition submitted by the dissident faction generated animated exchanges between Abdirazak and the Egyptian delegation at the Trusteeship Council of the United Nations, who seemed not quite impressed by the arguments raised in the petition[138]. There was no disposition among the members of the Council to interfere with the internal affairs of Somali politics, and no delegation made any attempt to seriously embarrass the Lega government. Even the USSR was very mild in their criticism, which was directed carefully at the Italians and not at the Somali government. "The demands of the petitioners were not, therefore, taken up, and they made little impression", commented the UK delegate to the United Nations.[139]

Realizing that his arguments were unlikely to cut much ice with the members of the Trusteeship Council, Abdirazak refused to be drawn into any general indictment of the Somali government. Instead he made a face-saving statement on July 25 on behalf of "all Somali petitioners or otherwise who are now present" in which he said that "all Somalis were at one in pursuit of certain general aims for the future of Somalia which would be achieved with the harmonious co-operation of all segments of the people."[140] Most Somali heaved a collective sigh of relief that wide-scale violence and chaos were mercifully avoided. Yet the country remained badly split, largely along ethnic lines.

After long and laborious efforts The Prime Minister finally presented the programme of his government to the National Assembly, but only after taking the precaution of ensuring that the vote in the Assembly should be by roll call rather than by a secret ballot. By having a roll call, the Prime Minister would not only apply pressure on those who promised him their support, but also have the benefit of knowing whom he could count on in the future. In fact, a group of deputies introduced a motion requesting the vote of confidence to be conducted by roll call and not through secret ballot[141], a move intended to save the government from being defeated and humiliated in a secret ballot. The

137 TNA FO 371/138390, confidential telegram from the UKDEL to FO, August 10, 1959.

138 For more information on what the dissident group presented to the UN and the intervention of the Egyptian delegate on the subject, see the Council's official records (24th session 1022nd meeting, July 22, 1959.

139 TNA FO 371/138390, Confidential telegram from the UKDEL, New York, to FO, August 10, 1959.

140 Ibid.

141 Diary Aden Abdulla, July 10, 1959.

motion was approved by 57 votes in favour and 20 against.[142]

By 67 votes in favour against 10 and 1 abstention, Parliament approved the government's programme on 1 August. The ten 'no' votes came from Abdirashid Ali, Dahir Nour Egal, Haji Mussa Bogor, Haji Mussa Samatar, Haji Said Mussa Osman, Ibrahim Haji Mussa, Yassin Nour, Mohamed Ossoble, Nour Hashi Alas and Sugulle Mohamed. Osman Mohamoud Adde abstained from voting.[143]

But, in spite of this show of support for the government, it is not to be supposed that the political crisis was over. Less than one year before the target date for independence, the ruling party appeared more badly divided than ever before. One of the most difficult issues requiring urgent attention was that regarding the 13 members expelled from the governing party in early July; the case loomed large in the mind of many. A self-appointed group of three eminent wise men volunteered to conduct a long and delicate process designed to bring the dissidents back to the fold. The troika included Aden Abdulla, Haji Bashir Ismail and Haji Yousuf Egal. The 13 sought an undertaking from the Prime Minister not to increase the number of members of the cabinet, with the understanding that none of them was seeking ministerial positions. The latter condition was obviously meant to dispel widely believed notions that members of the group were pursuing political ambitions.[144]

It was noted that Haji Mussa Bogor was absent from each meeting convened for the mediation process. Predictably, the readmission procedure proved unclear and controversial as the group maintained that the Central Committee had acted outside their statutory powers. It was argued that matters related to discipline were the competence of the party's Disciplinary Committee and not the Central Committee. On this ground, the 13 resisted the proposal put forward by the wise men of lodging an appeal against the expulsion order from the party, accepting instead to submit joint signed request for readmission. In addition, the dissidents pointed out that, since they had not left the party of their own volition, but had been expelled, they demanded to be reinstated with an apology from the Central Committee. In the end, under pressure from the wise men, the Central Committee of the party decided the case *ex aequo et bono* by readmitting the group into the party.

However, the long and delicate work of persuasion and reconciliation conducted by the three wise men soon ran into trouble when some of the dissidents, among

142 Ibid., .July 24, 1959.

143 *Corriere della Somalia*, Agosto 2, 1959.

144 Diary Aden Abdulla, September 19, 27, 28, October 21, 1959.

them Nour Hashi Alas, Sugulle Mohamed and Abdirazak Haji Hussein, resisted the call to take a fresh oath of allegiance to the party principles and "the former Minister of the Interior, Haji Mussa Bogor, remained irreconciled", comments Mr Kendall, British Consul General in Mogadisho[145]. Mussa rejoined the Lega of his own volition shortly before the 1964 general elections.

The readmission of the dissidents had removed a potential menace to law and order in the run-up to independence; it had also weakened any possible considerable internal influence of the Greater Somali League, the new party founded by Haji Mohamed Hussein. The readmission of the group, however, had generated a serious unexpected political crisis leading to the resignation from the party of an influential government Minister, Sheikh Ali Giumale, Minister of Health, Veterinary Services and Labour, and close friend of the Prime Minister, who retired to his political stronghold of Beledweyne in protest against the re-admission into the Lega of the dissident deputies. The Minister saw the readmission of the dissident group as illegal because not properly sanctioned by the party's disciplinary bodies[146]. Efforts to convince the Minister to reconsider his position proved difficult and it took considerable time to take him back to the fold.

While the Darod–Hawiye dispute was centre stage, further evidence of a worsening situation emerged with the publication of an anti-government manifesto, dated April 30, 1959, being circulated by hand around Mogadisho. It was signed by a Galkayo tribal Chief, Haji Sugulle Habasei, who demanded, among other things, new and free elections, a congress of chiefs and religious leaders, greater religious influence in politics and adoption of Arabic as the country's official language. The manifesto emphasized the refusal of any postponement of independence on the Somali's part[147]. As explained earlier, the issue of possible delayed independence was first raised by Abdullahi Issa himself, in his capacity as Lega envoy at the Trusteeship Council of the United Nations in 1953. Now that he was head of the government, he had the duty of dismissing the existence of any plan designed to postpone independence. It did not need an expert to realize that the manifesto, in which claims were made as to the 'discovery' of a Western plot to delay Somali independence, bore the hallmark of the Egyptian propaganda released by Radio Cairo. The manifesto was given no publicity in the press, but on May 23 the *Corriere della Somalia* published a letter signed by an

145 TNA FO 371/138316, confidential report of November 18, 1959 to the FO.
146 Ibid.
147 Ibid., letter no. 1017/59, app. A, May 20, 1959.

imposing number of leading Darod, including eleven deputies led by Abdirazak, totally disowning it as reactionary, unrepresentative of Darod opinion and possibly written not by a Somali, but by a treacherous outside hand.

A leading article appearing in the *Corriere della Somalia* on May 13, written by the Prime Minister under the challenging headline Down with Tribalism, further denounced the manifesto as an attack on Somali unity from a few unrepresentative reactionaries. "On the whole, the more educated Darod were strongly opposed to the Manifesto and it made the Darod deputies more willing to back Aden Abdulla in order to avoid a really serious inter-tribal feud", comments a British diplomatic source in Mogadisho.[148]

Further difficulties emerged for the Prime Minister when the Legislative Assembly failed to approve by the required two-third majority two of the three bills intended to confirm the freehold of lands on which the Italian Petrol Agency (AGIP), alongside two Arab concerns, had built various installations. The first bill, in respect of an Arab's store in Merca, was safely passed, but the other two, in respect of an Arab's cinema at Jenale and an AGIP petrol station and depot near Margherita (Jamama), failed to obtain the required majority under article 14 of the Trusteeship Agreement between Italy and the United Nations[149]. This to the great annoyance of the Prime Minister, "who was unused to such display of independence by the usually docile Assembly", comments a British source in Mogadisho.[150]

Abdullahi Issa headed two governments from 1956 to 1960 under the supervision of the Italian Administrator. To many, the achievements of his two pre-independence administrations had been very poor, undermined by continued internal bickering and personal antagonism among his ministers. The ministers, all from the Lega, were accused of tribal loyalties in dealing with public affairs of their respective competence, and of pursuing their own personal interests. Many of them were able to accumulate vast personal fortunes within a short period of becoming cabinet ministers.

The Times correspondent, in Mogadisho during the independence celebrations, described Issa as "calm, patient, and polite without the gift of oratory."[151] After independence, Issa served as Minister of Foreign Affairs in Abdirashid's

148 TNA FO 371/138310, confidential letter from the British Consulate Mogadisho, to the FO, May 20, 1959.

149 *Corriere della Somalia*, November 11, 1959.

150 TNA FO 371/138316 confidential report the FO, London, November 18, 1959.

151 *The Times*, June 29, 1960.

government, from 1960 to 1964, a function he performed amid frequent controversies and continued rifts with his Prime Minister over major foreign policy issues on which the two men often did not see eye to eye.

From 1964 Issa was appointed to head less important ministries in the Abdirazak and Egal governments. He served as Minister of Health and Minister of Trade and Commerce before sinking into oblivion following the military coup of October 1969. He was placed under detention together with the rest of the Cabinet, but no criminal charges were brought against him. Unlike other prominent party fellows who turned their back, he remained loyal up to the end to the Lega, a party he had joined in 1944. Apart from the poor performance of his administration, there were two barriers in his way to the premiership or presidency of the republic after independence. The first one stemmed from a long-standing, unwritten norm applied to the sharing of the top three state positions among the major Somali clans. Based on this norm, the positions of Head of State, Prime Minister and President of the National Assembly were assigned to representatives from the four major Somali ethnic groups: Darod, Hawiye, Issak and Rahanweyn. Consequently, following the election of Aden Abdulla as President of the Republic in 1961, Abdullahi Issa could not be chosen as Prime Minister: it was simply unthinkable that both positions should be filled by two men hailing from the same Hawiye lineage.

The second barrier was of a constitutional nature and related to his age, barring him from joining the race for the Presidency of the Republic. "The original text of the draft of the Constitution, prepared by the Minister of Constitutional Affairs, fixed the minimum age of the President of the Republic at 35 years. However, when the issue came for discussion, the Constituent Assembly amended the draft article bringing the minimum age of the President to 45 in line, as argued by some deputies, with Islamic practices", writes Mario D'Antonio, a legal advisor who attended the works of the technical committee in charge of drafting the Constitution.[152]

Abdullahi Issa was 38 at the time. "This age limit debars all Somaliland Ministers from the Presidential Office as well as Abdullahi Issa", commented the British Ambassador at Mogadisho.[153]

152 Mario D'Antonio, *La Costituzione somala, precedenti storici e documenti costituzionali,* Istituto Poligrafico dello Stato, Roma 1962, p. 93 (quoting Records of the Constituent Assembly no. 29 of June 9, 1960, p. 10).

153 TNA FO 371/146955 Confidential report of July 6, 1960 from British Embassy Mogadisho to FO.

Demand for early independence

American views on the issue

The Trusteeship Agreement between the Administering power and the United Nations stipulated that the trusteeship mandate end on 2 December 1960. However, events in the Trust Territory, beginning with the elections of March 1959 and culminating with the formation of the government, led to the emergence of voices within the ruling party calling for early termination of the trusteeship regime. In fact, in a move probably intended to embarrass the government, Abdirashid Ali, leader of the dissident faction of the party, submitted to the Legislative Assembly a motion calling for independence on January 1, 1960. Co-signing the motion were Mohamed Ossoble Adde, Ibrahim Haji Moussa, Sugulle Mohamed Mohamoud and Yassin Nour Hassan, all from the dissident group[154]. Explaining the motives for the introduction of the motion, Abdirashid referred to alleged Ethiopian intentions designed to block the planned union between Somalia and Somaliland.[155]

As a matter of fact, the Ethiopian government was deeply disturbed by the proposed unification of the Protectorate with the Trust Territory and remonstrated with Britain and the US regarding a widely publicized statement by Mr Lennox-Boyd (British Colonial Secretary at the time) about constitutional progress in Somaliland and a possible merger with Somalia. Ethiopia regarded the British Minister's statement as interference in 'African internal affairs' and an attempt to create blocs[156]. In a message to the Emperor of Ethiopia, the leaders of the three major Somali political parties—the Lega, the National Union Front (NUF) and the Somali National League (SNL)– categorically rejected the Ethiopian demarche. The government of Somalia, for its part, sent His Majesty Haile Selassie a most explicit message.[157]

Abdirashid's motion on early independence had obviously embarrassed the government, which would have found it difficult to vote against it. It was thus decided to adjourn the debate until August 22. In what seems to be a lack of co-ordination and a show of mistrust among ruling party deputies, a second motion, most probably with the government's blessing, was submitted one day later. This second motion, jointly introduced by Mohamed Sheikh Gabio, Hilowle Moallim,

154 ASMAE, AFIS, box 19, file 40. Minutes of Parliament meeting no. 42 of August 22, 1959.
155 Costanzo, op. cit., p. 62.
156 *Corriere della Somalia*, Febbraio 16, 1959.
157 Ibid.

Osman Mohamoud Ibrahim and Ali Sheikh Jess[158], requested Italy to grant early independence 'as soon as possible' without determining a date and citing the 'political maturity' of the Somali people and the development of what they called 'free institutions' as the reason for the initiative. The motion did not mention any external threat[159]. When it was put on vote, the first motion was rejected by 52 votes to 12 and 4 abstentions[160], while the second was unanimously approved on 25 August 1959, with one abstention[161]. The National Assembly made reference to the progress and political maturity achieved by Somalia, not to the crucial work still to be done before independence, the completion of the Constitution and the election of the Head of State being top of the agenda[162]. The motion requested the Italian government to pass the resolution to the General Assembly of the United Nations[163]. In a declaration made in Rome on August 30, 1959, Alberto Folchi, Italy's Foreign Affairs Undersecretary, confirmed that his government was prepared to consider favourably the request for the advancement of the date of Somalia's independence. However, he added: "It will be necessary, in particular, to complete beforehand the plan for the transfer of power to be presented to the Trusteeship Council of the United Nations; to ensure perfect political development of the territory in order to arrive at the day of independence with a Constitution drafted and approved; and, finally, to lay the foundations of future friendly relations between Italy and independent Somalia, subject to the ratification of both Parliaments."[164]

The United Arab Republic (Egypt), acting through the Egyptian member of the United Nations Advisory Council for Somalia (UNACS), Minister El-Zeyat, was determined to force the Somali government to ask for independence as early as possible. To do this, El-Zeyat tabled his own motion before the Fourth Committee of the General Assembly, suggesting October 15 as a suitable date "knowing fully well that the Somali Prime Minister, who is reputed to harbour anti-Egyptian sentiments, could not and would not allow earlier independence to appear to be linked with Egyptian championship of the Somali cause," comments a British intelligence report.[165]

158 ASMAE, AFIS, box 19, file 40. Minutes of Parliament meeting no. 42 of August 22, 1959.
159 Costanzo, op. cit., p. 63.
160 Diary Aden Abdulla, August 25, 1959.
161 *Corriere della Somalia*, Agosto 24-25, 1959.
162 Report of the UN Advisory Council for the Trust Territory of Somalia, 1958.
163 ASMAE, AFIS, box 9, file 10. Letter no. 341085, from Abdullahi Issa to Mario di Stefano, October 31 1959.
164 UN A/C.4/433, November 11, 1959.
165 TNA FO 371/138306 Dispatch from British Consulate Mogadisho, April 10, 1959.

In an endeavour to clarify the situation, the Prime Minister, in a letter of 1 October, 1959 addressed to the Administrator, announced: "After carefully examining the state of affairs, the Somali government, in an extraordinary session on 26 September, while reiterating the wishes of the Somali people to attain independence as soon as possible, has deemed it preferable that certain problems, including the preparation of the Constitution and the election of the Head of State, be first resolved. Therefore, the Council of Ministers, having taken all these into consideration, has come to the conclusion that, for the time being, no date could be set for the proclamation of an early independence."[166] Finally, the issue of early independence was discussed at the UN in November 1959 during the XIV session of the General Assembly and a decision was taken on the issue on 5 December 1959, fixing the date of independence for July 1, 1960 as suggested by the Somali government, with the undertaking to first complete the Constitution and the plan for transfer of power.[167]

The Italian Senate and Lower Chamber of Deputies adopted a bill ending Italy's rule in Somalia on July 1, 1960, six months ahead of the terms provided in article 24 of the Trusteeship Agreement between Italy and the United Nations Trusteeship Council of January 27, 1950. By Law no. 643 of June 28, 1960, the Italian Administration officially known as AFIS was set to terminate on July 1, 1960.[168]

However, while in principle supporting the idea of early termination of the trusteeship, Italy had shown strong reservations regarding the planned unification with the Protectorate of Somaliland, preferring instead to see Somalia remain alone after independence. In a meeting with Aden Abdulla and the Prime Minister in Mogadisho on August 3, 1959, the Italian Minister of Treasury, Paolo Emilio Taviani, on official visit to Somalia, confirmed his government's intention to give continued economic support to Somalia after independence, but made it clear that this policy might be subject to revision in the event of Somalia going ahead with the process of unification with the Protectorate of Somaliland. That was, without doubt, a clear case of diverging positions between Italians and Somalis over an important issue relating to Somali nationalism. Totally differing with his Italian guest, Aden Abdulla entered the following comment in his journals on August 4, 1959: "I think the Italians are wasting their time with us, as we will

166 UN A/C.4/433 November 11, 1959.

167 Doc, UNOR, A/R. 418 (XIV), December 5, 1959.

168 *Gazzetta Ufficiale della Repubblica Italiana,* no. 170, Luglio 13, 1960.

never renounce such a possibility for whatever motive."[169]

The Americans, on their part, expressed reservations over the earlier date of independence and made suggestions to the Somalis to reconsider that position. The early termination of the trusteeship regime was first raised by Ambassador Enrico Anzilotti during a conversation with officials from the Department of State. Anzilotti confirmed in the meeting that "Italy would find it difficult to refuse a request for independence before 1960 on account of plans for Somalia's Constitution and election of Head of State by the end of 1958, and of Somalia's wish to negotiate directly for foreign aid."[170] The United States, however, felt there were advantages in not moving too rapidly, on the grounds that the Somali government would not be able to act effectively for some time and would therefore need as much guidance as possible.

The issue of early termination of the trusteeship regime was further discussed in talks held by the President of the Legislative Assembly and the Prime Minister with US Ambassador Mr Bliss during the latter's visit to Somalia in October 1957. The Prime Minister expressed his government's eagerness to get in touch with other nations, and particularly the United States, and his plan to ask for independence in January 1959[171]. US views on the issue of early termination of the trusteeship were expressed by Ambassador Bliss: "the US hoped that Somalia would not anticipate independence because we believed that Somalia would profit by having the full period in which to develop its technicians and to assimilate techniques of government."[172]

Reacting to the position of the American Ambassador, the Prime Minister observed that two years made little difference. What was more important for his government was to directly deal with foreign nations for aid and, perhaps, arms[173]. Aden Abdulla was even more specific, saying that if the United States or any other power would increase its aid in the trusteeship period to take up the increasing slack being left by Italy, it might be possible for Somalia to wait until 1960, but that otherwise he also believed that independence in 1959 would probably be in Somalia's best interest[174]. It should be remembered that during

169 Diary Aden Abdulla, August 4, 1959.

170 Telegram from the Department of State to the Embassy in Italy, Washington, June 26, 1957 (615 Foreign Relations, 1955-1957, vol. XVIII).

171 230 Dispatch from the Consulate at Mogadisho to the Department of State, Mogadisho, October 18, 1957 (618 Foreign Relations, 1955-1957, vol. XVIII).

172 620 Foreign Relations, 1955-1957, vol. XVIII.

173 Ibid.

174 Ibid.

discussions on the future of Somalia at the United Nations in 1949, the United States of America supported the establishment of Italian trusteeship over Somalia, but making independence conditional on the progress and development of the Territory to be reviewed by the General Assembly and the Trusteeship Council of the United Nations with a view to determining whether it was ready for independence.[175]

The drafting of the Constitution

The Trusteeship Agreement provides no clear indications as to whether the Administering Authority was expected to prepare a constitutional charter for the Trust Territory before independence, or whether this was an issue to be tackled by the Somali government after independence.[176]

However, the Administration started drafting a Constitution, aiming to have it ready before the independence date. For this purpose, two committees were appointed: a Political Committee and a Technical Committee[177]. Chairing the Political Committee was the President of the Legislative Assembly, with other members including the Prime Minister, the Cabinet ministers, the Undersecretary, the two Vice-presidents of the Legislative Assembly, the leaders of the parliamentary groups, the two Secretaries of the Parliament, two functionaries residing in Mogadisho and designated by the Prime Minister, one representative from each political party, recognized and represented in the Legislative Assembly designated by the parties themselves.

The Technical Committee was chaired by Professor G.A. Costanzo, Dean of the Somali Institute of Law, Economics and Social Science, and included Professor Dino Fiorot of Padua University, Dr Giuseppe Finocchiaro, President of the Court of Justice, Dr Salvatore Spadaro, Magistrate of Accounts, Dr Carlo Fettrappa-Sandri, Head of the Cabinet of the Administrator, Dr Carlo Prisco, Attorney General, Dr Renato Angeloni, Counsellor of the Court of Justice, Dr Vincenzo Mellana, Appeal Judge of the Court of Justice, and Dr Mario Tucci, Deputy Attorney General. An expert designated by the United Nations Advisory Council, Paolo Contini, Senior Legal Advisor in the office of Legal Affairs of the United Nations Secretariat, was a member of the Technical Committee. The Advisory Council also asked the Secretariat to approach international

175 UN Doc. A/C.1/497 of October 10, 1949.

176 Costanzo, op. cit., p. 9.

177 Decree no. 140 of September 6, 1957.

governments and inquire whether they would submit nominations for another expert, particularly versed in Islamic law.[178]

In response to the inquiry made by the Secretariat, the governments of Egypt and Lebanon each proposed a candidate. The Advisory Council selected the one first proposed, Dr. A.F. Sayer Dayer, from the University of Ein Shams, Cairo, and the Technical Committee co-opted him as a member.

In its first meeting, the Technical Committee began considering the inclusion in the Committee of Somali nationals, despite their inadequate expertise in constitutional matters, on the grounds that no foreigner would genuinely represent the interest of Somalis; therefore, it was felt imperative to include Somali members in the work of the Committee. After informal approval by the Chairman of the Political Committee, seven Somalis were co-opted. They were: the Chief Kadi, two kadis of the Court of Justice, one government counsellor, two heads of department from the Ministry of Finance, one head of department from the Ministry of Economy.[179]

Between October 1957 and May 1959 the Technical Committee prepared a preliminary draft constitution of 141 articles, accompanied by a 316-page commentary[180]. The framers of the Constitution did not start with a blank sheet, but built on existing constitutions. The Committee examined a variety of recent and old models worldwide, including the French Constitution of 1946, the German Constitution of 1949 and the Italian Constitution of 1947; some Constitutions based on the Presidential model, such as those of the US and the Philippines of 1935; those of some Islamic countries in North Africa and the Near East; the Constitution of the former Egyptian Republic of 1956; the Constitution of the former Syrian Republic of September 1950 (parliamentarian model) and 1953 (presidential model); the Constitution of the Kingdom of Jordan of 1952; the Constitution of Lebanon of May 1926; the Constitution of Iraq of 1925; the Constitutions of Brazil, Eritrea, Ethiopia, Ghana, Greece, India, Indonesia, Iran, Mexico, Pakistan, and Portugal. The United Nations Charter and Universal Declaration of Human Rights were also consulted[181]. In reality, however, the Committee depended heavily on the Italian constitutional

178 UN Doc. T/1372, April 22, 1958, para.97, p. 34.

179 Sheikh Aboubakar Abdullahi Omar, Sheikh Mohamed Mohamoud Mohamed, Sheikh Mohamed Sheikh Ali Abukar, Mohamed Sheikh Gabio, Mohamud Iousuf Aden 'Muro', Sheikh Abdulle Mohamoud Mohamed, Aweys Sheikh Mohamed Moallim. Later on, two more Somali members were added: Omar Moallim Mohamed and Hassan Mohamed Hassan 'Waqoyi'.

180 P. Contini, *Somali Republic: an Experiment in Legal Integration*, Frank Cass & Co. Ltd, 1969, p. 3.

181 Costanzo, op. cit., p. 23.

model, considered the most suitable model in the Somali context on the grounds that it was the Constitution of the administering power which had established the legal system of the institutions existing in the Trust Territory. Furthermore, the Italian Constitution appeared suitable on account of the thoroughness of some of its sections, such as those concerning the principles governing the duties and rights of citizen and man.

At its first meeting on 11 October 1957, the technical committee decided to set up six sub-committees[182], each dealing with specific chapters of the Constitution: General principles and rights and duties of men and citizens, Legislative functions, Executive functions, Decentralization, Judicial functions, Constitutional guarantees. Each committee prepared draft articles on the chapter assigned to it and submitted it together with an explanatory report to the technical committee for discussion and approval.

The work of the Committee was carried out in three separate phases: in the first phase, 38 plenary meetings were held, as well as fifty-eight sub-committee meetings, ending in March 1958; the second phase, in which only 24 plenary meetings were held, was dedicated to revision of the proposals already submitted[183]. The entire final text of the Constitution was approved on 1 November 1958 and submitted one month later to the President of the National Assembly on December 2, 1958. Between April 4 and May 9, 1960 both drafts were examined in detail by a drafting political committee of fifty Somali members[184].

The Committee approved a new draft of 100 articles and submitted it to the expanded Constituent Assembly.

The Legislative Assembly becomes a constituent body

With the completion of the draft text of the Constitution by the Technical Committee, the Legislative Assembly has been transformed into a Constituent Assembly for the purpose of framing the Constitution of the future State of Somalia. Until independence, the Administering Authority retained ultimate responsibility for foreign affairs, defence and security, and the Administrator had veto power with respect to laws adopted by the Legislative Assembly. However, as provided by Law no. 6 of January 8, 1960, this power did not apply to the Constituent Assembly. Accordingly, the text of the Constitution was not subject

182 T/1372, 22 April, 1958, p. 35, para 100.
183 P. Contini, op. cit., p. 3.
184 Ibid., p. 3.

to the Administrator's approval.[185]

The Legislative Assembly, transformed into a Constituent Assembly, was to carry on its dual functions of approving the Constitution as a constituent body, and acting as Legislative Assembly to deal with routine work. In view of the fact that the Somali Legislative Assembly was almost entirely composed of Lega members, the UN Trusteeship Council recommended in 1959 that the composition of the Political Committee and Constituent Assembly be broadened to include representatives of all existing political parties and other important social and cultural organizations of the Territory, and to provide for the popular confirmation of the Constitution[186]. The issue generated heated debate in the Legislative Assembly between opponents and supporters of the proposal. The Somali government was highly suspicious of the proposal which it saw as a clear sign of the Trusteeship Council's long held reservations on the fairness of the 1959 general elections. The government and all those opposing the idea of changing the composition of the Constituent Assembly maintained that only the representatives elected by the people were mandated to make the Constitution for the country; this mandate was not given to any extra-parliamentary bodies or groups. They further argued that the UN proposal was not a legally binding document on the grounds that it was drafted not as a resolution but as a mere recommendation. By contrast, those in favour of the UN proposal argued that the Assembly elected in 1959 was expected to deal only with ordinary legislation, and as such it had no mandate to draft a Constitution; hence the need to include in the Constituent Assembly representatives of all existing political parties, in addition to social and cultural organizations.

However, a third opinion emerged during the discussions, calling for suspension of the discussions on the draft Constitution until full independence and union with British Somaliland were achieved. When the proposal was put to the vote, it was rejected by 30 votes against 15 in favour, with 13 abstentions.[187]

Pressured by different parties, the Legislative Assembly, by 33 votes against 14 and 13 abstentions, eventually accepted the UN recommendation to include two members of each existing political party in the Constituent Assembly[188]. As a result of this decision, twenty representatives appointed by political parties, cultural, economic and religious categories were included in the Constituent Assembly

185 Legge n° 6 gennaio 8, 1960, Bollettino Ufficiale, suppl. n° 1 al n°1, 25 gennaio 1960..

186 GA Resolution 1415 (XV).

187 *Corriere della Somalia*, Maggio 23, 1960.

188 Ibid.

and Political Committee. The following political parties and organizations were invited to designate their respective representatives: LGS, HDMS, GSL, UNS, PLGS, UNA; Organizzazione Generale Studenti Somali, Confederazione Somala dei Lavoratori, Federazione Sindacati della Somalia, Confederazione Commercianti; religious experts and Associazione Studenti Universitari.

It should be noted that, while the PLGS and the UNA designated their representatives, the other opposition parties declined the invitation on the grounds that their possible membership of the Political Committee would be neutralized by the inclusion of the Teachers' Union, Chamber of Commerce and religious fraternity, all of whom had been nominated by the government and were Lega supporters.[189]

On May 23 the Constituent Assembly began its debate on the political Committee's draft and, after 42 sessions lasting 31 working days, approved it on June 21, 1960, a little more than two weeks before the independence date of 1st July[190]. The Constitution was adopted by acclamation and, upon being issued by the provisional President of the Republic, came into force on July 1, 1960. Eighty-seven deputies were present during the approval of the final text of the Constitution[191]. It had taken one year and several sessions to complete the work. In fairness, some of the delays were the product of attempts to find a compromise with the conservative members of the Assembly.

The Somali Charter is composed of a preamble and 105 articles. The preamble, not included in the draft prepared by the Technical Committee because of its inherent political character, evokes in the name of God people's right to self-determination and expresses their will to co-operate with all people for the consolidation of liberty, justice and peace in the world. These are universal principles derived from the United Nations Charter. The Constitution follows a fairly usual pattern, providing for a legislative assembly (Article 49), a president as head of State (Article 70), and a prime minister (Article 83).

The Constitution lays down the powers of each of these bodies. The president is elected by the Legislative Assembly for a six-year term. He is the commander of the armed forces (Article 75 (f), and appoints and dismisses the prime minister, though this power is limited by the fact that the government must have the confidence of the assembly. The president may also dissolve the assembly

189 TNA FO371/1456955, confidential report (1017/60) from British Consulate Mogadisho, June 10, 1960.

190 D'Antonio, op. cit., p. xxvi.

191 Costanzo, op. cit., p.107.

after having heard the opinion of its president (Article 53); however, dissolution may not take place during the first year in office of the assembly or during the last year in office of the president (Article 53 (3). The National Assembly, consisting of deputies elected for five years, has the power to prepare laws and other legislative measures, amnesty and pardon, taxation and expenditure, budget and annual accounts, approval of treatises, declaration of war and parliamentary investigation (Article 72 of 1960 Constitution). The judicial power is vested in the judiciary, which is independent of the executive and legislative powers (Article 92 of 1960 Constitution).

Constitutional framework. The impact of Islamic doctrine

The form of government (federalist or unitary) the new nation would adopt was the subject of prolonged debate in the Constituent Assembly. The HDMS advocated a federal government, a principle enshrined in the statute of the party. In the course of the discussions on the draft Constitution at the Constituent Assembly, Abdullahi Haji Mursal, of HDMS, introduced an amendment calling for a federal system for the Somali Republic with the possibility for the Somali people to express their approval through a referendum.[192]

This preference derived from a deep-seated fear of dominance by the nomadic-pastoralists clans generally supporting the Lega. By contrast, the Lega advocated a unitary form of government, arguing that federalism would encourage clannishness. Federalism was anathema to the Lega. The federal system was seen as a dangerous principle that clan and regional groups could resort to, with potentially destructive effects on the unity of the country. In the end, political and numerical strength enabled the Lega to prevail and the unitary system was adopted. The 1960 Constitution also adopted the unicameral parliament instead of the bicameral system which exists in many countries. The rationale behind this choice rests on consideration of its advantages in terms of the time and expense involved in maintaining and operating the parliamentary structure.[193]

The Somali Constitution of 1960 was different from the Constitutions in force in other newly decolonized African countries, and was seen by experts in constitutional affairs as "a model of parliamentary government unique in Africa"[194]. Indeed, all other African countries had adopted the presidential

192 D'Antonio, op. cit., p. 4, quoting Records of the Constituent Assembly, no. 6, April 6, 1960, pp 5-6.

193 A. Morone, *'La crisi dello Stato in Somalia: una riconsiderazione storico-giuridica'*, Il Politico, Università di Pavia, Italy, 2002, anno LXVII, n° 2, p. 304, note 61.

194 Salvatore Foderaro, *La costituzione degli Stati africani,* Cedam, Padova, 1973, p. 467.

system, where the head of State has sweeping executive powers. By contrast, in Somalia the executive power is vested in the government headed by the prime minister (Article 77).

One does not need to be an expert to realize that the Somali Constitution derives its essence from that of Italy: a democratic instrument, without doubt, but based on a western model. "The Technical Committee which drew up the first draft consisted mostly of Italian jurists and officials, as well as Italian-trained Somalis. It is not surprising, therefore, that the form and substance of the Somali Constitution were strongly influenced by the Italian Constitution", comments Contini[195]. The Italian political system of parliament and elections, parties and programmes, was borrowed ready-made and superimposed on a foundation of social reality to which it did and does not correspond. The Constitution of the Italian Republic was the product of a long political and armed struggle against the fascist regime. All the democratic forces which took up arms against the fascist regime contributed to the preparation of the basic law.[196]

In the Somali case, the Constitution was prepared mainly by foreign experts, with little contribution by Somali elements. The organization of State institutions, the division of powers between the constitutional bodies of the State and the legal guarantees of civil and political rights of the citizens are the cardinal principles on which the Constitution is founded. However, these principles and others, such as equality of the citizens before the law (Art. 3 of the 1960 Constitution), human rights (Article 7 of 1960 Constitution) and freedom of religion (Article 29 of 1960 Constitution), are alien to Somali culture and traditions.

In the rural areas where the majority of the people live, the prevailing code of conduct is not the Constitution, but the Xeer, a set of unwritten norms and practices observed and complied with for centuries by the community in order to regulate the multitude of events that pertain to their daily lives and interaction. This customary law has the advantage of being a product of the community to which it applies and reflects existing realities. Some analysts bemoaned the scant attention paid to customary law in the writing of the Constitution. Nicolino Mohamed, a former top civil servant, is quoted as saying that "it was a serious mistake not to have created, like in Ghana, a Chamber of Elders" beside the NationalAssembly.[197]

The principles and norms contemplated in the Constitution are so complex

195 P. Contini, op. cit., p. 56.

196 The Italian Constitution was adopted in 1948.

197 Del Boca, op. cit., p. 283.

that even the most enlightened among the politicians who read and approved them often fell foul of them. It should also be noted that the Somali lawmakers often saw the Constitution as an instrument limiting their actions and political movements. Perhaps the best illustration of the general attitude of the Somalis vis-à-vis the Constitution and the law in general is provided by the statement made in Parliament by one MP: "Let us throw off this Constitution and the young man who authored it."[198]

As mentioned earlier, the Political Committee in charge of drafting the Constitution introduced few amendments to the text prepared by the Technical Committee. However, these amendments, very few as they may appear, included one important principle which left its mark on the essence and legal foundation of the Constitution. This was the adoption of the doctrine of Islam as the main source of the laws of the State, giving the new Constitution a clear Islamic character. All efforts were made by the Constituent Assembly to strike a balance between the need to preserve the Islamic doctrine as the main source of the laws of the State and the need to frame a modern and democratic Constitution. The importance of Islam in Somali society is reflected in several clauses of the Constitution. To start with, the very first article of the Constitution establishes that: "Islam shall be the religion of the State" (1960 Constitution, Article 1, paragraph 3). Article 6 ('The Republic within the International Order') reads: "The Somali Republic shall encourage solidarity among the people of the world, and in particular among Africans and Islamic people." Article 29 ('Freedom of Religion') reads: "Every person shall have the right to freedom of conscience and freely to profess his own religion and to worship subject to any limitations which may be prescribed by law for the purpose of safeguarding morals, public health or order. However, it shall not be permissible to spread or propagandize any religion other than the true faith of Islam." This provision is a result of an amendment, adopted by law, of the original provision reflected in Article 29 of the Constitution.[199]

The original text, which gave broader scope of freedom of religion, read: "Every person shall have the right to freedom of conscience and freely to profess his own religion, to practise it and impart its teaching, subject to any limitation which may be prescribed by law for the purpose of safeguarding morality, public health or order." The amendment came as an endeavour to

198 A clear reference to Mohamed Sheickh Gabio, the then Minister of Constitutional Affairs.

199 Legge n°16 del 29 giugno 1963.

control the spread of religious fanaticism and its inherent perils after a clergyman affiliated to the Mennonite Mission operating in Somalia was stabbed to death by a fanatic Somali. The Mennonite Mission, a Protestant mission based in the United States of America and operating schools and hospitals in Jamama, Jowhar and Mahaddai, was subjected to virulent attacks which eventually led in July 1962 to the murder in Mogadisho of a Protestant priest, Merlin Grove Russel, whose wife also suffered severe injuries in the attack.[200]

Article 35, dealing with education, makes teaching of Islam compulsory for pupils of Islamic faith in primary and secondary state schools, and the teaching of the Holy Koran is a fundamental element in primary and secondary State schools for Muslims.

One of the eligibility requirements for the President of the Republic is that he must be a Muslim citizen (Article 71 of the Constitution). There are two cardinal principles in the 1960 Constitution conferring supremacy to the Islamic doctrine over other sources of law. The first of these principles provides that "The doctrine of Islam shall be the main source ('fonte principale') of the laws of the State" (Article 50 of 1960 Constitution), and the second that "Laws and provisions having the force of law shall conform to the Constitution and to the general principles of Islam." (Article 98 (1) of the Constitution)

Consequently, a law might be declared null and void by the Constitutional Court not only if it contravenes a specific provision of the Constitution but also if it contravenes the general principles of Islam[201]. Although the Constitution (Articles 98-103) contained provisions for the creation of a Constitutional Court to review the constitutionality of laws, and of a High Court of Justice with jurisdiction for criminal proceedings against the president of the republic, the prime minister, and the other ministers, neither the Constitutional Court nor the High Court of Justice had, in practice, worked in Somalia. The reader may recall that, in addition to the Constitution, Somalia also abides by an unwritten power-sharing agreement, a sort of 'national pact' under which the top three State institutions, i.e. the offices of president, prime minister and speaker of parliament are evenly allocated to the major Somali clans (Darod, Hawiye, Issak and Rahanweyn). A similar 'gentlemen's agreement' exists in Lebanon, the only difference being that the power-sharing is based on confessional basis criteria between Christians, Sunni Muslims and Shi'ite Muslims.

200 The fanatic murderer, Sheikh Yassin, was sentenced to 20 years imprisonment.
201 P. Contini, op. cit., pp 58-59.

The Somaliland parties divided over the issue of the Union

The pressure for independence and union with Somalia had greatly increased following the February elections in the Somaliland Protectorate, which introduced, for the first time, a legislative council and a ministerial government. However, the matter had hardly been debated in either territory. Everyone had what can be termed an imprecise view of the union.

In the Protectorate, different views did exist between the Somali National League (SNL) and United Somali Party (USP) with regard to the timing and modality of the union with the Trust Territory. The SNL was the party of the Issak, and the USP the party of the Gadabursi, the Issa, the Dulbahanta and the Warsangeli tribes. The SNL was in favour of allowing time for the issue of the union to be debated and not precipitate it[202]. For Mohamed Haji Ibrahim Egal, leader of the SNL, "the ultimate aim would be complete union, if practicable, but at this stage, his party did not wish to commit themselves to the kind of unification arrangements which circumstances in the foreseeable future might make practicable."[203] Egal wanted the union to proceed slowly because, "if union came too soon, he and his colleagues would be at a disadvantage with the government of Somalia, because of lack of experience."[204] He wanted to form a 'supreme council' which would govern the two territories for five years. Both territories would have equal numbers of members in the Council, and the Legislative Council of the two territories would not be amalgamated, but function as two separate governing bodies for the two regions. During this limited period, the new Constitution for the united state would be framed[205]. Egal hoped for a common police service and a unified customs tariff, both legacies left by the British Military Administration (BMA), and expressed categorical rejection of federal arrangements on grounds of impracticability and poor cost effectiveness.

As H.F.T. Smith put it "Egal, with his typical 'imprecise' thinking on the union and on virtually everything else, was simply carried on by events. [...] The union marked the total absorption of Somaliland by Somalia."[206] An opposite view, held mainly by the leaders of the NUF headed by Michael Mariano, and by the

202 I.M. Lewis, op. cit., p. 162.

203 TNA FO 371/138316, Minutes of meeting with the Somali National League in the Chief Secretary's office in Hargeisa, December 8, 1959.

204 TNA FO 371/146966. Election in Somaliland Protectorate H.F.T. March 1, 1960.

205 Ibid., report from D. Hall to I. Watt, ESQ. February 10, 1960.

206 TNA FO 371/146981 Report dated December 8,1959 from R.H.T., Hargeisa to FO.

USP, advocated the union taking place immediately without any hindrance from present differences that could be addressed within a unitary system[207]. All political parties in the north expressed their preference for beginning negotiations with Somalia "from a position of constitutional equality", meaning after 1 July 1960.[208]

"Although the SNL representatives said that their ultimate aim was complete union, they were not ready, for the foreseeable future, to commit themselves beyond whatever form of unification might appear to be practicable and acceptable both to them and to the government of Somalia", comments I. Watt.[209]

If this was the feeling in the Protectorate, let us see now what the position of the political leaders was in the Trust Territory *vis-à-vis* the unification arrangements between the two territories. There is scant information leading to a clear picture of the thinking of the southern leaders on the issue. However, it is widely reported that top southern politicians had warned the northern leaders against a hasty decision on unification with the south[210]. Well-informed British sources in Mogadisho attribute to Aden Abdulla the conviction that at least in the initial stage "any union between the two territories must be a loose federation rather than total amalgamation."[211] It was further reported that Abdullahi Issa had telegraphed Mohamed Haji I. Egal, the Somaliland Prime Minister, urging him to postpone discussions on the Act of Union. "The Somaliland Legislative Assembly ignored this request and entirely approved all three stages of the Bill without substantial amendments intending, as they admitted, to present Somalia with a fait accompli", reveals a British secret document.[212]

"To many, the SNL showed themselves more realistic than the other parties who plumped straight away for all-out union", comments I. Watt in the secret report he prepared in Hargeisa on December 11, 1959[213]. If this was the position of the major political parties in the North, the question of public opinion *vis-à-vis* the union calls for answer. A very convincing one comes from I.M. Lewis: "Whatever the merits of the two schools of thought, and each clearly had much to commend it, the strength of the public nationalistic feeling was now such that

207 TNA FO 371/138316, Minutes of separate meetings with USP and NUF in the Chief Secretary's office in Hargeisa on December 8 and 11, 1959.

208 TNA FO 371/138316, Minutes of separate meeting in the Chief Secretary's office in Hargeisa, December 8, 1959.

209 TNA FO 371/138316 Report by Mr. I. Watt, Hargeisa, December 11, 1959.

210 Interview released by Abdi Hassan Boni to the London-based Somali language Universal TV, June 26, 2008.

211 TNA CO 371/13831, conversations between Aden Abdulla and British Consul on June 24, 1959.

212 TNA FO 371/146958 confidential report of July 9, 1960 from British Embassy Mogadisho to FO.

213 TNA FO 371/138316 Report by Mr. I. Watt, Hargeisa, December 11, 1959.

the latter view must prevail."[214]

The Legislative Council of the Somaliland Protectorate passed a resolution on April 6, 1960 demanding independence and union with Somalia by July 1. This was followed by unofficial talks about union between a Protectorate legislative delegation and a Legislative Assembly delegation of Somalia in Mogadisho from April 15 to April 23. On April 25, the delegations published a declaration for full and complete independence and union of the two territories, under one flag, one president, one parliament and one government by July 1, 1960. This union, the legality of which has recently come under scrutiny, was termed by one author as the 'Precipitate Union'[215]

To understand what went wrong with the process, we need to take one step back to 1960 and follow the evolution and sequence of events leading to the eventual merger between the northern and southern regions of Somalia. Although the union was, in principle, agreed in April 1960, the details of the instrument, particularly its legal effects, had received scant attention. During the weeks preceding independence for the two territories, politicians were busy with preparations for the celebrations, and in the hasty process, some important legal aspects were overlooked.

On June 27, the day after independence, the Somaliland Legislative Assembly passed the 'Union of Somaliland and Somalia Law'[216] incorporating the proposed Act of Union previously sent to Mogadisho to be signed by the representatives of Somalia. The proposed Act of Union that was intended to be signed by the representatives of the independent States of Somaliland and Somalia was not signed on July 1, 1960 by Somalia. Instead, after prolonged debate, on the evening of June 30, the Legislative Assembly of the Trust Territory adopted, 'in principle', the *Atto di Unione* (Act of Union)[217]. However, there were significant differences between the Act of Union approved by the independent State of Somaliland and the text adopted 'in principle' by the Legislative Assembly of the Trust Territory and requesting "the government of Somalia to establish with the government of Somaliland a definitive single text of the Act of Union to be submitted to the National Assembly for approval."

There was no time for the two governments to reach an agreement on a definitive text, as the Somaliland Legislative Assembly had requested. This was

214 I.M. Lewis, op. cit., p. 162.
215 Touval, op. cit., p. 110.
216 Law no. 1, June 27, 1960.
217 P. Contini, op. cit., p. 9.

supposed to precede the election of the provisional president of the republic. Article 2 of the Transitional and Final Provisions of the Constitution stipulates: "Immediately after signing the Act of Union of the two Somali Territories (Somalia and Somaliland), the New National Assembly (The National Assembly was to comprise the two legislative bodies of the two countries) shall elect [...] a Provisional President of the Republic..."

No single text was submitted to the National Assembly for approval. The absence of any union agreement between the two independent States presented serious legal lacunae which can be translated as the 'Union of Somaliland and Somalia Law' being devoid of any validity in Somalia; the approval, 'in principle', of the *Atto di Unione* by the Legislative Assembly of the Trust Territory was not of itself legally binding in Somaliland[218]. Despite the unresolved legal aspects, the President of the Assembly proclaimed the union and the members of the Assembly sealed it by standing ovation on July 1, 1960. In a bid to formalize the union, the Provisional President of the Republic signed a temporary decree-law, shorter than the *Atto di Unione*, which never came into force as it had never been submitted to the National Assembly within the statutory time limit of five days for the conversion into law (Article 63 of the 1960 Constitution).

"This Union was *de facto* rather than *de jure* since the act giving legal validity to the Union was not passed by the National Assembly until January 1961", comments a British Council document[219]. The new State was proclaimed as being unitary, with one government, one parliament and the capital at Mogadisho. The independent Republic of Somaliland was thus reduced to two administrative regions with equal status to each of the other six regions of the former Trust Territory of Somalia.

The trusteeship regime gave the Trust Territory several unique advantages compared to the British Protectorate of Somaliland. The Trusteeship Agreement required the administering power to develop the Territory's political institutions, to expand the education system and to improve the economic infrastructure. These were advantages that British Somaliland, which was to be incorporated into the new Somali State, did not have. The disparity between the two territories in economical development and political experience would cause serious difficulties when the time came to integrate the two States.

218 Ibid., p. 10.
219 TNA CO 1045/1145. Confidential annual report 1960-1961, British Council Mogadisho.

PART THREE

INDEPENDENCE COMES AT MIDNIGHT

Chapter IX

RIOTS ACCOMPANY THE CELEBRATIONS

By virtue of Law no. 643 of June 28, 1960, the Italian government officially sanctioned the independence of Somalia. AFIS thus formally ended its trusteeship administration in Somalia at 16hrs of 30 June 1960, six months before the time stipulated in the Trusteeship Agreement, when the last administrator, Mario Di Stefano, left Mogadisho on board a plane bound for Nairobi, Kenya[1]. At 6 o'clock in the afternoon, in all centres of Somalia, the Italian and UN flags were for the last time lowered. "Thus, in the most discrete manner, Italy leaves Africa and closes the last chapter of her colonial adventure, started 90 years ago on the Red Sea shores", comments Angelo del Boca[2]. "At midnight on the 30th of June 1960 the Somali flag was hoisted on the National Assembly building. The Provisional Head of State, His Excellence Aden Abdulla, appeared on the balcony of the Assembly where he was greeted by a very large crowd of happy and cheering Somalis."[3] Michele Pirone[4], who was in Mogadisho at the time, wrote "at midnight, 30 June 1960, when the hundreds of thousands

1 His Excellence Silvio Daneo, the Italian Ambassador, arrived at the airport as the Administrator left.

2 Del Boca, op. cit., p. 291.

3 TNA FO 271/146958 confidential report of July 8 from British Embassy, Mogadisho.

4 Pirone wrote extensively on Somali customary law and history. He was very conversant with Somali language and culture, having acquired vast experience during his long service in Somalia as a colonial officer..

of Somalis gathered in the Piazza della Solidarietà Africana saw the hoisting of the flag above the National Assembly building, 114 cannon salvoes, equal to the number of Suras in the Koran, saluted the event."[5] When calm returned, Aden Abdulla, in his capacity as provisional president of the republic, started reading, standing on the floodlit balcony of the National Assembly Building, the proclamation announcing the birth of a free and independent Somalia: "To you, Somalia, who, from this instant see the light, you have a face and a name, may God bless you and grant you long life." He then added "Today we are Somalis, today we are independent and sovereign. Today we finally have a State and a flag. It is a blessing from God; let us protect and preserve it." And after reading the proclamation, Aden Abdulla invited the crowd to turn their thought to "the millions of African brothers still languishing under the yoke of injustice and lack of understanding."[6]

Angelo del Boca describes the new Head of State, with undeniable accuracy, in the following words: "If there is a man who can claim the status of determined and coherent nationalist, in addition to being a moderate, this man is Aden Abdulla."[7] The President's speech was followed by that of Senator Giuseppe Medici, head of the Italian delegation, who read a brief but significant message from the Italian Head of State to the President of the Somali Republic: "Being aware of the significance and importance of today's celebrations, I have the privilege to notify you with sincere congratulations that Italy, in compliance with the Resolution adopted by the United Nations General Assembly, has ended at zero hour of today, 1 July 1960, the trusteeship administration assigned to her by the United Nations on November 21, 1949. I have therefore the honour of declaring that Italy extends, as from this moment, its recognition to Somalia as sovereign and independent. Italy is convinced that she is transferring sovereign powers to a State based on the democratic and modern institutions, albeit embryonic, of an adequate administration. I do moreover confirm that in the future also Somalia can count on the support and friendship of the government and the people of Italy."[8]

The last to speak on the occasion was Mr Constantine Stavropoulos, Deputy Secretary General of the United Nations, who said, among other things, that "independence could never have been achieved without the enthusiastic and

5 M. Pirone, op. cit., p. 149.
6 Del Boca, op. cit., p. 292.
7 Ibid., p. 292.
8 Ibid.

constructive spirit of the Somali people and Italy's enlightened leadership."[9]

All United Nations members, except for South Africa, Byelorussia and Ukraine, were invited to attend the independence celebrations. That procedure seemed normal on account of the fact that Somalia was a UN trust territory. However, the Prime Minister issuing an invitation to Israel raised diplomatic complications between Egypt and Somalia which could have undermined the serene atmosphere of the celebrations had they not been tactfully handled. It was reported by the Italian Ministry of Foreign Affairs that the Egyptian consul general based in Mogadisho formally protested to the Prime Minister, wielding threats of boycott of the celebrations by all Arab States if an Israeli delegation attended the celebrations[10]. According to Italian diplomatic sources in Cairo, the reasons for this were: (a) Arab countries might 'steal Egypt's thunder' and (b) reports had reached Cairo of resentment from both Somalia and the Somaliland Protectorate at the invitation extended to Israel[11]. In diplomatic terms, such invitations would not commit Somalia to establishing diplomatic relations with all those invited, and the Somalis found it difficult to understand the fuss the Egyptians were making out of the invitation extended to a member of the United Nations who took part in the debate on the future of Somalia in 1949 and voted in favour of Somali independence. However, in order to outmanoeuvre the Egyptian plot, the Prime Minister did not cancel the invitation, but appealed to the Italian government to convince the Israelis to withdraw their acceptance of the invitation.[12]

It was an open secret that relations between Egypt and the Somali government had never been cordial, undermined as they were by the activities of Egyptian agents present in Somalia either as consular staff or members of the Consultative Council of the United Nation, which was considered by the Somalis an unacceptable interference in their internal affairs. As we have seen, the Egyptians were active during the trusteeship mandate in trying to suppress the Somali language and culture in favour of the Arabic language and culture, the aim being that of 'arabizing' the whole of Somali society. To this the Somalis reacted vigorously in many ways in defence of their national identity, language and culture, and their firm stand *vis-à-vis* this foreign intervention contributed to

9 *The New York Times*, July, 1, 1960.

10 TNA FO 371/147048, Telegram of June 2, 1960, from Rome to FO.

11 Ibid., confidential telegram, dated June 3, 1960 from C.J. Audland to D.A.H. Wright, British Ambassador in Addis Abeba.

12 Jama Mohamed Ghalib, *The Cost of Dictatorship. The Somali Experience*, Lillian Barber Press, 1995, p. 49.

the deterioration of relations.

The Somali government took on the burden of offering free accommodation and some limited transport facilities to the foreign dignitaries invited. Therefore, owing to severe logistic constraints, sending countries were requested to limit the size of the official delegations attending the celebrations to 3 members. The Legislative Assembly which provided for additional revenue to support the creation of the national army also covered "any other matter concerned with independence."[13]

One expensive item under this provision was the construction of two elaborate hotels, each fitted with air conditioning and lifts, all set to be completed before the independence date to accommodate 400 important guests pouring in from around the world. The two new hotels, named Juba and Shabelle after Somalia's two rivers, were rushed to completion: construction works started early in February before financial provisions were authorized by the Assembly, and special prefabricated materials arrived from Italy, as did Italian technicians.

No head of State or government was among the representatives of the seventy-two countries invited to the celebrations[14]. Major western countries sent junior ministers, and the United Nations an undersecretary. Italy was represented by Senator Giuseppe Medici, Minister of Education, as head of delegation, accompanied by the Undersecretary for Foreign Affairs, Carlo Russo; Mr John Profumo, Minister of State for Foreign Affairs, was appointed British Special Ambassador to the celebrations. The American delegation was led by Mr F.M. Mueller, the Secretary of Commerce. Representatives from the British Commonwealth and Colonial Territories included: Kenya, Aden, Sierra Leone, Tanganyika, Uganda, Ghana and Nigeria.

After the conclusion of the celebrations, the 90 deputies from the former Trust Territory and the 33 parliamentarians from the former British Protectorate of Somaliland met in order to constitute the unified National Assembly and elect a provisional head of State for the Somali State. As expected, Aden Abdulla was elected (with 107 votes out of 115 deputies present and voting) for a period of one year, until the time when the Constitution would be approved by referendum. The choice was certainly a good one, and almost inevitable since Aden Abdulla was the only eligible politician of any standing over the constitutional age limit of 45.

13 Legge n°8 febbraio 6, 1960, 'Delega al Governo per l'emanazione di provvedimenti fiscali', Bollettino Ufficiale, suppl. n°1 al n° 2, 6 Febbraio 1960.

14 *The New York Times*, July, 1, 1960.

Ambassadors were to present their credentials to the Provisional Head of State from 17:00 on July 1, 1960 at 'Villa Somalia', the former residence of the Administrator and now residence of the Provisional Head of State. The Italian Ambassador was the first, followed by Britain, France, Germany and the USA.[15]

The great enthusiasm, however, was muted by the bloody incidents which accompanied the celebrations of independence: on the night between 30 June and 1 July 1960, clashes broke out in Mogadisho as thousands of protesters responding to the calls from the Greater Somali League Party converged in Piazza della Solidarietà Africana, the main square facing Parliament. Despite the ban, some four thousand protesters started their march towards the Parliament chanting slogans such as "Down with colonialism and imperialism", "We demand immediate, free and democratic elections", "Djibouti is part of Somalia"[16]. At the beginning, the police used water cannons and tear gas to disperse the crowd, but the protesters responded with stone throwing. When the events took this turn, the police charged the demonstrators, among them women and children, using live ammunition, while television and cameramen captured the ugly scene. The dramatic result of the confrontation was two persons killed and 17 injured. Demonstrations escalated in Mogadisho as the government cracked down hard, arresting 300 people in a single day including opposition leaders and other activists under the eyes of the international media present in Mogadisho to cover the event and of the foreign dignitaries invited to attend the celebrations.

The violent riots which accompanied the Congolese Independence Day in 1960 and plunged the country into deep chaos came to the mind of many. "Having got into a panic, the government took a serious decision which was not adequate to the events, by enforcing censorship on the press and then even blocking outgoing dispatches," comments Angelo del Boca[17]. Foreign correspondents arriving with their copy at the signal station "were confronted by Hassan Nur Elmi, a senior government official, who had been given the unenviable job of censoring telegrams", reported a British source in the Somali capital[18]. In order to circumvent the Somali government's veto on transmitting media report on the incidents to the outside world, a group of American and British journalists chartered a flight to Nairobi, from where they dispatched the first news on the

15 TNA FO371/146958, confidential report no. 1013/60 of July 8, 1960, from the British Embassy Mogadisho to FO.

16 Del Boca, op. cit., p. 294.

17 Ibid., p. 295.

18 TNA FO 371/146958/ confidential report no. 1013/60) of July 8, 1960 from the British Embassy Mogadisho to FO.

incidents in Mogadisho[19]. As for the Italian newsmen, "they chose the road of negotiation, which they carried out patiently with the government, but it was only at about one o'clock at night, thanks to the direct intervention of the President of the Republic Aden Abdulla, that they were allowed to send brief radio dispatches to Italy."[20]

On 1 July, the Italian delegation attending the independence celebrations was busy negotiating a number of treaties to be concluded between Italy and the Republic of Somalia. Having failed to reach agreement because of unacceptability to the Somalis of various clauses in the draft documents, only some of the 14 treaties and conventions were signed. These were: (1) Treaty of Friendship. This includes exchange of notes relating to diplomatic representation by Italy in countries where Somalia would not be represented. (2) Commercial Agreement for payment and economic co-operation. This regulates the participation of Italian capital in the economic development of Somalia. (3) Consular Convention, and (4) Air Services Agreement.[21]

It was agreed that the Somali government would assume all rights and obligations deriving from international instruments concluded by the Italian government on behalf of Somalia during the trusteeship regime, i.e. between December 2, 1950 and June 30, 1960. The exchange of letters was accompanied by a list of nineteen multilateral conventions entered into by Italy and extended to Somalia before the beginning of the trusteeship. This list was furnished by the Italian government for information purposes only, and the Somali government did not grant any undertakings with respect to those conventions.[22]

An important question that had to be settled was whether the new Republic would become successor of State with respect to treaties and other rights and obligations pre-dating the Union. The matter was dealt with in Article 4 of the Act of Union as follows: 1. "All rights lawfully vested in or obligations lawfully incurred by the independent government of Somaliland and Somalia or by any person on their behalf, shall be deemed to have been transferred to and accepted by the Somali Republic upon establishment of the Union." 2. "Whenever such rights and obligations arise from any international agreement their acceptance by the Somali Republic shall be subject to Article 67 of the Constitution."[23]

19 Del Boca, op. cit. p. 295.
20 Ibid., p. 296.
21 TNA FO371/146958.Telegram no. 427 of July 1, 1960 from British Embassy Mogadisho to FO.
22 P. Contini, op. cit., p. 15.
23 Law no. 2, January 31, 1961, "Act of Union".

Who is to blame for the meagre results?

Throughout the long years of colonial activities in Somalia, the European powers, namely Britain and Italy, paid little or no interest to native education and economic development. Although Italy's cautious penetration of Somalia started in early 1885, yet an effective administration, having authority over the entire territory, was only established in 1927, with the unification of the small Sultanate of Bargal to the rest of southern regions. Fascism considered Africans to be racially inferior, and therefore not deserving of the social, political and/or economic privileges granted to Europeans. However, a certain amount of educational development was considered necessary, and State-subsidized Catholic mission schools provided elementary education for Somalis. Of all the Italian colonies in Africa, Somalia received the least aid for genuine education. To obtain an education, Somalis had one of two choices: either the traditional Koranic Schools, or the highly suspect mission-run government schools. Statistics collected in 1934 shows a total student population in Somalia of only 1,265, enrolled at different educational levels, with all schooling activities concentrated in main centers like Mogadisho, Villabruzzi, Merca, Brava, Baidoa, Jilib and Kismayo.[24]

In 1939, a secular school was founded for the sons of supreme Somali chiefs[25]. "Those few Somalis who had been influenced by Italian culture had no educational opportunity beyond the elementary curriculum. The intermediate level was exclusively for Italians, and there was no higher education in the colony", comments Robert Hess.[26]

Italy's responsibilities are highlighted by Claudio Pacifico, on the basis of his diplomatic experience in Somalia, with the words: "Italy's failure to offer a genuine education to the Somalis during the long period of colonialism represents one of the gravest Italian responsibilities, with grave consequences felt up to the present time."[27]

As regards the post-war period, the most important undertakings Italy took on under the Trusteeship Agreement were: democratization and modernization of the country, economical and financial development, improvement of the educational system and shifting of power from the administration to a national

24 Hess, op. cit., p. 170.

25 George G. Dawson, 'Education in Somalia, Comparative Education Review, vol. 8, no. 2, Oct. 1964, p. 201.

26 Ibid., p. 188.

27 Claudio Pacifico, *Somalia: ricordi di un mal d'Africa Italiana*, Edimond, Città di Castello 1996, p. 50.

government. In the field of modernization, we have seen how the country made little progress and tribalism remained the basic element in Somali political and social life. For a variety of reasons, AFIS tried little to change this century-old Somali tradition. The administration used tribalism as an instrument to govern the country, the only system they perceived as viable to achieve results while respecting the target date for independence. "With a short time before it, the administration had been content to accept, by and large, the status quo, rather than institute changes which could increase its political difficulties," comments one author[28]. In the economic sector the country could not overcome its dependence on foreign assistance even to meet its ordinary budgetary commitments.

The only bright side of the AFIS management lay in the education sector, where a noticeable achievement was recorded. New State schools providing free education replaced the previous education system run by the Catholic missions with government subsidies. During the trusteeship period, education was governed by the principle that independence could only be based on 'education in the broadest sense.' On this basis, institutes of education at the elementary and intermediate levels were established in all important centres of the Territory, and Mogadisho, the capital, saw the opening of secondary and technical schools for the study of industrial, commercial, maritime and fishery-related subjects, as well as a teacher training college and a school of Islamic disciplines. An Agricultural Institute (Collegio Professionale Agrario) was established in the agricultural area of Genale, Lower Shabelle. Another programme offered evening literacy classes for adults and provided further training to civil servants.

Data collected in 1957 shows that some 51,000 children and adults of both sexes were enrolled in primary schools, 146 in junior and secondary schools, 336 in technical institutions and a few hundred more in higher educational institutions[29]. This figure represents a major breakthrough, compared to the situation in 1950, when Italy assumed the administration of the Trust Territory, where there were only 29 primary schools and some two thousand students receiving education[30]. The education system was complicated by the paucity of trained teachers at the beginning of the trusteeship mandate. In 1950 the total number of teachers in the primary school was 170, of which 35 female: 72 Italians, 62 Somalis and 32 Arabs[31]. To address this shortage of teachers, the Administration embarked on

28 Finkelstein, op. cit., p. 11.
29 I.M. Lewis, op. cit., p. 140.
30 Costanzo, '*L'educazione, chiave dello sviluppo della Somalia*', Affrica, anno XV, n° 3, 1960, p. 144.
31 Ibid., p. 142.

a bold programme whereby an increasing number of Somali teachers were sent to Italy to attend teacher training courses. Commenting on AFIS's education programme, Professor Giuseppe Costanzo explains that the Administration had three main objectives to achieve: (a) to provide the majority of Somalis with at least primary education, (b) to offer higher education to the small *intelligentsia* already existing, and (c) to promote the formation of a new, well-educated élite.[32]

For these meagre results in the educational sector, Italy received some accolades at the United Nations. The Liberian UN representative, on behalf of the African States, expressed its appreciation and sent a commendation to Italy and Somalia for the positive conclusion of the trusteeship regime. The representative of the United Arab Republic (Egypt), concluding the general show of appreciation for the Italians' work in Somalia, made the following statement: "The faithful implementation of the Trusteeship Agreement by Italy as the Administering Authority must be recognized and appreciated. We are fully aware of Italy's great task and the debt which civilization owes to its completion."[33] ." It was also said that, in enacting the trusteeship regime placed on Somalia, Italy had applied not only the "spirit, but possibly the 'letter' of the trusteeship agreement."[34]

Although Italy gained praise from the United Nations for its performance in Somalia, yet from the Somali point of view, advantages were far below expectations. In all sectors, the measures taken by the AFIS were inadequate and hastily implemented in the race against time to meet the approaching independence date. As a result, Italy left behind a weak democracy, an ordinary budget and balance of payment in the red, and a shaky public administration that was doomed to further deteriorate, and finally collapsed 9 years later. Few disagree that, in devising the resolution adopted in 1949, the United Nations had as their guiding consideration the need to find a politically acceptable compromise plan. Little attention was paid to the deplorable economic and social conditions of the Trust Territory despite warnings from different quarters, among which the Four Powers Commission of Investigation and successive UN visiting missions to the Territory.

One author with deep knowledge of the institute of international trusteeship commented that the decision of the United Nations "departed from the Western

32 Ibid.

33 General Assembly, 14th session, 846th plenary meeting, December 5, 1959, as reported in G. Costanzo, Problemi costituzionali della Somalia nella preparazione all'indipendenza (1957-1960), Giuffrè, Milano 1962, p.76.

34 George H. T.Kimble, Tropical Africa, vol. II, 'Society and Policy', Twentieth Century, New York 1969, p. 260.

principle of gradualism – a principle which assumes that full independence can be stable and secure only if the political bases of a state are derived from prolonged tutelage, constitutional maturity and basic popular consensus on the essentials of state unity and aims. It also ignored the Western tendency to assume that economic validity is a prerequisite to political stability."[35] In as short a period as the trusteeship regime, Italy cannot claim to have contributed to the economic and democratic developments of Somalia. In other words, the Italians withdrew from Somalia not on the basis of any solid progress, but because of the calendar. The only obligation that Italy satisfactorily fulfilled was the transfer of power to a local government. This turned out to be the easiest task among the obligations contemplated in the Trusteeship Agreement. The blame is to be apportioned between the Lega, the United Nations and the Italians, for their gross failure to realize that ten years were not a realistic time frame for laying down the foundations for a genuine state apparatus. It seems that each of these three stakeholders had its own agenda, not necessarily reflecting the best interest of the Trust Territory and its inhabitants.

At the United Nations, the Asian and Arab countries used Somalia as a test case to manifest their anticolonial policy; the Italians, for their part, wanted to ride the momentum generated by the UN decision so as to come out of the international isolation caused by fascism; the Lega dei Giovani Somali, with its competing tribal components, wanted to take more than a fair share of the spoils as quickly as possible. Despite these shortcomings, however, it would be wrong to conclude that the trusteeship regime was a negative experience; far from that. It brought to end a period encompassing two brutal overlapping events: the war and the British military occupation of Somalia. After a period of economic and social stagnation which characterized nearly a decade of British Military occupation, the trusteeship regime became something of a golden age for Somalia: with UN and Italian money pouring in and experienced Italian administrators who had come to see Somalia as their home, infrastructural and educational development blossomed. "The Trustee period was a boon to Somalia in the form of capital. As a former colonial power, Italy was more effective in transferring capital than it had been during the colonial period", comments one writer.[36]

The trusteeship regime brought with it radical social and economic changes and a stable petty bourgeois class emerged. The dormant economy started to

35 A.A. Castagno, op. cit., p. 339.
36 Rhymer, op. cit., p. 104.

prosper. Somalis became civil servants, teachers, soldiers, petty traders in coastal cities and small business owners. Mogadisho changed appearance, becoming a modern city with gardens and paved roads flanked by trees; new coffee bars, cinemas, restaurants and other public amenities such as night clubs and theatres mushroomed in every part of the Territory. Italians were able to maintain links with Somalis on a new basis of parity of status and esteem. The Italian administration also introduced fashion and Italian cuisine, as well as many Italian products. The major urban centres, basic public services, transport and the postal service were restored. In the words of one author, "Whatever the shortcomings of Italian rule before 1940, the Trusteeship Administration worked hard to remedy them."[37]

Who is the hero of independence?

Most African countries, former colonies of Great Britain and France, had acceded to political independence by 1960. Some of these countries did acquire their political independence through a peaceful process; others gained it through armed struggle led by liberation movements. Each of these liberation movements had a leader, a national figure, who led the revolt against foreign domination.

In countries such as South Africa, Zimbabwe and Kenya liberation was achieved at the end of a long political or armed struggle. Similarly, in Latin America as well as in Asia, most countries attained political independence following massive popular uprisings in many cases, and through armed struggle, with consequent heavy loss of human lives, in others. The African liberation movements were generally led by individuals who had spent long periods of time in exile in foreign countries where they acquired political experience and solid education backgrounds. Many of them attended Western universities and a led a middle-class life in some of those countries before the emergence of their national movements[38]. Many began as nationalists and sadly turned into uncrowned kings presiding over security States of monstrous proportions. A good number of these African leaders later became heads of States or government in their respective countries. Among these great men it is worth mentioning the fiery Kwame Nkrumah of Ghana, the charismatic Jomo Kenyatta of Kenya, the scholarly Julius Nyerere of Tanganyika (later Tanzania), the nationalistic Siaka

37 Seton-Watson, '*Italy's Imperial Hangover*', Journal of Contemporary History, vol. 15, no. 1 (Jan. 1980), p. 174.

38 Touval, op. cit., p. 83.

Stevens of Sierra Leone, the emotional Kenneth Kaunda of Zambia, and the excellent Nelson Mandela of South Africa. These iconic men and others were instrumental in shaping the destinies of their respective countries.

By contrast, the Somali political associations which came into existence in the Forties were political parties operating openly with the blessing of the occupying power; they were not armed liberation movements, as was the case in other parts of Black Africa. The British granted the Somalis the right to form political associations and were therefore seen by the Somalis as 'liberators' from the fascist regime. Logically, waging an armed struggle against an 'ally' was out of the question, and it would not have served any meaningful purpose.

The Somali political elite, destined to lead the country at the end of the trusteeship mandate, was the product of a superficial westernization achieved not through education or armed struggle, but simply by circumstance. They spoke only their native Somali language, had no important foreign contacts, and had barely travelled abroad. The consequence was that none of them could be called the father or mother of Somali nationalism or independence. None of the 13 'founding fathers' of the Lega commonly referred to as the 'pioneers of Somali independence' emerged as a national political leader. One of the questions most frequently asked is "Who is the leading light in the Lega dei Giovani Somali?"

As we have seen, in all countries of the world, every major national political party has a leading figure who symbolizes the unity and strength of the organization. The Lega seemed to have been an exception to this rule. Its office-bearers were subject to re-election every year, which often resulted in changes in leadership. There is therefore no leader recognized by the Somalis as a political father-figure on the national scale. The president of the party was a primus inter pares rather than an outstanding figure. There is no Mandela or Kenyatta in Somalia. A number of factors may help to explain this – though one could not disagree with the explanation offered by a British intelligence report, according to which "the intensely parochial tribal spirit has always militated against any leader rising above it."[39] Another author further explained: "These qualities abound among the Somalis who have aptly been described as belonging to an egalitarian society."[40]

In the life of Somalia, there are two historical events symbolizing the struggle for the independence of the country: these occurred on January 11, 1948 and

39 TNA FO 1015/140, Somali Intelligent Report, no. 2, of May 24, 1947.

40 P. Contini, op. cit., p. 90.

October 5, 1949 respectively. On January 11, 1948 in Mogadisho, in the presence of the delegation from the Four Power Commission of Investigation, elements affiliated to the Lega clashed with the rival Conferenza Somala campaigning for the return of Italy as administering authority. In the clash, 14 Somalis from the pro-Italian group and 52 unarmed Italian civilians lost their life at the hands of elements belonging to the Lega, who had converged in Mogadisho from as far as Ogadenia, reportedly with the help of British colonial officers[41]. The Lega suffered just one casualty, a young female by the name of Hawa Osman, alias 'Tacco'. Speculations apart, the woman's true identity and the circumstances surrounding her death remain shrouded in mystery. In the list of Somali casualties published in the official newspaper of the time, she is referred to as Hawa Ahmed and not as Hawa Osman. Today, Hawa 'Tacco' is remembered as national heroine: a simple statue marks the spot in Mogadisho where she fell, hit by a stray arrow.

The other date considered as a milestone in Somali history is October 5, 1949. On this day, the Lega staged a big demonstration in Mogadisho, the aim of which was to voice opposition to the possible return of Italy to Somalia. Somalia's future was being discussed at the United Nations in Lake Success. A number of people, 3 according to British accounts, were killed on that day when police used live ammunition to disperse the rally as people started hurling stones at them. Other sources put the death toll much higher than the figures provided by the colonial authorities. I have been given only two names among the victims of 5 October 1949: Abdi Yousuf and Jibril Dirie[42]. No record could be traced of the remaining individuals said to have been killed by the British forces, and the few individuals still alive who witnessed the event could not provide any useful information. A simple monument was erected in 1963 in Dhagahtur Square as a memorial to the casualties[43]. It was the military regime, however, which accorded them the dignified recognition they deserved by erecting this monument in their memory, exactly at the sites where the shootings took place.

41 Bullotta, op. cit., p. 184.

42 Personal interview with Mohamoud Yusuf Aden 'Muro' in Louein, Belgium, on August 9, 2009.

43 *Somali News*, December 27, 1963.

Sharmarke appointed Prime Minister

Problems of national integration

As widely predicted, President Aden, in his capacity as provisional head of state, had on July 6, 1960 nominated Abdirashid Ali, a rising political figure and leader of the dissident faction within the ranks of the Lega, to form the first government of the independent Republic of Somalia[44]. On July 5, 1960 Issa's government handed their resignation to the President of the Republic, as did Mohamed Haji Ibrahim Egal, former Prime Minister of the Independent State of Somaliland.

Elected in his tribal base of Gardo, Majertenia, the new Prime Minister was one of a handful of Somalis with a university degree. In fact, he returned from Italy in 1958 after completing a course in Political Science at Rome University with distinction. He was also among the few southerners who received elementary education during the fascist regime at the special 'Figli di capi' school in the late Thirties. A former civil servant during AFIS and British Administrations, the new Prime Minister had no experience in government but had the benefit of a solid parliamentary majority. He was one of the leading exponents of the ruling party, and a militant in the radical wing of the party, bitterly opposed to the return of Italy to Somalia. However, he soon changed his attitude when, in August 1959, in a public debate at the National Assembly, he praised the Italian government for "loyally and effectively respecting its obligations under the Trusteeship Agreement of the United Nations."[45]

Following long days of difficult negotiations, further complicated by personal and tribal equations, Sharmarke formed a 15-member government, a clan coalition dominated by the Lega but supported by the two clan-based Northern parties (SNL and USP) as junior partners. Of the fifteen ministerial positions, four were allocated to the Northern SNL-USP: Abdi Hassan Boni (USP) became Vice Prime Minister; Mohamed Haji Ibrahim Egal (SNL) Minister of Defence; Ali Garad Jama (USP) Minister of Education; Ahmed Haji Dualeh (SNL) Minister of Agriculture. It should be noted that Ahmed Haji Dualeh 'Keysi' had resigned from his ministerial and parliamentary positions, opting instead for the diplomatic service, reportedly over divergences with the government on the production and marketing of bananas. The remainder seats were distributed among southern

44 Decreto amministrativo no. 2 del 22 luglio 1960, Bollettino Ufficiale, suppl. n° 3 al n° 1, 30 luglio 1960.

45 Costanzo, op. cit., p. 62.

clans. Clan representation in the government was "within bounds in support of the unwritten rule of clan balance."[46]

Among Abdirashid's new ministers were a few 'holdovers' from Issa's pre-independence administration, including Abdullahi Issa, Sheikh Ali Jim'ale and Abdinour Mohamed Hussein, while Mohamed Haji Ibrahim Egal, Ali Garad Jama and Ahmed Haji Dualeh held office in the short-lived government of Somaliland. According to generally well-informed sources, Issa and Egal, the two former Prime Ministers, were initially reluctant to join Abdirashid's government, but "finally they succumbed as it gradually became plain that he could gain sufficient support to form a government without them."[47]

Entering the government for the first time was Abdulkadir Mohamed Aden 'Zoppo'. His inclusion in the government, despite his long-standing strong opposition to the Lega programme, was due to his leadership of the Rahanweyn group of 24 deputies and also to his defection from the HDMS, of which he had been secretary general for a long time. But after the formation of the government, days of manoeuvring were in fact required, in large part because, within the parliamentary majority, tribal interests and vote selling had to be placated if there was to be any hope of a reasonably strong and durable ministry emerging. "Because of the venality of an unknown, but certainly not small number of deputies, who would have few scruples in selling their vote to the highest bidder, the Prime Minister delayed the presentation of his programme to the Assembly until he felt sure of obtaining the necessary number of votes", comments a well-informed British source[48]. The same source adds that the opposition within the Assembly collapsed when the Lega called a meeting of all its deputies and instructed them to vote for the government. On August 13, 1960, the government presented its programme to the National Assembly, gaining a large vote of confidence: 97 votes in favour and 3 votes against[49]. The 3 'nays' were from Michael Mariano (National United Front), Yousuf Ismail Samatar (Somali National League) and Mohamed Aden Maho (HDMS)[50]. It was also reported that, in spite of clear instructions given by the party to its parliament members to

46 Aweys Osman Haji and Abdiwahid Osman Haji, Clan, Sub-clan and Regional Representation in the Somali Government Organization 1960-1990: Statistical Data and Findings, Washington D.C. 1998, p. 14.

47 TNA FO 371/146958 confidential document of July 23, 1960 from British Embassy Mogadisho to FO.

48 Ibid.

49 Government Activities from Independence until today, 11 July 1960-31 December 1963,presidence of Council of Ministers, Mogadisho 1964.

50 TNA FO 371/146958 confidential document of August 20, 1960 from British Embassy Mogadisho to FO.

vote for the government, twenty-one deputies absented themselves.

While the union between the two territories seemed to be going smoothly on the surface, beneath there were simmering problems of a legal, administrative and tribal nature whose solution remained a daunting task. Before the union, the two territories had been, for more than half a century, administered by two different European powers. The northern laws and institutions were those of a British dependency; in the south, the Italian system developed during the colonial and trusteeship periods prevailed. When the two regions were joined in July 1960, they had two different judicial systems, different currencies, different organizations and conditions of service for the army, police and civil servants.

The taxation and customs systems were different, and so were the two educational systems. The exchange rates of the two currencies also differed, and economic contacts between the two regions were virtually non-existent. The legal and the judiciary systems needed to be harmonized for the new republic to function properly. The northern legal system was based on English common law and the Indian penal code. In the south, the system was mainly modelled upon the Italian penal and civil code.

In order to assist the Somali government in this endeavour, a Consultative Commission for Integration (later re-named Consultative Commission for Legislation) was established in October 1960 by presidential decree; the commission was chaired by Paolo Contini, a UN expert, from its establishment until the end of 1964.[51]

In the field of integration, the government quickly achieved enormous progress. With the help of the United Nations Consultative Commission for Integration, the institutions of the two territories were quickly unified. Priority was given to unifying the civil service and the judiciary. A single legal system was approved. The fiscal and accounting systems were unified; the police and the national army were integrated. Another difference was represented by the dual language used in the administration (Italian in the south and English in the north). In the absence of an official Somali script, official and private business was conducted in two different languages, this linguistic barrier further hampering administrative efficiency. The Somalis who had been trained under the former British Protectorate, many of whom had been moved to Mogadisho, soon became contemptuous of the Italian administrative system, or lack thereof, and

51 Decreto amministrativo, 11 ottobre, 1960 n° 18 rep. Bollettino Ufficiale, suppl. n° 1 al n° 4, 14 ottobre 1960.

were keen on British methods to be introduced throughout the Republic. "They have sometime proclaimed their views with a lack of tact that has not endeared them to their southern compatriots", comments a British Council report.[52]

In the sphere of language, many thinking Somalis were convinced that English, as the language of commerce and technology and the principal means of communication with the rest of the world, would predominate over Italian in the long run, despite strong feelings among many Somalis in favour of preserving the Italian language for cultural and historical reasons.

In addition to the linguistic, legal as well as other differences referred to above, physical communication between the two regions constituted a major problem. There was no direct telephone line between Hargeisa and Mogadisho, and although the cities were connected by regular twice-weekly air flights, the journey by road normally took three days to complete during the dry season.[53]

The prospects of reducing this distance improved in 1962 when Ethiopia made a formal request for permission for weekly Ethiopian Airlines commercial flights from Addis Abeba to Mogadisho; the request was turned down by Abdirashid, Prime Minister at the time, because of the perceived fear that the Ethiopians' ultimate purpose might be to carry out intelligence activities in Somalia. However the then Minister of Foreign Affairs, Abdullahi Issa, looked on the request with favour because he had in mind a counter-proposal to Ethiopia for a land corridor linking Mogadisho with Hargeisa (via Fer-Fer, Shilabo, Warder and Aware) and one between Mogadisho and Burao. If Ethiopia accepted this *quid pro quo*, Somalia would benefit by a reduction of the long land journey to Hargeisa via Garowe[54]. Ethiopia also requested loading facilities at the port of Mogadisho for the equipment necessary to a German oil company operating in Ogaden. This second request was destined to be rejected too, this time not for security concerns, but on grounds of the non-existence of a transit accord between the two countries. On the issue of the land corridor, the President of the Republic saw eye to eye with the Foreign Minister on account of its potential benefits for Somalia.[55]

52 TNA CO 1045/1145, British Council annual report 196 0-61.
53 I.M. Lewis, op. cit., p. 171.
54 Diary Aden Abdulla, June 30, 1962.
55 Ibid.

Early signs of dissatisfaction

Wanle Weyn and the referendum on the Constitution

With the fading of the wave of nationalistic enthusiasm which accompanied the celebrations for independence and union, resentments surfaced in the north. The significant goodwill and optimism discernible in the early Sixties had evaporated. The mood was now one of deep hostility: a disillusioned and cynical public now railed against the northern political classes responsible for the precipitate union with the former Italian colony. Politicians as well as common Somalilanders soon realized how 'disingenuous' they had been to press for quick union with the south without giving careful thought to the consequences. Hargeisa lost its prestige as the capital of a former independent country, declining to mere headquarters of a region. Mogadisho became the centre of political and economic affairs and the seat of the National Assembly and the executive. The declining economy brought suggestions for a merger of the region's political parties that would form a strong common ground capable of defending the region's interests.

A first step in that direction was taken in September 1960 with the merger of SNL and USP. The amalgamated party assumed the name of Somali National League United Somali Party (SNL-UUP)[56]. One author described the merger as "very like two New York banks which merge but hang on to both their names."[57] This new mood in the north found expression in three different forms: firstly, in rejecting the referendum on the Constitution; secondly, in the aborted coup of December 1961, and thirdly, in the following very popular verse: "Adoo guri barwaaqa ah geel dhalay ku haaysta, geedi lama lalaabo oo abaar looma guuree, Anigeeysu geeystoo galabsaday xumaantee, wixii ila garaad ahoow gobanima ha tuurinaay", which roughly translates as: "If you live in a place full of pasture with milk-producing camels, you should not suddenly pack up and blindly move to a barren land. I have put myself in difficulties. O thinking people, don't throw away freedom and dignity."[58] The verse reflected a sense of deep regret stemming from the hasty decision on the part of the northerners to join the south, abandoning their land, where they believed they were well off, without advancing their condition in the slightest.

The Act of Union was based on a Constitution unfamiliar to the Northerners, who had never been associated with it at any stage of its long drafting cycle. When

56 *Somaliland News (Hargeisa)*, October 3, 1960.

57 Touval, op. cit., p. 119.

58 *The Somaliland Times*, issue 437, June 12-18, 2010.

they did get hold of the draft document, it was too late for them to examine and digest the complex legal document so as to bring any meaningful contributions. With Independence Day rapidly approaching, they were only able to contribute two articles: Art 88, barring civil servants and public employees from becoming political party leaders, and Art. 89, establishing a Civil Service Commission.

British diplomatic sources in Mogadisho suggest that A. Issa did not wish the Constitution to be advanced to the Constituent Assembly on grounds that Somaliland was not represented, but that he failed to win sufficient support in the Legislature[59]. On the ground, opposition to the government was most clearly displayed in the North. In effect, arriving in Hargeisa on September 11, 1960, some members of the NUF showed their disapproval to the government by turning their back on the Prime Minister.[60]

One of the first actions taken by the new government was organizing the referendum on the Constitution. The text of the Constitution was released in English, Italian and Arabic. Many reckon that this was of little benefit to the estimated 90% of the population who could not read and write any of these 3 foreign languages. On 20 June 1961, the Constitution, as contemplated by section III of the Transitional and Final Provisions, was submitted to a popular referendum and passed almost unanimously, 90.6% of the electorate being in favour.[61]

But what the government omitted to mention was how this strong support for the Constitution was mustered and the controversy surrounding the way the government had handled the voting process. Widespread rigging in the voting process was reported, especially in the south. In all but two provinces, Hiran and the Northern regions, the referendum was accepted. In the northern regions, with a predominant SNL presence, a huge campaign against the referendum was mounted, resulting in the rejection of the Constitution in those areas. The vote was a tribally divisive issue, with No votes highest in the Issak areas of former British Somaliland, and Yes votes in the Warsangheli, Gadabursi and Dulbahanta areas. The only area in southern Somalia where a No vote was registered against the Constitution was the central region of Hiran: the margin was wide, the count being 14,296 for and 23,553 against[62]. This result was a personal triumph for

59 TNA FO 371/146967 Confidential telegram from British Consulate , Mogadisho to FO.

60 TNA FO 371/146955 confidential report from British Embassy, Mogadisho to FO, December 7, 1960.

61 Somali Republic, Government activities from Independence until Today (July 1, 1960 - December 30, 1963) Presidency of Council of Ministers, Mogadisho, p. 16.

62 Data obtained from the research unit of Northern Somalis Peace and Unity (NSPU), May 18, 2006.

Sheikh Ali Giumale, who had campaigned for a 'no' vote.

The referendum revealed a dramatic split between north and south. Whereas the north voted solidly against the Constitution, the south strongly voted in favour, using all means available including fraud, a negative legacy of the trusteeship era. The opposition to the Constitution was based not on disagreement with the substance of the document, but rather on rivalry among political classes. The Northerners, shocked by the massive fraud, began referring to Southerners by the pejorative term 'Wanle-Weyn' (from the small southern town of Wanle-Weyn, Lower Shabelle, whose result of 68,994 Yes vs. 0 No was more outstanding even than the count in Mogadisho)[63]. "Stuffing ballot boxes for a Constitution expected to lay the legal foundation of the new Republic, though not unpredicted, was not a sign of good omen", comments Amina H. Aden.[64]

The Supreme Court confirmed the decision of the Central Electoral Office for the referendum in relation to complaints originating from the district offices of Merca, Afgooye, Beledweyne, Dusa Mareb, and El Bur. The Court rejected the complaints directly submitted by the GSL, SNL and USP. Following this decision, a proclamation of the regularity of the vote was made.[65]

Referendum results[66]:

TOTAL VOTES CAST	1,948,343
YES VOTES	1,756,216
NO VOTES	183,000
SPOILED BALLOT PAPERS	9,132

Soon after these inflated results were published, the southern regions were hit by the worst floods in living memory, which wrecked vast swathes of agricultural land, causing immense damage to the national economy. An anonymous person from Somaliland, mindful of the role the Ministry of Interior had played in fixing the vote, hurled the following curse at the Minister of the Interior: "Ilaahii Wanle-Weyn webiga ku daroow, Waziirka Gudahana Wadnaha gooy" which roughly means: "May Allah who dumped Wanle-Weyn into the flood now strike dead the Minister of the Interior." Legend has it that the then Minister of the

63 *Somali News*, June 23, 1961.

64 Amina H. Aden, 'Somalia: An Illusory Political Nation State', Comparative Studies of South Asia, Africa and the Middle East Spring 1994 14(1): 99-109.

65 Excerpt from Supreme Court proceedings, July 4, 1961.

66 Renato Angeloni, Diritto costituzionale somalo Milano, Giuffrè, 1964, p. 277.

Interior, Abdirazak Haji, was flown to America to receive treatment for a lung-related ailment at Walter Hospital in Washington, DC. To many Northerners this was Allah's answer to their prayers!

Controversy over the legality of the 'Precipitate Union'

British Somaliland became an independent State acquiring all the attributions of sovereignty on June 26, 1960, precisely four days before the former Trust Territory of Somalia became independent on July 1, 1960. Mohamed Haji Ibrahim Egal, the Prime Minister of the independent Somaliland, took the oath on the Quran to the new State and hoisted the blue and white starred flag.[67]

Britain, in its capacity as a former colonial power, accorded diplomatic recognition to the newly born Republic of Somaliland; however it did not establish an embassy in Hargeisa, but rather a consulate subordinated to the British Embassy in Mogadisho. A message from the Queen was delivered to Hargeisa by Mr T.E. Bromely, British Consul General in Mogadisho, on the occasion of Somaliland independence. The message read: "I, my government and my people of the United Kingdom wish you well on the day of independence. The connection between our people goes back some 130 years and British administration of the Protectorate for 60 years. I look forward to continuing and enduring friendship between our two countries."[68] Since Somaliland was a protectorate and not a colony, there was no need for a UK Act of Parliament to confer independence on the territory. Independence was thus conferred by royal proclamation[69]. A number of other foreign countries, including Egypt, Ghana, Libya and Israel, are known to have extended diplomatic recognition to the former British Protectorate of Somaliland.[70]

For many other countries, the imminent union with Somalia appeared to have made the question of recognition rather academic and devoid of practical meaning. The United States of America was most reluctant to go to the trouble and expense of independence celebrations and establishing an embassy in Hargeisa, in a country whose separate existence was going to be ephemeral. "The United States did not extend official recognition to the newly independent State of Somaliland on June 26, 1960 partly to avoid embarking on a lot of paperwork for a country with an estimated life of five days and for fear of

67 *The Times*, June 27, 1960.

68 Ibid., editorial: British Rule In Somaliland Is Ended.

69 TNA FO 371/146958 letter from I. Watt (CAA 270/6/018 to FO, July 15, 1960.

70 A short briefing paper by AH Nur, April 2011.

upsetting the Ethiopians", reveals a British source[71]. The US sent a short message of congratulations to the Somaliland Council of Ministers, delivered to Hargeisa by a diplomat from the American Consulate General in Mogadisho. Similar messages were sent to the Prime Minister, Mohamed Ibrahim Egal, by a number of foreign dignitaries including the Prime Minister of Somalia Abdullahi Issa, Mr P. Herton of the USA, Field Marshal Ayoub Khan, Dag Hammarskjold, Mario di Stefano, Haile Selassie, Nehru, and Chancellor Adenhauer.[72]

On July 1, the Legislative Assembly of Somalia and the Somaliland Legislative Council, sitting together for the first time as a national assembly, acclaimed the Act of Union between the two territories, thus creating the Republic of Somalia. It seemed that the constitutionality of the Act was not entirely clear, as no formal Act of Union had been signed. The two draft acts, one for each territory, contained important differences. "Neither side seemed likely to jeopardize the de facto union by querying its legality at the present time", commented the British Ambassador in Mogadisho.[73]

Examination and comparison of the two draft Acts of Union of Somaliland and Somalia reveals some important differences. I have briefly outlined them below.

The Somali draft divided Somaliland into two administrative regions and provided for existing laws in the two territories to continue until abrogated. Civil servants in both territories were to receive terms and conditions of service no less favourable than the terms current until unification of the two services. None of these issues were expressly addressed in the Somaliland draft. Further, according to the Somali draft, the president of the Somali Assembly would become the first president of the National (united) Assembly and the current Cabinet would constitute the first unified cabinet presided over by the Prime Minister; whereas the Somaliland draft stated that the current president would chair the National Assembly only for the purpose of taking the oath of allegiance and selecting the first president of the National Assembly, and made no mention of the Prime Minister, simply stating that the unified cabinet would be appointed in accordance with the Constitution. Finally, the Somali draft provided for international treaties and agreements stipulated by the two States to be placed before the National Assembly for ratification, whereas the Somaliland

71 TNA FO 371/146981, confidential report 15121/14460 from British Embassy Washington, D.C. to FO, London, June 8, 1960.

72 *The Somaliland News*, June 27, 1960.

73 TNA FO 371/146955, confidential report from British Embassy, Mogadisho to FO August 5, 1960.

draft stated that such agreements should automatically become binding upon the new unified State.[74]

The Act of Union immediately came under strong criticism from a number of northern lawmakers who challenged the legality of the procedure for its adoption in Parliament. As mentioned, the Act was approved by acclamation on July 1, 1960 at the National Assembly, without first being debated by members of Parliament in accordance with the law requiring a unanimous vote in the Assembly for approval by acclamation. Presiding over the Parliament session was the newly elected President of the National Assembly, Jama Abdullahi Ghalib, a Northerner. The irregularity was angrily brought to the attention of Aden Abdulla. "Today," Aden Abdulla wrote in his diary on January 18, 1961" I received four MPs from the North: Abdullahi Ahmed, Osman Garad, Ibrahim Idd and a fourth one; they were complaining that, against their views, the President of the Assembly had had the law of the Union approved by acclamation, without first opening debate on it."[75] The President further notes: "If this is what actually happened, it was a grave mistake, infringing the rule requiring unanimity in Parliament before the approval by acclamation." Aden Abdulla, apparently conscious of the legal and political consequences this new development might raise, quickly advised the Prime Minister to persuade the four parliamentarians to desist from taking any action. with regard to the way the Act was passed by the National Assembly.[76]

As a consequence, seven months later, steps were taken to redress the mistake: on 18 January 1961 a new Act of Union consisting of 10 articles and defining in more precise terms the legal effects of the union was submitted to the National Assembly, with retroactive effects as from July 1, 1960 and validity throughout the Republic[77]. The Act of Union between the former Trusteeship Territory of Somalia and the British Territory of Somaliland was signed by the provisional Head of State on January 31, 1961, after the said four lawmakers agreed with the Prime Minister to drop their reservations with regard to the previous irregularities[78]. Arguments and doubts about the legality of the union between the two countries were voiced from different quarters but, as Contini wrote, "There is no doubt that, on the first of July, a full and lawful union was formed by the will of the peoples of the two territories. However, the legal formalities

74 Ibid.
75 Diary Aden Abdulla, January 18, 1961.
76 Ibid.
77 Legge n°5 del 31 gennaio 1961, Bollettino Ufficiale, n°2, 1-2 febbraio 1961.
78 Diary Aden Abdulla, January 30, 1961.

had not been completed in time. The Act of Union of Somaliland and Somalia did not have any legal validity in the south and the approval 'in principle' of the Atto di Unione by the Legislative Assembly of Somalia was not sufficient to make it legally binding in that territory.

"Despite this anomaly," Contini concludes, "the union, for all practical purposes, was formalized, but its precise legal effects had not been laid down in any instrument having binding force in both parts of the State."[79] Haji N.A. Noor Muhammad, another legal expert, who served in Somalia as Supreme Court Judge[80], went further: "The doubts entertained regarding the union were set at rest by the Act of Union of 1961 and the union emerged stronger, with integration of laws and different legal systems prevailing in both parts of the Republic."[81]

Some of the provisions of the Act of Union were declaratory of already existing conditions. Thus Article 1 provided for Somaliland and Somalia, being united, to constitute the Somali Republic, 'which shall be an independent, democratic and unitary Republic.' An important institutional provision is considered in article 6, which established that the armies of the northern and southern regions (respectively 'Somaliland Scouts' and 'Esercito Nazionale Somalo') "shall constitute the national army of the Somali Republic and shall be under the Ministry of Defense."

The same article provided for the unification of the two police forces as the Police Force of the Somali Republic which, following the Italian system previously applied in the south, was placed under the authority of the Minister of the Interior. The Act of Union was based on the premise that, in the beginning, it would be undesirable to introduce drastic changes which might shake the freshly laid foundation of the Republic. Accordingly, it established that the courts and public bodies of the two territories would continue with their respective powers and jurisdictions until superseded by integrated legislations (Act of Union, Article 3 (2).

Following the same principle, provision was made for the laws extant in Somaliland and Somalia at the time of establishment of the union to remain in full force and effect until changed by future legislation (Article 3 (1). Officials of

79 P. Contini, op. cit., p. 10.

80 Vice-president of the Supreme Court of the Somali Republic, his services being provided to the Somali government by the United Nations under the OPEX Programme.

81 The Development of the Constitution of the Somali Republic, published by the Government of the Somali Republic, Ministry of Grace and Justice, 1969, p. 32.

the northern and southern regions were assured conditions of service no less favourable than those applicable to them at the time of the union (Article 3 (4). All persons who on July 1, 1960 were citizens of Somaliland and Somalia became ope legis (by law) citizens of the Somali Republic. The customs tariffs applicable in the two territories before the union remained unchanged. However, in the case of goods moving between the two regions, where the import duty in the territory to which the goods were proceeding was higher, a duty equal to the difference between the two rates was charged.

One author referred to the union between the two territories as "Siamese twins whose godparents were the United Nations, Britain and Italy."[82] The issue of the Union was considered an internal problem of the Somalis, in which the United Nations, the British and the Italians had no role to play.

Aden Abdulla wins the presidential election

Sharmarke re-confirmed

With the approval of the Constitution and the expiry of the one-year provisional period, the National Assembly was required to elect a new president under Article 70 of the Constitution itself. On 6 July 1961, the National Assembly started the process: the election was a two-horse race between Sheikh Ali Jim'ale and Aden Abdulla[83]. Neither of the two contenders could gain the two-third majority of the 123 deputies required to win an outright victory in the first two secret ballots; in the subsequent ballots, as per Art. 70, an absolute majority was required.

In the first ballot, both candidates got an equal number of 60 votes, with one single vote in dispute that held the balance. In the second ballot, Sheikh Ali Jim'ale received 61 votes, pulling slightly ahead of Aden Abdulla who had 59 votes. One vote was still disputed. The third ballot confirmed the victory of Aden Abdulla over Sheikh Ali Jim'ale by a wafer-thin margin of 62 votes out of the 123 cast by the deputies. Aden Abdulla was re-elected President of the Somali Republic on 6 July 1961 for the extended period of 6 years. The live radio broadcast of the election, followed with passion throughout the country, was a powerful instance of civic education. From his office at Villa Somalia, formerly the official residence of the Italian administrators, after learning of his election as President of the Republic, Aden Abdulla wrote the following entry in his diary

82 Majorie Perham, The Times, July 4, 1960

83 Aden Abdulla had been elected provisional president of the republic on July 1, 1960, a position he held until the approval of the Constitution by popular referendum on June 20, 1961.

for July 6, 1961: "May Allah, who sees my clean conscience and good intentions as well as I do, help me to serve my country and my people."[84]

Abdulla and Jim'ale had much in common—both belonged to the ruling party, both were elected from the same electoral district (Beledweyne), and both belonged to the same Hawiye clan family; but it would be wrong to conclude that they had the same leadership style[85]. The narrow victory of Aden Abdulla and the tight competition between the "two giants in the election contest"[86] shows how divided Parliament was and highlights the ruling party's inability to reach consensus on one candidate. While there seemed to have been none of the vote rigging that had troubled the general elections, it was widely rumoured that vote buying tactics had been used to influence the outcome of the election. Jim'ale received his support mainly from the Hawiye deputies, who blamed Osman for 'abandoning' his own ethnic group, the Hawiye, and from the Issak component, who felt that "Somaliland's (or rather the Isaac's) interests were being subordinated to those of Somalia", as Castagno comments[87]. However, to set the record straight, it should be added here that Aden Abdulla did not favour any one clan family to the detriment of any other, and those entertaining this idea certainly did not know the man. "Abdulla was a man capable of holding independent views, who in the decade of Trusteeship had emerged as the most respected statesman in Somalia and an astute arbitrator who could reach beyond partisan politics to reconcile conflicting factions."[88]

However, the election was not a controversy-free exercise: soon after the election, a group of 11 deputies, all from Sheikh Ali Giumale's camp, raised the possibility of presenting a motion in Parliament designed to invalidate the presidential election because of an alleged irregularity regarding a ballot paper that had been counted in favour of the winning candidate. They contended that the name on one of the ballots cast was 'Aden Osman' and not 'Aden Abdulla Osman', the full name of the elected President[89]. As time passed, however, the initiative to push the motion through Parliament ran out of steam and consequently never appeared on the actual agenda for discussion in the House,

84 Diary Aden Abdulla, July 6, 1961.

85 Sheikh Ali Jim'ale conceded defeat and congratulated Aden Abdulla soon after the results were announced.

86 *Somali News*, July 7, 1961.

87 A.A. Castagno, *Political Parties and National Integration in Tropical Africa*, University of California Press, Berkeley, 1964, p. 548.

88 A.A. Castagno, op. cit. p. 547.

89 Diary Aden Abdulla, July 14, 1961.

apparently overshadowed by the process of formation of the new government and by the single deputies beginning to vie for ministerial positions.

When a new head of state is elected, the incumbent prime minister is constitutionally required to submit the resignation of his entire government to the elected president. Abdirashid took this step on July 6, i.e. the same day of the election of the Head of State, but the President requested him to remain as a caretaking administrator.[90]

Art. 3 of the Constitution states that the "Prime Minister shall be appointed and dismissed by the President of the Republic", but does not provide any clear indications as to how the Prime Minister should be selected. Every time a new head of state is elected, or a new Parliament is inaugurated, the president will initiate a cycle of complex informal consultations with party leaders and key political figures in Parliament and outside. This is technically an exploratory phase during which public opinion is consulted regarding the person who might be best placed to form a government and obtain a confidence vote in Parliament. This is a well-established routine practice inherited by the Italian administration. The exploratory phase is followed by the designation of the Prime Minister, who accepts it 'with reservation', meaning that he will in turn initiate a process of consultation to ascertain whether he has sufficient backing from Parliament to form a government. After this he will report back to the President, either to formally accept or to decline the designation. The final phase of government formation is the appointment of the cabinet ministers, followed by the confidence vote in Parliament.

The persons or groups to be consulted include the country's leading politicians as well as prominent private citizens. Predictably, the opinions and preferences of the individuals consulted were rather varied. Abdirashid's candidature received strong support from the two main political parties in the country, the HDMS and the ruling party, the LGS.

The first person to be consulted was the President of the National Assembly, Jama Abdullahi Ghalib, together with his Deputy, Haji Bashir Ismail; both men supported the candidature of the outgoing Prime Minister, Abdirashid[91]. By contrast, the other two Vice-presidents of the National Assembly, Haji Omar Sheegooq and Haji Aboubakr Haji Farah, proposed the designation of Sheikh Ali Jim'ale as premier, on the grounds that he had won the confidence of more

90 Caretaker governments are expected to handle daily issues, but not to introduce controversial bills.
91 Diary Aden Abdulla, July 8, 1961.

than half of Parliament in the presidential election[92]. Sheikh Ali Jim'ale also received strong backing from Mohamed Haji Ibrahim Egal, Abdullahi Issa, Mohamed Gabio, Haji Aboubakr Abdulkadir and Sheikh Aboukar, all belonging to the faction who had lost the presidential election. For the President, however, the identification or categorization of Parliament groups on the basis of their voting preferences was wrong, since the presidential election was and should be carried out through secret ballot. In addition to this, the President rejected the idea that he represented the group who elected him, commenting: "This would establish a dangerous, unacceptable precedent."[93]

A bigger surprise was the name of national army Military Chief Gen. Daud Abdulla, emerging out of the consultations as a candidate for premiership. The General's candidature, forwarded by the outgoing Prime Minister, was rejected a priori by the President on the grounds that the General was "lacking political support in Parliament", besides being "much needed in his current position."[94] A number of small parties (Partito Liberale, Unione Africani, Unione [?] Mniferro, Partito Socialista, Partito Popolare and Lega Musulmana) were also consulted. While the Partito Liberale backed Sheikh Ali Giumale, the remaining parties either left the decision to the President or opted for Abdirashid[95]. As the general consensus emerging from the consultations appeared to be in favour of the outgoing Prime Minister, the President again called on Sharmarke to form a new cabinet. "I designated Abdirashid to form a new government and he accepted the designation 'with reservation'", the President announced[96], adding: "I am sure, as I was in July last year, that the Prime Minister designated is the best qualified man for this task."[97]

Following his designation, Abdirashid started consultations among the parliamentary groups of all parties in order to form the government. The Parliament, as we have seen, was split into two main factions: those who supported the election of Aden Abdulla and those who opposed him. The group led by Ali Jim'ale and Egal advanced conditions for their entry into the government, to the effect of asking that half of the cabinet posts be allotted to their group[98]. The second rival faction, consisting of about 60 MPs, counterattacked by calling for

92 Ibid.
93 Ibid.
94 Ibid.
95 Diary Aden Abdulla, July 10, 1961.
96 Ibid., July 11, 1961.
97 *Somali News*, July 14, 1961.
98 Diary Aden Abdulla, July 17, 1961.

the exclusion of Sheikh Ali Giumale, Mohamed Ibrahim Egal and Abdullahi Issa from the government unless they withdrew the motion invalidating the election of Aden Abdulla that their faction had earlier submitted to the President of the National Assembly.[99]

The designated Premier was soon faced with difficulties on how to satisfy each and every clan represented in Parliament during the allocation of portfolios. After weeks of intense discussions with different parliamentary groups, particularly with Sheikh Ali Giumale's, three cabinet posts went to the group who had lost the election: Abdirashid then returned to the Head of State on July 20 and withdrew the reservation with which he had first accepted his designation and the task of forming a government.[100]

A difficult start

On July 27 Abdirashid, for the second time, formed a coalition government between the political parties from the former British Somaliland (SNL-USP) and Trust Territory (SYL): composed of 28 members (16 ministers and 12 undersecretaries), this was in fact a coalition of clan representatives called ministers. Distribution of the portfolios between the various clans saw four plus the premiership going to the Darod; three to the Rahanweyn; three to the Issak; and four to the Hawiye. The Gadaboursi got a vice premiership. In a country where clan loyalties rather than ideology determine political support and access to resources, the public have never valued the importance of State institutions. The Prime Minister and MPs, therefore, were never seen as persons holding institutional office who would administer the country as a whole, but rather as individuals representing their own clan interests.[101]

There was a whiff of *déja-vu* in the fact that the Prime Minister's choice of appointees was criticized as much for their mediocrity as for their partisanship. A group of deputies led by Yassin Nour and Mohamoud 'Muro' accused the Prime Minister of betraying the principles according to which he had voted against Abdullahi Issa's government in 1959, and vowed that they would not support his government in Parliament.[102]

In a British consular memo of the time, Abdirashid is quoted to have once

99 Ibid., July 24, 1961.

100 *Somali News*, July 21, 1961.

101 This explains why every Somali government, depending on the PM's ethnic clan, was popularly referred to as Governo Sa'ad, Governo Majeerteen or Governo Issak.

102 Diary Aden Abdulla, August 6, 1961.

criticized the size of Abdullahi Issa's government: "The Prime Minister's proposal for a cabinet of 10 ministers and 5 undersecretaries was unnecessary extravagance for a country like Somalia … the proposed cabinet was being made up on strictly tribal lines as a result of the Prime Minister's wish to please everybody."[103] Rashid's government was not by any stretch of the imagination even approximating the President's expectations regarding competent cabinet ministers. Commenting on the formation of the government, Aden Abdulla wrote in his diary on July 27 1961: "With the number of cabinet ministers and the inclusion in the government of certain individuals, Abdirashid made me swallow a bitter pill; for fear of who knows what, he left some good men out. I am sorry, but this is a disappointment and a disservice to his honour."[104] The President also refers to Abdirashid waging a hostile campaign against Abdullahi Issa in 1959, on the grounds of the number of ministers in Issa's government and their poor qualifications to the job.

The Prime Minister faced his first challenge when a bill was introduced in Parliament on 14th August 1961, before discussion of the government programme and ahead of the confidence vote, directing him to fix the number of ministers at twelve and that of undersecretaries at 5. A row then broke out between Parliament and the government following the latter's request that the vote of confidence on its programme must take precedence over discussion of the bill, on the grounds of respect for the Constitution. With a vote of 57 to 55 and no abstentions, the National Assembly decided that the bill should be discussed before the vote of confidence[105]. Subsequently, with a 63-to-6 vote, Parliament passed the bill fixing the number of ministers at twelve and recommending five as the ideal number of undersecretaries.[106]

The beleaguered Premier presented his resignation to the President of the Republic on August 15, 1961, but the latter requested him to continue in office on the grounds that he still considered the Prime Minister the most suitable person to head the government, and that the delay caused by new consultations for the formation of a government "could not be afforded at the present moment."[107] To facilitate the Prime Minister's task of downsizing the cabinet, a

103 TNA FO371/138312, Memorandum from H.M. Consul (Commercial) M. Peters to H.M. Consul General, Mogadisho, June 24,1959.

104 Diary Aden Abdulla, July 27, 1961.

105 TNA FCO 141/6721, telegram no. 516, from Bromley to FO London, August 17, 1961.

106 Government Activities from Independence until today, 11 July 1960-31 December 1963, Presidency of Council of Ministers, Mogadisho, 1964, p. 18.

107 Ibid.

number of ministers (Abdi Hassan Boni, Osman Mohamed Ibrahim and Sheikh Omar Sheikh Hassan 'Lugey', respectively Vice Prime Minister, Minister of General Affairs & Personnel and Minister of Communications) volunteered to step down[108], followed by all 5 of the undersecretaries, who in solidarity with the PM jointly submitted their resignation. On 19 August, Abdirashid presented a lean cabinet to the Parliament and obtained a vote of confidence with a majority of 94 to 19 votes.[109]

The 19 MPs who voted against were: Salad Elmi 'Durua', Hassano 'Alio' Mursal, Hassano 'Mohamed' Nour, Mohamed Ahmed 'Ottavio', Haji Ali Ghedi Shador, Haji Mohamoud 'Borracco', Osman Mohamed Afrah, Osman Ahmed Roble, Haji Yousuf Iman, Haji Aboubakr Sheikh Omar, Mohamed Abdulle Assir, Haji Abdullahi Mursal, Ali Issa Ali, Mohamed Ali Farah, Hassan Ali Abdi, Sheikh Muktar Mohamed, Sheikh Ibrahim Omar, Mohamed Shuriye and another deputy, all from the Lega[110]. Opposition came mainly from deputies affiliated to the ruling party, their reasons for breaching party discipline and taking a stance against the government ranging from disappointment at failure to qualify as ministers to other grudges against some members of the government. One deputy is quoted as saying that he voted against the Abdirashid government because "some of his ministers, like Abdulkadir 'Zoppo' and Sheikh Abdulle, are intolerable."[111] Only three ministers from pre-independence governments (Sheikh Ali Giumale, Abdullahi Issa and Abdinour Mohamed Hussein) joined the new government.

In less than six months, the government faced fresh challenges from the same dissident faction within the ruling party, by way of a motion of non-confidence based on alleged poor performance. In an extraordinary session of the National Assembly in March 1962, a group of 31 MPs including Yassin Nour Hassan, Abdullahi Hussein 'Maggior', Ahmed Egag, Haji Mohamoud Ahmed 'Boracco', Abdullahi Haji Mohamoud 'Insania', Aden Shire Jama, Sheikh Omar Sheikh Hassan, Mohamed Ossoble Adde, Haji Ali Ghedi Shador, Osman Haji Mohamoud Afrah and Mahamed Dolli Hascio, all from the ruling party, tabled a motion of non-confidence stating that the government would not stand by its policy commitments. It is worth noting that for the second time Yassin Nour

108 Diary Aden Abdulla, August 16, 1961.

109 Government Activities from Independence until today, 11 July 1960-31 December 1963, Presidency of Council of Ministers, Mogadisho 1964, p. 19.

110 Diary Aden Abdulla, August 23, 1961.

111 Ibid., December 1, 1961.

put himself at the top of the list of MPs introducing the motion, together with Mohamed Ossoble Adde and Ahmed Egag, erstwhile supporters of the Prime Minister in the revolt within the ruling party against Abdullahi Issa's second government in 1959.

In a genuine democratic system, a vote of no confidence is put forward by the opposition in the hope of weakening or defeating the government. However, in Somalia the vote of no confidence is routinely put forward by disgruntled members of the ruling party, in clear contravention of logic and party discipline, not to introduce a viable political programme, but to gain positions. Party discipline was not a strong point of the ruling party. The government came under fire for allegedly squandering enormous sums of public money to enrich those who administered it, spending it on cars and missions abroad, not all of them indispensable. The main accusation contained in the motion was that the government had not undertaken the necessary measures towards perfecting the organization of the State, thus failing to carry out its political programme and honour the engagement conferred upon it by Parliament.[112]

Irrespective of the aims of the proponents of the motion of non confidence, the fact that ministers were constantly travelling abroad and the financial advantage they reaped from their peregrinations, calculated at Sh.So350 per diem, had already become a source of cutting jokes. At one time, the Undersecretary for Foreign Affairs was on mission for nearly 4 months and his Minister for 3 months and 15 days[113]. Other instances showing the pleasure that Somali politicians, including the deputies, took in spending time outside the country were (as reported by the independent English language monthly magazine *Dalka* in an editorial titled *Government in Exile*) a sizeable number of ministers, including the Prime Minister, finding themselves in Rome at the same time "apparently not on official business,"[114] or the fact that at one time the President of the National Assembly went on official visit to China for 25 days, accompanied by 20 lawmakers and a number of supporting staff, including interpreters and translators, on a mission that cost taxpayers an estimated Sh.So100, 000[115]. On the other hand, while members of the Cabinet were continuously on missions abroad, they rarely undertook missions within the country and, if they did, it was

112 *Somali News*, April 6, 1962.
113 Diary Aden Abdulla, November 5, 1961.
114 Yousuf Duhul (ed.), Dalka, facsimile edition, vol. 1 (1965), August 1, 1965.
115 Diary Aden Abdulla, August 31, 1966.

only to their respective constituencies.[116]

After long discussions, the National Assembly rejected the motion of no confidence by 82 to 28 votes. The result of the voting was a devastating blow and an embarrassment to the sponsors of the motion; but even more damaging to their reputation were the revelations made to Aden Abdulla by Abdulkadir 'Zoppo', Minister of Finance, who had allegedly uncovered a grubby financial deal in which the authors of the motions had offered Sh.So120,000 to HDMS members of Parliament in exchange for their support. According to 'Zoppo', the bribe was turned down.[117]

The dismissal of Minister Sheikh Ali Jim'ale

As reported earlier, a number of former members of the pre-independence government, such as Sheikh Ali Jim'ale and Abdullahi Issa, were included in the new Abdirashid administration. Issa and Jim'ale were co-opted into the cabinet, not only to balance the tribal equation, but also with the aim of mending the rift with the group whose presidential candidate lost the election. However, less than a year from independence, differences developed between the Minister of Health, Veterinary and Labour, Sheikh Ali Giumale, an influential political figure from Hiran, and the Prime Minister. Admittedly, the differences were, at bottom, of a personal nature, and soon developed into a lack of co-operation between the two[118]. Abdirashid often lamented the existence of what he called a 'gang' led by Haji Farah Ali and including certain members of the government, Abdullahi Issa and Mohamed Haji Ibrahim Egal among them, working to undermine his government[119]. It was an open secret that Abdullahi Issa, like his long-time ally Sheikh Ali Giumale, had difficult working relations with his Prime Minister. At one time, he even came under pressure from his group not to travel to Dar-as-Salaam to represent Somalia at the celebrations for the independence of Tanganyika, his absence being intended to embarrass the Prime Minister. "I resisted this pressure because I could not do that without first resigning from the government", Abdullahi Issa confessed in a private conversation with Aden Abdulla[120]. A paradoxical situation arose when, at a certain point, two civil servants, Said Issa and Abdurahman Nour Hersi, offered their good offices to

116 Ibid., July 10, 1962.
117 Ibid., April 6, 1962.
118 Ibid., December 30, 1961.
119 Ibid., February 25, 1962.
120 Ibid., January 1, 1962.

mediate in the dispute between the Prime Minister and his Minister for Foreign Affairs.[121]

"The Sheikh Ali Giumale/Abdirashid feud took a new twist on October 1961 when a *tête-à-tête* originally planned to solve their differences ended in acrimonious dispute and the PM vowed to sack the Minister, whereupon the latter threatened to display in the National Assembly the reasons why he was being sacked."[122] The following day, Abdirashid went to see the President with a copy of the decree revoking Giumale's appointment to the Ministry of Health, Veterinary Services &Labour.[123]

Thus by presidential decree, on the initiative of the head of the government, Minister Sheikh Ali Giumale, who had run against Aden Abdulla in the presidential election in 1961, was removed from office. However, the Head of the State countersigned the decree on November 30 only after giving the matter much thought and making repeated unsuccessful attempts to reconcile the two giants[124]. The Prime Minister also rejected mediation efforts conducted by a number of party figures[125]. For Abdirashid, it was either Giumale's removal or the resignation of the entire Cabinet[126], a scenario strongly reminiscent of the crisis which had brought about the resignation of Mussa Bogor in early 1959.[127]

Giumale's removal sparked off a widespread protest in the Hiran Region, particularly in his political base of Beledweyne, where people clamoured against their Minister's dismissal. Messages of solidarity also came from paramount chiefs, notables and religious leaders, as well as from Lega branches in Beledweyne and Bulo Burti—these were addressed to the Head of State and accused the Prime Minister of practising tribalism[128]. The dismissal of the Minister of Health also raised security concerns in Hiran, to the point that the Minister of the Interior, Abdirazak Haji, paid an unannounced visit to Beledweyne, from where he reported that the situation in the city was tense following the removal of Sheikh Ali Jim'ale earlier in the month. Haji took a tough line, warning the public in Bulo Burti and Beledweyne that the government would take grave measures against those who, in solidarity with Sheikh Ali Giumale, may stir up trouble in

121 Ibid., February 6, 1962.
122 Ibid., November 26, 1961.
123 Ibid., November 27, 1961.
124 Ibid. November 30. 1961.
125 Ibid.
126 Ibid., November 27, 1961.
127 Mussa Bogor stepped down in May 1959 as Minister of the Interior following a quarrel with Abdullahi Issa.
128 Diary Aden Abdulla, December 5, 1961.

the region.[129]

On the basis of purely tribal considerations, Ahmed Ghelle Hassan, from the same clan family as Sheikh Ali Giumale, was appointed Minister of Justice on the 6th March 1962: a move intended to assuage the Hawadle clan family, a predominantly Hawiye tribe in the Hiran region.

Records show that Ali Jim'ale was one of the few politicians who fully performed their mandate as parliamentarian, whether as member of the government or the opposition, and that he never lost touch with his roots and his constituency. A skilled politician and extraordinary orator well capable of captivating an audience, Jim'ale saw his popularity sky-rocket when campaigning against the referendum on the Constitution, the 'no' vote outnumbering the 'yes' in Hiran in 1961. In 1963 Sheikh Ali quit the Lega to establish, in close co-operation with Egal, a new party, the Somali National Congress (SNC), winning 22 seats in the 1964 general elections. The man known to his close friends as 'il Duca dell'Hiran' ('the Duke of Hiran') passed away at Beledweyne on November 24, 1979. That day Beledweyne mourned the loss of its distinguished son. I was among the thousands who attended his funerals, also honoured by an official government delegation.

Aborted coup. A farcical trial

The hastily formed union between the former British Protectorate of Somaliland and the Trust Territory of Somalia had generated immediate and widespread discontent in the Northern region over the economic decline there and the growing political influence of Mogadisho. This was not a happy union: troubling trends began to emerge as Northerners realized how wrong they had been to hasten the process leading to the merger with the southern regions.

The Northerners' high expectations of being treated as a country of longer-standing independence and senior partners joining their junior brothers were soon dashed when, in the distribution of power between the two regions, they not only lost the premiership but failed to gain any of the 'juicy' ministries in the first government after independence[130]. This was the beginning of a long struggle leading eventually to secession from the southern regions and proclamation of independence in 1991.

On December 9 and 10, 1961, only 10 days after the dismissal of Sheikh

129 Diary Aden Abdulla, December 23, 1961.

130 Hussein Ali Dualeh, *Search for a New Somali Identity,* self-published, 2002, p. 17.

Ali Giumale, a coup was attempted in Hargeisa and other main northern towns. A group of young British-trained officers locked their commanding officers in a bungalow and kept them there under guard. In a bid to cover up their real intentions, they told the non-commissioned officers (NCOs) that a military takeover was underway in Mogadisho and that their superiors were in a secret meeting communicating with the supreme command there. However, the rebellion was short-lived: within a few hours, after a brief battle, the forces loyal to the government arrested the twenty-one rebels (most of them young Sandhurst-trained officers from the North) and freed the commanders. In the course of the aborted mutiny, Sub Lt. Abdullahi Said was killed.[131]

Sub Lt. Hassan 'Walanwal', the leader of the plot, directed the arrest of Col. Mohamed Ainanshe and Major Osman Sobrie 'Sonkor'. According to some analysts, the rebellion was staged to protest against the senior military officers, all from the South, who had not been trained as military officers but as policemen. Although this may partially be true, a political motivation for the rebellion cannot be ruled out. In the Sixties, military coups were a common phenomenon in Africa as the continent struggled to consolidate its newly acquired independence and come to terms with the new realities. The military coup in the North did not take anyone by surprise: rather, it was seen as an event recurring everywhere in Africa, in which the military toppled corrupted civilian administration.

The rebels were charged with waging war against the State (an offence punishable by death under Section 121 of the Indian Penal Code)[132] and kept in total isolation for a long time. The Commander of the national army, General Daud, though in favour of allowing the inmates to receive visits from their families, wanted the case brought before a military tribunal to ensure long and deterrent punishment rather than bringing it before an ordinary court, "a circumstance not contemplated by the Constitution", as Aden Abdulla commented.[133]

This was the most complicated trial ever held in the Republic because of the irreconcilable differences between the legal traditions involved in the case. Since the offence had been committed in the north, the Regional Court of Hargeisa had territorial jurisdiction; however, for security reasons, the Supreme Court ruled that the Hargeisa Court should hold the trial in Mogadisho. Needless to say, the rebels' families, alongside northern politicians, campaigned against the

131 *Somali News*, December 12, 1961.
132 P. Contini, op. cit., p. 61.
133 Diary Aden Abdulla, January 6, 1962.

trial being held there.[134]

The prosecutor was an Italian judge, Severino Santiabichi, unfamiliar with Indian criminal law and with the English language. He had served as a judge in Somalia since the Trusteeship period, lectured in Criminal Procedure Law at the University of Mogadisho and was the author of a book on *diya*, or blood money, in Somali common law[135].After returning to Italy, he presided over the trial in Rome of the Red Brigades accused of kidnapping and killing the former Italian Prime Minister, Aldo Moro, in 1978.

The presiding judge was a Briton, unfamiliar with the Somali penal system and unable to speak either Italian or Somali. The defense counsel consisted of two Indian attorneys practising in Kenya, both unfamiliar with the Somali penal system and the language. The prosecution witnesses were all Somalis testifying in Somali, unfamiliar with the Italian language. Although the Hargeisa Court was moved to Mogadisho, the trial was governed by northern law which, at the time, consisted of the Indian penal code and criminal procedure.[136] Court proceedings were further complicated by the amount of translation from and into the three languages. The accused were allowed to hire foreign lawyers conversant with English law. As the funds collected by their immediate families proved insufficient to fully cover the lawyers' fees (amounting to Sh.So41,000), the government was called in to settle the balance (Sh.So29,060)[137], as provided by article 41 of the 1960 Constitution ("The State shall guarantee, under the conditions prescribed by law, free legal aid to the poor.").

Based on the evidence produced to the Court, the prosecutor requested the accused be sentenced. However, in a terse ruling, the judge threw out the case claiming that the defendants had committed no crime against the State and handing down the following verdict: "In no case has the prosecutor made the prima facie case requiring any accused to make his defence. All accused are acquitted."[138] All of the twenty-one accused were acquitted on a flimsy technicality based on the argument that they had not been identified nor even had their proper names and military ranks clearly mentioned. The Attorney General filed an appeal against the court ruling. The date for hearing the appeal was postponed several times until early 1965, when all the defendants benefited from an amnesty, and the

134 Diary Aden Abdulla, April 14 and 15, October 3, 1962.

135 Severino Santiabichi, *Il prezzo del sangue e l'omicidio nel diritto somalo*, Giuffrè, 1963.

136 P. Contini, op. cit. pp. and 60-61.

137 Diary Aden Abdulla, January 6, 1963.

138 P. Contini, op. cit., p. 65.

appeal was dropped.[139]

For the prosecutor, enough evidence had been produced to the Court to warrant a conviction of the defendants; but the Court held that the *prima facie* case had not been made. Consequently, the defendants were acquitted on the grounds that 'the witnesses had not pointed them out'. The prosecutor was convinced that the witnesses who appeared before the Court had known all the defendants for a long time, had worked with them and were therefore in a position to know them by name and military rank. What doubt, then, could arise as to their identification?

The prosecutor argued that the formal procedure for the identification of a person should be applied where a question on the identity of such person arises. He went on to say: "the least we can say is that the reasons on which the judge based the decision are childish." As Paolo Contini eloquently put it, "this trial was probably the clearest case of two legal traditions being unable or unwilling to understand each other."[140]

As the old saying goes, 'the onlooker gets the best of the fight'. In this case, the onlookers were the 'putschists'. Many of those who had carefully followed the proceedings openly questioned the judge's impartiality[141]. In a nutshell, the case was a sorry farce from start to finish. One of the young officers, Hussein Ali Dualeh[142], describes the state of anxiety he and his co-defendants felt in the few minutes before the verdict was delivered: "The day of judgment came. We were naturally apprehensive, though greatly heartened by our clairvoyant's prediction that we should all be released. The Judge entered the Court. We all stood up. He started reading his judgment which took no less than two hours. He accepted our defense lawyer's legal contention that the defendants have neither been identified nor had their proper names and ranks clearly mentioned. He ordered our immediate release."[143]

139 Ibid.

140 Ibid.

141 The judge, Mr Haslewood, was ordered to leave the country within twelve hours!

142 Dualeh served as Somali Ambassador in Kenya and Uganda during the military regime..

143 Dualeh, op. cit., p. 39.

The revolt of the Issak lawmakers

Unrest in the North

The crisis in the North stemmed from the government policy aimed at bringing northern import duties in line with those applied in the south. The legislation on import duty, introduced in 1963, had caused turmoil in the north and deepened the social crisis among northerners, already unhappy about the hasty union with former Italian Somaliland.

The increase of import duties in the north was not driven only by the necessity to unify the price regime, but by the main purpose of generating new income to offset the loss of annual contributions to the ordinary budget following the severing of diplomatic relations with Great Britain. Speaking during a stormy debate in the Parliament on the new legislation, the Minister of Finance said: "A rupture with the British would result in a budgetary deficit of Sh.So17.5 million and a reduction in foreign exchange takings equal to the same amount. We have decided to bear additional burdens in order to meet the situation. We propose to fill the budgetary and foreign exchange gaps by revising our customs tariffs to increase our revenues: this would add more than Sh.So10 million a year to our revenue. There were separate customs tariffs for the north and the south which were substantially different from each other. These have now been unified into a single customs tariff for the whole country."[144]

According to the Minister of Finance, export duties on a limited number of goods were increased to raise more revenue. The export tax on charcoal was increased to discourage exports and prevent and deter the destruction of the forests. Export duties on a very large number of goods, including incense and myrrh, were completely abolished. Imports of staple goods (cereals, dates, tea, coffee, vegetables, oil, medicine, etc), were taxed at lower rates, while luxury goods (tinned foods, confectionery, chocolates, firearms, motor vehicles, furniture, silk and fine fabrics) were taxed at higher rates.[145]

The government, after some initial resistance, eventually bowed to the mounting pressure and decided to review the level of import duty levied on petrol, and not on diesel as had been expected[146]. "For reasons which are difficult to understand," comments Lewis "the government failed to realize that most

144 *Somali News*, April 19, 1963.

145 Ibid.

146 Diary Aden Abdulla, May 12, 1963.

of the motor vehicles in the North use petrol and not diesel."[147] By the time the government recognized its blunder and took the initiative to revise its earlier decision and save whatever possible, the damage had already been done. "Predictably, this unpopular law had triggered widespread disorder and strikes in Hargeisa and other major centers in the north. On May 1, 1963 in Hargeisa a group of rioters, angered by the tariff increase, established a makeshift market and abandoned the former market place. The police interfered in the matter and, in dispersing the group of rioters, killed four people and injured 17 – all the casualties were civilians. Among the police force several servicemen were also seriouslyinjured."[148]

Because of the strike, shops and other businesses were closed and the transportation sector was brought to a standstill, resulting in tons of basic commodities left lying in the stores. The general situation in former British Somaliland remained volatile and represented a source of real concern for Mogadisho. The President of the Republic was also thrown into the fray, and embarked on a long tour of all major urban centers of the North, the general success of which must be partly attributed to his high personal reputation. The President pleaded with the Somalis not to act violently. "I have one more thing to add: for the gradual progress of the country towards economic, social and political development along democratic lines, we must have discipline. Without discipline, nothing can be achieved; lack of discipline and chaos will block the whole process and merely bring about what some would call a 'strong' regime, but I would simply call dictatorship."[149] However, it would be wrong to conclude that the increased price of basic commodities was the only matter troubling the northerners: there was also an added element which preoccupied northern politicians' minds and needed to be tackled.

In early 1961 in Hargeisa, the police commissioner, regional governor, chief justice, police superintendant and district commissioner all happened to belong to one particular ethnic group, the Darod. In the overwhelming Issak area of Hargeisa, the unusual number of Darod senior officials had generated an uneasy feeling. Whether this circumstance was a deliberate government policy was not clear, but there were no express norms forbidding government officials of the same ethnic tribe to serve at the same duty stations at the same time. This was a delicate matter, and Minister Egal requested that steps be taken to change the

147 I.M. Lewis, op. cit., note 11, p. 324.
148 *Somali News*, May 3, 1963.
149 *Somali News*, May 10, 1963.

tribal composition of the regional authorities in Hargeisa. "The Prime Minister and Minister Egal urged me to raise the matter with Abdirazak", reveals Aden Abdulla.[150]

The following day, the Head of State received the Minister of the Interior for consultations and raised with him the issue brought to his attention by the Prime Minister and his Minister of Education. The President also raised the thorny old problem of the Dusa Mareb, Bardera and Galkayo districts, whose administrative borders with Elbur, Lugh and Obbia had been delimited along tribal lines by the Italian administration.

While accepting, in principle, that the issue of the administrative boundaries of these three districts needed re-examining, the Minister rejected outright the idea of transferring civil servants unless there were plausible reasons for doing so. "Movement of civil servants from one place to another should not be effected merely to appease certain individuals, because by doing so you will anger others and consequently encourage tribalism", stated the Minister.[151]

There were many voices proposing the establishment of the office of 'resident minister' in the North with the responsibility of co-ordinating government activities in the region. Abdirazak also rejected this idea, suggesting instead that full power be accorded to regional governors. It was later decided to dispatch a special team of three cabinet ministers from the North to Hargeisa with a clear brief to redress the situation. The three ministers (Mohamed Haji Ibrahim Egal, Sheikh Ali Ismail and Ali Garad Jama) were given full powers to make proposals.

The mission, however, ended in failure as its members could not agree on certain aspects of the recommendations to be presented to the government. The Minister of Agriculture, Ali Garad Jama (from the Dulbahanta tribe/clan) disagreed with the other two members of the mission (both of ethnic Issak origin) on the disciplinary transfer of four senior staff. Without consulting the other members of the mission, Ali Garad made contact with Mogadisho from Hargeisa, expressing his displeasure at the disciplinary action proposed against the District Commissioner of Hargeisa, a fellow Dulbahanta. The position of the two Issak ministers was further undermined by the hasty decision taken by the Council of Ministers to appoint as governor of Mudug the very officer against whom disciplinary action had been recommended[152]. This prompted the resignation of the two SNL ministers.

150 Diary Aden Abdulla, August 23, 1961.
151 Ibid., August 24, 1961.
152 Mohamed Ahmed Abdulla 'Sakhran' was appointed governor of Mudug.

The SNL quits the coalition government

The SNL parliamentary group maintained that their withdrawal from the coalition had caused the fall of the government, which consequently had lost the power to present project laws to Parliament for discussion until the crisis might be solved[153]. Accordingly, on 25 October 1962 the SNL parliamentary group requested the Head of Parliament to suspend the ongoing discussion of a project law, claiming that no legislative acts could be discussed in Parliament until the crisis persisted. When the chairman of the session, Haji Bashir Ismail, rejected the proposal, the entire SNL group staged a walk-out. A group of Southern members of Parliament closed ranks with the SNL in a show of solidarity[154], a move apparently aimed at giving the crisis a national dimension. The government was shaken by a bout of infighting and resignations, which left the coalition unworkable and undermined the very foundation of the union between the two regions of Somalia. The Prime Minister resisted the idea of requesting a vote of confidence as the President of the Republic had suggested, arguing that "except for a handful of MPs, the majority of Parliament supported his government."[155] In a functioning democracy, loss of support from a junior partner in the coalition would have triggered the resignation of the entire government, but the Prime Minister remained defiant. However, the USP parliamentary group did not follow the SNL, thus splitting the northern parties along tribal lines.[156]

Intense negotiations started with the SNL, designed to resolve the crisis and convince the party to return to the fold. It has been suggested that an increase in ministerial representation for the northern regions may have contributed to a solution of the crisis[157]. This came as a proposal by the three vice-presidents of the National Assembly, who offered the SNL two more ministerial positions (vice prime minister without portfolio and undersecretary) in return for continued partnership in the coalition government[158]. Predictably enough, this proposal soon opened the floodgate for similar claims from the USP.[159]

153 Diary Aden Abdulla, October 24, 1962, entry covering discussions he had with 14 SNL deputies led by Egal..

154 Abdullahi Hussein Maggior and Mohamed Ossoble Adde, among others.

155 Diary Aden Abdulla, October 25, 1962.

156 Vice-PM Abdi Hassan Boni and Minister of Agriculture Ali Garad Jama (both USP) did not resign.

157 *Somali News*, February 8, 1963.

158 Meeting with Haji Aboukar Sheikh Omar, SNL parliamentarian from Borama, reported in Diary Aden Abdulla, January 3, 4, 1963.

159 Meeting with Abdi Hassan Boni and Ali Garad Jama reported in Diary Aden Abdulla, January 5, 1963; meeting with Abdi Hassan Boni, Haji Mussa Ahmed Scirua, Abdullahi Gablan, Osman Garad and

On the other hand, it soon emerged that not all members of the SNL parliamentary group agreed on a common strategy on how to solve the crisis. In fact, while the bulk of the group travelled to Hargeisa for a hastily convened congress, six SNL members of Parliament (Yousuf Ismail Samatar, Haji Aboukar Haji Farah, Haji Aboukar Sheikh Omar, Haji Ibrahim Osman Fod 'Basbas', Mohamed Sheikh Musse and Haji Ibrahim Nour Jama) chose to remain in Mogadisho and met with Aden Abdulla to inform him of their desire to enter the government "before a negative conclusion comes out of the Congress."[160]

Despite being warned of the risk of expulsion from the party, two SNL members did break ranks and made themselves available to join the government. It was now widely known that Haji Ibrahim Osman Fod 'Basbas' and Yousuf Ismail Samatar 'Ghandi' had been in secret contact with the Prime Minister and had set their sights on the two vacant cabinet posts.[161]

On the basis of the decision taken by the six SNL members to boycott the congress, the Prime Minister, ahead of the outcome of the SNL Congress and ignoring the President's call for caution, appointed Haji 'Basbas' and Yousuf Ismail Samatar as ministers (respectively of Industry and Commerce and of Education). "I withheld the decree of appointment of the two new ministers and, in vain, advised the Prime Minister to wait for new developments from Hargeisa in order to convince the splinter group to join their colleagues in Hargeisa", wrote Aden Abdulla in his diary for January 21, 1963.[162]

Meanwhile, far away in Hargeisa, a new and dangerous threat to the union between the two regions was arising. In fact, the President of the Republic received a cable from the SNL executive, reflecting the decision of the party Congress to question the validity of the Act of Union. The cable read: "The national conference of the two regions called by SNL wishes to present its loyal compliments to Your Excellency - It further wishes to thank you for the worthy attempts you have made to solve the present problems - It however considers its painful duty to reject your Excellency's proposal - It considers that the roots of the problems go much deeper than the mere increase of portfolios for the party's MPs: the Prime Minister, in the name of his government, has brought the fundamental principles of our union into question - It therefore wishes

Mohamed Yousuf Elmi, Aden Abdulla, reported in Diary Aden Abdulla, January 6, 1963.

160 Diary Aden Abdulla, January 20, 1963.

161 Yousuf Ismail Samatar was temporarily relieved from his functions as Secretary General of the SNL while the Congress was in session in Hargeisa (cf. telegram from SNL president Abdullahi Ahmed Weid to Aden Abdulla in Diary Aden Abdulla, January 19, 1963).

162 Diary Aden Abdulla, January 21, 1963.

to pose the following points for your serious consideration: One: legitimacy of the present government once it has lost the support and the good-will of these two regions - Two: legitimacy of discarding the original Act of Union - Three: sharing of the executive powers of the Republic between the two former territories - The conference further decided to send national delegation to Your Excellency after Ramadan unless a satisfactory solution is found before then - The conference wishes to inform Your Excellency that anyone who intends to participate in the present government would be automatically expelled from our party and disowned by the people of the two regions we have the honour of representing. The Chairman, National SNL Conference."[163]

The union between former British Somaliland and the former UN Trust Territory was entering unchartered waters, and the SNL decision sent shock waves across the country.

Following these new developments, the Head of the State was left with no alternative but to discontinue the mediation efforts he had started five months back. Venting his disappointment, on January 25–26 he wrote in his diary: "For five months I have been trying to mediate between the government and the SNL. I've had enough of Mohamed Haji Ibrahim Egal and company. From now on I will give free hand to Abdirashid to go ahead with whatever plan he might have in mind to solve the crisis."[164]

End of the crisis and formation of new government

At the end of inconclusive mediation efforts also involving the Head of the State, the Central Committee of the ruling party directed the Prime Minister to try and end the crisis by effecting a limited government reshuffle and relieving certain members of the government of their responsibilities.[165]

These measures fell short of the expected resignation of the entire Cabinet, as called for by the SNL. The ministers losing their jobs after the reshuffle were Sheikh Abdulla Mohamoud and Abdinour Mohamed Hussein (Minister of Trade and Commerce and Public Works respectively), who had been heavily criticized for poor performance. Undersecretaries Hussein Omar Hassan 'Hussein Jiis' and Sheikh Mohamed Issak Salad were also dropped. The initial list of undersecretaries to be dropped included Mohamed Sheikh Mohamed Dahir

163 Diary Aden Abdulla, January 25, 1963.

164 Ibid.

165 Diary Aden Abdulla, November 6, 1962.

(Health and Labour), "but, unexpectedly, for unexplained reasons, the Prime Minister spared the latter, venting his anger instead on Sheikh Mohamed Issak", comments Aden Abdulla[166]. Many thought that the Prime Minister should have got rid of Ali Garad Jama, Minister of Agriculture, who was believed to be part of the problem.

One of the most striking effects of the reshuffle was the shunting of Abdirazak Haji, considered the Prime Minister's right hand man, from the much coveted Portfolio of the Interior to the lesser Ministry of Public Works and Telecommunications.

In an interview released to the weekly newsletter *Somali News*, the Prime Minister admitted that the removal of Abdirazak from the Ministry of the Interior came following growing pressure from the Central Committee of the ruling party[167]. However, what the Prime Minister did not mention was the sustained pressure the Head of the State had received from a group of Hawiye MPs, all from the ruling party and led by veteran politician Haji Farah Ali, calling for the removal of his Minister of the Interior[168]. The Hawiye were not in fact the only group demanding the removal of Abdirazak: the SNL also viewed his presence in that ministry as problematic[169]. At one point in 1962, the President of the Republic inquired whether Abdullahi Issa would be willing to take up the responsibility of the Ministry of the Interior, but the latter rejected such an idea, stating that the task would be difficult for him[170]. However, if the removal of Abdirazak was aimed at reducing political tension, this objective was not achieved: recriminations and counter recriminations between the government and the dissident group within the ruling party continued unabated, leading eventually to an irreparable split and to the creation of a new opposition party deriving its support from the Hawiye and Issak clans.

Another noticeable change brought about by the reshuffle was the appointment of Mohamoud Abdi Nour 'Juje', who had not hitherto been part of the government, as Minister of the Interior.

With two ministries still unmanned, the government obtained a vote of confidence on November 11, 1962. On 2 February 1963 the vacant positions were filled, as predicted, by Yusuf Ismail Samatar for the Ministry of Education

166 Ibid.
167 Interview with Abdirashid, *Somali News*, November 9, 1962.
168 Diary Aden Abdulla, May 27, 1962.
169 Diary Aden Abdulla, January 4, 1963.
170 Diary Aden Abdulla, January 1, 1962.

and Haji Ibrahim Osman 'Haji Basbas' for the Ministry of Industry and Trade[171]. In a subsequent move, in 1963, Ahmed Ghelle Hassan would be included in the government. Of particular interest here is how the Prime Minister, in distributing the portfolios, kept a delicate balance among the rival clans represented in the National Assembly:

> Hilowle Moallim (Ogaden) replaced Hussein Omar Hassan 'Jiis' (Ogaden).
> Aden Shire Jama, Aden 'Low' (Marehan) replaced Sheikh Abdulla Mohamoud (Marehan).
> Abdurahman Haji Moumin (Gugun Dhabe) replaced Sheikh Mohamed Issak (Gugun Dhabe).
> Haji Ibrahim 'Basbas' (Habar Yonis) replaced Sheikh Ali Ismail (Habar Yonis).
> Yousuf Ismail Samatar (Issa Musse) replaced Mohamed Ibrahim Egal (Issa Musse).
> Ahmed Ghelle Hassan (Hawadle) replaced Sheikh Ali Jim'ale (Hawadle).
> Mohamoud Abdinour 'Juje', a non-Rahanweyn from Baidoa, replaced Abdinour Mohamed Hussein (Rahanweyn).

The rebellion of the Hawiye deputies

The birth of the Irir party

The rapid access to independence had subjected the social fabric of the ruling party to a series of dangerous stresses and strains, generating numerous currents of discontent within the party, mainly of a tribal nature. One peculiarity, or rather weakness, of the Somali political system was that the role of the opposition was played by factions within the governing party and not necessarily by opposition parties. Dissident groups within the ranks of the majority party who, for one reason or another, failed to get their slice of the power, would regularly join forces in an effort to build some bargaining power in the distribution of the cabinet posts. The first of such rebellions within the ranks of the Lega was the much-celebrated move staged by a group of deputies against Abdullahi Issa's second government in 1959. This was followed by a second rift in 1962, this time against Abdirashid, led by parliamentarians from the Issak clan and resulting in the withdrawal of the junior SNL party from the coalition.

171 Ibid.

In the same year, a third rebellion was recorded when eleven Hawiye MPs (Salad Elmi Durwa, Abdullahi Hussein Maggior, Mohamed Ossoble Adde, Mohamed Abdulle Assir, Haji Abdio Ebraw, Haji Abdissamed Moallim Ali, Osman Ahmed Roble, Assan Ali, Ali Issa Ali and Abdullahi Amin) broke away from the ruling party. The move followed the walk-out staged on the previous day by the same group during discussion on the vote of confidence for the government[172]. The group voiced their displeasure with the way the ruling party had handled the government crisis following the withdrawal of the SNL from the coalition. This third rebellion in the history of the Somali parliamentary system was led by Sheikh Ali Jim'ale and included Haji Farah Ali and others. All belonged to the faction who had lost the presidential election in 1961, and while they would miss no chance to raise complaints, their main concern was the Minister of the Interior, who as we have seen was considered the Prime Minister's right hand man. Repeated reconciliation efforts between Darod tribal leaders in the government, represented by the Prime Minister and including his Minister of the Interior, on the one side, and Hawiye tribal leaders within Parliament, including Haji Farah Ali, Sheikh Ali Jim'ale and Abdullahi Issa, on the other, ended in failure.

The dissident Hawiye group resisted the idea of being re-admitted to their former party, preferring instead to forge an alliance with the Issak of the north. This alliance, led by SNL members and headed by Mohamed Haji Ibrahim Egal, and also including some dissident former Lega parliamentarians from the South, wasted no time inaugurating a new political party in 1963, called the Somali National Congress (SNC). The new party had a tribal flavour that could further widen the country's tribal rift. Commenting on the formation of the new political party and its programme, Ahmed I. Samatar wrote: "...the only reason for its birth was the need to create an alternative vehicle to replace the leadership, or at least establish a stronger bargaining position for the dissident group."[173]

Referring to the uneasy political relations between Darod and Hawiye politicians, now approaching breaking-point, Aden Abdulla wrote in his diary for June 10, 1962: "I must talk seriously to Abdirashid about the mistrust between Somalis, particularly between Darod and Hawiye, which continues gaining ground like a devilish creeping shrub. At times they cast aspersions even on me on the basis of suspicion. We have to take action and study in depth how to

172 Diary Aden Abdulla, November 20, 1962.

173 Ahmed I. Samatar, *Socialist Somalia, Rhetoric & Reality*, Institute for African Alternatives, Zed Books Ltd, London 1988, p. 62.

uproot this dangerous leech."[174]

History records how, during the civilian regime, administrations spent most of their time struggling for survival because of squabbles within the ruling party, rather than focusing on more urgent and vital issues related to the well-being of the population at large. The birth of the new party added to the historical divide between major Somali clans. The Greater Somali League was thought to stand for the Darod, the HDMS traditionally represented the interests of the Dighil and Mirifle, the Lega was seen as a consortium of several Somali tribes and the SNC was considered to represent the Irir ethnic lineage.

Amid passionate campaigning, particularly intense in the Northern regions, the SNC performed strongly in the 1964 general elections, winning 22 seats nationwide. However the party fared poorly in the last general elections of 1969, winning only 11 members, all of whom joined the ruling party soon after the results of the elections were announced.

New Public Order Law. Scuffle in Parliament

A controversial Public Order Law was passed by the National Assembly in July 1963 at a time when the Lega felt threatened by the emergence of new opposition parties[175]. Lega-led Somali governments, with no exception, had scarcely been models of democracy, opting to push through Parliament a Public Order Law, a dismal piece of colonial legislation, to throttle the opposition. Formed of 77 articles, the law provided, *inter alia*, for tougher control on public meetings and associations. The bill generated a stormy debate and further doubts on the strength of Somali democratic institutions. The opposition accused the government of planning to use the law as a means to suppress freedom in the elections scheduled for 1964. This contrasted with the government's claim that the Public Order Law was more liberal than the legislations in force in both parts of the Republic prior to independence.

Defending the bill, the government further explained that political parties and associations could be dissolved only if they were found to violate the Constitution (Article 60 of Public Order Law), and that the power to dissolve them was vested exclusively in the Supreme Court. Furthermore, the law gave any person aggrieved by a measure taken by public order authorities the right to appeal to the Supreme Court (Article 62 of Public Order Law and articles 38

174 Diary Aden Abdulla, June 10, 1962.

175 Legge n° 21 agosto 26, 1963, Bollettino Ufficiale, suppl. n° 4 al n° 9 del 14 settembre 1963.

And 39 of the Constitution).

A state of emergency could be declared only in cases of serious disturbances of the public order, serious public calamity or danger of war or disorders. The power to proclaim a state of emergency was given only to the President of the Republic after authorization from the National Assembly (Articles 68 and 75 (g) of the 1960 Constitutions).

Ahead of the vote on the bill, tension mounted and the Somali Parliament was the scene of a brawl between a dozen opposition politicians and some members of the ruling party. A number of MPs (including Haji Mussa Bogor, Haji Mussa Samatar, Mohamed Ali Da'ar and Gianaco Giumale, the latter one of the Parliament Secretaries) came under physical attack, suffering head injuries in the fight[176]. The President of the National Assembly had taken the unprecedented measure of calling the police to restore order and forcibly evict the most turbulent MPs among the opposition group. The police, however, in compliance with Parliament internal procedure, refrained from taking any action inside the building.

Abdullahi Hussein 'Maggior', a deputy from El Bur, is reported to have declared: "This law will pass only over my dead body", and another lawmaker, Osman Ahmed Roble, representing Aden Yaval, snatched the draft law document from the government desk and tore it to shreds[177]. Two MPs, Ahmed Ismail 'Duqsi' and Sheikh Ali Ismail, both representatives of Burao, were temporarily detained at Mogadisho Police Station.

The Somali Parliament had been the theatre of similar brawls in the past when, in 1962, Haji Mohamoud 'Borraco', in the course of a Parliament session, threw a bunch of paper and photos at some formerly pro-Italian MPs, who later joined the Lega ranks. Missing the intended target, the papers landed on Aden Shire Jama 'Aden Low', the deputy from Dusa Mareb, who was sitting nearby. It was later learnt that Haji 'Borraco' had actually targeted Haji Mussa Samatar, deputy from Iskushuban, following statements made by the latter's group to Italian media in which they reportedly claimed that the ethnic Darod constituted the majority of the Somali tribes and were therefore destined to rule the country in the future.

In a bid to allay the tension, later on in the year, a big luncheon was organized at Juba Hotel to mark the beginning of a reconciliation process, alla somala,

176 Diary Aden Abdulla, July 16, 1963.
177 Ibid., July 10, 1963.

between the deputies involved in the brawl. This effort resulted in a request for authorization to prosecute the assailants being rejected by the National Assembly[178]. The Public Order Law was approved on July 13 by 72 votes in favour, 10 against and one abstention.[179]

The first and only state of emergency was proclaimed on February 8, 1964 in accordance with article 70 of the Public Order Law. This was necessitated by the growing tension between Ethiopia and Somalia, in the run-up to that year's general elections.[180]

It is worth mentioning that on December 9, 1958 the Legislative Assembly had passed a law tabled by a group of deputies belonging to the ruling party and giving sweeping powers to the police to arrest people for up to six months[181]. The measure was obviously conceived to curb the activities of the opposition parties in anticipation of the political elections scheduled for March 1959. Both the opposition parties and the UN Consultative Council expressed concern about passing such a law at a time when there was no threat of emergency in the Trust Territory. The bill was wisely vetoed by the Administrator and never came intoforce.[182]

In the meantime, Yassin Nour Hassan, a burly, ambitious young MP from Galkayo, was elected secretary general of the ruling party almost by acclamation, with 129 of the 136 members of the party Congress voting him.[183]

Vying for the office of secretary general were Mohamed Sheikh Gabio, Abdullahi Haji 'Insania' and Mohamed Haji Sobrie, the latter having served in the past as secretary general of the ruling party. Gabio, who was not a member of Parliament, became a 'stop-gap' secretary until the following party congress. Yassin replaced Sheikh Mohamoud Mohamed Farah 'Malingour', a member of the party's 'old guard'. However, his popularity soon dwindled on account of the party's internal political crisis, leading eventually to his resignation and expulsion. Yassin was expelled from the party on three different occasions. The first time was in July 1959 when, ignoring party directives, he and 12 other deputies voted against the government; the second time was on July 17, 1964 for refusing to adhere to the party line during the political crisis following Abdirazak's designation as Prime Minister, and the third time in 1966 for breach of party discipline. Each

178 Ibid., December 26-27, 1963.
179 *Somali News*, July 19, 1963.
180 *Somali News*, February 14, 1964.
181 UN Document T/1444, April 14, 1959, par. 98, p. 24.
182 Ibid., par. 102.
183 Diary Aden Abdulla, July 20, 1963.

expulsion order was followed by tribally brokered readmission to the party.

Yassin Nour is known to have played an important role in the process of reconciliation between Abdirashid and Egal, two political arch-rivals, resulting in the election of the former as Head of State in 1967 and in the formation of the first Egal government. Yassin was given the much coveted Ministry of the Interior in 1967 and reconfirmed in the position in 1969.

The controversial 1969 general elections, the last to take place in Somalia, were held under his authority. Arrested with all his fellow cabinet ministers following the military take-over in October 1969, Nour was brought before a special tribunal, found guilty of stealing public funds and given a prison sentence. However, like all the other ministers, he was released before serving the complete prison term following an amnesty. He took refuge in Saudi Arabia, where he continued to oversee the shady business deals he had initiated during his long tenure as a minister and parliamentarian.

Chapter X

FOUR WORRIES FACE THE NEW REPUBLIC

In addition to the problems of integration generated by the merger of the Northern and Southern regions, it was evident that other worries would continue to dog the country and its new leaders. These concerns fall under four different categories: the economy, tribalism in its various forms, the script for the Somali language and the so-called 'missing territories'.

Economy

Notions of political and national sovereignty are fictitious if there is no economic independence. By that token Somalia, although declared independent on 1 July 1960, was far from having achieved complete independence.

The most important export crop in post-independence Somalia was the banana, which, together with livestock and its by-products, constituted 90% of the country's export. Its production potential had not been fully utilized, and because of the high cost of storage, packing and shipping, Somali bananas could not compete on the world market.[1]

By 1935 the Italian government had established a Royal Banana Plantation Monopoly (Regia Azienda Monopolio Banane, or RAMB) to organize the

1 Bollettino Ufficiale della Repubblica, Legge n°1 del 1°gennaio 1967; budget for the 1967 financial year.

cultivation and export of Somali bananas under State authority. Seven Italian ships were at RAMB's disposal to encourage the Somali banana trade. RAMB was reinstated at the beginning of the Italian Trusteeship Administration in 1950 as the Banana Plantation Monopoly, better known as 'Azienda Monopolio Banana' (AMB), to encourage the revival of a sector that had been nearly demolished by the war.

The right to import bananas into Italy thus became the sole prerogative of the Italian Banana Monopoly. The Monopoly established contracts with banana producers which were formally due to expire in 1960 but in fact continued well after independence. Somali bananas were importable into Italy duty-free, and only subject to a 1% *ad valorum* administrative fee. Bananas imported into Italy from other areas were dutiable at a rate of 40% *ad valorum*[2]. Somali bananas cost more than those from other countries, and for this reason could only be traded on the Italian market; yet despite this they remained much sought after for their high quality.

The AMB was responsible for the distribution of Somali bananas in Italy. After delivery at Somali ports, bananas were transported to Italy in freighters hired by the AMB and sold to licensed wholesale distributors at a price designed to cover the CIF price of the fruit, the cost of land transport within Italy and AMB administrative expenses; to this was added a profit margin for the AMB, which was in fact an indirect tax imposed by the Italian government and ultimately paid by the consumer[3]. As a consequence, bananas from other countries (e.g. Guinea) were available on the Italian market at the price of 105-110 lire/kg, while Somali bananas arrived in Italy already costing 130 to 170 lire/kg.

As mentioned earlier, in the list of Somali exports, bananas were followed in order of importance by livestock, hides and skins, fish and some meat. In 1964, the total value of Somali exports was 257 million somalos, while the value of imports stood at 390 million somalos. The trade deficit was the result of heavy dependence upon imported goods for virtually all other national requirements, including foodstuffs, clothing, medicine and all types of manufactured goods and machinery. Although the Territorial Council approved in 1954 a law protecting foreign companies and capital, foreign companies gave no indication of being prepared to invest huge capital in Somalia. According to an analyst well familiar with Somali economy, the country offered little advantage on

2 TNA FO 371/131483Appendex "A" to letter of August 28, 1958 from British Consulate to FO.

3 Karp, op. cit., p. 90.

investment compared to other regions of Africa[4]. In order to attract more private entrepreneurs to invest in Somalia, the government passed in 1960 the Foreign Investment Law, offering foreign investors, among other fringes, the possibility to remit abroad annual profits equal to a maximum of 15% of the total investment[5]. Collection of revenue from imports, exports and stamp duty constituted the key source of income for the ordinary budget, and the funds generated were hardly sufficient to cover the government's administrative costs. Financing of development projects depended totally on foreign assistance.

The high proportion of nomadic population and the poor system of transport and communication left behind by the long period of colonial neglect represented a fundamental challenge for the new Somali nation in the effort to achieve economic and social development. The negative economic performance recorded in the first two years following independence is indicated by a budget deficit of over Sh.So60 million for the 1961 financial year and an estimated deficit of Sh.So38 million for the following year. A budget deficit occurs when a country's government spends more than it takes in from taxes or other form of revenue. Poor management of public funds was partly to blame for the chronic budget deficit. Worried by this recurring difficulty, Aden Abdulla commented: "The level of foreign contributions needed to cover the national budget deficit, without taking into account the economic development, is really high, and to tell the truth, we should take the blame."[6] Italy and Great Britain were expected to cover the budget deficit for 1962 in the proportion of Sh.So23M and Sh.So15M [?] respectively.[7]

The gloomy economic situation was also highlighted by Yassin Nour Hassan, Secretary General of the ruling party, during the XII Afro–Italian meeting held in Milan in 1963[8]: "Somalia lags behind all African countries in almost every aspect of development even though poverty has blighted the whole continent. In fact, it ranks last for GDP, and third-to-last for foreign trade, ahead of Burkina Faso and Niger, and only because these are land-locked."[9] Mogadisho was a city without a seaport, or an airport, with no asphalted roads, drainage system or drinking water supply plant. If this was the situation of the capital city, it was not

4 U.Triulzi, *L'Italia e l'economia somala dal 1950 ad oggi*, Africa, vol. XXVI, no. 4 (1971), p. 446.

5 Legge n° 10 Febbraio 18, 1960, art. 7.

6 Diary Aden Abdulla, February 1, 1961.

7 Diary Aden Abdulla, October 31, 1961.

8 *Corriere della Somalia*, nos. 98 & 99, 1963, as quoted in Del Boca, Nostalgia delle colonie, Mondadori 2001.

9 Del Boca, op. cit., p. 348.

hard to imagine the situation in more remote provinces. The country was without infrastructure; there was no railway system, the roads were highly inadequate and most of them were rendered impassable by floods during the rainy season. Even Radio Mogadisho's broadcasting signal did not quite reach the out-lying areas. Furthermore, despite having the longest coastline in Africa (about 3,025 km stretching along the Indian Ocean to the south-east and from the Gulf of Aden to the southern lip of the Red Sea in the north), Somalia was the only country in the continent without a modern seaport. In 1960, there were only two decent hotels in Mogadisho: two prefabs called Juba and Shabelle, hastily set up, as we have seen, shortly before the independence celebrations to accommodate the foreign dignitaries invited to attend the national event.

Tribalism, the silent killer

Linea Tomaselli

Although physical unification of the southern regions and northern sultanates of Somalia had been achieved through the coercive measures adopted by the Italian fascist regime in late 1920s, a true national unity was never achieved. Nomadic survival patterns and pervasive poverty worked against the formation of a national conscience. "The nomad has his own principles of association, law, justice, and government. His loyalty is to his clan, beyond those he owes no civic obligation or duties", writes Castagno[10]. Somali national identity is not very strong, and comes second after the much stronger and more important clan identity. For example, when a Somali is asked who he is, he says: "I am clan X or Y." It is hard to meet anyone who would say "I am a Somali."

Somali nationalists did not acknowledge from the start that the issue of 'differences' had to be addressed to guarantee peaceful coexistence in the geographical expression called Somalia. They chose instead to deny the existence of any differences and continue to believe that the Somalis were a 'perfectly homogeneous people' sharing one language, one religion and one culture. The Lega's patriotic nationalism was little more than an empty slogan and had little reality as a permanent and effective political sentiment. "Agnation is far more important than party solidarity", comments I.M Lewis[11]. Somalia lacked a national sense; it was never a nation, but groups of tribes in constant and bitter dispute.

10 A.A. Castagno, op. cit., p. 342.

11 I.M. Lewis, *'Modern Political Movements in Somaliland II'*, Africa Journal of the International African Institute, vol. 28, no. 4 (Oct. 1958) p. 348.

Such reality persists to this day and despite vociferous pleas for their abolition on the part of small sections of the community, the ties of clanship remain firmly rooted in Somali society.

The vast majority of the members of any one tribe are still to be found living together within their own tribal boundaries. Tribal loyalties have never given way to nationalistic loyalties, and no wholesale change should as yet be expected even among the 'detribalized' Somali diaspora, let alone among people living in Somali towns. Even within the large Somali community living in London, for instance, members of any one tribe can be found living within their own tribal groups. This explains why no Somali party had any political programme of its own except for the Greater Somalia issue, which the parties warmly welcome, at least on their banners. Even the Lega dei Giovani Somali, often referred to as a-tribal party, is nothing more than "a coalition of a large number of clans and lineage groups, engaged in continuous rivalry and competition", as Saadia Touval wrote.[12]

As Afyare Elmi[13] correctly points out, "The popular perception among Somalis is that each clan owns the traditional areas it inhabits. So only that clan would have a say in the political and economic issues that are related to that part of the country."[14] This popular conception was legitimized through past colonial rules, which have remained unaltered to this day. The most widely known of such rules is the one related to the long-standing question of clan boundaries in the areas of Galkayo and Dusa Mareb, in central Somalia, which gives each tribe settled there exclusive political, land and grazing rights within the areas assigned to them. In fact, the trusteeship administration traced on the ground, for security purposes, a line popularly known as 'Linea Tomaselli' (Tomaselli Line), named after the then Italian Governor of Mudug and separating the Darod from the Hawiye clans. The area east of the line was assigned to the Habargidir, and the area west of the line to the Marehan and Majerten clan families[15]. To this day Galkayo and Dusa Mareb, two strongholds of the Lega dei Giovani Somali, are ethnically divided cities. "The division of Galkayo city between Darod and Hawiye evokes memories of West Berlin and East Berlin as well as East and West Jerusalem", comments one writer.[16]

For the greater part of the Somali population, life continued according to the

12 Touval, op. cit., p. 89ifc.

13 Afyare is Assistant Professor at the University of Doha, Qatar.

14 Afyare Abdi Elmi, *Understanding the Somalia Conflagration: Identity, Political Islam and Peace Building*, Pluto Press 2010, p. 38.

15 Ordinance no. 6 of March 31, 1955.

16 Ismail A. Ismail, Governance, *the Scourge and Hope of Somalia*, Trafford, 2010, p. 442.

unchanged pattern of centuries. In practice, jurisdiction of the administrative range of the State was limited to the few towns that had resident district commissioners. Absence of State authority compelled the local communities to rely for conflict management and justice upon an informal system of protection involving a combination of tribal or clan militias and traditional authorities.

In 1914 Governor Giacomo De Martino appointed a number of traditional chiefs and kadis to administer the colony of Somalia. "They were the colonial government's instrument for the administration of the territory, acting as an intermediary between the government and the local population."[17] Following in the footsteps of the fascist regime, the trusteeship administration thus co-opted traditional chiefs for each major Somali tribe, who were divided into notables and paramount chiefs and requested to act as salaried intermediaries. Their wages ranged from Sh.So 60 for the less important chiefs to Sh.So1,000 for the most influential. The highest salary went to Sultan Mussa Yousuf Bogor of the Osman Mohamoud, resident at Iskushuban in Majertenia[18], followed by Islan Mohamed Mussa of the Issa Mohamoud, resident at Eyl, with a salary of Sh.So500[19], by Iman Omar Ali of the Abgal, resident at Itala (Adale), with a salary of Sh.So 400[20] and Abdurahman Ali Issa, the Sultan of the Bimal, with a salary of Sh.So 310[21]. In 1914, before the unification of Somalia, the highest paid chief was the Sultan of Begehedi, receiving a monthly stipend of 150 rupees[22]. The number of stipended persons, between chiefs and notables in the provinces, was 50 in Majertenia, 40 in Mudug, 11 in Hiran, 50 in Benadir, 23 in Upper Juba and 9 in Lower Juba.

One of the first steps taken by the newly established Somali government in 1956 was to formalize the practice of granting salaries to tribal chiefs[23]. An attempt made by the government in 1958 to abolish the system of traditional chiefs was quickly abandoned in the face of mounting pressure and protests from every corner of the country. Within a short time, the Somali government realized how wrong it had been to expect an anti-tribal resolution to root out a centuries-old institution. To do away with tribalism would have resulted in

17 Hess, op. cit., p. 108.
18 Decreto n°. 131 ottobre 18, 1950, Bollettino Ufficiale, suppl.n° 1 al n.8, Novembre 30, 1950.
19 Ibid.
20 Decreto n° 105 settembre 30, 1950.
21 Decreto n° 133 settembre 30, 1950.
22 Hess, op. cit., p. 198.
23 Decreto n° 78 maggio 18, 1956, Bollettino Ufficiale, suppl. n° 2 al n° 5; Decreto n° 33 del 23 settembre 1957, Bollettino Ufficiale, 1° ottobre 1957.

alienating the clan elders ('capi cabila') who operated in the rural constituencies, a reservoir of strong electoral backing for the ruling party.

The issue was again discussed in 1959 at the Central Committee of the governing party, and all agreed that in view of their political force and the enormous electoral and general influence of clan elders in their own communities, the policy of paying salaries to the traditional chiefs should be retained. The Committee recommended eliminating the disparity in economic treatment among the traditional chiefs. Retention of the warrant chiefs and their assimilation in the administration structure strengthened tribal solidarity rather than weakening it.

After independence, the Somali government continued with the colonial practices of leaving the nomadic population strictly to their own devices and using the services of tribal chiefs "while intervening from time to time to stop feuds and imposing arbitrary collective punishment on the wrongdoing clan."[24]

Collective responsibility of diya-paying group

Although Somalia had become independent and adopted a modern Constitution, yet certain practices inherited from the past colonial administrations remained in force. One of these practices was the collective responsibility of *diya*-paying. This was a colonial rule, introduced by the British in 1943, whereby "any tribe engaging in inter-clan fighting, riots and affray, resulting in wounding or death of any person might be liable to collective punishment imposed on inhabitants of a village area of a district or member of any tribe, sub-tribe, clan or community."[25]

Centuries-old tribal conflicts over scarce grazing and water resources often led to clashes between two clans in which people were killed. In Somali common law, *diya*, or blood money, normally amounting to one hundred camels for the life of a man, and fifty camels for that of a woman, is payable by the offender's *diya*-paying group. While the camel may still be used in rural areas as a means of paying *diya*, in urban areas diya is paid in cash. In case the *diya* was not paid promptly to the victim's tribe, the government intervened by confiscating the camels of the offender's entire tribe, the latter bearing joint civil responsibility with the single wrongdoer.

An attempt to abolish this practice was made at the Lega Congress of 1958, where it was decided that "the person found guilty of the crime of homicide should

24 I.M. Lewis, *'Modern Political Movements in Somalia - II*, Africa Journal of the International African Institute, vol. 28, no. 4, Oct. 1958, p. 356.

25 TNA WO 230/118 Proclamation no. 6 of 1943.

be held responsible for the crime, both criminally and civilly, and his tribe shall not in any way share this responsibility."[26] However, after independence, Lega-led governments had not only backed away from this decision, but reinforced the practice of collective punishment by enacting the Public Order Law in 1963[27]. The underlying principle of the Public Order Law was to prevent the group to which the offender belonged from removing its livestock to distant places to avoid paying compensation under common and Sh'aria law. Since non-payment of *diya* was highly likely to bring reprisals and bloodshed, the law gave the police authority to seize the cattle or other property belonging to the offender's group.[28]

The most dramatic case in modern times of collective punishment effected in 1966 under the Public Order Law was the confiscation of between 1,500 and 2,700 camels belonging to the Habargidir Ayr sub-clan as forced payment of *diya* in favour of the Hawadle clan and other tribes[29]. The case landed before the National Assembly, becoming a subject of heated exchange between the then Minister of the Interior, Abdulkadir Mohamed 'Zoppo', and Haji Farah Ali, a veteran politician from the opposition and former minister during the Trusteeship Administration. In fact, a group of Habargidir legislators addressed a formal question in writing to the Minister of the Interior, seeking clarification on the police raid on innocent villagers and the confiscation of their camels. Initially, the Minister dodged the question; however, pressed by the Speaker of the House, he eventually provided full clarification on the matter[30]. There seemed to be a clash between the Public Order Law allowing collective responsibility and the constitutional norms prohibiting it.[31]

However, the Supreme Court held that the collective punishment prohibited by article 43, paragraph 1 of the Constitution was the same measure as the regional courts of the former Trust Territory under Italian administration had the right to impose under article 82 of the Law of the Organization of the Judiciary approved by royal decree no. 937 of 11 June 1911. This law was enacted for the purpose of punishing the villagers and communities when crimes were committed in areas falling within the jurisdiction of the regional courts. In other words, what the

26 TNA FO 371/131464, deliberations of the General Assembly of the Somali Youth League Party for the year 1958, p. 5.

27 Art. 69, Legge n° 21 del 26 agosto 1963, Bollettino Ufficiale, suppl. n° 4 al n° 9, September 19, 1963.

28 P. Contini, op. cit., p. 69.

29 Diary Aden Abdulla, May 24, 1966.

30 By virtue of his association with the National Assembly, the author had the opportunity to personally witness this debate..

31 Article 43 of the 1960 Constitution.

Constitution prohibited was the collective punishment referred to above and not the collective responsibility of *diya* paying in cases of homicide[32]. The provisions of articles 23 and 24 of the Judicial Organization of 1935, allowing collective punishment of the villagers, were temporarily suspended for two years during the Trusteeship Administration[33]. The Supreme Court of Somalia, in a milestone judgment, ruled that even though considered a penal punishment under Sharia Law, *diya* is only a civil liability under Somali common law.[34]

It should be noted that immediately after the military take-over in 1969, the collective civil liability levied on *diya*-paying groups under the 1963 Public Order Law was abrogated. The new law established that "No one, except the person responsible for death or physical or moral injury, shall be liable to pay compensation."[35] This is an important legal development by which the military regime has abolished the centuries-old tradition known as *heer*.

Homogeneity of Somali society

The notion propagated by foreign scholars that Somali society is more homogeneous than others in Africa and constitutes a genuine nation-state in the European sense has recently been seriously questioned. Foreign scholars had built their conclusions on some characteristics shared by Somali society, without taking into considerations the differences existing within this society. As Saadia Touval puts it: "A nation is not merely a group of people who posses certain characteristics in common: in addition, they should constitute a society and communicate with one another on matters of common interest."[36] Traditional Somali society is compartmentalized into a myriad of small extended family units which tend by nature to be mutually hostile and unstable units. Apart from profound clan divisions, Somalis are also divided on the basis of their occupational position, class, and physical appearance. "These differences are as deeply rooted historically as those of clan identity, even if they are not as frequently evoked by Somalis in their political discourse."[37]

32 Haji N.A. Noor Muhammad, *The Development of the Constitution of the Somali Republic*, the Government of the Somali Republic, Ministry of Grace and Justice, April 1969, pp. 73-74.

33 Ordinanza n° 14 agosto 2,1954, Bollettino Ufficiale, suppl. n° 1 al n° 8, 16 agosto 1954.

34 Hussein Hersi & Ahmed Aden vs. Yusuf Deria Ali, Supreme Court, Civil Appeal no. 2 of 1964; judgment delivered on May 16th, 1964.

35 Art, 6, Legge n° 67 novembre 17,1970, Bollettino Ufficiale, Somali Democratic Republic, suppl. N Bis al n°11,.

36 Touval, op. cit., p. 25.

37 Catherine Besteman and Lee V. Cassanell, *The Struggle for Land in southern Somalia. The War behind the War*, HAAN, 1996, p. 14.

The existence of strong ethnic minorities, with different identity and origin, has long been denied or ignored by the Somali political class. A system of social stratification exists in the Somali social structure, under which certain groups are regarded as socially superior. Bantu people and lower-caste groups engaged in weaving, ironwork and menial tasks are relegated to an inferior social position. "Manual labour is in fact regarded as undignified by the nomadic tribal groups as is the low status assigned to farmers and artisans in the indigenous social structure. It is an attitude which impedes the social development of the population", concludes a United Nations report.[38]

The Bantu people are ethnically, linguistically and culturally distinct from the Somali nomad who, in general, disdains agriculture and upholds the values of a tribal lineage system that does not include the Bantu[39]. As a marginalized group, the Bantu have lacked true representation in politics, with limited access to government services, educational opportunities and professional positions in the private sector[40]. The Italian colonial authorities forcibly conscripted the Bantu into slave-like labour in order to establish large plantations and exploit the land potential of the Juba and Shabelle river valleys. This group of people, originally from East Africa, are still considered as second class citizens and referred to as *jareer* or *tima adag* ('kinky-haired') and *addoon* (slaves) because of their African origin. "Even as free or freed persons, they carried the stigma of their original slave status and their occupational position as farmers in a heavily pastoral society."[41]

The attitude of the Somalis towards the Bantu race is eloquently described by Gerald Hanley: "The Somalis never treated the Bantu as their equals, not even when they soldiered together in the same units. A great deal of it has to do with looks, facial features, and the Somali, lean and handsome and hawk-nosed, felt themselves to be more becoming than the Bantu. In fact, the Somalis resented being considered African at all, and they demanded different treatment in ration and uniform than that given to the Bantu."[42]

Until recently Somalis have generally objected to being regarded as 'Africans' because to them the term described subject Negroid peoples. The myth of Somali

38 A Trust Territory at the Half-way Point: Somaliland under Italian Administration, UN Department of Public Information, 1954.

39 Dan van Lehman and Omar Eon, *The Somali Bantu, Their History and Culture,* Center for Applied Linguistics, Washington , DC, February 2003, p. 4.

40 Ibid., p. 5.

41 Besteman & Cassanelli., op. cit., p. 16.

42 Gerald Hanley, Warriors: *Life and Death among the Somalis,* Redwood Books, 1971, pp. 150-51.

'superiority' has contributed to the notion that 'Somalia is in Africa, but not of Africa'. Only recently, with the growing political importance of Africa, have signs appeared of a change in this attitude, though the feeling remains strong among the Somali population at large[43]. The notion of the social inferiority of the Bantu emerges very clearly from Somali literature: to give one example, a marriage between a full-blooded Somali and a Bantu is to this day regarded as an appalling misalliance.

The claim that the Somalis share one language and culture has also come under scrutiny. To explain that the Somalis are not a homogenous society as some claim, Mohamed Haji Muktar wrote: "Somalia has always been divided into southern agro-pastoral clans and northern pastoral clans who have distinctly different cultural, linguistic and social structures. The monoculture about which most students of Somalia speak about is extrapolated mainly from the study of the northern part of the country." Mohamed Haji Muktar calls this notion "a myth."[44] Critics of the notion of cultural and linguistic homogeneity of Somali society focus on the existence of two major national languages, Maay and Maxaatiri, widely spoken in the country. Maxaatiri is mainly spoken by the nomadic population in the northern region, and Maay is the language of the agro-pastoralists in the South. Unlike Maay, Maxaatiri enjoyed national status, and the Rahanweyn felt demeaned that their tongue was considered tribal. Eventually, after bitter and protracted debates between supporters and detractors of the 'two-languages theory', the former won the battle and the two-language policy was enshrined in the provisional Constitution approved in August 2012. Both Maay and Maxaatiri now have equal rank as official languages of the Somali Republic.[45]

The Maay and Maxaatiri languages are so different from each other that speakers of one of these languages have difficulty understanding the other, except for some individuals living in urban areas, who interact with each other through schooling, work or business. To give one example, easy communication between a farmer from the Upper Juba province and a camel herder from the Togdheer province is impossible because of the language barrier. A further proof of this diversity is illustrated by the fact that the international aid workers who came to

43 Touval, op. cit., p. 25.

44 Mohamed Haji Muktar, *'The plight of the Agro-pastoral Society of Somalia,* Review of African Political Economy, vol. 23, issue 70, Dec. 1996, p. 543.

45 Article 5 of the provisional Constitution reads "The official language of the Federal Republic of Somalia is Somali (May and Maxatiri).

Somalia to help combat the drought found that their Maxaatiri interpreters could not speak or understand Maay-speaking Somalis[46]. It is also common knowledge that in most government offices in the Bay and Bakol provinces, and particularly in the Courts, the services of local interpreters conversant with the Maay language were widely used. Much comment was sparked by the case of a Governor of the Bakol province, a northerner who, in the face of communication difficulties with the local Maay speakers, had to hire an interpreter fluent in both Maay and Maxaatiri. There are also other minor languages known by the names of the tribes that speak them, such as Bravani, Reer Hamar and others, but because of the limited number of speakers, they are not comparable to Maxaatiri and Maay.

A nation in search of a written language

The Egyptian attempts to frustrate this plan

Somali, the mother tongue of the majority of the inhabitants of Somalia, was until fairly recently an unwritten language. The Somali language has been classified as part of the Afro–Asiatic family, eastern Cushitic branch. Problems of a political, religious and tribal nature, as well as foreign influence, have long frustrated the plan to adopt a script for the Somali language. Early efforts to select a common script met with considerable external opposition, particularly from Egypt, whose strategy was to give Somalia a false Arab identity.

The first Linguistic Committee was established in 1961, but failed to agree on a single alphabet amid discussions dominated by tribal, political and religious considerations. One school of thought advocated the use of the Arabic script, with the obvious aim of satisfying the conservative religious segment of society influenced by the Egyptian cultural mission in Somalia[47]. Opposing this, the more progressive and intellectual elements favoured the adoption of a modified Roman alphabet. A third school of thought, moved by nationalistic motivations, developed new scripts for the Somali language, known as 'Osmania' and 'Kadaria' after their inventors[48]. The Osmania script, invented in 1920 by Yassin Osman Kenedid, was used since the end of Second World War in private correspondence, and indeed became the script of the first Somali nationalists, even though its detractors considered it nothing more than a script for the 'Darod dialect'.[49]

46 Besteman & Cassanelli, op. cit., p. 17.
47 Touval, op. cit., p 98.
48 Yassin Osman Kenadid and Hussein Sheikh 'Kadare'.
49 A. Morone, *'L'Egitto di Nasser e la formazione dello Stato somalo,'* Rivista di storia dell' 800 e del 900,

On 1 August 1950, the United Nations Advisory Council for Somalia (UNACS) adopted a resolution[50] according to which the Somali language was to be taught in addition to Italian in schools throughout the Trust Territory of Somaliland under Italian administration. The Council advised the Administering Authority to seek technical assistance and guidance from the United Nations' Education, Scientific and Cultural Organization (UNESCO) on investigating the possibility of developing Somali as a national language with its own alphabet, and in determining what languages of instruction should be used in the future. However, unlike other colleagues, the Egyptian delegate, Mr Ragheb, abstained from voting on the resolution[51]. On the same subject, the Trusteeship Council of the United Nations, in its session of 1953, again stressed "the urgency to make Somali a written language in order to facilitate mass education."[52] At the Trusteeship Council, again, the unexpected happened when the Egyptian delegate, Mr Amal Nachaat, opposed this recommendation, favouring instead the adoption of Arabic as the national language for Somalia.

The Italian Foreign Ministry denounced the campaign being waged by the UNACS Egyptian delegate against the adoption of Somali as a national language. However, it should be emphasized that the Egyptians were not alone in campaigning against the United Nations' recommendation with regard to the Somali language. On 21 November 1950, the text of a telegram calling for the adoption of Arabic as the language of Somalis was published in the Mogadisho newspaper. The writer was Sherif Mohamed Abdurahman, of the Asciaraf Sarman tribe, a member of the Lega[53]. Another telegram against Somali and in favour of Arabic as the national language, signed by Mohamed Osman Bari, President of a little-known organization called 'Union of Somali Youth', appeared in *El-Gamhouria*, a semi-official Arabic-language Egyptian newspaper, on January 10, 1954. The message ended with the following words: "We hope that Egypt, leader of the Islamic countries and supporter of the liberals, will assist us to foil this imperialistic manoeuvre".[54]

The Egyptians never relented in their efforts to forestall the adoption of Somali as the country's official language. In fact, once more, when UNESCO drafted a

anno XIII, no. 4, Ottobre 2010, p. 660.

50 Resolution A/AC 33 /R. 9/Rev.1, August 1, 1950.

51 TNA FO 371/80887 secret report n 9/s, from the British Consulate FO, September 14, 1950.

52 ASMAE, AP, 1953, box 917.Telespresso no. 91/07071, from the Foreign Ministry, D.G. Somalia to the Italian Embassy in Cairo, on November 26, 1953.

53 TNA FO 371/80887, Secret report from the British Consulate, Mogadisho to FO November 24, 1950.

54 Telespresso no. 01368, from Jannelli to Mogadiscio, January 23, 1954 (copy is with the author).

five-year-plan for education in Somalia emphasizing the need for development of Somali as the national language, Dr. El Zeyyad, the Egyptian member of the United Nations Advisory Council, criticized the plan on the grounds that, however admirable the concept of a national language may be, such language should not have priority over a language of wider use—presumably Arabic.[55]

However unpalatable, the Egyptian policy designed to block all initiatives towards the development of a written form for Somali was in many ways understandable—not so the shocking and unexpected position taken on the issue by the Lega, the future government party .

In a surprise move, the leadership of the Lega, the very party which had previously advocated the adoption of Somali as a national language, reversed this long-held policy and came out in support of the use of Arabic instead, in a long petition addressed to the United Nations[56]. The petition, dated 3 May 1951, contained very disturbing and misleading information depicting the Somali people as 'backward' and the Somali language as 'underdeveloped', thus reducing Somali to the level of a rustic dialect. The text of the petition reads: "The Arabic language is uniform and is understood in all Muslim countries. From a questionnaire recently conducted by our secretariats all over Somalia, we discovered that there is no general agreement among the Somalis as to which one of the various dialects should become the national language. The people of each province or area insisted that their dialect should be made the national language. When they were, however, asked if they had any objection to the introduction of Arabic as the national language they expressed no objection whatsoever.

"The Somali language is underdeveloped and as such has a very limited vocabulary with no literature at all. It is extremely difficult to express ourselves adequately in the Somali language. It is difficult, if not impossible, for the Somalis to improve their language at the present time. Such improvement or development would require time and education and would require perhaps a few centuries.

"Since the Somali people are backward and the job of developing the Somali language is a gigantic task requiring the attention of highly educated and cultured men, such an attempt would be futile. And if the Somalis, in their present condition, cannot develop their language, it is also difficult to see how foreigners could tackle the problem in the course of a few years.

"On the other hand, the Arabic language is rated as very highly developed

55 TNA FO 371/138315 confidential report from British Consulate, Mogadisho to FO, November 4, 1959.

56 UNOR "T/PET". 11/40, May 3, 1951, p. 22.

and rich in its vocabulary and literature, expanding from day to day. The Arabic language is a growing, vital language. It is already highly developed and is expanding from day to day. The Arabic language is 'international', we might very well say. It is read and spoken all over the Muslim world including Somaliland. The Somali language, on the other hand, is narrow and confined to the Somali people inhabiting the Horn of Africa. In learning the Arabic language perfectly, the Somalis would embark on an ocean of culture which knows no limits. The Arabic language is already widely used in Somalia since the Somalis are all Muslims. The Holy Koran, written in Arabic, is taught to all Somali children from their tender years; the Somalis say their prayers in Arabic; Somali judges record all evidences and proceedings before them in Arabic; documents, private papers and letters are all written in Arabic. Thus already by an unconscious process, by the very fact that Somalis are Muslim, the *'lingua franca'* of Somalis is Arabic. The Arabic language is necessary for linking together Somalia with the Muslim countries culturally and politically. There is a union of thought and feeling between all Muslims all over the world; and the Arabic language helps to foster and strengthen the bonds between Muslim brothers who are all believers in Allah, His Holy Prophet Mohamed, and the Holy Koran."[57]

Other political parties joined the Lega and expressed acceptance of Arabic as the national language of the territory; however, this apparent unanimity was largely the result of none daring to fall behind the others. "Few are paying no more than lip service knowing that it is impracticable", comments a UN report[58]. This conclusion rings particularly true if we consider that most adherents of the Lega were sending their children to Italian schools in Somalia while publicly displaying skin-deep support for Arabic as the national language.

In 1957, six years since the petition was sent to the UN, the Somali government, in a *volte-face* that had obviously received the blessing of the Central Committee of the ruling party, printed a page of the official daily newspaper *Corriere della Somalia* in Somali, with a Roman character transliteration. This bold experiment generated such a violent reaction, particularly on the part of conservative religious leaders, that it was never repeated.

As expected, the pro-Arab lobby, still dormant but strong, denounced the use of the Roman script with the derogatory slogan "Latiin waa laa Diin" ("Latin is irreligious"), thus forcing the government to back down. Kamal El-din Salah,

57 Ibid.

58 UN Doc. T/1344, Rapport de la Mission de Visite des Nations Unies dans les territoirs sous tutelle de l'Afrique Orientale (1957), la Somalie sous administration italienne, pars. 40-41, p. 6.

the Mogadisho-based Egyptian delegate to the UN Consultative Council, had coined the slogan and likened "using the Roman alphabet to choosing the pagan alphabet of the colonialists." Convinced that this would ultimately keep Somalia apart from pan-Arabism and separate it culturally from the Islamic religion[59], Salah also ignored the Council's resolution on the matter, used his influence so that the mosques would preach against the Somali language and "threatened the Advisory Council Secretariat Staff."[60]

Through the propaganda activities of their consular agents in Mogadisho, the Egyptians further escalated their opposition to the Somali language by accusing the Somali Prime Minister of being in the service of the Italians[61]. "No one seemed to be questioning that Arabic was the language of the Koran, and a foreign language for Somalis – just like any other foreign language", commented the *Corriere della Somalia.*[62]

Despite the clear parliamentary mandate issued in 1959 and urging all necessary measures be taken to introduce a written Somali language and adopt it as the official language, "no government took the risk of making a decision because of concern that such a decision would set off widespread social disruption."[63]

The thorny issue of an alphabet for the Somali language was finally solved when in 1972, basing its decision on the work and recommendations of a technical committee, the military regime took the brave and wise decision of adopting a modified Roman alphabet as the basis for an official orthography for the Somali language. At the same time, and for the first time, Somali was recognized as the country's official language.[64]

Missing territories

The idea of uniting the so-called 'missing territories' is not a new concept. It was first conceived in 1943 and given top priority in the foreign policies of successive Somali governments. Somali irredentist claims found legal embodiment in Article 6 (4) of the 1960 Constitution. The map hanging on the walls of government

59 Letter n. 32/4/3/S, from Kamal Al-din Salah to Cairo, March 14, 1957, reported in Morone, L'ultima colonia: come l'Italia tornò in Africa 1950-1960, p. 174.

60 TNA FO 371/118675, telegram no. 1A, from British Consulate, Mogadisho to FO, January 6, 1956.

61 Letter n. 777/3//81/2, from African Department of the Egyptian Ministry of Foreign Affairs to Cabinet of the Minister, October 30, 1957, reported in Morone, op. cit., p. 174.

62 *Corriere della Somalia*, Giugno 20, 1952.

63 J.W. Johson, 'Orality, literacy and Somali oral poetry'Journal of African Cultural Studies, (November 1, June 2006) vol.18, p. 121.

64 Legge n° 60 ottobre 21, 1972, 'Alfabeto ufficiale per la lingua somala', Bollettino Ufficiale, suppl. n° 2 al n°10, October 23, 1972.

offices told the tale of Greater Somalia, to include a portion of Kenya known as NFD, a portion of Ethiopia known as Ogaden, and the entire former territory of French Somaliland, now Republique du Djibouti[65]. These are the lands inhabited by ethnic Somalis, one people 'divided' by old colonial lines. Somalis living in these three neighbouring countries are represented by three of the five points of the star on the Somali flag[66]. The other two points represent respectively the former Italian Trust Territory of Somalia and the former British Somaliland Protectorate, the latter now a *de facto* independent, stable and separate entity emerging from the ashes of the defunct Somali Republic.

The government's official position on unification was stated by the Prime Minister in his address to the Legislative Assembly in July 1959: "All means must be employed, within the framework of legality and the pursuit of peace, to obtain the union of all Somali territories and their reunification under the same flag. This constitutes for us not only a right, but also a duty which cannot be neglected, because it is impossible to want to distinguish between Somali and Somali."[67]

In the programme presented by the first government in 1956, mention was made only of the "unresolved border demarcations between Ethiopia and Somalia"[68], with no reference to the issue of national unification. During the discussion on the 1960 Constitution, political parties advanced different approaches on how to achieve this unification. Although the radical wing of the Lega and the Greater Somali League did not publicly advocate war as a means of unification, they did push for the Constitution to include an article calling for unification of Somali territories "by all means necessary."[69] However, the moderate majority in the political Committee, demanding "reunification of the dismembered nation by peaceful means", ultimately prevailed, and this was the wording adopted in Article 6 (4).

Apart from its rhetoric and generic nature, the statement does not offer any assurance regarding the method for achieving unification. Saadia Touval, a writer who can hardly be accused of harbouring anti-Somali sentiments, offers an

65 Ogaden became an autonomous region within the Federal Republic of Ethiopia in 1992, and Djibouti became an independent republic in 1977.

66 The Somali flag was established under 'Ordinanza n° 17 rep. del 6 settembre 1954' (Bollettino Ufficiale AFIS n° 10), Mogadisho, October 1, 1954.

67 Statement of the Prime Minister in the Legislative Assembly on 26 July 1959.

68 Statement delivered on 26 September 1956 before the Legislative Assembly by PM Abdullahi Issa in presenting his first government programme. Bollettino Ufficiale Afis, suppl. n° 2 al n° 11, November 13, 1956.

69 Touval, op. cit., p. 98.

eloquent comment in this regard: "Their ambiguity regarding method has been explained by the romantic, yet perhaps not invalid, proposition that independence and national unification have seldom been granted to nations for the asking; rather, they had to be won by fighting."[70] The scheme was an ambitious and almost impossible one. Many believed that successive Somali governments banged the nationalistic drum to divert the public's attention from the national problems the Somalis were suffering. A number of external as well as internal factors have equally contributed to making it, since its inception, a distant dream.

Externally, as expected, the strongest opposition to Somali nationalism came from three leading foreign powers greatly involved in the future of the Horn of Africa – namely Ethiopia, Britain and France. Emperor Haile Selassie declared that his country would never give up the Ogaden. The UK, even though in favour of unification of Somaliland with Somalia, reiterated its opposition to the area known as northern Frontier District (NFD) being detached from Kenya to join a united Somalia. As for France, its position was closely allied to that of Ethiopia, based on the common interest in the lucrative port of Djibouti and the railway line linking it to Ethiopia.[71]

Another key external factor working against the Greater Somalia scheme emerged in 1963 with the establishment of the Organization of African Union (OAU), now known as African Union, whose charter recognizes the inviolability of the existing African borders inherited by the colonial European powers. (Article 3 of the OAU Convention)

The intractability of this problem is reflected in a statement released by Premier Abdirashid: "Our misfortune is that our neighbouring countries, with whom, like the rest of Africa, we seek to promote constructive and harmonious relations, are not our neighbours. Our neighbours are our own kinsmen whose citizenship has been falsified by indiscriminate boundary 'arrangements'. They have to move across artificial frontiers to their pasture lands. They occupy the same terrain and pursue the same pastoral economy as ourselves. We speak the same language. We share the same creed, the same culture, and the same tradition. How can we regard our brothers as foreigners? Of course we all have a strong and very natural desire to be united. The first step was taken in 1960 when the Somaliland Protectorate was united to Somalia. This act was not an act of 'colonialism' or 'expansionism' or 'annexation'. It was a positive contribution

70 Ibid.

71 Djibouti finally gained its independence from France in 1977. It was immediately recognized by the Somali Republic and established diplomatic ties with the new republic.

to peace and unity in Africa."[72]

Internally, there was no national consensus or clear understanding of the benefits of the Greater Somalia project. In other words, a true populist-based Somali nationalism was never born. A fragmented tribal society in constant internal conflict cannot be expected to harbour nationalistic feelings. This sense of need for a 'greater Somalia' did not extend to the public at large. More immediate and pressing were the internal problems of a new nation with little cohesion of identity and interests.

A number of writers with deep knowledge of Somalia maintain that the nationalistic campaign found its strongest backing among northern and central pastoral clans, particularly those who had kinship bonds with people living beyond State borders. "The Rahanweyn and Hawiye feel little connection with those on the other side of the border. The settled and semi-sedentary population of the riverine and inter-river south had little interest in this irredentism scheme", comments Lee Cassanelli, adding that on the issue of Greater Somalia "the Hawiye and Dighil and Mirfle, in particular, are less ardent than they were at one time though they still pay lip service to the idea."[73] According to British diplomatic sources, "These two tribal groups, Dighil & Mirifle and Hawiye, while wishing to see the union of all Somalis, would ultimately not like to see 400,000 more Darod entering a united Somalia to swell the numerical advantage that tribe already possess."[74]

In addition to the external and internal factors described above, the weakness of the economy contrasted with the aspiration of uniting all Somali-inhabited territories in one nation, which would entail military and diplomatic expenditure such as to place an unbearable burden on state coffers.

The Organization of African Unity and African borders

Somalia isolated at the African Summit

This chapter does not purport to cover the full extent and dynamic of OAU involvement in the solution of the territorial disputes between its members, but only to give a brief account of the principles underlying the OAU's intrinsic

72 The Somali Peninsula, a New Light on Imperial Motives, Information Service of the Somali Government, 1962, p. vi.

73 Besteman and Cassanelli, op. cit., p. 18.

74 TNA FO 371/131463 confidential report 1018/58 from British Consulate Mogadisho to FO, April 1, 1958.

inability to settle the territorial disputes brought before it, in particular that involving Somalia and its immediate neighbours.

The issue of Somali irredentism was initially raised at the first Afro-Asian Solidarity Conference in Cairo (1957), when the Conference accepted the Somali resolution that all forms of colonialism in the Horn of Africa, which by implication included Ethiopia's rule over the Ogaden as well as British and French rule over Somali-inhabited areas, be eradicated.[75]

Somali aspirations found further support in the Ghanaian–Somali communiqué, released at the end of the state visit of Somali President Aden Abdulla to Ghana in 1961. The communiqué states that the two countries recognized "the imperative need to restore the ethnic, cultural and economic links arbitrarily destroyed by colonialism."[76] Encouraged by this strong support gained outside the OAU, Somalia requested the inclusion in the agenda of the preparatory meeting of foreign ministers to be held in Addis Abeba in May 1963 of an item entitled 'General consideration of the question of the territorial disputes between neighbouring African countries, and the need of establishing effective mechanism to examine and settle such territorial disputes'.[77]

However, and despite the joint communiqué of 1961, a few weeks before the Addis Abeba African Conference President Nkrumah of Ghana had circulated a message addressed to all African Head of States in which he stressed the inviolability of the existing borders between neighbouring African countries. His position was based on the argument that since Africa was taking the path of unity, it was not wise to make territorial claims and alter existing frontiers. A copy of this message was handed to Aden Abdulla on 3 March 1963 by the Ghanaian *chargé d'affaires* at Mogadisho. This message dampened the enthusiasm of President Aden Abdulla, a fervent nationalist who firmly believed in the right of self-determination for Somalis living in Ethiopia and Kenya. He recorded his disappointment and disagreement with Nkrumah in his diary on 3 March 1963: "No one can give up what belongs to him, and reality is the opposite of Nkrumah's position."[78]

While preparations were underway for the first African Summit convened to adopt the new African Charter, two new developments emerged that cast doubts

75 A.A. Castagno, *The Somali-Kenyan Controversy*, op. cit., pp.181-182.

76 Touval, op. cit., p.vi.

77 Proceedings of the Summit Conference of Independent African States, Addis Abeba, May 1963, vol. 1 Document AGENDA/CONF/5, May 15, 1963.

78 Diary Aden Abdulla, March 3, 1963.

over Somali participation to the planned summit. Firstly, the Somali government in March 1963 signalled its decision not to take part in the Lagos meeting of African foreign ministers, as a reaction to the concept of inviolability of the borders between African States contained in the charter. Secondly, a diplomatic storm between Ethiopia and Somalia was sparked off by the treatment of Abdurrahman Hussein, a Somali diplomat based in Addis Abeba.[79]

The Ethiopians claimed that this diplomat, from ethnic Ogaden, was an Ethiopian national. He was refused permission to leave the Embassy premises, which created a tug-of-war between the two countries. Reacting to the treatment reserved to the Somali diplomat, President Aden Abdulla sent a message to the African Heads of State, informing them of his government's decision not to participate in the planned African Conference to be held in Addis Abeba in May 1963 "unless the Ethiopian government recedes from its position and guarantees Abdurahman and his family safe return to Somalia." Following mediation efforts made by the USA government, the diplomat was later allowed to leave[80]. It should be mentioned that Abdurahman was at the centre of another diplomatic rift between Ethiopia and Somalia when, in 1961, he was denied an entry visa to Ethiopia as a member of a Somali delegation travelling to Addis Abeba to attend a conference sponsored by the United Nations African Economic Development Organization.

Once the reason for boycotting the Conference was removed, and in consideration of growing pressure from a number of African leaders including Presidents Tubman of Liberia, Nkrumah of Ghana and the Prime Minister of Uganda Milton Obote, the Somali government reversed its earlier decision, giving formal communication to this effect to the Emperor Haile Selassie as well as those African heads of State who had expressed concern over the Somali boycott of the Conference[81]. However, it would be wrong to conclude that the decision to attend the Conference was made solely on the basis of the positive outcome of the diplomatic row. Political anxieties, too, have hastened and reinforced the government's change of course. In fact, there is good reason to believe that, after the precipitous decision of severing relations with Britain, the government became increasingly aware that they could not afford to commit another political blunder by absenting themselves from the First Summit Conference of

79 In later years Abdurahman, a strikingly tall and slim man, became Somali ambassador in Dar-as-Salaam and Nairobi.

80 *Corriere della Somalia*, Aprile 24, 1963.

81 Diary Aden Abdulla, April 6, 1963.

Independent African States.

At the Summit Conference, Somali territorial claims were received with scant enthusiasm. In fact, the address in which the Somali Head of State presented the Somali territorial dispute with Kenya and Ethiopia to the summit provoked a dramatic incident and brought forth a sharp reply from the Prime Minister of Ethiopia, Aklilu Habte Wolde[82]. The Ethiopian delegate expressed surprise that "a brother State should have felt it necessary to exhibit in public our petty differences." In a subsequent statement, Ato Habte Wolde added: "If we are to get new boundaries and maps on the basis of race and religion, in a few years many States of Africa will cease to exist. We must respect the present frontiers and maps, good or bad."[83]

The chairman of that plenary session, President Houphouet-Boigny of Cote d'Ivoir, was even tougher when he described the Somali President's speech as breaking the procedure of the meetings. Other heads of State spoke of the border problems in a more general way. President Kwame Nkrumah of Ghana, for instance, reversing the position on the border issues that he had voiced in an informal meeting with the Somali President on the eve of the Conference[84], stated before the African gathering: "There is hardly one African State without a frontier problem with its adjacent neighbours. It would be futile for me to enumerate them because they are already familiar to us all. But let me suggest to Your Excellencies that this fatal relic of colonialism will drive us to war against one another. Unless we succeed in arresting the danger through mutual understanding on fundamental issues and through African unity which will render existing borders obsolete and superfluous, we shall have fought in vain for independence. Only African unity can heal this festering sore of boundary disputes between various states."[85]

President Modiba Keyta of Mali supported the idea that the existing borders should be respected: "If all of us present here are truly animated by the ardent desire to achieve African unity, we must take Africa as it is, and we must renounce any territorial claims if we do not wish to introduce what we might call black imperialism in Africa. African unity demands each one of us respect the legacy that we have received from the colonial system, that is to say: maintenance of the

82 Proceedings... vol., I, section 2, documents CIAS/GEN/INF/25 and CIAS/GEN/INF/43.

83 *Somali News*, May 31, 1963.

84 Diary Aden Abdulla, May 23, 1963.

85 Speech delivered by K. Nkrumah at the Conference of African Head of States and Governments at Addis Abeba, May 1963 , Proceedings... , vol. 1, Section 2, document CIAS/GEN/INF 36, p. 7, par. 33.

present frontiers of our respective states."[86] In fact, article III, paragraph 3 of the OAU Charter merely proclaims the principle of "respecting the sovereignty and territorial integrity of each State and its inalienable right to independent existence."[87] Aden Abdulla makes this entry in his diary while still in Addis Abeba: "Modiba Keyta seems to be the most annoyed by my speech against Ethiopia."[88]

Although the OAU had acknowledged the imperfections of the national borders of African countries from the outset, the Assembly of Heads of State and Government held in Cairo in 1964 adopted a resolution which solemnly declared: "All member states pledge themselves to respect the borders existing on their achievement of their nation independence."[89] Somali reaction to this was swift and strong: the National Assembly passed a motion condemning the OAU Resolution on African boundaries.

Many resolutions adopted by the OAU continually strengthened the territorial inviolability of African States and their respective frontiers. Resolution A.G.H./16.1 of July 21, 1964, to cite just one, incorporates the rule of *uti possidetis juris*, a principle of international law according to which newly formed states should have the same borders as they had before their independence.

The Organization was involved in four border disputes: between Morocco and Algeria; Somalia and Ethiopia; Somalia and Kenya, and Ghana and Upper Volta (today Burkina Faso). The first dispute, brought before it a few months after its establishment, was the one involving Morocco and Algeria. Morocco claimed Mauritania as part of its territory. It is worth mentioning that Morocco and Somalia attached to their signatures of the OAU Charter a reservation on the clause stipulating that existing colonial frontiers should not be construed as recognition of existing borders.[90]

Later on, realizing that the long-standing policy based on territorial claims was not gaining ground, the Somalis changed direction to pursue the more defendable principle of self-determination for the concerned people. The Somalis appeared to have finally realized that the word 'territorial claim' was too strong and legally controversial an expression, and returned to advocating the right of self-determination for all Somalis living in neighbouring countries. This departure from the extant policy towards the 'missing territories' was first suggested by

86 Proceedings vol., 1. section 2, document CIAS/GEN/INF 33, p. 2.

87 The National Assembly approved the OAU Charter by unanimous vote on July 4, 1963.

88 Diary Aden Abdulla, May 24, 1963.

89 Res. A.G.H/16.1, July 21, 1964.

90 Touval, *'The Organization of African Unity and African Borders,'* International Organization, vol. 21, issue 01, December 1967, p. 107.

Aden Abdulla, who saw the advantage of advocating the principle of self-determination for the concerned population. He writes in his diary: "To justify our policy and canvass large international support, it is necessary to reiterate that our difficulties with our neighbours are not based on territorial claims, but on the search for justice to the Somalis kept under force by those countries."[91] However, the principle of self-determination has become subject to different interpretations. For the Kenyans and Ethiopians it is a principle applicable only to people under colonial rule and not to minorities within independent African States. The Somalis, on the other hand, argued that the United Nations General Assembly Resolution 1514 (XV) refers in its preamble and its operative part to self-determination as a principle of universal application.

The United Nations' 1960 declaration on the guaranteeing of independence to colonial countries and peoples (Resolution 1514) states that "any attempt aimed at partial and total disruption of the national unity and territorial integrity of a country is incompatible with the purpose and principles of the Charter of the United Nations."[92] From a strictly Somali point of view, claims over the missing territories certainly had a historical foundation, but the neighbouring countries were not ready to relinquish sovereignty over vast provinces, which they saw as a loss of importance and prestige. The result was that, only three years from the date of independence, Somalia's relations with its African neighbours were spoiled beyond repair and diplomatic ties with a major European power, Great Britain, were severed. Many believe that it had been obvious since the Addis Abeba African Summit of 1963 that Somalia had lost any chances of obtaining satisfaction through Pan-Africanism.[93]

Somalis were never popular with other Africans, and major powers in the world were not ready to endorse their aspirations. United Kingdom and Italy, the two nations that had in the past, to some degree, encouraged the idea of Greater Somalia, which was of course in their own interest, now dropped their support for the scheme, aligning themselves with the position of the OAU on the disputed African borders. Most OAU members were alienated by Somali irredentism and feared that if Somalia were successful in detaching the Somali populated portions of Ethiopia and Kenya, its example might inspire their own

91 Meeting of Aden Abdulla with Abdirashid Ali and Abdullahi Issa, March 24, 1963, vide Diary Aden Abdulla March 24, 1963; meeting with Mohamed Ali Da'ar, before his goodwill mission to a number of African countries, Diary Aden Abdulla, March 28, 1963.

92 Resolution1514 (XV), December 14, 1960.

93 A.A. Castagno, *The Somali-Kenyan Controversy*, op. cit., p. 183.

restive minorities[94]. The question of French Somaliland was not raised explicitly in the form of a border or territorial dispute at the African summit: formally it was a question of decolonization.

Despite the difficult relations, Somalia supported the Ethiopian proposal to establish at Addis Abeba the seat of the Organization of African Unity (OAU), contested by Senegal.

The referendum on the future of NFD

Somalia severs diplomatic relations with Britain

Events in Kenya prior to the country's independence had led to increasing activity by Somali political parties in the northern Frontier District (NFD), and their demand for secession from Kenya and union with Somalia were given wide publicity in the Republic.[95]

Available records show, however, that not everyone in the NFD was in favour of uniting with the Somali Republic. The Northern Province People's Progressive Party (NPPPP), the Northern Province Democratic Party (NPDP), the People's National league (PNL) and the National Political Movement of Nairobi were organized to champion the cause of NFD unification with the Somali Republic. On the other hand, the Northern Province People's National Union, the Galla Political Union of Nairobi and the United Ogaden Somali Association of Nairobi and Garissa were set up to oppose any union with Somali Republic. "The former were better organized and represented the aspirations of the majority of the people in the area", comments Castagno.[96]

The Northern Frontier District covers an area of 102,000 square miles and is comprised of six administrative districts: Garissa, Wajir, Mandera, Moyale, Marsabit and Isiolo. The Somalis are mainly concentrated in the east of the NFD, in the Garissa, Wajir and Mandera Districts.

Following growing pressure from the Somali NFD parties in Kenya, particularly the People's Progressive Party led by Aden Lord, the Somali National Assembly passed a resolution on 13 November 1961 in support of union of the province with the Republic[97]. The likely consequences of this course of action is explained

94 Ibid.

95 I.M. Lewis, *'Pan-Africanism and Pan-Somalism,'* Journal of Modern African Studies, 1, 2 (1963), p. 154.

96 A. A. Castagno, *The Somali-Kenyan Controversy*, op. cit., p. 175.

97 Diary Aden Abdulla, November 13, 1961.

by an author very much conversant with Somali affairs in these clear words: "The Somali government was now being forced to adopt a course bound to lead to conflict with the Kenyan nationalists as well as with Ethiopia, and likely to increase the Republic's difficulties in finding Pan-African support for her aims."[98] In March the Prime Minister made a strongly anti-imperialist speech, attacking Ethiopia and France and warning the British government that "it would be held responsible if the 'mistakes' of the past were added to and the inhabitants of the NFD were refused the right to freely decide their own destiny."[99]

During the Lancaster House Constitutional Conference on Kenya's independence (February-April 1962) the issue of Somali self-determination was raised by members of the NFD and Somali delegations who demanded that the NFD question be addressed before Kenyan independence[100]. Despite opposition from the Kenyan African National Union (KANU) and Kenyan African Democratic Union (KADU) to the secession of the northern Frontier District, British Colonial Secretary Reginald Maudling responded to the NFD-Somali request by announcing on April 6, 1962 that a Commission would be appointed to inquire into the state of public opinion in the NFD. However, the British government made it clear that a final settlement of the NFD problem would have to be acceptable to Kenya's African leaders.

Meanwhile, the government of the Republic sought to promote better relations with Kenyan African leaders. Accordingly, KANU was invited to send delegates to the Republic's Independence Day on 1 July. Kenyatta himself came later on a short visit, followed by a six-day visit by Ronald Ngala and members of KADU for informal talks. Both leaders were treated with full honour and awarded the Star of Somali Solidarity. However, no progress was made with Kenyatta, although Ngala, as might have been expected on the basis of his party's regional policy, appeared to be more flexible.

In this spirit of optimism on the part of Somalia, the British Government appointed a commission to ascertain and report on the wishes of the population in the NFD. The Commission was headed by Mr G.CM. Onyuke, a Q.C. from Nigeria, and Maj. General M.P. Bogert, from Canada was the Deputy Head. Specifically, the Commission's brief was to enquire whether the Kenya Somalis

98 I.M. Lewis, *'Pan-Africanism and Pan-Somalism',* Journal of Modern African Studies, 1, 2 (1963,) p. 155.

99 *Somali News*, March 25, 1962.

100 The Somali delegation, composed of M.I. Egal, Mohamoud 'Juje', Abdulkadir 'Zoppo', Mohamoud Yousuf 'Muro', was not officially part of the Lancaster House Constititional Conference.

wished to remain in Kenya or join the Somali Republic. In December 1962, the Commission's report was conclusive: the inhabitants expressed the wish to secede and join the Republic of Somalia. 86% of the whole NFD favoured the region's secession from Kenya after the latter's independence, with the object of ultimately joining the Somali Republic[101]. Despite these quite unequivocal findings, the wishes of the Somali inhabitants of NFD were ignored and the new constitutional arrangements for Kenya, announced on 8 March 1963 by British Commonwealth and Colonial Secretary Duncan Sandys, provided only for the creation of a seventh new region embracing the predominantly Somali areas of the NFD.

Kenya's prominent leaders such as Jomo Kenyatta and Tom Mboya vehemently rejected the transfer of any part of Kenya to Somalia and threatened war to preserve Kenya's territorial integrity. In a statement released in Addis Abeba in early 1961, Mr Tom Mboya not only rejected the Somali claim but stated that "Kenya will reopen the issue of the cession of Jubaland to Italy in 1925."[102] In a clear reference to the Somali territorial claim, Mr Ngala, Principal Minister and member of the Kenya African National Union (KANU), stated that "the Masai are divided between Kenya and Tanzania and there are other tribes living along the two sides of the Kenya-Ugandan border."[103]

The wishes of the Somali inhabitants of the NFD were ignored in favour of those of Kenyan nationalists who opposed a partition of the colony. As I.M. Lewis eloquently put it, "Britain had evidently decided that, whatever interests she might have in maintaining friendship with the Republic, and whatever responsibilities she might be held to owe to her Somali subjects in Kenya, or to her former subjects in the northern Regions of the Republic, these were not such as to justify endangering the long-standing *entente* with Ethiopia and alienating the new Commonwealth territory of Kenya."[104]

Somali nationalism suffered a blow from which it never recovered. In a surprise move, however, news came from Britain to the effect that Her Majesty's government was considering fresh proposals to be shared with the Somali government. In fact, the British Ambassador in Mogadisho gave the Somali Prime Minister this message: "I immediately reported to the Foreign Office the conversation about the NFD which I had with your Excellency on March 12. I

101 HL Deb vol. 248 cc600-36 600, 03 April 1963.
102 Diary Aden Abdulla, October 11, 1961.
103 Ibid.. October 26, 1961.
104 I.M. Lewis, op. cit., pp. 193-194.

should like to inform Your Excellency at once of the contents of a communication I have just received from the Foreign Office. This communication states that a proposal is under urgent consideration and that the Foreign Office hopes to be able to communicate with Your Excellency about it within the next two or three days."[105]

Despite the assurances the Ambassador received from his government, the hoped-for proposal never came from Britain. "With remarkable restraint and a pardonable ignorance of British diplomatic history, Abdirashid permitted himself the observation that he doubted if any other British diplomat had even been similarly treated", comments I.M. Lewis.[106]

Tens of thousands of protesters took part in anti-Western demonstrations in Mogadisho. A climate of 'nationalist agitation' which had little relation to the country's severe economic and social problems appears to have been created by the government. Foreign embassies, including those of Britain, America, Ethiopia and even Italy were attacked by angry mobs causing damage to the buildings. The Ethiopian and American Embassies in particular were the target of much anger, and two Somali protesters were fired at and wounded by Ethiopian security personnel when they tried to climb the wall of the Ethiopian Embassy. The Embassy demanded reparation of the damage caused to the building by the protesters[107]. The Somali government reportedly also paid 20,000 Birr as compensation for the attack on the Ethiopian Embassy in Mogadisho in 1963.[108] Reacting to the British decision over the future of the NFD, the Somali government submitted a motion to the National Assembly calling for the severing of diplomatic relations with Britain "for failing to recognize the wishes expressed by the overwhelming majority of the people inhabiting the NFD." The motion was passed by 70 votes to 14.[109]

The outcome of this vote shows that most parliamentarians supported the motion but did not perhaps fully realize the adverse economic effects that might arise from such a decision. With no access to valuable natural resources such as oil, copper or uranium to enhance its position, Somalia had no economic leverage to influence a major power such as Britain in ways analogous (to cite only one outstanding example) to the Arab oil-producing countries altering some major

105 Diary Aden Abdulla, March 16, 1963.

106 I.M. Lewis, op. cit., p. 193.

107 Diary Aden Abdulla, February 24, 1963.

108 Yihun, op. cit., p. 139.

109 J. Drysdale, *The Somali Dispute*, Pall Mall Press, London, 1964, p. 144.

power's policy towards Israel[110]. The question to be answered is why Somalia severed relations with Britain, a move highly likely to produce a boomerang effect. The answer lay with the government's need to assuage growing popular indignation *vis-à-vis* the British decision.

John Drysdale makes the following comment on the prevailing atmosphere during the meeting in which Britain was informed of the formal severance of relations between the two countries: "without rancour and with great courtesy the Foreign Minister, Mr Abdullahi Issa, handed to the British Ambassador[111] on 18th March 1963 the formal note breaking off diplomatic relations." Non-essential British diplomatic staff and their families left Mogadisho immediately[112]. It is worth mentioning that the Somali Consulate in Aden, still under British rule, remained open, while the Consulate in Nairobi was closed and staff evacuated despite the absence of any decision from the British government to that effect.

The government divided over the rupture with Britain

There were mixed reactions in Somalia over the decision to sever relations with Great Britain. Many believed that the decision was taken hastily, without due consideration being given to its political and economic consequences, and that it deprived the government of a valuable channel of communications with Britain regarding the future of the NFD before the Independence of Kenya. It was further argued that continued relations with Britain would have kept the door open for dialogue on finding possible alternative solutions to the contention.

The members of the Cabinet were also divided over the issue of rupture of diplomatic relations with Britain. Disagreement between Abdirashid and his Foreign Minister surfaced immediately following the referendum on the future of the NFD. The Foreign Minister vigorously resisted any move likely to lead to the deterioration of relations with Great Britain for fear that such a move might ultimately harm Somali interests.[113]

The divergence between the Prime Minister and his Minister of Foreign Affairs over the NFD issue further widened when in June 1963 media reports from Nairobi quoted the Minister of Foreign Affairs, after his meeting with Jomo

110 Susan Gitelson, *Why Do Small States Break Diplomatic Relations with Outside Powers? Lessons from the African Experience*, International Studies Quarterly, vol. 18, no. 4 (Dec. 1974), pp. 451-84.

111 The British Ambassador of the time was Mr Pyman..

112 The American Embassy protected British interests in Somalia, while the Italian Embassy in Britain was charged with protecting Somali interests in Britain.

113 Diary Aden Abdulla, February 23, 1963.

Kenyatta in Nairobi, as saying that "The leaders of both countries are equally interested in the NFD issue and in the East African Federation [...] the frontier problem will cease to exist once the federation is achieved."[114] Such statement attributed to the Minister was interpreted by the PM as undermining the NFD cause and consequently exonerating Great Britain of its responsibility to solve the NFD problem prior to the independence of Kenya, a circumstance denied by the Minister.

This disagreement fuelled widespread speculations that the Foreign Minister was considering stepping down[115]. As a result of the rupture, the British lost the BBC relay station transmitter at Berbera, over flight and landing rights at Mogadisho Airport for British military aircrafts between Nairobi and Aden, and the licence of Aden Airways. Except for a small number of British Council scholarships, UK economic assistance to Somalia was suspended. Before the rupture, the amount of much-needed British assistance was equal to almost £2M [?]per annum.[116]

Somalia had voluntarily relinquished generous British annual aid, a self-inflicted and severe blow to an already weak economy. The impact of the suspension of British aid was soon felt—so much so that, in a frenetic search for income to cover the budget deficit created by the loss of British aid, the Minister of Finance is reported to have approached the US Embassy in Mogadisho. However, the Americans made it clear that providing such kind of assistance under their programme was not a possibility, expressing instead their readiness to provide food supplies and military equipment.[117]

Amid this confusion, rumours started circulating about the British government's intention to open negotiations with the Somali government on the future of the NFD, provided that Somalia renounced the three districts of Isiolo, Marsabit and Moyale. The same unconfirmed reports further suggested that the British government would be ready to seriously consider the possibility of placing the 7th Province of Kenya (which in fact is NFD) under UN trusteeship[118]. However, in a surprise move, Great Britain placed the province under the direct rule of the British governor of Kenya and not under the Kenyatta government. "I learned with satisfaction today from the press that Her Majesty's government

114 Ibid., June 5, 1963.

115 Ibid., July 4, 1963.

116 TNA FCO 31/223, Confidential tele no 5098 of December 22, 1967, addressed to Nairobi; Government of Somali Republic, Activities from Independence until Today, December 31, 1963, p. 88.

117 Diary Aden Abdulla, April 5, 1963.

118 Diary Aden Abdulla, May 9, 1963.

of Britain and Northern Ireland has placed the 7th province of Kenya (NFD) under the direct rule of the governor of Kenya, substracting it from the control of the Kenyan government led by Jomo Kenyatta", comments Aden Abdulla.[119]

A hastily convened conference held in Rome between 25 and 29 August 1963 to discuss the request of the Somalis in Kenya's Northern Frontier District to be allowed to secede from Kenya and join Somalia ended in failure. It should be noted that the Somali delegation to the Conference in Rome was led by the Prime Minister himself, and among the members of his delegation the absence of the Foreign Minister was very conspicuous.[120]

The British representative present at the Rome talks explained that his government's decision not to grant secession was in line with the consensus of African opinion expressed in Addis Abeba on the issue of the borders between African States (Article 3 of the OAU Convention).

A Somali proposal to the effect that, pending a final solution, the disputed area should be placed either under joint Somali–Kenyan or United Nations administration received scant attention. Britain's strategy was to delay the matter until Kenya became independent in the hope that this would push the burden of negotiation onto the new government to be formed soon after.

On his return from the inconclusive talks in Rome, an angry Sharmarke called for general mobilization. As reported by *The New York Times*, he declared upon arriving at Mogadisho airport that he "would not hesitate to scrap civil government and hand over full government to the military in the interest of the unity [...] Our democratic system, though theoretically admirable, is not adapted to the present situation"; and called for a united front of all Somalis within and outside the Republic, "even at the cost of general mobilization."[121]

In what was taken as an allusion to the United States, Mr Sharmarke expressed regret that there had been no response to Somalia's appeal to nations friendly to Britain and France to use their good offices "to obtain justice for Somalis still under foreign rule. [...] Nevertheless", he concluded, "Somalia is not isolated. Many nations are ready to help unconditionally."[122] Observers had no doubts that he was referring to pledges given to him during official visits to a number of foreign countries, including the Soviet Union, the United Arab Republic, India,

119 Diary Aden Abdulla, June 1, 10, 1963.

120 It was an open secret that the two men held divergent views about the NFD dossier, as well as severance of relation with Britain.

121 'Somali Premier Asks Army Rule', *The New York Times*, September 08, 1963.

122 Ibid.

Pakistan and communist China, before the Rome talks. The Premier accusingly stated that in the past 75 years Britain had bartered the Somali peoples and territories seven times in favour of other countries. "By evading a solution of the Northern Frontier District issue in Kenya," he said, "Britain has perpetrated one more act of injustice and hostility against the Somali Republic."

When Kenya became independent in December 1963, NFD Somalis began a long guerrilla war against the new government. The Somalis called them freedom fighters and the Kenyans called them *shiftas*, a term applied to bandits and cattle rustlers. The Somali government officially denied Kenya's charges that the guerrillas were trained in Somalia, equipped with arms and directed from Mogadisho. But it could not deny that the *Voice of Somalia* radio station influenced the level of guerrilla activity by means of its broadcasts beamed into Kenya.

In contrast, Somalia's relations with Italy after independence remained good, and Italian influence continued in the modernized sectors of social and cultural affairs. Although their number had dropped to about 2,000 on the date of independence, the Italian community in Somalia controlled, in various ways, almost 70% of Somali economy.[123]

Italy was an important market for Somali goods, particularly, as we have seen, for bananas produced on the large Italian-owned commercial farms in the river valleys. Italy's sponsorship enabled Somalia to become an associate of the European Economic Community (EEC), which gave it another source of economic and technical aid and assured preferential status for Somali exports on West European markets.[124]

The Soviet arms deal

Soon after independence, Somalia wasted no time in aggressively pursuing irredentist aims by embarking on a programme of military build-up and consequently diverting huge amounts of resources from productive investments[125]. The necessity of acquiring arms to levels strictly necessary for internal security and defensive purposes is not in question; but the emphasis on foreign policy used as a way of distracting attention from domestic difficulties was a constant trait of the Somali political class after independence. In its efforts to secure

123 G. Vedovato, 'La Somalia, Stato indipendente', Rivista di studi politici internazionali, anno XXVII, n° 3, 1960, p. 325.

124 Legge n° 25 Dicembre 14, 1963, concerning ratification of the Convention of Association between the European Economic Community and the Association of African States and Madagascar of July 20, 1963.

125 In 1967, 20 % of the national budget went to the Army.

military assistance, the Somali government established ties with the Soviet Union and China soon after independence. At the outset, despite Somalia's approaches, the Western powers fell short of making an offer.

In October 1963, during a state visit to Italy by the President of the Somali Republic and members of his delegation, the Italians briefed their Somali guests on the ongoing consultations between Italy, the United States and the Federal Republic of Germany on the issue of military aid to Somalia. However the Italians, acting on an intelligence report, enquired as to whether the Somali government was already negotiating the same issue with the Russians. The Italians were particularly interested to learn what Somalia's attitude would be *vis-à-vis* the Russians in the event the three Western powers should accept the Somali request and make an offer. The Somali leader's response was clear and concise: "I don't see why Somalia would not opt for the Western offer, if that offer was at the same level or more favourable than the Soviet's. The West has beaten around the bush for long time but they are still in time to meet our needs."[126]

The Italians saw Russian penetration in Somalia as a loss of prestige for the West in the former Trust Territory. Italian concerns triggered an unplanned meeting between Ambassador Giovanni Fornari (Head of Political Affairs of the Italian Ministry of Foreign Affairs) and Aden Abdulla at the latter's hotel in Rome, in the presence of Ambassador Mohamed Sheikh Hassan. Fornari's visit was connected to his scheduled trip to Bonn for the meeting of the three Western powers over military aid to Somalia. Ambassador Fornari wondered whether his visit would serve any purpose, since according to intelligence reports from Mogadisho Somalia had already ratified an agreement with the Soviet Union. Aden Abdulla's retort was quick and categorical: "I am not the one sending you to Bonn[127]. [...] If the West were ready to draw up an urgent plan of military aid within a clear timescale, the Somali government might be in a position to thank the Soviets for their favourable disposition and decline their offer." The Italian diplomat used the occasion to raise the spectre of the political and economic problems that Somalia might face: "Fornari was trying to frighten me by referring to potential adverse political and economic repercussions Somalia might suffer in the event we accepted Soviet military assistance."[128]

The President, however, took exception to the Italian diplomat's concerns, for he felt that the responsibility for any steps taken by the Somali government

126 Diary Aden Abdulla, October 3, 1963.
127 Ibid., October 15, 1963.
128 Ibid.

would fall squarely on the Western powers who for over three years, either in bad faith or in their own interest, failed to meet Somalia's urgent military needs[129]. In the meantime, news started trickling into Italy of the departure of 60 Somali army officers to the Soviet Union for training purposes, some of whom were reportedly expected to go to Italy for the same purposes. Taken by surprise, while still in Rome, Aden Abdulla made the following long entry in his diary for October 17, 1963 "Abdirashid has forgotten that I had warned him not to get into commitment with the Soviets before my return from the state visit to Italy, during which time I will be gauging what the Italians and their Western allies think about providing military assistance to Somalia. Abdirashid did not think that after all I am the one who should sign the agreement, even though the idea of refusing to sign it never even crossed my mind."[130]

The Americans became deeply troubled by the pro-communist statements attributed to the Somali Prime Minister during his official visit to China. These concerns prompted an immediate meeting between Aden Abdulla and Mr Torbert, the US Ambassador in Mogadisho, during which the American diplomat raised with the President the concerns of his government *vis-à-vis* the 'communist danger' in connection with the statements of the Prime Minister and his Minister of Information. The Somali President, in turn, raised with the Ambassador the issue of Somalia's outstanding request for Western military assistance, and his frustration and irritation with Western powers were palpable: "Mr Ambassador, give us the arms we need for our puny army or leave us to get them from elsewhere."[131]

On 19 October, one day before leaving Rome for Mogadisho, Aden Abdulla was again contacted by the Italian authorities for an unscheduled meeting with President Antonio Segni at the Palazzo del Quirinale, the official residence of the Italian Head of State. It was in that meeting that the level of Western military aid to Somalia was finally disclosed. The three Western powers offered Somalia arms for a 6,000-strong national army: a package worth $18m, far below the level of assistance already offered by the Soviet Union. "If the Somali government were ready to accept this offer, the material would start arriving in Mogadisho no later than the coming December", Aden Abdulla was told[132]. The Soviet–Somali Agreement, on the other hand, provided for the expansion and training of the

129 Ibid., October 15, 1963.
130 Ibid., October 17, 1963.
131 Ibid., September 12-13, 1963.
132 Ibid., October 19, 1963.

Somali national army from 2,000 to 10,000, and included the supply of MIG-15 aircraft and T-34 tanks. In addition, Somali cadets were to be trained in the USSR. According to experts, the Soviet Army's package was ten times greater than the total of the Somali estimated defense budget for 1964 £ 3,900,000.[133]

Upon his return to Mogadisho on October 21, the Head of State received detailed briefings from General Daud Abdulla, commander of the national army, on the latter's recent mission to the Soviet Union where, acting under a letter of credentials from the government, he initialled an agreement with the Soviet Union on military assistance for a 10,000-strong Somali national army. The Sh.So 200M [?] worth of military equipment stipulated included 23 military planes (20 of which jet fighters), 100 tanks, some cannons and other military equipment. Daud concluded his briefing by announcing that "the same agreement has been signed by the Parliament Speaker, Jama Abdullahi Ghalib."

"This latter point is highly damaging of me and I am therefore not minded to tolerate it, since, apart from the clear bad faith and lack of consideration shown to me by hastily concluding an agreement with the Russians, I am convinced that no one may sign any documents on my behalf when I am away on mission. [...] It is high time that one of us, Abdirashid or I, should go."[134] Aden Abdulla noted in his diary.

When he met the Prime Minister on the following day, the President did not immediately raise the legal issues surrounding the agreement signed by the PM, but briefed him instead on the outcome of his discussions with the Italian authorities. In order to avoid a possible deterioration of relations with the West, the President recommended that the Prime Minister open additional talks with the Western powers and accept their offer if it should prove acceptable.

The exercise on the part of the Speaker of functions constitutionally conferred to the Head of State also aroused legal arguments. Under the 1960 Somali Constitution, the power to ratify international treaties is vested in the Head of State (Article 75 (e) of the Constitution of 1960). The President of the Parliament did not dispute this, but claimed that "he came under pressure from the Prime Minister to sign the document because he was made to believe that the matter was urgent."[135] This circumstance was, however, denied by the Prime Minister, who declared he had even warned Jama Abdullahi that the latter would

133 Robert G. Patman, *The Soviet Union in the Horn of Africa, the Diplomacy of Intervention and Disengagement,* Cambridge University Press, 1990, p. 49.

134 Diary Aden Abdulla, October 22, 1963.

135 Ibid., October 22-23, 1963.

"take all the responsibilities arising out of signing the agreement."[136]

Rejection of Western military aid

The Somali government was now faced with the difficult choice between the two offers of military assistance laid on the table respectively by the West and the Soviet Union, the latter already signed though legally questionable, and the former not yet concluded.

Abdirashid and Daud were, *a priori*, known to favour Soviet military aid, mainly on grounds of its appealing size compared with that offered by the three Western powers, which was considered inadequate. The Western offer obviously fell short of the more ambitious Somali plan to organize at least a 20,000-strong national army. In October, a last-ditch meeting with the Western military attachés in Mogadisho aimed at getting a better deal proved inconclusive. The Prime Minister, the Minister of Defence and the Commander of the national army met the military attachés of Italy, the United States and the Federal Republic of Germany. In presenting their aid programme, the three Western countries seemed unwilling to increase the level of military aid, and warned the Somali government that their offer was not to be taken as complementary to the Russian offer, as the Somali government evidently wished to do.

On November 3, 1963, the Somali Prime Minister informed the Ambassadors of the United States, Italy and Germany that his government found itself compelled to reject their tripartite military aid programme. The reasons given for this were: (a) inadequate quality and quantity of the arms; (b) failure of the proposed package to cover Somali naval and air requirements; (c) failure of the proposed structure of military organization to satisfy Somali defensive requirements, and (d) the programme's lack of uniformity and likelihood to cause training difficulties. The Prime Minister added that in view of its expressed non-alignment policy, his government was unable to accept the further condition that all future arms supplies to Somalia should come from the West[137]. The Somali government stressed that acceptance of Soviet military aid did not imply any modification to its foreign policy of non-alignment[138]. Abdullahi Issa, the Minister of Foreign Affairs, declared that the Somali government had accepted Soviet military assistance in preference to Western aid for the simple reason that

136 Diary Aden Abdulla 7-8 November 1963.

137 TNA CO 822/3057, Developments in the Somali Republic October 1963, including information up to November 1963.

138 Ibid.

the Western powers concerned had attached conditions to their offers, namely that Somalia would not accept any military aid from the East. "This as any other condition was unacceptable to a sovereign country like Somalia", stressed the Minister.

After their offer was rejected, the USA, Italy and Germany each replied individually, stating the following points: (a) the programme had been rejected without any examination by the Somalis; and (b) the condition that the Somali government should not obtain aid from other sources was purely a practical one (given the impossibility of maintaining side by side two very different military systems) and not intended to impair the Somali policy of non-alignment.[139]

As there had been no disagreement that the President of the National Assembly had acted ultra vires (i.e. beyond his power), and as the government did in fact opt for the Soviet offer, the agreement with the Soviets had to be signed afresh by the President of the Republic and the matter was finally put to rest.

The reaction of the Western countries (particularly Germany, Italy and the US) to the new development was, as may be expected, one of bitter shock and consternation. The ambassadors of the three Western states in Mogadisho met separately with the Somali President to express their concern over the Somali-Soviet military agreement, which they considered exceeded the needs of the country. The US *Chargé d'Affaires* Mr Rogers relayed to the President his country's "embarrassment over the agreement Somalia entered onto with the Soviet Union for military assistance instead of taking the military assistance package offered by the West."[140] The American diplomat expressed his personal view, warning of the danger inherent in diverting huge financial resources to keeping such a vast military machinery as was being offered by the Soviet Union operational and regularly supplied with spare parts, to the detriment of the economic and social sectors. Having also referred to the alarm that Soviet military assistance to Somalia may raise in neighbouring countries, Rogers nonetheless ended his meeting with the Somali Head of State on a positive note: "whatever decision your government may wish to take, it will not affect the relations between our two countries, and the United States will continue its economic assistance to Somalia."[141]

It is worth mentioning that in 1962, the Americans threatened so suspend the delivery of 3 aircraft they had pledged to supply to Somalia if Somali pilots were

139 Ibid.

140 Diary Aden Abdulla, October 24, 1963.

141 Ibid.

sent to the Soviet Union for training. This had sparked a strong reaction from the Prime Minister, who made it clear that he would not accept any conditions imposed by foreign powers.[142]

The German Ambassador Herr Kopf, whose country was a major contributor in providing training and logistics to the Somali police force, met the President shortly before taking up his new post as ambassador in Jeddah, Saudi Arabia. Kopf did not conceal his worries on the impact that communist ideology might have on the young Somali officers being sent to Russia for military training, and on the danger that they may in the future act to undermine the Somali civilian government[143]. The Ambassador expressed his conviction that contact with Soviet military officers had developed in some Somali officers a Marxist perception on important issues that contrasted with the democratic outlook of most of the country's civilian leaders.

The Italian Prime Minister sent a message to his Somali counterpart in relation to the matter. A copy of the letter was given to the President by the Italian Ambassador in Somalia, Gastone Belcredi, who, as Aden Abdulla wrote, struck "the familiar old note of Western concern with the possible negative repercussions of the massive Soviet military assistance on relations with the neighbouring countries and on the Somali budget[144] [...] this is the result of years of hesitation by the West addressing the Somali request for military assistance, and they are now overreacting in the face of the new developments."[145]

It would however be wrong to believe that opposition and criticism over the military deal with the Soviets only came from the Western side; in fact, influential Somali personalities also voiced concern over the matter. One of these was the chief of police, General Mohamed Abshir, who having closely followed the negotiations from his vantage point expressed strong opposition to acceptance of Soviet military aid, recommending instead the Western package be taken. In Abscir's view, the country's scant financial resources would make it difficult to maintain and keep operational such military force under strong communist influence. Furthermore, the General believed that in the long run "the army may represent a threat of subversion to the democratic institutions of the Republic."[146] Abshir's words proved prophetic – except that what the army toppled when it

142 Ibid., August 21, 1962.
143 Ibid., November 21, 1963.
144 Ibid., November 25, 1963.
145 Ibid., October 24, 1963.
146 Ibid., October 23, 1963.

seized power in 1969 was not a structure of functioning democratic institutions, but a corrupt and unpopular administration. In other words, the military did little more than lay the ghost of an institution that was already dead.

On 22 January 1964, the first consignment, which included a dozen MIG 17 and a hundred between T34 and armored tanks plus some hundred Soviet military trainers, started pouring into Somalia.[147]

Ironically, the Soviet Union shifted massive military support from Somalia to Ethiopia and then played a key part in the military defeat of its former ally in the Ogaden conflict of 1977-'78. A Somali attack on Ethiopia in 1977 ended in disaster; an Ethiopian counter-offensive backed by Cuban troops wreaked havoc on the Somali army and led gradually to the collapse in 1991 of the last national Somali regime. On November 13, 1977, Mogadisho "boldly suspended by abrogation its 1974 Friendship Treaty with Moscow, terminating Soviet access to all naval support facilities, expelling Soviet advisors and severing diplomatic relations with Cuba."[148]

A few brief background notes on the Somali National Army are in order. The army was established on 6 April, 1960[149]. A small contingent police force known as 'Gruppo Mobile' or 'mobile group' was the first nucleus of the army. Prior to the creation of the Ministry of Defence in July 1960, the national army was temporarily put under the office of the Prime Minister.[150]

The idea of a national army had popular appeal for questions of prestige and of the perceived employment prospects that it offered. The first recruitment of 2,000 volunteers for the national army was spread across the six regions. It should be mentioned that in March 1958 a motion was presented to Parliament calling for the creation of an Armed Corps, as distinct from the police, and the introduction of universal military training. The motion was opposed by the Administrator on the grounds of the expenses involved, and referred back to the government for further study[151]. By Decree no. 20 of April 12, 1960, the Administrator appointed Lieutenant Colonel Daud Abdulla Hersi, former police officer, Commander in Chief of the army.[152]

147 Waldemar A. Nielson, The Great Powers and Africa, Pall Mall Press, London 1969, pp 213-214.

148 Richard Remnek, Soviet Policy in the Horn of Africa: The Decision to intervene, Centre for Naval Analysis, January 1980, p. 3.

149 Legge n°183, Bollettino Ufficiale, 12 Aprile 1960.

150 Art.3 of Decree no.15, April 6, 1960.

151 TNA FO 371/138306 Dispatch no. 15 1019 of April 10, 1959. from British Consulate, Mogadisho.

152 *Corriere della Somalia*, Maggio 2, 1960.

The 1963 municipal & 1964 political elections

The dissolution of Mogadisho Local Council

Under law no. 19 of 14 August, 1963, municipal elections were held for the third time throughout the Republic on November 26, 1963[153]. The law established four categories of local administration, based on the size and importance of a town, with the number of councillors to be elected ranging from eleven to twenty-five, elected for a four-year term.

As in earlier elections, the 1963 municipal elections were characterized by a spate of violence and general unrest in many parts of the country. All the instances of violence had one factor in common, namely illegality and election fraud being attributed mainly to the regional and district authorities but also to the managers of the polling stations.

In this charged atmosphere, election-related violence directed at the District Commissioner of Hargeisa and the Governor of Lower Juba was recorded[154]. Denunciations from the opposition parties over obstacles reportedly placed by the regional authorities on the free exercise of their political rights mounted, and eventually reached the attention of the President of the Republic.[155]

In every region of the country, violent clashes occurred between competing tribal groups. One such high-profile incident, and perhaps the most serious, was the attempted killing in December of the acting Governor of Mudug, Mohamed Ahmed Abdulla 'Sakhran', who escaped assassination in broad daylight in the centre of Galkayo. Following this incident, the Acting Governor imposed a three-month ban (from 19 January to 10 April 1964) on all political activities by the opposition parties, namely the SNC and SDU, in Galkayo. But while all the rigours of the law were applied to the SNC, the SDU only received a warning. The Minister of the Interior later intervened, instructing the Acting Governor to suspend the measures applied to the two parties, and was commended for this by President Aden Abdulla.[156]

Despite the questionable practices adopted by the local authorities to restrict the activities of the opposition parties, the ruling party was heavily defeated in

153 The first and second elections were organized in the former Trust Territory in 1954 and 1958 respectively.

154 Diary Aden Abdulla, November 30, 1963.

155 Meeting between Aden Abdulla, Egal, Haji Farah and Abdullahi Ahmed Weyd (SNC) with regard to difficulties the party encountered in Merca and Coriolei (reported in Diary Aden Abdulla, September 14, 1963).

156 Diary Aden Abdulla, December 25-26, 1963.

15 major urban centres, including Mogadisho, by the SNC. In Mogadisho, for instance, the ruling party obtained 16,283 votes against 21,773 for the SNC. On the basis of these results, the Lega dei Giovani Somali would get 8 councillors and the SNC 11, out of 25 councillors.

Kenadid Ahmed Yousuf (LGS) and Ahmed Mudde Hassan (SNC) ran for the much-coveted post of sindaco (mayor) of the capital. After a number of unsuccessful rounds of voting in which the two candidates failed to receive the required majority, Ahmed Mudde was elected on draw as sindaco of the city on January 2, 1964. Seemingly shocked by the opposition's success, the government tried to block the SNC mayorship of Mogadisho through questionable means. The law granted the Minister of the Interior power to dissolve the local council where it failed to "perform its functions or persistently [...] defaults in performing the duties imposed on it by law, or exceeds or abuses its powers." (Art. 44 of law n. 19 of August 14, 1963) Using these legal provisions as expedient, the government decided on January 2, 1964 to dissolve the Municipal Council of Mogadisho. On the same day, the Minister of the Interior issued a decree dissolving the Council on the grounds that it "had chosen as Mayor the person who had served in the same capacity during the previous administration in 1962, which was dissolved on the grounds of serious administrative irregularities without giving any assurances of being able to perform its functions."[157] Many doubted that the government's move was on solid legal ground. The President of the Republic, who was consulted on the issue prior to the dissolution of the City Council, warned against such a move, which he viewed as "inappropriate and imprudent", expressing his doubts that such a decree could be legally justifiable.[158]

The elected mayor and a number of councillors petitioned the Supreme Court for the annulment of the Minister's decree. The Court held that the "inability of the City Council should be evaluated a posteriori, whereas the grounds stated in the Decree were based on a priori judgment of how the Council would perform its functions in the future." Accordingly, the Supreme Court annulled the Minister's decree, and the same Minister reinstated the dissolved Local Council.[159]

In 1964, the third general elections were held in a far from conducive atmosphere. The ballot for the 123-member parliament was the first since the merger of the former two states of Somaliland and Somalia in July 1960. In a bid

157 Ministerial Decree no. 9 of January 2, 1964.

158 Diary Aden Abdulla, January 2, 1964.

159 Ahmed Mudde Hussein & others vs. The Minister of the Interior (Supreme Court Full Bench, Judgment of March 7, 1964).

to defuse the political tension generated by the ill-handled administrative elections of November 1963, a group of Darod and Hawiye leaders/parliamentarians affiliated to the ruling party promoted the initiative of a merger between the newly created SNC and the Lega. The sponsors of this initiative included Abdullahi Issa (Hawiye), Haji Mussa Bogor (Darod), Ahmed Mohamed 'Ottavio' (Hawiye), Haji Bashir Ismail (Darod), Osman Mohamed Afrah (Hawiye) and Yassin Nour Hassan (Darod). The tribal composition of the team was clear and well balanced. The plan was to merge the two parties before the general elections set for March 1964. As time was short, a proposal was made to the President of the Republic to put back the date of the elections, tentatively by one month, for the plan to be refined and finalized[160]. It was reported that the SNC, in principle, welcomed the plan, provided it was endorsed by the respective Central Committees of the two parties; the Lega leadership, however, appeared less keen on a full merger, preferring instead the option of discussing the matter after the elections.[161]

The 1964 elections are remembered in the country's history for the difficult security conditions in which they were held, with border skirmishes breaking out between Ethiopia and Somalia a few days before the polling day. The government's decision to go ahead with the election process despite the uncertain climate of the time was applauded by the public at large. Instead of suspending the operation, the government capitalized on the circumstances to galvanize the public to vote massively, under the famous slogan "the ballot in one hand and the gun in the other" attributed to Premier Abdirashid.

As had happened in the past, this election was seriously flawed by lack of reliable data on the number of eligible voters. An attempt to address this problem was made when a bill was introduced by a group of MPs requesting the government to carry out a census of the population in 1963 and one before the elections scheduled for 1964. While the first article of the bill was approved, the remaining two, regarding the time frame set for the census to be completed and the financial resources for the operation, did not attract enough support; consequently the bill did not pass.

Voters were allowed to express their preference in whichever electoral district they may be on the day of voting. The difficult task of determining whether a person was eligible to vote was left with the electoral officers. In the absence of an electoral certificate or any other identity documents, and again, in a bid to

160 Diary Aden Abdulla, January 15, 1964.
161 Ibid., January 25, 1964.

avoid a vote being cast more than once, each voter's left hand was marked with indelible ink upon entering the polling station.

As part of the process of unification of the different legislations existing in the two regions, the National Assembly approved a law by which the northern region extended the right to vote to all persons over 18 years of age, including women, by a vote of 52 in favour and 42 against. In the former Protectorate of Somaliland, under the 1958 law concerning the Legislative Council, women had no right to vote, and men could only vote if they were over 21. Another change introduced by the new electoral law involved the abolition of a clause stating that a candidate to the Legislative Council in Somaliland had to own property or capital[162]. To avoid the obvious political difficulty inherent in any revision, distribution of seats between the two territories was left unchanged, with 90 for the southern regions and 33 for the northern regions. Voters chose from a list rather than electing one candidate, and seats were allocated in proportion to the number of votes, using the ranking order in each party list.

Each list had to be accompanied by the signature of at least five hundred supporting voters and by a deposit of Sh.So5,000 (equivalent to US$ 700.00 at the time) as security. Where a list failed to obtain at least the votes necessary for the election of one deputy, one half of the deposit was forfeited to the State. (Article 11 (2) of the electoral law). The country was divided into 47 constituencies. Eighteen political parties competed in the 1964 general elections.

The difficult quest for free and fair elections

While the election law was being discussed in Parliament, a more urgent problem emerged which demanded prompt attention: how to ensure the correct application of the law and run fair and free elections, avoiding a repetition of the past illegal practices? The entire electoral process, as we have explained, was 'vulnerable' to fraud. Antiquated rules, some dating back to Trusteeship time, had left behind a deeply flawed system. Cheating had become so brazen that few Somalis expected fair elections, and there was widespread mistrust in the government's ability or willingness to ensure this. In fact, in the run-up to the March polls, the opposition parties, in particular the SDU, urged the President of the Republic to create a caretaker administration to oversee the elections.[163]

162 *Somali News*, May 31, 1963.

163 Meeting between Aden Abdulla and the SDU party executive, represented by Haji Mohamed Hussein and Yousuf Osman Samatar 'Berda-Ad' and others. January 7, 1964 (reported in Diary Aden Abdulla, January 7, 1964).

The President sent repeated messages to the government demanding 'assurances' that the poll would not be 'engineered'. He spoke very loudly of the need for free elections. "I received Abdirashid, the Prime Minister, together with the Minister of Grace and Justice, Ahmed Ghelle Hassan. In the presence of the latter, I urged the Prime Minister and his government to give solid assurances of regularity in the coming political elections or to step down, since I could not accept any repetition of the irregularities of the past political elections", he wrote in his diary of 6–7 January 1964.

This strong pronouncement, however, led to a conflict with the Prime Minister, who expressed his readiness to resign from office. "As usual, the Prime Minister said that he was ready to resign, but the message I was trying to pass on was the need to work together with the aim of averting electoral frauds, paying attention to my suggestions and not losing sight of the ballot boxes."[164] The repeated calls from the President for free and fair polls also raised concerns among some Lega members, who feared that these calls for justice may have adverse effects on the ruling party and, consequently, on their re-election to Parliament.

In his well-written diary, Aden Abdulla transcribed *verbatim* a heated exchange he had had with two prominent members of the governing party. "I received in my office Sheikh Mohamoud Mohamed 'Malingur' and Abdurahman Haji Moumin, both members of the Central Committee of the Lega, who had the impudence of accusing me for allegedly defending the party of Sheikh Ali Jim'ale and company, and consequently 'damaging' the Lega dei Giovani Somali". The conversation with the two deputies, particularly with Malingour, became very heated at times. "I invited the two gentlemen to read the provisions contained in Article 70 (3) of the Constitution, dealing with the oath of loyalty to the Head of the State, and warned them that if their intention was to deny the other parties their right for the convenience of the Lega, they were wasting their time with me as I would never let such a thing to occur. [...] There is nothing I desire more than the Lega winning and becoming strong, but not at the price they want." The President was rebuked for 'exceeding' his authority as president of a parliamentary regime.[165]

As the election date was drawing near, the President addressed the same strong message to an audience of provincial governors convened at the presidential mansion. Present at the meeting were Abdurahman Ahmed Ali (Hargeisa), Omar

164 Diary Aden Abdulla, January 7, 1964.
165 Ibid.

Mohamed Gouled (Lower Juba) Osman Omar Sheegoow (Hiran) and Ahmed Haji Aden Gouled (Majertenia). The governors of Burao and Upper Juba were not present. Abdulla exhorted the governors to try to ensure fairer, 'one man, one vote' elections in the areas under their respective administrative jurisdiction.[166]

One of the flaws of the electoral law of 1964 was the excessive power given to polling station chairmen, often blamed for rigging elections. To remedy this flaw, the President of the Republic suggested the deployment of police with the task to keep an eye on the ballot boxes throughout the process of vote casting up to the counting of votes. Electoral law prohibits security forces from entering polling stations unless asked to do so by the chairman (Art. 34 (2) of the electoral law).

Pursuing his efforts aimed at improving the electoral law, the President of the Republic addressed a letter to both the government and the presidency of the National Assembly, calling their attention to the need of redrafting some articles of the law in order to ensure its maximum improvement. He stressed a number of provisions, in particular the articles barring civil servants from eligibility to the National Assembly (which in his view meant exclusion for many qualified persons), the provisions governing electoral propaganda, and the casting and counting of votes.

As a result, the government accepted the proposal allowing civil servants to stand for election: those who failed would automatically go back to their previous jobs; those who won would choose whether to serve as a parliamentarian or a civil servant within 15 days from the date of election. Abdulla's suggestion to have police constantly monitor the ballot boxes was unfortunately not followed, and polling station chairmen retained the same powers by which many had abused the system and committed fraud in past elections. Once again vote rigging, bribing of polling station officers and intimidation of political opponents characterized the election process; however the 1964 general election, despite its shortcomings, saw a reduced level of vote rigging in comparison to the 1959 elections.

The first encouraging results came with the remarkable gains made by the opposition parties which secured together a total of 54 seats in the 123 seats of the National Assembly, a level of representation equal to nearly half of the seats of the Parliament and never reached before. Many had predicted that the opposition would have made gains at the election, but few had expected such levels of success.

166 Ibid., January 18, 1964.

Two men should be credited for the relatively smooth running of the 1964 political elections— one is President Aden Abdulla, who knew what sort of Somalia he wanted and publicly denounced the questionable policy of his former party, which had perfected the dark art of rigging; another was Mohamoud Abdinour 'Juje', the Minister of the Interior. Together they gave new hope to many Somalis embarrassed by the fact that their country had become a byword for swindling and electoral fraud. Indeed, presidential intervention alone was not enough to provide an absolute guarantee against election rigging as long as unscrupulous and corrupt civilian authorities and police officers remained part of the problem.

The President received strong support in his efforts from his long-time friend and future Prime Minister, Abdirazak Haji, who proposed selecting "well-qualified and honest staff from the capital as polling station chairmen, particularly those destined to operate in outlying districts."[167] Sadly, not everyone in the government or in the ruling party seemed to value Abdulla's cry for impartiality and justice in the election process, and some went as far as accusing him of harbouring anti-Lega sentiments and being biased in favour of the SNC. "My interventions in this sense have been interpreted simply as a move against the Lega and in favour of the SNC; this interpretation is in bad faith and does not remotely tally with my intentions," he wrote.[168]

Despite all the security measures taken by the government to ensure a smooth voting process, the elections were not incident-free. At Dusa Mareb (Mudug), which had been a flash-point for years, violence broke out where aggrieved clan elements attacked the town on March 28, just two days before the elections. In the ensuing armed confrontations between rival tribal groups and between clans and the security forces, 13 people were killed. In Iskushuban (Majertenia), another high-tension area, a local paramount chief was among a number of people killed in election-related troubles.

The elections and the Somali–Ethiopian boundary clashes

On attaining independence, the Somali Republic not only inherited the old Italo–Ethiopian border dispute, but enshrined in its Constitution the aspiration of bringing the Ogaden region into the Republic (Article 6 (4) of the 1960 Constitution). Relations between Ethiopia and Somalia have always been anything

167 Ibid., March 13, 1964.
168 Ibid., January 30, 1964.

but friendly. Following the Somali Republic's emergence as an independent State formed by the amalgamation between the independent State of Somaliland and the Trust Territory in July 1960, the Ethiopians strengthened their military presence in the disputed Haud and Reserved Area. In 1960 Ethiopia terminated grazing rights in the Ogaden, nullifying the Treaty of London that had permitted Somali herders to move freely in and out of the region. Relations between Somalia and Ethiopia quickly deteriorated. The termination of grazing rights was a blow not only to Somali pan-nationalism, but to the very livelihood of Somali herders.

Repeated border incidents, of which the most serious occurred at Danot, a watering centre in Haud (about 120 mile south of Burao) when Ethiopian authorities refused to allow a party of nomads from the Republic to draw water, led to tribal skirmishes in the area, which were suppressed by Ethiopian ground and air forces. In September, an Ethiopian spy ring was uncovered in the northern region of Somalia and was alleged to have been sent there to stir up trouble during the President's visit in the area[169]. Since the establishment of the Republic, both sides have, in practice, respected the existing frontiers – although the uneasy situation led to two undeclared wars and numerous skirmishes along the provisional border.

In mid-January 1964, few weeks before the general elections in Somalia, the Third Division of the Ethiopian Army, under the Command of Gen. Amman Andom, launched air and ground attacks against Somali territory at numerous points along the Somali–Ethiopian boundary, including a bombing raid on Hargeisa[170]. General Andom, an Eritrean, became Acting Head of State of Ethiopia following the coup that deposed Emperor Haile Selassie on September 12, 1974. He was later executed following disagreements with Colonel Menghistu, the Ethiopian strongman, in November 1974. "Initially, Somalia did well in their counterattacks against the Ethiopians, but advantage in number and especially in air power won the day for Addis Abeba", comments Marcus.[171]

According to well-informed sources, the Somali army was estimated then at only 4,000. The Ethiopian forces included about 10,000 men in the Imperial Guard, about 26,000 regular soldiers, and a number of irregulars in the Territorial Army, in addition to its small air force equipped with jet fighters and a relatively

169 Ibid., September 23, 1962.

170 Peter J. Schraeder, *From Irredentism to Secession. The Decline of Pan-Somali Nationalism*, University of California Press, p. 12.

171 Harold G. Marcus, *A History of Ethiopia*, updated edition, University of California Press 2002, p. 174.

modern mechanized unit[172]. The elections went ahead despite the tension with Ethiopia.

A ceasefire agreement between Somalia and Ethiopia was subsequently negotiated on March 31, 1964; this was however accomplished not through OAU but with the help of Lieutenant General Ibrahim Aboud, the Sudanese military ruler, who acted as intermediary between the two parties[173]. Meanwhile Kenya and Ethiopia concluded a mutual military pact in 1964 in response to what the two countries perceived as continued threat from Somalia. A similar arrangement was made between Britain and Kenya under the so-called Bamburi Agreement, an oral statement made by Mr Duncan Sanday in 1964 to the effect that the British would possibly come to the aid of Kenya if she were attacked by Somalia, further formalized in 1967 in a message from PM Harold Wilson to President Kenyatta.

The key point of the message read: "The Kenyan government may be sure that, if Kenya was the victim of outright aggression by Somalia, the British government would give the situation most urgent consideration. While, therefore, the British government cannot in advance give the Kenyan government any assurance of automatic assistance, the possibility of the British going to Kenya's assistance in the event of an organized and unprovoked attack by Somalia is not precluded."[174] From the wording of the statement, one can conclude, however, that this understanding is not comparable to the existing military pact between Ethiopia and Kenya.

Election results

A landmark Supreme Court ruling on election results

The country was divided into 47 constituencies, in 10 of which[175] no election was held as only the ruling party presented its lists of candidates. Twenty-one political parties competed in the elections, which took place throughout the country on March 30, 1964. When the votes were counted, the following results emerged:

172 A.A. Castagno, "The Somali-Kenyan Controversy, p. 187.

173 Touval, 'The Organization of African Unity and African Borders', International Organization, vol. 21, issue 01, December 1967, p. 11.

174 TNA FCO 31/1725 Harold Wilson's letter of September 6,1974 .

175 Aden Yaval, Bender Beila, Bosaso, Candala, Gardo, Eyl, Garowe, Dinsor, Iskushuban and Zeila.

PARTY	NO. OF SEATS
LEGA DEI GIOVANI SOMALI	69
SOMALI NATIONAL CONGRESS	22
SOMALI DEMOCRATIC UNION	15
PARTITO COSTITUZIONALE INDIPENDENZA SOMALA	9
OTHER PARTIES	8

In some main cities, where a relatively free and fair voting had taken place, support for the ruling party hit rock bottom and the party lost seats to the opposition. In Mogadisho, the governing party was humiliated, coming an ignominious fourth behind the SNC, SDU and the SANU-HIZBIA coalition, its worst ever result in the capital.

Also in the capital, the party lost the two parliamentary seats and the mayorship. Similarly, in important centres like Hargeisa, Beledweyne and Merca, the Lega fared badly. By 1966 however, the Lega's parliamentary group jumped from 69 to 78, followed by another wave of deputies defecting from their party to join the Lega, to the point that, by July 1967, the governing party counted 105 members in the National Assembly.[176]

The newly elected third legislature convened its first section on May 26, 1964; the first item on the agenda was the election of the speaker of the parliament and his deputies. The first part of the proceedings was presided over by the oldest member, 58 year-old Mohamed Ossoble Adde. By 82 votes against 38 received by Ali Garad Jama, the outgoing Minister of Agriculture, Ahmed Sheikh Mohamed Absie was elected President of the National Assembly. In the same day, Haji Bashir Ismail (78 votes), Sheikh Mukhtar Mohamed Hussein (75 votes) and Ahmed Qumane (68 votes) were elected Vice-presidents.[177]

Responding to Somali tribal logic, after the elections the top three State bodies were divided among the major clans. The Issak retained presidency of the National Assembly: Ahmed Sheikh Mohamed Absie, like his predecessor, was Issak. The premiership went again to the Darod: Abdirazak Haji was a Darod like his predecessor. The Hawiye were represented by the incumbent Head of State. The big losers were the Rahanweyn, a major tribe in southern Somalia.

Petitions were lodged to the Supreme Court against the election results,

176 Tripodi, op. cit., p. 109.

177 *Somali News*, May 26, 1964.

coming from a number of electoral districts: Adale, Aden Yaval, Erigavo, Las Anod, Hargeisa, Alula, Balad, Beledweyne, Merca, Berbera, Bosaso, Garadag, Kandala, Kismayo, Dusa Mareb, Odweyne, Iskushuban and Wanleweyn.

The Supreme Court rejected all these petitions as unacceptable, except the one from Merca. In the case of this district, because of irregularities in one of the polling stations, the chairman of the district electoral office annulled the elections held in the whole district and called for new polls[178]. This was challenged by the interested parties and appealed in the Supreme Court with the argument that under the Election Law the chairman of the district central electoral office had no authority to set aside elections for the district. The Court held that the chairman of the central electoral office had no other power except to correct the results of the counting by subtracting the 300 invalid votes assigned to the SYL. On this ground the Court annulled the chairman's decision and directed him to allot one seat to the SDU and one seat to the SNC[179]. The order was carried out within two days from publication of the judgment, and Haji Mohamed Hussein (SDU) and Haji Farah Ali (SNC) took their seats in the National Assembly[180]. The Lega candidate lost the case to the opposition parties.

This was an important judicial case involving a decision of the Supreme Court of Somalia resulting in seating in the National Assembly. However, no clear explanation was given as to why only the Merca case had received judicial review to the exclusion of other cases where the election results had been contested. The defeated Lega candidate was Abdullahi 'Insania', a leading figure in the political movements advocating the return of Italy to Somalia as an administering power, while both Haji Mohamed and Haji Farah were among the five-member group who met the Four Power Commission of Investigations in 1948, representing the Lega. The 1964 elections brought about a change of government: Abdirashid, who had been in office since July 1960, was not reconfirmed as Prime Minister, and submitted the resignation of his government on May 26, 1964. A long and uneasy 'cohabitation' between the President and his Prime Minister had thus come to an end. That the President's confidence in his Prime Minister had reached its lowest ebb is confirmed by the long and detailed diary entry for October 1, 1963, in which Abdulla writes of his intention to replace the Prime Minister at the next opportune occasion: "The reasoning of this man on matters of freedom, his

178 Haji N.A. Noor Muhammad, 'Judicial review of Administrative Action in the Somali Republic, Journal of African Law, vol. 10, no. 1 (Spring. 1966), p. 1.

179 For a more detailed analysis, see the Supreme Court ruling published in Somali News, July 10, 1964.

180 Supreme Court judgment, dated July 9th 1964 and delivered by Dr. Giuseppe Papale, Acting President.

attitude, particularly towards the SNC, irritates me. I made all efforts to convince him that I have no interest to protect anyone or any organizations in particular, and that my interest is to see that the rights enshrined in the Constitution are respected. However, I have the impression that he doesn't want to understand. He harbours the idea that I am a gullible man who takes for granted all claims coming from the opposition. Abdirashid is a hopeless reactionary, and so, for me, as a Prime Minister he's dead in the water. I am sorry for him. It is too late to replace him with another person at this stage. I pray that God Almighty give me the fortitude to be patient with him up to the election in March."[181] The notion that Abdirashid was still 'the man best suited to the position', held by the President in 1961, was now untenable for him.[182]

Abdirashid's years of government had not been great in terms of achievements. A number of factors seem to have haunted him, hindering efforts to deliver great service: the continued bickering within his own ruling party, keeping him often under attack; the severe floods and famine which hit the country in 1961 with devastating effects on agriculture and livestock; his excessive attention to building up a strong, but expensive national army. His critics grumbled that his policies amounted to giving priority to military expenditure to the detriment of the social sector which was suffering from chronic neglect; the issue of the missing territories led to growing tension with the neighbouring countries as well as with major Western donors; his administration had not proved capable of introducing democratic and economic reforms; the northern regions remained unstable, as evidenced by rejection of the referendum on the Constitution which generated the aborted coup of 1961; his administration also failed to tackle the scourge of corruption. All these factors had left the economy in ruins and the country at the mercy of foreign aid.

181 Diary Aden Abdulla, October 1, 1963.

182 *Somali News*, July 14, 1961.

Chapter XI

REZAK REPLACES RASHID

"Rizaq miyaa Rashid ka roon, inta kale ma rootiyaa?"

Translation

"Is Rizak better than Rashid, are the rest worthless?"

In line with the legacy of the Italian Administration, after each general election the Head of the State embarks on an intensive process of consultations aimed at gauging the mood and the orientation prevailing among the political forces in the country, before the designation of the future Prime Minister.

Immediately after the election results were released, messages were sent to the President by single individuals, suggesting the reconfirmation of Abdirashid, considered a *'salvatore della patria'* or saviour of the country[1]. It was an open secret that the President had long been seriously considering the designation of Abdirazak as alternative to Abdirashid. He was waiting for the right time for a change of premier, and the right time came with the general elections of March. However, Aden Abdulla also knew the weak spot of the future Prime Minister. In his diary for April 17, he wrote: "I have always admired and liked Abdirazak Haji Hussein, even if I know he is resentful and vengeful towards those he thinks are his enemies, a serious flaw, unbecoming for a Prime Minister. Notwithstanding this, I have always held the conviction that he is *'un'àncora di salvezza per la Somalia'*, a life-saving last hope for Somalia."[2]

In 1963, after venting his disappointment with Abdirashid's performance,

1 Diary Aden Abdulla, April 8, 1964.

2 Ibid., April 17, 1964.

Abdulla wrote in his diary for 12 November: "This chap (Abdirazak) has the makings of a statesman; I need to nominate him Prime Minister at the next occasion. He is full of energy and he is honest. His weak point is the obstinacy and the tendency to demonize his political adversaries. But, to make up for that, he is honest and can be a good friend. [...] If Abdirazak made efforts to gain the confidence of his adversaries instead of treating them harshly, I do believe that he would be a good Prime Minister."[3] Abdirazak rarely missed a chance to rub his opponents' noses in the dirt, often using crude rhetoric. On account of his alleged harsh manners, during his time as Minister of the Interior he came under repeated criticism from both Hawiye and Issak MPs, who sought his removal from office. On one occasion, for instance, a group of 10 Hawiye deputies met Aden Abdulla at the Presidential Palace to voice their dissatisfaction with Abdirashid's government: at the end of the meeting, it turned out that the main complaints were directed at the Minister of the Interior.

When he first learned during the informal consultations that he might be asked to form a new government, "Abdirazak seemed worried about my intention to designate him as Prime Minister. Probably, he thinks he could not exclude Abdirashid and Abdullahi Issa from the government, because he fears that being excluded they might turn out to be an obstacle to his policies for cleaning up the situation they have created. He suggested other candidates, Kenadid Ahmed Yousuf for instance, and agrees that there is no case for re-enlisting Abdirashid."[4]

All of a sudden, however, the political process had been overshadowed by unconfirmed voices about an alleged military coup planned "in the event Abdirashid was not reconfirmed", a prospect which, had it materialized, would have undermined the democratic republican institutions built up during the past decade.

It should be noted that in the early Sixties few Somalis seemed to be worried about the scourge of a military coup as experienced in a number of African countries of recent independence. The top Somali military officers, formed and educated on loyalty to the constitutional order in line with Italian military tradition, did not seem intentioned to interfere in political matters which they considered the exclusive domain of the civilian establishment.

Speculations of an imminent military coup were categorically ruled out by the Commander of the national army, Gen. Daud Abdulla. "The Army and I owe

3 Ibid., November 12, 1963.
4 Ibid., April 25, 1964.

allegiance to the Republic and its President." This solemn statement, made by Gen. Daud in a meeting with Aden Abdulla at the Presidential Palace on May 30, 1964, was aimed at dispelling any doubts that the army might be harbouring ambitions to interfere with the constitutional prerogative of the head of State to designate a Prime Minister of his choice, whether Abdirazak or Abdirashid. However, General Daud is reported to have stated before taking leave: "Mr President, the devil you know is better than the one you don't" – a thinly veiled suggestion to re-designate Abdirashid as Prime Minister.[5]

Understandably, the process of informal consultation was long and drawn out. The first to be seen were the former Prime Ministers Abdullahi Issa and Mohamed Haji Ibrahim Egal, and the outgoing Premier, Abdirashid. While Issa fell short of giving any indication with regard to the future Prime Minister, Egal, although not explicitly indicating anyone, made it clear that between Razak and Rashid he would prefer the latter[6]. Abdirashid also refrained from expressing any preference, but requested the President not consider him as candidate. "I would be grateful to you for ever if you would drop my name from the list of prospective PM candidates", he is reported to have said.[7]

It was then the turn of the President of the National Assembly and his three Vice-presidents. While Ahmed Mohamed Absie and Ahmed Qumane made no suggestions, Haji Bashir and Sheikh Muktar endorsed the candidature of the outgoing Prime Minister. Sheikh Mukhtar, although he recognized Abdirashid's weaknesses, remained convinced that there was no better candidate and that Abdirazak should be excluded *a priori*. "I know Abdirazak very well as an extremely vengeful person and this is why Abdirashid is preferable", he is reported as saying.[8]

The Central Committee of the ruling party and its parliamentary group also endorsed Abdirashid's candidacy. This decision was formally handed to the President on June 3, 1964 by a group of Central Committee members led by Yassin Nour Hassan and including Mohamed Sheikh Gabio, Mohamed Ibrahim 'Wanle', Ali 'Sciopero' and Abdi Hassan Boni. However, as Aden Abdulla reveals, "the group tried to 'addolcire la pillola amara' (sweeten the bitter pill) by stating that the party was well aware of the President's prerogative to designate as Prime Minister the person he thinks appropriate for the job and, therefore, the decision

5 Ibid., May 30, 1964.
6 Ibid., May 31, 1964.
7 Ibid.
8 Ibid., June 1, 1964.

of the party was a mere proposal."[9]

The opposition parties SNC, SDU and HDMS, expressed no particular preference for any candidate[10]. Proposals for the reconfirmation of Abdirashid "for a temporary period of even three months" in order to safeguard the unity of the ruling party came from a well-known group of wise men[11] but were rejected outright by the President because considered impracticable.

Il dado è tratto (The die is cast)

Who is the 'imposed' Prime Minister?

The long awaited news came on Monday 7 June, 1964, when the President made official his decision to designate Abdirazak Haji as Prime Minister. However, this defiant decision did not please the Central Committee of the ruling party and the majority of its parliamentary group:

"I received Abdirazak at 10am to designate him to form a government. He accepted the designation with 'reservation' [...] The new Prime Minister accepted the designation with caution, fearing that he might not be supported by Parliament; but more than this, and even though, when friendship and politics get in conflict, the former has no chance at all, he was tormented by the idea of splitting from his erstwhile friend, Abdirashid," comments the President.[12]

One anonymous Somali, certainly from Mogadisho, who had obviously been expecting a different outcome, expressed his surprise with the famous remark: "*Rizaq miyaa Rashid ka roon, inta kale ma rootiyaa?*" which roughly translates: Is Razak better than Rashid, are the rest worthless?

Abdirashid and Abdirazak had as a common denominator their origins in the Majerten clan-family and a long militancy in the ranks of the ruling party. Yet in all other aspects they could not have been more different: while Abdirashid was one of the few Somali MPs with a university education and long experience in administration, Abdirazak, although he enjoyed a formidable reputation as an orator, was a self-made man without formal education who had served as a radio and telegraph operator in the British Gendarmerie. One of Abdirashid's qualities was his ability to compromise, which had served him well in dealing with an often fractious Parliament; by contrast, the designated Premier was widely

9 Ibid., June 3, 1964.
10 Ibid., 3-4 June 1964.
11 Haji Dirie, Sherif Mohamoud Abdurahman, Haji Osman 'Illivi' and Omar Abdalla Banafunzi.
12 Diary Aden Abdulla, June 7, 1964.

seen as a confrontational man who treated friends and foes alike in a rather abrasive manner. Abdirashid was also known for his close ties with influential religious sects based in the capital, which further enhanced his stature as a political campaigner. In addition to this, the two political giants disliked each other thoroughly, as well as disagreeing about policy, and that made their battle in the National Assembly all the more spectacular.[13]

Predictably, the designation of Abdirazak split the ruling party in two, with a new rebellious faction loyal to Rashid emerging. The President, though well aware of the designated Prime Minister's unpopularity, chose to exercise his prerogatives under article 78 (3) of the Constitution and to go ahead with his decision. Much of the turmoil within the ruling party stemmed from the power struggle between the Prime Minister and his erstwhile confidant and long-time political ally. The once cozy personal relationship between the two political giants began to turn sour. In a real functioning democracy, the designation of a candidate from the same ruling party as the Prime Minister should be seen as a routine succession rather than a move likely to split the party.

It is significant to remember that this was not the first time the President had designated a Prime Minister of his choice without the endorsement of the Central Committee of the ruling party: in 1960, immediately after independence, and again later in 1961, he designated Abdirashid Ali instead of Abdullahi Issa, who had been proposed by the Central Committee with the support of more than half of the Parliament[14]. But while the 1961 designation of Abdirashid had raised only minor difficulties, that of Abdirazak in 1964 had sent a wave of strong opposition through Parliament, rippling through the ruling party and the public at large. This fact haunted Razak throughout his troubled tenure as Prime Minister until he was voted out of office in 1967. The question of who the man chosen as Premier actually was, and why he was contested by the Issak, the Hawiye and even by a wider section of his own Darod clan family calls for an answer.

A rough sketch of the Prime Minister gives the picture of a man hailing from a nomadic family from Mudug, who, like many of his generation, had had no opportunity to receive a formal education. He served as a NCO for the British Military Administration in the 40s, during which time he joined the Lega dei Giovani Somali, becoming leader of the party in 1956. He began his

13 By virtue of his association with the National Assembly, the author was able to witness, on a number of occasions, some heated exchanges between the two in the National Assembly Hall.

14 Diary Aden Abdulla, May 1, 1964.

parliamentary career in 1959, elected on the Lega ticket from the Eyl district, and in 1964 from Garowe (both districts are in the Majertenia province). In the troubled 1969 general elections, he moved to Galkayo district, the centre of his clan family, where he won by a slender margin the election he had entered as an opposition candidate.

Abdirazak was a maverick politician: his non-conformist attitude was on display when, asked about his views on the main permanent legacy of the Italian administration in Somalia after ten years of Trusteeship regime, he retorted caustically: "Espresso and macchiato."[15] Unlike other members of his party, he was deeply suspicious of the aid Italy would give Somalia after 1960. "Personally," he said "I would prefer this aid be channelled to Somalia through the UN [...] the same should go for any aid coming from other countries, in order to avert any hidden agenda designed to place influence on our country which I fear, but will be inevitable."[16]

Abdirazak, at the time Head of the Somali University Institute and soon to become Minister of the Interior, was obviously out of tune with many of his party fellows who, on the eve of independence, were releasing favourable comments on AFIS's record in Somalia. For instance, Aden Abdulla, President of the National Assembly and future Head of State, had this to say: "We must sincerely admit that Italy has done its duty. [...] At the beginning there was a period characterized by mutual mistrust and even by fighting; however, in the last six years, a sincere collaboration has come into being between us and the Italian administration."[17]

Abdullahi Issa's words were even kinder to Italy: "The Somali government must recognize that the efforts made by Italy and the considerable sacrifices endured by the Italian people in favour of Somalia are worthy of the highest recognition."[18] Abdirashid Ali Sharmarke, future Prime Minister and President of the Republic, also commended the work done by Italy in Somalia during the trusteeship regime, expressing his appreciation during the debate in the National Assembly on August 17, 1959 on the motion he had submitted for an early independence.[19]

However, after becoming Prime Minister, Abdirazak, interviewed by the same

15 Interview with Angelo Del Boca, at Mogadisho, on 27 June 1960 (Del Boca, op. cit., p. 288).

16 Ibid.

17 Interview released by Aden Abdulla to Angelo del Boca on June 25, 1960, (Del Boca, op. cit., p. 287).

18 Interview released by Abdullahi Issa to Angelo del Boca on June 26, 1960, (ibid.).

19 Costanzo, op. cit., p. 48.

journalist who met him in Mogadisho on June 27, 1960, described the Italian work in Somalia as "meritorious and praiseworthy", adding that "Somali frontiers are open for all Italians ready to collaborate with us, not only in the economic field but in all others."[20]

A second question calls for an answer: why was this man chosen in the first place, and why did the political class of the time oppose him? He was chosen because of his personality and his way of administering State affairs in a style distinguishing him from his predecessors, often accused of condoning, or at least not being tough enough on, corruption and top-level widespread maladministration since 1956. The Somali political class was known to be corrupt and inefficient, inclined only to keep the status quo and resistant to any reforms and innovations which they feared might undermine their positions. In a country of unabashed kleptocrats, the designated Prime Minister shone like a beacon of probity. His opponents saw him as a threat to their dubious business interests; and feared that he might undermine their illegal economic interests, in the same way as the mafia fears the interference of the police and the judiciary. He was chosen by the President, against all odds, because of his reform policy and also for making the anti-corruption drive the centrepiece of his term of office. In fact, his first order of the day was to request the members of his government to sign an undertaking not to engage in any professional, commercial, industrial or financial activities during the period of office[21]. A few optimists, however, did believe that the new administration could seriously challenge a political culture that had dominated Somalia since the installation of the trusteeship system 14 years back.

The Parliament rejects Abdirazak

After lengthy and difficult negotiations with politicians and tribal leaders, Abdirazak finally formed his first government consisting of 13 ministers, all nominally affiliated to the majority party but in practice representing their respective clan families who had endorsed them in the elections. The members of the government were sworn in on June 15, 1964, except for Abdullahi Issa, who seemed reluctant to take up his new post as Minister of Health, Veterinary and Labour, which he considered inadequate to his political stature[22]. Issa later

20 Del Boca, op. cit., pp. 370-371.
21 Art. 80 (2) of 1960 Constitution.
22 Diary Aden Abdulla, June 15, 1964.

accepted his new responsibility and was sworn in on June 18, 1964.[23]

The Cabinet included a number of deputies who defected from their original political parties to join the governing party. These were Aden Issak, Sheikh Hassan Abdullahi and Ismail Dualeh Warsama (SNC); Mohamoud Issa Jama (MNS), and Yousuf Aden Bowkah (USP). Like his predecessors, Abdirazak faced a delicate task in assembling a cross-tribal team of ministers that could win a confidence vote in Parliament. However, in the distribution of ministerial posts the Prime Minister departed from the usual practice of strict tribal balancing, giving the northerners important portfolios such as Foreign Affairs, Finance, Defence and Agriculture, on the grounds that they had presented more professionally qualified representatives than the southerners had. However, as we will explain, this spirit of innovation would soon die down.

Among the clans discontented by not being represented in the government were the Abgal, a major clan with two ministers in the outgoing Abdirashid administration[24], and the Hawadle, who had failed to win representation for the first time since 1956. Of the outgoing cabinet ministers, only Abdulkadir 'Zoppo' and Abdullahi Issa were retained, respectively as Minister of the Interior and Minister of Health & Labour. The former Minister of the Interior, Mohamoud 'Juje', was excluded from the government, reportedly vetoed by Abdulkadir 'Zoppo', the influential Minister of the Interior and his arch-rival politician from Upper Juba, who in the same way had excluded 'Juje' from Abdirashid's first government (1960-1962). The Head of State attempted to persuade the Prime Minister to include Mohamoud 'Juje' in the government, but this clashed with 'Zoppo''s agenda, and the new Prime Minister felt that 'Zoppo' was needed in the government, as his influence on the strong Upper Juba parliamentarian group was thought instrumental for the purpose of gaining a vote of confidence.[25]

Against this background, complicated by a serious rift within the Lega parliamentary group, the first Abdirazak government was humiliated in Parliament on July 14, 1964 by a vote of no confidence, with 59 negative vote and 57 in favour. Out of the 116 voting MPs, five did not vote (Abdirashid Ali and Sheikh Hassan Abdullahi of the LGS; Haji Farah Ali and Abdullahi Gire of the SNC; and Mustaffa Sceikh of the SDU), and two were on official mission abroad (Ali Omar Sheegoow to Bruxelles and Ahmed Yousuf Dualeh to Cairo).

The vote cut heavily across party lines. While 48 Lega MPs voted in favour

23 Ibid., June 18, 196.

24 Ali Mohamed Hirave 'Hagarrei' and Mohamoud Ahmed Mohamed 'Kutuba-hor'.

25 Diary Aden Abdulla, June 13-14, 1964.

of the government, 33 members of the same party voted against, including the secretary general, Yassin Nour. Four Lega deputies were absent. The major opposition party, the SNC, cast 18 votes against the government, but some of its members voted in favour and two were absent. Eight SDU deputies voted 'no', two voted 'yes' and one was absent. The 6 members of the other parties (HDMS and Partito Repubblicano Somalo or PRS) all supported the government.[26]

Article 82 of the 1960 Constitution provides that upon a vote of no confidence by the Assembly, all members of the government shall resign. Accordingly the government did resign, but the Prime Minister was requested to continue to preside over a caretaker government. For the first time, a Somali parliament that people had thought would be the government's lapdog showed real bite and denied confidence. A 34-strong dissident faction within the ruling party joined hands in a coalition with the opposition parties represented by SNC and SDU to defeat the government. However, this rejection stemmed more from enmity against the Prime Minister and spite for the President of the Republic than from any considerations as to the substance of the government's programme.

The Central Committee of the ruling party decided to take disciplinary measures involving expulsion from the party of four of its members for breach of party line. They were Yassin Nour Hassan, Secretary General of the party, Sheikh Muktar Mohamed, Abdullahi Mohamed Qablan, member of the Central Committee and Chief Whip of the Lega parliamentary group, and Abdi Hassan Boni. Following the expulsion of Yassin Nour, Mohamed Sheikh Gabio had been elected as a 'stop-gap' secretary of the party[27]. This new development is strongly reminiscent of a similar situation in 1959, when after the general elections the Prime Minister, together with a group of 13 other dissidents, mounted a vigorous campaign against the government led by Abdullahi Issa. The rejection of the government not only caused a domestic political crisis, but also overshadowed the First Ordinary Session of the African States Conference in Cairo. Without a proper government in place, the President of the Republic felt it was inappropriate to attend an international conference, and consequently cancelled his attendance as Head of the Somali delegation. On the President's behalf, the Minister of Foreign Affairs read the following message to the Chairman of the Summit: "Mr President, I have asked Ahmed Yousuf Dualeh, my special representative to the First Ordinary Session of the Head of States and

26 *Somali News*, July 17, 1964.
27 Ibid., July 31, 1964.

Governments, to convey to Your Excellency my very deep regret that neither my Prime Minister not I are able to personally attend the First Ordinary Session of Head of State and Government of the OAU. We are precluded from attending in virtue of the recent constitutional developments in our country which have necessitated the formation of a new government."[28]

The difficult negotiations

Following the denial of confidence to the government, the President of the Republic had started afresh on the long and drawn-out process of informal consultations across the political spectrum. The Head of the State met a number of cross-party politicians, starting with Mohamed Haji Ibrahim Egal, Abdullahi Issa and Abdirashid Ali, three former Prime Ministers.

For Mohamed Ibrahim Egal, the only option left open for the President was to designate a Prime Minister drawn from the opposition to form a coalition government, "since the Lega has postponed without good reason their scheduled party congress meant to find a solution to the crisis."[29] In contrast, Abdullahi Issa thought a reconciliation process within the ruling party was needed before proceeding with the designation of a Prime Minister: an idea welcomed by the President, who encouraged Issa "to link up with the President of the National Assembly to that effect, while Abdirashid refrained from giving any indications as to who might be designated as Prime Minister."[30]

Although the governing party was still divided between supporters and detractors of Abdirazak, the general orientation emerging from the consultations seemed to indicate that support to Abdirashid was dwindling. A number of lawmakers affiliated to the dissident faction of the Lega (including Haji Yousuf Egal, Osman Ahmed Roble, Jama Nour Ali, Hassan Aden Haji, Ahmed Mohamed Ali 'Allora', Sheikh Mohamed Yousuf, Haji Hassano Mohamed Nour, Abdi Hassan Boni, Abdullahi 'Qablan' and Haji Mussa Bogor) proposed, as a way to solve the crisis and reconcile party members, to drop both Rashid and Razak in favour of a third candidate[31], while a delegation from the Central Committee of the Lega led by Gabio, the new *pro tempore* Secretary General, did not seem to be clearly rejecting the idea of designating Abdirazak. The President was asked to hold back on his decision for a few more days in order to give a chance to these

28 Ibid., July 24, 1964.
29 Diary Aden Abdulla, July 19, 1964.
30 Ibid.
31 Ibid., July 21, 1964.

efforts to cool down tensions within the party[32]. This was a sharp shift from just a month earlier, when the Central Committee of the party had shunned Abdirazak in favour of Abdirashid. Some MPs held that it was legally or morally not correct to advance the candidature of someone who had been rejected by the Parliament[33]. The President, however, seemed unconvinced by these arguments, and continued to believe that the candidate he had chosen was the best MP available. "I see no reason why I should drop Abdirazak," he comments, "and I cannot find among the deputies anyone who has the qualities of the designated Prime Minister."[34]

Opposition parties assumed different positions on the candidate for Prime Minister. The SDU, led by Omar Abdurahman, expressed no preference for any particular candidate, for they were much more interested in the programme of the executive than the person heading it[35]. The HDMS, led by Haji Muqtar and Sheikh Mohamed Omar, both members of Parliament, expressed preference for Abdirazak's candidature[36]. The SNC, the second largest group in the Parliament, led by Sheikh Ali Giumale, advanced a list of 13 names as potential Prime Ministers, among them lawmakers as well as technocrats. The lawmakers included Abdulkadir Mohamed 'Zoppo', Mohamoud Issa Jama and Abdullahi Issa (SYL), Haji Bashir Ismail, Aden Shire Jama, Mohamed Sheikh Hassan and Yassin Nour Hassan (SYL dissidents), Mohamed Haji Ibrahim Egal, Ismail Dualeh Warsame, Mohamed Hassan Nour 'Giasti', Ali Mohamed Ossoble 'Wardhiigley' and Haji Abdurahman Sheikh Hassan (SNC). Among the technocrats were civil servants like Hussein Nour Elmi and Mohamed Awale Liban.

The Central Committee worked in tandem with the party's parliamentary group in exploring ways and means of reconciling party members: this eventually resulted in the revocation of the disciplinary measures taken against the four members in July. A brief announcement published in the government daily *Corriere della Somalia* carried a headline reading *The Central Committee has pardoned the members expelled from the party*[37]. This was a Somali-style (*alla somala*) solution.

At the end of the consultations, on Thursday 6 August, the President again designated Abdirazak asking him to form a new government: "Two things

32 Ibid., July 22, 1964.

33 Aden Abdulla's discussions with Abdullahi Ossoble Siad, reflected in Diary Aden Abdulla, July 18-19, 1964, and with Mohamed Ali Da'ar on the following day.

34 Diary Aden Abdulla, July 19, 1964.

35 Ibid., July 22-23, 1964.

36 Ibid.

37 *Corriere della Somalia*, Agosto 5, 1964.

appeared to be tormenting the Prime Minister: firstly, whether or not to include Mohamoud 'Juje' in the Cabinet as a reward for the latter's breaking away from the dissident faction and, secondly, his intention to lure away Ismail Dualeh Warsame from his party, the SNC, in exchange for a cabinet post, and to cause other kinsmen of his, the Habar Je'lo, to do the same."[38]

Understandably, the new Prime Minister was fully conscious of the uphill struggle he was facing and of the task he was expected to perform. The humiliating defeat he had suffered in Parliament, an experience he was not ready to repeat, appeared to have disheartened him. "The confusion of the last months seems to have shaken him; he looks almost disoriented"[39], notes Aden Abdulla. The designated premier soon embarked on long and uneasy negotiations with his opponents within the ruling party, who showed no sign of relenting in their hostility to him.

The Central Committee and the dissident parliamentary group of the Lega seemed incapable of reaching consensus on the formation of the government. At a certain point, out of frustration with this, the Prime Minister aired the idea of forming a coalition government with non-Lega political parties[40]. Twenty days later, on August 26, 1964, after negotiations with various tribal leaders-cum- MPs, the designated Prime Minister "*ha sciolto la riserva*", or dropped the reservation with which he had accepted the responsibility to form a new government.[41]

Formation of Abdirazak's second government

On August 31, 1964, 24 days after his designation, the Prime Minister presented to the Head of State a list containing 3 more members than the previous one and consisting of 15 ministers and 7 undersecretaries, all drawn from the ruling party. They were sworn in at Villa Somalia before the Head of State[42]. Almost all ministers kept their previous portfolio, except for Mohamoud Issa Jama, former Minister of Agriculture, who was replaced by Ismail Dualeh Warsame. Joining the cabinet for the first time were Mohamoud Abdinour 'Juje' and Abdurahman Haji Moumin, as Minister without Portfolio in the Prime Minister's Office and Minister of Justice respectively[43]. Ali Omar Sheegoow, former Minister of

38 Diary Aden Abdulla, August 6, 1964.

39 Ibid., August 7, 1964.

40 Telephone conversation between the Prime Minister and the President, reported in Diary Aden Abdulla, August 15, 1964.

41 Diary Aden Abdulla, August 26, 1964.

42 Ibid., August 31, 1964.

43 Mohamoud 'Juje' was later (in February 1965) appointed Minister of Communications and Transport.

Justice in the first Abdirazak government, became Minister without Portfolio for Planning. With Abdurahman Haji Moumin's inclusion in the government, Hawiye expectations were partially met, while the Abgal and the Hawadle continued to feel underrepresented. They were given one undersecretary each: Ahmed Ghelle Hassan (Hawadle and former Minister of Justice in the Abdirashid government) and Islao Osman Nur Amir (Abgal).

The inclusion of Mohamoud 'Juje' in the government came as a recognition for the key role he had played in the solution of the crisis and for his breaking away from the ranks of the anti-Abdirazak faction within the ruling party. Mohamoud 'Juje' and Abdullahi Issa were from the old guard of pre-independence administrations, but they were both relegated to less appealing positions. Actually, until the last minute, the Prime Minister had been inclined to drop Issa and replace him with Haji Farah Ali, his kinsman. "I insisted, without however putting undue pressure on him, that he should think hard before dropping Abdullahi Issa and, if it was necessary to do so, he should have a clear conversation with him in the presence of Haji Farah and 'Ottavio', Abdullahi's kinsmen."[44] The Prime Minister describes Abdullahi Issa as "an eternal rival to every head of government, with the tendency to undermine every government even if he is a member of it."[45]

Finally, after the prolonged crisis which had started in April, by a majority of 91 to 23 with one abstention, the Lega-dominated Parliament approved the government's programme late in the night of September 28. No explanation seems possible as to what arguments might have changed the Central Committee's anti-Abdirazak stance. However, anti-Abdirazak forces did not relent, remaining ever ready to exploit any mistake or blunder on the government's part.

Upon taking office, the Prime Minister had promised that, unlike his predecessors, he would run an exemplary government with 'clean' ministers, making the anti-corruption drive the centrepiece of his term of office. However, in less than two years since its inauguration, the government was hit by a wave of alleged corruption scandals involving three Cabinet ministers and one undersecretary of State and eventually resulting in their dismissal.

The ministers allegedly involved in the corruption cases were Osman Mohamoud Adde, Minister of Commerce and Industry; Awil Haji Abdullahi, Minister of Finance; Ismail Dualeh Warsama, Minister of Agriculture; and Islao

44 Diary Aden Abdulla, August 25-26, 1964.

45 Ibid., August 11, 1964.

Osman Nour Amer, Undersecretary of Agriculture. Actually, for the record, it should be stated that Awil Haji, alias Anthony James, tendered his resignation without being asked[46], while the other two ministers were sacked[47]. Protected by the immunity they enjoyed as members of Parliament, they could not be arrested or held to account.[48]

Coming under growing pressure, and in order to survive, Premier Abdirazak seemed to be losing much of his initial combativeness and enthusiasm, and soon reverted to the ugly old practice of tribal representation he had often denounced as he filled the vacated ministerial posts.

In a government reshuffle, Awil Haji Abdullahi (Issak, Habar Yonis) was replaced by Sheikh Hassan Abdullahi (Issak, Habar Yonis); Osman Mohamoud Adde (Majerten, Osman Mohamoud) was replaced by Haji Bashir Ismail (Majerten, Osman Mohamoud); Ismail Dualeh Warsama (Issak, Habar Je'lo) was replaced by Ahmed Ismail 'Duqsi' (Issak, Habar Je'lo); and Islao Osman Nour Amer (Abgal) was replaced by Osman Ahmed Roble (Abgal).

Abdirazak's fragile administration was further rocked by the unexpected resignation of the Undersecretary of State for Finance, Abdullahi Mohamed Ahmed 'Qablan', who apparently disagreed with the Prime Minister's way of conducting state affairs[49]. In his letter of resignation, addressed to the Prime Minister, Qablan (MP for Las Qoray) gave the following reasons: "My reason is that I don't agree with the policy followed by Your Excellency as far as the internal, foreign, and social and economic affairs are concerned. I doubt very much Your Excellency's policy concerning finance and the economy shall ever produce results to the interest of this country, especially the attitude of the government towards the projects financed with the loans from the USSR and the banana exports business." The Prime Minister responded by stating that at no time, during 19 months as Undersecretary, had Qablan brought to his attention any proposal or suggestion with regard to the issues raised in his resignation letter, and cast strong doubt on Qablan's motives, alleging that frustration at failing to attain the rank of minister in the recent government reshuffle was a more plausible explanation for his decision to resign.[50]

The ruling party elected Abdirazak as Secretary General in a conference held

46 *Somali News*, January 3, 1966.
47 Ibid., January 11, 1966.
48 Art. 85 (4), 1960 Constitution.
49 *Somali News*, April 22, 1966.
50 Diary Aden Abdulla, April 18, 1966.

on November 18, 1964. Despite launching the concept of the Prime Minister becoming 'leader of the party', Mohamed 'Gabio' was dropped and Mohamed Jama Badmah, a moderate parliamentarian from the north, was elected vice-secretary general in his place. 'Gabio' was given the less prestigious position of administrative secretary, probably because he was not, at the time, a member of the Parliament. This was the first time in Somalia that the dual responsibility of government and party leadership was combined in one man's hand[51]. Three years later, by 121 votes against 10, Abdirazak was again elected Secretary General of the party on February 28, 1967.[52]

Law on retail trade and the exodus of Arabs

Abdirazak's new government may have passed its first test by obtaining the vote of confidence, but a daunting task was looming on the horizon for his administration. In fact, the anti-Abdirazak faction in the Parliament missed no occasion of opposing the government, with or without convincing reason, by introducing private bills aimed at embarrassing and weakening the Prime Minister and his administration. In 1965, for instance, the National Assembly passed a controversial draft law[53] known as 'Legge Da'ar' after the name of the MP who introduced it, debarring non-Somali citizens from engaging in retail trade within Somalia[54]. The bill was approved by an absolute majority of 84 votes, more than two thirds of the voting members of the Parliament.

The President of the Republic, worried about the strong reactions and heightened tension the law had provoked within and outside Somalia, wrote in his diary for 9 and 10 December 1964: "The qualified majority approving the bill makes absolutely fruitless my submission to the Parliament for further re-examination of the decision [...] What shall we do with the thousands of Arab nationals engaged in commercial business, 70–80% of whom have Somali mothers and who do not know where to go? What will be the reaction of the independent Arab countries and Yemen, and what will be the destiny of the thousands of Somali nationals working/living in Aden, Hijjaz, Yemen, and Kuwait?"[55]

51 *Somali News*, November 29, 1964.
52 Diary Aden Abdulla, March 2, 1967.
53 *Somali News*, January 15, 1965.
54 Mohamed Ali Da'ar, a strikingly tall and slim man elected from the electoral district of Eyl, Majertenia, served as Undersecretary of the Ministry of Foreign Affairs in the Abdirashid government..
55 Diary Aden Abdulla, December 9-10, 1964.

If promulgated by the President of the Republic, the bill would have been "tantamount to an order of expulsion of the thousands of little non-Somali shop owners, mainly of Yemeni origin, who have been in Somalia for generations. Such a wholesale eviction would have the most unfortunate consequences on the Republic's relations with countries like Aden where a substantial Somali community live", as noted in a leading article in the monthly *Dalka* on July 1, 1965[56]. As feared, news of the bill triggered a mass exodus of Arabs from Somalia, and in the process, many of them hastily sold their properties below market price. Consequently, relations between Somalia and Aden deteriorated, as reflected in the virulent attacks levelled at Somalia in the Aden press at the time.[57]

The President of the Republic, exercising his power under the Constitution, returned the bill to Parliament for reconsideration with a motivated message. A final decision on retail trade law was still pending, when a new motion calling for the immediate Somalization of the posts of President of the Supreme Court and Public Prosecutor was introduced by a group of MPs led by Salad Elmi Mohamoud 'Durua'[58]. It was well known that at that time the country lacked professionally trained Somalis capable of taking up such sensitive positions as listed in the motion. "Graduation in Law is not in itself everything needed to fill such high posts. Experience is equally important", declared the Prime Minister during parliamentary debating of the motion[59]. This private member bill was rejected by 57 against, 34 in favour and 2 abstentions.

But Razak's woes were far from over. In May 1966, a group of dissident MPs within the ruling party submitted to the Parliament another draft law directing the government to take steps for nationalization of the coastal depot (*deposito costiero*) belonging to the Italian oil company AGIP in Mogadisho. The bill was introduced by Ali Garad Jama at a time when the government was engaged in serious negotiations with AGIP on ways and means for Somalia to start importing oil directly from the Soviet Union. "The proponent of the bill appears to ignore the fact that this coastal depot belongs to a company whose capital comes partially from Somali shareholders", comments Aden Abdulla[60]. The growing pace of bills presented by single MPs and designed chiefly to hit foreign-owned private companies became a source of embarrassment for the government. The

56 *Dalka*, facsimile edition, vol.1 (1965), July 1, 1965.
57 Ibid.
58 SNC Deputy elected from Belet Uen.
59 *Somali News*, January 8, 1965.
60 Diary Aden Abdulla, May 4, 1966.

Minister of Finance, in particular, hardly concealed his worries over the negative effects this and similar bills may have on relations with Italy[61], the country that had been offering Somalia generous annual financial contributions in cash to cover the chronic budget deficit since independence, in addition to offering hefty financial aid and technical assistance in development projects, and to granting preference to imports of Somali bananas. "In spite of all this, there are lawmakers continuing to advance proposals for the expropriation of the AGIP Coastal Depot, SEIS Electric Company, the plot of land housing the Italian cemetery in Mogadisho, the combined value of which could not be more than the financial aid we receive annually from Italy", commented Aden Abdulla.[62]

A new bill providing for Somalization of the managerial posts of all private companies operating in Somalia was introduced in May by a group of MPs led by Mohamed Ali Da'ar. The bill, which affected foreign-owned private companies, most of them Italian, was approved by the Parliament in May by a large majority[63]. The arguments in support of these bills were highly nationalistic, and few MPs may have been willing to vote against them. Once approved, they became a source of embarrassment for the government, which now found it defaulting on the international obligations it had accepted under bilateral agreements. All these bills were in substance designed to scare away potential and actual foreign private investors operating in Somalia, with the ultimate aim to cause the collapse of the government. "The sponsors of the private bills are the same persons: Abdullahi Qablan, Yassin Nour, Ahmed 'Allora', Osman Sheikh Ahmed, Mohamed Abdi 'Galansce', Haji Mussa Samatar and others, supported by the SDU."[64] The dissidents within the ruling party and the opposition, as mentioned earlier, targeted areas of activities in which they considered the government was vulnerable.

The President of the Republic, exercising his power under the Constitution (Article 61 (3) of 1960 Constitution), returned the bill on private companies to the Parliament with a motivated message, citing political and legal grounds and requesting MPs to reconsider. In his message the President said, among other things: "The law is in contrast with international agreements concluded by Somalia with friendly countries". He cited, in particular, Article 5 of the Friendship Agreement with Italy, approved by Law No. 28 of October 30, 1961

61 Ibid., May 8, 1966.
62 Ibid., May 21, 1966.
63 Ibid., May 27, 1966.
64 Ibid., November 22, 1966.

which reads "the citizens of each country will be guaranteed in the territory of the other country protection and security for persons and their properties, and will be assured of the same rights, privileges and treatments which the citizens of the country enjoy within the law."[65] The President also stressed the adverse consequences of the bill on the badly needed foreign investment in Somalia. On December 31, 1966, the National Assembly voted on the Somalization Bill that the President had returned in July 1966. The vote was 67 for the bill and 31 against[66]. The bill fell short of the required two-third majority, and consequently never became law.

The mutinous mood within the ruling party flared up again when in June 1966 the National Assembly rejected two government-sponsored bills, delegating to the government the power to issue four codes (Civil, Health, Navigation, Civil Procedure) and bringing up to date four other codes (Labour, Penal, Traffic and Criminal Procedure). The Labour Code Bill was concerned with amendments to the provisions governing temporary appointment of personnel[67]. The paradox was that these non-controversial government-sponsored bills were defeated in a secret ballot, by 51 votes against and 38 in favour, after being approved earlier in openvoting.[68]

"It seems that many MPs are determined to make life difficult for the government in the run-up to the presidential elections due in 12 months time, since I no longer have the power to dissolve Parliament and call for early parliamentary elections under Article 53 (3)", the President comments[69], further venting his frustration by adding: "Judging on how things are going in Parliament, the situation is very critical for Abdirazak's government. Two years ago I took the decision to give the country a brave and honest Prime Minister, and so far I've not regretted that, but now I am sick and tired of continuing to fight those irresponsible and corrupt so-called representatives of the people. Those MPs who, in the secret ballot, voted in a manner different from the way they voted publicly, are cowards."[70] The President refers to those MPs as 'franchi tiratori' or 'snipers', an expression widely used in Italian political jargon to define a member of Parliament who votes against his party in a secret ballot. The secret ballot is a tricky instrument often used by MPs to embarrass the government.

65 *Somali News*, December 30, 1966.
66 TNA FCO 31/221 Confidential report no. A 249, from US Embassy, Mogadisho, January 15, 1967.
67 *Somali News*, June 1, 1966.
68 *Corriere della Somalia*, Giugno 22, 1966.
69 Diary Aden Abdulla, June 23, 1966.
70 Ibid., June 24, 1966.

The following case better illustrates how the secret ballot was far from being a transparent system. In July, the Central Committee of the ruling party and the Lega parliamentary group endorsed the candidature of Aden Shire Jama 'Aden Low' to the post of Vice President of the National Assembly, vacated by Haji Bashir Ismail following his appointment as member of the government. According to an unwritten norm, since Haji Bashir belonged to the Darod ethnic clan, it was accepted that his post should go to a Darod fellow member of the Parliament. There were two contenders for the post: Aden Shire and Mohamed Ali Da'ar, both from the same Darod family. The former received the endorsement of 32 votes against 22 in favour of the second[71]. Mediation efforts carried out by Darod MPs to persuade one of the two rivals to withdraw his candidature in favour of the other ended in failure[72]. What surprised many was that, although Aden Shire was the official candidate of the ruling party, he was yet defeated in a secret ballot in Parliament by his rival candidate, resulting in 52 votes for Ali Da'ar and 48 for Aden 'Low'.

Removal of the President of the National Assembly

In keeping with long-standing tradition, each of the three top elected State positions, namely, President of the Republic, Prime Minister and President of the National Assembly, are allocated evenly to politicians hailing from one of the major Somali clans represented in Parliament. During the second legislature, 1959–1964, the important position of President of the National Assembly was held by a Northerner, Jama Abdullahi Ghalib, who in 1964, following the general elections and in keeping with this practice, was replaced by another Northerner, Ahmed Sheikh Mohamed Absie, from Berbera[73]. Halfway through his tenure, allegations emerged of mismanagement of National Assembly funds on his part. A parliamentary committee was established towards the end of 1965 to investigate the matter[74]. Following a joint decision taken by the Central Committee of the Lega dei Giovani Somali and its parliamentary group, the Speaker was expelled from the party for 'failing to abide by the party's rules':[75] a clear reference to his objection to submitting the resignation demanded by the party.

Soon after his expulsion, he was also removed from the post of President

71 *Corriere della Somalia*, Luglio 23, 1966.
72 Diary Aden Abdulla, July 23, 1966.
73 Elected on a Lega ticket from Berbera, he received 82 votes on May 26, 1964..
74 Under the Chairmanship of Deputy Abdi Bulle Aden, elected from Bur Hakaba.
75 *Somali News*, February 10, 1966.

of the National Assembly through a motion presented by 51 MPs, all from the ruling party, for reasons vaguely termed as 'inefficiency' in performing his functions. This was the first time a President of the National Assembly in exercise was subjected to such a drastic measure. The proponents of the motion invoked articles 55 and 57 of the Constitution as well as rules 74 and 2 of the Standing Committee of the Assembly. In an effort to challenge the legality of the motion, the President of the Assembly suspended the extraordinary session of the Parliament convened to discuss the matter on 26 February, 1966, arguing that the constitutional provisions on which the motion was based did not apply to the removal of the President of the National Assembly. The matter was then referred to legal experts[76] as well as to the Standing Committee of the National Assembly, the body competent to decide on conflicts of opinion concerning interpretation and application of the Standing Rules[77]. The Board deliberated that articles 2 and 74 of the Standing Rules did not preclude the National Assembly discussing the motion and acting upon it as necessary.

The National Assembly was convened in ordinary session on March 2, 1966, and the motion was one of the items on its agenda. The National Assembly, chaired by the beleaguered Speaker himself, passed the motion during its session of March 4 by 85 votes in favour, 33 against and 1 abstention. Voting was by way of secret ballot[78].

Apparently, all Lega MPs voted compact in favour of the motion, while the negative votes mainly came from the opposition. It was not clear why it should be so urgent to convene an extraordinary session of the Parliament just to remove the Speaker and expel him from the party at a time when the parliamentary investigation commission was still busy investigating him for alleged maladministration. The parliamentary group of the SDU accused the Prime Minister, who was also the secretary general of the ruling party, of orchestrating the move which precipitated the Speaker's removal.[79]

On March 8, Sheikh Muktar Mohamed Hussein[80], one of the 3 Vice-presidents of the National Assembly, was elected to replace Absie with a majority of 69 votes. His closest contender, Mohamed Haji Ibrahim Egal, of the SNC, received 42 votes[81]. Rashid Sultan Abdullahi, the MP for Hargeisa, was elected Vice-

76 Diary Aden Abdulla, February 27, 1966.
77 *Somali News*, March 4, 1966.
78 Ibid., March 4, 1966.
79 Diary Aden Abdulla, January 30, 1966.
80 Elected from the electoral district of Oddur.
81 *Somali News*, March 11, 1966.

president of the Parliament to fill the position vacated by Sheikh Muktar.

The removal of Absie was the highest-profile case since independence involving the head of one of the top three institutions of the State, and understandably left Absie feeling as if he had been singled out in a country full of inefficient and corrupt politicians. Of course, Absie's administration left enough room for criticism, his performance in office, his leadership qualities and style contrasting starkly with those of Aden Abdulla, who had served as President of the National Assembly between 1956 and 1960.

The investigations carried out by the parliamentary commission appear to have revealed a black hole between Sh.So400,000 and Sh.So490,000 in the National Assembly's budget[82]. With the forced departure of Absie, the top three positions (Presidency of the Republic, Presidency of the Parliament and Premiership) were all now covered by southerners. Egal, belonging to the same clan and sub-clan as the outgoing President of the Parliament, seemed to be the natural candidate to take up the job according to the unwritten tribal formula followed in filling vacated elective posts. However, there was a requirement Egal could hardly fill: as a member of the SNC he belonged to an opposition party, and the Lega wanted for the Presidency of the National Assembly someone from their party.

Civil service reform. 'Busta rossa'

As mentioned earlier, the Prime Minister made anti-corruption measures and reform of the public administration the centrepiece of his term of office. Reforms aimed at streamlining the workings of the State were laudable, but the steps taken by Abdirazak's government to terminate the contracts of State personnel were seen by many as arbitrary.

In order to safeguard the security of tenure of career civil servants, the law provides that their appointment can be terminated by the government only for reduction of staff, physical or mental incapacity, unsatisfactory service, disciplinary action and conviction for certain offences.

The government claimed that the employees targeted for dismissal fell under three different categories: (a) those considered corrupt, (b) the incompetent, and (c) those suspected of divulging state secrets. Some of these behaviours are criminal offences.

The key question is why the individuals suspected of wrongdoing were not

82 Conversations between Aden Abdulla and Abdi Bulle Aden, Chairman of the Parliamentary Enquiry Committee (Diary Aden Abdulla, May 6, 1966).

charged under the relevant laws and brought to justice. The Prime Minister seemed to be fighting his crusade against corruption in the public administration single-handedly. Letters of dismissal were soon handed to many civil servants without proper legal procedure, and in certain cases even sent to deceased persons (of which the government had obviously kept no accurate record).

On account of the colour of the envelope containing the dismissal letters, the scheme became popularly known as 'Busta rossa' or 'red envelope'. The Prime Minister saw the move as a crucial step in eradicating corruption; however his critics viewed it as an arbitrary exercise in sidelining dangerous opponents. "The layoffs were not the product of a transparent, objective, and therefore methodical process", comments Ismail A. Ismail. "His action was said to be politically motivated and he was immediately castigated for 'purging' his predecessor's supporters from public service."[83] "The move appeared to be a whim, rather than a well-defined set of criteria", comments Mohamed Osman[84]. The Prime Minister started his reform process from the top of the administration rather than from the bottom. In other words, the reforms failed to extend to the 'field' administration and to affect the regional governors and district commissioners who were in effect the instrument through which the government ruled the country, in addition to serving as middlemen between the government and the population, the bulk of which lived outside Mogadisho[85]. When it was pointed out to him that civil servants had no work security because the government was now able to dismiss them on a whim, the Prime Minister replied that only those who had obtained positions of responsibility through favouritism and nepotism need worry about their career. Abdirazak was obviously unaware that he was pushing his agenda too far and too fast.

A civil servant was given the right to challenge any administrative decision concerning him, first through the competent minister and then by appealing to the Supreme Court[86]. Forty-three among the civil servants whose appointments were terminated thus appealed to the Supreme Court challenging the government's authority to terminate their appointments. In Dr Mohamed Farah Kid et al. vs. The Prime Minister[87], the Supreme Court, on its own motion, raised the question of article 35 of the Civil Servant Law authorizing the public administration to

83 Ismail A. Ismail, op. cit., pp. 160-161.
84 Mohamed Osman Omar, op. cit., p. 71.
85 Ismail A. Ismail, op. cit., p. 163.
86 Art.34 of Civil Service Law n. 7 of March 15, 1962.
87 Supreme Court Full Bench Judgement of December 16, 1965.

change the status of civil servants in temporary exemption from the application of the safeguards laid down in article 88, paragraph 5 of the Constitution providing that "The status of civil servant shall be established by law". This issue was referred to the Constitutional Court, which had however not been set up[88]. All senior civil servants dismissed without proper procedure were reinstated in their positions by the successive Administration, led by Premier Egal.

By mid 1966, it became clear that the government was struggling, and that in-fighting within the ruling party made execution of the governmental programme very difficult. The Prime Minister's authority was seriously undermined when the Parliament rejected four draft laws prepared by the government. This rejection of non-controversial government legislation was a show of no confidence in the government, leading the embattled Prime Minister to resign. In his letter of resignation to the President of the Republic, Abdirazak stated: "Mr President, as a result of the unclear and unconceivable manner in which the bills have been rejected, I tend to be convinced that my government can hardly carry out its complex and delicate task in the face of the obscure and mysterious climate prevailing in the National Assembly."[89] However, the President invited Abdirazak to withdraw the resignation and seek instead a fresh confidence vote from Parliament. In July, the government requested and obtained a renewed vote of confidence. Out of 108 MPs present, 72 voted in favour of the motion, 23 against and 13 abstained[90]. However, not every MP from the ruling party voted for the government. In fact, a group of 13 deputies abstained from voting, thus contravening the party's directives. Haji Mussa Bogor, Haji Mussa Samatar, Osman Mohamoud Adde, Ismail Dualeh, Ahmed Mohamed 'Allora', Awil Haji Abdullahi, Abdullahi Mohamed 'Qablan', Mohamed Ahmed Haji Salah, Yassin Nour Hassan, Ahmed Gure Mamoun, Mohamed Abdi Jibril 'Galansce', Islao Nour Osman and Ali Alio Mohamed all abstained from voting.

The 13 MPs were expelled from the party for violation of the party line[91]. For reasons that were never explained, no action was taken against two other members of the Lega, Haji Abdullahi Mohamed Ismail (Candala) and Osman Ahmed Hirabe (Afgooye), who were absent from voting.[92]

The manoeuvering by deputies to gain personal advantage from the impending

88 P. Contini, op. cit., p. 31.
89 *Somali News*, July 1, 1966.
90 Diary Aden Abdulla, July 13, 1966.
91 Ibid., July 19, 1966.
92 Ibid.

presidential election was a chief factor in the breakdown of strict party discipline. The dissident faction within the ranks of Lega lawmakers was pursuing the clear political objective of causing the premature departure of the Prime Minister, on the assumption that if he remained in office up to the presidential election scheduled for June 30 1967, the chances for re-election of Aden Abdulla, and consequently of Abdirazak, would be good. "A government led by Abdirazak would represent a threat to their chances in the general elections of 1969."[93]

Two influential MPs, Haji Mussa Boqor and Yassin Nour, led the rebellious faction who had vowed to undermine the Prime Minister at all cost. Haji was a veteran politician, son of the last Sultan of the Osman Mohamoud, and over time had shown considerable political ability to forge alliances within his party. Yassin had served as secretary general of the ruling party from 1963 to 1964, and as an ultra-ambitious young parliamentarian had vowed to get rid of the Prime Minister, believing that the latter's presence made it difficult for him to become a minister. Like Abdirazak, he belonged to the Omar Mohamoud, Majerten sub-clan[94]. Yassin Nour eventually succeeded in his plan, becoming minister for his clan in 1967, a position that had been held by Abdirazak since 1960.

In the meantime, a new unexpected element was added to the political conundrum the government was facing. Early in 1967, less than one year before the presidential election set for June 1967, renewed speculations on alleged military plans to overthrow the constitutional order again came to the surface. However, while in 1964 there had been no clear indication as to who might be behind these plans, this time the new commander of the national army[95], General Mohamed Siad Barre, in a detailed report to the Prime Minister, gave the names of three senior army officials he suspected of plotting to overthrow the regime, citing their 'stubbornness and behaviour'. Lieutenant Colonels Mohamed Farah Aidid, Mohamed Nour and Major Ali Matan, in charge of the Operation Services, the Artillery and the Air Force respectively, were the army officers General Siad thought might have been harbouring subversive plans[96]. Rumours of an impending military takeover were rife, to the point that, a week before Siad Barre's report to the Prime Minister, Mohamed Haji Ibrahim Egal had shared with Aden Abdulla an intelligence report indicating that Siad Barre

93 Conversations between Haji Yousuf Egal and Aden Abdulla on July 5, 1966 (Diary Aden Abdulla, July 5, 1966).

94 Diary Aden Abdulla, November 19, 1966.

95 By Presidential Decree of June 24, 1965, no. 138, following the death of Daud Abdulla, General Siad Barre became Commander of the National Army..

96 Diary Aden Abdulla, April 30, 1966.

himself, with his colleagues, might be drawing up plans for a military coup, "in the event the President they like is not elected in the 1967 presidential election."[97] This was probably a reference to Abdirashid.

It was further alleged that, within the national army, two rival groups of military officers, the Darod clan on one side, and the Issak–Hawiye clans on the other, were conspiring to overthrow the constitutional order. Allegedly, each of these two groups was prepared to pre-empt the other in staging the coup. But these rumours were once more dismissed by Gen. Siad Barre as 'alarmist propaganda.'[98]

Siad Barre appears to have succeeded in dispelling from the mind of the gullible politicians of the time any idea of the threat posed by the army under his command; but he never abandoned the plan of ascending to power. He was just buying time, waiting for the right moment to act: and the occasion he was awaiting came in October 1969.

Abdirazak left office following the election of Abdirashid as President of the Republic in June 1967. Although Abdirazak became secretary general of the ruling party in 1964 in addition to filling his position as Prime Minister, his administration, from start to finish, maintained strained relations with a generally hostile Parliament that often kept the government on the defensive.

The situation Abdirazak had faced during his tenure is eloquently explained by I.M. Lewis: "In the National Assembly the government was severely harassed at every possible opportunity by the ousted Prime Minister [Abdirashid] and his faction [...] this covert sabotage was facilitated by the Assembly practice of normally voting by secret ballot, thus making it extremely difficult for Abdirazak to control his ill-disciplined party."[99]

As a result of this difficult relationship with Parliament, coupled with the damage done to its image by a series of corruption scandals involving a number of cabinet ministers, the government led by Abdirazak, like the previous administration, was left with little time to address the specific economic needs of the country.

Just one year before the presidential election of June 1967, the Prime Minister started showing signs of fatigue and seemed to lack the determination and stamina he had displayed at the beginning of 1964. In the face of growing parliamentary

97 Ibid., April 24, 1966.

98 Mohamed Siad gave this report to the Prime Minister at the latter's residence in the presence of Aden Abdulla (Diary Aden Abdulla, January 15, 1967)..

99 I.M. Lewis, op. cit. p. 202.

opposition to his administration, he felt unable to sack certain ministers that had allegedly been involved in corruption for fear of the tribal outcry a similar measure may entail. His promise to inaugurate a new era of ethical and clean politics, exemplified by his catchphrase "*l'uomo giusto al posto giusto*" (the right man in the right place), and to create an administration that would advance the agenda of good governance, remained unfulfilled, albeit certainly through no fault of his own. Only six months before the presidential election, tired and with his authority already waning further, Abdirazak revealed to the President his intention to step down. However, the President persuaded him to stay on up to the end of his mandate, but advised him to reduce his working schedule and take some 9 to 10 hours' rest everyday.[100]

Until the end, and despite the political difficulties, Aden Abdulla continued to harbour the conviction that his embattled Prime Minister remained the best among the politicians of the time. "No one is free from flaws, but I am still convinced that Abdirazak is the best available man for honesty, courage and determination. Sadly, he is not in good health and has not reached the statutory age to become Head of State," wrote Aden Abdulla in his diary for November 29, 1966[101]. Arrested in October 1969 by the military regime, though not a member of the government, Abdirazak was later released and appointed Permanent Representative of Somalia at the United Nations in New York, but soon quit this position owing to differences with the government.[102]

A democratically elected African president steps down quietly

Abdirashid elected Head of State

Unlike the rest of Africa, Somalia had adopted the parliamentary system of government, meaning that the President of the Republic is elected by the Parliament, not by the people, for the duration of six years (Article 70 of the 1960 Constitution). By virtue of this system, the executive power was vested not in the President of the Somali Republic but in the government led by the Prime Minister (Articles 77 and 83 of 1960 Constitution). The mandate of the first President of the Republic was set to expire in July 1967. When the time for the election came, there were only two candidates running for the Presidency of the Republic: the incumbent and the former Prime Minister, Abdirashid Ali. By

100 Diary Aden Abdulla, November 23, 1966.

101 Ibid., November 29, 1966.

102 Abdirazak passed away in America on 31 January 2014.

decision of the party, members of the Lega parliamentary group were allowed to vote in favour of the presidential candidate of their own choice, meaning that there was no official party candidate and no party line to respect. However, shortly before the date of the presidential election, a legal argument emerged as to the eligibility of the incumbent to seek re-election, on grounds of constitutional provisions: "A person cannot be elected consecutively for more than one term" (Art. 71 of 1960 Constitution). The argument was based on the fact that Aden Abdulla had been elected in 1960 for one year as provisional President of the Republic before being elected for a complete term of 6 years in 1961. The matter was submitted to legal experts who concluded that Article 71 of the Constitution should be interpreted "as applying to the case of a person elected for two full terms in office and not for shorter terms." [103]

Unexpectedly, however, soon after the legal argument was put to rest, the presidential election was nearly overshadowed by an external event taking place in an area sited beyond Somali borders: a war that had broken out between the State of Israel and a coalition of Arab States in the Middle East. This war, which began on June 6, 1967, four days before the Somali presidential election, is known in military history as the Six-Day War. The Arabs call it 'the 1967 war' or 'An-naksah' (the Setback). It has been said that for Israel this war was a question of sheer survival, for the Arabs it was a matter of credibility.

Citing the military confrontation in the Middle East as a justification, the President of the National Assembly and the Prime Minister advanced the idea of putting off the presidential election at least to June 20, arguably to monitor the situation in the Middle East. The President, however, did not share this idea: "No, no, no, I see no link between what is happening in the Middle East and the presidential election here in Somalia."[104] On the one hand, the government received unanimous support from the National Assembly for its policy over the Arab–Israeli conflict, including the decision to intervene militarily against Israel[105], a move seen by many as an empty promise and a dangerous adventure.

Since Somalia had become independent in 1960, its foreign policy was determinedly non-interventionist and its Constitution repudiates war as a means of settling international disputes (Art. 6 (2) of 1960 Constitution). Its armed forces had seen little action at home and even less abroad. While nobody has

103 Meeting between Aden Abdulla and Sheikh Muktar, President of the National Assembly (Diary Aden Abdulla, April 2, 1967).
104 Diary Aden Abdulla, June 6, 1967.
105 Ibid., June 7, 1967.

provided an explanation of what irremissible national interest pushed Somalia to join a war it had nothing to do with, the risk involved was high, because Israel was legally entitled to militarily attack Somalia as a belligerent party. This blunder became more evident when the government sent a long letter to Ethiopia requesting authorization to overfly its air space in order to transport combat troops destined to fight on the Arabs' side. This request was ridiculed, coming as it did at a time when Ethiopia was refusing over flight rights even to Somali commercial aircrafts making service between Mogadisho and Hargeisa. Ethiopia is known to have taken a neutral stand vis-à-vis the military conflict taking place in the Middle East.

No one in the National Assembly showed the wisdom or courage to voice dissent, despite the abundant arguments available. As to the public at large, nobody seemed to take seriously the bravado displayed by a government who was at the time on the brink of being voted out of office. A show of moral solidarity for the Arabs is understandable, but fighting on their side was dangerous stupidity. Records show that in 1956, following the Anglo-Franco-Israeli aggression against Egypt, the Somali government reacted in a reasonable manner that was much less risky to the country. The government introduced a motion to the Legislative Assembly condemning the aggression and expressing solidarity with the government and the people of Egypt; the motion was adopted by acclamation in November 1956[106]. The solidarity shown by the Somali public to the Egyptian people, seen as victims of aggression, was so strong that by the end of December 1956 an amount of Sh.So 83,000 was collected for the Port Said victims. "Lists of subscribers were published in the government newspaper, the *Corriere della Somalia*, each time under a heading referring to the Martyrs of PortSaid."[107]

Finally, when the legal arguments on Article 71 of the Constitution and the ill-conceived attempt to postpone the election because of the war in the Middle East were put to rest, the 123-man Assembly held a 3-hour session on June 10, 1967 to elect the President. The law provides for the President of the Republic to be elected by secret ballot, with a two-third majority on the first and second ballots, or an absolute majority in subsequent ballots. The incumbent and his former Prime Minister faced each other in a close competition which saw the former Premier winning, at the third secret ballot, with 73 to 50 votes. In the

106 *Corriere della Somalia*, Novembre 2, 1956.

107 TNA FO 371/125676, summary report for the month December 1956, from British Consulate, Mogadisho to FO.

first and second rounds, Abdirashid obtained 63 and 67 votes respectively, while Aden Abdulla got 57 and 55 in the first and second round respectively. Three papers were invalidated in the first ballot and one in the second[108]. On June 10, 1967 Aden Abdulla bowed out following defeat by his erstwhile political ally and former Prime Minister Abdirashid Ali Sharmarke.[109]

In actual fact Aden Abdulla had done little to engage in vigorous campaigning for re-election, and had not sought support from individual lawmakers or made any concessions or promises in exchange for votes. In a rare heart-to-heart with his close friend and confidant, Mohamed Ali Dhorre 'Agaweyne'[110], he explained the reasons why he would not seek re-election: "I do not consider myself indispensable: my advice and ideas are not appreciated, therefore I feel useless as Head of State. Consequently, I do not see why I should prolong my stay at the Palace. Seven years are a long enough time to weigh up the pros and cons.[111] Such modesty is rare in a political climate of bombast and self-promotion.

On May 20, less than 30 days before the presidential election, Aden Abdulla received a group of legislators from the Issak clan. The group, led by Mohamoud Issa Jama and Mohamed Haji Dualeh, offered Abdulla the support of the Issak in Parliament in exchange for the assurance that one of them would be appointed Prime Minister—namely Mohamed Ibrahim Egal, in the event he won the election. But Aden Abdulla was not a man to trade commissions behind closed doors [...] "I told them that I am not accustomed to making such undertakings (*non è del mio costume di fare simili promesse*), meaning not that I am ruling out *a priori* the possibility of what they want to achieve, but rather that I will stick to my ways, leaving them the freedom to act in the way they deem is in the interest of the country."[112]

It is reported that the same group of Issak MPs made the same offer, with the same condition, to Abdirashid, who accepted the deal at once. Abdirashid kept his word, designating Mohamed Haji Ibrahim Egal as Prime Minister after winning the election. This circumstance is confirmed by American Embassy sources in Mogadisho referring to conversations in which Egal, among other things, is quoted as saying that "Sharmarke had summoned him telling him that

108 *Somali News*, June 20, 1967.

109 The parliamentary seat vacated by Abdirashid as MP from the Gardo constituency was taken by Abdi Einab..

110 Elected twice from Obbia, he served as Undersecretary of the Ministry of Education in the Abdirashid government and Undersecretary of Public Works in Abdirazak's government..

111 Diary Aden Abdulla, July 8, 1966, November 7, 1966.

112 Ibid., May 20, 1967.

he owed his election mainly to Egal and because of this debt of gratitude and for general reasons, he proposed to appoint him Prime Minister."[113]

There was no conflict over ideological or political issues, whether domestic or international, as both men were from the same political party. However the outgoing President and the incoming were different in personality and background, as well as in their style of doing politics and managing State affairs. Aden Abdulla was known to conduct State affairs by strict observance of the Constitution and the law rather than through political alliances: he was a man above the parties, capable of taking unpopular decisions without compromising on matters of principle. His former Prime Minister, on the other hand, did know how to forge political alliances within and outside Parliament. The election of Abdirashid was made possible not only by his active campaigning, but also by his ability to capitalize on the government's unpopularity.

Displaying a marked degree of faith and foresight, Aden Abdulla not only conceded defeat but, even though his term of office was not due to expire until July 6, 1967, he wrote to the President of the National Assembly asking Parliament to accept early transfer of power from June 30 at 6 pm, in order to allow the newly elected President of the Republic to preside over the celebrations marking Independence Day on 1 July[114]. Abdulla's request was acclaimed by the Parliament.[115]

It was the first time Africa had experienced an orderly transfer of power from one leader to another. The second case of an African Head of State to peacefully leaving office was that of President Leopold Seder Senghor of Senegal, who stepped down in 1981 and passed the torch to his successor. Aden Abdulla's decision to step down before the expiry of his presidential mandate was hailed in all quarters as a sign of great statesmanship, and Abdirashid was sworn in to replace him in a climate of impressive calmness and respect for the Constitution. In view of this, 15 MPs led by Mohamed Ibrahim Egal put forward a motion proposing that the outgoing President be greeted in the name of the nation with a unanimous vote of thanks as a token of the great esteem in which he was held by all his countrymen everywhere. The motion was approved by acclamation[116]. Undoubtedly, Abdulla was a unique personality. As a politician, "he was well

113 TNA FCO 31/222, telegram of June 15, 1967 from Nairobi to Commonwealth Office, quoting report from the American Embassy at Mogadisho.

114 *Somali News*, June 28, 1967.

115 Ibid.

116 Ibid., June 28, 1967.

ahead of his time", as noted by Abdirazak, who knew him very well[117]. During his tenure as Head of State, Aden Abdulla gave proof of a rare sense of statesmanship, moderation and impartiality in a country in which the loyalty of the politicians is to their clans and not to State institutions. With Abdirashid Ali at the helm of the State, the three top elective positions were in the hands of the Issak, Darod and Rahanweyn; the Hawiye remained out of the equation for the first time since 1956.

Aden Abdulla left a hole none of his successors managed to fill[118], and although he completed his term of office and passed the torch with dignity, the two heads of State who succeeded him unfortunately both left their positions prematurely and in tragic circumstances. Abdirashid Ali, the second President of the Republic, was brutally murdered in October 1969, while the third President, General Mohamed Siad Barre, who came to power through a military coup, fled the capital in 1991 before completing his second seven-year term.[119]

117 Conversation between Abdirazak Haji Hussein and the author, New York, 1982.

118 He passed away in 2007.

119 President Barre was re-elected President for a new seven years term in May 1986.

Chapter XII

A NORTHERNER APPOINTED PRIME MINISTER

Egal's 'détente' policy

The 1967 presidential election saw alliances between uneasy political bedfellows. After the ritual informal consultations, Sharmarke designated his erstwhile opponent, Mohamed Haji Ibrahim Egal, as his Prime Minister[1]. The new Prime Minister was not a political novice in the Somali arena, having led the short-lived State of Somaliland in June 1960[2], and had a long record of fierce and personal antagonism towards the President of the Republic. Egal was the man who in 1962 caused the collapse of the coalition government (SYL–SNL–USP) led by Abdirashid: his resignation as Minister of Education was followed by a protracted political stalemate which shook the very foundation of the country's unity; in the same year he spearheaded the much publicized walk-out of SNL MPs from the National Assembly which eventually led to the formation of the SNC party in 1963. In the fluid world of Somali politics, former allies easily become rivals and vice versa, depending on circumstances. "The two men, Egal and Rashid, were reconciled through the mediation efforts of mutual friends, like Ismail Nahar and the veteran SYL campaigner Haji Mussa

1 Decree no. 108 of July 18, 1967.

2 After the collapse of the Somali State in 1991, Egal was elected as President of the self-declared independent Somaliland. He passed away in Pretoria, south Africa, on May 3, 2002.

Boqor," reveals Jama Mohamed Ghalib[3]. It goes without saying that, before his designation, Egal had chosen to repudiate his party, the SNC, to join the ruling party, which was a prerequisite to qualify for the premiership. Official record on the exact date on which he crossed the floor is not available, but some sources suggest that it was in 1967, while others put it as early as 1966.

The new Prime Minister, a British educated politician known for his pragmatism and leaning towards the West, had two key objectives to achieve before forming the government: (a) to readmit to the ruling party the 13 deputies expelled in July 1966, and (b) to allow willing SNC members to join the ruling party. This last issue was made necessary by the Lega rejecting the idea of forming a coalition executive with other parties, as Egal had proposed.

The Central Committee, after long discussions, took a favourable stand *vis-à-vis* the two issues, thus clearing the way for Egal to form the government. As a result, the expelled members were readmitted to the party, and ten SNC parliamentarians were accepted to join the Lega. They were: Haji Farah Ali, Ali Mohamed 'Wardhiigley', Haji Abdurahman 'Gariare', Haji Yusuf Iman, Abdullahi Jire, Said Farah Abdi, Salad Elmi Durwa, Mohamed Haji Bile, Abdullahi Ga'al Sobrie and Mohamed Ossoble Adde[4]. By July 1967, of the originally 22 SNC lawmakers, only a handful had remained loyal to the party—among them its veteran leader, Sheikh Ali Giumale.

Encouraged by this initial success, Egal formed his first government, raising the number of cabinet members from thirteen to eighteen and including representatives of every major clan family[5]. The new government, drawn from the ruling party, had no fewer than 7 Northerners, including the PM, with five ministers without portfolio and nine undersecretaries. The Prime Minister reserved the Foreign Affairs portfolio for himself. Only Aden Issak, Mohamoud 'Juje' and Ali Omar Sheegoow had been part of the previous Abdirazak administration.

It is significant to remember that, for the first time since 1956, Abdullahi Issa was left without a ministerial post, replaced by his kinsman Haji Farah Ali, who combined the two offices of Minister of Finance and that of Deputy Prime Minister[6]. Other former SNC party members were given cabinet posts as

3 Ghalib, op. cit., p. 66.

4 *Corriere della Somalia*, Luglio 12, 1967.

5 Haji and Haji, op. cit. , pp. 46-48.

6 The veteran parliamentarian appears to have been rewarded on account of his active support of Abdirashid's election as President.

a reward for supporting Abdirashid in the presidential election. They included: Ali Mohamed 'Wardhiigley', Abdullah Jire, Haji Yusuf Iman, Ismail Dualeh, Mohamed Ossoble Adde, Mohamed Haji Bile, and Salad Elmi Durwa. Among the nine undersecretaries, two had served as ministers in Abdirashid's government (namely Abdinour Mohamed Hussein and Ahmed Ghelle Hassan).

In August 1967, the National Assembly confirmed Egal's appointment almost unanimously, with a vote of confidence of 119 against one, with the abstention of three[7]. No Prime Minister in modern Somali history had ever enjoyed such strong support from such a tribal gathering, elevated to the rank of Parliament.

Premier Egal was quick to inaugurate a new and pragmatic approach in dealing with the issue of the so-called missing territories. Somali politicians assumed that this question dominated popular opinion and that any government would fall if it did not demonstrate a militant attitude towards neighbouring countries administering Somali-inhabited territories. Premier Egal held the strong conviction that previous administrations had neither gained international support for the Somali Republic nor contributed to the internal economic and social development of the country, but rather caused Somalis to become isolated in Africa, making no friends but only enemies. Somalia had not achieved the respectable international status necessary to conduct a meaningful foreign policy capable of dealing with the external world. The cause of this situation was a deliberate ignorance of internal African affairs and of changing world affairs, and Egal realized that time was running out for his politically isolated country. In fact, when Mohamed Haji Ibrahim Egal was chosen in 1967 as Prime Minister of Somalia, the country was a pariah State, ostracized by its neighbours and shut off from the mainstream of the East African Community Organization (EAC). Egal's bravest act was to face up to the fact that the notion of Greater Somalia and a strict policy of nationalism would not lead anywhere. Taboo flew out of the window: Egal decried irredentism, once the mainspring of foreign policy, as useless. Only friendship with the West and the neighbouring countries could end isolation. His deeds matched his words, and he was able to bring to an end tensions with the neighbouring countries and to restore diplomatic ties with them.

Egal was very securely in office, and he felt that the government could afford to explore new solutions despite the obvious political risks involved. On entering office, he felt he could change the policy if he conducted the change gradually

7 *Somali News*, August 12, 1967.

and discreetly[8]. The previous government led by Abdirazak, in view of its narrow majority in Parliament, "sounded relatively moderate in private, but it could hardly afford to appear very moderate before the Parliament or the public."[9] Egal, though not a democrat, was more pragmatic than his southern brothers, and understood that armed confrontation and open hostility were not the only available means to tackle the outstanding disputes with neighbouring countries. Egal took the lead in pursuing what was dubbed as a policy of *détente* towards neighbouring countries.

Before embarking on his new foreign policy, Premier Egal sought and obtained a full parliamentary mandate to continue with his initiatives towards finding a peaceful solution to the problems of the Somali inhabited territories held by Kenya and Ethiopia. In fact, by 89 votes against one, with the abstention of four MPs, the National Assembly passed a motion supporting the government's policy vis-à-vis the Somali territories[10]. The section of the motion dealing with operational matters reads: "The National Assembly expresses its approval of the initiative recently undertaken by the government at Kinshasa, Addis Abeba and Arousha, with the intention of creating an atmosphere of understanding and mutual confidence so as to reach peaceful settlement of disputes between Somalia and its bordering countries. It encourages the government to continue the activities already initiated and to take further positive steps for the satisfactory settlement of outstanding disputes safeguarding the rights of the people directly interested."

It would, however, be wrong to believe that Parliament gave Egal *carte blanche*—the premier was in fact required to seek ratification from the Assembly of any specific agreements reached with Kenya and Ethiopia[11]. The motion's preamble reflected two key phrases in the government's policy statement of August 8, 1967, namely that governments would 'continue the policy of earlier governments' and 'induce foreign countries to grant self-determination to the Somali territories still under alien rule.'

The new overture of real *détente* with neighbouring States received discreet encouragement from the United States of America. "Over the past few months,

8 TNA FCO' 31/223, Talk with the Prime Minister of Somalia and others about the resumption of diplomatic relations, by Malcolm MacDonald, British Special Representative in Kenya, on December 30, 1967.

9 TNA FCO 31.223, Report A 127 of October 23, 1967.

10 *Somali News*, November 24, 1967.

11 TNA FCO 31/223 Note on the memorandum of understanding concluded between Kenya and Somalia at Arousha on October 28, 1967 by John Drysdale.

with our quiet applause, Egal has begun peace talks with Haile Selassie and Kenyatta, pulled back the Somali guerrillas raiding the border areas and cut his military spending", reads a State Department document[12]. The new policy towards neighbouring countries was earlier sanctioned at the Assembly of the Head of States and Government of the Organization of the African Unity in Kinshasa.[13]

The first peace talks between Kenya and Somalia were held in Arousha in October 1967. This was the second time in two years Arousha had been used as a venue for peace talks between Kenya and Somalia. On the first occasion, in December 1965, President Kenyatta was invited to Arousha by President Nyerere to meet Somali President Aden Abdulla, who was then on state visit in Tanzania. After a series of meetings at presidential and ministerial level facilitated by President Julius Nyerere, the Conference ended in deadlock because of the Somali government's unwillingness to state categorically that it renounced territorial claims on Kenya. However, "In an attempt to retrieve the position at the eleventh hour, the Somali delegation, which included also the then Premier Abdirazak Haji drafted a joint declaration, but the Kenyan government declined to accept", wrote Drysdale. "The declaration", Drysdale adds "reaffirmed the Somali government's respect for the principle of territorial integrity of States", and stated that the Somali government did not "profess any policy of territorial expansionism and pledged its co-operation in bringing about peace and order in the area in question."[14]

In 1967, through President Kenneth Kaunda of Zambia's efforts at mediation, the Somali Premier met with Kenyan President Jomo Kenyatta in Arousha. Their talks paved the way for resumed trade and diplomatic relations based on a 'Memorandum of Understanding' in which Kenya and Somalia agreed to examine possibilities for ending hostilities referred to as minor issues[15]. The Memorandum of Understanding at Arousha provided for the appointment of a working committee consisting of Kenya, Somalia and Zambia "to examine ways and means of bringing about a satisfactory solution to major and minor

12 347: Memorandum from the President's Special Assistant (Rustow) to President Johnson Washington, March 13, 1968.

13 AHG/ST.1: Declaration on Kenya-Somalia Relations, Fourth Ordinary Session in Kinshasa, Congo, from 11 to 14 September 1967.

14 TNA FCO 31/222, Drysdale Note on the Memorandum of Understanding concluded between Kenya and Somalia at Arousha on October 28, 196, published in African Research Limited.

15 MOU signed by the President of Kenya and the Somali Prime Minister on October 28, 1967 in Arousha and witnessed by the President of Zambia.

differences between Kenya and Somalia." Before the Arousha Agreement, a declaration known as the Kinshasa Declaration was made at the Head of States and Government Meeting of the Organization of African Unity in Kinshasa in September: both governments agreed to respect each other's sovereignty and territorial integrity, to maintain security on the borders, discontinue hostile media broadcasts and accept Zambian President Kenneth Kaunda's offer of mediation[16]. A similar policy was pursued with Ethiopia.[17]

The United States followed Egal's *détente* policy very closely and expected him to see it through. If, however, the Somali government had reversed this policy and returned to its former attitude of hostility towards its neighbouring countries, the United States government would have been 'very tough' with Somalia, trying to ensure maximum isolation for the country.[18]

Opposition to Egal's policy

Egal's policy of *détente* became as divisive at home as it was accommodating abroad. The trend of opposition was spearheaded by former Prime Minister Abdirazak Haji, who, as we have seen, had sanctioned in 1965 a joint declaration based on similar terms, which had been rejected by the Kenyan government: "There was no basis on which to launch a successful attack, particularly since he himself (Abdirazak) had recommended the same provision in his draft communiqué at the first Arousha meeting", comments J. Drysdale[19]. A number of Somali newspapers were also critical of the Somali-Kenya Memorandum signed at Arousha. The monthly Italian language newspaper, *La Tribuna*[20], for instance, described it as a 'sell-out' of Somali aspirations. The Central Committee of the Lega passed a resolution critical of the Memorandum, as a result of which Egal closed the party's HQs in Mogadisho.[21]

On the other hand, there were many who defended the government's political

16 AHG/ST.1: Declaration on Kenya-Somalia Relations, Fourth Ordinary Session in Kinshasa, Congo, from 11 to 14 September 1967.

17 Addis Abeba Agreement September 1967; Mogadisho Agreement February 1968; Addis Abeba Agreement September 1968.

18 TNA FCO31/223, confidential report from the British Embassy at Washington to J.D.N. Hartland-Swann, Esq., north and East Africa Department, FO, November 13, 1967.

19 TNA FCO 31/222, Drysdale Note on the Memorandum of Understanding between Kenya and Somalia at Arousha on October 28, 1967, published in Africa Research Limited, p. 5.

20 *La Tribuna*, which was owned by Ismail Giumale, raged against the government on every conceivable issue..

21 TNA FCO 31/223, confidential report from the British Embassy in Washington to J.D. Hartland-Swann, Esq., north and East Africa Department, FO, November 13, 1967.

ouvertures towards the neighbouring African States. Speaking at the National Assembly during the debate on the issue, Salad Abdi Mohamoud, a lawmaker from Gardo and former minister during the trusteeship regime, made the following important statement: "Every independent State is entitled to sovereignty and territorial integrity, and since there is a recognition of dispute between Somalia and Kenya in the Memorandum, the signing of the document by the present government cannot rightly be interpreted as having given away any of the rights of the Somali people."[22]

The interpretation supported by some that the Somali government had waived claims on Kenya territory should be read in the context of the Somali Prime Minister's foreign policy statement in Mogadisho, in which Egal declared: "We in the Somali Republic make no claims on the territory of any of our neighbours. We do not wish to annex the territory of any state whatsoever or to expand into such territory [...]. We do intend to champion the cause of the Somali territories under foreign domination, in order that they attain sovereign independent status through the process of self-determination[23]. The matter was made even clearer when Egal, departing from the printed text of his speech to the Parliament, said: "We, the Somali Republic, declare our support to the Somalis who are waging their struggle for independence. We are with them and still give them moral and material support at all times and at all international gatherings and we shall not in any way retreat from this."[24] In reality, Egal did not repudiate the principle enshrined in the Constitution to reunite the Somali inhabited territories under one State. There was strong emotional and constitutional support in Somalia for these claims and it was doubtful that any political leader could successfully make such a renunciation. What Egal was trying, after the political failure of earlier Somali governments, was to achieve the same objectives through negotiations and not through military support to the Somali guerrilla movements.

The ruling party became deeply divided over the Arousha Understanding. Amid general disorientation and lack of discipline following the closure of Lega HQs in Mogadisho[25], 12 members of the Central Committee, led by former Premier Abdirazak, met at Abdirazak's residence and passed a further resolution

22 TNA FCO 31/222, Drysdale Note on the Memorandum of Understanding between Kenya and Somalia at Arousha on October 28, 1967, published in Africa Research Limited.
23 *Africa Confidential*, no. 19, September 22, 1967.
24 Ibid.
25 TNA FCO 31/223, confidential report from the British Embassy in Washington to J.D. Hartland-Swann, Esq., north and East Africa Department, FO, November 13, 1967.

expelling Egal from the party[26]. In addition, three other members were expelled from the Central Committee: Mohamed 'Yero' (Deputy from Wanleweyn), Ahmed Ali 'Giudicino' (Deputy from Oddur) and Ali Ghedi Shador (Deputy from El-Der)[27]. This was a big blow to Egal's prestige, and he worked quickly to regain the upper hand, challenging the legality of the disciplinary measures taken against him on the grounds that the Committee lacked the necessary quorum of at least 13 out of the 23 members. On November 25, the Central Committee met again and passed a resolution reinstating Egal and expelling Abdirazak[28]. The in-fighting that characterized the ruling party caused Abdirashid to appoint a Conciliation Committee with the task of narrowing the differences between Egal and Abdirazak. The Conciliation Committee consisted of 16 members, including, among others, the former President Aden Abdulla, the Speaker of the Parliament, Sheikh Muktar, Mohamed Sheikh Gabio and Ugaz Yassin. The Committee, endorsed by a meeting of the full party, decided to relieve Abdirazak of the post of President of the Central Committee, although he was allowed to remain in the party.[29]

After losing the leadership of the party, amid open confrontation with the Prime Minister, Abdirazak turned his back on the governing party and founded a new political party, the Democratic Action Party. History repeats itself: Abdirazak followed in the footsteps of some of his former party fellows (Haji Mohamed Hussein, Haji Farah Ali and Sheikh Ali Jim'ale to name but few) who quit the ruling party and established opposition political parties.

Many of my generation remember Abdirazak's firebrand rhetoric during the weekly meetings at his party HQs in Mogadisho inciting people to rise up against the government. Though Abdirazak was not, perhaps, Somalia's most popular politician, he was beyond doubt the ablest exponent of what remained of the old guard. His new party did not attract many followers, mainly because the man was not new in the Somali political arena: his long association with Lega-led administrations and his scant talent for public relations represented a handicap for him, and therefore his chances of winning national support had not increased. In the last general elections of 1969, his party won only 2 seats nationwide.

26 *The Nationalist*, 23 November 1967.

27 Diary Aden Abdulla, November 16, 1967.

28 TNA FCO 31/223, Confidential letter no. 10280, from British Embassy, Washington to FO, November 30, 1967.

29 TNA FCO 31/223, confidential report from the British Embassy at Washington to J.D.N. Hartland-Swann, Esq., north and East Africa Department, FO, December 6, 1967.

Somalia resumes diplomatic relations with Britain

When Egal took on the premiership in 1967, Somalia had no diplomatic relations with Great Britain, a major donor country extending generous annual financial aid to help with the Somali ordinary budget. "A critic of the Somalia break with Britain in 1963, Egal comes to power in a government at odds with another major European power, France, and two relatively strong African neighbour States who enjoy particularly close relations with Britain and United States of America respectively," reads a declassified document from the American Embassy in Mogadisho[30]. According to certain foreign media reports, Egal was one of a handful of lawmakers who, in 1963, abstained when a vote was taken on breaking off diplomatic relations with Britain[31]. Egal was widely regarded as a pro-British politician, and as such was expected to restore diplomatic relations with Britain at once upon becoming Prime Minister in 1967. However, he did not act immediately "in order to create an image for himself as a good Somali, not unduly under British or any other Western influence."[32] He also wished to buy a little more time to persuade his followers to support him with certain other radical changes in government policy. He received a much-needed boost from Parliament, who gave him full mandate to begin negotiations with Britain designed to restore the interrupted ties.

Although both sides, Britain and Somalia, were keen to resume relations, each appeared undecided as to who should first make the formal request to restore relations. The Prime Minister was of the opinion that, in view of the developments started in Kinshasa and the ongoing negotiations with Kenya, Her Majesty's government should take the initiative and make a formal request to the Somali government[33]. Egal wished to be able to use British initiative as something that he could present to the Parliament, something Britain did not object to[34]. In fact, in a diplomatic note delivered in October 1967 to the Acting Prime Minister and Minister of Foreign Affairs, Haji Farah Ali, the British government expressed its readiness for resumption of Anglo–Somali relations[35].

30 FRUS 1964-68, vol. XXIV: 340. Telegram from the USA Embassy in Somalia to the Department of State, July 27, 1967.

31 *Africa Confidential*, no. 15 July 21, 1967, p. 5.

32 TNA CO 31/223, Malcolm MacDonald, Talks with the Prime Minister of Somalia and others about resumption of diplomatic relations, p 1, pars 4-5,December 27, 1967.

33 TNA CO 31/222, Photostat copy of a letter from the Somali Prime Minister's Office to John Drysdale October 8, 1967.

34 Ibid., confidential letter from FO to R.J.R. Owen, Esq., October 19, 1967.

35 Ibid.

The decision was further discussed and agreed upon through informal *tête-a-tête* talks between Prime Minister Egal and a top British envoy, Malcolm MacDonald, the British Special Envoy in Kenya, who was in Mogadisho towards the end of 1967, officially on a birdwatching trip. During this meeting, on December 27, 1967, Egal and MacDonald had unofficial, personal and frank discussions on the likely benefit Somalia might derive from restoration of diplomatic relations between the two countries.

The discussions are reflected in long notes prepared by the British envoy, covering in detail all the points raised in the conversations and showing how Somali expectations might have been unrealistic. In his detailed description of his discussions with the Somali Prime Minister, MacDonald wrote: "When I arrived to the Prime Minister's office on Wednesday afternoon, the Minister of State and the Secretary General of the Ministry of Foreign Office were also present. After a few minutes Egal dismissed them both, saying he would like to talk to me alone. Britain indeed had been very keen, in the course of the negotiations, not to arouse expectations in Somalia's mind of immediate major economic benefit deriving to them from restoration of diplomatic ties between the two countries. The Prime Minister was now ready to resume relations, but in that connection, he had a serious problem. Somalia was a poor country, very short of money. If he resumed relations with Britain, his colleagues in the cabinet, his supporters in the National Assembly, would expect from him to secure, in return, a large financial aid on similar scale as that given by Britain before the relations were broken off. Egal was well aware that, if the Somali government did not receive such considerable aid as a result of a restoration of diplomatic relations, his positions as Prime Minister could distinctly weaken. Egal, however, made it clear that he did not seek to lay down any pre-condition for resumption of diplomatic relations, but he hoped that the British Government would recognize the facts of his position as he had stated to me."[36]

MacDonald summed up his response to Egal in three concise and clear points: (1) the British objected to any pre-condition to resumption of relations; talk about aid should take place after, and not before resumption of relations. (2) In view of its present economic and financial difficulties, Britain was not in a position to contemplate extending any budgetary or development aid at all to Somalia; and (3) Britain would do its best to make available British Council scholarships for Somali students in 1968/1969 and afterwards. Britain was, however, ready to

36 TNA FCO31/223, Talks with the Prime Minister of Somalia and others, p. 2, par. 7, December 27, 1967.

consider any proposal of a modest scale that the Somali government wished to make for technical aid[37]. This firm response dealt a devastating blow to Egal's high expectations. However, Egal was a consummate diplomat: while feeling deeply disappointed, yet he accepted the inevitable with good grace, and before the meeting ended, the two parties agreed that diplomatic relations between the two countries should resume by January 5, 1968 at ambassadorial level[38]. Egal then wondered whether he and MacDonald would agree on the following formula concerning aid: (a) restoration of diplomatic relations should be without pre-conditions; (b) negotiations on financial aid could start after the resumption of diplomatic relations; (c) HMG would then be ready to consider sympathetically any suggestions the Somali government wished to make. Egal wished MacDonald to make no mention of anything related to British inability to give budgetary or development aid, a suggestion the British Envoy had disagreed with, proposing instead his own formula: (a) resumption of diplomatic relations without pre-conditions, (b) discussions about financial aid to start after the exchange of Ambassadors; (c) HMG would then be ready to consider any suggestions which the Somali government might wish to make on the merit of the case from the British as well as the Somali point of view; (d) HMG would have to face facts, and the unavoidable facts were Britain's 'present very serious economic and financial position'. In Mr MacDonald's mind, this meant that major aid would be impossible, and that any future aid would have to be on a modest scale. Egal had no other option but to accept the bitter formula.[39]

During his 'bird-watching' stay in Mogadisho, the British envoy met Abdirashid on December 28 at Villa Somalia. In his detailed notes on his conversations with the Somali President, MacDonald states: "Abdirashid comments that he was responsible for breaking off the relations, and that he had now come round to the view that the long and historic friendly relations between Somalia and Britain should resume."[40] Abdirashid had a reputation for leaning politically towards the Eastern bloc countries. However, after his election as President in 1967, he seemed to adopt a more conciliatory political approach with the West, matching the openly pro-Western attitude of his Prime Minister.

Like his Prime Minister, Abdirashid also held the expectation that the

37 Ibid.
38 Ibid.
39 Ibid.
40 TNA FCO 31/223 talks with the Prime Minister of Somalia on December 27, 1967 about the resumption of diplomatic relations, p. 7, par. 24.

resumption of relations could bring substantial economic benefits for Somalia; but this great hope soon vanished in the face of the frank and tough talk of his visitor. The British diplomat took the same firm attitude he had displayed with the Prime Minister, reiterating that, as far as HMG was concerned, there was no direct advantage for Somalia in the restoration of diplomatic ties. "Egal expressed understanding of this", comments MacDonald, "and the President nodded his head, though only in dubious acceptance."[41] Abdirashid missed the opportunity to remind MacDonald that "Britain had alienated Somali territories as many as seven times in the course of 75 years", a statement he had made before the extraordinary session of the National Assembly on March 11, 1963[42]. Gone was the militant attitude he displayed towards Britain and the neighbouring countries in 1963 when he was Prime Minister. This rather subdued stance was in stark contrast with Abdirazak's strong views vis-à-vis the restoration of diplomatic ties with Britain when he was President of the Council of Ministers. It emerged that, in a private meeting with Mr Roy Lewis, the Commonwealth Correspondent of *The Times*, the former Prime Minister advanced two bold conditions which, in his view, should be fulfilled before Somalia took the initiative to remedy the rupture. The first condition was that the HMG should make a public announcement undertaking not to give military and logistic support to further the Kenyan war against Somalia. The second condition was that HMG should announce a willingness to give Somalia substantial capital aid and technical assistance as "compensation for the injury which the United Kingdom has done Somalia by confusing her into breaking off diplomatic relations with the United Kingdom in March 1963."[43]

As for Kenya, diplomatic relations with this country had been restored without difficulties. The Somali Ambassador, Mr Abdirahman Ahmed Salah, presented his credentials in February, 1968[44]. The first Ambassador of Kenya to Somalia, Mr Henry Mulla, presented his credentials on May 29, 1968[45]. Initially a young Kenyan Muslim, of no diplomatic experience, Sheikh Balale, was designated as the Kenyan first Ambassador to Somalia. However Egal, in order not to cause offence by refusing, sent Ali Omar Sheegoow, the Minister of State for Foreign

41 TNA FCO 31/223 talks with the Prime Minister of Somalia on December 27, 1967 about the resumption of diplomatic relations, p. 7, par. 24.

42 *Somali News*, March 15, 1963.

43 TNA FCO 31/221, Interview of Roy Lewis, Commonwealth correspondent of 'The Times', with Abdirazak, reported in letter POL 92/250/1 from British Embassy Mogadisho to FO, March 9, 1967.

44 *East African Standard*, July 25, 1968.

45 TNA FCO 31/223, Report from British Embassy, Mogadisho, to FO, June 5, 1968.

Affairs, on secret mission to Kenyatta to ask him to withdraw the nomination and send instead 'a really high diplomat' to Mogadisho.[46]

The peace dividend

The immediate results of Egal's overture *vis-à-vis* the neighbouring countries were, with respect to Ethiopia, the end of the state of emergency imposed by Ethiopia in 1964, the restoration of civil administration in Ogaden and the restoration of over flight rights for Somali Airlines on flights to the northern regions, in addition to the resumption of free access by Somali pastoralists to their traditional grazing land. An agreement signed between Ethiopia and Somalia provided for direct telephone and telegraph links between Addis Abeba and Mogadisho.[47]

With regard to Kenya, emergency regulations in the north East Province (NFD) were lifted with effect from Saturday, March 15, 1969[48]. Kenya also granted landing rights at Nairobi airport for the Somali Airlines fleet, which had been withdrawn in 1966[49], and gave an undertaking to back Somalia's application for membership of the East African Community, thus bringing "nearer the concept of the enlarged economic family of Nations stretching from the Horn down to the Zambezi", commented the *East African Standard*[50]. From the economic point of view, the normalization of ties with the two neighbouring countries was generally beneficial to Somalis settled along the common border, who had been living in a state of emergency since the 1964 ceasefire agreement brokered by the Organization of African Unity (OAU).

A jubilant Egal, returning to Mogadisho from Nairobi, released the following statement at Mogadisho airport: "It has been a painful history of the African sister States of Kenya and Somalia that they inherited from their colonial past a problem that has affected for a period the amicable and fraternal relationship that should exist between African countries, especially between those who share as many common affinities as Kenya and Somalia."[51] Questions remained, however, about just how faithful the new partners would be to each other.

At the same time, Egal ably allied himself with the West to counterbalance Soviet influence in Somalia. Among the tangible results of his new policy was

46 Ibid., Confidential letter from British Embassy, Mogadisho to FO, February 16, 1968.
47 *Somali News*, March 7, 1969.
48 Ibid., March 21, 1969.
49 Ibid., April 26, 1968.
50 *East African Standard*, July 30, 1968.
51 *Somali News*, February 28, 1969.

substantial financial aid from the USA and concession to Italian and German companies to explore newly discovered uranium deposits in some areas of Somalia[52]. The Americans were able to get off to a good start with the new government by announcing on June 24, a $12.9 million long-term, low-interest loan to Somalia to be used as follows: $8.5 million for improvements to Mogadisho Water Supply; $ 2 million for Credito Somalo Bank and $ 2.4 million for phase II of Kismayo Port[53]. These loans were pledged long before the change of government; however, the fact that the Americans did go through with them clearly represented something of an expression of confidence for the new government.

Egal is also credited to have pushed harder than his two southern predecessors for better relations with Italy, a major donor country. When Amintore Fanfani, the Italian Foreign Minister, paid the first official visit by an Italian Foreign Minister to Somalia (from 11 to 15 January 1968), he was welcomed by an 'unprecedented warm reception.' The Christian Democrat leader, who was popular in Somalia, was greeted at the airport by a cheering crowd of thousands, many of them waving the Italian tricolour. Nothing of the sort had happened a few days earlier, when US Vice-president Hubert Humphrey came on an official visit to Mogadisho and was welcomed only by handful of not particularly enthusiastic people; his car was closely guarded by Somali security forces and by FBI agents. Fanfani, of course, had not come empty-handed: in his top-level meeting on January 13 with Somali authorities, he announced that Italy was ready to offer an additional 12 billion Lire in economical, financial and technical assistance from January 1968, under the new law on co-operation[54]. In addition to this, during his visit, Fanfani handed over to the Somali authorities the new police hospital built with Italian funds and announced the plan for the construction of two bridges on Webi Shabelle, as well as promising financial assistance to Italian banana growers adversely affected by the closure of the Suez Canal.

Secret State Department reports suggest that the Prime Minister had taken a number of steps to cut down the Somali national army and put a stop to shifta activities in neighbouring countries. According to the same American reports, General Siad Barre's submission of a draft budget for the financial year 1968, which included a request for a 7% increase in funds, totalling $10.5 million, was

52 Del Boca, op. cit., p. 356.

53 TNA FCO 31/222, Confidential report from British Embassy, Washington to I.J.D. Hartland-Swann, Esq., North & East Africa Department, FO, June 30, 1967.

54 Del Boca, op. cit., p. 372.

rejected. Egal, instead, told the army to submit a revised budget of not more than $7.5 million, expect even further cuts and plan on the basis that it would remain a force of not more than 9,000 men. He then ordered the disbandment of the 3,000 or so men who were recruited before the Djibouti referendum, and instructed the army to call off the shifta in Ethiopia and Kenya and to prevent future guerrilla activities[55]. In 1967, military expenditure amounted to Sh.So52,000,000, representing 20% of the total ordinary budget of 246,000,000.[56]

According to American intelligence sources at Mogadisho, Premier Egal intended from the beginning to progressively reduce Armed Forces expenditure and use the army for 'civic action' and economic development projects[57]. Understandably, the Somali national army, one of the strongest in Africa, saw the new ouverture as a factor diminishing its importance and as threat to its expansion. A confidential British diplomatic report from Washington also indicates how the State Department was worried about possible reaction from the Somali national army to this treatment, although they seemed to be fairly confident that Egal had the authority and prestige "to ram his new policy down the throat of the military leaders."[58] ." While casting serious doubt about any trouble that might come to Egal from the older British and Italian trained officers, the Americans nevertheless believed there was some real dissatisfaction among the younger Russian and Egyptian trained officers. They concluded, however, that these young officers were not yet sufficiently numerous to be able to stage a successful coup, even if they tried to do so. In the final analysis, the Americans certainly showed a lack of perceptiveness when they discounted General Siad as the "potential leader of a military coup."[59]

Foreign aid to Somalia 1964-69

Because of its non-aligned policy and strategically important position, Somalia found itself in a position that enabled her to easily resort for assistance to both the West and East alike. If foreign aid were meant to help solve the economic predicament of a developing country, Somalia would have been the first to draw advantage of the generosity of foreign donors and come out of its chronic

55 TNA FCO 31/222, confidential report from British Embassy, Washington, quoting State Department sources in Mogadisho, to D.J. Speares Esq., North & East Africa Department, FO, August 29, 1967.

56 Diary Aden Abdulla, January 11, 1967.

57 TNA FCO 31/222, telegram no. 2749 from British Embassy, Washington to FO, August 24, 1967.

58 Ibid., confidential report from British Embassy, Washington, D.C. bearing the signature of R.J. Owen and addressed to D.J. Speares, Esq., North & East African Department, FO, August, 29, 1967.

59 Ibid.

poverty. However, as shown by figures supplied by international institutions, this was not the case and Somalia was destined to survive, for years to come, with foreign aid.

The International Bank of Reconstruction and Development gave a dramatic account of the high rate of aid Somalia had received, compared with other underdeveloped countries. According to this international institution, during 1964-69 Somalia received an annual average of about $15 per capita of her estimated population of 3 million[60]. This rate of aid is more than three times the figure of $4.5 per capita, which is the average annual aid to other less developed countries during 1964–7[61]. Another peculiarity of foreign aid to Somalia was that about 85% of the country's total development expenditure, up to the end of 1969, was externally financed, compared to other developing countries where foreign resources accounted for only about 10% of total investment expenditure.[62]

The first concerted attempt at economic and social development was undertaken right after independence under the 'First Five-Year Plan 1963-67'. The plan was to spend a total of 1,400 million Somali Shillings (the exchange rate, which had been stable throughout this period, was $1=Sh.So7.14)[63] on a number of projects, some of them already in existence and others yet to be established. The development initiatives included: expanding the productive capacity of the existing factory of Jowhar[64]; development of meat packing, fish processing, milk and dairy production and the textile industry; construction or improvement of a number of roads; building of three seaports at Kismayo, Berbera and Mogadisho; expansion of irrigation for crops and fodder; founding of a number of state farms. In the allocation of funds to the various services, the social services appear to have been relegated to a lesser scale, as only 6.5% and 3.0% were earmarked respectively for Education and Health.

"Unfortunately," writes O. Mehmet "the period 1964–67 was not a good period for the young Republic afflicted by two major setbacks, one to be attributed to nature, therefore, beyond its control, the second of its making. Generally, nature was not generous as poor rains in 1964 and the following year reduced grain

60 This population figure is not based on a reliable population census.

61 International Bank for Reconstruction and Development, World Bank Atlas, Population, Per Capita Product and Growth Rates, Washington, D.C., 1969, quoted in Ozay Mehmet, '*Effectiveness of Foreign Aid, the Case of Somalia*', *Journal of Modern African Studies*, vol. 9, no. 1 (May 1971), p. 31.

62 O. Mehmet, op. cit., p. 31.

63 Ibid., p. 33.

64 Originally an Italian sugar factory, this was turned into a mixed enterprises in 1963 with the Somali government holding a controlling share of the stock. After the coup of October 1969 it was completely taken over by the State.

production and grazing over wide areas, causing famine among 70,000 nomads and heavy losses of livestock."[65] The second setback, of the country's making, was the increase in the military expenditure following armed confrontation along the border with Ethiopia in 1964.

The first decade in the life of independent Somalia, starting as it had with an ambitious programme of economic and social development, ended with little tangible progress towards these objectives. Indeed, evidence suggests that living standards, on average, were lower at the close of the decade than at its beginning[66]. Critics said that the bulk of this foreign assistance was used for the upkeep of a bloated administration and for a 500% increase in the size of the Somali army[67]. However, it would be unfair not to recognize that some of the foreign aid went into infrastructural investment and development projects.

The main projects realized with EEC funds include Mogadisho General Hospital (Digfer) and the tract of road linking Afgooye to Shalambod. American aid funds were utilized for basic infrastructural investment, such as construction of a deep-water port in Kismayo[68], water and electricity for the town, a feasibility study for the port of Mogadisho and work on the capital's water supply. American assistance also covered agricultural projects, particularly developing experimentation and a demonstration farm in Afgooye, and a soil laboratory and farming training centre at Baidoa. Projects realized with Chinese funds included the National Theatre of Mogadisho, the Hargeisa water supply project, Somalia Cigarette Manufacture, Benadir Hospital in Mogadisho, Mogadisho Stadium, the Beledweyne–Burao Road and Fanole Farm. The Federal Republic of Germany financed the construction of a tract of the Kismayo–Jilib road and the Technical Institute of Burao, among other projects.

Top on the list of donor countries was Italy, who had been giving Somalia substantial budgetary support and development aid, the bulk of it in grants[69]. The United Nations had been helping Somalia in various important programmes with aid amounting to about Sh.So155 million, by far the larger part of which was a grant[70]. USSR funds were used to build Wajit Hospital for the treatment of

65 O. Mehmet, op. cit., p. 34.

66 The World Bank Atlas report (cf. note 64 above) reveals that Somalia's per capita GNP declined at an average rate of 1.6% annually during 1961-7. (World Bank Atlas..., p. 36).

67 David Laitin and Said S. Samatar, *Somalia, Nation in Search of a State*, Dartmouth Publishing Co., 1987, p. 108.

68 Decree no 3 of October 7, 1962.

69 First five-year development plan (1963-68).

70 Law no. 1 of January 1, 1967, 'Budget for the Financial Year 1967', p. 13.

tuberculosis disease, the State Printing in Mogadisho, Radio Mogadisho Station and the Port of Berbera. Little progress was made in Soviet funded agricultural projects: the state farm of Tog-Wajale and Jilib failed badly due to lack of local funds to pay the wages of workers and other recurrent expenses.

The Prime Minister admitted the failure of the Soviet-financed projects, citing as a reason lack of funds on the Somali side to ensure the continuation of the projects. In particular, the Wajit TB Hospital, a 50-bed hospital opened in July 1964, had been adversely affected by a shortage of drugs, because of gross negligence imputable to the Somali Ministry of Health. The poor management of drugs supply eventually resulted in the closure of the hospital, pushing the patients to leave en masse.[71] By the end of 1969 only 12.5% of all development projects were completed, with 51.6% being under construction and the remaining 35.9% still awaiting implementation[72]. The government blamed several factors for the underperformance: lack of skilled manpower and qualified personnel in the development projects, inefficiency of government departments, failure on the government's part to raise the required local contribution and insufficient allocation of working capital, obstructing performance of the completed projects[73]. The recipient and the donors are equally to blame for the delay in the implementation of the projects. In the words of O. Mehmet, "These delays resulted partly from time-taking negotiations with donors concerning financial arrangements, partly from long feasibility studies, and partly from exceedingly slow-moving autocratic machinery."[74]

Despite the infusion of funds, experts and enthusiasm imported from abroad, things did not go as planned in Somalia. Aid obviously fostered dependency rather than laying the foundation for a genuinely independent state. The development plans, not unlike those made during colonial times, were essentially directed to satisfying the interests of the ruling class (the bureaucracy and the merchants). "The only sector registering growth" writes Calchi Novati "was the public sector."[75] The weakness of the productive sectors, aggravated by total neglect of the agricultural sector, condemned Somalia to heavy dependence on foreign aid. The government expenditure for agriculture during the period 1964–69 oscillated between a minimum of 0.7% and a maximum of 2.3%, against 3.4%

71 Diary Aden Abdulla, January 31, 1966.

72 Law no. 24 of February 25, 1970, 'Budget for the Financial Year 1970, Bollettino Ufficiale, May 5, 1970, suppl. n°1 al n° 5.

73 O. Mehmet, op. cit., 35.

74 Ibid cit, 43.

75 Calchi Novati, op. cit., p. 131.

for public health, 2.9% for education and 16.7% for defence[76]. As for geographic distribution of the projects, the lion's share went to the southern regions, while larger areas in the northern regions had virtually no development activities at all. A partial explanation for this state of affairs may be related to the higher population density in the southern regions, which also possess more fertile land. It is a fact, however, that the nomadic population lives primarily in the northern regions and that livestock, together with bananas, is a major product for export.

The 1969 political elections

Under legislation issued on June 6, 1968, the 1969 elections, the third and last elections in the country, were held in March of that year, and for the first time combined voting for municipal and National Assembly posts.[77]

The major feature of these elections was doubtlessly the appearance of a mass of small political parties. Whereas twenty-one political parties had contested the general elections of 1964, this time sixty-four parties, representing sixty-four clans and sub-clans, most of which created just before the poll and all seeking a slice of the national pie[78], entered the field, with 2,214 candidates for the 123 available seats[79]. Most of the organizations contending for the election as political parties were not in reality parties in the true sense of the word, but rather temporary clan groupings, devoid of any clear political programme, formed solely for the purpose of putting up candidates with the ultimate aim of joining the ruling party after the elections. As Saadia Touval eloquently puts it, "Politics in the Horn, like the politics of industrial societies, consist of competing among groups for influence in the management of public affairs. The distinction lies in the character of the groups. In developed industrial societies the competing groups are made of individuals united by common economic or social interests or perhaps a common ideology. Among the Somalis they are determined by common ancestry."[80]

The country was divided into 48 electoral districts, out of which 5 had no contest at all, since only the ruling party had registered and presented lists of candidates who were automatically proclaimed elected before the counting of

76 Ibid.

77 Law no. 13 of 6 June, 1968, ' Political Elections and Local Council Elections', Bollettino Ufficiale, suppl. n° 6 al n° 6, June 28, 1968.

78 *Somali News*, March 7, 1969.

79 Bulo Burti district, with its 26 political parties contending in the elections, held the record for the highest level of political parties in a single constituency.

80 Touval, op. cit., p. 90.

the ballots. Compared to the past elections, the number of 'uncontested' seats has dropped significantly. The five 'uncontested' electoral districts were Aden Yaval, Bender Beila, Bur Hakaba, Jerriban and Zeila, all won by the ruling party.[81]

The electoral law had introduced two new innovations with respect to 1964: (a) Under Article 9 of the Law, the system of proportional representation was modified by assigning each constituency an electoral quotient determined by dividing the total number of votes cast by the number of seats assigned to each constituency. Consequently, only parties which reached the electoral quotient were allocated seats. The government claimed that changes to the system were designed to discourage the proliferation of small parties contending the elections; (b) Under Article 9 of the Law, all public servants, civilians or otherwise, who wished to stand as candidates were ineligible from running for the election unless they resigned from government employment at least 180 days before the date of voting "on the basis of the existing tradition in former Somaliland."[82] As a result, many prominent civil servants and military officers resigned their posts to stand as candidates. By contrast, in the southern region, by prevailing tradition civil servants were allowed to stand as candidates on the assumption that they represented the best educated and most qualified members of the population and they would be able to improve the quality of the legislature. Accordingly, a number of civil servants had been elected to the National Assembly in 1959 and 1964, and had been placed on leave without pay for the duration of their elective office.

One obvious flaw of the electoral law was the lack of electoral certificates which allowed voters to cast their votes in the electoral district where they found themselves on the day of voting. Illiterate villagers and town dwellers had an equal say in choosing their candidates. No one knew how many voters (or indeed people) there were in any of the country's provinces. This shortcoming encouraged irregular movements of the population from districts where only one list ('*lista unica*') was presented to cast their vote in other electoral districts.

Again, like in 1964, no attempt was made to review the constituency boundaries inherited from past colonial administrations. The security deposit for the election of MPs was raised from Sh.So1,000 in 1964 to Sh.So 5,000, to be forfeited and credited to State revenue in case the list failed to obtain the necessary votes for the election of at least one deputy. To prevent voters casting their ballot more

81 *Somali News*, April 4, 1969.
82 P. Contini, op. cit., p. 27.

than once, their left hand was marked with indelible ink before voting, a familiar system that had been in use since 1959.

In a highly polarized political environment, few expected the build-up to the elections to be anything other than violent. Scores of people are thought to have died in the post-election violence, though authoritative figures are hard to come by. Official reports said that about 25 people died during the elections, but it is understood that this was a somewhat conservative estimation. Owing to censorship, no reference to the killings appeared in the local papers at the time. Most of the troubles arose because of complicated divisions of the territory into tribal boundaries, inaugurated during the trusteeship regime, with no attempt made after independence to rectify the situation. Alula, Iskushuban, Galkayo, Dusa Mareb, Merca, and Lugh Ferrandi, to mention just a few, had been flash-points for years during election times.

A few weeks before the general elections, changes involving the leadership of the governing party had taken place. A brief notice appeared in the government-owned weekly *Somali News*, announcing the sudden resignation of Ali 'Hagarey', who was also the Minister of State for the Presidency of the Council of Ministers, from his post of secretary general of the ruling party. The announcement added that the leader of the party, Premier Egal, had nominated Sheikh Mohamoud 'Malingur' as the new secretary general.[83]

The government rallied all its resources and "the much respected police commander, General Mohamed Abscir resigned from his post, refusing to agree that police transport should be employed to carry SYL voters to the polling stations."[84]

In anticipation of the general elections, the government appointed new regional governors and district commissioners. The regional authorities, particularly those hailing from the south, were notorious for their expertise in election fraud. "The new appointees were widely seen as mercenaries who were appointed on ad hoc basis to rig the elections for the candidate favoured by the government", comments Ismail A. Ismail, one of the most experienced district commissioners of the time.[85]

Like the past political of 1964, the 1969 elections were characterized by large voter turnout and gerrymandering. Few months before the elections, Yassin Nour, who was once said to be the richest man under 40 in Somalia and who

83 *Somali News*, March 7, 1969.

84 I.M. Lewis, op. cit., p. 204.

85 Ismail, A. Ismail, op. cit., p. 195.

had been running the powerful Ministry of Interior as his fief since 1967, issued a decree upgrading Jerriban, a small watering point east of Galkayo, to the level of electoral district, moving two seats from the more populated Galkayo constituency. Jerriban became an uncontested constituency for the Minister of the Interior, where only the Lega list was allowed. In 1963, the government led by Abdirashid took similar measures by elevating the small watering point of El-Deer to district level and allocating to it two seats detached from El Bur, a more populated district.

The final results of the elections were released on April 7, 1969 by the Central Electoral Office, chaired by the President of the Appeal Court, Judge G. Marotta-Gigli[86]. There was a reduction in the number of people who voted compared with previous elections: 879,554 people recorded votes, compared with 913,069 in 1964 and more than 1,300,000 in the administratives of 1963.[87]

All together, 63 political parties contested the elections, of which 27 were represented in the 1969-74 House. Egal's SYL party won the general elections, securing a second term for the Prime Minister and scooping up 73 of the 123 seats (about 90% of the seats in Parliament), followed by the SNC with 11 seats, SANU 6, HDMS 3 and PLGS 3. The remaining 22 small parties managed to obtain 1 or 2 seats each, totalling 27 seats.[88]

Whatever Somali voters may have wanted, it was axiomatic that the Lega did not lose elections. So, gross irregularities in the 1969 election should come as no surprise. The Lega was an extraordinarily powerful, hard to defeat money machine. The methods it had adopted to attain these results were certainly not democratic and even illegal, but it would be a grave mistake to judge them too harshly on this account. The Somalis who led the nation and had a thin veneer of culture were all born in the bush, brought up in the bush and taught the law of the bush before they came into contact with the foreign imposed democratic values.

86 Bollettino Ufficiale della Repubblica Somala, suppl. n° 3 al n° 6, Mogadiscio, Aprile 8, 1969.
87 *Somali News*, April 4, 1969.
88 Ibid.

The 'carefully managed' vote gave the following result:

LEGA DEI GIOVANI SOMALI (LGS)	73 SEATS
SOMALI NATIONAL CONGRESS (SNC)	11 SEATS
SOMALI AFRICAN NATIONAL UNION (SANU)	6 SEATS
PARTITO COSTITUZIONALE INDIPENDENZA SOMALA (HDMS)	3 SEATS
PARTITO LIBERALE GIOVANI SOMALI (PLGS)	3 SEATS
OTHER MINOR PARTIES OBTAINED A TOTAL OF	27 SEATS

Petitions to the Supreme Court

Electoral appeals were filed before the Supreme Court for remedy against the non-acceptance of lists for election issued by some Regional Courts under article 14, paragraph 3 of the Political and Local Council Elections Law. The Article reads: "The representatives may file a petition in writing on questions of law before the Regional Court territorially competent against the order rejecting the presentation of the list within three days from the date of such rejection, and the Court shall decide within three days from the date of the filing of the petition. An appeal shall be filed with the Supreme Court against the decision of the Regional Court rejecting the petition within three days from such decision. The Supreme Court shall decide the appeal at least thirty days prior to the date of voting and such decision shall be final."

Discontent was exacerbated when the Supreme Court, under its newly appointed President Abdul Rahman Sheikh Ali, the first Somali President to hold this position[89], rejected on a technicality, i.e. on procedural grounds, a number of electoral petitions and complaints filed by political parties against decisions taken by local authorities. Although a judicial system for Somalia, entirely separate and independent from the Italian judiciary, was established in 1956, until 1968 the highest judicial posts were still held by Italians, owing to the lack of qualified Somali judges. Abdirahman replaced Mr Aldo Peronaci, a widely respected Italian judge who had clashed with Egal over legal and protocol matters[90]. Like other expatriate judges, Mr Peronaci was seen as a neutral judge, unlikely to toe the government's line and with no interest to favour one political party against another. The foreign nationals who had sat as Supreme Court judges in the past

89 Ordinance no. 5 of February 2, 1956.

90 Peronaci was appointed president of the Supreme Court by Presidential Decree no. 70 of March 1, 1965.

had thoroughly examined election results, handing down decisions not in favour of Mr Egal's party[91]. Many believe that Judge Peronaci was removed before the elections to spare the government from being embarrassed.

A Division Bench of the Supreme Court consisting of Mr Abdul Rahman Sheikh Ali, Mr Mohamoud Sheikh Ahmed and Sheikh Mohamed Sheikh Ali declared inadmissible all the appeals filed by the Popular Movement for Democratic Action (PMDA) of Bur Hakaba, by the Socialist National Congress (SNC), Hargeisa branch, by the Hizbia Destour Mustaqil Somali (HDMS), Bur Hakaba branch, by Somali Youth League (SYL), Mogadisho Branch, by the (SNC) Baidoa branch, by the Central Committee of the SYL, Bosaso branch. The appeals were all declared inadmissible on the following grounds: (a) the legal grounds for appeal required under article 14 (3) of the election law were not presented on time; (b) Even if the grounds had arrived on time, the appeals would still remain inadmissible inasmuch as not signed by the representatives of the list within the terms of article 14 (3) as read with article 12 (5) of the electoral law[92]. Despite this well-articulated Court ruling, many openly questioned the impartiality of the judges, a direct slight against an institution which suffered problems of credibility and fairness.

The most celebrated legal case among the electoral appeals referred to above was the PMDA appeal against the order of rejection by the Baidoa Regional Court, dated February 1969, of the petition filed by the same party against the non-acceptance of its list for election in the district of Bur Hakaba. Much was said about this, and the issue of the non-acceptance of the PMDA list for the election of Bur Hakaba became the subject of lively debate among the Somali public at large. The facts of the case are as follows: the district commissioner of Bur Hakaba, who happened to be the same person who had produced one million votes in Wanleweyn during the referendum on the Constitution in 1961 and who was reputed to be an expert in 'fixing' elections, rejected the PMDA list, the party of Abdulkadir 'Zoppo'. It was widely rumored that the district commissioner held grudges against Zoppo stemming from alleged ill-treatment he suffered at his hands when Zoppo was Minister of Internal Affairs. In Somalia, facts and fiction are not easy to separate, but one rumour which gained widespread currency suggested that the government purposely posted

91 The corrections made to the 1964 Merca election results and the annulment of the 1959 Lugh elections are two cases in point..

92 Judgment delivered by Mr Abdul Rahman Sheikh Ali. For a full explanation of the Court ruling, see Somali News, February 28, 1969.

this particular commissioner at Bur Hakaba just to bar the former minister from competing in his tribal power base. The reader may wish to learn more about why the government wanted to vex the former minister. To understand this we need to take one step back to the 1967 presidential election. The election of the President had split the ruling party into two rival groups, one in support of the incumbent and the other in favour of Abdirashid. Abdulkadir 'Zoppo' joined the faction supporting the incumbent, and in the subsequent political developments he quit the ruling party to join the newly-established MPDA led by Abdirazak.

Zoppo, a cunning politician, had a record-breaking number of switches of loyalty from one political party to anther. It is on record that, during his political career, he changed sides three times: the first time in the late 40s, when he repudiated the Lega to join the Hizbia Dighil Mirifle (HDM); the second time in 1959, when he rejoined the Lega, turning his back on the HDM to become a minister, and the third time in 1968 when he joined the MPDA.

In a functional democracy, affiliation to political parties and expression of one's own opinion would be seen as legitimate exercise of one's rights. However, the government did not see things that way. In their eyes, Abdulkadir 'Zoppo' had committed two 'grave acts' that they interpreted as inimical to them, firstly joining the anti-Rashid faction in the presidential election of 1967 and later joining the MPDA.

Barely six months since the elections were held the entire political scene was suddenly thrown into turmoil by the military, and Egal and his party had little time to enjoy their stolen victory. Judge Abdurahman was arrested by the military junta and suspended from service with effect from November 1, 1969, "pending unspecified criminal case against him"[93] : a legally questionable action since judges cannot be prosecuted for handing down verdicts, however unpopular they may be. Abdurahman's arrest becomes even more bizarre if one considers that the judge who replaced him as President of the Supreme Court, Mohamoud Sheikh Ahmed Mussa, was sitting in the Division Bench of the Supreme Court who had examined the rejected appeal cases[94]. Many, however, compared the meticulous approach of the 1964 Supreme Court with the rushed proceedings of the 1969 Court, viewed by some as a rubber-stamping of the validity of the election results.

93 Decreto del Presidente del Consiglio Rivoluzionario Supremo n° 2 del 9 dicembre 1969.

94 Ibid., no. 1.

A single-member opposition

As stated earlier, it was in the field of foreign policy that Egal chiefly broke new ground. He did in fact appear to have good foreign policy advisors, but for domestic affairs he heavily relied on bad advisors who pushed him to make the fatal mistakes which eventually brought his premature downfall in 1969.

Mohamed Haji Ibrahim Egal could have gone down in history either as a leader who guided Somalia towards stability, or as the man who scotched its chances of better future. Sadly he chose the infamy and displayed some of his southern brothers' ugly traits. But, while the southern political classes were experts in electoral fraud and had been in that 'business' since 1954, Egal was a novice, and as such, he handled the election clumsily by just blindly following in the footsteps of his southern big brothers.

In the run-up to the general elections, the Prime Minister, who was also the party leader, travelled extensively throughout the country on a campaign. Never had a Prime Minister before him toured the country during an election year; but while this might have appeared as the beginning of a season of openness and innovation, Egal's real, sinister intention was eventually revealed by the way the elections were conducted. His critics say that he was deeply involved in manipulation of the elections in the northern regions, hand-picking deputies of his choice, albeit not among nationally well-known figures, their only necessary qualification being that of loyalty to the Prime Minister. Instead of consolidating the impartiality of the 1959 elections in the Somaliland Protectorate, Egal succumbed to the partisan system inherited from the trusteeship mandate. Despite all his courage, skill and brains, he was always better at preaching democracy than practising it.

As for the southern regions, critics say that they became a fiefdom of Yassin Nour, the Minister of the Interior, who oversaw the most controversial political elections ever organized in Somalia. Somalis had grown used to electoral irregularities since the time of the United Nations trusteeship regime, but were still shocked by the scale of the vote rigging in 1969, the likes of which had never been experienced in the past.

Within a few weeks from the election, all but one of the new MPs who were not members of the Lega had joined the ruling party: a total of 60 newly deputies elected from a myriad of small parties. Some of them cabled their adhesion while they were still in their respective outpost electoral districts and before returning to Mogadisho. All were attracted by the advantages of being inside rather than outside the ruling party. Such transmigrations from one party to another are not without historical precedent in Somali politics. The tendency of members to switch their alliance to the ruling party has come to define a significant element of Somali institutional politics since the general elections of 1956. Somalia was heading towards the gradual establishment of a one-party State, as the case was in all Africa. Similar instances of 'crossing the floor' were also experienced in the 1964 general elections, but not to the scale experienced in 1969, which annulled parliamentaryopposition.[95]

The single opposition member who resisted the temptation to join the ruling party was Abdirazak Haji Hussein, who became, as Tripodi put it, "a rare example in the history of democracy."[96] I.M. Lewis goes further than Tripodi, giving an unflattering description of the massive movement of deputies crossing the floor: "The unedifying stampede of deputies left Abdu ar-Razak Haji Hussein sitting alone as sole opposition member of the National Assembly!"[97] However, what Tripodi and Lewis seem to overlook is that, in Somalia, the role of the political opposition has always been played by factions within the ruling party, and not by the opposition parties alone. Circumstances did not allow, but there were good reasons to believe that, in the course of the legislature (1969–1974), other deputies affiliated with the ruling party would have joined ranks with Abdirazak to oppose the government.

Abdirazak's track record as a parliamentarian shows that he had been a thorn in the side of each administration, unless he was member of it—he led the much-celebrated rebellion within the Lega against Abdullahi Issa's government in 1959; in 1967, after losing office, he led the faction within the ruling party opposing the policy of *détente* inaugurated by Egal towards the neighbouring countries, and eventually formed a party of his own, using it as a platform to attack the government's reputation and inflame public opinion during the weekly meetings at the party's HQs in Mogadisho. But despite the powerful oratory he displayed in public, he never managed to seriously worry his former party or cut deeply into its constituency. For a long time the Lega represented the springboard for anyone in search of political power; leaving it became like leaving the mafia, with the sole difference that former Lega members were merely relegated in political limbo, rather than risking physical elimination as mafia members would.

95 Michele Pirone, '*Previsioni sulle prossime elezioni in Somalia*', Africa, Roma, n° 3, 1969.
96 Tripodi, op. cit., pp. 110-111.
97 I.M. Lewis, op. cit., p. 204.

The first business of the Fourth Legislature when it convened on May 8, 1969 after the elections was to elect a president and the members of the presidency of the National Assembly. By 114 votes Sheikh Muktar Mohamed was elected President of the House. Before the voting took place, Hon. Sheikh Ali Jim'ale withdrew his candidature for the office. In the same session, Ahmed Qumane (110 votes), Haji Yousuf Egal (108 votes) and Haji Farah Ali (107 votes) were elected vice-presidents.[98]

Meanwhile, the President of the Republic had begun consultations with the country's leading politicians concerning the designation of a Prime Minister following the government's resignation after the general elections; but the Prime Minister was asked to remain in office together with his cabinet ministers for routine administrative functions until the new government was formed[99]. As widely anticipated, Egal had been designated for the second time to form a new government.

Egal's second government, consisting of twenty cabinet ministers, was formed; the Prime Minister reserved for himself, as in 1967, the Foreign Affairs portfolio[100]. Egal included in his government 4 ministers without portfolio, one more than his first government of 1967; they were known as Ministers of State[101]. Seven of his ministers (Abdullahi Mohamed Hired, SNC; Hared Farah PLGS; Jama Ganni SDU; Ismail Jim'ale PLGS; Soufi Mohamed HDMS; Elmi Duale, PAS; Sheikh Abdullahi Sheikh Ibrahim, OSU[102], were elected on a non-Lega ticket in the general elections of March 1969.

It is also significant to mention that, before the general elections, a change in the top echelon of the police force had been effected, by which the much respected Police Chief, General Mohamed Abshir, resigned from his post after "refusing to agree that police transport should be employed to carry SYL voters to the polling stations."[103] Abscir was later transferred to the Foreign Service as Ambassador[104]. The former deputy chief of the police force, General Jama Ali Korshel, promoted major general, took over as chief of police[105], and General Hussein Kulmie, former aide de camp of the president, became deputy chief of

98 *Somali News*, May 8, 1969.
99 Ibid., May 9, 1969.
100 Presidential Decree no. 86 of May 22, 1969.
101 Elmi Duale to Foreign Affairs, Osman Ahmed Roble to the office of the Prime Minister, Hared Farah Nour to Somali Affairs and Sheikh Abdullahi Sheikh Ibrahim to Religious Affairs and Awqaf.
102 *Corriere della Somalia*, April 9, 1969.
103 I.M. Lewis, op. cit., p. 204.
104 Presidential Decree no. 64 of April 22, 1969.
105 Presidential Decree no. 65 of April 22, 1969.

police[106]. Abshir was later separated from the service following his resignation[107]. These changes did not involve the national army, under General Mohamed Siad, despite widely circulating speculations that Premier Egal was seriously considering sending the Commander to Russia, officially for military training, but practically to remove him from command. However, General Siad Barre, who was well aware of Egal's thinking and of his weaknesses, outmanoeuvred the latter's plan by staging a military coup which toppled the ineffective civilian government and by this dramatically altered the country's history.

The slow agony of a regime

The military takeover

In the late 1960s, Somalia saw not only regional but also growing internal conflicts. Rivalries between clans caused the fragmentation of political parties into smaller and smaller units. This explains why in March 1969 over 60 political parties contended in the elections.

In the absence of a clear political programme in election times, Somalis began to spit ethnic vitriol at one another, emerging from the 1969 elections far more polarized than ever before along tribal lines. The Courts were bent, public institutions were dysfunctional and the economy, dominated by Italian-era banana production, was sick. Much of the hope with which Somalis greeted independence in July 1960 had evaporated: too little had changed for the better. Political leaders focused on the conflict with neighbouring countries, relegating social and economic problems to the bottom of their priorities list. The following figures, extracted from the national budget for 1967, show how the crucial social sectors were neglected. The allocation in the 1967 national budget for the Ministry of Defence was 19.95%, against 6.99% and 7.02% for Health and Education respectively: very inadequate when compared to 18% in Kenya and Tanganyika and 27% in Uganda.[108]

Angelo del Boca described the lack of direction and sense of general despair the country was going through few months before the military coup: "By the summer of 1969, nine years after independence, in Somalia, the country U Thant[109]

106 Presidential Decree no. 66 of April 22, 1969.

107 Decree no. 184 of September 17, 1969.

108 Five Year Plan 1963-67, pp. 2-3; George G. Dawson, op. cit. p. 213.

109 U Thant, a Burmese diplomat, served as Secretary General of the U. N. from November 1962 to December 1971.

liked to define as the 'darling child of the United Nations', nothing remains of the characteristics that made her an example. The democracy is a mere memory. The multiparty is a mockery; the neutrality, a faded option; and in the Parliament, confusion reigns."[110]

The President and the Prime Minister were largely responsible for all this, but that does not exempt the public at large from its share of responsibility. The fact that the government was losing its grip gradually was becoming a lot more evident. The Premier and the President did not seem particularly concerned about official corruption and nepotism, although these practices were conceivably normal in a society based on kinship and clanship. The question that arose was whether a polls victory obtained by unethical means would enable the ruling elite to govern until the end of the legislature, or throw the country back into tribal enmities and chaos. Neither of these two scenarios happened: a military solution sadly became the option.

Rumours of a military coup were rife, but the government and the President showed no sign of alarm. The opposition remained largely divided without a common programme, fragmented, as had always been the case, along tribal lines. A foundering regime had weakened itself by discontenting everyone. The election fraud was only one of the fuses that could detonate an explosion at any moment. Another was the rampant corruption in the public administration, which wasted vast amount of public money, including aid from foreign governments, and fuelled anger among the mass of Somalis, who resented economic deprivation and the opulence enjoyed by the political elite. Public unease mounted, faith in the regime waned, and the optimistic mood quickly gave way to cynicism. By 1969, after nearly a decade of independence, Somalia was effectively bankrupt, shackled to foreign aid for survival and prone to sliding into a dictatorial regime.

On October 15, Radio Mogadisho gave the shocking news that the President of the Republic had been shot dead at about 12:45 in Las Anod by a rogue policeman. The President was visiting the northern provinces of the country that had been hit by famine and drought. It is significant to recall that a year earlier the President had survived an assassination attempt when he narrowly avoided a grenade while being driven from the airport to Villa Somalia. It soon emerged that the earlier assailant was a close relative of the rogue soldier who gunned down the President in October 1969.

It is hard to believe but, during the critical two weeks preceding his assassination,

110 Del Boca, op. cit., p. 377.

the President of the Republic, together with the Speaker of Parliament, was on mission to the northern regions; at the same time, the Prime Minister was on state visit to the United States of America. The military had obviously exploited these circumstances to stage the coup, which most probably would not have taken place had the three top State authorities not been absent from the capital. "There could have been no better situation for the army and its Soviet advisors to hatch a *coup d'état*," comments one writer.[111]

In the absence of reliable information, the tragic event had generated a jumble of contradictory accounts on the motives that might be behind the killing of the President. Among these, the one linking the criminal act to the way the general elections were conducted had gained the widest currency. According to this account, the killer appeared to have acted in reaction to the political violence which had caused the death of dozens of people, including some of his close relatives, in the electoral district of Iskushuban (Majertenia). The accused denied this account before the court, citing instead different motives for his brutal action.

The public, still in shock after the brutal murder of their beloved Head of State, also had to come to terms with an ugly hiccup in the burial arrangements when Murursade tribesmen, claiming traditional title to the burial site, demanded payment in exchange for permission to perform the burial rituals. Left with no choice, and pressed by the volatile situation, the government yielded to the tribesmen's diktaat. It is believed that a sum of Sh.So30,000 was paid to the tribesmen, but this account should be taken with a pinch of salt.

A sense of lack of State authority was felt in the first hours following the death of the President, particularly when rumours started circulating that it had proven impossible to even send news of the tragic event to the Prime Minister, who was on State visit in the USA. After the official visit, Egal appears to have taken some days off at Las Vegas, as a guest of American film star William Holden. "The Somali Embassy in Washington took the trouble to seek the FBI's assistance in order to locate the whereabouts of our Prime Minister" wrote Mohamed Aden Sheikh[112]. When the 'missing' Premier was eventually located and informed of what had happened, he hastily returned from Washington to Mogadisho. Soon after his arrival, he and his party's leadership started the selection process for a presidential candidate. The choice finally fell on Haji Mussa Bogor, a consummate politician and close associate of the slain President. The election was set to take

111 Mohamed Diriye Abdullahi, *Culture and Customs of Somalia*, 2001, p. 29.

112 Mohamed Aden Sheikh, *La Somalia non e' un' isola dei Caraibi. Memoria di un pastore somalo* in Italia, Diabesis, 2010, p. 57.

place in compliance with article 74 of the Constitution on the following day on October 21, 1969. But, on October 21, no election took place, and the National Assembly did not meet as planned, because, as Lewis wrote: "When, at a late-night meeting at the party HQs on October 20, the party caucus reached agreement to present this nominee as their official candidate, thus virtually ensuring his election as President and Mohamed Haji Ibrahim Egal's re-appointment as Premier, those army officers who were closely watching development decided to act."[113]

Tanks rolled into the streets of the capital. Twenty-four hours after the state funeral of the slain Somali President, a self-styled revolutionary council seized power without bloodshed, and would rule the country for almost 21 consecutive years, led by military officers who had donned civilian garb. This military takeover was quickly dubbed a 'revolution'. Explaining the difference between revolutionary movements and military takeover, Bernard Lewis wrote: "The word 'revolution' has been much misused in the modern Middle East, being applied to, or claimed for, many events which would more appropriately be designated by the French *coup d'etat*, or the Italian *colpo di Stato*. [...] Interestingly, the English language does not provide an equivalent term."[114]

The immediate aftermath

At a time when almost all African States had experienced some sort of a military coup or plot, Somali civilian leaders seemed not to have given much thought to that danger, choosing to believe that a military coup was not a method of changing the government of their country.

The slaying of the President on October 15 by a rogue soldier appears to have increased the pressure on the military to speed up the takeover. The military takeover was welcomed with open arms by the public at large, not because the army looked best, but because the population was sick of the corrupt and inept civilian administrations led by the Lega party since 1956. "The parliamentary regime collapsed like an empty sack, and by all accounts to the vivid joy of most of the population" comments Basil Davidson.[115]

Many had lived off the patronage of the civilian-led government when it was in power, but no group or individual lifted a finger to defend it; everyone melted away into the mass of people who welcomed the military takeover. Out

113 I.M. Lewis, op. cit., pp. 206-7.

114 Bernard Lewis, The Crisis of Islam, Holy War and Unholy Terror, The Modern Library, New York 2003, p. 21.

115 'Notes on the Revolution in Somalia', The Socialist Register,' vol. 12, 1975 p. 208.

of desperation, all Somalis accepted the same unelected regime, and the resultant government was a form of military dictatorship leading them into uncharted water.

The new rulers put the Prime Minister and his Cabinet ministers under house arrest at the presidential Villa situated at Afgooye, some 30 km south-west of the capital, and imposed a curfew on the capital. The new military junta soon blamed the civilian government for everything, from corruption and incompetence to mismanagement of the national economy and electoral fraud. They were correct in their description, and the accusations levelled against the former government members would not be hard to prove if seriously investigated. "The degeneration of the political system and widespread corruption paved the way for Siad Barre's military dictatorship", comments one author.[116]

The bloodless revolution staged by the military in 1969 suspended the Constitution and the other constitutional organs (judiciary, parliament, political parties, elections and trade unions)[117]. The first official proclamation of the Supreme Revolutionary Council "in the name of the people" was published in the Charter of 21 October 1969; and Law No. 1 of the same date had abrogated all norms deemed incompatible with or contrary to the spirit of the 'revolution'. The right to *habeas corpus* contemplated under the article 66 of the Somali Penal Code was temporarily suspended[118]. Existing international treaties were to be honoured, but national liberation movements and Somali unification were to be supported. The country's name was immediately changed into "Somali Democratic Republic", a formulation that in Africa usually, albeit not always, signifies an intention to move to the left.

Meanwhile, the trial of *Askari* Abdulkadir Abdi Mohamed, regimental roll (matricola) 4745, later identified as Said Yusuf Ismail, which was pending before the Regional Court of Burao, territorially competent to hear the case, was transferred, for security reasons, to the National Security Court in Mogadisho.[119]

It should be noted that, as well as *Askari* Said, a number of other persons were arrested for alleged involvement in the killing of the President: Mohamoud Yousuf Ismail, a radio telegrapher, based at Eyl; Sheikh Nureddin Ali Olow, councillor of the Supreme Court; Ainab Farah Miraf, a businessman resident at

116 Tripodi, op. cit., p. 57.

117 Law n. 43 of August 6, 1970, Bollettino Ufficiale, suppl. n°3 al n°.

118 Law n. 12 of March 3, 1970.

119 Decree of the Revolutionary Council no. 10 of 28 October 1969; Decree of the Supreme Revolutionary Council no. 9, January 10, 1970.

Las Anod; Ten. Beddel Hersi Farah, commander of the Las Anod police station at the time of the incident; Ten. Abdi Rabi Raghe, an officer of the Drawishta Boliska Unit, based at Burao. The arrest of this group was effected on the basis of confessions made by the principal defendant to the police.

The case, whose investigation was assigned to a team of police investigators led by the Prosecutor General of the time, Abdi Farah Basciane, was presented to the Court as that of a politically motivated crime committed through a conspiracy of the co-defendants.[120]

The main defendant pleaded guilty of murder, but denied acting on grounds of personal grudges towards the former President, stating that he had acted in the general interest of the country and the people. In his sworn testimony before the Court, the main defendant said that he was troubled by the former President's "lack of loyalty to the people, for doing nothing to advance the progress of the country, and for not showing interest to the territories under foreign domination", and that in the Burao region (Katuma) "as a result of the rigged political elections, people are killing each other, as is the case also in other areas of the country. [...] The discovery of uranium deposits announced by the former Premier Egal was dismissed by the BBC—so I became convinced that Abdirashid and Egal were fooling the people. [...] In the face of this reality, I decided to save the country from catastrophe because, as a citizen and soldier, I took the oath to be faithful and defend my country from internal as well as externalenemies."[121]

Defense attorneys for the defendant[122] argued that the defendant deserved leniency, as his act had accelerated and ignited the first spark of the revolution of 21 October. "The defendant's act, though deplorable from a moral and religious perspective, is justified by its aim. Said's name will be inseparable from the revolution of October 21, 1969 which has salvaged the country from chaos and corruption," further argued the defense counsel. Reference was made to the Egyptian revolution of 1952 and that of Russia of 1917 which, due to external factors, took place slightly ahead of their scheduled date.

The accused was found guilty of murder under article 434 of the Somali Penal Code (SPC) and sentenced to death on October 8, 1970, just less than one year since the tragic event at Las Anod. His five co-defendants were acquitted[123]. The

120 Abdi Farah Basciane was later found guilty of false evidence under Art .291 of the Somali Penal Code.

121 National Security Court ruling no. 37/70 Reg. Sent. no. 63/70 Reg. Gen., pp 20-22.

122 Abdulaziz Nour Hersi and Mohamed Jama Habeb.

123 National Security Court ruling no. 37/70 Reg. Sent. no. 63/70 Reg. Gen. , p. 24.

trial's outcome seemed to be quite clear-cut. However, plenty of lurid speculation surrounds Saidi's decision to gun down the President. The theory that the defendant was alone in the preparation and execution of the criminal plan to kill the President is too simplistic to be convincing. The story seems to be missing a chapter, and many questions remain: what is the real story of the assassin's time in the police force; why was he moved to Las Anod shortly before he shot the President; what role might have been played by possible instigators, widely rumoured at the time to be among the President's rival politicians: the answers have not been unearthed.

The deposed Prime Minister, along with some of his ministers was brought before a special Court whose three judging panel were members of the military Supreme Revolutionary Council (SRC). Never before had a Somali politician been put on trial: the climate of impunity and the myth of unaccountability for ministers was thus brought to an end.

Ironically, the trial was held at the building which was once the seat of the National Assembly, now converted into a courtroom, where the deputies were expected to meet on October 21, 1969 for the election of the new President of the Republic. Many had doubted that the new military rulers, who had all until recently been loyal to the deposed government, would allow the trial to go ahead: but even when it did, only charges of embezzlement of public funds were brought against some of the ministers. The Prime Minister was given the maximum prison sentence of 30 years charged with embezzlement of public funds under article 241 of Somali Penal Code on October 15, 1974. The Court ruled also the confiscation of his private mansion, "Villa Baidoa" in Mogadisho[124]. The investigation fell short of extending to cases involving bribery, abuse of power, political corruption and election fraud. Only cases of petty theft of public funds were hastily investigated, as a result of which the PM and a handful of his ministers were held accountable and received sentences. None of them served their full prison terms, all of them benefitting from amnesty. They were soon rehabilitated and rewarded with highly remunerative public positions, despite the provisions in the Penal Code barring any person convicted of serious crime from holding public office. Some of the ministers convicted of embezzlement, including Egal, were appointed diplomats and managers of State bodies[125]. One valid reason for this leniency towards the former rulers may possibly be traced to

124 National Security Court Ruling no. 161/74, p, 14.

125 Egal was appointed ambassador in New Delhi, India.

the past association of the top military members of the Revolutionary Council with the civilian administration. The Somali military had been hollowed out by a legacy of corruption so bad that senior officers were repeatedly accused of taking part in the rigging of the last political elections.

The military ruled the country for over 20 years, in the course of which, except perhaps in the first few years, their celebrated merits were few and very modest, in the face of dramatic failures in foreign policy and a military adventure against Ethiopia which proved to be a fatal miscalculation. Like the civilian regime they ousted in 1969, they too soon ran out of ideology and sense of direction.

BIBLIOGRAPHY

Abdi Sheik-Abdi, "Somali Nationalism: Its Origins and Future". The Journal of Modern African Studies, Vol, 15, No. 4, (Dec., 1977), pp, 657–665.

Abdisalam M. Issa- Salwe, "The Collapse of the Somali State", Haan Associates, London, 1994.

Aden Abdulla Osman, Diary, 1958, 1959, 1961, 1962, 1963, 1964, 1966, 1967.

Afyare Abdi Elmi, "Understanding the Somalia Conflagration, Identity Political Islam and Peace Building", Pluto Press 2012.

Agreement for the regulations of mutual relations (with annexure, schedule and exchange of letters) on 1944.

Ahmed Baha'al-Din, "Mu'amaratun fi Ifriqia" (Plot in Africa) Cairo, Isa al-Babi al Halabi, 1958.

Ahmed I. Samatar, "Somalia as Africa's First Democrats: Premier Abdirazak H. Hussein and President Aden A. Osman", <Bildhaan>, 2, 2002.

Ahmed I. Samatar, Socialist Somalia, Rhetoric and Reality, Zed Books Ltd, London 1988.

Ali Jimale Ahmed, "The Invention of Somalia". The Red Sea Press Inc., 1995.

Angeloni Renato, The Somali Penal Code with comments and annotations based on preliminary studies, Milano – Giuffre' Editore - 1967.

Arnera Alfredo, "I Carabilnieri in Somalia Durante l'Amministrazione Fiduciaria Italiana in Somalia", "Il Carabiniere, No. 5 (1980).

Aweys Osman Haji and Abdiwahid Osman Haji, in "Clan, Sub-clan and Regional Representation in the Somali Government Organization 1960–1990: Statistical Data and Findings", Washington D.C. 1998.

Barnes C., "The Somali Youth League, Ethiopian Somaliland the Greater Somalia Idea, 1946–48. <Journal of Eastern African Studies, I, 2007, 2.

Battera F., "Dalla tribu' allo Stato nella Somalia nord-orientale: Il caso dei Sultanati di Hobyo e Majeerteen,. 1880–1930", Edizione Universita' di Trieste, Trieste 2004.

Bigi Ferdinando, "Situazione e Prospettive Economiche della Somalia alla vigilia dell' Indipendenza" in Africa, Anno XV, No. 3, 1960.

Braine Bernard, "Storm Clouds over the Horn of Africa". International Affairs (Royal Institute of International Affairs 1944–), Vol. 34, No. 4. (Oct., 1958), pp, 435-443.

British Military Administration, "The First to be freed, His Majesty's Stationary Office, London 1944.

Bullotta Antonia., La Somalia sotto due Bandiere, Garzanti, Milano 1949.

C. Grove Haines, "The Problem of the Italian Colonies" Middle East Journal, Vol. 1, No. 4 (Oct. 1947) pp, 417–431.

Calchi Novati , G.P., Il Corno D'Africa Nella Storia e nella Politica Etiopia, Somalia e Eritrea fra nazionalismi, Sottosviluppo e Guerra. Sei, Torino, 1994.

Calchi Novati G,P "Gli incidenti di Mogadiscio e il del Gennaio 1948, rapporti italo-inglesi e nationalism somalo , in <Africa>, XXXV, 1980, pp, 327–356.

Calchi Novati G.P. "Una rilettura degli incidenti di Mogadiscio del Gennaio 1948 e il difficile rapport fra Somali e italiani, in <studi Piacentini>, 15, 1994, pp 223–234.

Castagno A.A. " Somali Republic, in J.S. Coleman , C.G. Rosberg, (eds) Political Parties sand National integration in Tropical Africa , University of California Press, Berkeley 1964, pp, 512–559.

Castagno A.A. "The Republic of Somalia Africa's most homogenous State? , in <Africa> Special Report>, V. 1960, 7, p. 9.

Castagno A.A. "The Somali-Kenyan Controversy: Implications for the Future". The Journal of Modern African Studies, Vol 2 No 2, (Jul., 1964), pp, 165–188.

Castagno, A. A., Somalia in <International Conciliation>, 552, March 1959, pp, 339-400.

Catherine Besteman and Lee V. Cassanelli. "The Struggle for the Land in Southern Somalia" Haan Publishing, London 1996.

Contini Paolo. "The Somali Republic: An Experiment in Legal Integration", Frank Cass & Co. Ltd 1969.

Costanzo, G.A., "Problemi Costituzionali della Somalia nella Preparazione all'indipendenza" (1957-1960), Giuffre', Milano 1962.

D'Antonio Mario, "La Costituzione Somala, Precedenti storici e documenti costituzionali", Istituto Poliografico dello Stato, Roma 1962.

De Vecchi, Cesare-Maria "Orizzonte d' Iimpero, Cinque Anni in Somalia" A.

Mondadori – Milano, 1930.

Del Boca Angelo, "Gli Italiani in Africa Orientale, I. Dall'unita' alla Marcia su Roma", Arnoldo Mondadori Editore S.p.A, Milano 2001.

Del Boca Angelo, "Gli Italiani in Africa Orientale, IV, Nostalgis delle Colonie", Arnoldo Mondadori editore S.p.A, Milano 2001.

Del Boca, Angelo, "Gli Italiani In Africa Orientale, II, La conquista dell'Impero", Arnoldo Mondadori Editore S.p.A, Milano 2001.

Drysdale, J., "The Somali dispute", Pall Mall Press, London 1964.

F.E. Stafford, "The Ex-Italian Colonies" International Affairs (Royal Institute of International Affairs 1944–), Vol. 25, No. 1. (Jan., 1949).

Fornari Giovanni, "La Somalia nei primi due anni di Amministrazione Fiduciaria Italiana" in La Comunita' Internazionale, Luglio 1952, Vol, VII no. 3, p, 391).

Gasbarri Luigi, "L'AFIS (Amministrazione Fiduciaria Italiana della Somalia, 1950–1960) Una pagina di Storia Italiana da ricordare, in Africa", Anno XLI, No. 1, Marzo 1986, pp 73–88).

George G. Dawson, "Education in Somalia" Comparative Education Review, Vol. 8, No 2, (Oct., 1964), pp, 199–214.

Gerald Hanley, Warriors Life and death among the Somalis, Eland, London, 1993.

Haji N.A. Noor Muhammad, "Judicial Review of Administrative Action in the Somali Republic" Journal of African Law, Vol, 10, No. 1, (spring, 1966), pp 9–20.

Harper Mary, "Getting Somalia Wrong? Faith, and Hope in a Shattered State". Zed Books Ltd 2012.

Hess, R . Italian Colonialism in Somalia, Chicago University Press, Chicago 1966.

I.M. Lewis, "A Modern History of the Somali, Nation and State in the Horn of Africa, (4th edition) 2002.

I.M. Lewis, "Modern Political Movements in Somaliland I" Africa: Journal of the International African Institute, Vol.28, No. 3 (July, 1958), pp, 244–261.

I.M. Lewis, "Modern Political Movements in Somaliland II" Africa Journal of the International African Institute Vol. 28, No. 4 (Oct., 1958), pp 344–363.

I.M. Lewis, "The Politics of the 1969 Somali Coup". The Journal of Modern

African Studies, Vol. 10, No. 3 (Oct., 1972) pp, 383–408.

I.M. Lewis," Pan-Africanism and Pan-Somalism" The Journal of Modern African Studies, Vol. 1, No. 2, (Jun., 1963), pp, 147-161.

Ismail Ali Ismail, "Governance, the Scourge and Hope of Somalia" Trafford Publishing 2009.

Jama Mohamed Ghalib, "The Cost of Dictatorship: The Somali Experience", Lilian Barber Press, New York1995.

Johnson, J.W. "Orality, Literacy, and Somali Oral Poetry, in <Journal of African Cultural Studies> , XVIII, 2006, 1, pp, 119-136.

Karp, Mark, "Economics of Trusteeship in Somalia" New York University Press, January 1960.

Lawrence S. Finkilstein, Carnegie Endowment for International Peace Paper prepared for a Seminar held on February 25–26, 1955).

Lewis Bernard, "The Crisis of Islam, Holy War and Unholy Terror". The Modern Library, New York 2003.

Martino Enrico, "Due Anni in Somalia", Mogadiscio 1955.

Mesfin Wolde Mariam, "The Background of the Ethio–Somalian Boundary Dispute" Cambridge University Press 2009.

Mohamed Aden Sheikh, "La Somalia non e' un' Isola dei Caraibi, Memoria di un Pastore Somalo in Italia", Edizione Diabesis, 2010.

Mohamed Haji Muktar, "The Plight of the Agro-pastoral Society of Somalia" in Review of African Political Economy, 1996, p, 453).

Mohamed Osman Omar, "Somalia Between Devils and Deep Sea", Somali publication, 2004.

Mohamed Osman Omar, "Somalia Past and Present" , Somali publication, 2006.

Mohamed Osman Omar, "Somalia, a Nation driven to despair", Somali publication, Mogadisho, 2002.

Mohamed Osman Omar, "The Road to Zero, Somalia's Self–destruction". Haan Associates 1992.

Mohamed Osman Omar, "The Scramble in the Horn of Africa" (History of Somalia 1827–1977), Somali publication, Mogadisho 2001.

Morone A.M., "L'Onu e l'Amministrazione fiduciaria italiana in Somalia. Dall'idea all'istituzione del trusteeship", Istituto Poligrafico, in < Italia Contemporanea, 242, pp, 45–64 marzo 2006.

Morone A.M., "La nuova italia e le ex colonie nell'opera e nelle carte di

Giuseppe Brusasca", in <I sentieri della ricerca, 7–8, 2008, pp, 205–240.

Morone A.M.," L'Egitto di Nassere e la formazione dello Stato somalo: influenze politiche, interazioni culturali e identita' nazionale" , in <Contemporanea>, XIII, 2010, 4, pp, 649-679.

Morone, A.M., "L'ultima colonia. Come l'Italia e' tornata in Africa 1950–1960", Editori Laterza & Figli, 2011.

Mwakikagile Godfrey "The Modern African State: Quest for Transformation" 2001, p, 110.

Nuredin Haji Scikei, "Somalia un'Invenzione Italiana" in Affricana, Rivista di Studi Extraeuropei, 2001.

Ogenga Otunnu in "Factories affecting the Treatment of Kenyan-Somalis and Somali Refugees in Kenya: A Historical Overview". Refugee, Vol. 12, No. 5 (November- December 1992, p, 21.

Ozay Mehmet, "Effectiveness of Foreign Aid-The Case of Somalia", The Journal of Modern African Studies, Vol. 9, No, 1 (May, 1971), pp, 31–47.

Pacifico Claudio, "Ricordi di un Male d'Africa Italiano" Edimond SRL Citta' di Castello (Pc) 1996.

Palumbo Patrizia, "A Place in the Sun" (Africa in Italian Colonial Culture from Post-unification to the present) Regents of University of California 2003.

Pirone Michele. " Appunti di Storia dell' Africa" Edizione Ricerche , Roma 1961.

Puccioni Dino, "Si stara' a Vedere" Topografia ABC, Firenze 1998.

Rapport du government italien a l'Assemblee' Generale des Nationes Unies sur l'Administration de la Somalie placee' sous la tutelle de l'Italie, 9 vol. Istituto Poligraaphico dello Stato, Roma 1951–1959.

Remo Roncati , "Alcide de Gasperi (Partecipare alla Ricostruzione del mondo) Rubbettino Editore 2012.

Rennel of Rodd "British Military Administration of occupied Territories in Africa, during the years 1941–1947.

Rhymer Scott, "The Reluctant Imperialist: Italian Colonization in Somalia" 2005, p, 104).

Rivlin Benjamin, "The Italian Colonies and the General Assembly". International Organization, Vol. 3, No. 3 (Aug,. 1949), pp. 459–470.

Rossi Gianfranco. " L'Africa italiana verso l'indipendenza" (1941–1949), Giuffre', Milano 1985.

Salah Mohamed Ali," Huddur and the History of Southern Somalia", Nahda Bookshop Publisher 2005.

Saul Kelly, "Cold War in the Desert, Britain, the United States and the Italian Colonies", 1954–52, p, 150.

Seton-Waston Christopher, "Italy's Imperial Hangover" Journal of Contemporary History, Vol, 15, No. 1 Imperial Hangovers. (Jan., 1980), pp, 169–179" Sage Publications, Ltd 2007.

Sforza Carlo," Cinque Anni a Palazzo Chigi", Roma 1952, pp, 97–99).

Stephen H. Longrigg, "Disposal of Italian Africa", International affairs (Royal Institute of International affairs 1944–) Vol. 21, no. 3, (Jul., 1945), pp, 363–369.

"The Somali Peninsula, a New Light of Imperial Motives", Published by the Information Services of the Somali Government, 1962.

Touval Saadia, (1967) The Organization of African Unity and African Borders, International Organization, 21, pp, 102–127.

Touval Saadia," Somali nationalism, International Politics and the drive for unity in the Horn of Africa". Harvard University Press 1960.

Tripodi Paolo "Back to the Horn: Italian Administration and Somalia's Troubled Independence". The International Journal of African Historical Studies, Vol 32, No 2/3. (1999).

Tripodi, Paolo, "The Colonial Legacy in Somalia: Rome and Mogadishu from Colonial Administration to Operation Restore Hope". Macmillian Press Ltd on 1999 & St. Martin's Press, Inc. 1999.

Triulzi U, "L'Italia e l'Economia Somala dal 1950 ad oggi" in Affrica, Vol. XXVI, December 1971, p, 442).

Trusteeship Agreement of the Territory of Somaliland under the Italian Administration, adopted by the Trusteeship Council, January 27, 1950).

Ungari Andrea, Umberto Zanotti Bianco and the Mogadishu Events of 1948". Association for the Study of Modern Italy 2010 Vol. 15 No. 2, May 210, pp, 161–176.

United Kingdom of Great Britain and Northern Ireland and Italy (Exchange of notes constituting an agreement regarding the transfer to Italy of the provisional administration of Somalia) 1952.

Venturini Gabiella, "Italy and the United Nations" Hamline Law Review", 1966, p, 627.

W.E. Crosskill, "The Two Thousand Mile War" Robert Hall-London, 1980.

Ware G., "Somalia from Trust Territory to Nation, 1950–1960", Phylon (1960–), Vol, 26, No. 2 . (2nd Qtr. 1965), pp, 173–185.

Zanotti –Bianco Umberto and the Mogadisho events of 1948, Modern Italy Vol. 15, No. 2, May 2010, p, 165.

APPENDIX 1

1. *1950*. Signor Fornari, the first Administrator of Somalia, while reviewing Italian troops on parade in Beledweyne. Behind him is seen Signor Tomaselli, the Governor of Mudug.

2. *1954* Promotion Ceremony of newly appointed Somali Police officers. From Left to Right: Chief Administrator of Somalia; Enrico Martino, Lieutenant Colonel; Umberto Ripa Di Meana, Lieutenant; Mohamed Siad Barre.

3. *1954*. Promotion Ceremony of newly appointed Somali Police officers. From Left to Right: Chief Administrator of Somalia; Enrico Martino, Lieutenant; Mohamed Abshir, Lieutenant; Hussein Kulmie, Lieutenant; Mohamed Ibrahim Liiqliiqato, Lieutenant; Mohamed Siad Barre

4. *1959* Portrait Picture of three young cadets at the Modena Military Academy in Italy. From Left to Right: Cadet Mohamud Ghelle Yousuf, Cadet Mohamoud Muuse Hersi, Cadet Mussa Hassan Sheikh.

APPENDIX 2

1. *1st April 1950.* Handover ceremony. The handover ceremony from the British Administration to the Italian Trusteeship of Somalia.

2. *6th September 1954.* Ceremony of the hoisting of the Somali Flag. Speech of Chief Administrator Enrico Martino.

3. *6th September 1954.* Ceremony of the hoisting of the Somali Flag. The first time the Somali flag was hoisted at the seat of the Government in Mogadishu. In this picture you can see the Somali flag on the far right and the Italian flag in the middle and on the left the United Nations flag.

4. *6th September 1954.* Speech of Sultan Abdurahman Ali Issa, member of the Territorial Council

5. *6th September 1954.* Ceremony of the hoisting of the Somali Flag. Speech of Aadan Abdulla Osman, Vice President of the Territorial Council.

APPENDIX 3

1. *May 1953*. Murdered Member of Territorial Council. Ustad Osman Hussein; Member of Territorial Council was assassinated in Mogadishu just before his trip to UN headquarters in New York.

2. *1955*. Enrico Anzilotti. The Italian Ambassador and third Administrator of Somalia from 1955 to 1958.

3. *1956*. Sisters, Sirad & Maryan Yousuf. First Somali Female Elementary Teachers to have graduated from Italy.

4. *1954*. Giuseppe Bettiol. Member of the Italian Parliament and Lecturer Somali National University.

5. *1956–57?*. Mohamed Sheikh Osman Edmondo & Dr Chiti. Mohamed was member of Territorial Council & Dr Chiti was officer of Italian Administration in Mogadishu at a meeting held in Hague.

L'Amministratore alla Scuola di Polizia passa in rivista la Compagnia d'onore

6. *1955*. Ambassador Enrico Anzilotti (3rd Italian Administrator) and General Umberto Ripa Di Meana; Head of Somali Police force visiting the Somali Police Academy in Mogadishu.

APPENDIX 4

1. *1950–1959*. Dr Gualtiero Benardelli. Chief of Political & Civil Affairs office based in Mogadishu, Somalia.

2. *1935*. Sultan Olol Dinle. Sultan of the Shabele who participated the Italian-Ethiopian war.

THE HAND-OVER IS COMPLETED

Nine Years of British Administration over the territory of Somalia ended this morning, in accordance with the decision taken by the United Nations in General Assembly at Lake Success on 20th November, 1949.

Above the Headquarters of the Administration building in the capital, Mogadishu, now flies the Tricoloured flag of the Republic of Italy, to whom the United Nations have entrusted the task of guiding the peoples of the territory towards independence which is to be achieved in ten Years time.

ITALY ASSUMES TRUSTEESHIP OF SOMALIA

The Union Jack is Lowered

The Flag of the Italian Republic Unfurls

Guards of Honour Salute Both Colours

A PROCLAMATION BY H.E. POMPEO GORINI

Spettacoli del giorno

3. *1st of April 1950. Corriere Della Somalia* News Paper. Headlines read; 'The Hand-Over is Complete' as Italy assumes Trusteeship of Somalia from the British Administration.

4. *1935.* Sultan Olol Dinle & Genaral Graziani preparing for the battle ahead against the Ethiopian forces.

INDEX

A

I

J

K

L

M

N

www.ingramcontent.com/pod-product-compliance
Lightning Source LLC
Chambersburg PA
CBHW031114020426
42333CB00012B/87
9781912411481